W9-BRS-470

MODERN GUNS
Identification & Values

6th Revised Edition

Russell C. Quertermous
Steven C. Quertermous

COLLECTOR BOOKS
A Division of Schroeder Publishing Co., Inc.

The current values in this book should be used only as a guide. They are not intended to set prices, which vary from one section of the country to another. Auction prices as well as dealer prices vary greatly and are affected by condition as well as demand. Neither the Author nor the Publisher assumes responsibility for any losses that might be incurred as a result of consulting this guide.

For the purpose of estimating values, the firearm's condition is the first and foremost consideration. Conditions of guns evaluated in this guide are considered to be in accordance with the National Rifle Association (NRA) definitions, taken from its magazine, *The American Rifleman*. This evaluation system is generally accepted in the firearms trade.

New Discontinued—same as new, but discontinued model. The following definitions will apply to all second hand articles.
Perfect—in new condition in every aspect: **Excellent**—new condition, used but little, no noticeable marring of wood or metal, bluing perfect (except at muzzle or sharp edges); **Very Good**—in perfect working condition, no appreciable wear on working surfaces, no corrosion or pitting, only minor surface dents or scratches; **Good**—in safe working condition, minor wear on working surfaces, no broken parts, no corrosion or pitting that will interfere with proper functioning; **Fair**—in working condition, but well worn, perhaps requiring replacement of minor parts or adjustments, no rust but may have corrosion pits; which do not render article unsafe or inoperable.

Values in this guide are for guns in the following conditions:
New (retail); present suggested retail prices still in production. Excellent and Very Good; or Very Good and Good, for all second hand items.

The illustrations included are from gun manufacturer's promotional photos, advertisements, catalogs, and brochures. Since they are from a number of sources, relative size cannot be determined by comparing photos.

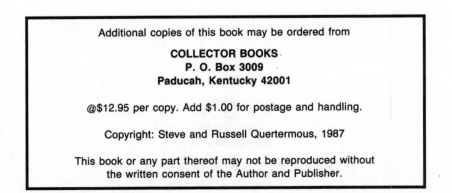

Additional copies of this book may be ordered from

COLLECTOR BOOKS
P. O. Box 3009
Paducah, Kentucky 42001

@$12.95 per copy. Add $1.00 for postage and handling.

Copyright: Steve and Russell Quertermous, 1987

This book or any part thereof may not be reproduced without the written consent of the Author and Publisher.

CONTENTS

ACKNOWLEDGMENTS

The companies included for the use of catalogs, advertisements and promotional material.

A special thanks to the following gun manufacturers for additional photos, information and assistance: Beretta Arms Co. Inc. for material on Beretta handguns and shotguns; Browning for material on Browning handguns, rifles and shotguns; Charter Arms Corporation for material on Charter Arms handguns; Colt Industries, Firearms Division for material on Colt handguns and rifles; Commercial Trading Imports, Inc. for material on Baikal shotguns; Harrington & Richardson, Inc. for material on Harrington & Richardson handguns, rifles and shotguns; Heckler & Koch for material on Heckler & Koch rifles and handguns; Interarms for material on Mark X rifles, Valmet rifles, Whitworth rifles, Walther handguns and rifles, Star handguns and Astra handguns; Ithaca Gun Co. for material on Ithaca shotguns; Iver Johnson Arms, Inc. for material on Iver Johnson handguns, Kleinguenther Inc. for materials on Kleinguenther rifles; Mannlicher for materials on Mannlicher rifles and shotguns; Marlin for material on Marlin and Marlin-Glenfield rifles and shotguns; O.F. Mossberg & Sons Inc., for material on Mossberg and New Haven rifles and shotguns; Remington for material on Remington rifles, shotguns and handguns; Richland Arms Co. for material on Richland shotguns; Savage Arms for material on Savage rifles and shotguns, Stevens rifles and shotguns, Fox shotguns, and Anschutz rifles; Sears, Roebuck & Co. for material on Sears rifles and shotguns and Ted Williams rifles and shotguns; Smith & Wesson for material on Smith & Wesson handguns, rifles and shotguns; Speer Inc. Advertising for material on Mossberg firearms; Sterling Arms Corporation for material on Sterling handguns; Universal Firearms for material on Universal rifles; Weatherby, Inc. for material on Weatherby rifles and shotguns; Winchester-Western for material on Winchester rifles and shotguns; U.S. Repeating Arms for material on Winchester rifles and shotguns.

Petersen Publishing Company for the use of the following photographs from *Guns and Ammo Annual*, 1977, 1982 and *Hunting Annual* 1983:

SHOTGUNS:

Beretta BL4, 680 Trap, 685, MKII Trap, GR-2; 410, AL-2; Bernardelli Game Cock; Browning Super Light, Citori Trap, B-SS, BPS, 2000; Charles Daly Field III, Auto Superior; Fox FA-1; Franchi Standard; Harrington & Richardson 176, 1212; Ithaca 37 Standard, 37 DV Deluxe, 37 Bicentennial, 51 Deluxe Trap, 51 Magnum, 51 Deerslayer; Mannlicher Oxford, Mossberg 500 ATP8, 500 AHTD, Slugster, Richland 200; Smith & Wesson 916, 1000, 3000; Valmet 412K; Weatherby Orion, Athena, 92, 82; Winchester 1200 Defender

RIFLES:

Anschutz 1422D, 520/61; Browning BAR; Harrington & Richardson 750; Heckler & Koch 770, 940; Mossberg 321K, 341, 353, 800, 810; New Haven 453T; Remington 541 S, 700 ADL; Sako Classic, Safari; Stevens 35, 125; Valmet 412, M62/S, M-71/S; Walther KKJ, KKM, UIT, Moving Target; Winchester 70 XTR Featherweight, 70 Western, 70XTR Sporter Magnum, Super Xpress

HANDGUNS:

Beretta 951; Browning Challenger II, Challenger III; Charter Arms Explorer II, Bulldog Tracker; Colt S-4 Targetsman, Target S-3; Dan Wesson 9-2, 44V; Heckler & Koch HK4, P9S; Iver Johnson TP22; Llama Comanche; Ruger Redhawk; Smith & Wesson 30, 1953 22/32, 25-1955, 10, 31, 27, 28, 58, 38, 547 M & P, 586; Sterling MKII 400

Stackpole Books for the use of the following photographs from W.H.B. Smith's *Books of Pistols and Revolvers* and *Book of Rifles*: Astra 1911-Patent, 1915 Patent, 1924, 300, 600, 400; Bayard 1908, 1923, 1930; Beretta 1915, 1923, 1931; Browning, FN, 1900, 1903 Military, 1910, 1922; CZ 22, 1945; Colt 1900, 1902, 1905, Model M, 1911; Fiala Single Shot; Harrington & Richardson 32; Japanese Military pistols; Lignose 2A, 2 Pocket; MAB C; Mauser 2; Sauer 1913, WTM, H; Savage 1907, 1915, 1917; Smith & Wesson 32 & 35, No. 3 Frontier, Doubled Action Frontier, Military & Police 32-20, New Century; Star 1919; Steyr Solothurn, Vest Pocket; Walther 5, 4, 7, 9; Webley & Scott 1906, Mark I; Military rifles

Shotguns

AYA

AYA Matador
Gauge: 10, 12, 16, 20, 20 magnum
Action: Box lock; top lever break-open; hammerless; selective single trigger and automatic ejector
Magazine: None
Barrel: Double barrel, 26″, 28″, 30″ any choke combination
Finish: Blued; checkered walnut pistol grip stock and beavertail forerm
Approximate wt.: 7 lb.
Comments: Made from 1953 until 1963. Replaced by Matador II.
Estimated Value: **Excellent:** **$375.00**
            Very good: **$285.00**

AYA Matador II
Same as the Matador with ventilated rib. Produced since the discontinuation of the Matador.
Estimated Value: **Excellent:** **$425.00**
            Very good: **$320.00**

AYA Bolero
Same as the Matador except non-selective single trigger and extractors; 28 and 410 gauges. Made from the mid 1950's until 1963.
Estimated Value: **Excellent:** **$350.00**
            Very good: **$275.00**

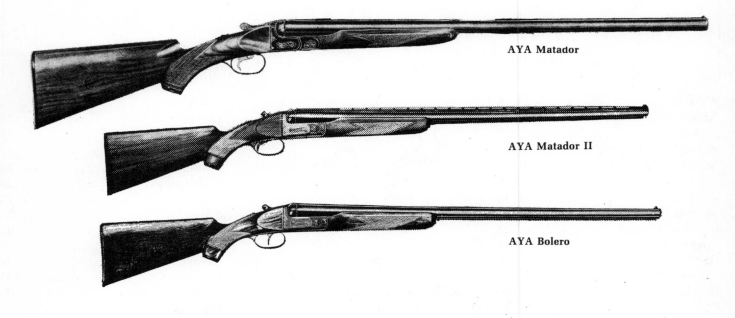

AYA Matador

AYA Matador II

AYA Bolero

Armalite

Armlite AR-17

Armalite AR-17
Gauge: 12
Action: Semi-automatic; gas operated; hammerless
Magazine: 2-shot
Barrel: 24″ aluminum alloy; interchangeable choke tubes; improved modified and full chokes
Finish: Gold anodized or black anodized; plastic stock and forearm
Approximate wt.: 5½ lb.
Comments: Barrel and receiver housing made of high tensile aluminum alloy. Made from about 1963 to 1965. Approximately 2000 manufactured.
Estimated Value: **Excellent:** **$675.00**
            Very good: **$500.00**

Baikal Model IJ-27IC and IJ-27EIC
Gauge: 12, 20
Action: Box lock; top lever break-open; hammerless; selective single trigger
Magazine: None
Barrel: Over and under double barrel; 26″, 28″, 30″ improved cylinder & modified or modified & full chokes; ventilated rib
Finish: Blued; engraved receiver; hand checkered walnut pistol grip stock and forearm
Approximate wt.: 7½ lb.
Comments: Made in Soviet Union; IJ-37EIC has selective ejectors, add $40.00.
Estimated Value: Excellent: $325.00
Very good: $240.00

Baikal Model IJ-27EIC Silver
Same as the Model IJ-27EIC with silver inlays and fancy engraving.
Estimated Value: Excellent: $425.00
Very good: $315.00

Baikal Model IJ-12
Less fancy but similar to the IJ-27IC. No engraving, no recoil pad; 28″ barrel only. Imported in the early 1970's.
Estimated Value: Excellent: $225.00
Very good: $165.00

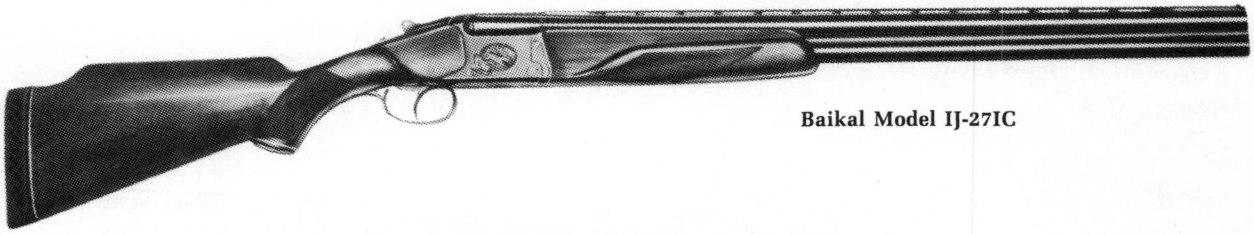

Baikal Model IJ-27IC

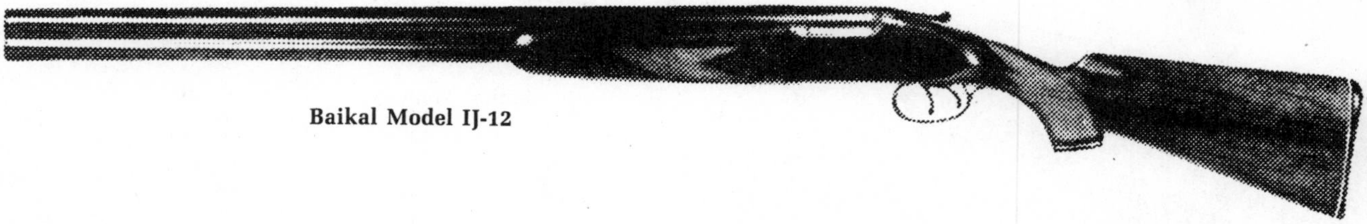

Baikal Model IJ-12

Baikal TOZ-66

Baikal TOZ-66
Gauge: 12
Action: Box lock; top lever break-open; exposed hammers
Magazine: None
Barrel: Double barrel; 28″ chrome lined, variety of chokes
Finish: Blued; checkered wood pistol grip stock and short tapered forearm; engraving
Approximate wt.: 8 lb.
Comments: Imported during the 1970's.
Estimated Value: Excellent: $250.00
Very good: $185.00

Baikal Model TOZ-34E Souvenir
Gauge: 12, 20, 28
Action: Box lock; top lever break-open; hammerless
Magazine: None
Barrel: Over and under double barrel; 26″ or 28″ improved cylinder & modified or modified & full; ventilated rib on 12 and 20 gauge; solid rib on 28 gauge
Finish: Blued; select walnut, hand checkered pistol grip stock and forearm; engraved receiver
Approximate wt.: 7 lb.
Comments: Imported from the Soviet Union. It features selective ejectors and cocking indicators.
Estimated Value: Excellent: $600.00
Very good: $450.00

8 Shotguns

Baikal Model IJ-18 and IJ-18E

Gauge: 12, 20
Action: Box lock; top lever break-open; hammerless; single shot; cocking indicator
Magazine: None
Barrel: 26″, 28″ modified, 30″ full choke
Finish: Blued; checkered walnut-stained hardwood, pistol grip stock and tapered forearm; engraved receiver
Approximate wt.: 6 lb.
Comments: IJ-18E has selective ejector, add $6.00.
Estimated Value: Excellent: $60.00
                 Very good: $45.00

Baikal IJ-58MA and 58MAE

Gauge: 12, 20 magnum
Action: Box lock; top lever break-open; hammerless
Magazine: None
Barrel: Double barrel; 26″ improved cylinder & modified, 28″ modified & full chokes; chrome lined
Finish: Blued; checkered walnut pistol grip stock and short tapered forearm; engraved receiver. IJ-58MAE has selective ejectors, add $28.00.
Approximate wt.: 7 lbs.
Comments: Imported in 1970's.
Estimated Value: Excellent: $230.00
                 Very good: $175.00

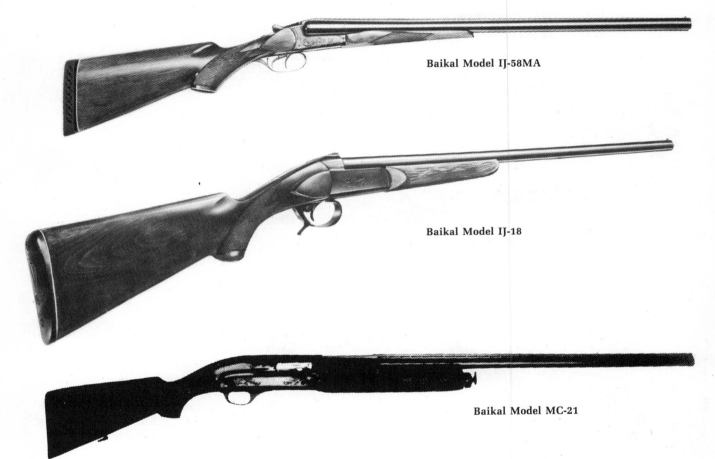

Baikal Model IJ-58MA

Baikal Model IJ-18

Baikal Model MC-21

Baikal Model MC-8

Gauge: 12
Action: Box lock; top lever break-open; hammerless
Magazine: None
Barrel: Over and under double barrel; trap, skeet, 26″ or 28″, modified or full chokes; chrome lined barrels
Finish: Blued; checkered walnut Monte Carlo pistol grip stock and forearm; engraved receiver
Approximate wt.: 8½ lb.
Comments: Imported during the 1970's
Estimated Value: Excellent: $1,800.00
                 Very good: $1,300.00

Baikal Model MC-21

Gauge: 12
Action: Semi-automatic; hammerless; side ejection
Magazine: 5-shot tubular
Barrel: 26″ improved cylinder, 28″ modified, 30″ full chokes; ventilated rib
Finish: Blued; checkered walnut, pistol grip stock and forearm; engraved receiver.
Approximate wt.: 7½ lbs.
Comments: Imported in the 1970's.
Estimated Value: Excellent: $325.00
                 Very good: $250.00

Baikal Model MC-5

Baikal Model MC-5
Gauge: 20
Action: Box lock; top lever break-open; hammerless; double triggers
Magazine: None
Barrel: Over and under double barrel; 26″ or 28″ improved cylinder & modified or skeet chokes; ribbed
Finish: Blued; checkered walnut pistol grip or straight stock and forearm; engraved receiver.
Approximate wt.: 5¾ lbs.
Comments: Imported during the 1970's.
Estimated Value: Excellent: $850.00
                   Very good: $650.00

Baker

Baker Batavia Leader

Baker Black Beauty Special
Similar to Baker Batavia Leader except higher quality wood and finish. Add $75.00 for automatic extractors.
Estimated Value: Excellent: $675.00
                   Very good: $500.00

Baker Black Beauty Special

Baker Batavia Leader
Gauge: 12, 16, 20
Action: Side lock; hammerless
Magazine: None
Barrel: 26″, 28″, 30″, 32″ double barrel; any standard choke combination
Finish: Blued; walnut pistol grip stock and forearm
Approximate wt.: 7-8 lbs.
Comments: Made from about 1900 to 1930. Add $75.00 for automatic extractors.
Estimated Value: Excellent: $425.00
                   Very good: $320.00

Beretta

Beretta Companion FS-1
Gauge: 12, 16, 20, 28, 410
Action: Underlever; hammerless; single shot
Magazine: None
Barrel: 26″, 28″ full choke
Finish: Blued; checkered walnut pistol grip stock and forearm
Approximate wt.: 5 lbs.
Comments: A folding shotgun made from about 1960 to the late 1970's.
Estimated Value: Excellent: $110.00
                   Very good: $ 80.00

Beretta Mark II Trap
Gauge: 12
Action: Box lock; top lever break-open; hammerless; single shot
Magazine: None
Barrel: 32″, 34″ full choke; ventilated rib
Finish: Blued; checkered walnut Monte Carlo pistol grip stock and forearm; recoil pad; engraving
Approximate wt.: 8 lbs.
Comments: Made from the mid 1970's to early 1980's.
Estimated Value: Excellent: $450.00
                   Very good: $340.00

Beretta Mark II Trap

Beretta Companion FS-1

Beretta BL-1

Gauge: 12
Action: Box lock; top lever break-open; hammerless; double triggers
Magazine: None
Barrel: Over and under double barrel; chrome steel; 26″-30″ improved cylinder & modified or modified & full chokes
Finish: Blued; checkered walnut semi-pistol grip stock and forearm
Approximate wt.: 7 lbs.
Comments: Made from about 1969 to early 1970's.
Estimated Value: Excellent: $400.00
               Very good: $310.00

Beretta BL-2

Similar to the BL-1 with selective single trigger.
Estimated Value: Excellent: $475.00
               Very good: $360.00

Beretta BL-3

Similar to the BL-2 with ventilated rib; engraving.
Estimated Value: Excellent: $600.00
               Very good: $450.00

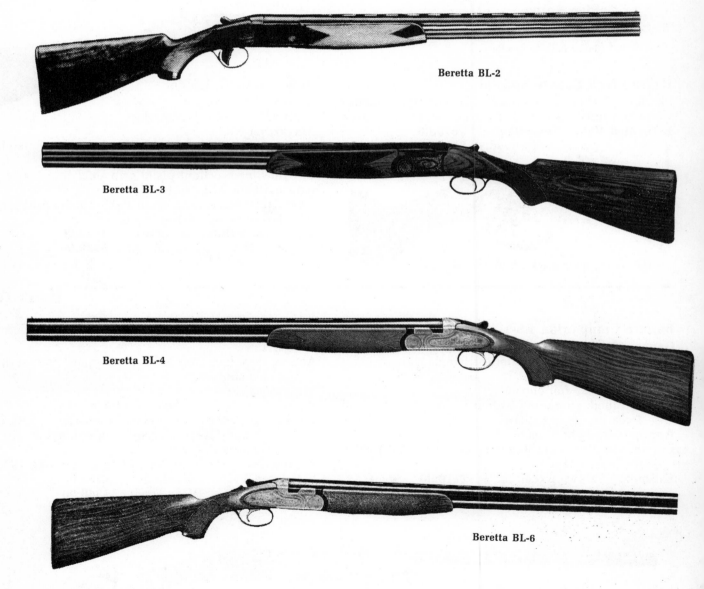

Beretta BL-2

Beretta BL-3

Beretta BL-4

Beretta BL-6

Beretta BL-4 and BL-5

Similar to the BL-3 with deluxe engraving and checkering; automatic ejectors. Add $200.00 for BL-5.
Estimated Value: Excellent: $700.00
               Very good: $540.00

Beretta BL-6

The finest of the BL line. Highest quality checkering and engraving. Similar to the BL-4.
Estimated Value: Excellent: $1,200.00
               Very good: $ 900.00

Beretta Silver Snipe

Gauge: 12, 20, regular or magnum
Action: Box lock; top lever break-open; hammerless
Magazine: None
Barrel: 26"-30" improved cylinder & modified, modified & full, full, or skeet chokes; ribbed; over and under double barrel
Finish: Blued; nickel receiver; checkered walnut pistol grip stock and forearm
Approximate wt.: 7½ lbs.
Comments: Made from mid 1950's to late 1960's. Add $25.00 for single selective trigger.
Estimated Value: Excellent: $500.00
  Very good: $360.00

Beretta Silver Snipe

Beretta Golden Snipe

Similar to the Silver Snipe with ventilated rib; automatic ejectors. Discontinued in the mid 1970's.
Estimated Value: Excellent: $550.00
  Very good: $400.00

Beretta Asel

Gauge: 12, 20
Action: Box lock; top lever break-open; hammerless; automatic ejector; single trigger
Magazine: None
Barrel: Over and under double barrel; 25", 28", 30" improved cylinder & modified or modified & full chokes
Finish: Blued; checkered walnut pistol grip stock and forearm
Approximate wt.: 7 lbs.
Comments: Made from the late 1940's to mid 1960's.
Estimated Value: Excellent: $950.00
  Very good: $720.00

Beretta Model S56E

Beretta Model S56E

Similar to Model S55B with scroll engraving on the receiver; selective automatic ejectors.
Estimated Value: Excellent: $675.00
  Very good: $550.00

Beretta Model S55B

Gauge: 12, 20, regular or magnum
Action: Box lock; top lever break-open; hammerless
Magazine: None
Barrel: Over and under double barrel; chrome lined; ventilated rib; 26" improved cylinder and modified; 28" or 30" modified & full; 30" full in 12 gauge
Finish: Blued; checkered walnut pistol grip stock and beavertail forearm; recoil pad on magnum
Approximate wt.: 6-7 lbs.
Comments: Made from late 1970's to early 1980's.
Estimated Value: Excellent: $600.00
  Very good: $440.00

Beretta Model 680 Trap

Beretta Model 680 Competition Skeet

Gauge: 12
Action: Top lever, break-open; hammerless; automatic ejector; single selective trigger
Magazine: None
Barrel: Over and under double barrel; 26" or 28" skeet choke barrels; ventilated rib
Finish: Blued; checkered walnut pistol grip stock and forearm; silver grey receiver with engraving; gold-plated trigger
Approximate wt.: 7 lbs.
Comments: Interchangeable barrel capacity; price includes luggage-style case.
Estimated Value: Excellent: $1,175.00
  Very good: $ 885.00

Beretta Model 680 Trap

Similar to the Model 680 Skeet with a Monte Carlo stock, recoil pad; 30" or 32" improved modified & full choke barrels.
Estimated Value: Excellent: $1,175.00
  Very good: $ 890.00

Beretta Model 680 Mono Trap

Similar to the Model 680 Trap with a single high ventilated rib barrel; 32" or 34" full choke barrel.
Estimated Value: Excellent: $1,175.00
  Very good: $ 900.00

Beretta Model 625

Gauge: 12, 20, regular or magnum
Action: Box lock; top lever break-open; hammerless; double barrel: mechanical extractor
Magazine: None
Barrel: 26″ improved cylinder/modified; 28″ or 30″ modified/full; double barrel
Finish: Blued; grey receiver; checkered walnut pistol grip or straight stock and tapered forearm
Approximate wt.: 6 to 7 lbs.
Comments: Introduced in the mid 1980's.
Estimated Value: New (retail): $935.00
Excellent: $700.00
Very good: $525.00

Beretta Model 626

Similar to the Model 625 with selective automatic ejectors.
Estimated Value: New (retail): $1,225.00
Excellent: $ 915.00
Very good: $ 690.00

Beretta Model 685

Beretta Model 685

Gauge: 12, 20, regular or magnum
Action: Top lever, break-open; hammerless; single selective trigger
Magazine: None
Barrel: Over and under double barrel; 26″ improved cylinder & modified, 28″ or 30″ modified & full, 30″ full & full; ventilated rib
Finish: Blued; checkered walnut pistol grip stock and fluted forearm; silver grey receiver with light engraving
Approximate wt.: 8 lbs.
Comments: Currently available.
Estimated Value: New (retail): $875.00
Excellent: $655.00
Very good: $490.00

Beretta Model 686

Gauge: 12, 20, regular or magnum
Action: Top lever, break-open; hammerless; single selective trigger; selective automatic ejectors
Magazine: None
Barrel: Over and under double barrel; 26″ improved cylinder & modified, 28″ or 30″ modifed & full, or 30″ full & full; ventilated rib; multi-choke tubes available
Finish: Blued; checkered walnut pistol grip stock and fluted forearm; silver grey receiver with engraving; recoil pad on magnum
Approximate wt.: 8 lbs.
Comments: Currently available. Add 10% for multi-choke tubes.
Estimated Value: New (retail): $1,025.00
Excellent: $ 765.00
Very good: $ 575.00

Beretta GR-2

Beretta GR-2
Gauge: 12, 20
Action: Box lock; top lever, break-open; hammerless
Magazine: None
Barrel: Double barrel; 26″-30″; variety of choke combinations
Finish: Blued; checkered walnut semi-pistol grip stock and forearm
Approximate wt.: 6 to 8 lbs.
Comments: Made from the mid 1970's to late 1970's.
Estimated Value: Excellent: $475.00
                    Very good: $350.00

Beretta GR-3
Similar to the GR-2 with single selective trigger.
Estimated Value: Excellent: $550.00
                    Very good: $420.00

Beretta GR-4
Similar to the GR-3 with automatic ejector; engraving and deluxe wood work.
Estimated Value: Excellent: $650.00
                    Very good: $490.00

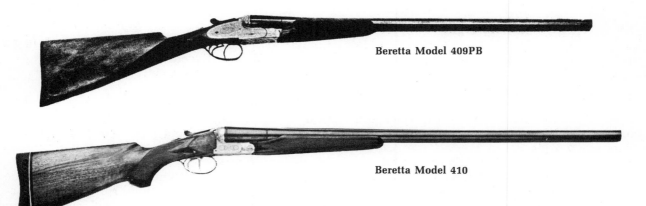

Beretta Model 409PB

Beretta Model 410

Beretta Model 409PB
Gauge: 12, 16, 20, 28
Action: Box lock; top lever, break-open; hammerless; double triggers
Magazine: None
Barrel: Double barrel 27½″, 28½″, 30″ improved cylinder & modified or modified & full chokes
Finish: Blued; checkered walnut straight or pistol grip stock and small tapered forearm; engraved
Approximate wt.: 6 to 8 lbs.
Comments: Made from mid 1930's to mid 1960's.
Estimated Value: Excellent: $550.00
                    Very good: $425.00

Beretta Model 410E
Similar to the 409PB with higher quality finish and engraving; automatic ejector.
Estimated Value: Excellent: $675.00
                    Very good: $500.00

Beretta Model 411E
Similar to 410E with higher quality finish.
Estimated Value: Excellent: $950.00
                    Very good: $720.00

Beretta Model 410
Gauge: 10 magnum
Action: Box lock; top lever, break-open; hammerless; double triggers
Magazine: None
Barrel: Double barrel; 27½″, 28½″, 30″ improved cylinder & modified or modified & full chokes
Finish: Blued; checkered walnut stock and short tapered forearm
Approximate wt.: 10 lbs.
Comments: Made from the mid 1930's to early 1980's.
Estimated Value: Excellent: $950.00
                    Very good: $700.00

Beretta Model 410E

Beretta Model 424

Beretta Silver Hawk Featherweight

Beretta Silver Hawk Featherweight

Gauge: 12, 16, 20, 28
Action: Box lock; top lever, break-open; hammerless
Magazine: None
Barrel: Double barrel; 26″-32″ variety of chokes; matted rib
Finish: Blued; checkered walnut pistol grip stock and forearm
Approximate wt.: 7¼ lbs.
Comments: Made from the mid 1950's to late 1960's.
Estimated Value: Excellent: $490.00
　　　　　　　　　Very good: $350.00

Beretta Silver Hawk Featherweight Magnum

Similar to the Silver Hawk Featherweight in 10 or 12 gauge magnum; chrome lined 30″ or 32″ barrels; ventilated rib; recoil pad.
Estimated Value: Excellent: $550.00
　　　　　　　　　Very good: $400.00

Beretta Model 424

Gauge: 12, 20
Action: Box lock; top lever, break-open; hammerless; double trigger
Magazine: None
Barrel: Double barrel; chrome lined; matted rib; 26″ or 28″ improved cylinder & modified or modified & full chokes
Finish: Blued; checkered walnut straight grip stock and forearm
Approximate wt.: 6 lbs.
Comments: Produced in the late 1970's to mid 1980's.
Estimated Value: Excellent: $675.00
　　　　　　　　　Very good: $510.00

Beretta Model 426

Gauge: 12, 20 magnum
Action: Top lever, break-open; hammerless; single selective trigger; selective automatic ejector
Magazine: None
Barrel: Double barrel; 26″ improved cylinder & modified or 28″ modified & full; solid rib
Finish: Blued; checkered walnut pistol grip stock and tapered forearm; silver grey engraved receiver; silver pigeon inlaid
Approximate wt.: 8 lbs.
Comments: Currently available. Discontinued mid 1980's.
Estimated Value: Excellent: $ 840.00
　　　　　　　　　Very good: $ 625.00

Beretta Silver Pigeon

Beretta Silver Pigeon

Gauge: 12
Action: Slide action; hammerless
Magazine: 5-shot tubular
Barrel: 26″-32″, various chokes
Finish: Blued; engraved and inlaid with silver pigeon; chrome trigger; checkered walnut pistol grip stock and slide handle
Approximate wt.: 7 lbs.
Comments: Made from about 1960 for 6 years.
Estimated Value: Excellent: $275.00
　　　　　　　　　Very good: $200.00

Beretta Gold Pigeon

Similar to the Silver Pigeon with heavy engraving; gold pigeon inlaid; ventilated rib; gold trigger.
Estimated Value: Excellent: $575.00
　　　　　　　　　Very good: $455.00

Beretta Ruby Pigeon

Similar to the Gold Pigeon with deluxe engraving and ruby eye in inlaid pigeon.
Estimated Value: Excellent: $650.00
　　　　　　　　　Very good: $500.00

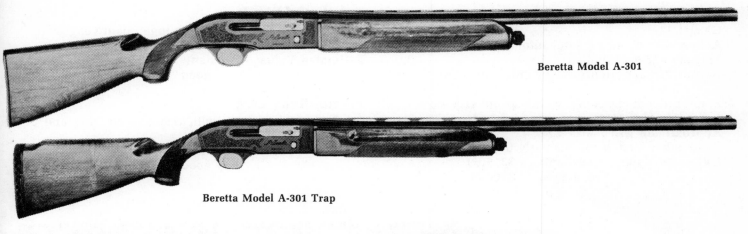

Beretta Model A-301

Beretta Model A-301 Trap

Beretta Model A-301

Gauge: 12, 20 regular or magnum
Action: Gas operated, semi-automatic; hammerless
Magazine: 3-shot tubular
Barrel: 26″ improved cylinder; 28″ modified or full; 30″ full in 12 gauge; ventilated rib; chrome molybdenum
Finish: Blued; checkered walnut pistol grip stock and forearm; decorated alloy receiver; recoil pad on magnum model
Approximate wt.: 6¼-7 lbs.
Comments: Made from the late 1970's to early 1980's. Add $45.00 for magnum.
Estimated Value: Excellent: $365.00
Very good: $275.00

Beretta Model A-301 Trap

Similar to the A-301 with Monte Carlo stock, recoil pad and gold plated trigger; 12 gauge only; 30″ full choke.
Estimated Value: Excellent: $375.00
Very good: $290.00

Beretta Model A-301 Skeet

Similar to the A-301 Trap with a 26″ skeet choke barrel.
Estimated Value: Excellent: $365.00
Very good: $285.00

Beretta Model A-301 Deer Gun

Similar to the A-301 with a 22″ slug barrel; adjustable open sights.
Estimated Value: Excellent: $365.00
Very good: $280.00

Beretta AL-2

Beretta AL-3

Beretta AL-1

Gauge: 12, 20 regular or magnum
Action: Gas operated, semi-automatic; hammerless
Magazine: 3-shot tubular
Barrel: 26″-30″ skeet, improved cylinder, modified or full chokes; ventilated rib
Finish: Blued; checkered walnut pistol grip stock and forearm
Approximate wt.: 6½-7¾ lbs.
Comments: Made from the late 1960's to mid 1970's.
Estimated Value: Excellent: $275.00
Very good: $200.00

Beretta AL-2

Similar to the AL-1 with ventilated rib; recoil pad; chrome lined bores.
Estimated Value: Excellent: $325.00
Very good: $250.00

Beretta AL-3

Similar to the AL-2 with light engraving.
Estimated Value: Excellent: $350.00
Very good: $260.00

Beretta Silver Lark

Gauge: 12
Action: Gas operated, semi-automatic; hammerless
Magazine: 5-shot tubular
Barrel: 26"-32", improved cylinder, modified or full chokes
Finish: Blued; checkered walnut pistol grip stock and forearm
Approximate wt.: 7 lbs.
Comments: Made from the early to late 1960's.
Estimated Value: Excellent: $275.00
Very good: $200.00

Beretta Gold Lark

Similar to the Silver Lark with high quality engraving and ventilated rib.
Estimated Value: Excellent: $375.00
Very good: $280.00

Beretta Ruby Lark

Similar to Silver Lark with deluxe engraving and a stainless steel barrel.
Estimated Value: Excellent: $500.00
Very good: $385.00

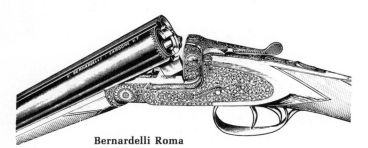

Beretta Model A302 Mag-Action

Beretta Model A302 Mag-Action

Gauge: 12, 20 regular or magnum
Action: Gas operated, semi-automatic
Magazine: 3-shot tubular
Barrel: 26" improved cylinder; 28" modified or full; 30" full; ventilated rib
Finish: Blued; checkered walnut pistol grip stock and fluted forearm
Approximate wt.: 7 lbs.
Comments: Interchangeable barrel capacity, 2¾" or 3" chambering. Introduced in 1982. Add 5% for multi-choke model with four choke tubes.
Estimated Value: New (retail): $585.00
Excellent: $435.00
Very good: $330.00

Beretta Model A302 Skeet

Similar to the Model A302 Mag-Action except 26" skeet choke barrel.
Estimated Value: New (retail): $599.00
Excellent: $450.00
Very good: $335.00

Beretta Model A302 Trap

Similar to the Model A302 Mag-Action with Monte Carlo stock and 30" full choke barrel.
Estimated Value: Excellent: $435.00
Very good: $330.00

Beretta Model A302 Slug

Similar to the Model A302 Mag-Action with a 22" slug barrel; adjustable front sight, folding leaf rear sight; swivels.
Estimated Value: New (retail): $599.00
Excellent: $450.00
Very good: $330.00

Bernardelli

Bernardelli Roma

Bernardelli Roma

Gauge: 12, 16, 20
Action: Anson & Deeley type; top lever break-open; hammerless; double trigger; automatic ejector
Magazine: None
Barrel: Double barrel, 27½" or 29½" modified & full choke
Finish: Blued; checkered walnut straight or pistol grip stock and forearm
Approximate wt.: 5 to 7 lbs.
Comments: Produced in three grades from the mid 1940's. Add $50.00 for single trigger.

Estimated Value:	Roma 3	Roma 4	Roma 6
Excellent:	$800.00	$1,000.00	$1,200.00
Very good:	$600.00	$750.00	$900.00

Bernardelli Game Cock

Bernardelli Game Cock Deluxe
Same as the Game Cock with light scroll engraving; single trigger; automatic ejector.
Estimated Value: Excellent: $760.00
Very good: $575.00

Bernardelli Game Cock Premier
Same as the Game Cock with more engraving; selective single trigger; automatic ejector.
Estimated Value: Excellent: $875.00
Very good: $650.00

Bernardelli Game Cock
Gauge: 12, 20
Action: Box lock; top lever break-open; double trigger; hammerless
Magazine: None
Barrel: Double barrel, 25″ improved & modified or 28″ modified & full chokes
Finish: Blued; checkered walnut straight stock and fore-arm; light engraving
Approximate wt.: 6½ lbs.
Comments: Produced in the early 1970's.
Estimated Value: Excellent: $690.00
Very good: $520.00

Bernardelli Italia

Bernardelli Italia
Gauge: 12
Action: Top lever break-open; exposed hammer; double trigger
Magazine: None
Barrel: Double barrel; chrome lined 30″ modified & full chokes
Finish: Blued; engraved receiver; checkered walnut straight grip stock and forearm
Approximate wt.: 7 lbs.
Comments: Still in production.
Estimated Value: Excellent: $860.00
Very good: $650.00

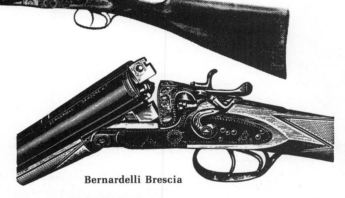

Bernardelli Brescia

Bernardelli Brescia
Same as the Italia but available in 28″ barrels or 20 gauge in 26″ barrels; modified & improved cylinder bore.
Estimated Value: Excellent: $750.00
Very good: $560.00

Bernardelli Holland

Bernardelli Holland
Gauge: 12
Action: Side lock; top lever break-open; hammerless; double trigger; automatic ejector
Magazine: None
Barrel: Double barrel, 26″ to 32″ any choke combination
Finish: Blued; straight or pistol grip stock and forearm; engraving.
Approximate wt.: 7 lbs.
Comments: Produced from the mid 1940's to the early 1970's.
Estimated Value: Excellent: $2,000.00
Very good: $1,500.00

Bernardelli Holland Deluxe

Bernardelli Holland Deluxe
Same as the Holland with engraved hunting scene.
Estimated Value: Excellent: $2,500.00
Very good: $1,900.00

Bernardelli St. Uberto

Gauge: 12, 16
Action: Box lock; top lever break-open; double triggers; hammerless
Magazine: None
Barrel: Double barrel; 26″ to 32″, any choke combination
Finish: Blued; checkered walnut straight or pistol grip stock and forearm
Approximate wt.: 7 lbs.
Comments: Made from the mid 1940's to present. Add 40% for automatic ejectors.
Estimated Value: New (retail): $795.00
　　　　　　　　　Excellent:　$595.00
　　　　　　　　　Very good:　$445.00

Bernardelli St. Uberto

Breda

Breda Autoloading

Breda Autoloading

Gauge: 12, 12 magnum
Action: Semi-automatic; hammerless
Magazine: 4-shot tubular
Barrel: 25½″ or 27½″
Finish: Blued; checkered walnut straight or pistol grip stock and forearm; available with ribbed barrel; engraving on grades 1, 2 and 3
Approximate wt.: 7¼ lbs.
Comments: Engraved models worth more, depending on grade and quality of engraving. Add 30% for magnum.
Estimated Value: Excellent:　$350.00
　　　　　　　　　Very good:　$275.00

Browning

Browning BT-99 Trap

Browning Superposed

Browning BT-99 Trap

Gauge: 12
Action: Top lever, break-open; automatic ejector; hammerless; single shot
Magazine: None
Barrel: 32″ or 34″ full, modified or improved modified choke; high post ventilated rib
Finish: Blued; wide rib; checkered walnut pistol grip stock and forearm, some with Monte Carlo stock; recoil pad; some engraving; Pigeon grade is satin grey steel with deep relief hand engraving.
Approximate wt.: 8 lbs.
Comments: Introduced in the early 1970's
Estimated Value: New (retail): $876.50
　　　　　　　　　Excellent:　$660.00
　　　　　　　　　Very good:　$490.00

Browning Superposed Field Grade

Gauge: 12; 20 added following World War II; 28 and 410 added in early 1960's
Action: Non-selective trigger; twin single triggers; selective trigger
Magazine: None
Barrel: Browning over and under double barrel; 26½″, 28″, 30″, 32″, choice of chokes; ventilated or matted rib
Finish: Blued; hand-checkered European walnut pistol grip stock and forearm; fluted comb; recoil pad; engraving
Approximate wt.: 6 to 8 lbs.
Comments: This gun first appeared in 1931 and has been made in a dozen different grades. More inlays and engraving is added on higher grades. Some expensive, highly decorative grades are currently produced. Belgium made until 1973. Add $500.00 for Grade I.
Estimated Value: Excellent:　$800.00 - $1,500.00
　　　　　　　　　Very good:　$650.00 - $1,200.00

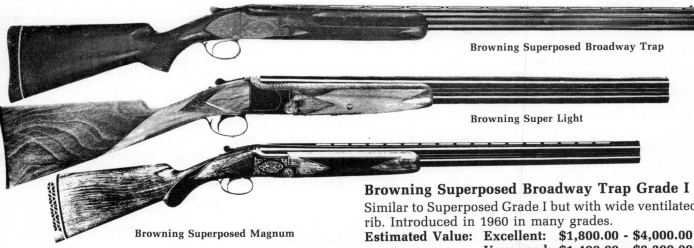

Browning Superposed Broadway Trap

Browning Super Light

Browning Superposed Magnum

Browning Super Light

Similar to Grade I Superposed except: lightweight; 26½″ barrel; straight grip stock. Introduced in the late 1960's in many grades.
Estimated Value: Excellent: $2,000.00 - $4,500.00
Very good: $1,500.00 - $3,500.00

Browning Superposed Broadway Trap Grade I

Similar to Superposed Grade I but with wide ventilated rib. Introduced in 1960 in many grades.
Estimated Value: Excellent: $1,800.00 - $4,000.00
Very good: $1,400.00 - $3,200.00

Browning Superposed Magnum Grade I

Same gun as the Superposed Grade I except chambered for 3″ magnum 12 gauge and with recoil pad.
Estimated Value: Excellent: $1,600.00 - $3,600.00
Very good: $1,200.00 - $2,800.00

Browning Citori Grade I

Browning Citori Grade I

Gauge: 12, 20, 28, 410; regular and magnum
Action: Top lever, break-open; hammerless; single selective trigger; automatic ejector
Magazine: None
Barrel: Over and under double barrel; 26″ or 28″, variety of choke combinations in 420, 28 or 20 gauge; 26″, 28″ or 30″ variety of choke combinations in 12 gauge; ventilated rib
Finish: Blued; checkered walnut stock and forearm; Hunting Model has pistol grip stock and beavertail forearm; Sporter has straight stock and lipped forearm; engraved receiver; high polish finish on Hunt- ing Model, oil finish on Sporter; Upland Special has straight stock.
Approximate wt.: 6½ to 7¾ lbs.
Comments: Similar to the Browning Superposed. Introduced in the early 1970's and currently produced. In 1982 a Superlight Model was added in 12 or 20 gauge with straight stock and scaled-down forearm. Add 3% for 410 or 28 gauge; 3% for Superlight; 4% for "Invector" choke tubes; 6% for Upland Special.
Estimated Value: New (retail): $836.50
Excellent: $625.00
Very good: $470.00

Browning Citori Grade II

Similar to the Citori Grade I with select walnut stock, satin gray receiver engraved with Canada Goose and Ringneck Pheasant scenes. Add 5% for 410 or 28 gauge.
Estimated Value: Excellent: $975.00
Very good: $730.00

Browning Citori Grade III

Similar to the Grade II with grey receiver, scroll engraving and mallards and ringnecks decoration; 20 gauge, 28 gauge and 410 bore have quail and grouse.
Estimated Value: New (retail): $1,185.00
Excellent: $ 890.00
Very good: $ 665.00

Browning Citori Grade V

Similar to the Citori Grade II with hand-checkered wood, hand-engraved receiver with Mallard Duck and Ringneck Pheasant scenes. Add 5% for 410 or 28 gauge; 3% for "Invector" choke tubes.
Estimated Value: Excellent: $1,475.00
Very good: $1,100.00

Browning Citori Grade VI

Similar to the Grade V Citori with grey or blued receiver, deep relief engraving, gold plating and engraving of ringneck pheasants, mallard drakes and English Setter.
Estimated Value: New (retail): $1,730.00
Excellent: $1,300.00
Very good: $ 975.00

Browning Citori Sideplate

Similar to the Citori Grade V in 20 gauge Sporter style only; 26″ improved cylinder & modified or modified & full choke; sideplates and receiver are decorated with etched upland game scenes of doves, Ruffed Grouse, quail, pointing dog; trigger guard tang is decorated and engraved. Introduced in 1981. Discontinued in 1984.
Estimated Value: Excellent: $1,475.00
Very good: $1,100.00

Browning Citori Trap

Browning Citori Skeet

Similar to the Citori with 26″ or 28″ skeet choke barrels; high post target rib. Add 50% for Grade II or Grade III decoration; 100% for Grade IV or Grade V.

Estimated Value: New (retail): $937.50
Excellent: $700.00
Very good: $525.00

Browning Citori Trap

A trap version of the Citori in 12 gauge only; high post target rib; 30″, 32″ or 34″ barrel; Monte Carlo stock. Add 50% for Grade II or Grade III decoration; 100% for Grade V or Grade VI.

Estimated Value: New (retail): $937.50
Excellent: $700.00
Very good: $525.00

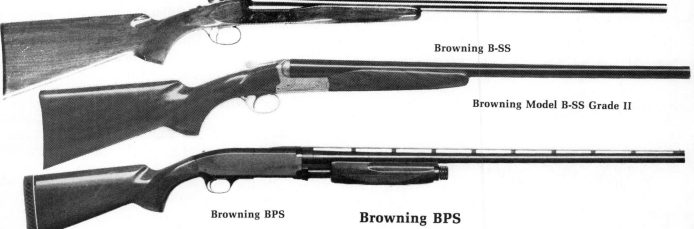

Browning B-SS

Browning Model B-SS Grade II

Browning BPS

Browning B-SS

Gauge: 12, 20
Action: Top lever, break-open; hammerless; automatic ejector
Magazine: None
Barrel: Double barrel; in 12 gauge, 30″ full & full or modified & full chokes; in 12 and 20 gauge, 28″ modified & full chokes; 26″ modified & full or improved cylinder & modified chokes
Finish: Blued; checkered walnut pistol grip stock and forearm
Approximate wt.: 7-7½ lbs.
Comments: Made from the early 1970's to present. Add 5% for barrel selector.

Estimated Value: New (retail): $775.00
Excellent: $580.00
Very good: $435.00

Browning Model B-SS Grade II

Similar to the B-SS with engraved satin grey frame featuring a pheasant, duck, quail and ducks. Discontinued 1984.

Estimated Value: Excellent: $850.00
Very good: $650.00

Browning B-SS Sidelock

Similar to the Model B-SS with sidelock action, engraved grey receiver, double triggers, small tapered forearm and straight grip stock.

Estimated Value: New (retail): $1,627.50
Excellent: $1,220.00
Very good: $ 915.00

Browning BPS

Gauge: 12, 20; 2¾″ or 3″
Action: Slide action; concealed hammer; bottom ejection
Magazine: 4-shot; 3-shot in magnum
Barrel: 26″ improved cylinder bore, 28″ modified choke, 30″ or 32″ full choke; ventilated rib; 20 gauge added in 1982 with variety of chokes; invector choke tubes available
Finish: Blued; checkered walnut pistol grip stock and forearm; trap model has Monte Carlo stock
Approximate wt.: 7½ lbs.
Comments: Produced since the late 1970's. Add 5% for Trap Model.

Estimated Value: New (retail): $385.95
Excellent: $290.00
Very good: $220.00

Browning BPS Upland Special

Similar to the BPS with a straight grip stock, 22″ barrel and "Invector" choke tubes. Introduced in 1984.

Estimated Value: New (retail): $385.95
Excellent: $290.00
Very good: $220.00

Browning BPS Buck Special

Similar to the BPS with a 24″ barrel for slugs, rifle sights. Add 5% for strap and swivels.

Estimated Value: Excellent: $300.00
Very good: $225.00

Browning BPS Youth and Ladies

Similar to the Model BPS in 20 gauge only with 22″ barrel, compact stock and recoil pad. Introduced in 1986.

Estimated Value: New (retail): $385.95
Excellent: $290.00
Very good: $220.00

Browning B.A.A.C. No. 1 Regular

Gauge: 12
Action: Semi-automatic, hammerless
Magazine: 4-shot
Barrel: 28″
Finish: Blued; walnut straight stock and grooved forearm
Approximate wt.: 7¾ lbs.
Comments: This gun was sold in the U.S. from 1902 to 1905. Made in Belgium.
Estimated Value: Excellent: $300.00
Very good: $230.00

Browning B.A.A.C. No. 2 Trap

Trap grade version of the No. 1 with some checkering.
Estimated Value: Excellent: $325.00
Very good: $250.00

Browning B.A.A.C. Two Shot

Similar to the No. 1 in 2 shot model.
Estimated Value: Excellent: $250.00
Very good: $200.00

Browning B.A.A.C. No. 0 Messenger

A short, 20″ barrel, version of the No. 1, made for bank guards, etc.
Estimated Value: Excellent: $260.00
Very good: $195.00

F.N. Browning Automatic

Similar to the B.A.A.C. No. 1 sold only overseas. Some models carried swivels for sling. Produced until Browning's American sales began in 1931.
Estimated Value: Excellent: $325.00
Very good: $275.00

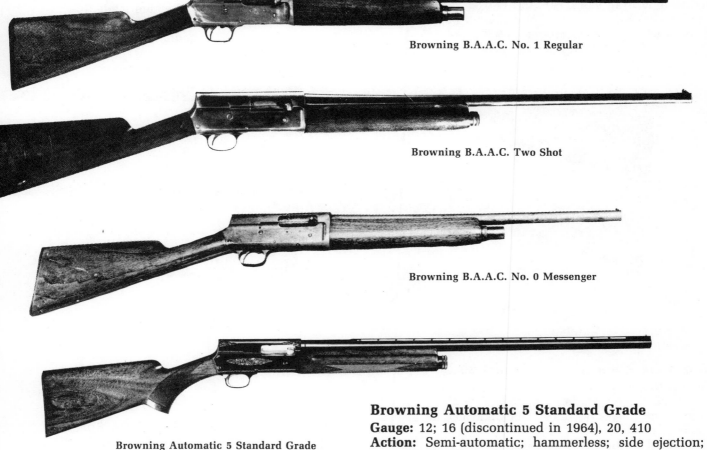

Browning B.A.A.C. No. 1 Regular

Browning B.A.A.C. Two Shot

Browning B.A.A.C. No. 0 Messenger

Browning Automatic 5 Standard Grade

Browning Automatic 5 Grades II, III, IV

Basically the same shotgun as the Standard Grade with engraving and improved quality on higher grades. Discontinued in the early 1940's. Add $25.00 for rib.

Estimated Value:	Gr. II	Gr. III	Gr. IV
Excellent:	$700.00	$850.00	$1,000.00
Very good:	$550.00	$600.00	$ 800.00

Browning Automatic 5 Standard Grade

Gauge: 12; 16 (discontinued in 1964), 20, 410
Action: Semi-automatic; hammerless; side ejection; recoiling barrel
Magazine: 4-shot, bottom load; 3-shot model also available
Barrel: 26″-32″ full choke, modified or cylinder bore; plain, raised matted rib or ventilated rib.
Finish: Blued; checkered walnut, pistol grip stock and forearm.
Approximate wt.: 7 to 8 lbs.
Comments: Made from about 1931 to 1973 in Belgium. Add 13% for ventilated rib.
Estimated Value: Excellent: $530.00
Very good: $460.00

Browning Automatic 5 Light 12

Browning Automatic 5 Light 20

Browning Automatic 5 Light 20

Basically the same as the Standard Grade except: 20 gauge only; a lightweight 26″ or 28″ barrel. Made from the late 1950's to present. Add 6% for "Invector" choke tubes; add 35% for Belgian made.

Estimated Value: New (retail): $559.95
Excellent: $420.00
Very good: $315.00

Browning Automatic 5 Trap

Basically the same as the Standard Grade except 12 gauge only; trap stock; 30″ full choke; ventilated rib; made in Belgium until 1971. Add 35% for Belgian made.

Estimated Value: Excellent: $550.00
Very good: $440.00

Browning Automatic 5 Light 12

Basically the same as the Standard Grade except 12 gauge only and light weight. Made from about 1948 to present. Add 6% for "Invector" choke tubes; add 35% for Belgian made.

Estimated Value: New (retail): $559.95
Excellent: $420.00
Very good: $315.00

Browning Automatic 5 Light Skeet

Similar to the Light 12 and Light 20 with 26″ or 28″ skeet choke barrel. Add 35% for Belgian made.

Estimated Value: Excellent: $420.00
Very good: $315.00

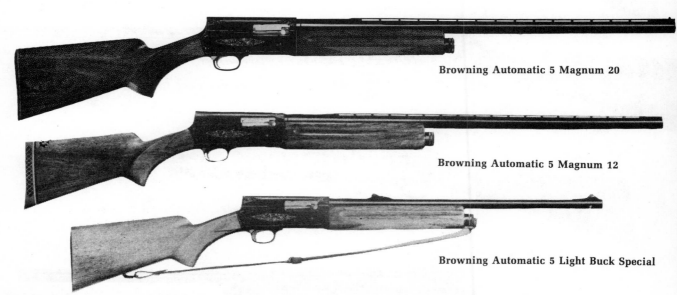

Browning Automatic 5 Magnum 20

Browning Automatic 5 Magnum 12

Browning Automatic 5 Light Buck Special

Browning Automatic 5 Magnum 20

Similar to the Standard Model except 20 gauge magnum; 26″ or 28″ barrel. Made from the late 1960's to present. Add 6% for "Invector" choke tubes; add 35% for Belgian made.

Estimated Value: New (retail): $569.95
Excellent: $425.00
Very good: $320.00

Browning Automatic 5 Magnum 12

Similar to the Standard Model except 12 gauge magnum, equipped with recoil pad. Made from the late 1950s to present. Also equipped with a 32″ full choke barrel. Add 6% for "Invector" choke tubes; add 35% for Belgian made.

Estimated Value: New (retail): $569.95
Excellent: $425.00
Very good: $320.00

Browning Automatic 5 Light Buck Special

Similar to the Standard Model, 12 or 20 gauge; special 24″ barrel choked and bored for slug. Made from the early 1960's to present. Add 4% for strap and swivels; add 35% for Belgian made.

Estimated Value: Excellent: $425.00
Very good: $320.00

Browning Automatic 5 Buck Special Magnum

Same as the Buck Special, for 3″ magnum shells, in 12 and 20 gauge. Add 4% for strap and swivels; add 35% for Belgian made.

Estimated Value: Excellent: $440.00
Very good: $330.00

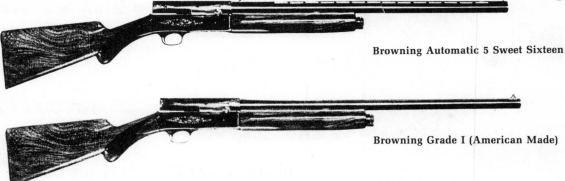

Browning Automatic 5 Sweet Sixteen

Browning Grade I (American Made)

Browning Automatic 5 Sweet Sixteen

A lightweight 16 gauge version of the Standard Model with a gold plated trigger. Made from about 1936 to 1975. Add 8% for ventilated rib. Made in Belgium.
Estimated Value: Excellent: $600.00
Very good: $475.00

Browning Grade I (American Made)

Similar to Browning Standard Grade. Made by Remington from 1940 until about 1948. World War II forced the closing of the F. N. plant in Belgium.
Estimated Value: Excellent: $275.00
Very good: $225.00

Browning Special (American Made)

Similar to Grade I with a matted or ventilated rib.
Estimated Value: Excellent: $325.00
Very good: $275.00

Browning Special Skeet (American Made)

Same as the Grade I with a Cutts Compensator.
Estimated Value: Excellent: $280.00
Very good: $230.00

Browning Utility (American Made)

Similar to Grade I with Poly Choke.
Estimated Value: Excellent: $260.00
Very good: $220.00

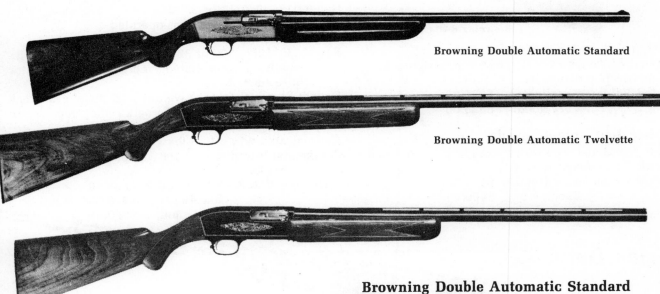

Browning Double Automatic Standard

Browning Double Automatic Twelvette

Browning Double Automatic Twentyweight

Browning Double Automatic Twelvette

Basically the same as the Standard with lightweight aluminum receiver. Made until the early 1970's.
Estimated Value: Excellent: $340.00
Very good: $255.00

Browning Double Automatic Twentyweight

A still lighter version of the Standard with 26½″ barrel. Made until the early 1970's.
Estimated Value: Excellent: $375.00
Very good: $280.00

Browning Double Automatic Standard

Gauge: 12
Action: Semi-automatic, short recoil, side ejection; hammerless; 2 shot
Magazine: 1-shot
Barrel: 30″ or 28″ full choke; 28″ or 26″ modified choke; 28″ or 26″ skeet; 26″ cylinder bore or improved cylinder
Finish: Blued; checkered walnut pistol grip stock and forearm
Approximate wt.: 7¾ lbs.
Comments: Made from the mid 1950's to the early 1960's. Add 8% for ventilated rib.
Estimated Value: Excellent: $350.00
Very good: $265.00

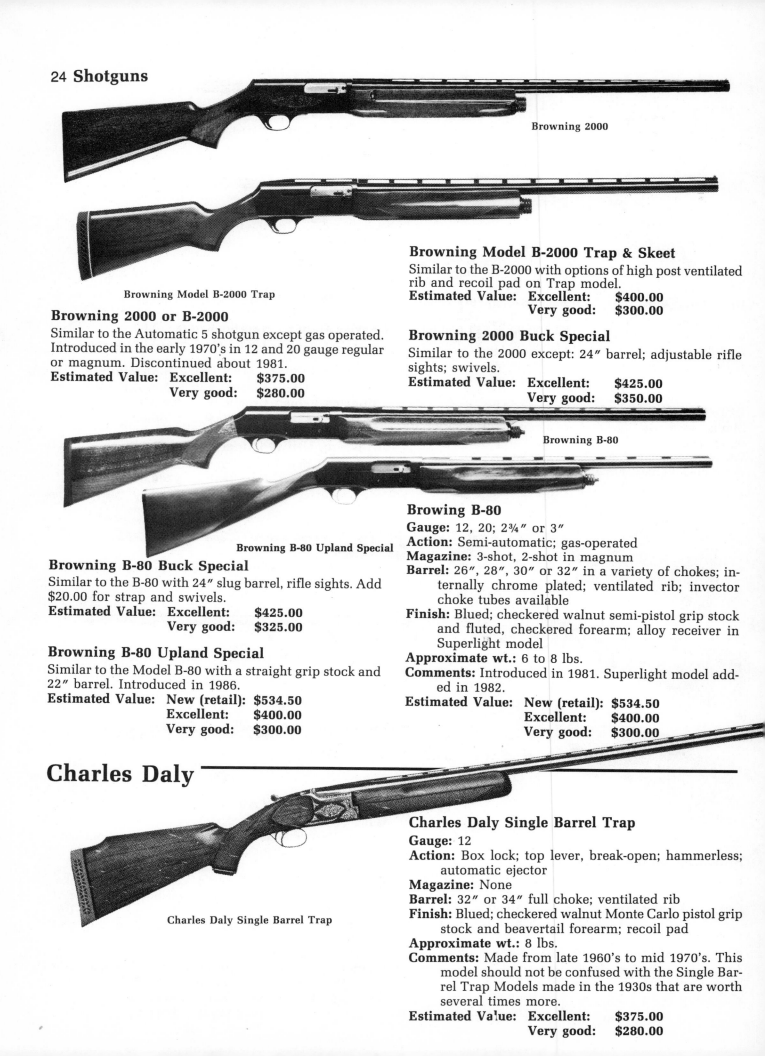

Browning 2000

Browning Model B-2000 Trap

Browning 2000 or B-2000

Similar to the Automatic 5 shotgun except gas operated. Introduced in the early 1970's in 12 and 20 gauge regular or magnum. Discontinued about 1981.
Estimated Value: Excellent: $375.00
Very good: $280.00

Browning Model B-2000 Trap & Skeet

Similar to the B-2000 with options of high post ventilated rib and recoil pad on Trap model.
Estimated Value: Excellent: $400.00
Very good: $300.00

Browning 2000 Buck Special

Similar to the 2000 except: 24″ barrel; adjustable rifle sights; swivels.
Estimated Value: Excellent: $425.00
Very good: $350.00

Browning B-80

Browning B-80 Upland Special

Browning B-80 Buck Special

Similar to the B-80 with 24″ slug barrel, rifle sights. Add $20.00 for strap and swivels.
Estimated Value: Excellent: $425.00
Very good: $325.00

Browning B-80 Upland Special

Similar to the Model B-80 with a straight grip stock and 22″ barrel. Introduced in 1986.
Estimated Value: New (retail): $534.50
Excellent: $400.00
Very good: $300.00

Browing B-80

Gauge: 12, 20; 2¾″ or 3″
Action: Semi-automatic; gas-operated
Magazine: 3-shot, 2-shot in magnum
Barrel: 26″, 28″, 30″ or 32″ in a variety of chokes; internally chrome plated; ventilated rib; invector choke tubes available
Finish: Blued; checkered walnut semi-pistol grip stock and fluted, checkered forearm; alloy receiver in Superlight model
Approximate wt.: 6 to 8 lbs.
Comments: Introduced in 1981. Superlight model added in 1982.
Estimated Value: New (retail): $534.50
Excellent: $400.00
Very good: $300.00

Charles Daly

Charles Daly Single Barrel Trap

Charles Daly Single Barrel Trap

Gauge: 12
Action: Box lock; top lever, break-open; hammerless; automatic ejector
Magazine: None
Barrel: 32″ or 34″ full choke; ventilated rib
Finish: Blued; checkered walnut Monte Carlo pistol grip stock and beavertail forearm; recoil pad
Approximate wt.: 8 lbs.
Comments: Made from late 1960's to mid 1970's. This model should not be confused with the Single Barrel Trap Models made in the 1930s that are worth several times more.
Estimated Value: Excellent: $375.00
Very good: $280.00

Charles Daly Hammerless Double

Gauge: 10, 12, 16, 20, 28, 410
Action: Box lock; top lever, break-open; hammerless; automatic ejector (except Superior)
Magazine: None
Barrel: Double barrel; 26″, 28″, 30″, 32″; choice of choke combinations
Finish: Blued; checkered walnut pistol grip stock and short tapered forearm; engraving
Approximate wt.: 4 to 8 lbs.
Comments: Manufactured in differing grades, alike except for quality of finish and amount of engraving. Made from 1920 to 1935.

Estimated Value:	Excellent	Very Good
Diamond	$3,000.00	$2,250.00
Empire	$2,200.00	$1,650.00
Superior	$1,500.00	$1,150.00

Charles Daly Commander 100

Gauge: 12, 16, 20, 28, 410
Action: Box lock; top lever, break-open; hammerless; automatic ejector
Magazine: None
Barrel: Over and under double barrel; 26″, 28″, 30″ improved cylinder & modified or modified & full chokes
Finish: Blued; checkered walnut straight or pistol grip stock and forearm; engraved
Approximate wt.: 5 to 7½ lbs.
Comments: Made from the mid 1930's to about 1939.
Estimated Value: Excellent: $600.00
Very good: $450.00

Charles Daly Commander 200

This is a fancier version of the Commander 100 with select wood, more engraving and a higher quality finish.
Estimated Value: Excellent: $700.00
Very good: $525.00

Charles Daly Field Grade

Charles Daly Superior Grade

Charles Daly Diamond Grade

Charles Daly Diamond Grade

Similar to the Superior with select wood and fancier engraving.
Estimated Value: Excellent: $650.00
Very good: $490.00

Charles Daly Superior Grade

Similar to the Field Grade but not chambered for magnum.
Estimated Value: Excellent: $575.00
Very good: $430.00

Charles Daly Field Grade

Gauge: 12, 20, 28, 410, 12 magnum, 20 magnum
Action: Box lock; top lever, break-open; hammerless; single trigger.
Magazine: None
Barrel: Over & under double barrel; 26″, 28″, 30″, various choke combinations; ventilated rib.
Finish: Blued; engraved; checkered walnut, pistol grip stock & forearm; 12 gauge magnum has recoil pad.
Approximate wt.: 6 to 8 lbs.
Comments: Manufactured since the early 1960's.
Estimated Value: Excellent: $550.00
Very good: $410.00

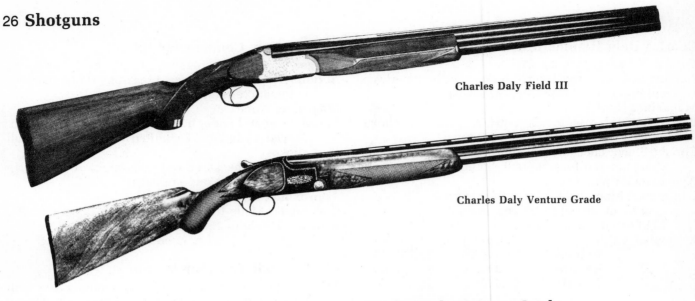

Charles Daly Field III

Charles Daly Venture Grade

Charles Daly Field III
Similar to the Field Grade with some minor changes; double trigger. Currently available.
Estimated Value: New (retail): $450.00
Excellent: $337.00
Very good: $255.00

Charles Daly Superior II
Similar to the Field III but higher quality. Currently available.
Estimated Value: New (retail): $624.00
Excellent: $470.00
Very good: $350.00

Charles Daly Venture Grade
Gauge: 12, 20
Action: Box lock; top lever, break-open; hammerless; automatic ejector
Magazine: None
Barrel: Over and under double barrel; 26″, 28″, 30″, various chokes; ventilated rib
Finish: Blued; checkered walnut pistol grip stock and forearm
Approximate wt.: 7 to 8 lbs.
Comments: Made since the early 1970's to mid 1980's. Add $25.00 for Skeet model; $35.00 for Trap model.
Estimated Value: Excellent: $400.00
Very good: $300.00

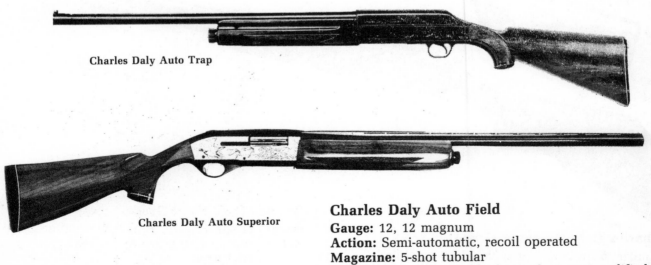

Charles Daly Auto Trap

Charles Daly Auto Superior

Charles Daly Auto Field
Gauge: 12, 12 magnum
Action: Semi-automatic, recoil operated
Magazine: 5-shot tubular
Barrel: 26″ improved cylinder or skeet, 28″ modified or full, 30″ full, chokes; ventilated rib
Finish: Blued; checkered walnut pistol grip stock and forearm
Approximate wt.: about 7½ lbs.
Comments: Made from the mid 1970's to present.
Estimated Value: New (retail): $386.00
Excellent: $290.00
Very good: $215.00

Charles Daly Auto Superior
Similar to the Auto Field but higher quality.
Estimated Value: Excellent: $300.00
Very good: $225.00

Cogswell & Harrison

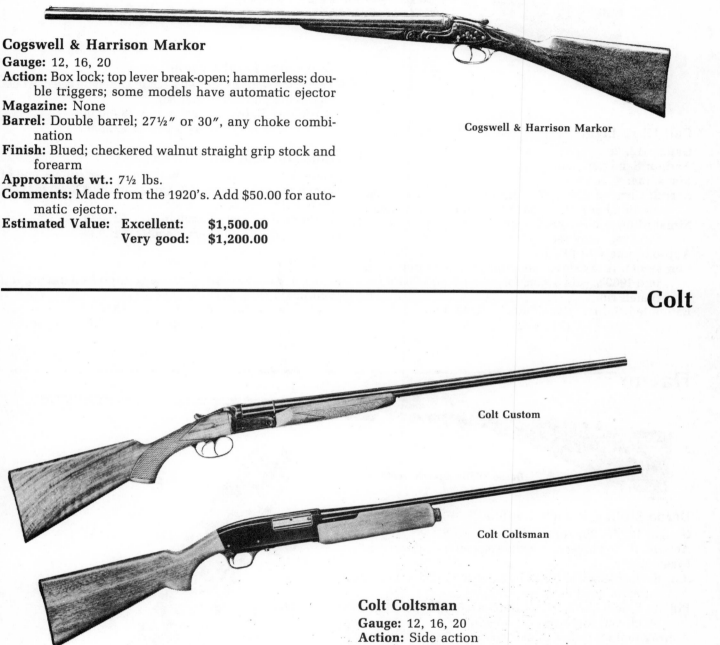

Cogswell & Harrison Markor

Gauge: 12, 16, 20
Action: Box lock; top lever break-open; hammerless; double triggers; some models have automatic ejector
Magazine: None
Barrel: Double barrel; 27½″ or 30″, any choke combination
Finish: Blued; checkered walnut straight grip stock and forearm
Approximate wt.: 7½ lbs.
Comments: Made from the 1920's. Add $50.00 for automatic ejector.
Estimated Value: Excellent: $1,500.00
                 Very good: $1,200.00

Cogswell & Harrison Markor

Colt

Colt Custom

Colt Coltsman

Colt Coltsman

Gauge: 12, 16, 20
Action: Side action
Magazine: 4-shot
Barrel: 26″ improved, 28″ modified, 30″ full chokes
Finish: Blued; plain walnut pistol grip stock and slide handle
Approximate wt.: 6½ to 7 lbs.
Comments: Made from the early to mid 1960's in takedown models.
Estimated Value: Excellent: $190.00
                 Very good: $140.00

Colt Coltsman Custom

A fancier version of the Coltsman with checkering and a ventilated rib.
Estimated Value: Excellent: $225.00
                 Very good: $170.00

Colt Custom

Gauge: 12, 16
Action: Box lock; top lever, break-open; hammerless; double trigger; automatic ejector
Magazine: None
Barrel: Double barrel; 26″ improved & modified, 28″ modified & full or 30″ full chokes
Finish: Blued; checkered walnut pistol grip stock and tapered forearm
Approximate wt.: 7 to 8 lbs.
Comments: Produced in the early 1960's.
Estimated Value: Excellent: $375.00
                 Very good: $280.00

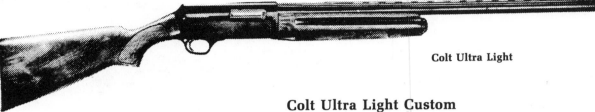

Colt Ultra Light

Colt Ultra Light

Gauge: 12, 20
Action: Semi-automatic
Magazine: 4-shot
Barrel: Chrome lined, 26″ improved or modified, 28″ modified or full, 30″, 32″ full chokes; rib available
Finish: Blued; checkered walnut pistol grip stock and forearm; alloy receiver
Approximate wt.: 6½ lbs.
Comments: A takedown shotgun produced during the mid 1960's. Add $15.00 for solid rib; $25.00 for ventilated rib.
Estimated Value: Excellent: $240.00
Very good: $180.00

Colt Ultra Light Custom

This is the same as the Ultra Light Auto with select wood, engraving and ventilated rib.
Estimated Value: Excellent: $300.00
Very good: $225.00

Colt Magnum Auto

Same as the Ultra Light Auto in magnum gauges and of heavier weight. Add $15.00 for solid rib; $25.00 for ventilated rib.
Estimated Value: Excellent: $250.00
Very good: $190.00

Colt Magnum Auto Custom

Same as Magnum Auto with select wood, engraving and ventilated rib.
Estimated Value: Excellent: $310.00
Very good: $230.00

Darne

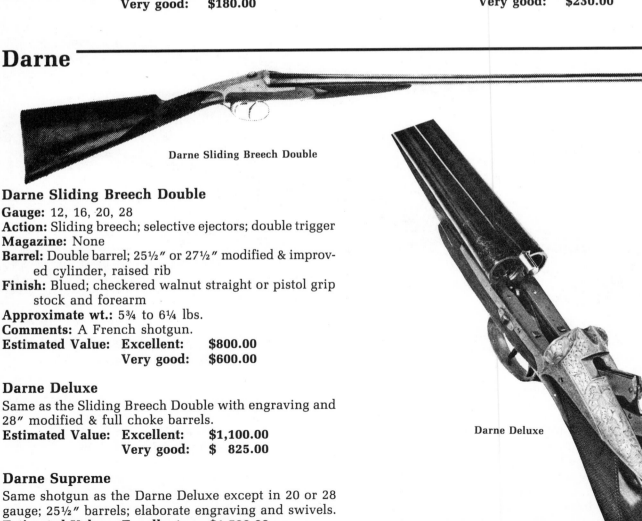

Darne Sliding Breech Double

Darne Sliding Breech Double

Gauge: 12, 16, 20, 28
Action: Sliding breech; selective ejectors; double trigger
Magazine: None
Barrel: Double barrel; 25½″ or 27½″ modified & improved cylinder, raised rib
Finish: Blued; checkered walnut straight or pistol grip stock and forearm
Approximate wt.: 5¾ to 6¼ lbs.
Comments: A French shotgun.
Estimated Value: Excellent: $800.00
Very good: $600.00

Darne Deluxe

Same as the Sliding Breech Double with engraving and 28″ modified & full choke barrels.
Estimated Value: Excellent: $1,100.00
Very good: $ 825.00

Darne Deluxe

Darne Supreme

Same shotgun as the Darne Deluxe except in 20 or 28 gauge; 25½″ barrels; elaborate engraving and swivels.
Estimated Value: Excellent: $1,500.00
Very good: $1,200.00

Davidson

Davidson Model 69SL

Davidson Model 73 Stagecoach
Gauge: 12, 20 magnum
Action: Box lock; top lever break-open; exposed hammers
Magazine: None
Barrel: Double barrel; 20″ improved cylinder & modified or modified & full chokes; matted rib
Finish: Blued; checkered walnut pistol grip stock and forearm; sights; engraved receiver
Approximate wt.: 7 lbs.
Comments: Made from early to late 1970's.
Estimated Value: Excellent: $200.00
Very good: $150.00

Davidson Model 69 SL
Gauge: 12, 20
Action: Side lock
Magazine: None
Barrel: Double barrel; 26″-30″, variety of chokes
Finish: Blued or nickel; checkered walnut pistol grip stock and forearm; gold trigger; bead sights; engraved
Approximate wt.: 6 to 7 lbs.
Comments: Made from early 1960's to late 1970's.
Estimated Value: Excellent: $210.00
Very good: $155.00

Davidson Model 63B

Davidson Model 63B
Gauge: 12, 16, 20, 28, 410
Action: Box lock; top lever break-open; double triggers
Magazine: None
Barrel: Double barrel; 26″, 28″; 25″ in 410; 30″ in 12 gauge; improved cylinder & modified, modified & full, full & full chokes
Finish: Blued or nickel; checkered walnut pistol grip stock and forearm; bead sights; some engraving
Approximate wt.: 6 to 7 lbs.
Comments: Produced in Spain
Estimated Value: Excellent: $185.00
Very good: $145.00

Davidson Model 63B Magnum

Davidson Model 63B Magnum
Same as Model 63B in 10, 12, or 20 gauge magnum. Available with 32″ barrel in 10 gauge.
Estimated Value: Excellent: $240.00
Very good: $190.00

Fox

Fox Trap (Single Barrel)
Gauge: 12
Action: Box lock; top lever break-open; hammerless; automatic ejector; single shot
Magazine: None
Barrel: 30″, 32″ trap bore; ventilated rib
Finish: Blued; checkered walnut half or full pistol grip stock and large forearm; some with recoil pad; decorated receiver; after 1931 Monte Carlo stock. Grades differ in quality of craftsmanship and decoration. ME Grade was made to order with inlaid gold and finest walnut wood.
Approximate wt.: 7 to 8 lbs.
Comments: Made until the early 1940's. Prices for grades made before 1932 are about 20% less.

Fox Trap (Single Barrel)

Estimated Value:	Grade	Excellent	Very Good
	JE	$1,600.00	$1,200.00
	KE	$2,000.00	$1,400.00
	LE	$2,500.00	$1,800.00
	ME	$5,500.00	$4,000.00

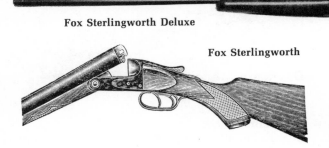

Fox Sterlingworth Deluxe

Fox Sterlingworth

Fox Sterlingworth

Gauge: 12, 16, 20
Action: Box lock; top lever break-open; hammerless; double trigger or selective single trigger; some with automatic ejector
Magazine: None
Barrel: Double barrel; 26″-30″; full & full, modified & full, cylinder & modified chokes
Finish: Blued; checkered walnut pistol grip stock and forearm
Approximate wt.: 5¾ to 8 lbs.
Comments: Made until the early 1940's. Add $50.00 for selective single trigger; $75.00 for automatic ejector.
Estimated Value: Excellent: $500.00
Very good: $375.00

Fox Sterlingworth Deluxe

This is a fancy model Sterlingworth with ivory bead; recoil pad; 32″ barrels; selective single trigger. Add $75.00 for automatic ejector.
Estimated Value: Excellent: $575.00
Very good: $430.00

Fox Sterlingworth Skeet

Basically the same as the Sterlingworth with skeet bore; 26″ or 28″ barrels; straight grip stock. Add $75.00 for automatic ejector.
Estimated Value: Excellent: $550.00
Very good: $410.00

Fox Skeeter

Similar to Sterlingworth with 28″ skeet bored barrels; ventilated rib; ivory bead; recoil pad, 12 or 20 gauge; automatic ejector.
Estimated Value: Excellent: $1,000.00
Very good: $ 750.00

Fox Model B

Fox Hammerless Doubles

These are very similar to the Sterlingworth models, in varying degrees of increased quality. All have automatic ejectors except Grade A. Add $50.00 for selective single trigger; $125.00 for ventilated rib.

Estimated Value:	Grade	Excellent	Very Good
	A	$ 700.00	$ 525.00
	AE	$ 800.00	$ 600.00
	BE	$ 900.00	$ 650.00
	CE	$1,200.00	$ 875.00
	DE	$2,000.00	$1,500.00
	FE	$5,000.00	$3,750.00

Fox Super Fox

Gauge: 12
Action: Box lock; top lever break-open; hammerless; double trigger; automatic ejector
Magazine: None
Barrel: Double barrel; 30″ or 32″ full choke
Finish: Blued; checkered walnut pistol grip stock and forearm
Approximate wt.: 7¾ to 9¾ lbs.
Comments: This is a long range gun produced from the mid 1920's to early 1940's.
Estimated Value: Excellent: $500.00
Very good: $400.00

Fox Model B, BE

Gauge: 12, 16, 20, 410
Action: Box lock; top lever break-open; hammerless; double triggers; plain extractor
Magazine: None
Barrel: Double barrel; 24″-30″ full & full, modified & full, cylinder & modified chokes; ventilated rib
Finish: Blued; checkered walnut pistol grip stock and forearm; case hardened receiver on current model
Approximate wt.: 7½ lbs.
Comments: Made from the early 1940's to present. 16 gauge discontinued in late 1970's. Model BE has automatic ejector.
Estimated Value: New (retail): $369.00
Excellent: $275.00
Very good: $210.00

Fox Model B Lightweight

Same as the Model B with 24″ cylinder bore and modified choke barrels in 12 and 20 gauge.
Estimated Value: Excellent: $250.00
Very good: $200.00

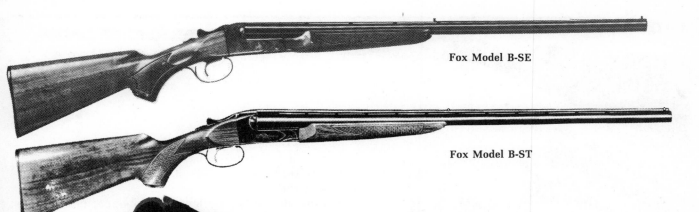

Fox Model B-SE

Fox Model B-ST

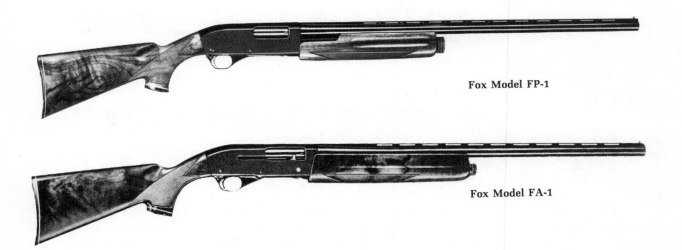

Fox Model BDL

Fox Model B-DL & B-DE
Similar to the B-ST with chrome frame and beavertail forearm. Made from the early 1960's to early 1970's.
Estimated Value: **Excellent:**   **$350.00**
                        Very good: **$275.00**

Fox Model B-SE
Basically the same as the Model B with automatic ejectors and a single trigger. In production from 1968 to the present.
Estimated Value: **New (retail):**   **$467.06**
                    Excellent: **$350.00**
                    Very good: **$260.00**

Fox Model B-ST
This is the same as Model B with gold plated nonselective single trigger. Made from the mid 1950's to mid 1960's.
Estimated Value: **Excellent:**   **$325.00**
                        Very good: **$250.00**

Fox Model FP-1

Fox Model FA-1

Fox Model FP-1
Gauge: 12; 2¾″ or 3″
Action: Slide action, hammerless
Magazine: 4-shot tubular; 3-shot with 3″ shells
Barrel: 28″ modified, 30″ full choke; ventilated rib
Finish: Blued; checkered walnut pistol grip stock and slide handle; rosewood cap with inlay
Approximate wt.: 7¼ lbs.
Comments: Produced from 1981 to 1983
Estimated Value: **Excellent:**   **$260.00**
                        Very good: **$200.00**

Fox Model FA-1
Gauge: 12; 2¾″
Action: Semi-automatic, gas operated
Magazine: 3-shot tubular
Barrel: 28″ modified; 30″ full choke; ventilated rib
Finish: Blued; checkered walnut pistol grip stock and forearm; rosewood cap with inlay
Approximate wt.: 7½ lbs.
Comments: Produced from 1981 to 1983.
Estimated Value: **Excellent:**   **$285.00**
                        Very good: **$220.00**

Franchi

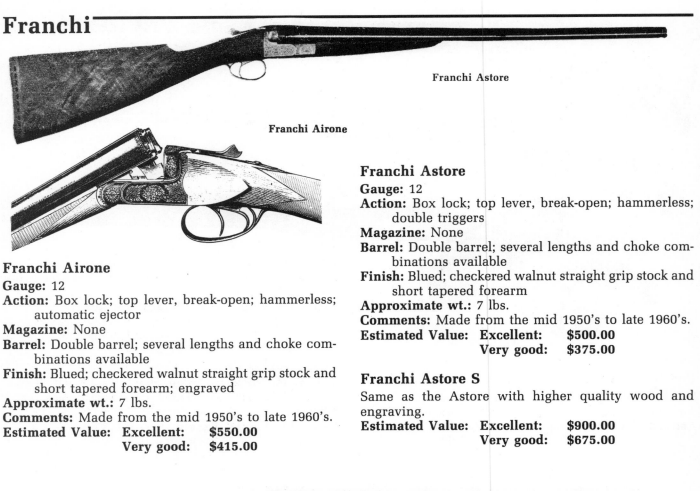

Franchi Astore

Franchi Airone

Franchi Airone

Gauge: 12
Action: Box lock; top lever, break-open; hammerless; automatic ejector
Magazine: None
Barrel: Double barrel; several lengths and choke combinations available
Finish: Blued; checkered walnut straight grip stock and short tapered forearm; engraved
Approximate wt.: 7 lbs.
Comments: Made from the mid 1950's to late 1960's.
Estimated Value: **Excellent:** **$550.00**
Very good: **$415.00**

Franchi Astore

Gauge: 12
Action: Box lock; top lever, break-open; hammerless; double triggers
Magazine: None
Barrel: Double barrel; several lengths and choke combinations available
Finish: Blued; checkered walnut straight grip stock and short tapered forearm
Approximate wt.: 7 lbs.
Comments: Made from the mid 1950's to late 1960's.
Estimated Value: **Excellent:** **$500.00**
Very good: **$375.00**

Franchi Astore S

Same as the Astore with higher quality wood and engraving.
Estimated Value: **Excellent:** **$900.00**
Very good: **$675.00**

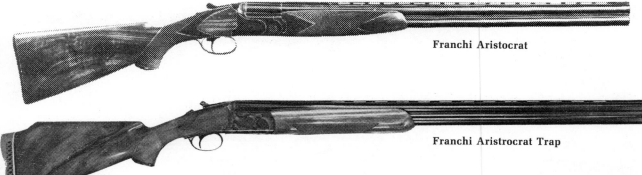

Franchi Aristocrat

Franchi Aristrocrat Trap

Franchi Aristocrat

Gauge: 12
Action: Box lock; top lever, break-open; hammerless; automatic ejector; single trigger
Magazine: None
Barrel: Over and under double barrel; 24″ cylinder bore & improved cylinder; 26″ improved cylinder & modified, 28″, 30″ modified & full chokes; ventilated rib
Finish: Blued; checkered walnut pistol grip stock and forearm; engraved
Approximate wt.: 7 lbs.
Comments: Made from the early to late 1960's.
Estimated Value: **Excellent:** **$525.00**
Very good: **$390.00**

Franchi Aristocrat Trap

Similar to the Aristocrat with Monte Carlo stock; chrome lined barrels; case hardened receiver; 30″ barrels only.
Estimated Value: **Excellent:** **$540.00**
Very good: **$400.00**

Franchi Aristocrat Skeet

Same as the Aristocrat Trap with 26″ skeet barrels.
Estimated Value: **Excellent:** **$550.00**
Very good: **$410.00**

Franchi Aristocrat Silver King

Similar to the Aristocrat with higher quality finish; select wood; engraving.
Estimated Value: **Excellent:** **$625.00**
Very good: **$460.00**

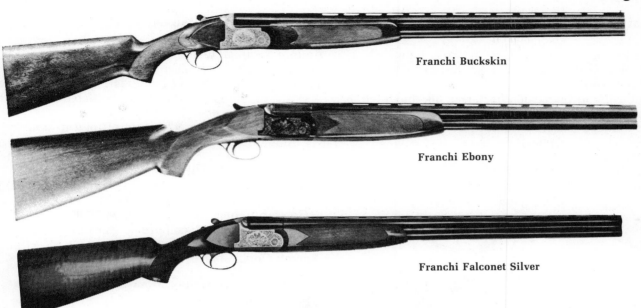

Franchi Buckskin

Franchi Ebony

Franchi Falconet Silver

Franchi Falconet Buckskin & Ebony

Gauge: 12, 20
Action: Box lock; top lever, break-open; hammerless
Magazine: None
Barrel: Over and under double barrel; 24″-30″ barrels in several choke combinations; ventilated rib; chrome lined
Finish: Blued; colored frame with engraving; epoxy finished checkered walnut pistol grip stock and forearm
Approximate wt.: 6-7 lbs.
Comments: Made from about 1970 to late 1970's. Buckskin and Ebony differ only in color of receiver and engraving.
Estimated Value: **Excellent:** **$545.00**
              Very good: **$410.00**

Franchi Falconet Silver

Same as the Buckskin and Ebony except: 12 gauge only; pickled silver receiver.
Estimated Value: **Excellent:** **$575.00**
              Very good: **$430.00**

Franchi Falconet Super

Similar to the Falconet Silver except slightly different forearm; 12 gauge only; 27″ or 28″ barrels. Currently manufactured.
Estimated Value: **Excellent:** **$650.00**
              Very good: **$485.00**

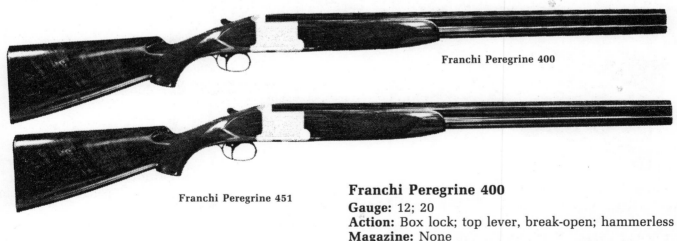

Franchi Peregrine 400

Franchi Peregrine 451

Franchi Peregrine 400

Gauge: 12; 20
Action: Box lock; top lever, break-open; hammerless
Magazine: None
Barrel: Over and under double barrel; 26½″, 28″ in various chokes; chrome lined; ventilated rib
Finish: Blued; checkered walnut pistol grip stock and forearm
Approximate wt.: 7 lbs.
Comments: Made from the mid to late 1970's.
Estimated Value: **Excellent:** **$425.00**
              Very good: **$320.00**

Franchi Peregrine 451

Similar to the 400 except: alloy receiver; light weight.
Estimated Value: **Excellent:** **$475.00**
              Very good: **$365.00**

Franchi Diamond

Gauge: 12
Action: Box lock; top lever, break-open; hammerless; single selective trigger; automatic extractors
Magazine: None
Barrel: Over and under double barrel; 28″ modified & full choke; ventilated rib
Finish: Blued; checkered walnut pistol grip stock and forearm; silver plated receiver
Approximate wt.: 6¾ lbs.
Comments: Currently produced.
Estimated Value: Excellent: $640.00
                  Very good: $480.00

Franchi Standard Model, 48AL

Gauge: 12, 20, 28
Action: Semi-automatic; recoil operated
Magazine: 5-shot tubular
Barrel: 24″, 26″ improved cylinder, modified or skeet, 28″ modified or full chokes; ventilated rib on some models; chrome lined
Finish: Blued; checkered walnut pistol grip stock with fluted forearm
Approximate wt.: 5 to 6¼ lbs. One of the lightest autoloaders available.
Comments: Manufactured in Italy from about 1950 to present; 28 gauge discontinued.
Estimated Value: New (retail): $375.95
                  Excellent: $285.00
                  Very good: $210.00

Franchi Standard Model

Franchi Slug Gun

Franchi Standard Magnum

Franchi Hunter

Franchi Hunter Magnum

Franchi Hunter, 48AL

Similar to the Standard Model; 12 or 20 gauge; higher quality wood; engraving; ventilated rib.
Estimated Value: New (retail): $395.00
                  Excellent: $300.00
                  Very good: $225.00

Franchi Hunter Magnum

Same as the Hunter with recoil pad and chambered for magnum shells.
Estimated Value: Excellent: $325.00
                  Very good: $250.00

Franchi Standard Magnum, 48AL

Similar to the Standard with recoil pad; chambered for magnum shells; 12 or 20 gauge.
Estimated Value: New (retail): $395.00
                  Excellent: $300.00
                  Very good: $250.00

Franchi Slug Gun, 48AL

Similar to the Standard Model with a 22″ cylinder bore barrel; sights; swivels; alloy receiver. Made from the mid 1950's to early 1980's; 12 or 20 gauge.
Estimated Value: Excellent: $300.00
                  Very good: $230.00

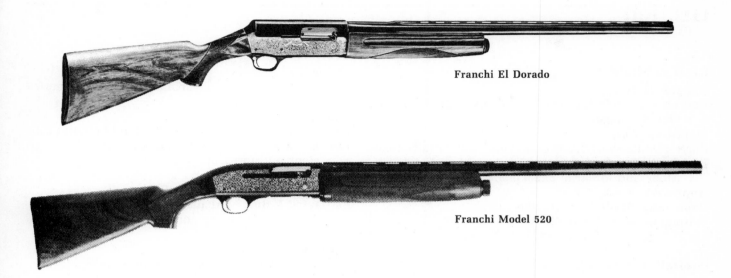

Franchi El Dorado

Franchi Model 520

Franchi Eldorado

Similar to the Standard Model with heavy engraving; select wood; gold trigger; ventilated rib.
Estimated Value: **Excellent:** **$400.00**
Very good: **$300.00**

Franchi Model 500

Similar to the Standard except: gas operated; 12 gauge only; made for fast takedown.
Estimated Value: **Excellent:** **$300.00**
Very good: **$225.00**

Franchi Model 520

Similar to the Model 500 with deluxe features.
Estimated Value: **Excellent:** **$350.00**
Very good: **$280.00**

Franchi Model 530 Trap

Similar to the Model 520 with Monte Carlo stock; high ventilated rib; 3 interchangeable choke tubes.
Estimated Value: **Excellent:** **$525.00**
Very good: **$400.00**

Greener

Greener Empire

Gauge: 12 or 12 magnum
Action: Box lock; top lever, break-open; hammerless
Magazine: None
Barrel: Double barrel; 28″, 30″, 32″, any choke
Finish: Blued; checkered walnut straight or semi-pistol grip stock and forearm
Approximate wt.: 7½ lbs.
Comments: Made from before 1900 until the mid 1960's.
Estimated Value: **Excellent:** **$1,200.00**
Very good: **$ 900.00**

Greener Empire Deluxe

Same as the Empire Model only fancier.
Estimated Value: **Excellent:** **$1,500.00**
Very good: **$1,225.00**

Greener Empire

Greener General Purpose

Gauge: 12
Action: Martini action; single shot
Magazine: None
Barrel: 26″, 30″, 32″ modifed or full choke
Finish: Blued; checkered walnut straight grip stock and forearm.
Approximate wt.: 6 to 7 lbs.
Comments: Made from the early 1900s to the early 1960s.
Estimated Value: **Excellent:** **$275.00**
Very good: **$210.00**

Greifelt

Greifelt Model 22

Gauge: 12, 16
Action: Box lock; top lever, break-open; hammerless; double trigger
Magazine: None
Barrel: Double barrel; 28″ or 30″ modified or full choke
Finish: Blued; checkered walnut straight or pistol grip stock and forearm; cheekpiece
Approximate wt.: 7 lbs.
Comments: Made from the late 1940's.
Estimated Value: Excellent: $1,175.00
Very good: $ 885.00

Greifelt Model 22E

Same as Model 22 with automatic ejector
Estimated Value: Excellent: $1,250.00
Very good: $ 950.00

Greifelt Model 103

Gauge: 12, 16
Action: Box lock; top lever, break-open; hammerless; double triggers
Magazine: None
Barrel: Double barrel; 28″ or 30″ modified and full
Finish: Blued; checkered walnut straight or pistol grip stock and forearm; cheekpiece
Approximate wt.: 7 lbs.
Comments: Made from late 1940's.
Estimated Value: Excellent: $1,125.00
Very good: $ 850.00

Greifelt Model 103E

Same as Model 103 with automatic ejector.
Estimated Value: Excellent: $1,200.00
Very good: $ 900.00

Greifelt Model 22

Harrington & Richardson

Harrington & Richardson No. 3

Gauge: 12, 16, 20, 410
Action: Box lock; top lever, break-open; hammerless; single shot; automatic extractors
Magazine: None
Barrel: 26″-32″ full choke
Finish: Blued; walnut semi-pistol grip stock and tapered forearm
Approximate wt.: 5½ to 6½ lbs.
Comments: Made from about 1908 intil World War II.
Estimated Value: Excellent: $60.00
Very good: $50.00

Harrington & Richardson No. 5

Gauge: 20, 28, 410
Action: Box lock; top lever, break-open; exposed hammer; single shot; automatic extractors
Magazine: None
Barrel: 26″, 28″ full choke
Finish: Blued; walnut semi-pistol grip stock and tapered forearm
Approximate wt.: 4½ lbs.
Comments: Made from about 1908 until World War II.
Estimated Value: Excellent: $60.00
Very good: $50.00

Harrington & Richardson No. 3

Harrington & Richardson No. 5

Harrington & Richardson No. 6

Harrington & Richardson No. 6

Similar to the No. 5 in 10, 12, 16 and 20 gauge; heavier design and barrel lengths of 28″-36″. Weighs 5 to 8 lbs.
Estimated Value: Excellent: $65.00
Very good: $55.00

Harrington & Richardson No. 8

Similar to the No. 6 with different style forearm and in 12, 16, 20, 24, 28 and 410 gauges.

Estimated Value: Excellent: $65.00
Very good: $55.00

Harrington & Richardson No. 8

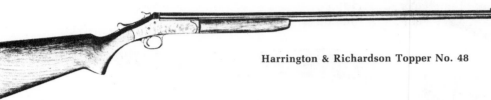

Harrington & Richardson No. 7

Harrington & Richardson No. 7 or No. 9

Similar to the No. 8 with smaller forearm and more rounded pistol grip. Not available in 24 gauge.

Estimated Value: Excellent: $60.00
Very good: $50.00

Harrington & Richardson Topper No. 48

Harrington & Richardson Topper No. 48

Similar to the No. 8. Made from the mid 1940's to the late 1950's.

Estimated Value: Excellent: $65.00
Very good: $55.00

Harrington & Richardson Topper No. 488 Deluxe

Similar to the No. 48 with chrome frame; recoil pad; black lacquered stock and forearm.

Estimated Value: Excellent: $60.00
Very good: $55.00

Harrington & Richardson Topper Jr. 480

Youth version of the No. 48; 410 gauge; 26″ barrel; smaller stock.

Estimated Value: Excellent: $55.00
Very good: $45.00

Harrington & Richardson Topper Jr. 580

Similar to the Topper Jr. 480 with color finish similar to 188 Deluxe.

Estimated Value: Excellent: $50.00
Very good: $40.00

Harrington & Richardson Folding Model

Harrington & Richardson Folding Model

Gauge: 28, 410 with light frame; 12, 16, 20, 28, 410 with heavy frame

Action: Box lock; top lever, break-open; exposed hammer; single shot

Magazine: None

Barrel: 22″ in light frame; 26″ in heavy frame; full choke

Finish: Blued; walnut semi-pistol grip stock and tapered forearm; sight

Approximate wt.: 5½ to 6¾ lbs.

Comments: This shotgun has a hinged frame; barrel folds against stock for storage. Made from about 1910 until World War II.

Estimated Value: Excellent: $90.00
Very good: $70.00

Harrington & Richardson Topper No. 148

Gauge: 12, 16, 20, 410

Action: Box lock; top lever, break-open; hammerless; single shot; automatic extractor

Magazine: None

Barrel: 28″-36″ full choke

Finish: Blued; walnut semi-pistol grip stock and forearm; recoil pad

Approximate wt.: 5 to 6½ lbs.

Comments: Made from the late 1950's to early 1960's

Estimated Value: Excellent: $60.00
Very good: $45.00

Harrington & Richardson Topper 188 Deluxe

Similar to the No. 148 with black, red, blue, green, pink, yellow or purple lacquered finish; chrome plated frame; 410 gauge only.

Estimated Value: Excellent: $55.00
Very good: $40.00

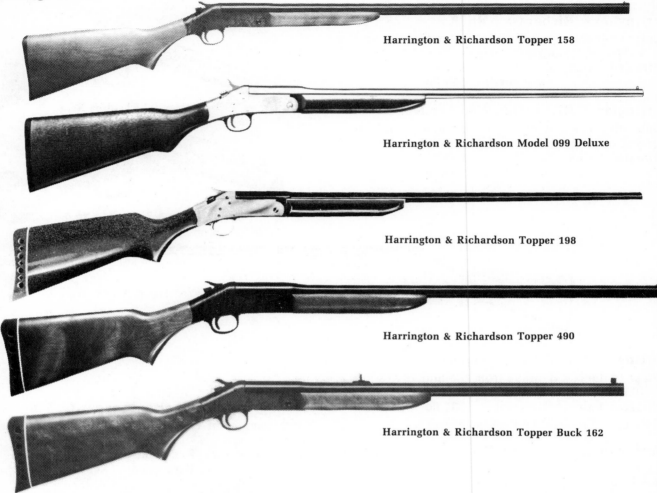

Harrington & Richardson Topper 158

Harrington & Richardson Model 099 Deluxe

Harrington & Richardson Topper 198

Harrington & Richardson Topper 490

Harrington & Richardson Topper Buck 162

Harrington & Richardson Topper 158 or 058

Gauge: 12, 16, 20, 28, 410; currently 20 gauge only
Action: Box lock; side lever, break-open; exposed hammer; single shot
Magazine: None
Barrel: 28″ - 36″, variety of chokes
Finish: Blued; plain wood, straight or semi-pistol grip stock & tapered forearm; recoil pad on early models
Approximate wt.: 5½ to 6½ lbs.
Comments: Made from the early 1960's to mid 1970's as Model 158, mid 1970's to 1985 as 058. Also available is 058 combination with 22″ rifle barrel in 22 Hornet or 30-30 Win. (Add 20%.)
Estimated Value: Excellent: $ 90.00
                         Very good: $ 65.00

Harrington & Richardson Model 099 Deluxe

Similar to the Model 158 with electro-less matte nickel finish. Introduced in 1982, discontinued in 1984.
Estimated Value: Excellent: $70.00
                         Very good: $55.00

Harrington & Richardson Topper 198 or 098

Similar to the Model 158 or 058 except: 20 or 410 gauge only; black lacquered stock and forearm; nickel plated frame. Discontinued 1982.
Estimated Value: Excellent: $75.00
                         Very good: $55.00

Harrington & Richardson Model 258 Handy Gun

Similar to the Model 058 combination shotgun/rifle with nickel finish, 22″ barrel; 20 gauge with 22 Hornet, 30-30, 44 magnum, 357 magnum, or 357 Maximum rifle barrel; includes case. Produced in the mid 1980's.
stimated Value: Excellent: $150.00
                        Very good: $115.00

Harrington & Richardson Topper 490 and 490 Greenwing

A youth version of the Model 158 and 058 with 26″ barrel; shorter stock; 20, 28 and 410 gauges only. Greenwing has higher quality finish.
Estimated Value: Excellent: $65.00
                         Very good: $50.00

Harrington & Richardson Topper 590

Similar to the 490 with chrome plated frame and color lacquered stock and forearm. Production ended in the mid 1960's.
Estimated Value: Excellent: $60.00
                         Very good: $45.00

Harrington & Richardson Topper Buck 162

Similar to the Model 158 and 058 with a 24″ cylinder bore barrel for slugs; equipped with sights.
Estimated Value: Excellent: $ 90.00
                         Very good: $ 65.00

Harrington & Richardson Golden Squire 159

Harrington & Richardson Model 176

Harrington & Richardson Golden Squire 159
Gauge: 12, 20
Action: Box lock; top lever, break-open; exposed hammer; single shot; automatic ejectors
Magazine: None
Barrel: 28″, 30″ full choke
Finish: Blued; wood straight grip stock and lipped forearm; recoil pad
Approximate wt.: 6½ lbs.
Comments: Made in the mid 1960's.
Estimated Value: **Excellent:** $75.00
Very good: $55.00

Harrington & Richardson Golden Squire Jr. 459
Similar to the 159 with a 26″ barrel and shorter stock.
Estimated Value: **Excellent:** $65.00
Very good: $45.00

Harrington & Richardson Model 176
Gauge: 10, 12, 16, 20 magnum
Action: Box lock; top push lever, break-open; exposed hammer; single shot
Magazine: None
Barrel: 32″ or 36″ full choke in 10 or 12 gauge; 32″ full choke in 16 or 20 gauge
Finish: Blued; case hardened frame; plain hardwood Monte Carlo pistol grip stock and forearm; recoil pad
Approximate wt.: 8 to 10 lbs.
Comments: Produced from the late 1970's to mid 1980's. All guns except 10 gauge discontinued in 1982.
Estimated Value: **Excellent:** $ 95.00
Very good: $ 70.00

Harrington & Richardson Model 176 Slug
Similar to the Model 176 with a 28″ cylinder bore slug barrel; rifle sights; swivels. Produced from 1982 to 1985.
Estimated Value: **Excellent:** $110.00
Very good: $ 80.00

Harrington & Richardson Model 088

Harrington & Richardson 404

Harrington & Richardson Model 088
Gauge: 12, 16, 20, 410, regular or magnum
Action: Box lock; top lever, break-open; exposed hammer; single shot
Magazine: None
Barrel: 28″ modified or full in 12 gauge; 28″ modified in 16 gauge; 26″ modified or full in 20 gauge; 25″ full in 410
Finish: Blued; case hardened frame; plain hardwood semi-pistol grip stock and forearm
Approximate wt.: 6 lbs.
Comments: An inexpensive line of all purpose shotguns produced from the late 1970's to mid 1980's.
Estimated Value: **Excellent:** $70.00
Very good: $55.00

Harrington & Richardson Model 088 Jr.
Similar to the Model 088 with a scaled-down stock and forearm; 25″ barrel in 20 or 410 gauge.
Estimated Value: **Excellent:** $70.00
Very good: $55.00

Harrington & Richardson Model 404
Gauge: 12, 20, 410
Action: Box lock; top lever, break-open
Magazine: None
Barrel: Double barrel; 26″, 28″ variety of choke combinations
Finish: Blued; checkered wood semi-pistol grip stock and forearm
Approximate wt.: 5¾ to 7½ lbs.
Comments: Made from the late 1960's to early 1970's.
Estimated Value: **Excellent:** $180.00
Very good: $135.00

Harrington & Richardson Model 404C
Similar to the 404 with Monte Carlo stock.
Estimated Value: **Excellent:** $190.00
Very good: $145.00

Harrington & Richardson Model 1212

Harrington & Richardson Model 1212

Gauge: 12
Action: Box lock; top lever, break-open; single selective trigger
Magazine: None
Barrel: Over and under double barrel; 28″ improved modified over improved cylinder; ventilated rib
Finish: Blued; decorated frame; checkered walnut pistol grip stock and forearm
Approximate wt.: 7 lbs.
Comments: Introduced in the late 1970's. Manufactured in Spain for H & R.
Estimated Value: Excellent: $275.00
             Very good: $200.00

Harrington & Richardson Model 1212 Waterfowl

Similar to the Model 1212 in 12 gauge magnum; 30″ full choke over modified barrel; ventilated recoil pad.
Estimated Value: Excellent: $290.00
             Very good: $210.00

Harrington & Richardson Gamester 348

Gauge: 12, 16
Action: Bolt action; repeating
Magazine: 2-shot
Barrel: 28″ full choke
Finish: Blued; plain wood semi-pistol grip stock and forearm
Approximate wt.: 7 lbs.
Comments: Made from about 1950 to 1954.
Estimated Value: Excellent: $65.00
             Very good: $55.00

Harrington & Richardson Gamester 349 Deluxe

Similar to the 348 Model with adjustable choke; 26″ barrel; recoil pad.
Estimated Value: Excellent: $80.00
             Very good: $65.00

Harrington & Richardson Huntsman 351

Gauge: 12, 16
Action: Bolt action; repeating
Magazine: 2-shot tubular
Barrel: 26″ adjustable choke
Finish: Blued; plain Monte Carlo semi-pistol grip stock and forearm; recoil pad
Approximate wt.: 7 lbs.
Comments: Made from the mid to late 1950's.
Estimated Value: Excellent: $70.00
             Very good: $55.00

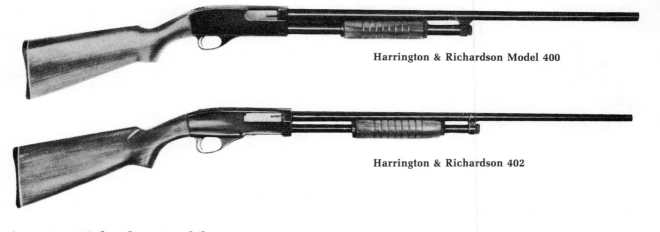

Harrington & Richardson Model 400

Harrington & Richardson 402

Harrington & Richardson Model 400

Gauge: 12, 16, 20
Action: Slide action; hammerless; repeating
Magazine: 5-shot tubular
Barrel: 28″ full choke
Finish: Blued; semi-pistol grip stock and grooved slide handle; recoil pad on 12 and 16 gauges
Approximate wt.: 7½ lbs.
Comments: Made from the mid 1950's to the late 1960's.
Estimated Value: Excellent: $140.00
             Very good: $100.00

Harrington & Richardson Model 401

Similar to the 400 with adjustable choke. Made to the early 1960's.
Estimated Value: Excellent: $145.00
             Very good: $105.00

Harrington & Richardson Model 402

Similar to the 400 in 410 gauge only.
Estimated Value: Excellent: $140.00
             Very good: $110.00

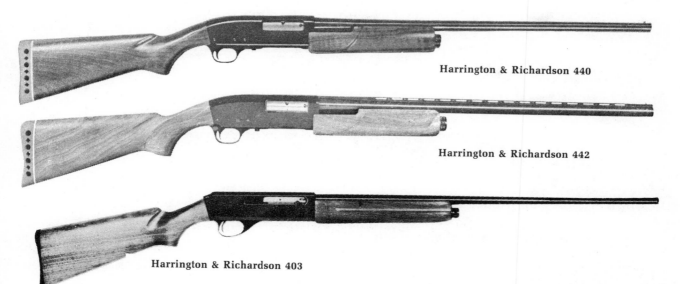

Harrington & Richardson 440

Harrington & Richardson 442

Harrington & Richardson 403

Harrington & Richardson Model 403
Gauge: 410
Action: Semi-automatic
Magazine: 4-shot tubular
Barrel: 26″ full choke
Finish: Blued; wood semi-pistol grip stock and fluted forearm
Approximate wt.: 5¾ lbs.
Comments: Made from the mid 1960's.
Estimated Value: Excellent: $200.00
Very good: $160.00

Harrington & Richardson Model 440
Gauge: 12, 16, 20
Action: Slide acton; hammerless; repeating
Barrel: 4-shot clip
Barrel: 24″-28″ variety of chokes
Finish: Blued; walnut semi-pistol grip stock and forearm; recoil pad
Approximate wt.: 7 lbs.
Comments: Made from the early to mid 1970's.
Estimated Value: Excellent: $145.00
Very good: $115.00

Harrington & Richardson Model 442
Similar to the 440 with a ventilated rib and checkering.
Estimated Value: Excellent: $160.00
Very good: $120.00

High Standard

High Standard Shadow Indy

High Standard Shadow Seven

High Standard Shadow Seven
Gauge: 12
Action: Box lock; top lever, break-open; hammerless; single selective trigger; automatic ejectors
Magazine: None
Barrel: Over and under double barrel, 27½″, 29½″, variety of chokes; ventilated rib
Finish: Blued; checkered walnut pistol grip stock and forearm; gold plated trigger
Approximate wt.: 8 lbs.
Comments: Made to the late 1970's.
Estimated Value: Excellent: $500.00
Very good: $375.00

High Standard Shadow Indy
Similar to Shadow Seven with higher quality finish; chrome lined barrels; engraving; recoil pad.
Estimated Value: Excellent: $600.00
Very good: $450.00

High Standard Flite-King Field

High Standard Flite-King Special

High Standard Flite-King Deluxe Rib

High Standard Flite-King Trophy

High Standard Flite-King Brush

High Standard Flite-King Skeet

High Standard Flite-King Trap

High Standard Flite-King Field

Gauge: 12, 16, 20, 410
Action: Slide action; hammerless; repeating
Magazine: 5-shot tubular; 4-shot tubular in 20 gauge
Barrel: 26″ improved cylinder; 28″ modified; 30″ full chokes
Finish: Blued; plain walnut semi-pistol grip stock and grooved slide handle
Approximate wt.: 6 to 7¼ lbs.
Comments: Made from the early 1960's to late 1970's
Estimated Value: Excellent: $140.00
                                Very good: $110.00

High Standard Flite-King Special

Similar to Flite-King Field with an adjustable choke and 27″ barrel. No 410 gauge.
Estimated Value: Excellent: $145.00
                                Very good: $115.00

High Standard Flite-King Deluxe Rib

Similar to the Flite-King Field with ventilated rib and checkered wood.
Estimated Value: Excellent: $165.00
                                Very good: $125.00

High Standard Flite-King Trophy

Similar to the Deluxe Rib model with an adjustable choke and 27″ barrel. No 410 gauge.
Estimated Value: Excellent: $170.00
                                Very good: $130.00

High Standard Flite-King Brush

Similar to Flite-King Field with an 18″ or 20″ cylinder bore barrel; rifle sights. 12 gauge only.
Estimated Value: Excellent: $185.00
                                Very good: $140.00

High Standard Flite-King Skeet

Similar to the Deluxe Rib model with a skeet choke; 26″ ventilated rib barrel. Not available in 16 gauge.
Estimated Value: Excellent: $180.00
                                Very good: $135.00

High Standard Flite-King Trap

Similar to the Deluxe Rib model with a 30″ full choke barrel; ventilated rib; recoil pad; trap stock. 26″ barrel on 410 gauge.
Estimated Value: Excellent: $190.00
                                Very good: $145.00

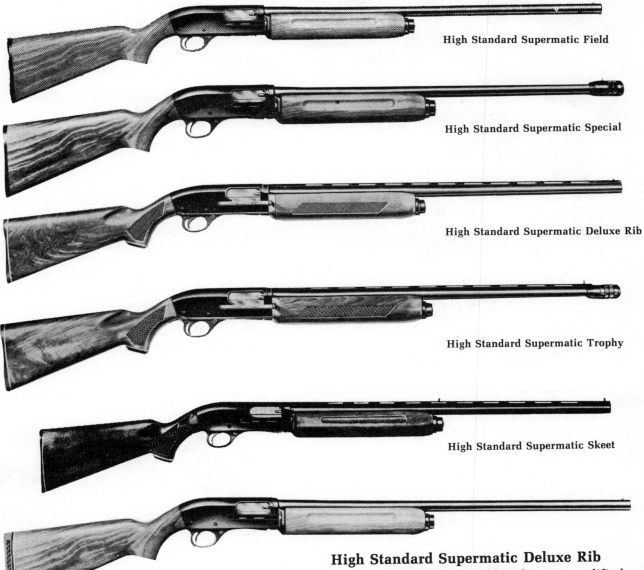

High Standard Supermatic Field

High Standard Supermatic Special

High Standard Supermatic Deluxe Rib

High Standard Supermatic Trophy

High Standard Supermatic Skeet

High Standard Supermatic Duck

High Standard Supermatic Field

Gauge: 12, 20, 20 magnum
Action: Semi-automatic, gas operated; hammerless
Magazine: 4-shot tubular; 3-shot tubular in 20 magnum
Barrel: In 12 gauge: 26″ improved; 28″ modified or full, 30″ full chokes. In 20 gauge: 26″ improved; 28″ modified or full chokes
Finish: Blued; plain walnut semi-pistol grip stock and fluted forearm
Approximate wt.: 7 to 7½ lbs.
Comments: Available from about 1960 to late 1970's; 20 gauge magnum from 1963 to late 1970's.
Estimated Value: **Excellent:** **$170.00**
                                        Very good: **$135.00**

High Standard Supermatic Special

Similar to the Supermatic Field with adjustable choke and 27″ barrel.
Estimated Value: **Excellent:** **$175.00**
                                        Very good: **$145.00**

High Standard Supermatic Deluxe Rib

Similar to Supermatic Field with a 28″ modified or full choke barrel, (30″ in 12 gauge); checkered wood and ventilated rib.
Estimated Value: **Excellent:** **$200.00**
                                        Very good: **$150.00**

High Standard Supermatic Trophy

Similar to the Supermatic Field with a 27″ barrel; adjustable choke; ventilated rib; checkering.
Estimated Value: **Excellent:** **$190.00**
                                        Very good: **$140.00**

High Standard Supermatic Skeet

Similar to Field Model with a 26″ ventilated rib barrel; skeet choke; checkered wood.
Estimated Value: **Excellent:** **$200.00**
                                        Very good: **$155.00**

High Standard Supermatic Duck

Similar to the Supermatic Field in 12 gauge magnum with a 30″ full choke barrel and recoil pad. Made from the early 1960's to mid 1960's.
Estimated Value: **Excellent:** **$200.00**
                                        Very good: **$160.00**

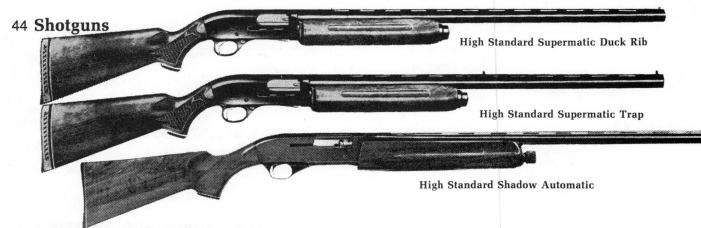

High Standard Supermatic Duck Rib

High Standard Supermatic Trap

High Standard Shadow Automatic

High Standard Supermatic Duck Rib

Similar to the Supermatic Duck with checkered wood and ventilated rib.

Estimated Value: Excellent: $210.00
Very good: $160.00

High Standard Supermatic Trap

Similar to the Supermatic Field in 12 gauge only; 30″ full choke; ventilated rib; checkered trap stock and forearm; recoil pad.

Estimated Value: Excellent: $200.00
Very good: $160.00

High Standard Shadow Automatic

Gauge: 12, 20, regular or magnum
Action: Semi-automatic; gas operated; hammerless
Magazine: 4-shot tubular
Barrel: 26″, 28″, 30″; variety of chokes; rib
Finish: Blued; walnut pistol grip stock and forearm; sights; recoil pad available
Approximate wt.: 7 lbs.
Comments: Made to the late 1970's.
Estimated Value: Excellent: $225.00
Very good: $170.00

Hunter

Hunter Fulton

Gauge: 12, 16, 20
Action: Box lock; top lever, break-open; hammerless; double or single trigger
Magazine: None
Barrel: Double barrel; 26″ to 32″ any choke
Finish: Blued; checkered walnut pistol grip stock and forearm
Approximate wt.: 6½ to 7½ lbs.
Comments: Made from the early 1920's until shortly after World War II in the United States. Add $50.00 for single trigger.
Estimated Value Excellent: $600.00
Very good: $450.00

Hunter Fulton

Hunter Special

Very similar to Hunter Fulton but somewhat higher quality. Add $50.00 for single trigger.
Estimated Value: Excellent: $650.00
Very good: $490.00

Ithaca

Ithaca Victory

Gauge: 12
Action: Box lock; top lever, break-open; hammerless; single shot
Magazine: None
Barrel: 34″ full choke; ventilated rib; trap grade.
Finish: Blued; engraving; checkered pistol grip stock and forearm
Approximate wt.: 8 lbs.
Comments: Made from the early 1920's to World War II. Other grades in higher quality available, valued up to $4,000. Prices here are for standard grade. Made in 5 grades.
Estimated Value: Excellent: $1,100.00
Very good: $ 825.00

Ithaca Victory

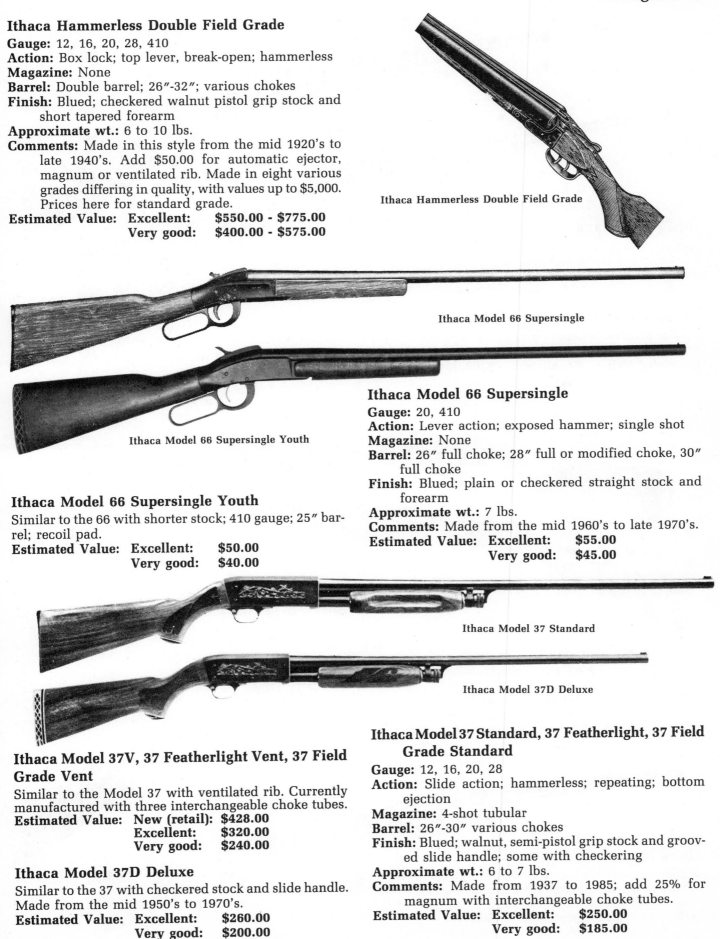

Ithaca Hammerless Double Field Grade
Gauge: 12, 16, 20, 28, 410
Action: Box lock; top lever, break-open; hammerless
Magazine: None
Barrel: Double barrel; 26″-32″; various chokes
Finish: Blued; checkered walnut pistol grip stock and short tapered forearm
Approximate wt.: 6 to 10 lbs.
Comments: Made in this style from the mid 1920's to late 1940's. Add $50.00 for automatic ejector, magnum or ventilated rib. Made in eight various grades differing in quality, with values up to $5,000. Prices here for standard grade.
Estimated Value: Excellent: $550.00 - $775.00
                    Very good: $400.00 - $575.00

Ithaca Hammerless Double Field Grade

Ithaca Model 66 Supersingle

Ithaca Model 66 Supersingle Youth

Ithaca Model 66 Supersingle Youth
Similar to the 66 with shorter stock; 410 gauge; 25″ barrel; recoil pad.
Estimated Value: Excellent: $50.00
                    Very good: $40.00

Ithaca Model 66 Supersingle
Gauge: 20, 410
Action: Lever action; exposed hammer; single shot
Magazine: None
Barrel: 26″ full choke; 28″ full or modified choke, 30″ full choke
Finish: Blued; plain or checkered straight stock and forearm
Approximate wt.: 7 lbs.
Comments: Made from the mid 1960's to late 1970's.
Estimated Value: Excellent: $55.00
                    Very good: $45.00

Ithaca Model 37 Standard

Ithaca Model 37D Deluxe

Ithaca Model 37V, 37 Featherlight Vent, 37 Field Grade Vent
Similar to the Model 37 with ventilated rib. Currently manufactured with three interchangeable choke tubes.
Estimated Value: New (retail): $428.00
                    Excellent: $320.00
                    Very good: $240.00

Ithaca Model 37D Deluxe
Similar to the 37 with checkered stock and slide handle. Made from the mid 1950's to 1970's.
Estimated Value: Excellent: $260.00
                    Very good: $200.00

Ithaca Model 37 Standard, 37 Featherlight, 37 Field Grade Standard
Gauge: 12, 16, 20, 28
Action: Slide action; hammerless; repeating; bottom ejection
Magazine: 4-shot tubular
Barrel: 26″-30″ various chokes
Finish: Blued; walnut, semi-pistol grip stock and grooved slide handle; some with checkering
Approximate wt.: 6 to 7 lbs.
Comments: Made from 1937 to 1985; add 25% for magnum with interchangeable choke tubes.
Estimated Value: Excellent: $250.00
                    Very good: $185.00

Ithaca Model 37R

Ithaca Model 37R Deluxe

Ithaca Model 37R

Similar to the 37 with a solid raised rib. Slightly heavier. Discontinued in the late 1960's.
Estimated Value: Excellent: $265.00
**   Very good: $195.00**

Ithaca Model 37R Deluxe

Similar to the 37D Deluxe with a raised solid rib. Made to the early 1960's.
Estimated Value: Excellent: $300.00
**   Very good: $225.00**

Ithaca Model 37DV Deluxe Vent

Similar to the 37D with ventilated rib. Currently manufactured.
Estimated Value: New (retail): $464.00
**   Excellent: $350.00**
**   Very good: $260.00**

Ithaca Model 37DV Deluxe

Ithaca Model 37S Skeet

Ithaca Model 37S Skeet

Similar to the 37 with extended slide handle and ventilated rib. Made to the mid 1950's.
Estimated Value: Excellent: $300.00
**   Very good: $225.00**

Ithaca Model 37T Trap

Similar to the 37S with trap stock; recoil pad; choice wood.
Estimated Value: Excellent: $300.00
**   Very good: $230.00**

Ithaca Model 37T Trap

Ithaca Model 37T Target

Available in skeet or trap version with high quality finish and select wood. Replaced the 37S and 37T Trap. Made from the mid 1950's to about 1961.
Estimated Value: Excellent: $325.00
**   Very good: $245.00**

Ithaca Model 37 T Target

Ithaca Model 37 Supreme, 37 Featherlight Supreme
Similar to the 37T Target. Currently manufactured.

Estimated Value:	New (retail):	$769.00
	Excellent:	$575.00
	Very good:	$430.00

Ithaca 37 Bicentennial

Ithaca Model 37 Ducks Unlimited
A commemorative version of the Model 37; 12 gauge only; 30″ full choke barrel; engraved receiver; ventilated rib; made in 1977.

| Estimated Value: | Excellent: | $300.00 |
| | Very good: | $240.00 |

Ithaca Model 37 Bicentennial
Limited to 1976, these shotguns have special engraving on the receiver, select wood and recoil pad.

| Estimated Value: | Excellent: | $475.00 |
| | Very good: | $375.00 |

Ithaca Model 37 Deerslayer

Ithaca Model 37 Deerslayer
Similar to the Model 37 with a 20″ or 26″ barrel and rifle sights. Made from the 1960's to present; 12 or 20 gauge.

Estimated Value:	New (retail):	$450.00
	Excellent:	$335.00
	Very good:	$250.00

Ithaca Model 37 Deerslayer Super Deluxe
Similar to the Model 37 Deerslayer with higher quality finish. Discontinued 1985.

| Estimated Value: | Excellent: | $325.00 |
| | Very good: | $245.00 |

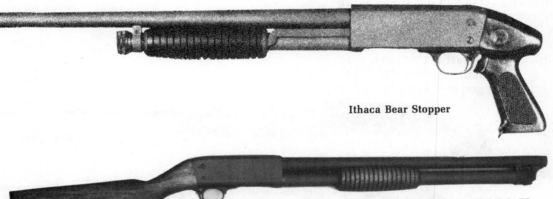

Ithaca Bear Stopper

Ithaca Model 37 M&P

Ithaca Model 37 DSPS; DSPS II
A law enforcement version of the Model 37 Deerslayer; grooved slide handle; available in regular, parkerized, or chrome finishes. Add 5% for 8-shot magazine; 15% for chrome finish (discontinued 1985); 5% less for DSPS II.

Estimated Value:	New (retail):	$397.00
	Excellent:	$300.00
	Very good:	$225.00

Ithaca Model 37 M&P
Similar to the Model 37 for law enforcement use; 18″ or 20″ cylinder bore barrel; non-glare tung oil finish; parkerized or chrome finish metal; 5 or 8-shot magazine. Add 5% for 8-shot magazine; 10% for chrome (discontinued 1985); 7% for hand grip.

Estimated Value:	New (retail):	$380.00
	Excellent:	$285.00
	Very good:	$215.00

Ithaca Bear Stopper
A short barrelled version of the Model 37; 18½″ or 20″ barrel; 12 gauge; one-hand grip and grooved slide handle; 5- or 8-shot magazine; blued or chrome finish. Add 5% for 8-shot; 10% for chrome. Produced in early 1980's.

| Estimated Value: | Excellent: | $275.00 |
| | Very good: | $205.00 |

Ithaca Model 37 Camo Vent

Similar to the Model 37 Field Grade Vent with a rust-resistant camo finish in spring (green) or fall (brown); sling and swivels; 12 gauge, 26″ full choke barrel. Introduced in 1986.

Estimated Value: New (retail): $500.00
Excellent: $375.00
Very good: $280.00

Ithaca Model 37 Ultra Deerslayer

Similar to the Ultra Featherlight with a 20″ barrel for slugs; sights; recoil pad; swivels.

Estimated Value: Excellent: $310.00
Very good: $235.00

Ithaca Model 37 Ultra Featherlight

Ithaca Model 37 Basic Featherlight

Similar to the Model 37 without cosmetic finish; no checkering; finished in non-glare tung oil; grooved slide handle; "vapor blasted" metal surfaces with a non-glare finish; add 2% for ventilated rib, 30% for magnum. Introduced in 1979, discontinued in the mid 1980s.

Estimated Value: Excellent: $250.00
Very good: $195.00

Ithaca Model 37 Ultra Featherlight, Ultralite

A 20 gauge lightweight version of the Model 37; 25″ ventilated rib barrel; recoil pad, gold trigger; special grip cap. Introduced in 1979. Currently available with interchangeable choke tubes.

Estimated Value: New (retail): $522.00
Excellent: $390.00
Very good: $295.00

Ithaca English-Ultrafeatherlight

Gauge: 12, 20
Action: Slide action; hammerless; repeating
Magazine: 3-shot tubular
Barrel: 25″ full, modified or improved cylinder bore; ventilated rib
Finish: Blued; checkered walnut straight grip stock and slide handle; waterfowl scene on receiver
Approximate wt.: 4¾ lbs.
Comments: A lightweight English stock version of the Model 37 series. Introduced in 1982. Currently available with interchangeable choke tubes.

Estimated Value: New (retail): $522.00
Excellent: $390.00
Very good: $295.00

Ithaca Model 300

Ithaca Model 900 Deluxe Slug

Ithaca Model 900 Deluxe

Similar to the 300 except: ventilated rib on all models; gold filled engraving; nameplate in stock; gold trigger.

Estimated Value: Excellent: $250.00
Very good: $200.00

Ithaca Model 900 Deluxe Slug

Similar to the 900 Deluxe with a 24″ barrel for slugs; rifle sights.

Estimated Value: Excellent: $240.00
Very good: $190.00

Ithaca Model 300

Gauge: 12, 20
Action: Semi-automatic; recoil operated; hammerless
Magazine: 3-shot tubular
Barrel: 26″ improved cylinder; 28″ modified or full, 30″ full chokes
Finish: Blued; checkered walnut pistol grip stock and forearm
Approximate wt.: 6½ to 7 lbs.
Comments: Made about 1970 to 1973. Add $10.00 for ventilated rib.

Estimated Value: Excellent: $220.00
Very good: $165.00

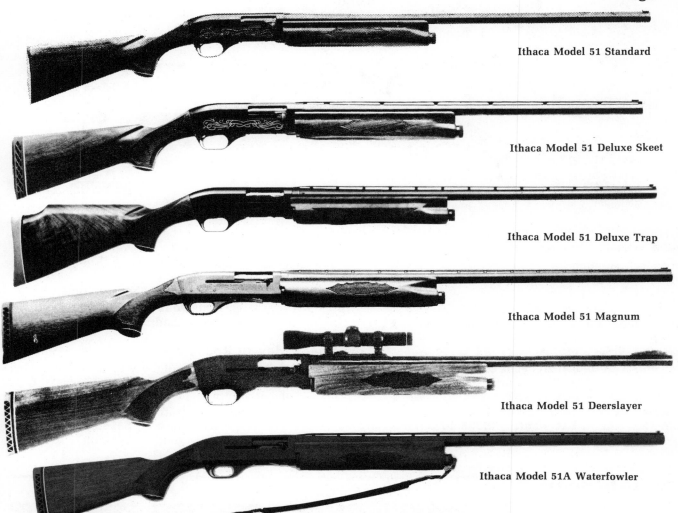

Ithaca Model 51 Standard

Ithaca Model 51 Deluxe Skeet

Ithaca Model 51 Deluxe Trap

Ithaca Model 51 Magnum

Ithaca Model 51 Deerslayer

Ithaca Model 51A Waterfowler

Ithaca Model 51 Standard, 51 Featherlight, 51A

Gauge: 12, 20
Action: Gas operated, semi-automatic
Magazine: 3-shot tubular
Barrel: 26″-30″, various chokes; some with ventilated rib
Finish: Blued; checkered walnut, pistol grip stock and forearm; decorated receiver
Approximate wt.: 7½ lbs.
Comments: Manufactured until 1986.
Estimated Value: Excellent: $350.00
Very good: $260.00

Ithaca Model 51 Deluxe Skeet, 51A Supreme Skeet

Similar to the 51 with recoil pad; ventilated rib; 28″ or 29″ skeet choke barrel, 26″ after 1985.
Estimated Value: New (retail): $858.00
Excellent: $645.00
Very good: $480.00

Ithaca Model 51 Deluxe Trap, 51A Supreme Trap

Similar to the Model 51 except: 12 gauge only; select wood; 28″ or 30″ barrel; recoil pad. Add 5% for Monte Carlo stock.
Estimated Value: New (retail): $869.00
Excellent: $650.00
Very good: $490.00

Ithaca Model 51 Magnum

Similar to the 51 but chambered for magnum shells; ventilated rib.
Estimated Value: Excellent: $390.00
Very good: $310.00

Ithaca Model 51 Deerslayer

Similar to the Model 51 with 24″ barrel for slugs; sights; recoil pad; 12 gauge only.
Estimated Value: Excellent: $350.00
Very good: $260.00

Ithaca Model 51 Ducks Unlimited

A commemorative version of the Model 51; 12 gauge only; 30″ full choke barrel; iridescent sight; engraved receiver; ventilated rib. Made in 1979.
Estimated Value: Excellent: $400.00
Very good: $285.00

Ithaca Model 51A Waterfowler, 51A Turkey Gun

Similar to the Model 51A with matte-finish metal and flat-finish walnut. The Turkey model has a 26″ ventilated rib barrel, the Waterfowler has a 30″ ventilated rib barrel. Introduced in 1984. Add 10% camo finish with vent rib.
Estimated Value: New (retail): $625.00
Excellent: $465.00
Very good: $350.00

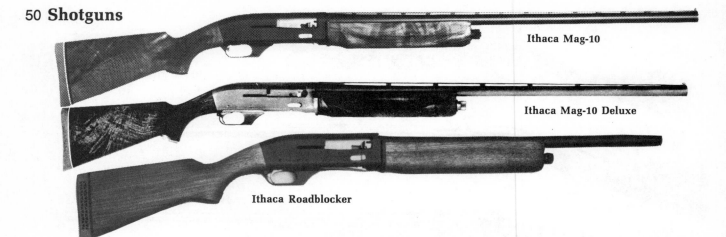

Ithaca Mag-10

Ithaca Mag-10 Deluxe

Ithaca Roadblocker

Ithaca Mag-10 Deluxe

Gauge: 10 magnum
Action: Semi-automatic, gas operated
Magazine: 3-shot tubular
Barrel: 32″ full choke; ventilated rib
Finish: Blued; checkered walnut pistol grip stock and forearm; recoil pad; swivels
Approximate wt.: 11½ lbs.
Comments: Currently manufactured. Deduct 15% to 20% for Ithaca Mag-10 Standard. Add 10% for camo finish with ventilated rib.
Estimated Value: New (retail): $924.00
Excellent: $695.00
Very good: $520.00

Ithaca Mag-10 Supreme

Similar to the Magnum 10 Deluxe with higher quality finish and select wood.
Estimated Value: New (retail): $1,124.00
Excellent: $ 840.00
Very good: $ 630.00

Ithaca Mag-10 Roadblocker

A law enforcement version of the Mag-10 with a 20″ barrel; plain stock; "vapor blasted" metal finish. Add 5% for ventilated rib.
Estimated Value: New (retail): $741.00
Excellent: $555.00
Very good: $415.00

Iver Johnson

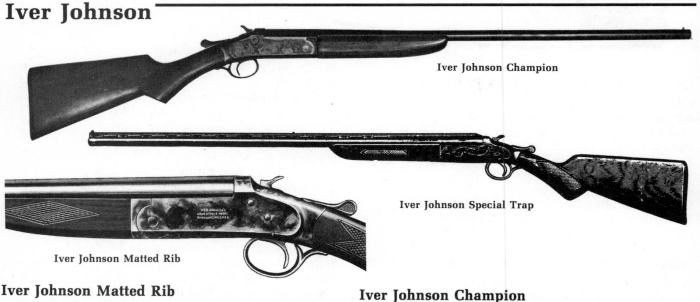

Iver Johnson Champion

Iver Johnson Special Trap

Iver Johnson Matted Rib

Iver Johnson Matted Rib

Similar to the Champion with a matted rib and checkering. Discontinued in the late 1940's.
Estimated Value: Excellent: $90.00
Very good: $70.00

Iver Johnson Special Trap

Similar to the Champion with a 32″ ribbed barrel; checkered stock; 12 gauge only. Manufactured until the early 1940's.
Estimated Value: Excellent: $150.00
Very good: $110.00

Iver Johnson Champion

Gauge: 12, 20, 410
Action: Box lock; top lever, break-open; hammerless; single shot; automatic ejectors
Magazine: None
Barrel: 26″-30, full choke
Finish: Blued; hardwood semi-pistol grip stock and short tapered forearm
Approximate wt.: 7 lbs.
Comments: Made from about 1910 to late the 1970's.
Estimated Value: Excellent: $65.00
Very good: $50.00

Iver Johnson Skeeter

Iver Johnson Hercules

Gauge: 12, 16, 20, 410
Action: Box lock; top lever, break-open; hammerless
Magazine: None
Barrel: Double barrel, 26″-32″ modified & full or full & full chokes
Finish: Blued; checkered walnut pistol grip stock and tapered forearm
Approximate wt.: 6 to 8 lbs.
Comments: Made from about 1920 to 1949. Available with some extras. Prices are for Standard grade. Add $75.00 for single trigger or automatic ejectors.
Estimated Value: Excellent: $350.00
Very good: $265.00

Iver Johnson Hercules

Iver Johnson Skeeter

Similar to the Hercules with addition of 28 gauge; 26″-28″ barrels; wide forearm. Add $75.00 for automatic ejectors; $75.00 for single selective trigger.
Estimated Value: Excellent: $450.00
Very good: $340.00

Iver Johnson Silver Shadow

Iver Johnson Super Trap

Iver Johnson Silver Shadow

Gauge: 12
Action: Box lock; top lever, break-open; hammerless
Magazine: None
Barrel: Over and under double barrel; 28″ modified & full choke; ventilated rib
Finish: Blued; checkered walnut pistol grip stock and forearm
Approximate wt.: 8¼ lbs.
Comments: Manufactured in Italy for Iver Johnson. Add $75.00 for single trigger.
Estimated Value: Excellent: $300.00
Very good: $225.00

Iver Johnson Super Trap

Gauge: 12
Action: Box lock; top lever, break-open; hammerless
Magazine: None
Barrel: Double barrel; 32″ full choke; ventilated rib
Finish: Blued; checkered walnut pistol grip stock and forearm; recoil pad
Approximate wt.: 8½ lbs.
Comments: Production stopped on this model during World War II. Available with some extras. Prices for Standard grade; add $35.00 for non-selective single trigger; $75.00 for selective single trigger or automatic ejectors.
Estimated Value: Excellent: $550.00
Very good: $410.00

Kessler

Kessler 3-Shot

Gauge: 12, 16, 20
Action: Bolt action; hammerless; repeating
Magazine: 2-shot detachable box
Barrel: 26″, 28″ full choke
Finish: Blued; plain pistol grip stock and forearm; recoil pad
Approximate wt.: 6 to 7 lbs.
Comments: Made for a few years only in the early 1950's.
Estimated Value: Excellent: $75.00
Very good: $55.00

Kessler Lever Matic

Gauge: 12, 16, 20
Action: Lever action
Magazine: 3-shot
Barrel: 26″, 28″, 30″, full choke
Finish: Blued; walnut straight stock and forearm; recoil pad
Approximate wt.: 7 lbs.
Comments: Produced for only a few years in the early 1950's.
Estimated Value: Excellent: $150.00
Very good: $110.00

Kleinguenther

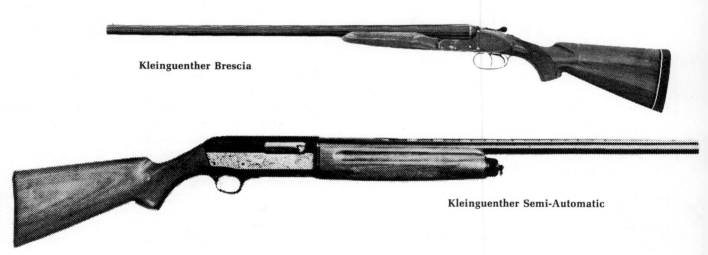

Kleinguenther Condor

Kleinguenther Condor

Gauge: 12, 20
Action: Double lock; top lever break-open; hammerless; selective single trigger; automatic ejectors
Magazine: None
Barrel: Over and under double barrel; ventilated rib; 26″ improved & modified or skeet; 28″ modified or modified & full; 30″ modified & full or full in 12 gauge
Finish: Blued; checkered walnut pistol grip stock and forearm; recoil pad
Approximate wt.: 7½ lbs.
Comments: An Italian shotgun produced in the 1970's.
Estimated Value: Excellent: $550.00
                      Very good: $415.00

Kleinguenther Condor Skeet

A skeet version of the Condor with a wide rib.
Estimated Value: Excellent: $575.00
                      Very good: $430.00

Kleinguenther Condor Trap

A trap version of the Condor with a Monte Carlo stock, wide rib; available in 32″ barrel.
Estimated Value: Excellent: $590.00
                      Very good: $440.00

Kleinguenther Brescia

Kleinguenther Semi-Automatic

Kleinguenther Brescia

Gauge: 12, 20
Action: Box lock; top lever, break-open; hammerless; double trigger
Magazine: None
Barrel: Double barrel; chrome lined, 28″ improved or modified or modified & full chokes
Finish: Blued; checkered walnut pistol grip stock and tapered forearm
Approximate wt.: 7½ lbs.
Comments: Manufactured in Italy.
Estimated Value: Excellent: $275.00
                      Very good: $205.00

Kleinguenther Semi-Automatic

Gauge: 12
Action: Semi-automatic; hammerless; side ejection
Magazine: 3-shot tubular
Barrel: Chrome lined; 25″ skeet, 26″ improved cylinder, 28″ and 30″ full chokes; ventilated rib
Finish: Blued; smooth walnut pistol grip stock and grooved forearm; engraved
Approximate wt.: 7½ lbs.
Comments: Made from the early to mid 1970's.
Estimated Value: Excellent: $300.00
                      Very good: $225.00

L.C. Smith

L.C. Smith Single Barrel

Gauge: 12
Action: Box lock; top lever, break-open; automatic ejectors, hammerless
Magazine: None; single shot
Barrel: 32″, 34″ choice of bore; ventilated rib
Finish: Blued; checkered walnut pistol grip stock and forearm; recoil pad
Approximate wt.: 8 lbs.
Comments: Produced by Hunter Arms until about 1946 and Marlin from about 1946 to 1950.
Estimated Value:

L.C. Smith Single Barrel

	Olympic	Specialty	Crown
Excellent:	$1,450.00	$2,000.00	$3,200.00
Very good:	$1,050.00	$1,450.00	$2,500.00

L.C. Smith Double Barrel (Hunter Arms)

Gauge: 12, 16, 20, 410
Action: Side lock, top lever break-down; hammerless; automatic ejectors; double or single trigger
Magazine: None
Barrel: 26″-32″ double barrel, any choke
Finish: Depending on grade, checkered walnut pistol, semi-pistol or straight grip stock and forearm; blued barrels
Approximate wt.: 6½ to 8½ lbs.
Comments: Produced by Hunter Arms until about 1946 and Marlin from 1946 to 1950. Prices for field grade. Others considerably higher due to higher quality of workmanship and finish. Add $50.00 for single trigger.
Estimated Value: Excellent: $625.00
Very good: $550.00

L.C. Smith Double Barrel (Hunter Arms)

L.C. Smith Field Grade (Marlin)

L.C. Smith Field Grade (Marlin)

Same as the Deluxe Model with standard checkered walnut pistol grip stock and forearm and extruded ventilated rib. Made from about 1946 to 1950.
Estimated Value: Excellent: $475.00
Very good: $360.00

L.C. Smith Deluxe (Marlin)

Gauge: 12, regular or magnum
Action: Top lever break-open; hammerless; side lock; double triggers
Magazine: None
Barrel: Double barrel; 28″ modified and full chokes; floating steel ventilated rib
Finish: Top quality, hand-fitted, hand-checkered walnut pistol grip stock and beavertail forearm; blued; case hardened side plates
Approximate wt.: 6¾ lbs.
Comments: Made from about 1968 to mid 1970's.
Estimated Value: Excellent: $500.00
Very good: $375.00

Lefever

Lefever Long Range

Lefever Trap

Lefever Nitro Special

Lefever Long Range

Gauge: 12, 16, 20, 410
Action: Box lock; top lever, break-open; hammerless; single shot
Magazine: None
Barrel: 26″, 28″, 30″, 32″; any choke
Finish: Blued; plain or checkered walnut pistol grip stock and forearm; bead sight
Approximate wt.: 5 to 7 lbs.
Comments: Made from the early 1920's to the early 1940's.
Estimated Value: Excellent: $175.00
Very good: $135.00

Lefever Trap

Gauge: 12
Action: Box lock; top lever, break-open; hammerless; single shot
Magazine: None
Barrel: 30″ or 32″ full choke; ventilated rib
Finish: Blued; checkered walnut pistol grip stock and forearm; recoil pad
Approximate wt.: 8 lbs.
Comments: Made from the early 1920's to the early 1940's.
Estimated Value: Excellent: $360.00
Very good: $275.00

Lefever Nitro Special

Gauge: 12, 16, 20, 410
Action: Box lock; top lever, break-open; hammerless; double triggers
Magazine: None
Barrel: Double barrel; 26″, 28″, 30″, 32″; any choke
Finish: Blued; checkered walnut pistol grip stock and forearm
Approximate wt.: 5½ to 7 lbs.
Comments: Made from the early 1920's to late 1940's. Add $75.00 for single trigger.
Estimated Value: Excellent: $450.00
Very good: $340.00

Lefever Excellsior

Similar to Nitro-Special with light engraving and automatic ejector.
Estimated Value: Excellent: $500.00
Very good: $375.00

Mannlicher

Mannlicher Gamba Oxford

Mannlicher Gamba Oxford

Gauge: 12, 20, 20 magnum
Action: Top lever break-open; hammerless; single or double trigger
Magazine: None
Barrel: Double barrel; 26½″ improved cylinder & modified or 27½″ modified & full
Finish: Blued; engraved receiver; checkered walnut straight grip stock and tapered forearm
Approximate wt.: 5½ to 6½
Comments: Add $140.00 for single trigger.
Estimated Value: Excellent: $1,325.00
Very good: $ 995.00

Mannlicher Gamba Principessa

Gauge: 28
Action: Top lever break-open; hammerless; single or double trigger
Magazine: None
Barrel: Double barrel; 26″ improved cylinder & modified or 28″ modified & full
Finish: Blued; case hardened received with engraved scrollwork; checkered walnut straight grip stock and tapered forearm; beavertail forearm available; recoil pad
Approximate wt.: 5½ lbs.
Comments: Add $130.00 for single trigger.
Estimated Value: Excellent: $1,175.00
Very good: $ 880.00

Marlin

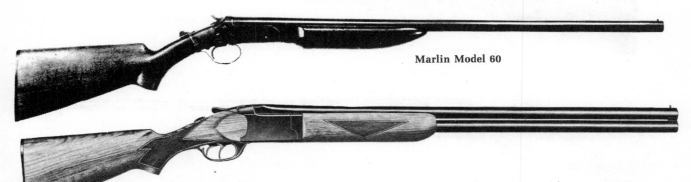

Marlin Model 60

Marlin Model 90

Marlin Model 60

Gauge: 12
Action: Box lock; take down breech-loaded; automatic ejector; exposed hammer; single shot
Magazine: None
Barrel: 30″ or 32″ full choke; matted top; 2¾″ chamber
Finish: Blued; walnut pistol grip stock and beavertail forearm
Approximate wt.: 6½ lbs.
Comments: This shotgun was made in 1923, a combination of Marlin and Hopkins & Allen parts. Less than 1,000 were manufactured.
Estimated Value: Excellent: $150.00
                       Very good: $115.00

Marlin Model 410

Gauge: 410
Action: Lever action; exposed hammer
Magazine: 5-shot tubular
Barrel: 22″ or 26″, 2½″ chamber
Finish: Blued; walnut pistol grip stock and beavertail forearm
Approximate wt.: 6 lbs.
Comments: A solid frame lightweight shotgun produced from about 1929 to 1932.
Estimated Value: Excellent: $375.00
                       Very good: $280.00

Marlin Model 90

Gauge: 12, 16, 20, 410 (also .22 caliber and .222)
Action: Top lever break down; box lock; double trigger (single trigger available prior to World War II); hammerless; non-automatic extractors
Magazine: None
Barrel: Over and under double barrel, 26″, 28″ or 30″ rifle; shotgun barrels available in 26″; 2¾″ chamber, 3″ chamber in 410; full, modified, skeet or improved cylinder bore
Finish: Blued; plain or checkered walnut pistol grip stock and forearm; recoil pad
Approximate wt.: 6 to 7½ lbs.
Comments: This shotgun or combination was manufactured from about 1937 to 1958. Add $40.00 for 410 gauge; $50.00 for single trigger.
Estimated Value: Excellent: $400.00
                       Very good: $300.00

Marlin Model 55 Hunter

Gauge: 12, 16, 20
Action: Bolt action; repeating
Magazine: 2-shot clip
Barrel: 26″ or 28″ full choke; "Micro Choke" available; 2¾″ or 3″ chamber
Finish: Blued; walnut pistol grip stock and forearm; recoil pad optional
Approximate wt.: 7¼ lbs.
Comments: Made from about 1950 to 1965.
Estimated Value: Excellent: $85.00
                       Very good: $60.00

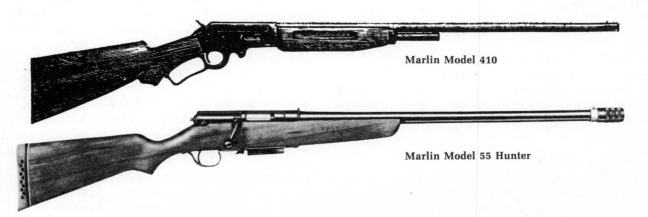

Marlin Model 410

Marlin Model 55 Hunter

Marlin Model 55G

Marlin Glenfield 50

Marlin Glenfield 60G

Marlin Model 55 Swamp Gun

Marlin Model 55 Goose Gun

Marlin 55G, Glenfield 55G and Glenfield 50

The same basic shotgun as the Marlin Model 55 Hunter. It was produced from about 1961 to 1966 as the 55G and Glenfield 55G and in 1966 it became the Glenfield 50.

Estimated Value: Excellent: $85.00
Very good: $65.00

Marlin Glenfield 60G

Same shotgun as the Marlin Model 59.

Estimated Value: Excellent: $70.00
Very good: $55.00

Marlin Model 55 Swamp Gun

The same shotgun as the Model 55 except barrel is shortened with "Micro Choke", recoil pad is standard and it has swivels. It weighs about 6½ lbs. and is chambered for 3" 12 gauge magnum shells. It was produced for two years beginning in 1963.

Estimated Value: Excellent: $90.00
Very good: $70.00

Marlin Model 55 Goose Gun

Same shotgun as the Model 55 except: swivels; extra long 36" barrel; chambered for 3" 12 gauge magnum shells; weighs 8 lbs.; recoil pad standard. It has been in production since 1966.

Estimated Value: New (retail): $180.95
Excellent: $135.00
Very good: $100.00

Marlin Model 59

Marlin Model 55S Slug Gun

Marlin Model 59, 60G, 61G

Gauge: 410
Action: Bolt action; self-cocking
Magazine: None; single shot
Barrel: 24″ full choke; chambered for 2½″ or 3″ shells
Finish: Blued; walnut pistol grip or semi-pistol grip stock and forearm
Approximate wt.: 5 lbs.
Comments: This takedown model was produced from about 1959 to 1961. It was replaced by Model 60G in 1962 which was replaced by the Model 61G in 1963. In 1966 it was discontinued.
Estimated Value: Excellent: $70.00
                       Very good: $55.00

Marlin Model 55S Slug Gun

Basically the same as Model 55, this gun has rifle sights and a 24″ barrel that is chambered for 2¾″ and 3″ shells. It has swivels and a recoil pad. In production since 1973.
Estimated Value: Excellent: $100.00
                       Very good: $ 75.00

Marlin Model 5510 Supergoose 10

Marlin Model 5510 Supergoose 10

Gauge: 10 gauge magnum
Action: Bolt action
Magazine: 2-shot clip (2⅞″ shells must be loaded singly)
Barrel: 34″ full choke; chambered for 2⅞″ or 3½″ shells
Finish: Blued; black walnut semi-pistol grip stock and forearm; swivels; recoil pad
Approximate wt.: 10½ lbs.
Comments: This is a more powerful version of the Marlin Goose Gun. Produced from 1976 to 1986.
Estimated Value: Excellent: $195.00
                       Very good: $150.00

Marlin Model 1898

Gauge: 12 (2¾″)
Action: Slide action; exposed hammer; side ejection
Magazine: 5-shot tubular
Barrel: 26″, 28″, 30″ or 32″
Finish: Blued; walnut pistol grip stock and grooved slide handle
Approximate wt.: 7¼ lbs.
Comments: This shotgun was produced in many grades beginning in 1898. Price for grade A (Field Grade.)
Estimated Value: Excellent: $300.00
                       Very good: $225.00

Marlin Model 1898

Marlin Model 19

Marlin Model 19 and 19G

Similar to the Model 1898 with slight improvements. Made from 1906-1907; 19G produced until 1915.
Estimated Value: Excellent: $250.00
                       Very good: $190.00

Marlin Model 24

Marlin Model 21 "Trap Model"

Marlin Model 26

Marlin Model 16

Marlin Model 16

Gauge: 16 (2¾")
Action: Slide action; exposed hammer
Magazine: 5-shot tubular
Barrel: 26" or 28"
Finish: Blued; walnut pistol grip stock and forearm; some checkered, some with grooved slide handle
Approximate wt.: 6¼ lbs.
Comments: This takedown model was made from about 1904 to 1910.
Estimated Value: Excellent: $300.00
Very good: $225.00

Marlin Model 24

An improved version of the Model 19 made from 1908 to 1915.
Estimated Value: Excellent: $260.00
Very good: $195.00

Marlin Model 21 "Trap Model"

This shotgun is very similar to the Model 24 with trap specifications.
Estimated Value: Excellent: $275.00
Very good: $205.00

Marlin Model 26

Very similar to the Model 24 except: stock is straight grip; solid frame. Made from about 1909 to 1915.
Estimated Value: Excellent: $240.00
Very good: $180.00

Marlin Model 17

Marlin Model 30

Marlin Model 30 and 30G

Gauge: 16 and 20
Action: Slide action; exposed hammer
Magazine: 5-shot tubular
Barrel: 25", 26", 28" modified choke, 2¾" chamber
Finish: Blued; checkered walnut straight or pistol grip stock, grooved or checkered slide handle
Approximate wt.: 6¾ lbs.
Comments: Made from about 1910 to 1915. In 1915 it was called the Model 30G.
Estimated Value: Excellent: $280.00
Very good: $210.00

Marlin Model 17 and 17G

Gauge: 12
Action: Slide action; exposed hammer
Magazine: 5-shot tubular
Barrel: 30" or 32" full choke; others available by special order
Finish: Blued; walnut straight grip stock and grooved slide handle
Approximate wt.: 7½ lbs.lbs.
Comments: This solid frame shotgun was made from about 1906 to 1915; from 1908 to 1915 as Model 17G.
Estimated Value: Excellent: $300.00
Very good: $225.00

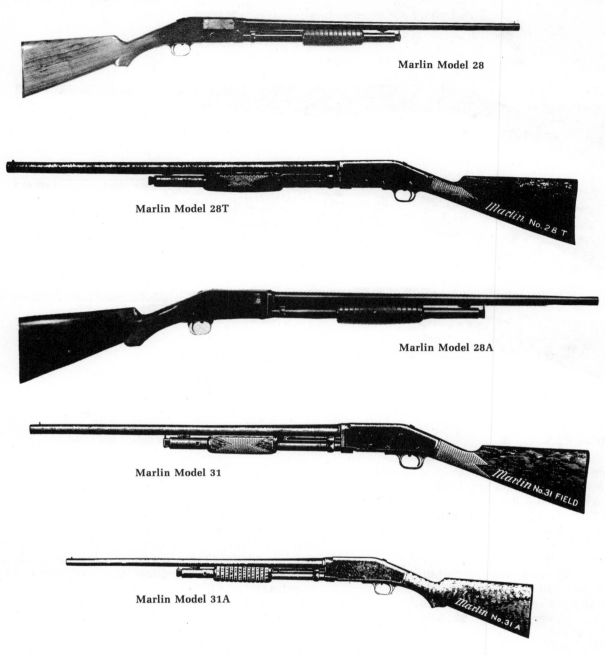

Marlin Model 28

Marlin Model 28T

Marlin Model 28A

Marlin Model 31

Marlin Model 31A

Marlin Model 28, 28T, 28TS

Gauge: 12
Action: Slide action; hammerless; side ejection
Magazine: 5-shot tubular
Barrel: 26″ or 28″ cylinder bore or modified choke; 30″ or 32″ full choke
Finish: Blued; checkered walnut pistol grip stock and slide handle
Approximate wt.: 8 lbs.
Comments: This takedown shotgun was produced from about 1913 to just before World War I. The Model 28T and 28TS were Trap grade guns with an available straight stock. Add $100.00 for 28T, 28TS.
Estimated Value: Excellent: $325.00
  Very good: $245.00

Marlin Model 28A

Basically the same as the Model 28. Made from about 1920 to 1922; replaced by the Model 43A.
Estimated Value: Excellent: $300.00
  Very good: $225.00

Marlin Model 31

This shotgun is much like the Model 28 except: 20 or 16 gauge. Made from about 1915 to 1917.
Estimated Value: Excellent: $360.00
  Very good: $270.00

Marlin Model 31A

Very similar to the Model 28A in 20 gauge only. Replaced by the Model 44A.
Estimated Value: Excellent: $290.00
  Very good: $220.00

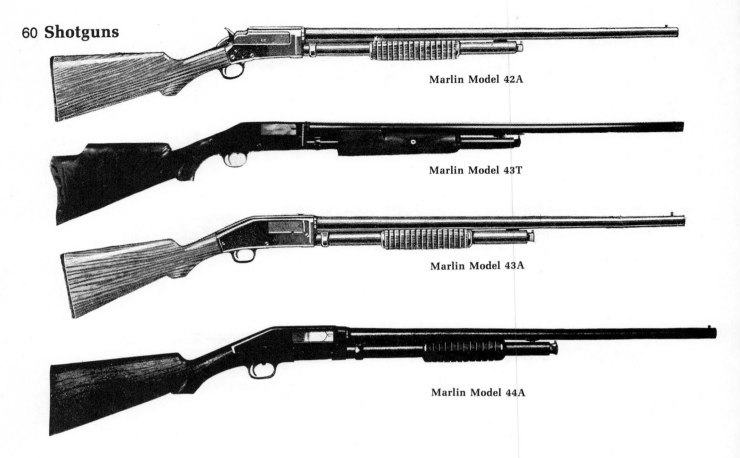

Marlin Model 42A

Marlin Model 43T

Marlin Model 43A

Marlin Model 44A

Marlin Model 42A

Gauge: 12
Action: Slide action; exposed hammer; side ejection
Magazine: 5-shot tubular; bottom load
Barrel: 26″ cylinder bore, 28″ modified, 30″ and 32″ full choke; 2¾″ chamber; round matted barrel
Finish: Blued; black walnut semi-pistol grip stock, grooved slide handle
Approximate wt.: 7½ lbs.
Comments: A takedown shotgun manufactured from about 1922 to 1934.
Estimated Value: Excellent: $280.00
  Very good: $210.00

Marlin Model 49

This shotgun is similar to the Model 42A. It was given away with stock in the corporation. It was produced from about 1925 to 1928.
Estimated Value: Excellent: $375.00
  Very good: $275.00

Marlin Model 43A

Gauge: 12
Action: Slide action; hammerless; side ejection
Magazine: 5-shot tubular
Barrel: 26″ cylinder bore, 28″ modified, 30″ and 32″ full choke; 2¾″ chamber
Finish: Blued; walnut pistol grip stock and grooved slide handle
Approximate wt.: 8 lbs.
Comments: Made from about 1923 to 1930. It was a new style takedown.
Estimated Value: Excellent: $240.00
  Very good: $180.00

Marlin Model 43T and 43TS

Same basic shotgun as the Model 43A except it has checkered Monte Carlo stock and forearm with recoil pad. The Model 43TS had a choice of many options and the value thereof is dependent on the number and type of extras.
Estimated Value: Excellent: $300.00
  Very good: $225.00

Marlin Model 44A

Gauge: 20
Action: Slide action; hammerless; side ejection
Magazine: 4-shot tubular; bottom load
Barrel: 25″ or 28″ cylinder bore, modified or full choke; 2¾″ chamber
Finish: Blued; walnut pistol grip stock and grooved slide handle
Approximate wt.: 6 lbs.
Comments: A takedown model produced from about 1923 to 1935.
Estimated Value: Excellent: $280.00
  Very good: $210.00

Marlin Model 44S

Same basic shotgun as the Model 44A except it came with either straight or pistol grip checkered stock and forearm.
Estimated Value: Excellent: $275.00
  Very good: $205.00

Marlin Model 63A

Gauge: 12
Action: Slide action; hammerless; side ejector
Magazine: 5-shot tubular
Barrel: 26″ cylinder bore, 28″ modified choke, 30″ or 32″ full choke
Finish: Blued; plain walnut pistol grip stock and grooved slide handle
Approximate wt.: 8 lbs.
Comments: An improved version of the Model 43A. Made from about 1931 to 1935.
Estimated Value: Excellent: $275.00
Very good: $200.00

Marlin Model 63T and 63TS

The Model 63T was basically the same shotgun as the Model 63A except it was only produced in 30″ or 32″ barrel and had a checkered straight stock. The Model 63TS could be ordered to the buyers specifications. Prices are for standard trap gun.
Estimated Value: Excellent: $325.00
Very good: $240.00

Marlin Model Premier Mark I

Marlin Model Premier Mark II

Marlin Model Premier Mark IV

Marlin Model Premier Mark I

Gauge: 12
Action: Slide action; hammerless; side ejection
Magazine: 3-shot tubular
Barrel: 26″ cylinder bore, 28″ modified, 30″ full choke; ventilated rib available; 28″ slug barrel with rifle sights available; 2¾″ chamber
Finish: Blued; walnut pistol grip stock and forearm; recoil pad optional
Approximate wt.: 7 lbs.
Comments: Made from about 1960 to 1963.
Estimated Value: Excellent: $150.00
Very good: $115.00

Marlin Model Premier Mark II

This is basically the same shotgun as the Premier Mark I except the stock and forearm are checkered and the receiver is engraved.
Estimated Value: Excellent: $205.00
Very good: $155.00

Marlin Model Premier Mark IV

This is basically the same shotgun as the Mark II except the wood is more elaborate and the engraving heavier.
Estimated Value: Excellent: $270.00
Very good: $200.00

Marlin Model 120 Magnum

Marlin Model 120T

Marlin Deluxe 120 Slug Gun

Similar to the Marlin 120 with a 20″ slug barrel and rifle sights. Produced from the late 1970's to 1986.

Estimated Value: **Excellent:** **$275.00**
Very good: **$210.00**

Marlin Model 120T

This is basically the same shotgun as Model 120 with a Monte Carlo stock and 30″ full choke or 30″ modified trap choke barrel. This gun was offered from 1973 to the late 1970's.

Estimated Value: **Excellent:** **$280.00**
Very good: **$210.00**

Marlin Model 120 Magnum

Gauge: 12 gauge magnum
Action: Slide action; hammerless
Magazine: 5-shot tubular (4-shot with 3″shells)
Barrel: 26″ cylinder bore, 28″ modified or 30″ full choke
Finish: Blued; ventilated rib; checkered walnut, pistol grip stock and forearm; recoil pad
Approximate wt.: 7¾ lbs.
Comments: This gun was first offered in 1971. In 1973 a 40″ MXR Magnum barrel and a choked 26″ slug barrel were offered for the first time. Discontinued in 1986.

Estimated Value: **Excellent:** **$275.00**
Very good: **$210.00**

Marlin Glenfield 778

Marlin Glenfield 778 Slug

Similar to the Glenfield 778 with a 20″ slug barrel and rifle sights.

Estimated Value: **Excellent:** **$200.00**
Very good: **$150.00**

Marlin Glenfield 778

Gauge: 12, regular or magnum
Action: Slide action; hammerless; repeating
Magazine: 5-shot tubular; 4-shot with 3″ magnum
Barrel: 26″ improved cylinder; 28″ modified; 30″ full choke; ventilated rib available; 38″ MXR full choke barrel available without rib
Finish: Blued; checkered hardwood, semi-pistol grip stock and fluted slide handle; recoil pad
Approximate wt.: 7¾ lbs.
Comments: Made from about the late 1970's to early 1980's. Add $50.00 for ventilated rib or MXR barrel.

Estimated Value: **Excellent:** **$175.00**
Very good: **$130.00**

Mauser

Mauser Model 496 Trap

Mauser Model 496 Competition

Mauser Model 496 Competition

Similar to the Model 496 with select wood; higher ventilated rib.

Estimated Value: **Excellent:** **$625.00**
Very good: **$475.00**

Mauser Model 496 Trap

Gauge: 12
Action: Box lock; top lever, break-open; hammerless; automatic ejectors; single shot
Magazine: None
Barrel: 32″ modified or 34″ full chokes; ventilated rib
Finish: Blued; checkered walnut Monte Carlo pistol grip stock and tapered forearm; engraved; recoil pad
Approximate wt.: 8½ lbs.
Comments: Imported in the 1970's.
Estimated Value: **Excellent:** **$500.00**
Very good: **$375.00**

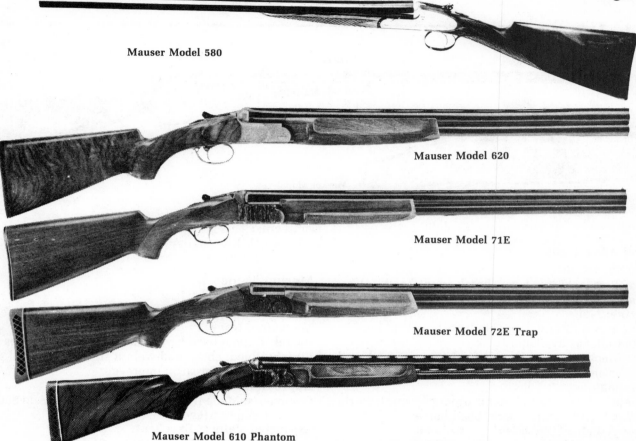

Mauser Model 580

Mauser Model 620

Mauser Model 71E

Mauser Model 72E Trap

Mauser Model 610 Phantom

Mauser Model 580

Gauge: 12
Action: Side lock; top lever break-open; hammerless
Magazine: None
Barrel: Double barrel; 28″-30″, various chokes
Finish: Blued; checkered walnut straight stock and tapered forearm; engraved
Approximate wt.: 7¾ lbs.
Comments: Imported in the 1970's.
Estimated Value: Excellent: $825.00
Very good: $620.00

Mauser Model 620

Gauge: 12
Action: Box lock; top lever, break-open; hammerless; automatic ejectors; single trigger
Magazine: None
Barrel: Over and under double barrel; 28″, 30″ improved cylinder & modified or modified & full or skeet chokes; ribbed
Finish: Blued; plain walnut pistol grip stock and forearm; recoil pad
Approximate wt.: 7½ lbs.
Comments: Imported from the early to mid 1970's.
Estimated Value: Excellent: $875.00
Very good: $650.00

Mauser Model 71E

Similar to the Model 620 with double triggers and no recoil pad; 28″ barrel.
Estimated Value: Excellent: $420.00
Very good: $315.00

Mauser Model 72E Trap

Similar to the Model 71E with large recoil pad; engraving; wide rib; single trigger.
Estimated Value: Excellent: $575.00
Very good: $430.00

Mauser Model 610 Phantom

Gauge: 12
Action: Box lock; top lever, break-open; hammerless
Magazine: None
Barrel: Over and under double barrel; ventilated rib between barrels and on top barrel; 30″, 32″ various chokes
Finish: Blued; case hardened frame; checkered walnut pistol grip stock and forearm; recoil pad
Approximate wt.: 8 lbs.
Comments: Made in the mid 1970's.
Estimated Value: Excellent: $900.00
Very good: $675.00

Mauser Contest

Gauge: 12
Action: Top lever break-open; automatic ejectors; single selective trigger
Magazine: None
Barrel: Over and under double barrel; 27½″ improved cylinder & improved modified
Finish: Blued; engraved grey sideplates; checkered walnut pistol grip stock and lipped forearm
Approximate wt.: 7½ lbs.
Comments: Add $500.00 for trap model.
Estimated Value: Excellent: $1,000.00
Very good: $ 750.00

Merkel

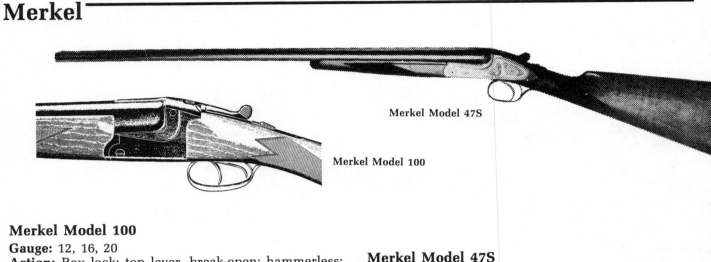

Merkel Model 47S

Merkel Model 100

Merkel Model 100

Gauge: 12, 16, 20
Action: Box lock; top lever, break-open; hammerless; double triggers
Magazine: None
Barrel: Over and under double barrel; several lengths and chokes available
Finish: Blued; checkered walnut pistol grip stock and forearm
Approximate wt.: 8½ lbs.
Comments: A German shotgun produced until World War II. Add $50.00 for ribbed barrel.
Estimated Value: Excellent: $725.00
Very good: $550.00

Merkel Model 47S

Gauge: 12, 16, 20
Action: Side lock; top lever break-open; hammerless
Magazine: None
Barrel: Double barrel; various lengths and chokes
Finish: Blued; checkered walnut straight or pistol grip stock and forearm; engraved
Approximate wt.: 8 lbs.
Comments: Made from the 1930's to 1970's. Add $50.00 for single trigger.
Estimated Value: Excellent: $1,500.00
Very good: $1,125.00

Mossberg

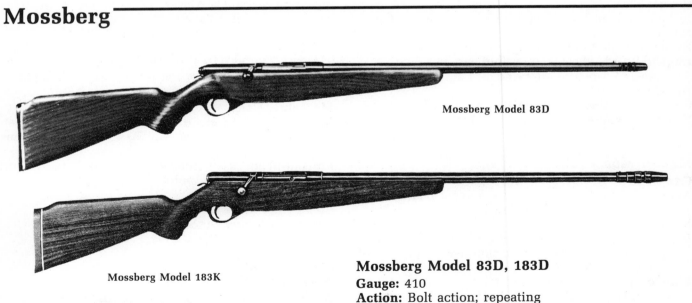

Mossberg Model 83D

Mossberg Model 183K

Mossberg Model 183K

Similar to the 183D with adjustable choke and recoil pad. Made from the early 1950's to mid 1980's.
Estimated Value: Excellent: $110.00
Very good: $ 80.00

Mossberg Model 83D, 183D

Gauge: 410
Action: Bolt action; repeating
Magazine: 2-shot, top loading; fixed magazine
Barrel: 23″ on 83D, 24″ on 183D; interchangeable choke fittings
Finish: Blued; hardwood Monte Carlo semi-pistol grip one-piece stock and forearm
Approximate wt.: 5½ lbs.
Comments: Made as the 83D from about 1940 to 1947 and as the 183D from 1948 until the early 1970's.
Estimated Value: Excellent: $80.00
Very good: $60.00

Mossberg Model 185K

Mossberg Model 190K

Mossberg Model 85D

Mossberg Model 190D

Mossberg Model 195D

Mossberg Model 385K

Mossberg Model 190K

Similar to the 183K in 16 gauge. Made from the mid 1950's to early 1960's.

Estimated Value: **Excellent:** **$80.00**
Very good: **$60.00**

Mossberg Model 195K

Similar to the 183K in 12 gauge. Made from the mid 1950's to early 1960's.

Estimated Value: **Excellent:** **$90.00**
Very good: **$70.00**

Mossberg Model 185K

Similar to the 183K in 20 gauge. Made from about 1950 to early 1960's.

Estimated Value: **Excellent:** **$85.00**
Very good: **$65.00**

Mossberg Model 190D

Similar to the 185D in 16 gauge. Made from the mid 1950's to early 1960's.

Estimated Value: **Excellent:** **$85.00**
Very good: **$65.00**

Mossberg Model 195D

Similar to the 185D in 12 gauge. Made from the mid 1950's to early 1970's.

Estimated Value: **Excellent:** **$90.00**
Very good: **$70.00**

Mossberg Model 385K

Gauge: 20
Action: Bolt action; repeating
Magazine: 2-shot detachable box
Barrel: 26″ adjustable choke
Finish: Blued; wood Monte Carlo semi-pistol grip one-piece stock and tapered forearm; recoil pad
Approximate wt.: 6½ lbs.
Comments: Made from the early 1960's to early 1980's.
Estimated Value: **Excellent:** **$100.00**
Very good: **$ 75.00**

Mossberg Model 85D, 185D

Gauge: 20
Action: Bolt action; repeating
Magazine: 2-shot detachable box
Barrel: 25″ on 85D, 26″ on 185D; interchangeable choke fittings
Finish: Blued; hardwood pistol grip one-piece stock and forearm
Approximate wt.: 6½ lbs.
Comments: Made as the 85D from about 1940 to 1948 and as the 185D from 1948 to the early 1970's.
Estimated Value: **Excellent:** **$95.00**
Very good: **$75.00**

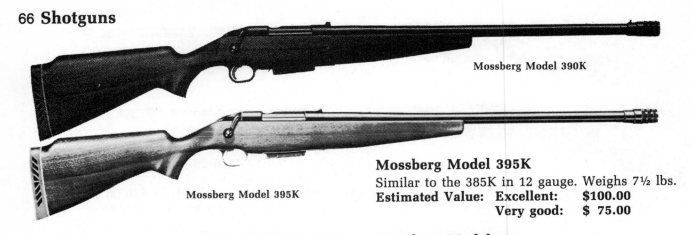

Mossberg Model 390K

Mossberg Model 395K

Mossberg Model 395K
Similar to the 385K in 12 gauge. Weighs 7½ lbs.
Estimated Value: Excellent: $100.00
Very good: $ 75.00

Mossberg Model 585
Similar to the Model 385K with improved safety. Produced in mid 1980's.
Estimated Value: Excellent: $120.00
Very good: $ 90.00

Mossberg Model 595
Similar to the Model 395K with improved safety. Introduced in 1984. Available with 28″ adjustable choke barrel or 38″ waterfowl barrel. Add $20.00 for Waterfowl model.
Estimated Value: Excellent: $120.00
Very good: $ 90.00

Mossberg Model 390 K
Similar to the 385K with a 28″ barrel in 16 gauge. Discontinued in the late 1970's.
Estimated Value: Excellent: $95.00
Very good: $75.00

Mossberg Model 395 SPL
Similar to the Model 395K with a 38″ full choke barrel for waterfowl; swivels. Introduced in 1982.
Estimated Value: Excellent: $115.00
Very good: $ 90.00

Mossberg Model 200D

Mossberg Model 200K

Mossberg Model 3000 Field
Gauge: 12, 20; regular or magnum
Action: Slide action, hammerless, repeating
Magazine: 4-shot tubular, 3-shot in magnum
Barrel: 26″ improved cylinder, 28″ modified or full, 30″ full; ventilated rib; "Multi choke" available
Finish: Checkered walnut pistol grip stock and slide handle
Approximate wt.: 6¼ to 7½ lbs.
Comments: Introduced in the mid 1980's. Add $25.00 for "Multi choke".
Estimated Value: New (retail): $359.95
Excellent: $265.00
Very good: $200.00

Mossberg Model 3000 Waterfowler
Similar to the Model 3000 with 30″ full choke barrel and Parkerized, oiled finish or camo finish with "Speedfeed" storage stock (add $45.00). Add $30.00 for "Multi choke".
Estimated Value: New (retail): $385.95
Excellent: $290.00
Very good: $215.00

Mossberg Model 3000 Slug
Similar to the Model 3000 with a 22″ slug barrel and rifle sights. Add $35.00 for black finish with "Speedfeed" storage stock.
Estimated Value: New (retail): $332.95
Excellent: $250.00
Very good: $185.00

Mossberg Model 200D
Gauge: 12
Action: Slide action; hammerless; repeating; slide handle is metal cover over wood forearm
Magazine: 3-shot detachable box
Barrel: 28″ interchangeable choke fittings
Finish: Blued; wood Monte Carlo semi-pistol grip one-piece stock and forearm
Approximate wt.: 7½ lbs.
Comments: Made from the mid to late 1950's.
Estimated Value: Excellent: $100.00
Very good: $ 75.00

Mossberg Model 200K
Similar to the 200D with adjustable choke.
Estimated Value: Excellent: $110.00
Very good: $ 85.00

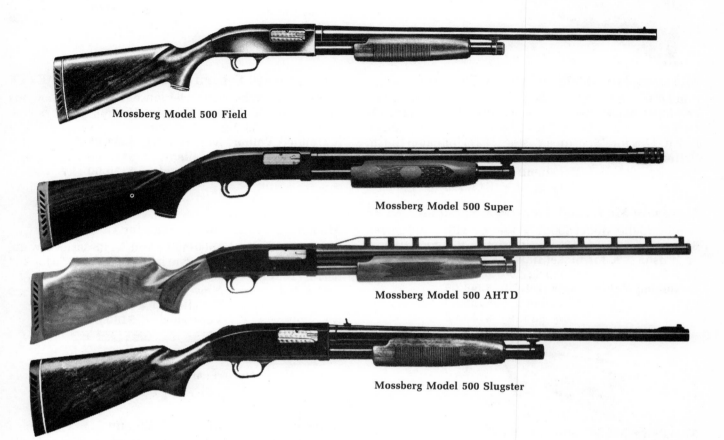

Mossberg Model 500 Field

Mossberg Model 500 Super

Mossberg Model 500 AHT D

Mossberg Model 500 Slugster

Mossberg Model 500 Field

Gauge: 12, 16, 20
Action: Slide action; hammerless; repeating
Magazine: 6-shot tubular
Barrel: 26″ adjustable choke or improved cylinder; 28″ modified or full; 30″ full choke in 12 gauge only; available with "Accu-Choke" after 1984. Vent rib available
Finish: Blued; walnut, pistol grip stock and grooved slide handle; recoil pad; camo finish and "Speedfeed" stock available in 1986.
Approximate wt.: 6-8 lbs.
Comments: Manufactured from about 1960 to present. Add 9% for vent rib; add 9% for "Accu-Choke"; add 35% for camo finish and "Speedfeed" stock.
Estimated Value: New (retail): $228.95
Excellent: $175.00
Very good: $130.00

Mossberg Model 500 Super

Similar to the 500 Field with checkered stock and slide handle & ventilated rib. 12 gauge magnum.
Estimated Value: Excellent: $200.00
Very good: $150.00

Mossberg Model 500 Hi-Rib Trap AHTD, AHT

Similar to 500 with high rib barrel and Monte Carlo stock. AHT full choke; AHTD had adjustable choke; 28″ or 30″ barrel.
Estimated Value: New (retail): $353.95
Excellent: $270.00
Very good: $200.00

Mossberg Model 500 Slugster

Similar to 500 with 18″ or 24″ slug barrel and rifle sights. Add 20% for removable choke.
Estimated Value: New (retail): $248.95
Excellent: $190.00
Very good: $140.00

Mossberg Model 500 ALDR, CLDR, ALDRX

Similar to 500 in 12 gauge (ALDR) and 20 gauge (CLDR) with removable choke. Add $50.00 for additional slugster barrel (ALDRX).
Estimated Value: Excellent: $200.00
Very good: $150.00

Mossberg Model 500 ALMR Duck Gun

Similar to the 500 in 12 gauge with 30″ or 32″ vent rib barrel for 3″ magnum. Discontinued in the early 1980's.
Estimated Value: Excellent: $190.00
Very good: $140.00

Mossberg Model 500 Security & Persuader ATP8

Mossberg Model 500 Security & Persuader ATP6

Similar to the Model 500, built in several models for law enforcement use. 12 gauge, 6-shot, 18½″ barrel. Add 17% for Parkerized finish; 9% for rifle sights; 26% for nickel finish; 17% for "Speedfeed" stock; 22% for camo finish.

Estimated Value: New (retail): $231.95
Excellent: $175.00
Very good: $130.00

Mossberg Model 500 Security & Persuader ATP8

Similar to the Model 500 ATP6 series with a 20″ barrel, 8-shot capacity. Add 8% for rifle sights; 16% for Parkerized finish; 24% for nickel finish; 4% for accessory lug; 16% for "Speedfeed" stock; 20% for camo finish.

Estimated Value: New (retail): $248.95
Excellent: $185.00
Very good: $140.00

Mossberg 500 Security & Persuader CTP6, ETP6

Similar to the other 500 series law enforcement shotguns in 20 gauge (CTP6) or 410 bore (ETP6); 18½″ barrel; 6-shot. Add $5.00 for 20 gauge.

Estimated Value: New (retail): $231.95
Excellent: $175.00
Very good: $130.00

Mossberg Model 500 Persuader Cruiser

Similar to the Model 500 ATP6 and ATP8 series law enforcement shotguns with one-hand grip. Add 6% for 20″ barrel; 26% for nickel finish.

Estimated Value: New (retail): $231.95
Excellent: $175.00
Very good: $130.00

Mossberg Model 500 ER

Mossberg Model 500 ER, ELR

Similar to the 500 Field in 410 gauge; 26″ barrel; skeet version has checkering and ventilated rib. Discontinued in the early 1980's.

Estimated Value: Excellent: $190.00
Very good: $140.00

Mossberg Model 500 Regal

Similar to the Model 500 with deluxe finish, crown design on receiver. Introduced in 1986. Add $20.00 for "Accu-Choke".

Estimated Value: New (retail): $266.95
Excellent: $200.00
Very good: $150.00

Mossberg Model 500 APR Pigeon

Similar to the 500 Field except; engraving; ventilated rib. Made from the late 1960's to the late 1970's.

Estimated Value: Excellent: $260.00
Very good: $190.00

Mossberg Model 500 APTR Trap

Similar to the 500 APR with a 30″ full choke barrel; Monte Carlo stock. Discontinued in the late 1970's.

Estimated Value: Excellent: $275.00
Very good: $200.00

Mossberg Model 5500

Mossberg Model 5500

Gauge: 12 regular or magnum
Action: Gas operated semi-automatic
Magazine: 4-shot tubular
Barrel: 26″ improved cylinder, 28″ modified, 30″ full; 28″ "Accu-Choke" with interchangeable tubes; ventilated rib available; 25″ on youth model.
Finish: Blued; checkered hardwood semi-pistol grip stock and forearm; aluminum alloy receiver; small stock on youth model.
Approximate wt.: 7½ lbs.
Comments: Produced from the early to mid 1980's. Add $20.00 for "Accu-Choke"; $15.00 for magnum.
Estimated Value: Excellent: $330.00
Very good: $250.00

Mossberg Model 5500 Slugster

Similar to the Model 5500 with 18½″ or 24″ slug barrel, rifle sights and swivels.

Estimated Value: Excellent: $335.00
Very good: $255.00

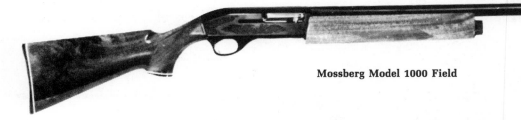

Mossberg Model 1000 Field

Mossberg Model 1000 Super

Gauge: 12 or 20, regular or magnum
Action: Gas-operated semi-automatic
Magazine: 3-shot tubular
Barrel: 26″, 28″, 30″ "Multi choke"; ventilated rib
Finish: Blued; checkered walnut pistol grip stock and forearm; recoil pad; scrolling on receiver
Approximate wt.: 6¾ to 7¾ lbs.
Comments: Introduced in the mid 1980's.
Estimated Value: New (retail): $534.95
Excellent: $400.00
Very good: $300.00

Mossberg Model 1000 Super Waterfowler

Similar to the Model 1000 Super with dull wood and Parkerized finish; 12 gauge only.
Estimated Value: New (retail): $561.95
Excellent: $420.00
Very good: $315.00

Mossberg Model 1000 Super Slug

Similar to the Model 1000 Super with 22″ slug barrel.
Estimated Value: New (retail): $525.95
Excellent: $395.00
Very good: $295.00

Mossberg Model 1000 Super Skeet

Similar to the Model 1000 Super with 25″ barrel.
Estimated Value: New (retail): $657.95
Excellent: $495.00
Very good: $370.00

Mossberg Model 1000 Field

Similar to the Model 1000 Super with alloy receiver; various chokes available including a 26″ skeet barrel; add $30.00 for "Multi choke"; Junior model has 22″ barrel with "Multi choke" (add $25.00).
Estimated Value: New (retail): $438.95
Excellent: $330.00
Very good: $245.00

Mossberg Model 1000 Slug

Similar to the Model 1000 Field with 22″ slug barrel, rifle sights.
Estimated Value: New (retail): $429.95
Excellent: $320.00
Very good: $240.00

Mossberg Model 1000 Trap

Similar to the Model 1000 Field with a 30″ "Multi choke" barrel, recoil pad, Monte Carlo stock and high-rib barrel.
Estimated Value: New (retail): $559.95
Excellent: $420.00
Very good: $315.00

Mossberg Model 712 Camo

Similar to the Model 712 with camo finish and "Speedfeed" storage stock. Add $20.00 for "Accu-choke".
Estimated Value: New (retail): $389.95
Excellent: $290.00
Very good: $220.00

Mossberg Model 712 Regal

Similar to the Model 712 with deluxe finish, crown design on receiver. Introduced in 1986. Add $20.00 for "Accu-choke".
Estimated Value: New (retail): $365.95
Excellent: $275.00
Very good: $200.00

Mossberg Model 712

Gauge: 12, regular or magnum
Action: Gas-operated semi-automatic
Magazine: 4-shot tubular, 3-shot in magnum
Barrel: 30″ full, 28″ modified, 24″ "Accu-choke", 24″ slug; ventilated rib available
Finish: Alloy receiver with anodized finish; checkered walnut finish semi-pistol grip stock and forearm; recoil pad; junior model has 13″ stock
Approximate wt.: 7½ lbs.
Comments: This shotgun was designed to handle any 12 gauge shell interchangeably. Introduced in 1986. Add $15.00 for slug model with rifle sights; $15.00 for ventilated rib; $40.00 for "Accu-choke".
Estimated Value: New (retail): $314.95
Excellent: $235.00
Very good: $180.00

New Haven (Mossberg)

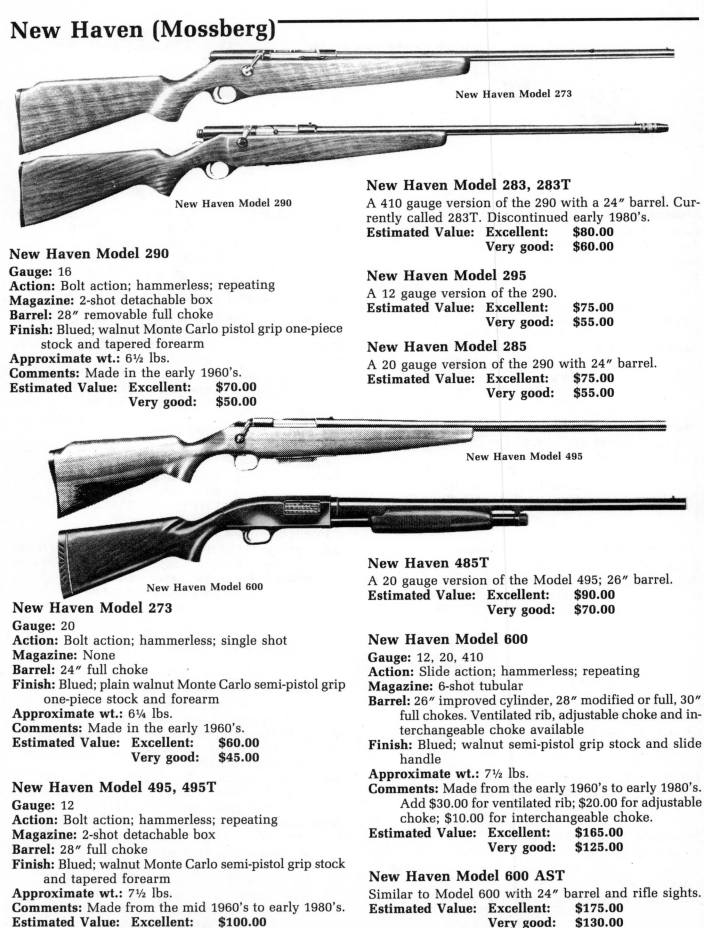

New Haven Model 273

New Haven Model 290

New Haven Model 290

Gauge: 16
Action: Bolt action; hammerless; repeating
Magazine: 2-shot detachable box
Barrel: 28″ removable full choke
Finish: Blued; walnut Monte Carlo pistol grip one-piece stock and tapered forearm
Approximate wt.: 6½ lbs.
Comments: Made in the early 1960's.
Estimated Value: Excellent: $70.00
Very good: $50.00

New Haven Model 495

New Haven Model 600

New Haven Model 273

Gauge: 20
Action: Bolt action; hammerless; single shot
Magazine: None
Barrel: 24″ full choke
Finish: Blued; plain walnut Monte Carlo semi-pistol grip one-piece stock and forearm
Approximate wt.: 6¼ lbs.
Comments: Made in the early 1960's.
Estimated Value: Excellent: $60.00
Very good: $45.00

New Haven Model 495, 495T

Gauge: 12
Action: Bolt action; hammerless; repeating
Magazine: 2-shot detachable box
Barrel: 28″ full choke
Finish: Blued; walnut Monte Carlo semi-pistol grip stock and tapered forearm
Approximate wt.: 7½ lbs.
Comments: Made from the mid 1960's to early 1980's.
Estimated Value: Excellent: $100.00
Very good: $ 75.00

New Haven Model 283, 283T

A 410 gauge version of the 290 with a 24″ barrel. Currently called 283T. Discontinued early 1980's.
Estimated Value: Excellent: $80.00
Very good: $60.00

New Haven Model 295

A 12 gauge version of the 290.
Estimated Value: Excellent: $75.00
Very good: $55.00

New Haven Model 285

A 20 gauge version of the 290 with 24″ barrel.
Estimated Value: Excellent: $75.00
Very good: $55.00

New Haven 485T

A 20 gauge version of the Model 495; 26″ barrel.
Estimated Value: Excellent: $90.00
Very good: $70.00

New Haven Model 600

Gauge: 12, 20, 410
Action: Slide action; hammerless; repeating
Magazine: 6-shot tubular
Barrel: 26″ improved cylinder, 28″ modified or full, 30″ full chokes. Ventilated rib, adjustable choke and interchangeable choke available
Finish: Blued; walnut semi-pistol grip stock and slide handle
Approximate wt.: 7½ lbs.
Comments: Made from the early 1960's to early 1980's. Add $30.00 for ventilated rib; $20.00 for adjustable choke; $10.00 for interchangeable choke.
Estimated Value: Excellent: $165.00
Very good: $125.00

New Haven Model 600 AST

Similar to Model 600 with 24″ barrel and rifle sights.
Estimated Value: Excellent: $175.00
Very good: $130.00

Noble

Noble Model 420

Noble Model 420

Gauge: 12, 16, 20
Action: Box lock; top lever, break-open; hammerless; double triggers
Magazine: None
Barrel: Double barrel, 28″ modified & full choke
Finish: Blued; checkered walnut pistol grip stock and forearm
Approximate wt.: 6¾ lbs.
Comments: Made from the late 1950's to the early 1970's.
Estimated Value: Excellent: $210.00
                   Very good: $160.00

Noble Model 420 EK

A fancy version of the Model 420 with automatic ejectors; select walnut; recoil pad; engraving; sights; gold inlay. Made in the late 1960's.
Estimated Value: Excellent: $275.00
                   Very good: $205.00

Noble Model 450E

Very similar to Model 420EK. Made from the late 1960's to the early 1970's.
Estimated Value: Excellent: $280.00
                   Very good: $210.00

Noble Model 40

Noble Model 50

Basically the same gun as the Model 40 without recoil pad or "Multi-Choke".
Estimated Value: Excellent: $125.00
                   Very good: $ 95.00

Noble Model 40

Gauge: 12
Action: Slide action; hammerless
Magazine: 5-shot tubular
Barrel: 28″ with multi-choke
Finish: Blued; plain walnut, pistol grip stock and grooved slide handle; recoil pad
Approximate wt.: 7½ lbs.
Comments: Made from the early to mid 1950's.
Estimated Value: Excellent: $140.00
                   Very good: $110.00

Noble Model 60

Noble Model 60 ACP

Very similar to Model 60 with a ventilated rib. Made from late 1960's to early 1970's.
Estimated Value: Excellent: $140.00
                   Very good: $110.00

Noble Model 60

Gauge: 12, 16
Action: Slide action; hammerless
Magazine: 5-shot tubular
Barrel: 28″ with variable choke
Finish: Blued; plain walnut, pistol grip stock and grooved slide handle; recoil pad
Approximate wt.: 7½ lbs.
Comments: Manufactured in takedown version from the mid 1950's to late 1960's.
Estimated Value: Excellent: $130.00
                   Very good: $100.00

Noble Model 60 AF

Noble Model 160 Deer Gun

Noble Model 66 RCLP

Noble Model 65

Noble Model 70

Noble Model 602

Noble Model 602 CLP

Noble Model 60 AF

A fancier version of the Model 60 with special steel barrel; select wood; fluted comb. Made only during the mid 1960's.

Estimated Value: Excellent: $145.00
Very good: $115.00

Noble Model 160 Deer Gun, 166L Deer Gun

Very similar to the Model 60 with a 24″ barrel; sights; swivels. Made in the mid 1960's as 160 and from late 1960's to early 1970's as 166L.

Estimated Value: Excellent: $150.00
Very good: $120.00

Noble Model 65

Basically the same as the Model 60 without the recoil pad or adjustable choke.

Estimated Value: Excellent: $120.00
Very good: $ 90.00

Noble Model 66 RCLP

Similar to the Model 60 ACP with a fancier checkered stock.

Estimated Value: Excellent: $145.00
Very good: $110.00

Noble Model 70 and 70X

Gauge: 410
Action: Slide action; hammerless
Magazine: 5-shot tubular
Barrel: 26″ modified or full choke
Finish: Blued; checkered walnut pistol grip stock and slide handle
Approximate wt.: 6 lbs.
Comments: Made from the late 1950's to late 1960's as Model 70 and from the late 1960's to early 1970's as 70X.

Estimated Value: Excellent: $150.00
Very good: $115.00

Noble Model 602

Similar to the Model 70 in 20 gauge and 28″ barrel; weighs 6½ lbs. Grooved slide handle.

Estimated Value: Excellent: $155.00
Very good: $120.00

Noble Model 602 CLP, 602 RCLP, 602 RLP

The 602 CLP is same as 602 with adjustable choke and recoil pad; 602 RCLP is same as 602 with recoil pad; 602 RLP is same as 602 with recoil pad and ventilated rib. Add $20.00 for ventilated rib.

Estimated Value: Excellent: $160.00
Very good: $125.00

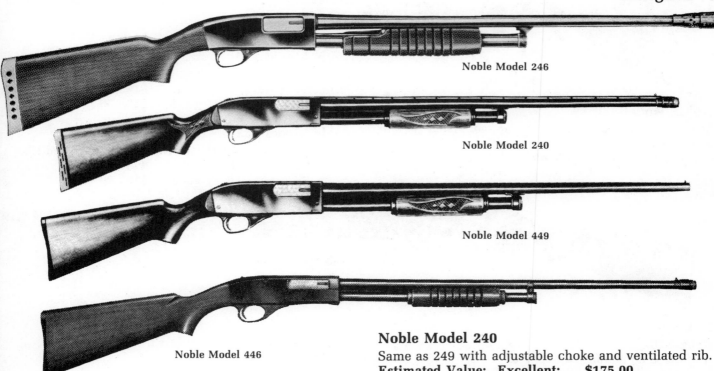

Noble Model 246

Noble Model 240

Noble Model 449

Noble Model 446

Noble Model 249

Gauge: 20
Action: Slide action; hammerless
Magazine: 5-shot tubular
Barrel: 28″ modified or full choke
Finish: Blued; checkered walnut pistol grip stock and slide handle; recoil pad
Approximate wt.: 6½ lbs.
Comments: Produced in the early 1970's.
Estimated Value: **Excellent:** $150.00
Very good: $115.00

Noble Model 246

Same as 249 with adjustable choke.
Estimated Value: **Excellent:** $160.00
Very good: $120.00

Noble Model 243

Same as 249 with ventilated rib.
Estimated Value: **Excellent:** $165.00
Very good: $125.00

Noble Model 240

Same as 249 with adjustable choke and ventilated rib.
Estimated Value: **Excellent:** $175.00
Very good: $130.00

Noble Model 449

Similar to Model 249 without recoil pad and in 410 bore.
Estimated Value: **Excellent:** $160.00
Very good: $120.00

Noble Model 446

Similar to Model 246 without recoil pad and in 410 bore.
Estimated Value: **Excellent:** $165.00
Very good: $125.00

Noble Model 443

Similar to Model 243 without recoil pad and in 410 bore.
Estimated Value: **Excellent:** $170.00
Very good: $130.00

Noble Model 440

Similar to Model 240 without recoil pad and in 410 bore.
Estimated Value: **Excellent:** $180.00
Very good: $135.00

Noble Model 390 Deer Gun

Noble Model 390 Deer Gun

Similar to Model 339 with a 24″ slug barrel; sights; swivels.
Estimated Value: **Excellent:** $160.00
Very good: $120.00

Noble Model 339

Gauge: 12, 16
Action: Slide action; hammerless
Magazine: 6-shot tubular
Barrel: 28″ modified or full choke
Finish: Blued; checkered walnut pistol grip stock and slide handle
Approximate wt.: 7½ lbs.
Comments: Made in the early 1970's.
Estimated Value: **Excellent:** $155.00
Very good: $115.00

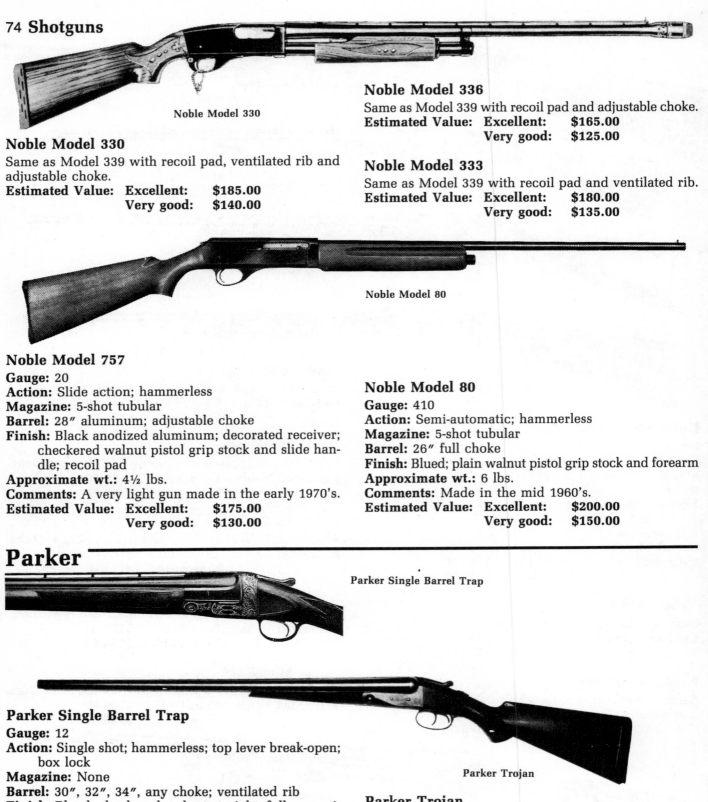

Noble Model 330

Noble Model 330

Same as Model 339 with recoil pad, ventilated rib and adjustable choke.

Estimated Value: Excellent: **$185.00**
Very good: **$140.00**

Noble Model 336

Same as Model 339 with recoil pad and adjustable choke.

Estimated Value: Excellent: **$165.00**
Very good: **$125.00**

Noble Model 333

Same as Model 339 with recoil pad and ventilated rib.

Estimated Value: Excellent: **$180.00**
Very good: **$135.00**

Noble Model 80

Noble Model 757

Gauge: 20
Action: Slide action; hammerless
Magazine: 5-shot tubular
Barrel: 28″ aluminum; adjustable choke
Finish: Black anodized aluminum; decorated receiver; checkered walnut pistol grip stock and slide handle; recoil pad
Approximate wt.: 4½ lbs.
Comments: A very light gun made in the early 1970's.
Estimated Value: Excellent: **$175.00**
Very good: **$130.00**

Noble Model 80

Gauge: 410
Action: Semi-automatic; hammerless
Magazine: 5-shot tubular
Barrel: 26″ full choke
Finish: Blued; plain walnut pistol grip stock and forearm
Approximate wt.: 6 lbs.
Comments: Made in the mid 1960's.
Estimated Value: Excellent: **$200.00**
Very good: **$150.00**

Parker

Parker Single Barrel Trap

Parker Trojan

Parker Single Barrel Trap

Gauge: 12
Action: Single shot; hammerless; top lever break-open; box lock
Magazine: None
Barrel: 30″, 32″, 34″, any choke; ventilated rib
Finish: Blued; checkered walnut straight, full or semi-pistol grip stock
Approximate wt.: 6½ to 7½ lbs.
Comments: Grades differ according to workmanship, checkering and engraving. Made from about 1917 to 1941. Manufacture of Parker guns was taken over by Remington in 1934 and this gun was called Remington Parker Model 930. There is a wide range of values for this gun. Prices for pre-1934 models.
Estimated Value: Excellent: **$3,000.00 - $12,000.00**
Very good: **$2,000.00 - $10,000.00**

Parker Trojan

Gauge: 12, 16, 20
Action: Top lever break-open; hammerless; box lock
Magazine: None
Barrel: Double barrel; 26″, 28″, 30″, full & full or modified & full chokes
Finish: Blued; checkered walnut pistol grip stock and forearm
Approximate wt.: 6½ to 8 lbs.
Comments: Made from about 1915 to 1939.
Estimated Value: Excellent: **$600.00 - $1,200.00**
Very good: **$475.00 - $1,000.00**

Parker Hammerless Double

Gauge: 10, 12, 16, 20, 28, 410
Action: Box lock; top lever, break-open; hammerless; selective trigger and automatic ejectors after 1934
Magazine: None
Barrel: Double barrel; 26″, 28″, 30″ , 32″; any choke combination
Finish: Blued; checkered walnut straight, full or semi-pistol grip stock and forearm
Approximate wt.: 6½ to 8½ lbs.
Comments: Grades vary according to workmanship, checkering and engraving. Manufacture of Parker guns was taken over by Remington in 1934 and this gun was called Remington Parker Model 920 until it was discontinued in 1941. Prices for pre-1934 models.
Estimated Value: Excellent: $2,100.00 - $50,000.00
Very good: $1,200.00 - $20,000.00

Parker Hammerless Double G.H.E.

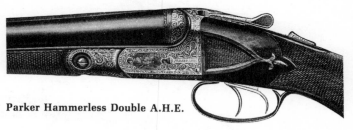

Parker Hammerless Double A.H.E.

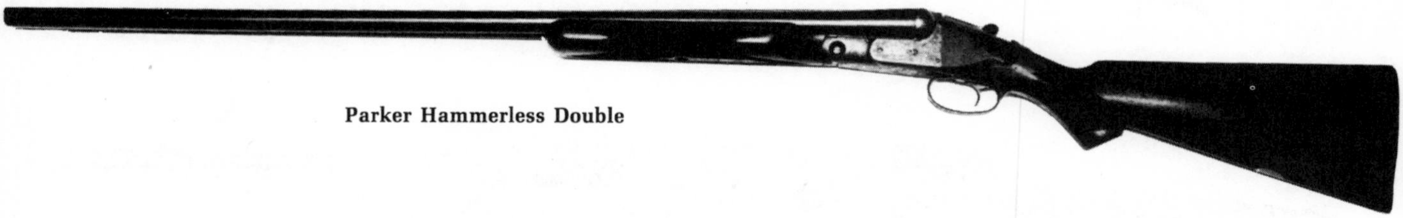

Parker Hammerless Double

Pedersen

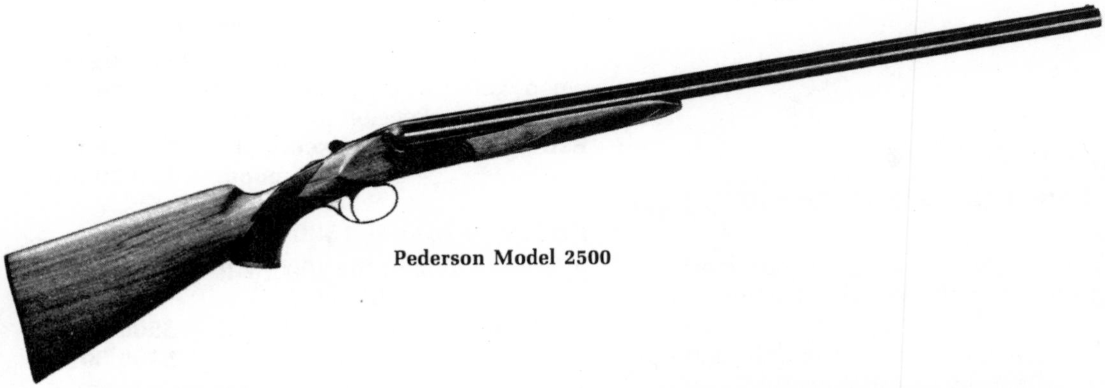

Pederson Model 2500

Pedersen Model 2000 Grade II

Gauge: 12, 20
Action: Box lock; top lever, break-open; hammerless; automatic ejectors; single selective trigger
Magazine: None
Barrel: Double barrel; length to customer's specifications
Finish: Blued; checkered walnut pistol grip stock and tapered forearm; engraved
Approximate wt.: 7½ lbs.
Comments: Made in the mid 1970's.
Estimated Value: Excellent: $1,500.00
Very good: $1,200.00

Pedersen Model 2000 Grade I

Similar to Grade II with fancier engraving, gold filling on receiver, select walnut.
Estimated Value: Excellent: $1,800.00
Very good: $1,450.00

Pedersen Model 2500

A field version of the 2000; no engraving.
Estimated Value: Excellent: $375.00
Very good: $300.00

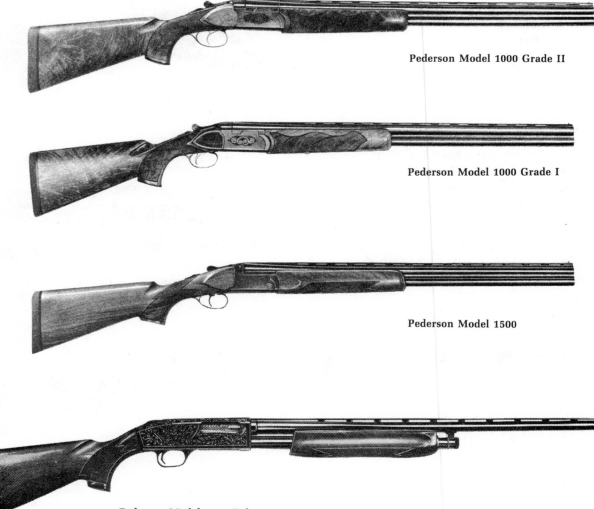

Pederson Model 1000 Grade II

Pederson Model 1000 Grade I

Pederson Model 1500

Pederson Model 4000 Deluxe

Pedersen Model 1000 Grade III

Gauge: 12, 20
Action: Box lock; top lever, break-open; hammerless; automatic ejectors; single selective trigger
Magazine: None
Barrel: Over and under double barrel; length made to customers specifications; ventilated rib
Finish: Blued; checkered walnut pistol grip stock and forearm; recoil pad
Approximate wt.: 7½ lbs.
Comments: Produced in the 1970's.
Estimated Value: Excellent: $650.00
Very good: $520.00

Pedersen Model 1000 Grade II

Similar to Grade III with engraving and fancier wood; made to customer's specs. Add $15.00 for magnum.
Estimated Value: Excellent: $1,725.00
Very good: $1,400.00

Pedersen Model 1000 Grade I

Similar to Grade II with extensive engraving, select wood, gold filling on receiver; made to customers specs; in hunting, skeet or trap models.
Estimated Value: Excellent: $2,100.00
Very good: $1,750.00

Pedersen Model 1500

A field version of the 1000 with standard barrel lengths only (26", 28", 30" or 32")
Estimated Value: Excellent: $500.00
Very good: $400.00

Pedersen Model 4000 Deluxe

Gauge: 10, 12, 410
Action: Slide action; hammerless; side ejection
Magazine: Tubular
Barrel: 26", 28", 30", variety of chokes; ventilated rib
Finish: Blued; checkered walnut pistol grip stock and slide handle; recoil pad; floral engraving on receiver
Approximate wt.: 6¾ lbs.
Comments: Made in the mid 1970's.
Estimated Value: Excellent: $350.00
Very good: $275.00

Premier

Premier Regent

Gauge: 12, 16, 20, 28, 410
Action: Box lock; top lever, break-open; hammerless; double triggers
Magazine: None
Barrel: Double barrel; 26″, 28″ modified & full chokes; matte rib
Finish: Blued; checkered walnut pistol grip stock and tapered forearm
Approximate wt.: 7 lbs.
Comments: Produced in the 1970's.
Estimated Value: Excellent: $220.00
                Very good: $180.00

Premier Brush King

Similar to Regent 12 and 20 gauge only; 22″ improved cylinder and modified choke barrels; straight stock. Still in production.
Estimated Value: Excellent: $245.00
                Very good: $200.00

Premier Magnum

Similar to Regent except: 10 gauge magnum with 32″ barrels or 12 gauge magnum with 30″ barrels; both gauges in full and full choke; recoil pad; beavertail forearm. Add $25.00 for 20 gauge magnum.
Estimated Value: Excellent: $250.00
                Very good: $200.00

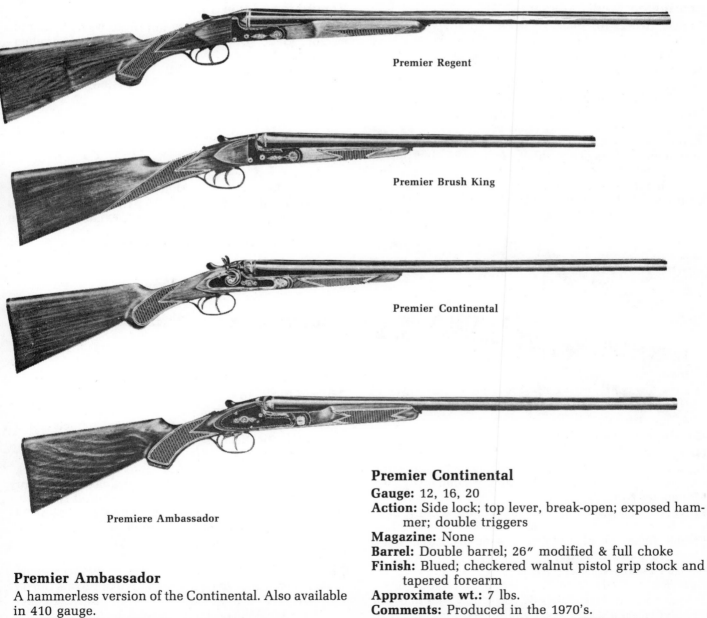

Premier Regent

Premier Brush King

Premier Continental

Premiere Ambassador

Premier Ambassador

A hammerless version of the Continental. Also available in 410 gauge.
Estimated Value: Excellent: $225.00
                Very good: $190.00

Premier Continental

Gauge: 12, 16, 20
Action: Side lock; top lever, break-open; exposed hammer; double triggers
Magazine: None
Barrel: Double barrel; 26″ modified & full choke
Finish: Blued; checkered walnut pistol grip stock and tapered forearm
Approximate wt.: 7 lbs.
Comments: Produced in the 1970's.
Estimated Value: Excellent: $275.00
                Very good: $200.00

Remington

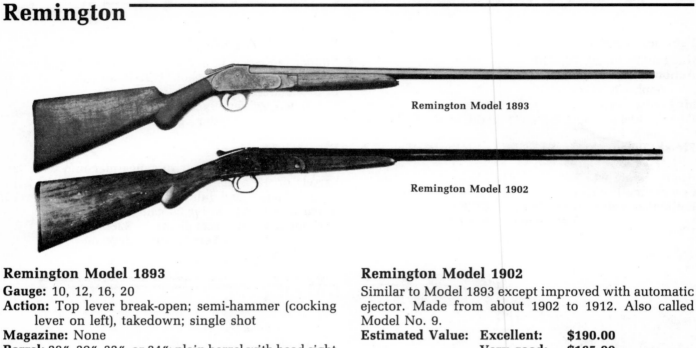

Remington Model 1893

Remington Model 1902

Remington Model 1889

Remington Model 1894

Remington Model 1893

Gauge: 10, 12, 16, 20
Action: Top lever break-open; semi-hammer (cocking lever on left), takedown; single shot
Magazine: None
Barrel: 28″, 30″, 32″, or 34″; plain barrel with bead sight at muzzle in standard chokes
Finish: Blued; case hardened receiver; smooth walnut, pistol grip stock and forearm
Approximate wt.: 5½ to 6½ lbs.
Comments: Made from about 1893 to 1906. Approximately 25,000 were produced. Also known as the Model No. 3 and the '93.
Estimated Value: Excellent: $175.00
                         Very good: $130.00

Remington Model 1902

Similar to Model 1893 except improved with automatic ejector. Made from about 1902 to 1912. Also called Model No. 9.
Estimated Value: Excellent: $190.00
                         Very good: $165.00

Remington Parker 930

Remington took over production of the Parker shotguns from 1934 to 1941; single shot hammerless.
Estimated Value: Excellent: $1,500.00 - $2,500.00
                         Very good: $1,000.00 - $2,000.00

Remington Model 1889

Gauge: 10, 12, 16
Action: Top lever break-open; side lock; breech loading black powder; exposed hammer; double trigger
Magazine: None
Barrel: Double barrel; 28″-32″ full, modified or cylinder bore; Damascus or steel
Finish: Blued; checkered walnut semi-pistol grip stock and short forearm
Approximate wt.: 7½ to 9 lbs.
Comments: Made from about 1889 to 1909 in seven grades. Approximately 30,000 produced. Prices are for Standard Grade.
Estimated Value: Excellent: $500.00
                         Very good: $375.00

Remington Model 1894

Gauge: 10, 12, 16
Action: Top lever break-open; concealed hammer; triple lock; double triggers; some models have automatic ejectors
Magazine: None
Barrel: Double barrel; 26″-32″ tapered barrels; full, modified or cylinder bore; ordnance steel or Damascus barrels with concave matted rib
Finish: Blued; checkered walnut straight or semi-pistol grip stock and short tapered forearm; special engraving and inlays on higher grades
Approximate wt.: 7½ to 8½ lbs.
Comments: Made from about 1894 to 1910 in seven grades. Receivers marked Remington Arms Co. on left side. Prices for Standard Grade. Deduct $125.00- $150.00 for Damascus barrels.
Estimated Value: Excellent: $700.00
                         Very good: $525.00

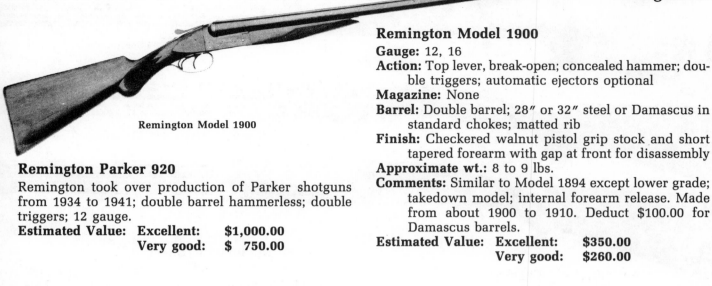

Remington Model 1900

Remington Parker 920

Remington took over production of Parker shotguns from 1934 to 1941; double barrel hammerless; double triggers; 12 gauge.

Estimated Value: Excellent: $1,000.00
Very good: $ 750.00

Remington Model 1900

Gauge: 12, 16
Action: Top lever, break-open; concealed hammer; double triggers; automatic ejectors optional
Magazine: None
Barrel: Double barrel; 28″ or 32″ steel or Damascus in standard chokes; matted rib
Finish: Checkered walnut pistol grip stock and short tapered forearm with gap at front for disassembly
Approximate wt.: 8 to 9 lbs.
Comments: Similar to Model 1894 except lower grade; takedown model; internal forearm release. Made from about 1900 to 1910. Deduct $100.00 for Damascus barrels.

Estimated Value: Excellent: $350.00
Very good: $260.00

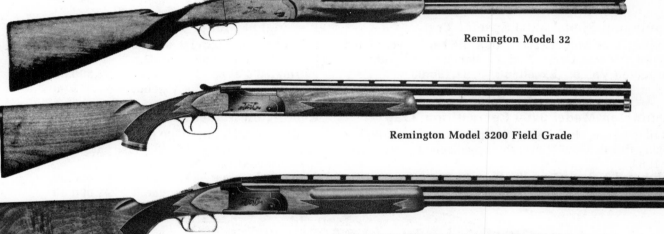

Remington Model 32

Remington Model 3200 Field Grade

Remington Model 3200 Magnum

Remington Model 32

Gauge: 12
Action: Top lever break-open; concealed hammer; single selective trigger; automatic ejectors
Magazine: None
Barrel: Over and under double barrel; 26″-32″ plain, solid or ventilated rib; full & modified choke standard but any combination available
Finish: Blued; engraved receiver; checkered walnut pistol grip stock and forearm
Approximate wt.: 7¾ to 8½ lbs.
Comments: One of the first modern American over and under double barrel shotguns produced. Made from about 1932 to 1942. Made in about six grades, high grades with fancier wood and engravings. Add $35.00 for solid rib; $50.00 for ventilated rib.

Estimated Value: Excellent: $650.00
Very good: $485.00

Remington Model 3200 Field Grade

Gauge: 12
Action: Top lever break-open; concealed hammer; selective single trigger; automatic ejectors
Magazine: None
Barrel: 26″-30″ over and under double barrel; ventilated rib; modified & full or improved cylinder & modified chokes
Finish: Blued; pointing dogs engraved on receiver; checkered walnut pistol grip stock and matching forearm
Approximate wt.: 7¾ to 8¼ lbs.
Comments: A modern version of the Model 32 started back in production in the early 1970's. Still available in Trap and Skeet models. Other models valued higher than Field Grade.

Estimated Value: Excellent: $850.00
Very good: $675.00

Remington Model 3200 Magnum

Similar to the Model 3200 Field Grade except: chambered for 12 gauge magnum; 30″ barrels in full & full or modified & full chokes; receiver decorated with engraved scrollwork.

Estimated Value: Excellent: $900.00
Very good: $700.00

Remington Model 3200 Special Trap

Remington Model 3200 Competition Trap

Remington Model 3200 Skeet

Remington Model 3200 Special Trap

Similar to the Model 3200 with a 32″ barrel; ventilated rib only; Monte Carlo stock available; recoil pad.
Estimated Value: Excellent: $1,100.00
Very good: $ 825.00

Remington Model 3200 Competition Trap

Similar to the Model 3200 Special Trap with a higher quality finish. Monte Carlo stock available. Discontinued in 1983.
Estimated Value: Excellent: $1,300.00
Very good: $ 975.00

Remington Model 3200 Skeet

Similar to the Model 3200 with a 26″ or 28″ skeet barrel; ventilated rib only; recoil pad; Monte Carlo stock.
Estimated Value: Excellent: $1,100.00
Very good: $ 825.00

Remington Model 3200 Competition Skeet

Similar to the Model 3200 Skeet with a higher quality finish. Discontinued in 1983.
Estimated Value: Excellent: $1,300.00
Very good: $ 975.00

Remington Model 3200 Pigeon

Similar to the Model 3200 Competition Skeet with 28″ improved modified and full choke barrels for live birds. Discontinued in 1983.
Estimated Value: Excellent: $1,320.00
Very good: $1,000.00

Remington Model 1908

Remington Model 10

Remington Model 1908

Gauge: 12
Action: Slide action; hammerless; bottom ejection; repeating
Magazine: 5-shot tubular
Barrel: 26″-32″ steel barrel in full, modified or cylinder bore
Finish: Blued; plain or checkered walnut straight or pistol grip stock and forearm
Approximate wt.: 7½ to 8 lbs.
Comments: Made from about 1908 to 1910 in six grades with fancy checkering and engraving on higher grades. Marking on top of barrel "Remington Arms Co." and patent date. About 10,000 made.
Estimated Value: Excellent: $360.00
Very good: $280.00

Remington Model 10

Gauge: 12
Action: Slide action; hammerless; bottom ejection; repeating
Magazine: 5-shot tubular
Barrel: 26″-32″ steel barrel in full, modified or cylinder bore
Finish: Blued; plain or checkered walnut straight or pistol grip stock and forearm
Approximate wt.: 7½ to 8 lbs.
Comments: Made from about 1910 to 1928, an improved version of the Model 1908. Made in seven grades with fancy checkering and engraving on higher grades. Also produced in 20″ barrel riot gun. Solid rib optional from 1910-1922; ventilated rib optional from 1922-1928. Prices are for Standard Grade.
Estimated Value: Excellent: $280.00
Very good: $210.00

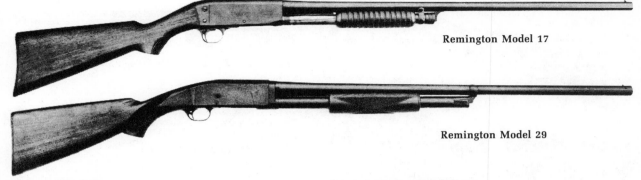

Remington Model 17

Remington Model 29

Remington Model 17

Gauge: 20
Action: Slide action; hammerless; bottom ejection; repeating
Magazine: 3-shot tubular
Barrel: 26″-32″ steel in full, modified or cylinder bore; matted sighting groove on receiver or optional solid rib; 20″ barrel on riot gun
Finish: Blued; plain or checkered walnut pistol grip stock and forearm
Approximate wt.: 7½ to 8 lbs.
Comments: Made from about 1917 to 1933 in seven grades. Higher grades have higher quality finish.
Estimated Value: **Excellent:** **$275.00**
⠀⠀⠀⠀⠀⠀⠀⠀⠀⠀**Very good:** **$205.00**

Remington Model 29

Gauge: 12
Action: Slide action; hammerless; bottom ejection; repeating
Magazine: 5-shot tubular
Barrel: 26″-32″ steel in full, modified or cylinder bore; optional solid or ventilated rib; 20″ barrel on riot gun
Finish: Blued; plain or checkered walnut pistol grip stock and forearm
Approximate wt.: 7½ to 8 lbs.
Comments: Made from about 1929 to 1933 in nine grades. Higher grades have higher quality finish. Prices are for Standard Grade.
Estimated Value: **Excellent:** **$240.00**
⠀⠀⠀⠀⠀⠀⠀⠀⠀⠀**Very good:** **$190.00**

Remington Model 31

Remington Model 870 AP

Remington Model 31

Gauge: 12, 16, 20
Action: Slide action; hammerless; side ejection; repeating
Magazine: 3-shot tubular or 5-shot tubular
Barrel: 26″, 32″ steel; full, modified, cylinder or skeet chokes; optional solid or ventilated rib
Finish: Blued; sighting groove on receiver; plain or checkered pistol grip stock and forearm; forearm checkered or grooved
Approximate wt.: 6½ to 8 lbs.
Comments: Made from about 1931 to 1949 in eight grades. Higher grades differ in quality of finish. Prices for Standard Grades. Add $20.00 for solid rib; $25.00 for ventilated rib.
Estimated Value: **Excellent:** **$200.00**
⠀⠀⠀⠀⠀⠀⠀⠀⠀⠀**Very good:** **$150.00**

Remington Model 31 R Riot Gun

Similar to Model 31 in 12 gauge only with 20″ plain barrel.
Estimated Value: **Excellent:** **$225.00**
⠀⠀⠀⠀⠀⠀⠀⠀⠀⠀**Very good:** **$170.00**

Remington Model 31 Skeet

Similar to Model 31 except: 12 gauge only; 26″ barrel; solid or ventilated rib; skeet choke. Add $20.00 for ventilated rib.
Estimated Value: **Excellent:** **$425.00**
⠀⠀⠀⠀⠀⠀⠀⠀⠀⠀**Very good:** **$320.00**

Remington Model 870 AP

Gauge: 12, 16, 20
Action: Slide action; hammerless; side ejection; repeating
Magazine: 4-shot tubular
Barrel: 26″, 28″, 30″ in 12 gauge; 26″ or 28″ in 16 and 20 gauge; full, modified or improved cylinder bore; plain or ventilated rib
Finish: Blued; plain or fancy; fluted comb, pistol grip stock and grooved slide handle
Approximate wt.: 6½ to 8 lbs.
Comments: Made in many styles, grades and variations from about 1950 to 1964. Higher grades have higher quality finish. Prices for standard grade. Add $25.00 for ventilated rib.
Estimated Value: **Excellent:** **$250.00**
⠀⠀⠀⠀⠀⠀⠀⠀⠀⠀**Very good:** **$185.00**

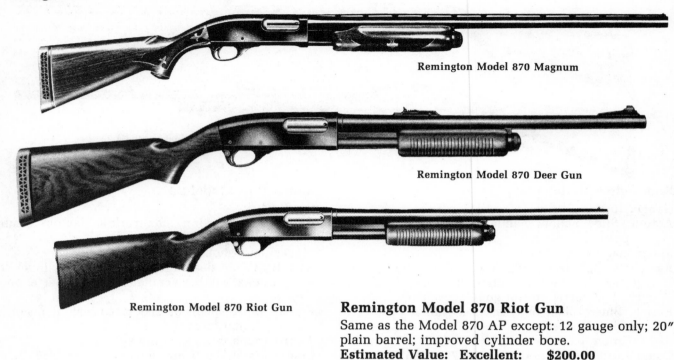

Remington Model 870 Magnum

Remington Model 870 Deer Gun

Remington Model 870 Riot Gun

Remington Model 870 Riot Gun

Same as the Model 870 AP except: 12 gauge only; 20″ plain barrel; improved cylinder bore.
Estimated Value: **Excellent:** $200.00
                Very good: $150.00

Remington Model 870 Magnum

Similar to Model 870 AP except: 12 gauge magnum; 30″ full choke barrel; recoil pad. Made from about 1955 to 1964. Add $25.00 for ventilated rib.
Estimated Value: **Excellent:** $260.00
                Very good: $195.00

Remington Model 870 Deer Gun

Similar to the Model 870 AP except: 12 gauge only; 26″ barrel for slugs; rifle type adjustable sights. Made from about 1959 to 1964.
Estimated Value: **Excellent:** $230.00
                Very good: $180.00

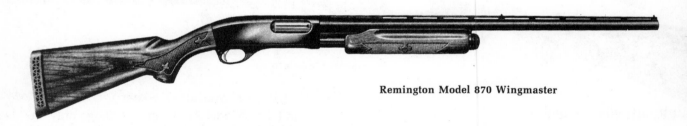

Remington Model 870 Wingmaster

Remington Model 870 Special Purpose

Similar to the Model 870 with oil-finish wood and Parkerized metal; recoil pad and nylon camo strap; 12 gauge only; venitlated rib, 30″ barrel. Introduced in 1985. Add $30.00 for 26″ "Rem Choke".
Estimated Value: **New (retail):** $444.95
                Excellent: $335.00
                Very good: $250.00

Remington Model 870 SP Deer Gun

Similar to the 870 Special Purpose with 20″ improved cylinder barrel and rifle sights. Introduced in 1986.
Estimated Value: **New (retail):** $420.95
                Excellent: $315.00
                Very good: $235.00

Remington Model 870 Wingmaster Field Gun

Gauge: 12, 16, 20 from 1964 to present; 28 and 410 added in 1969
Action: Slide action; hammerless; side ejection; repeating
Magazine: 4-shot tubular
Barrel: 26″-30″ in 12 gauge; 26″ or 28″ in 16 and 20 gauge; 25″ in 28 and 410 bore; full, modified or improved cylinder bore; plain barrel or ventilated rib
Finish: Blued; checkered walnut, pistol grip stock with matching slide handle; recoil pad.
Approximate wt.: 5½ to 7¼ lbs.
Comments: Improved version of the Model 870AP. Made in many grades and styles from about 1964 to present. Left hand models available and also lightweight models. Prices for standard grades. Add $30.00 for left hand model.
Estimated Value: **New (retail):** $475.00
                Excellent: $355.00
                Very good: $265.00

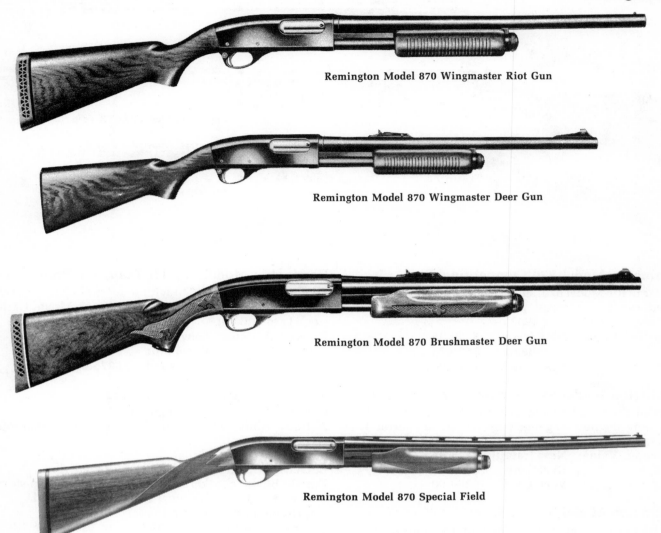

Remington Model 870 Wingmaster Riot Gun

Remington Model 870 Wingmaster Deer Gun

Remington Model 870 Brushmaster Deer Gun

Remington Model 870 Special Field

Remington Model 870 Wingmaster Riot Gun, Police

Similar to the Model 870 Wingmaster except: 12 gauge only; 18″ or 20″ improved cylinder barrel; plain stock and grooved slide handle; designed for law enforcement use. Add $25.00 for rifle sights.

Estimated Value: New (retail): $359.95
Excellent: $270.00
Very good: $200.00

Remington Model 870 Wingmaster Magnum

Same as the Model 870 Field Grade except: 12 or 20 magnum gauge only; full or modified choke. Add $30.00 for left hand model; add $30.00 for "Rem Choke".

Estimated Value: New (retail): $495.00
Excellent: $370.00
Very good: $275.00

Remington Model 870 Wingmaster Deer Gun

Same as the Model 870 Wingmaster except: 12 gauge only; 20″ barrel; rifle sights. Produced from 1964 to present.

Estimated Value: New (retail): $397.95
Excellent: $300.00
Very good: $225.00

Remington Model 870 Brushmaster Deer Gun

Same as the Model 870 Wingmaster Deer Gun except: 12 and 20 gauge; checkered stock and slide handle; recoil pad. Left hand version introduced in 1983.

Estimated Value: New (retail): $420.95
Excellent: $315.00
Very good: $235.00

Remington Model 870 Special Field

Similar to the Model 870 with a straight grip stock, 21″ ventilated rib barrel; 12 or 20 gauge; 3″ chamber. Introduced in 1984. Add $30.00 for "Rem Choke".

Estimated Value: New (retail): $475.95
Excellent: $355.00
Very good: $265.00

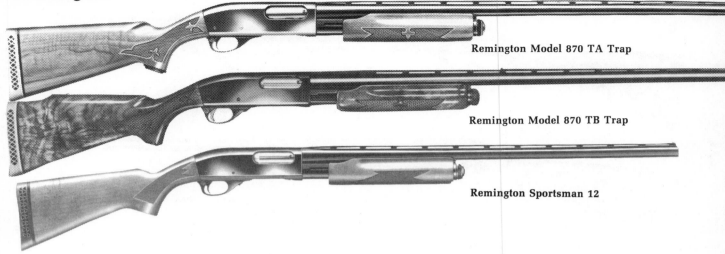

Remington Model 870 TA Trap

Remington Model 870 TB Trap

Remington Sportsman 12

Remington Model 870 Competition Trap

Similar to the Model 870; single shot; 30″ full choke; ventilated rib barrel; recoil pad; non-glare matte finish receiver. Introduced in 1982.

Estimated Value: New (retail): $759.95
Excellent: $570.00
Very good: $425.00

Remington Model 870 Wingmaster Limited 20

A scaled-down, lightweight version of the Model 870 for the young shooter; 20 gauge only; 21″ or 23″ barrel. Introduced in 1982.

Estimated Value: New (retail): $445.95
Excellent: $335.00
Very good: $250.00

Remington Model 870SA Skeet

Similar to the Model 870 in skeet choke; ventilated rib only; recoil pad. Made from the late 1970's to early 1980's; 25″ or 26″ barrel.

Estimated Value: Excellent: $275.00
Very good: $220.00

Remington Model 870 TB Trap, TA Trap

Similar to the Model 870 with a 30″ full choke barrel; ventilated rib only; recoil pad; choice of Monte Carlo stock (add $10.00).

Estimated Value: New (retail): $483.95
Excellent: $360.00
Very good: $275.00

Remington Sportsman 12 Pump

Gauge: 12 regular and magnum
Action: Slide action; hammerless; side ejection; repeating
Magazine: 4-shot tubular
Barrel: 28″ modified, 30″ full; ventilated rib
Finish: Blued; checkered walnut semi-pistol grip stock and slide handle; steel receiver; recoil pad.
Approximate wt.: 6½-7½ lbs.
Comments: Introduced in 1984. Add $25.00 for "Rem Choke".

Estimated Value: New (retail): $305.95
Excellent: $230.00
Very good: $170.00

Remington Autoloading

Remington Autoloading Riot Gun

Remington Autoloading Riot Gun

Similar to the Standard Grade except: 20″ barrel and weighs 6¾ lbs.

Estimated Value: Excellent: $200.00
Very good: $160.00

Remington Autoloading

Gauge: 12
Action: Semi-automatic; concealed hammer
Magazine: 5-shot tubular
Barrel: 26″, 28″ steel; full, modified or cylinder bore
Finish: Blued; matted sight groove; plain or checkered straight or pistol grip stock and forearm
Approximate wt.: 7¾ lbs.
Comments: Made from about 1905 to 1910 in six grades. Prices for Standard Grade.

Estimated Value: Excellent: $220.00
Very good: $175.00

Remington Model 11

Remington Model 11 Sportsman

Remington Model 11 Riot Gun

Remington Model 11

Gauge: 12 only to 1931; 12, 16, 20 1931-1948
Action: Semi-automatic; concealed hammer; side ejection; repeating
Magazine: 4-shot, bottom load
Barrel: 26″ or 28″ to 1931; 26″, 28″, 30″, 32″ 1931-1948; full, modified or cylinder
Finish: Blued; wood semi-pistol grip stock; straight grip on Trap grades; checkering and fancy wood on higher grades
Approximate wt.: 7½ to 8½ lbs.
Comments: Made from about 1911 to 1948 in six grades. Optional solid or ventilated rib available; rounded grip ends on stock from 1911 to 1916. Prices are for Standard Grade. Ad $15.00 for ribbed barrel.
Estimated Value: Excellent: $260.00
Very good: $200.00

Remington Model 11 Sportsman

Same as the Model 11 with a 2-shot magazine. Made from about 1931 to 1948 in six grades. Prices for the Standard Grade. Add $15.00 for solid rib; $25.00 for ventilated rib.
Estimated Value: Excellent: $325.00
Very good: $250.00

Remington Model 11 Riot Gun

Same as the Model 11 except with a 20″ plain barrel.
Estimated Value: Excellent: $240.00
Very good: $180.00

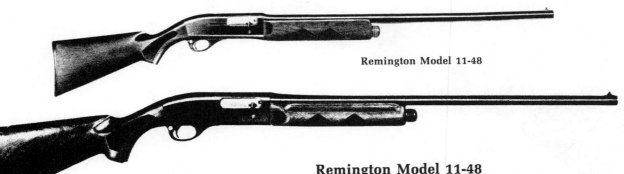

Remington Model 11-48

Remington Model 48

Remington 11-48 Riot Gun

Same general specifications as the Model 11-48 except: 12 gauge only; 20″ plain barrel. Made from about 1954-1968.
Estimated Value: Excellent: $240.00
Very good: $190.00

Remington Model 48

Similar to the Model 11-48 except: 2-shot magazine; 12, 16, 20 gauge. Made from about 1948-1959 in several grades to replace the Model 11 Sportsman. Prices for Standard Model. Add $30.00 for ventilated rib.
Estimated Value: Excellent: $215.00
Very good: $170.00

Remington Model 11-48

Gauge: 12, 16, 20; 28 after 1952; 410 after 1954
Action: Semi-automatic; hammerless; side ejection; take down; cross bolt safety
Magazine: 4-shot tubular; 3-shot in 28 and 410 gauge
Barrel: 26″, 28″, 30″ in 12, 16 and 20 gauge; 25″ in 28 and 410 bore; full, modified or improved cylinder
Finish: Checkered walnut pistol grip stock with fluted comb, matching semi-beavertail forearm; higher grades are fancier
Approximate wt.: 6½ to 7½ lbs.
Comments: Made from about 1949 to 1968 in about seven grades. Replacing the Model 11, it had an improved action and the rear of the receiver was rounded off flush with the stock. Prices for Standard Model. Add $30.00 for ventilated rib.
Estimated Value: Excellent: $265.00
Very good: $215.00

Remington Sportsman 58

Remington Sportsman 58 Magnum

Similar to the Sportsman 58 except: 12 gauge magnum; 30″ barrel; recoil pad. Made from the late 1950's to early 1960's. Add $30.00 for ventilated rib.

Estimated Value: Excellent: $240.00
Very good: $180.00

Remington Sportsman 58 Rifled Slug Special

Same as the Sportsman 58 except: 12 gauge only; 26″ barrel for slugs; equipped with rifle sights.

Estimated Value: Excellent: $250.00
Very good: $185.00

Remington Sportsman 58

Gauge: 12, 16, 20
Action: Semi-automatic; hammerless; side ejection; solid breech; gas operated sliding bolt; fixed barrel
Magazine: 2-shot tubular
Barrel: 26″, 28″, 30″; plain or ventilated rib; full, modified, improved cylinder or skeet chokes
Finish: Blued; checkered walnut pistol grip stock with fluted comb and matching semi-beavertail forearm
Approximate wt.: 6½ to 7½ lbs.
Comments: Made from about 1956 to 1963. Prices for Standard Model. Add $30.00 for ventilated rib.
Estimated Value: Excellent: $260.00
Very good: $195.00

Remington Model 878 Automaster

Remington Sportsman 12 Auto

Gauge: 12
Action: Gas-operated semi-automatic
Magazine: 4-shot tubular
Barrel: 28″ modified, 30″ full; ventilated rib; "Rem Choke" available
Finish: Checkered hardwood semi-pistol grip stock and forearm
Approximate wt.: 7¾ lbs.
Comments: Introduced in the mid 1980's. Add $30.00 for "Rem Choke".
Estimated Value: New (retail): $454.95
Excellent: $340.00
Very good: $255.00

Remington Model 878 Automaster

Gauge: 12
Action: Semi-automatic; gas operated; hammerless
Magazine: 2-shot tubular
Barrel: 26″-30″ full, modified, improved cylinder or skeet chokes
Finish: Blued; plain or checkered walnut pistol grip stock and forearm
Approximate wt.: 7 lbs.
Comments: Made similar to the Sportsman 58 to fill in the sales line with a lower priced, plain, standard grade shotgun. Made from about 1959 to 1962 in two grades. Prices for Standard Model. Add $30.00 for ventilated rib.
Estimated Value: Excellent: $240.00
Very good: $180.00

Remington Model 1100 Field Grade

Gauge: 12, 16, 20; 28 and 410 after 1970
Action: Semi-automatic; gas operated sliding bolt; fixed barrel; solid breech; hammerless; takedown
Magazine: 4-shot tubular
Barrel: 26″, 28″ in 16 and 20 gauge; 26″, 28″, 30″ in 12 gauge; 25″ in 28 and 410; full, modified, improved cylinder and skeet chokes; ventilated rib available
Finish: Blued; checkered wood pistol grip stock with fluted comb and matching forearm; engraved receiver
Approximate wt.: 6½ to 7½ lbs.
Comments: An improved, low-recoil shotgun to replace the 58, 11-48 and 878. Made from about 1963 to present in several grades. Add $30.00 for left hand model, $30.00 for "Rem Choke".
Estimated Value: New (retail): $560.95
Excellent: $420.00
Very good: $315.00

Remington Model 1100 SP Deer Gun

Similar to the Model 1100 Special Purpose with a 21″ improved cylinder barrel and rifle sights. Introduced in 1986.
Estimated Value: New (retail): $559.95
Excellent: $315.00
Very good: $235.00

Remington Model 1100 Magnum

Similar to the Model 1100 except: 12 or 20 gauge magnum; 28 or 30″ barrel; full or modified chokes; recoil pad. Add $30.00 for left hand model; $30.00 for "Rem Choke".
Estimated Value: New (retail): $610.95
Excellent: $460.00
Very good: $345.00

Remington Model 1100 Field Grade

Remington Model 1100 Magnum

Remington Model 1100 Deer Gun

Remington Model 1100 LT 20

Remington Model 1100 Special Purpose

Similar to the Model 1100 with oil-finished wood and Parkerized metal; recoil pad and nylon camo strap; 12 gauge only; ventilated rib barrel. Introduced in 1985. Add $30.00 for 26″ "Rem Choke".
Estimated Value: New (retail): $610.95
Excellent: $460.00
Very good: $345.00

Remington Model 1100 Deer Gun

Similar to the Model 1100 with a 22″ plain barrel and adjustable rifle sights; bored for rifle slugs; 12 or 20 gauge lightweight. Left hand version introduced in 1983.
Estimated Value: New (retail): $560.95
Excellent: $420.00
Very good: $315.00

Remington Model 1100 LT 20

A scaled-down version of the Model 1100 for young shooters; 20 gauge only; introduced in 1980.
Estimated Value: New (retail): $560.95
Excellent: $420.00
Very good: $315.00

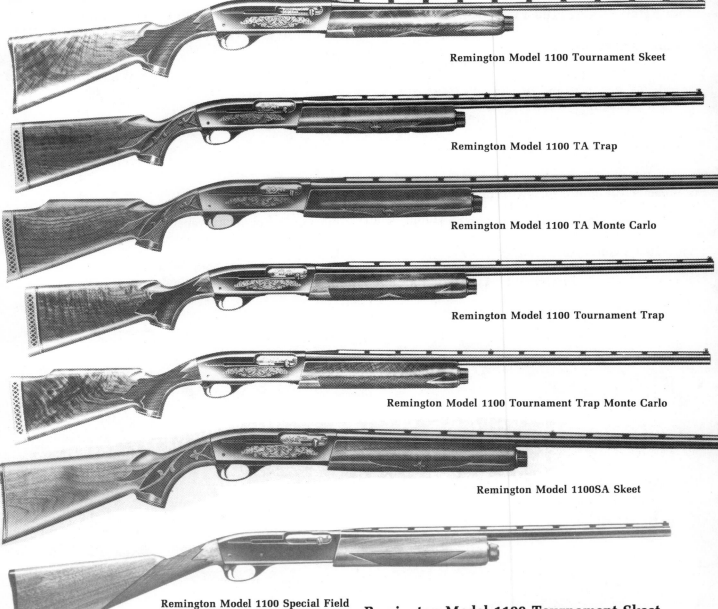

Remington Model 1100 Tournament Skeet

Remington Model 1100 TA Trap

Remington Model 1100 TA Monte Carlo

Remington Model 1100 Tournament Trap

Remington Model 1100 Tournament Trap Monte Carlo

Remington Model 1100SA Skeet

Remington Model 1100 Special Field

Remington Model 1100 Special Field

Similar to the Model 1100 with straight grip stock and 21″ ventilated rib barrel; 12 gauge or LT 20 Model, 2¾″ chamber. Introduced in 1983. Add $30.00 for "Rem Choke".

Estimated Value: New (retail): $590.00
Excellent: $440.00
Very good: $330.00

Remington Model 1100SA Skeet

Similar to the Model 1100 with a 25″ or 26″ skeet choke barrel; ventilated rib only; scroll receiver; made from the late 1970's to present. Add $30.00 for left hand model.

Estimated Value: New (retail): $625.95
Excellent: $470.00
Very good: $350.00

Remington Model 1100 Tournament Skeet

Similar to the Model 1100SA Skeet with higher quality finish.

Estimated Value: New (retail): $740.95
Excellent: $555.00
Very good: $415.00

Remington Model 1100TA Trap

Similar to the Model 1100 with a 30″ full or modified trap barrel; ventilated rib only; recoil pad; choice of Monte Carlo stock (add $10.00). Add $30.00 for left hand model.

Estimated Value: New (retail): $635.95
Excellent: $475.00
Very good: $360.00

Remington Model 1100 Tournament Trap

Similar to the Model 1100 TA Trap with higher quality finish. Add $10.00 for Monte Carlo stock.

Estimated Value: New (retail): $755.95
Excellent: $565.00
Very good: $425.00

Richland

Richland Model 200

Richland Model 200

Gauge: 12, 16, 20, 28, 410
Action: Box lock; top lever, break-open; hammerless; double trigger
Magazine: None
Barrel: Double barrel; 22″ improved cylinder and modified in 20 gauge; 26″, 28″ improved and modified or modified and full chokes
Finish: Blued; checkered walnut pistol grip stock and tapered forearm; cheekpiece; recoil pad
Approximate wt.: 6 to 7 lbs.
Comments: Manufactured from the early 1960's to mid 1980's.
Estimated Value: Excellent: $255.00
Very good: $190.00

Richland Model 202

This is the same shotgun as the Model 200 with an extra set of barrels. Produced until the mid 1970's.
Estimated Value: Excellent: $375.00
Very good: $290.00

Richland Model 707 Deluxe

Richland Model 711 Long Range Waterfowl

Richland Model 707 Deluxe

Gauge: 12, 20
Action: Box lock; top lever, break-open; hammerless; double trigger
Magazine: None
Barrel: Double barrel; 26″, 28″, 30″ variety of chokes
Finish: Blued; checkered walnut pistol grip stock and tapered forearm; recoil pad
Approximate wt.: 7 lbs.
Comments: Made from the mid 1960's to the mid 1970's.
Estimated Value: Excellent: $300.00
Very good: $225.00

Richland Model 711 Long Range Waterfowl

Gauge: 10, 12, magnum
Action: Box lock; top lever, break-open; hammerless; double trigger
Magazine: None
Barrel: Double barrel; 30″, 32″ full choke
Finish: Blued; checkered walnut pistol grip stock and tapered forearm
Approximate wt.: 8 to 10 lbs.
Comments: Made from the early 1960's to present. Made in 10 gauge magnum only from 1981 to 1983.
Estimated Value: New (retail): $395.00
Excellent: $295.00
Very good: $220.00

Richland Model 747

Gauge: 12 or 20, magnum
Action: Box lock; top lever, break-open; hammerless; single selective trigger.
Magazine: None
Barrel: Over & under double barrel; 22″ or 26″ improved cylinder & modified, 28″ modified & full.
Finish: Blued; grey receiver; checkered walnut pistol grip stock and forearm; ventilated rib on top and between barrels.
Approximate wt.: 7 lbs.
Comments: Introduced in the mid 1980's.
Estimated Value: New (retail): $450.00
Excellent: $340.00
Very good: $255.00

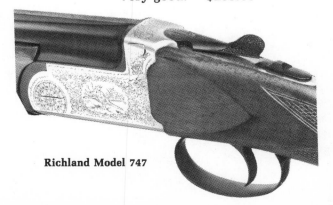

Richland Model 747

Richland Model 808
Gauge: 12
Action: Box lock; top lever, break-open; hammerless; non-selective single trigger
Magazine: None
Barrel: Over and under double barrel; 26″ improved cylinder & modified; 28″ modified & full; 30″ full & full
Finish: Blued; checkered walnut pistol grip stock and forearm; ribbed barrel
Approximate wt.: 7 lbs.
Comments: Made from the early to late 1960's.
Estimated Value: Excellent: $360.00
                    Very good: $270.00

Richland Model 844
Gauge: 12 magnum
Action: Box lock; top lever, break-open; hammerless; non-selective single trigger
Magazine: None
Barrel: Over and under double barrel; 26″ improved cylinder & modified; 28″ modified & full; 30″ full & full
Finish: Blued; checkered walnut pistol grip stock and forearm
Approximate wt.: 7 lbs.
Comments: Made in the early 1970's.
Estimated Value: Excellent: $290.00
                    Very good: $220.00

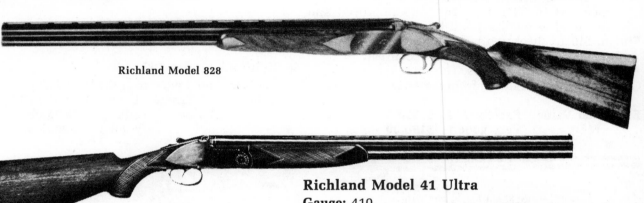

Richland Model 828

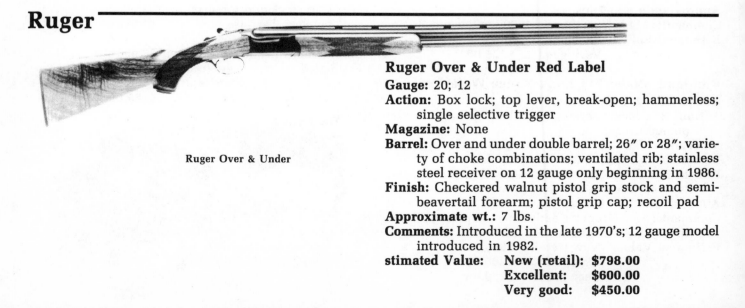

Richland Model 808

Richland Model 828
Gauge: 28
Action: Box lock; top lever, break-open; hammerless
Magazine: None
Barrel: Over and under double barrel; 26″ improved & modified; 28″ modified & full chokes
Finish: Blued; case hardened receiver; checkered walnut pistol grip stock and forearm; ribbed barrel
Approximate wt.: 7 lbs.
Comments: Made in the early 1970's.
Estimated Value: Excellent: $350.00
                    Very good: $260.00

Richland Model 41 Ultra
Gauge: 410
Action: Box lock; top lever, break open; hammerless; over and under double barrel; single non-selective trigger
Magazine: None
Barrel: Over and under double barrel; 26″ chrome lined, modified and full; ventilated rib
Finish: Blued; grey engraved receiver; checkered walnut pistol grip stock and forearm
Approximate wt.: 6 lbs.
Comments: A lightweight 410 shotgun first announced in 1985.
Estimated Value: New (retail): $289.00
                    Excellent: $215.00
                    Very good: $160.00

Ruger

Ruger Over & Under

Ruger Over & Under Red Label
Gauge: 20; 12
Action: Box lock; top lever, break-open; hammerless; single selective trigger
Magazine: None
Barrel: Over and under double barrel; 26″ or 28″; variety of choke combinations; ventilated rib; stainless steel receiver on 12 gauge only beginning in 1986.
Finish: Checkered walnut pistol grip stock and semi-beavertail forearm; pistol grip cap; recoil pad
Approximate wt.: 7 lbs.
Comments: Introduced in the late 1970's; 12 gauge model introduced in 1982.
stimated Value: New (retail): $798.00
                    Excellent: $600.00
                    Very good: $450.00

SKB

SKB 100

SKB 200

SKB 200 Skeet

SKB 280

SKB 500

SKB Model 100

Gauge: 12, 12 magnum, 20
Action: Box lock; top lever, break-open; hammerless; single selective trigger
Magazine: None
Barrel: Double barrel; 26″, 28″ improved cylinder & modified or 30″ full & full choke in 12 gauge
Finish: Blued; checkered hardwood pistol grip stock and short tapered forearm
Approximate wt.: 6 to 7 lbs.
Comments: Made from the mid 1960's to present.
Estimated Value: Excellent: $300.00
Very good: $225.00

SKB Model 200

Similar to the SKB 100 with engraved silverplate frame; wide forearm; select walnut; automatic selective ejectors. Add $21.00 for magnum.
Estimated Value: Excellent: $425.00
Very good: $320.00

SKB Model 200 Skeet

Similar to the 200 with 25″ skeet choke barrels and recoil pad.
Estimated Value: Excellent: $450.00
Very good: $340.00

SKB Model 280

Similar to the 200 without silver frame. Has straight grip stock.
Estimated Value: Excellent: $500.00
Very good: $375.00

SKB Model 500

Gauge: 12, 12 magnum, 20, 28, 410
Action: Box lock; top lever, break-open; hammerless
Magazine: None
Barrel: Over and under double barrel; 26″ improved cylinder & modified; 28″, 30″ modified & full; ventilated rib; chrome lined
Finish: Blued; checkered walnut pistol grip stock and forearm; recoil pad on magnum; front sight; engraved receiver
Approximate wt.: 6½ to 8 lbs.
Comments: Made from the mid 1960's to present. Add $20.00 for magnum.
Estimated Value: Excellent: $400.00
Very good: $300.00

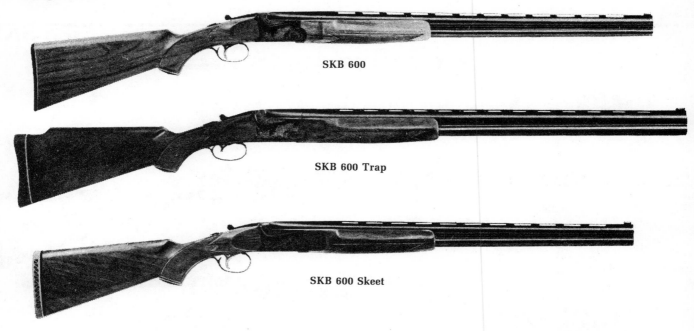

SKB 600

SKB 600 Trap

SKB 600 Skeet

SKB Model 500 Skeet

Similar to the Model 500 with 26″ or 28″ skeet choke barrels.

| Estimated Value: | Excellent: | $450.00 |
| | Very good: | $340.00 |

SKB Model 600

Similar to the 500 with select wood; trigger mounted barrel selector; silverplate frame; middle sight.

| Estimated Value: | Excellent: | $500.00 |
| | Very good: | $375.00 |

SKB Model 600 Trap

Similar to the 600 with regular or Monte Carlo stock; 12 gauge only; recoil pad, 30″ or 32″ full choke barrels.

| Estimated Value: | Excellent: | $525.00 |
| | Very good: | $395.00 |

SKB Model 600 Skeet

Similar to the 600 with 26″ or 28″ skeet choke barrels and recoil pad.

| Estimated Value: | Excellent: | $525.00 |
| | Very good: | $400.00 |

SKB Model 680

Similar to the 600 with a straight grip stock.

| Estimated Value: | Excellent: | $650.00 |
| | Very good: | $490.00 |

SKB Model 700

Similar to the 600 with higher quality finish and more extensive engraving.

| Estimated Value: | Excellent: | $700.00 |
| | Very good: | $525.00 |

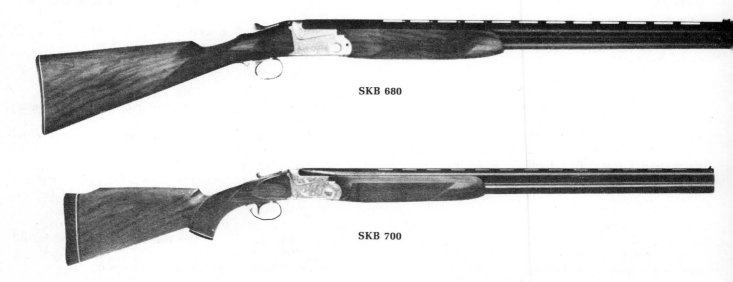

SKB 680

SKB 700

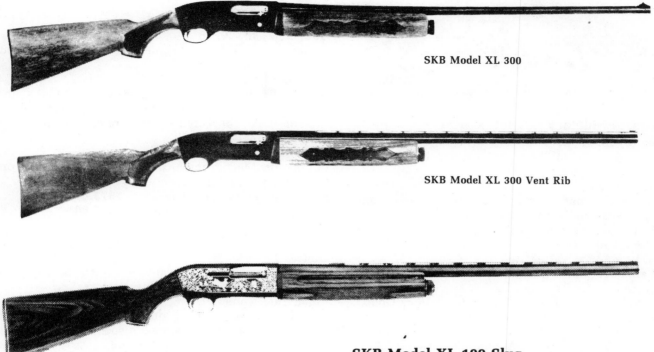

SKB Model XL 300

SKB Model XL 300 Vent Rib

SKB Model XL 900

SKB Model 7300

Gauge: 12, 20, regular or magnum
Action: Slide action; hammerless
Magazine: 4-shot tubular
Barrel: 26″ improved cylinder; 28″ modified; 28″ or 30″ full; ventilated rib; 24″ slug barrel available
Finish: Blued; checkered pistol grip stock and slide handle; recoil pad
Approximate wt.: 7 lbs.
Comments: Made in the late 1970's.
Estimated Value: **Excellent:** **$270.00**
                 Very good: **$200.00**

SKB Model XL 300

Gauge: 12, 20
Action: Gas operated; semi-automatic; hammerless
Magazine: 5-shot tubular
Barrel: 26″ improved cylinder or skeet; 28″ modified or full; 30″ modified or full chokes
Finish: Blued; decorated receiver; checkered walnut pistol grip stock and forearm
Approximate wt.: 6 to 7 lbs.
Comments: Made from the early to late 1970's.
Estimated Value: **Excellent:** **$260.00**
                 Very good: **$200.00**

SKB XL 300 Vent Rib

Similar to the XL 300 with front sights and ventilated rib.
Estimated Value: **Excellent:** **$285.00**
                 Very good: **$215.00**

SKB Model XL 100 Slug

A no-frills slug gun with 20″ barrel; rifle sights; swivels; similar to the XL 300.
Estimated Value: **Excellent:** **$235.00**
                 Very good: **$175.00**

SKB Model XL 900

Similar to the XL 300 Vent Rib with engraved silverplated receiver; gold trigger and name plate.
Estimated Value: **Excellent:** **$315.00**
                 Very good: **$235.00**

SKB Model XL 900 Slug

Similar to the XL 900 with a 24″ barrel for slugs; rifle sights; swivels.
Estimated Value: **Excellent:** **$310.00**
                 Very good: **$230.00**

SKB Model XL 900 Trap

Similar to the XL 900 with middle sight; no silver receiver; recoil pad; choice of regular or Monte Carlo stock.
Estimated Value: **Excellent:** **$300.00**
                 Very good: **$220.00**

SKB Model XL 900 Skeet

Similar to the XL 900 Trap with skeet stock and skeet choke barrel.
Estimated Value: **Excellent:** **$330.00**
                 Very good: **$250.00**

SKB Model XL 900 MR

Similar to the XL 900 for 3″ magnum shells; recoil pad; deduct $35.00 for slug model.
Estimated Value: **Excellent:** **$350.00**
                 Very good: **$260.00**

Sarasqueta

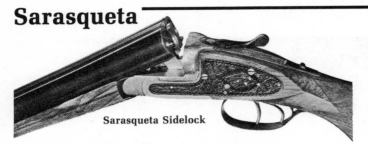

Sarasqueta Sidelock

Sarasqueta Sidelock Grades 4 to 12

Gauge: 12, 16, 20, 28
Action: Side lock; top lever break-open; hammerless; double triggers
Magazine: None
Barrel: Double barrel; standard barrel lengths and chokes available to customer specifications
Finish: Blued; checkered walnut straight or pistol grip stock and forearm
Approximate wt.: Varies
Comments: A Spanish shotgun. Grades differ as to quality and extent of engraving.

Estimated Value:	Grade	Excellent:	Very Good
	4	$ 400.00	$ 315.00
	5	$ 450.00	$ 360.00
	6	$ 480.00	$ 385.00
	7	$ 540.00	$ 430.00
	8	$ 800.00	$ 640.00
	9	$ 960.00	$ 765.00
	10	$1,100.00	$ 890.00
	11	$1,440.00	$1,150.00
	12	$1,800.00	$1,440.00

Sarasqueta Folding Shotgun

Gauge: 410
Action: Box lock; top lever, break-open; exposed hammer
Magazine: None
Barrel: Double barrel; 26″ choice of chokes
Finish: Blued; case-hardened frame; walnut pistol grip stock and forearm
Approximate wt.: Varies
Comments: A "folding" shotgun produced in the 1970's.
Estimated Value: Excellent: $120.00
           Very good: $ 90.00

Sarasqueta Model 2 and 3

Gauge: 12, 16, 20, 28
Action: Box lock; top lever break-open; hammerless; double trigger
Magazine: None
Barrel: Double barrel; standard barrel lengths and chokes available to customer's specifications
Finish: Blued; checkered walnut straight grip stock and forearm
Approximate wt.: Varies
Comments: Made from the mid 1930's. Grades differ only in engraving style.
Estimated Value: Excellent: $375.00
           Very good: $300.00

Sarasqueta Over & Under Deluxe

Gauge: 12
Action: Side lock; top lever break-open; hammerless; double triggers; automatic ejectors
Magazine: None
Barrel: Over and under double barrel; lengths and chokes made to customer's specifications
Finish: Blued; checkered walnut pistol grip stock and forearm
Approximate wt.: Varies
Comments: Made from the mid 1930's.
Estimated Value: Excellent: $1,200.00
           Very good: $ 850.00

Sarasqueta Folding Shotgun

Sauer

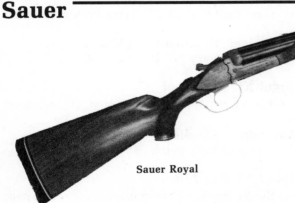

Sauer Royal

Sauer Royal

Gauge: 12, 20
Action: Box lock; top lever, break-open; hammerless; automatic ejectors; single selective trigger
Magazine: None
Barrel: Double barrel; 28″ modified & full, 26″ improved & modified in 20 gauge; 30″ full in 12 gauge
Finish: Blued; engraved frame; checkered walnut pistol grip stock and tapered forearm; recoil pad
Approximate wt.: 6 to 7 lbs.
Comments: Produced in Germany from the mid 1950's to late 1970's.
Estimated Value: Excellent: $850.00
           Very good: $640.00

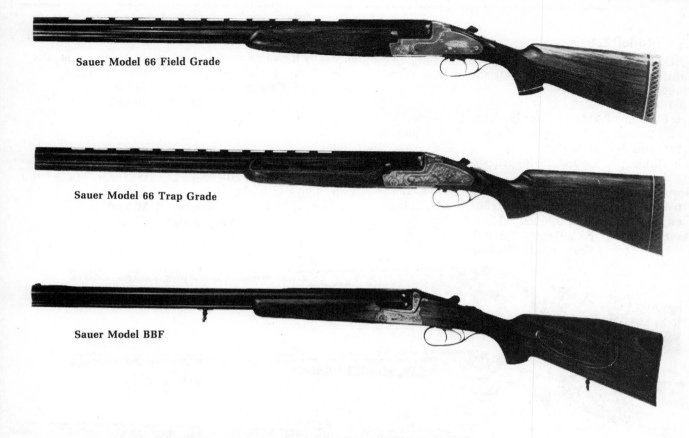

Sauer Model 66 Field Grade

Sauer Model 66 Trap Grade

Sauer Model BBF

Sauer Model 66 Field Grade

Gauge: 12
Action: Purdey action; hammerless; single selective trigger; automatic ejector
Magazine: None
Barrel: Over and under double barrel; 28″ modified & full choke; ventilated rib
Finish: Blued; checkered walnut pistol grip stock and forearm; recoil pad; engraving
Approximate wt.: 7 lbs.
Comments: Made from fthe mid 1950's. Prices are for Grade I. Fancier Grades II and III differ in quality and extent of engraving.
Estimated Value: **Excellent:** **$1,350.00**
                   Very good: **$1,020.00**

Sauer Model 66 Trap Grade

Basically the same as the Field Grade with 30″ barrels and a trap stock. Also produced in three grades.
Estimated Value: **Excellent:** **$1,500.00**
                   Very good: **$1,125.00**

Sauer Model 66 Skeet

Basically the same as the Trap Model with 25″ barrel in skeet choke.
Estimated Value: **Excellent:** **$1,450.00**
                   Very good: **$1,090.00**

Sauer Model BBF

Sauer Model BBF

Gauge: 16
Caliber: 30-30, 30-06, 7 x 65
Action: Kersten lock; Blitz action; top lever break-open; hammerless; double trigger
Magazine: None
Barrel: Over and under rifle-shotgun combination; 25″ Krupp barrels; rifle barrel and full choke shotgun barrel
Finish: Blued; checkered walnut Monte Carlo pistol grip stock and forearm; engraved; sights; swivels
Approximate wt.: 6 lbs.
Comments: Made from the mid 1950's. Also available in deluxe model with extensive engraving.
Estimated Value: **Excellent:** **$1,600.00**
                   Very good: **$1,200.00**

Savage

Savage Model 220

Gauge: 12, 16, 20, 28, 410
Action: Top lever break-open; single shot; hammerless; automatic ejector
Magazine: None
Barrel: Full choke; 28″, 30″, 32″ in 12 and 16 gauge; 26″, 28″, 30″, 32″ in 20 gauge; 28″ and 30″ in 28 gauge; 26″ and 28″ in 410 bore
Finish: Blued; plain wood, pistol grip stock and forearm
Approximate wt.: 6 lbs.
Comments: Made from 1930's until late 1940's. Reintroduced in the mid 1950's with 36″ barrel. Replaced by 220L in mid 1960's.
Estimated Value: Excellent: $70.00
Very good: $60.00

Savage Model 220P

Basically the same as 220 except no 410 gauge, has "Poly-Choke" and recoil pad.
Estimated Value: Excellent: $75.00
Very good: $60.00

Savage Model 220L

Similar to Model 220 except has side lever. Made from mid 1960's to early 1970's.
Estimated Value: Excellent: $60.00
Very good: $50.00

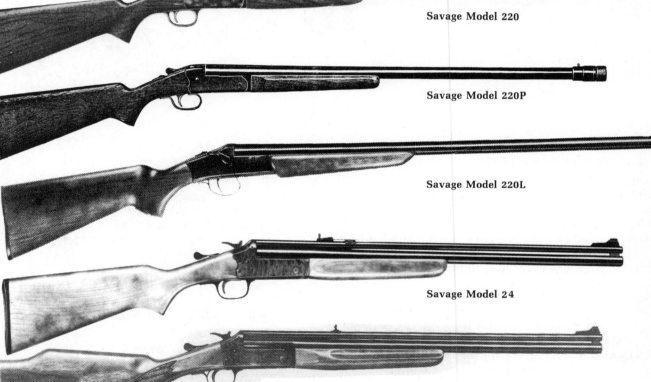

Savage Model 220

Savage Model 220P

Savage Model 220L

Savage Model 24

Savage Model 24D

Savage Model 24V, 24VS

Similar to the Model 24 except caliber 357, 222, 223, 30-30, or 22 Hornet over 20 gauge shotgun barrel. Introduced in 1979. Add $30.00 for satin nickel finish (24VS) and extra pistol grip stock. 357 and 22 Hornet calibers discontinued in mid 1980's.
Estimated Value: New (retail): $272.00
Excellent: $205.00
Very good: $150.00

Savage Model 24D

Deluxe version of the Model 24. Discontinued in mid 1980's.
Estimated Value: Excellent: $160.00
Very good: $140.00

Savage Model 24 Combination

Gauge: 20, 410
Caliber: 22 short, long, long rifle; 22 magnum
Action: Top lever break-open; exposed hammer; single trigger; bottom opening lever in mid 1980's.
Magazine: None
Barrel: Over and under double barrel; 24″ rifle barrel over shotgun barrel
Finish: Blued; checkered walnut finish hardwood pistol grip stock and forearm; sporting rear and ramp front sights; case hardened receiver
Approximate wt.: 6 lbs.
Comments: Made from the early 1950's to present.
Estimated Value: New (retail): $187.50
Excellent: $140.00
Very good: $105.00

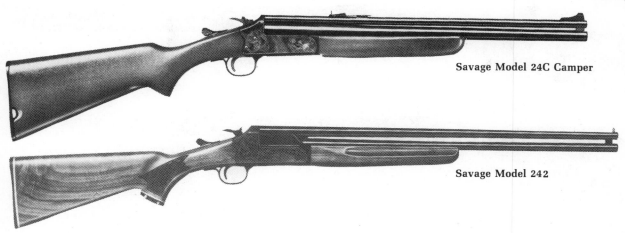

Savage Model 24C Camper

Savage Model 242

Savage Model 24C Camper, 24CS

A shorter version of the Model 24; 20″ barrel; 5¾ lbs.; 22LR over 20 gauge barrel; buttplate opens for ammo storage area. Add $45.00 for satin nickel finish (24CS) and extra pistol grip stock.

Estimated Value: New (retail): $208.39
Excellent: $155.00
Very good: $115.00

Savage Model 242

Similar to the Model 24 with 410 gauge over and under shotgun barrels; full choke; bead sights; introduced in 1979.

Estimated Value: Excellent: $150.00
Very good: $120.00

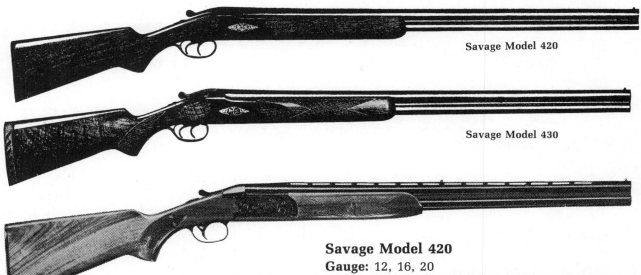

Savage Model 420

Savage Model 430

Savage Model 333

Savage Model 333

Gauge: 12, 20
Action: Top lever break-open; hammerless; single trigger
Magazine: None
Barrel: Over and under double barrel; 26″ to 30″; variety of chokes; ventilated rib
Finish: Blued; checkered walnut pistol grip stock and forearm
Approximate wt.: 6¼ to 7¼ lbs.
Comments: Made from the early to late 1970's.
Estimated Value: Excellent: $500.00
Very good: $375.00

Savage Model 420

Gauge: 12, 16, 20
Action: Box lock; top lever, break-open; hammerless; double triggers or non-selective single trigger
Magazine: None
Barrel: Over and under double barrel; 26″ to 30″ modified & full or cylinder bore & modified chokes
Finish: Blued; plain walnut pistol grip stock and forearm
Approximate wt.: 6¾ to 7¾ lbs.
Comments: Made from the mid 1930's until World War II. Add $25.00 for single trigger.
Estimated Value: Excellent: $360.00
Very good: $270.00

Savage Model 430

Same as Model 420 with special checkered walnut stock and forearm; matted upper barrel; recoil pad. Add $25.00 for single trigger.
Estimated Value: Excellent: $390.00
Very good: $295.00

Savage Model 330

Savage Model 333T Trap

Savage Model 28A

Savage Model 28D Trap

Savage Model 30

Savage Model 330
Similar to 333 without ventilated rib.
Estimated Value: Excellent: $450.00
Very good: $340.00

Savage Model 333T Trap
Similar to 333 with Monte Carlo stock and recoil pad in 12 gauge, 30″ barrel.
Estimated Value: Excellent: $525.00
Very good: $395.00

Savage Model 28A & B Standard
Gauge: 12
Action: Slide action; hammerless; solid breech; side ejection
Magazine: 5-shot tubular
Barrel: 26″, 28″, 30″ or 32″ cylinder, modified or full choke; raised rib on 28B
Finish: Blued; checkered wood pistol grip stock and grooved slide handle
Approximate wt.: 7½ lbs.
Comments: Made from the late 1920's until mid 1930's. Add $10.00 for matted rib.
Estimated Value: Excellent: $180.00
Very good: $135.00

Savage Model 28C Riot
Basically the same as 28A except with a 20″ cylinder bore barrel. This was for use by police, bank guards, etc., for protection.
Estimated Value: Excellent: $160.00
Very good: $120.00

Savage Model 28D Trap
Basically the same as 28B except: special straight checkered walnut stock and checkered slide handle; 30″ full choke barrel.
Estimated Value: Excellent: $200.00
Very good: $160.00

Savage Model 28S Special
Basically the same as 28B except: ivory bead front sight; checkered pistol grip stock; checkered forearm.
Estimated Value: Excellent: $210.00
Very good: $170.00

Savage Model 30
Gauge: 12, 20, 410
Action: Slide action; hammerless
Magazine: 4-shot tubular
Barrel: 26″, 28″, 30″; cylinder bore, modified or full choke; ventilated rib
Finish: Blued; decorated receiver; walnut pistol grip stock and grooved slide handle
Approximate wt.: 6½ lbs.
Comments: Made from late 1950's to late 1960's.
Estimated Value: Excellent: $190.00
Very good: $140.00

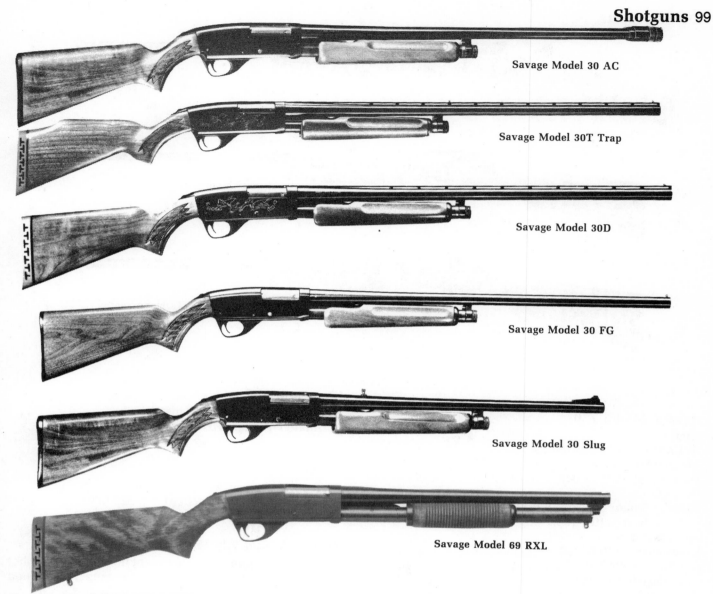

Savage Model 30 AC

Savage Model 30T Trap

Savage Model 30D

Savage Model 30 FG

Savage Model 30 Slug

Savage Model 69 RXL

Savage Model 30 FG (Field Grade)

Similar to Model 30 with plain receiver, no ventilated rib and horizontal groove in slide handle.

Estimated Value: Excellent: $150.00
                  Very good: $110.00

Savage Model 30 FG Slug Gun

Same as Model 30 FG with 22″ barrel and rifle sights, 12 gauge. Introduced in 1971, discontinued in the late 1970's.

Estimated Value: Excellent: $160.00
                  Very good: $120.00

Savage Model 30D (Deluxe)

1970's version of the Model 30 with recoil pad and horizontal groove in slide handle. Discontinued in the late 1970's.

Estimated Value: Excellent: $175.00
                  Very good: $130.00

Savage Model 30 AC

Same as Model 30 with adjustable choke.

Estimated Value: Excellent: $170.00
                  Very good: $125.00

Savage Model 30T Trap

Fancy version Model 30 in 12 gauge; 30″ full choke barrel; Monte Carlo stock; grooved slide handle; recoil pad. Introduced in mid 1960's.

Estimated Value: Excellent: $180.00
                  Very good: $135.00

Savage Model 69R, 69N, 69RXL

Gauge: 12, regular and magnum
Action: Slide action; hammerless; top tang safety
Magazine: 6-shot tubular, 4-shot on 69R
Barrel: 18¼″ cylinder bore, 20″ on 69R
Finish: Blued; walnut stock and grooved slide handle; recoil pad, swivels; 69N has satin nickel finish.
Approximate wt.: 6½ lbs.
Comments: A law enforcement shotgun introduced in 1982. Add $75.00 for model 69N. 69R and 69N discontinued in mid 1980's.

Estimated Value: New (retail): $208.39
                  Excellent: $155.00
                  Very good: $120.00

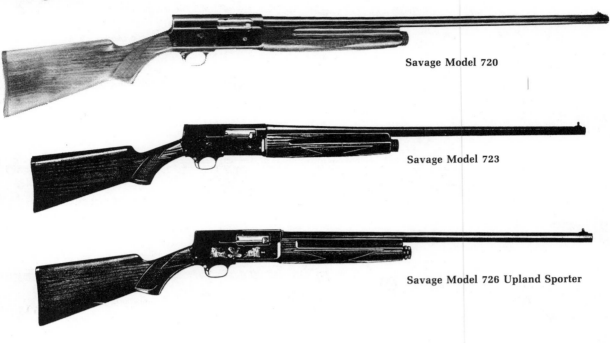

Savage Model 720

Savage Model 723

Savage Model 726 Upland Sporter

Savage Model 720

Gauge: 12
Action: Browning patent; semi-automatic; hammerless
Magazine: 4-shot tubular
Barrel: 28″, 30″ or 32″ cylinder bore, modified or full choke
Finish: Blued; checkered walnut pistol grip stock and forearm; after 1940, engraved receiver
Approximate wt.: 8½ lbs.
Comments: Originally a Springfield shotgun, this takedown model was made from about 1930 until the late 1940's. In the early 1940's, Model 720R (Riot Gun) was introduced with a 20″ barrel.
Estimated Value: Excellent: $220.00
Very good: $160.00

Savage Model 720-P

Basically the same as 720 with "Poly-Choke" produced from the late 1930's to 1940's; 3 or 5 shot; 12 gauge only.
Estimated Value: Excellent: $225.00
Very good: $165.00

Savage Model 721

Same as 720 with matted rib.
Estimated Value: Excellent: $225.00
Very good: $165.00

Savage Model 722

Same as 720 except with ventilated rib.
Estimated Value: Excellent: $230.00
Very good: $165.00

Savage Model 723

Same as 720 except no 32″ barrel; available in 16 gauge. Weights about 7½ lbs.
Estimated Value: Excellent: $200.00
Very good: $150.00

Savage Model 724

Same as 723 except with matted rib.
Estimated Value: Excellent: $210.00
Very good: $155.00

Savage Model 725

Save as 723 except with ventilated rib.
Estimated Value: Excellent: $225.00
Very good: $165.00

Savage Model 726 Upland Sporter

Basically the same a the 720 except no 32″ barrel; 2-shot tubular magazine; available in 16 gauge; decorated receiver.
Estimated Value: Excellent: $220.00
Very good: $160.00

Savage Model 727 Upland Sporter

Same as Model 726 except with matted rib.
Estimated Value: Excellent: $230.00
Very good: $165.00

Savage Model 728 Upland Sporter

Same as Model 726 except with ventilated rib.
Estimated Value: Excellent: $245.00
Very good: $185.00

Savage Model 740C Skeet Gun

Basically the same as Model 726 with a skeet stock and "Cutts Compensator". Discontinued in the late 1940's.
Estimated Value: Excellent: $240.00
Very good: $180.00

Savage Model 745 Lightweight

Similar to Model 720 with light alloy receiver. Made from late 1930's to 1940's; 3 or 5 shot; 12 gauge only.
Estimated Value: Excellent: $245.00
Very good: $175.00

Savage Model 775

Savage Model 775-SC

Savage Model 750

Savage Model 750 AC

Savage Model 755

Gauge: 12, 16
Action: Semi-automatic; hammerless
Magazine: 4-shot tubular; 3-shot tubular
Barrel: 26″ cylinder bore; 28″ full or modified; 30″ full choke
Finish: Blued; checkered walnut pistol grip stock and forearm
Approximate wt.: 8 lbs.
Comments: Made from the late 1940's until late 1950's; top of receiver flush with stock.
Estimated Value: Excellent: $210.00
Very good: $160.00

Savage Model 775 Lightweight

Similar to 755 with alloy receiver. Produced until mid 1960's.
Estimated Value: Excellent: $200.00
Very good: $150.00

Savage Model 755 - SC

Similar to 755 with Savage "Super Choke".
Estimated Value: Excellent: $220.00
Very good: $165.00

Savage Model 775 - SC

Basically the same as Model 755 with Savage "Super Choke" and 26″ barrel.
Estimated Value: Excellent: $225.00
Very good: $170.00

Savage Model 750

Gauge: 12
Action: Browning patent; semi-automatic; hammerless
Magazine: 4-shot tubular
Barrel: 26″ cylinder bore; 28″ full or modified
Finish: Blued; checkered walnut pistol grip stock and forearm; decorated receiver
Approximate wt.: 7¼ lbs.
Comments: Made from the early to late 1960's.
Estimated Value: Excellent: $280.00
Very good: $210.00

Savage Model 750 SC

Similar to the Model 750 with Savage "Super Choke". Made from 1962 for two years.
Estimated Value: Excellent: $300.00
Very good: $225.00

Savage Model 750 AC

Model 750 with adjustable choke. Made during mid 1960's.
Estimated Value: Excellent: $250.00
Very good: $190.00

Sears

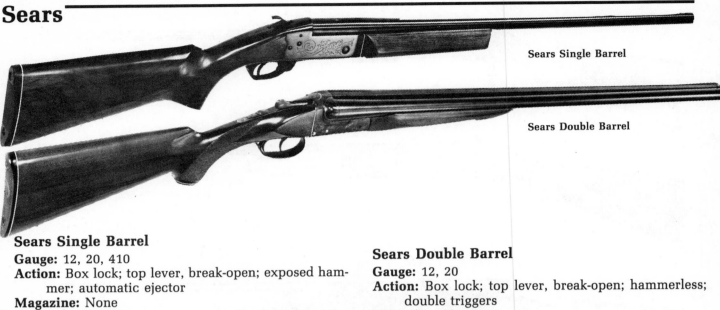

Sears Single Barrel

Sears Double Barrel

Sears Single Barrel

Gauge: 12, 20, 410
Action: Box lock; top lever, break-open; exposed hammer; automatic ejector
Magazine: None
Barrel: Full choke; 26″ in 410; 28″ in 20; 30″ in 12
Finish: Blued; wood pistol grip stock and forearm
Approximate wt.: 7 lbs.
Comments: Manufactured in the 1970's and 1980's.
Estimated Value: Excellent: $50.00
Very good: $40.00

Sears Double Barrel

Gauge: 12, 20
Action: Box lock; top lever, break-open; hammerless; double triggers
Magazine: None
Barrel: 28″ double barrel side by side; variety of chokes
Finish: Blued; epoxied black frame; walnut pistol grip stock and forearm
Approximate wt.: 7½ lbs.
Comments: Made to the early 1980's.
Estimated Value: Excellent: $175.00
Very good: $135.00

Sears Ted Williams Over & Under

Gauge: 12, 20
Action: Box lock; top lever, break-open; hammerless; automatic ejectors, selective trigger
Magazine: None
Barrel: Over and under double barrel; 26″, 28″ in standard chokes; ventilated rib; chrome lined
Finish: Blued; engraved steel receivers; checkered walnut pistol grip stock and forearm; recoil pad
Approximate wt.: 6¾ lbs.
Comments: Produced to the late 1970's.
Estimated Value: Excellent: $385.00
Very good: $285.00

Sears Ted Williams Over & Under

Sears Bolt Action

Gauge: 410
Action: Bolt action; repeating
Magazine: 3-shot detachable clip
Barrel: 24″ full choke
Finish: Blued; wood pistol grip stock and forearm
Approximate wt.: 5½ lbs.
Comments: Made to the late 1970's.
Estimated Value: Excellent: $75.00
Very good: $55.00

Sears Model 140

Gauge: 12, 20
Action: Bolt action; repeating
Magazine: 2-shot detachable clip
Barrel: 25″ adjustable choke
Finish: Blued; wood pistol grip stock and forearm
Approximate wt.: 7 lbs.
Comments: Made to the late 1970's.
Estimated Value: Excellent: $80.00
Very good: $60.00

Sears Model 140

Sears Bolt Action

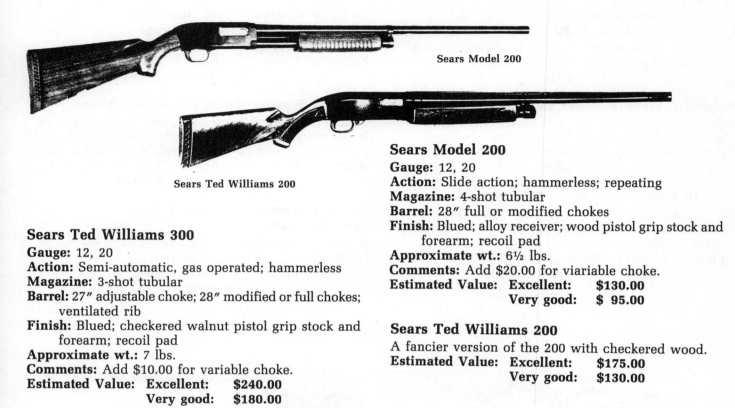

Sears Model 200

Sears Ted Williams 200

Sears Model 200

Gauge: 12, 20
Action: Slide action; hammerless; repeating
Magazine: 4-shot tubular
Barrel: 28″ full or modified chokes
Finish: Blued; alloy receiver; wood pistol grip stock and forearm; recoil pad
Approximate wt.: 6½ lbs.
Comments: Add $20.00 for viariable choke.
Estimated Value: **Excellent:** $130.00
 Very good: $ 95.00

Sears Ted Williams 200

A fancier version of the 200 with checkered wood.
Estimated Value: **Excellent:** $175.00
 Very good: $130.00

Sears Ted Williams 300

Gauge: 12, 20
Action: Semi-automatic, gas operated; hammerless
Magazine: 3-shot tubular
Barrel: 27″ adjustable choke; 28″ modified or full chokes; ventilated rib
Finish: Blued; checkered walnut pistol grip stock and forearm; recoil pad
Approximate wt.: 7 lbs.
Comments: Add $10.00 for variable choke.
Estimated Value: **Excellent:** $240.00
 Very good: $180.00

Smith & Wesson

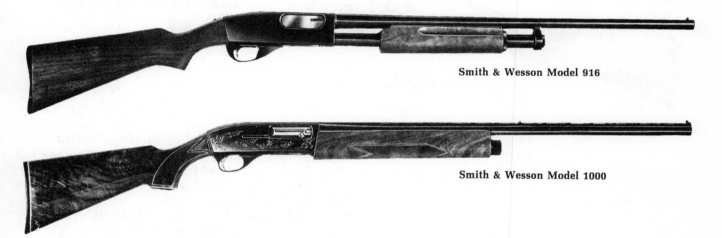

Smith & Wesson Model 916

Smith & Wesson Model 1000

Smith & Wesson Model 916

Gauge: 12
Action: Slide action; hammerless; side ejection
Magazine: 5-shot tubular
Barrel: 20″ cylinder bore; 26″ improved cylinder, 28″ modified, full or cylinder bore; ventilated rib on some models
Finish: Blued; satin finish receiver; walnut semi-pistol grip stock and grooved slide handle; recoil pad available
Approximate wt.: 7 lbs.
Comments: Made from the early 1970's to about 1980. Add $20.00 for Deer Model.
Estimated Value: **Excellent:** $150.00
 Very good: $120.00

Smith & Wesson Model 1000

Gauge: 12, 20, regular and magnum
Action: Semi-automatic, gas operated; hammerless; side ejection
Magazine: 3-shot tubular
Barrel: 26″, 28″, 30″; variety of chokes; ventilated rib
Finish: Blued; engraved alloy receiver; steel receiver on magnum; checkered walnut pistol grip stock and forearm; sights.
Approximate wt.: 7½ lbs.
Comments: Manufactured from the early 1970's to mid 1980's. Add $46.00 for magnum; $30.00 for "Multi-Choke" system.
Estimated Value: **Excellent:** $380.00
 Very good: $285.00

Smith & Wesson Model 1000 Super 12

Similar to the Model 1000 with "Multi-Choke" system; designed to use magnum shells. Introduced in 1984.
Estimated Value: Excellent: $450.00
Very good: $335.00

Smith & Wesson Model 1000 Trap

Similar to the Model 1000 with Monte Carlo stock; steel receiver; 30"multi-choke barrel; other trap features.
Estimated Value: Excellent: $450.00
Very good: $340.00

Smith & Wesson Model 1000S, Superskeet

Similar to the Model 1000 with 25" skeet choke barrel; muzzle vents and other extras. Add $200.00 for Superskeet model.
Estimated Value: Excellent: $380.00
Very good: $285.00

Smith & Wesson Model 1000 Slug

Similar to the Model 1000 with a 22" slug barrel, rifle sights, and steel receiver.
Estimated Value: Excellent: $380.00
Very good: $285.00

Smith & Wesson Model 1000 Waterfowler

Similar to the Model 1000 with a steel receiver; dull oil-finish stock; 30" full choke barrel; Parkerized finish; swivels; recoil pad; camoflage sling. Introduced in 1982.
Estimated Value: Excellent: $435.00
Very good: $325.00

Smith & Wesson Model 1000 Super 12 Waterfowler

Similar to the Model 1000 Waterfowler with the "Multi-Choke" system. Introduced in 1984.
Estimated Value: Excellent: $470.00
Very good: $350.00

Smith & Wesson Model 3000

Smith & Wesson Model 3000 Police

Smith & Wesson Model 3000

Gauge: 12, 20, regular or magnum
Action: Slide action; repeating; hammerless
Magazine: 3-shot tubular
Barrel: 26" improved cylinder; 28" modified or full, 30" full; ventilated rib
Finish: Blued; checkered walnut pistol grip stock and fluted slide handle; recoil pad
Approximate wt.: 7 lbs.
Comments: Currently produced. Add $25.00 for "Multi-Choke" system.
Estimated Value: Excellent: $300.00
Very good: $225.00

Smith & Wesson Model 3000 Waterfowler

Similar to the Model 3000 with steel receiver; 30" full choke barrel; Parkerized finish; dull, oil-finished wood; camouflaged sling and swivels. Introduced in 1982. Add $25.00 for "Multi-Choke" system.
Estimated Value: Excellent: $320.00
Very good: $240.00

Smith & Wesson Model 3000 Slug

Smiliar to the Model 3000 with a 22" slug barrel; rifle sights; swivels.
Estimated Value: Excellent: $270.00
Very good: $200.00

Smith & Wesson Model 3000 Police

Similar to the Model 3000 with 18" or 20" slug or police cylinder barrel; blued or Parkerized finish; bead or rifle sights; walnut finish, hardwood stock and grooved slide handle or plastic pistol grip and slide handle or folding stock. Add $25.00 for rifle sights; $10.00 for plastic pistol grip; $70.00 for folding stock.
Estimated Value: Excellent: $250.00
Very good: $185.00

Stevens

Stevens Model No. 93

Stevens Models No. 93, 97 Nitro Special
Gauge: 12, 16
Action: Top lever break-open; exposed hammer; single shot; Model 97 has automatic ejector
Magazine: None
Barrel: Special steel; 28″, 30″ 32″
Finish: Blued; nickel plated, case hardened frame; plain walnut pistol grip stock and lipped forearm
Approximate wt.: 7 to 7½ lbs.
Comments: Made from the early 1900's until World War I.
Estimated Value: Excellent: $70.00
  Very good: $55.00

Stevens Model No. 97 Nitro Special

Stevens Models No. 100, 110, 120
Gauge: 12, 16, 20
Action: Top lever break-open; automatic ejector; exposed hammer; single shot
Magazine: None
Barrel: 28″, 30″, 32″
Finish: Blued; case hardened frame; walnut pistol grip stock and forearm; No. 100 no checkering; 110 and 120 checkered walnut
Approximate wt.: 6 to 7 lbs.
Comments: Produced around the turn of the century for about 1 or 2 years.
Estimated Value: Excellent: $75.00
  Very good: $60.00

Stevens Model No. 120

Stevens Model No. 140
Similar to Model 120 except it is hammerless and has an automatic safety.
Estimated Value: Excellent: $100.00
  Very good: $ 75.00

Stevens Models No. 160, 165, 170
Gauge: 12, 16, 20
Action: Break-open; exposed hammer; single shot; automatic ejector except on 160
Magazine: None
Barrel: 26″, 28″, 30″, 32″
Finish: Blued; case hardened frame; checkered walnut pistol grip stock and forearm except 160 which is plain
Approximate wt.: 6 to 7 lbs.
Comments: Made around the turn of the century for about 5 years.
Estimated Value: Excellent: $65.00
  Very good: $50.00

Stevens Model No. 140

Stevens Model No. 170

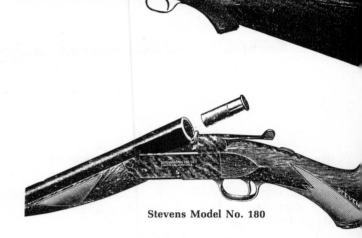

Stevens Model No. 182 Trap Gun

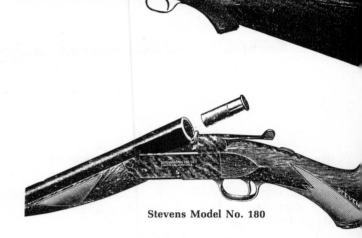
Stevens Model No. 180

Stevens Model No. 180

Gauge: 12, 16, 20
Action: Top lever break-open; hammerless; automatic ejector; single shot
Magazine: None
Barrel: 26", 28", 30" modified; 32" or 36" full choke
Finish: Blued; case hardened frame; checkered walnut pistol grip stock and forearm
Approximate wt.: 6½ lbs.
Comments: Produced from around 1900 until World War I.
Estimated Value: Excellent: $90.00
Very good: $70.00

Stevens Model No. 185, 190, 195

Gauge: 12
Action: Top lever break-open; hammerless; automatic shell ejector; automatic safety; single shot
Magazine: None
Barrel: Round with octagon breech; 30" or 32"
Finish: Blued; case hardened frame; checkered walnut pistol grip stock and forearm; frame engraved on No. 190, 195
Approximate wt.: 7 to 8 lbs.
Comments: These guns differ in quality of finish and engraving. Produced briefly around the turn of the century.
Estimated Value: Excellent: $150.00
Very good: $110.00

Stevens Model No. 970

Similar to the 185, this 12 gauge was made from around 1910 until World War I.
Estimated Value: Excellent: $80.00
Very good: $60.00

Stevens Model No. 182 Trap Gun

Similar to Model No. 180 except: Trap grade; 12 gauge only; matted top of barrel; scroll work on frame. Made from around 1910 to World War I.
Estimated Value: Excellent: $150.00
Very good: $110.00

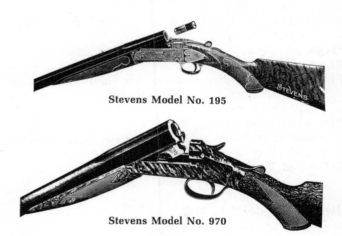
Stevens Model No. 195

Stevens Model No. 970

Stevens Model No. 85 Dreadnaught

Gauge: 12
Action: Top lever break-open; exposed hammer
Magazine: None, single shot
Barrel: 28", 30", 32" full choke
Finish: Blued; case hardened frame; plain walnut pistol grip stock and lipped forearm
Approximate wt.: 7½ lbs.
Comments: Made from around 1910 to mid 1920's.
Estimated Value: Excellent: $65.00
Very good: $50.00

Stevens Model No. 89 Dreadnaught

Same as the No. 85 with automatic ejector. Made until mid 1930's.
Estimated Value: Excellent: $70.00
Very good: $55.00

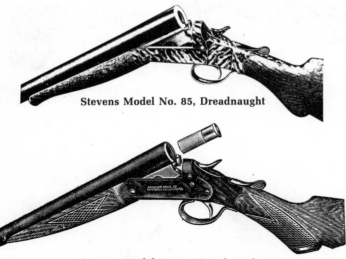
Stevens Model No. 85, Dreadnaught

Stevens Model No. 89 Dreadnaught

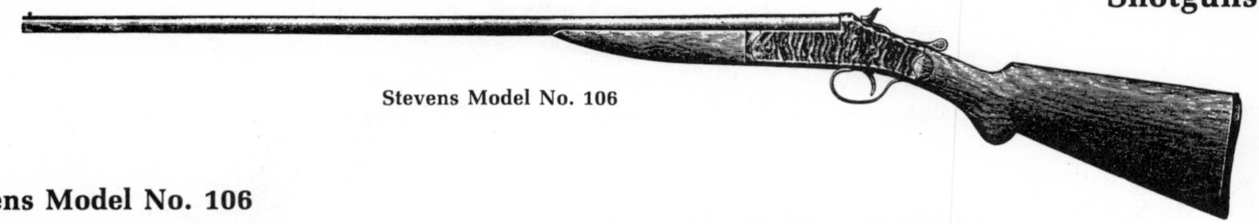

Stevens Model No. 106

Stevens Model No. 106

Gauge: 410
Action: Top lever break-open; exposed hammer; single shot
Magazine: None
Barrel: 26″ or 30″
Finish: Blued; case hardened frame; plain walnut pistol grip stock and forearm
Approximate wt.: 4½ lbs.
Comments: This lightweight, light-gauge gun was made from around 1910 until the 1930's.
Estimated Value: Excellent: $65.00
Very good: $50.00

Stevens Model No. 108

Same as the No. 106 with automatic ejector.
Estimated Value: Excellent: $75.00
Very good: $60.00

Stevens Springfield Model No. 958

Very similar to Model No. 108. Made from mid 1920's to early 1930's.
Estimated Value: Excellent: $70.00
Very good: $55.00

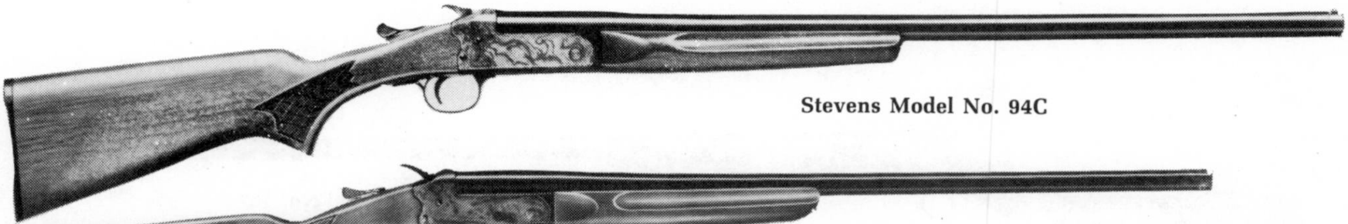

Stevens Model No. 94C

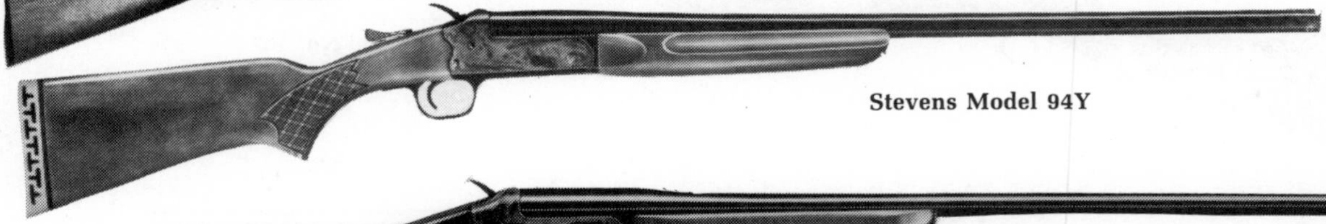

Stevens Model 94Y

Stevens Model 9478

Stevens Model 9478-10

Stevens Model No. 94C, 94

Gauge: 12, 16, 20, 410
Action: Top lever break-open; exposed hammer
Magazine: None
Barrel: 26″, 28″, 30″, 32″, 36″ full choke
Finish: Blued; case hardened frame; checkered walnut semi-pistol grip stock and grooved forearm
Approximate wt.: 6 to 8 lbs.
Comments: Made from mid 1960's to mid 1980's. Add $7.00 for 36″ barrel.
Estimated Value: Excellent: $65.00
Very good: $50.00

Stevens Model No. 94Y

Similar to 94C in youth version. Shorter stock; recoil pad, 26″ barrel; 20 gauge modified or 410 full choke.
Estimated Value: Excellent: $70.00
Very good: $55.00

Stevens Model 9478

Similar to the Model 94C with lever release on the trigger guard; no checkering. Add $8.00 for 36″ barrel.
Estimated Value: Excellent: $65.00
Very good: $50.00

Stevens Model 9478-10, Waterfowl

Similar to the Model 9478 with a 36″ full choke barrel; 10 gauge only; recoil pad.
Estimated Value: Excellent: $ 95.00
Very good: $ 70.00

Stevens Model 9478-Y

Similar to the Model 9478 in 410 full or 20 modified gauges; 26″ barrel; short stock with rubber buttplate.
Estimated Value: Excellent: $60.00
Very good: $45.00

Stevens Models No. 105, 107, 115, 125
Gauge: 12, 16, 20, 28
Action: Top lever break-open; exposed hammer; single shot; automatic ejector on all but Model 105
Magazine: None, single shot
Barrel: 26″ or 28″
Finish: Blued; case hardened frame; checkered walnut pistol grip stock and forearm except No. 107 (plain)
Approximate wt.: 5½ lbs.
Comments: A lightweight series of shotguns produced until about World War II for Model 105; 1950's for Model 107 and 1920's for Models 115 and 125.
Estimated Value: Excellent: $65.00
Very good: $50.00

Stevens Model No. 105

Stevens Springfield Model No. 95
Very similar to Model 107. Made from the mid 1920's until the early 1930's.
Estimated Value: Excellent: $60.00
Very good: $45.00

Stevens Model No. 107

Stevens Model No. 115

Stevens Model No. 125

Stevens Model No. 116

Stevens Model No. 116, 117
Very similar to the Model No. 115 with automatic ejector. Model No. 117 is equipped with Lyman sights. Made from the early 1930's until World War II.
Estimated Value: Excellent: $80.00
Very good: $60.00

Stevens Model No. 250

Gauge: 12
Action: Top lever break-open; exposed hammer; double trigger
Magazine: None
Barrel: 28″, 30″, 32″ double barrel
Finish: Blued; checkered walnut pistol grip stock and forearm
Approximate wt.: 8 lbs.
Comments: Made around the turn of the century for about 5 years.
Estimated Value: Excellent: $225.00
Very good: $165.00

Stevens Models No. 260 and 270

Similar to Model 250 with special Damascus or twist barrels; available in 16 gauge. Manufactured briefly around the turn of the century.
Estimated Value: Excellent: $200.00
Very good: $150.00

Stevens Models No. 350, 360, 370

Gauge: 12, 16
Action: Top lever break-open; hammerless; double trigger
Magazine: None
Barrel: Double barrel, matted rib, 28″, 30″, 32″
Finish: Blued; checkered walnut pistol grip stock and forearm
Approximate wt.: 7½ to 8½ lbs.
Comments: Produced around the turn of the century for about 5 years.
Estimated Value: Excellent: $175.00
Very good: $130.00

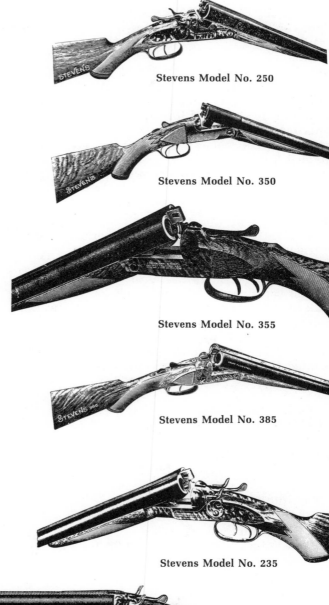

Stevens Model No. 250

Stevens Model No. 350

Stevens Model No. 355

Stevens Model No. 385

Stevens Model No. 235

Stevens Model No. 255

Stevens Models No. 355, 365, 375, 385

Gauge: 12, 16
Action: Top lever break-open; hammerless; double trigger
Magazine: None
Barrel: Double barrel; Krupp steel; matted rib; 28″, 30″, 32″
Finish: Blued; checkered walnut straight or pistol grip stock and forearm; 355 and 365 plain; 375 some engraving; 385 engraved frame
Approximate wt.: 7 to 8½ lbs.
Comments: Made from the early 1900's. 355 discontinued in World War I; all others before World War I.
Estimated Value: Excellent: $200.00
Very good: $150.00

Stevens Model No. 235, 255, 265

Gauge: 12, 16
Action: Top lever break-open; exposed hammers; double triggers; box lock
Magazine: None
Barrel: Double barrel; matted rib; 28″, 30″, 32″
Finish: Blued; checkered walnut pistol grip stock and forearm; case hardened frame; No. 255 has checkered buttplate
Approximate wt.: 7 to 8½ lbs.
Comments: Made from around 1907 until the 1920's; 255 stopped around World War I.
Estimated Value: Excellent: $210.00
Very good: $160.00

Stevens Riverside Model No. 215

Gauge: 12, 16
Action: Top lever break-open; exposed hammer; double trigger
Magazine: None
Barrel: Double barrel; 26″, 28″, 30″, 32″; matted rib; left barrel full choke, right barrel modified
Finish: Blued; case hardened frame; checkered walnut pistol grip stock and forearm
Approximate wt.: 7½ to 8½ lbs.
Comments: Made from around 1910 to World War II.
Estimated Value: Excellent: $200.00
  Very good: $150.00

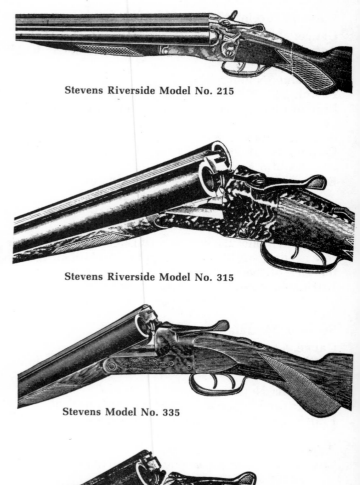

Stevens Riverside Model No. 215

Stevens Riverside Model No. 315

Stevens Riverside Model No. 315

Gauge: 12, 16
Action: Top lever break-open; hammerless; double trigger
Magazine: None
Barrel: Double barrel; 26″, 28″, 30″, 32″; matted rib; right barrel modified, left full choke
Finish: Blued; case hardened frame; checkered walnut semi-pistol grip stock and forearm
Approximate wt.: 7 to 7½ lbs.
Comments: Made from around 1910 until the late 1930's.
Estimated Value: Excellent: $195.00
  Very good: $150.00

Stevens Model No. 335

Stevens Model No. 335

Similar to the 315. Produced from around 1910 to the late 1920's.
Estimated Value: Excellent: $180.00
  Very good: $135.00

Stevens Model No. 345

Very similar to the No. 335 in 20 gauge. Made from around 1910 until the mid 1920's.
Estimated Value: Excellent: $200.00
  Very good: $150.00

Stevens Model No. 345

Stevens Model No. 330

Stevens Model No. 330

Gauge: 12, 16, 20, 410
Action: Top lever break-open; hammerless; double trigger; takedown
Magazine: None
Barrel: Double barrel; 26″-32″; right modified, left full choke; both full choke in 410
Finish: Blued; case hardened frame; checkered black walnut pistol grip stock and forearm
Approximate wt.: 5¾ to 7¾ lbs.
Comments: Made from the mid 1920's until the mid 1930's.
Estimated Value: Excellent: $185.00
  Very good: $140.00

Stevens Springfield Model No. 315

Stevens Model 311-R

Stevens Model 311,
Stevens Springfield Model No. 311
Springfield Hammerless

Gauge: 12, 16, 20, 410
Action: Top lever break-open; hammerless; double trigger; takedown
Magazine: None
Barrel: Double barrel; 24″-32″; right barrel modified, left full choke, except 32″ 12 gauge is full choke; matted rib
Finish: Blued; case hardened frame; smooth walnut semi-pistol grip stock and forearm
Approximate wt.: 5½ to 7¾ lbs.
Comments: Made from the early 1930's to present. Add $30.00 for selective single trigger. 16 gauge discontinued in late 1970's.
Estimated Value: New (retail): $278.00
Excellent: $210.00
Very good: $155.00

Stevens Springfield Model No. 315

A higher quality version of the Model 311; discontinued.
Estimated Value: Excellent: $200.00
Very good: $150.00

Stevens Model 311-R

A law enforcement version of the Model 311 with 18¼″ cylinder bore barrel; recoil pad; 12 gauge only. Introduced in 1982.
Estimated Value: New (retail): $278.00
Excellent: $210.00
Very good: $155.00

Stevens Model No. 530

Gauge: 12, 16, 20, 410
Action: Top lever break-open; hammerless; box lock; double trigger
Magazine: None
Barrel: Double barrel; 26″-32″; right modified choke, left full choke, except 32″ 12 gauge and 410 are both full choke
Finish: Blued; case hardened frame; checkered walnut pistol grip stock and forearm; recoil pad on early model
Approximate wt.: 6 to 7½ lbs.
Comments: Made from mid 1930's until early 1950's.
Estimated Value: Excellent: $185.00
Very good: $140.00

Stevens Model No. 530 ST

Same as 530 with non-selective single trigger.
Estimated Value: Excellent: $200.00
Very good: $150.00

Stevens Model No. 530M

Same as 530 with plastic stock. Discontinued in late 1940's.
Estimated Value: Excellent: $160.00
Very good: $120.00

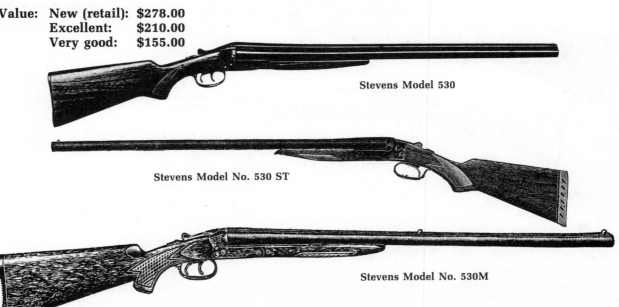

Stevens Model 530

Stevens Model No. 530 ST

Stevens Model No. 530M

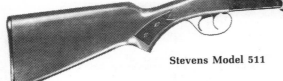

Stevens Model 511

Stevens Model 511

Gauge: 12, 20 regular or magnum
Action: Box lock; top lever, break-open; double trigger
Magazine: None
Barrel: Double barrel; 28″ modified & full choke
Finish: Blued; checkered hardwood semi-pistol grip stock and small forearm; case hardened frame
Approximate wt.: 7¾ lbs.
Comments: Produced in the late 1970's.
Estimated Value: Excellent: $200.00
Very good: $150.00

Stevens-Springfield Model No. 22-410

Stevens Model No. 240

Stevens-Springfield Model No. 22-410

Gauge: 410 and 22 caliber rifle
Action: Top lever break-open; exposed hammer; single trigger; separate extractors
Magazine: None
Barrel: Over and under double barrel; 22 rifle over 410 shotgun; 24″
Finish: Blued; case hardened frame; plastic semi-pistol grip stock and forearm; open rear, ramp front sights
Approximate wt.: 6 lbs.
Comments: Made from late 1930's until about 1950. Later produced as Savage.
Estimated Value: Excellent: $125.00
Very good: $ 95.00

Stevens Model No. 240

Gauge: 410
Action: Top lever break-open; exposed hammer; double trigger; takedown
Magazine: None
Barrel: Over and under double barrel; both barrels 26″ full choke
Finish: Blued; checkered plastic or wood pistol grip stock and forearm
Approximate wt.: 6½ lbs.
Comments: Made from the late 1930's until World War II.
Estimated Value: Excellent: $250.00
Very good: $185.00

Stevens Model No. 58

Stevens Model No. 59

Stevens Model No. 58

Gauge: 410
Action: Bolt-action
Magazine: 3-shot detachable box
Barrel: 24″ full choke
Finish: Blued; plain walnut one-piece pistol grip stock and forearm
Approximate wt.: 5½ lbs.
Comments: Made from late 1930's to late 1970's. Later versions have checkering.
Estimated Value: Excellent: $70.00
Very good: $55.00

Stevens Model No. 59

Similar to No. 58 except with a 5-shot tubular magazine. Discontinued in the early 1970's.
Estimated Value: Excellent: $80.00
Very good: $60.00

Stevens-Springfield Model 38

Stevens-Springfield Model 39

Stevens Model No. 258

Stevens-Springfield Model No. 37

Stevens Model No. 124

Stevens-Springfield Model 38
Similar to Steven Model No. 58.
Estimated Value: Excellent: $65.00
                    Very good: $50.00

Stevens-Springfield Model 39
Similar to Stevens Model No. 59
Estimated Value: Excellent: $70.00
                    Very good: $55.00

Stevens Model No. 258
Gauge: 20
Action: Bolt action; repeating
Magazine: 2-shot detachable box
Barrel: 26″ full choke
Finish: Blued; plain walnut one-piece pistol grip stock and forearm
Approximate wt.: 6¼ lbs.
Comments: This takedown shotgun was produced from the late 1930's until the mid 1960's.
Estimated Value: Excellent: $70.00
                    Very good: $55.00

Stevens Model No. 254
A single shot version of the Model 258.
Estimated Value: Excellent: $50.00
                    Very good: $40.00

Stevens-Springfield Model 238
Similar to Stevens Model 258.
Estimated Value: Excellent: $65.00
                    Very good: $50.00

Stevens-Springfield Model 237
Similar to Stevens Model No. 254.
Estimated Value: Excellent: $50.00
                    Very good: $40.00

Stevens-Springfield Model No. 37
Similar to Stevens-Springfield Model 237 except 410 bore.
Estimated Value: Excellent: $65.00
                    Very good: $50.00

Stevens Model No. 124
Gauge: 12
Action: Semi-automatic; side ejection; hammerless
Magazine: 2-shot tubular
Barrel: 28″ improved cylinder, modified or full choke
Finish: Blued; checkered plastic pistol grip stock and forearm
Approximate wt.: 7 lbs.
Comments: Made from late 1940's until mid 1950's.
Estimated Value: Excellent: $110.00
                    Very good: $ 85.00

Stevens Model No. 520

Stevens Model No. 522

Stevens Model No. 525

Stevens Models No. 520, 521, 522

Gauge: 12

Action: Browning patent; slide action; takedown; side ejection; hammerless

Magazine: 5-shot tubular

Barrel: 26″-32″; full choke, modified or cylinder; matted rib on 521

Finish: Blued; walnut pistol grip stock and grooved slide handle; checkered straight grip on 522

Approximate wt.: 8 lbs.

Comments: Made from early 1900's until World War II; 522 discontinued in the 1920's.

Estimated Value: **Excellent:** **$175.00**
                      Very good: **$130.00**

Stevens Models No. 525, 530, 535

Similar to 520 except fancier grades; 525 is custom built; 530 custom built with engraved receiver and rib; 535 custom built, heavily engraved. Discontinued by World War I.

Estimated Value: **Excellent:** **$225.00**
                      Very good: **$170.00**

Stevens Model No. 535

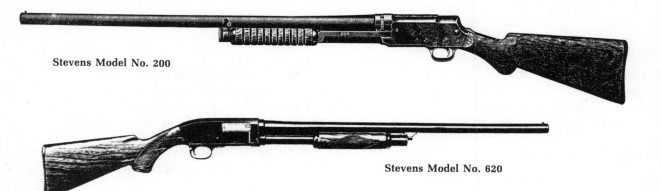

Stevens Model No. 200

Stevens Model No. 620

Stevens Model No. 200

Gauge: 20

Action: Pedersen patent slide action; hammerless; side ejection; takedown

Magazine: 5-shot tubular

Barrel: 26″-32″; full choke, modified or cylinder bore

Finish: Blued; walnut pistol grip stock and grooved slide handle

Approximate wt.: 6½ lbs.

Comments: Made from around 1910 until World War I.

Estimated Value: **Excellent:** **$175.00**
                      Very good: **$130.00**

Stevens Model No. 620

Gauge: 12, 16, 20

Action: Slide action; hammerless; side ejection

Magazine: 5-shot tubular

Barrel: 26″-32″; full choke, modified or cylinder bore

Finish: Blued; checkered walnut pistol grip stock and slide handle

Approximate wt.: 6 to 7¾ lbs.

Comments: A takedown shotgun made for about 30 years beginning in the late 1920's.

Estimated Value: **Excellent:** **$185.00**
                      Very good: **$140.00**

Stevens Model No. 620-P

Stevens Model No. 77

Stevens Model No. 820-SC

Stevens Model 79

Stevens Model No. 620-P

Same as Model No. 620 with "Poly-Choke".
Estimated Value: Excellent: $190.00
                   Very good: $150.00

Stevens Model No. 621

Same as No. 620 with matted rib. Discontinued after about 10 years.
Estimated Value: Excellent: $190.00
                   Very good: $145.00

Stevens Model No. 77

Gauge: 12, 16
Action: Slide action; hammerless; side ejection
Magazine: 5-shot tubular
Barrel: 26″ or 28″ improved cylinder, modified or full choke
Finish: Blued; plain walnut pistol grip stock and grooved slide handle
Approximate wt.: 7 lbs.
Comments: Made from the mid 1950's to early 1970's.
Estimated Value: Excellent: $170.00
                   Very good: $130.00

Stevens Model No. 77-SC

Same as 77 with Savage "Super Choke" and recoil pad.
Estimated Value: Excellent: $185.00
                   Very good: $140.00

Stevens Model No. 820

Gauge: 12
Action: Slide action; hammerless; side ejection
Magazine: 5-shot tubular
Barrel: 28″ improved cylinder, modified or full choke
Finish: Blued; plain walnut semi-pistol grip stock and grooved slide handle
Approximate wt.: 7½ lbs.
Comments: Produced for about 5 years beginning in 1949.
Estimated Value: Excellent: $165.00
                   Very good: $125.00

Stevens Model No. 820-SC

Same as No. 820 with Savage "Super Choke".
Estimated Value: Excellent: $200.00
                   Very good: $150.00

Stevens Model 79

Gauge: 12, 20, 410, regular and magnum
Action: Slide action; hammerless; side ejection; repeating
Magazine: 4-shot tubular; 3-shot in magnum
Barrel: 28″ modified or 30″ full in 12 gauge; 28″ modified or full in 20 gauge; 26″ full in 410
Finish: Blued; checkered hardwood semi-pistol grip stock and fluted slide handle
Approximate wt.: 7 lbs.
Comments: Produced in the late 1970's.
Estimated Value: Excellent: $120.00
                   Very good: $ 90.00

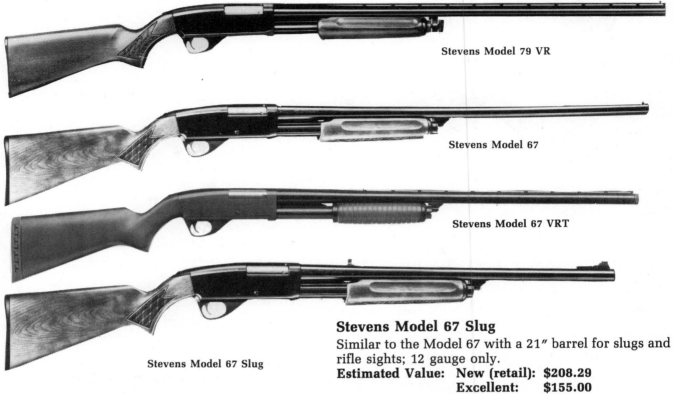

Stevens Model 79 VR

Stevens Model 67

Stevens Model 67 VRT

Stevens Model 67 Slug

Stevens Model 79 VR

Similar to the Model 79 with a ventilated rib.
Estimated Value: **Excellent:** $150.00
Very good: $115.00

Stevens Model 79 Slug

Similar to the Model 79 with a 21″ barrel for slugs; rifle sights.
Estimated Value: **Excellent:** $160.00
Very good: $120.00

Stevens Model 67, 67T

Gauge: 12, 20, or 410, regular or magnum
Action: Slide action; hammerless; side ejecting; repeating
Magazine: 4-shot tubular; 3-shot in magnum.
Barrel: 28″ modified or full; 26″ full in 410; 30″ full in 12 gauge; 67T has interchangeable choke tubes in 12 and 20 gauge only.
Finish: Blued; hardwood, semi-pistol grip stock and fluted or grooved slide handle; some with recoil pad.
Approximate wt.: 6¾ lbs.
Comments: Produced in the late 1970's to present. Add $16.00 for 67T.
Estimated Value: **New (retail):** $198.61
Excellent: $150.00
Very good: $110.00

Stevens Model 67 Slug

Similar to the Model 67 with a 21″ barrel for slugs and rifle sights; 12 gauge only.
Estimated Value: **New (retail):** $208.29
Excellent: $155.00
Very good: $115.00

Stevens Model 67T-Y, 67VRT-Y

Gauge: 20
Action: Slide action; hammerless; repeating
Magazine: 4-shot
Barrel: 22″ with three interchangeable choke tubes; ventilated rib on 67VRT-Y
Finish: Blued; hardwood, semi-pistol grip stock and grooved slide handle
Approximate wt.: 6 lbs.
Comments: Introduced in 1985. Designed for the young shooter with a shorter 12″ pull stock. Deduct $16.00 for plain barrel (67T-Y).
Estimated Value: **New (retail):** $229.29
Excellent: $170.00
Very good: $130.00

Stevens Model 67VRT-K

Similar to the Model 67VR-T except: laminated camo stock. Introduced in 1986.
Estimated Value: **New (retail):** $250.29
Excellent: $190.00
Very good: $140.00

Stevens Model 67 VR, 67 VR-T

Similar to the Model 67 with a ventilated rib (67 VR). 67 VR-T has ventilated rib and interchangeable choke tubes. Add 7% for interchangeable choke tubes in 12 or 20 gauge only.
Estimated Value: **New (retail):** $214.75
Excellent: $160.00
Very good: $120.00

Universal

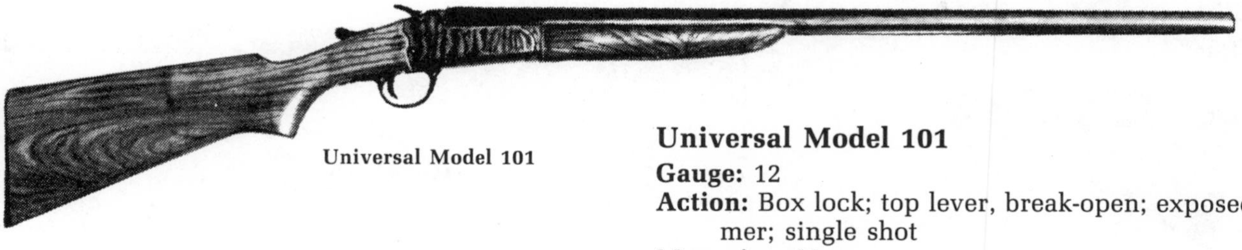

Universal Model 101

Universal Model 101
Gauge: 12
Action: Box lock; top lever, break-open; exposed hammer; single shot
Magazine: None
Barrel: 28″, 30″ full choke
Finish: Blued; plain wood pistol grip stock and tapered forearm
Approximate wt.: 7½ lbs.
Comments: Manufactured in the late 1960's.
Estimated Value: Excellent: $70.00
Very good: $55.00

Universal Single Wing
Similar to the Model 101 with automatic ejector. Made from the early to mid 1970's.
Estimated Value: Excellent: $75.00
Very good: $60.00

Universal Model 202

Universal Double Wing

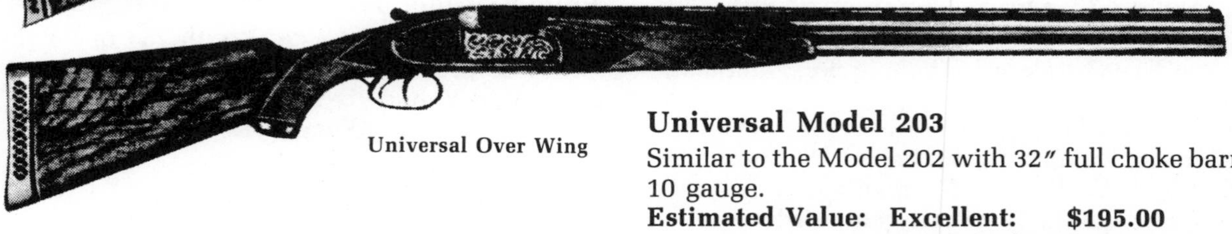

Universal Over Wing

Universal Model 203
Similar to the Model 202 with 32″ full choke barrels and 10 gauge.
Estimated Value: Excellent: $195.00
Very good: $150.00

Universal Model 2030
Similar to the Double Wing with 32″ full choke barrels and 10 gauge.
Estimated Value: Excellent: $200.00
Very good: $150.00

Universal Model 202
Gauge: 12, 20, 410
Action: Box lock; top lever, break-open; hammerless; double triggers
Magazine: None
Barrel: Double barrel; 26″ improved cylinder & modified; 28″ modified & full chokes
Finish: Blued; checkered walnut pistol grip stock and forearm
Approximate wt.: 7 lbs.
Comments: Manufactured in the late 1960's. Add $20.00 for 410 bore.
Estimated Value: Excellent: $175.00
Very good: $135.00

Universal Double Wing
Similar to the Model 202 with recoil pad. Made from 1970 to 1975; 12 or 20 gauge magnum.
Estimated Value: Excellent: $190.00
Very good: $145.00

Universal Over Wing
Gauge: 12, 20
Action: Box lock; top lever, break-open; hammerless
Magazine: None
Barrel: Over and under double barrel; 26″, 28″, 30″; ventilated rib
Finish: Blued; checkered walnut pistol grip stock and forearm; sights; recoil pad; engraving available
Approximate wt.: 8 lbs.
Comments: Made from about 1970 to 1975. Add $50.00 for single trigger.
Estimated Value: Excellent: $300.00
Very good: $225.00

Universal Auto Wing

Universal Duck Wing

Universal Duck Wing

Similar to the Auto Wing with 28″ or 30″ full choke barrel. Teflon coated. Discontinued in the early 1970's.
Estimated Value: Excellent: $275.00
Very good: $210.00

Universal Auto Wing

Gauge: 12
Action: Semi-automatic; hammerless
Magazine: 5-shot tubular
Barrel: 26″, 28″, 30″; variety of chokes; ventilated rib
Finish: Blued; checkered walnut pistol grip stock and forearm; sights
Approximate wt.: 8 lbs.
Comments: Made from about 1970 to 1975.
Estimated Value: Excellent: $250.00
Very good: $190.00

Valmet

Valmet Model 412KE

Valmet Model 412 KE

Gauge: 12, 20
Action: Top lever break-open; hammerless; automatic ejectors
Magazine: None
Barrel: Over and under double barrel; 26″ improved cylinder & modified; 28″ modified & full; 30″ modified & full in 12 gauge; ventilated rib
Finish: Blued; checkered walnut pistol grip stock and forearm; Monte Carlo stock with recoil pad; swivels
Approximate wt.: 7 lbs.
Comments: Made in Finland with interchangeable barrels available that make the shotgun a combination shotgun/rifle or a double rifle. Produced from the early 1980's to mid 1980's.
Estimated Value: Excellent: $560.00
Very good: $420.00

Valmet Model 412K

Similar to the Model 412KE with extractor and 36″ barrel. Introduced in 1982.
Estimated Value: Excellent: $560.00
Very good: $420.00

Valmet Model 412KE Trap

Similar to the Model 412KE with 30″ improved modified & full choke barrel.
Estimated Value: Excellent: $560.00
Very good: $420.00

Valmet Model 412KE Skeet

Similar to the Model 412KE with 26″ or 28″ cylinder bore & improved cylinder bore or skeet choke barrels.
Estimated Value: Excellent: $560.00
Very good: $420.00

Valmet Model 412K Combination

Similar to the Model 412K with a 12 gauge improved modified barrel over a rifle barrel in caliber 222, 223, 243, 30-06, 308; 24″ barrels. Introduced in 1982.
Estimated Value: Excellent: $625.00
Very good: $470.00

Valmet 12 Gauge

Gauge: 12
Action: Box lock; top lever, break-open; single selective trigger
Magazine: None
Barrel: Over and under double barrel; 26″ improved cylinder & modified; 28″ modified & full; 30″ modified & full or full & full chokes
Finish: Blued; checkered walnut pistol grip stock and wide forearm
Approximate wt.: 7 lbs.
Comments: Made from the late 1940's to the late 1960's in Finland.
Estimated Value: Excellent: $425.00
Very good: $320.00

Valmet Model 412S

Valmet Model 412S Combination

Valmet Model 412S

Gauge: 12, 20; regular or magnum
Action: Top lever, break-open; hammerless; automatic ejectors; extractor on 36" model.
Magazine: None
Barrel: Over & under double barrel; 26" cylinder bore & improved cylinder, improved cylinder or modified; 28" cylinder bore & modified or modified & full; 30" improved modified & full, modified & full; 36" full; ventilated rib.
Finish: Blued; checkered walnut pistol grip stock and forearm, adjustable for barrel differences; buttplate adjusts to fit shooter.
Approximate wt.: 7 lbs.
Comments: A shooting system with interchangeable barrels and adjustable buttplate; produced in Finland. Introduced in 1984.
Estimated Value: New (retail): $799.00
                 Excellent: $600.00
                 Very good: $450.00

Valmet Model 412S Combination

Similar to the Model 412S with a 24" 12 gauge improved/modified barrel over a 222, 223, 243, 30-06, or 308 caliber rifle barrel.
Estimated Value: New (retail): $879.00
                 Excellent: $660.00
                 Very good: $495.00

Weatherby

Weatherby Regency

Weatherby Regency

Gauge: 12, 20
Action: Box lock; top lever, break-open; hammerless; automatic ejectors; single selective trigger
Magazine: None
Barrel: Over and under double barrel; 26", 28", 30"; variety of chokes; ventilated rib
Finish: Blued; checkered walnut pistol grip stock and fluted forearm; recoil pad
Approximate wt.: 7 to 7½ lbs.
Comments: Made from the early 1970's to the early 1980's.
Estimated Value: Excellent: $810.00
                 Very good: $610.00

Weatherby Regency Skeet

Similar to the Regency in skeet chokes with a 26" or 28" barrel.
Estimated Value: Excellent: $825.00
                 Very good: $620.00

Weatherby Regency Trap

Similar to the Regency with a wide ventilated rib barrel; 30" or 32" full and full, full and improved modified, or full and modified chokes; choice of regular or Monte Carlo stock; 12 gauge only.
Estimated Value: Excellent: $860.00
                 Very good: $620.00

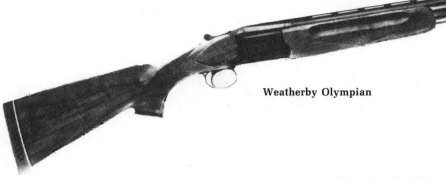

Weatherby Olympian

Weatherby Olympian Skeet

Similar to the Olympian with 26″ or 28″ skeet choke barrel.

Estimated Value: Excellent: $720.00
Very good: $540.00

Weatherby Olympian Trap

Similar to the Olympian; ventilated rib between barrels; 30″ or 32″ full & modified or full & improved modified chokes; Monte Carlo or regular stock.

Estimated Value: Excellent: $745.00
Very good: $560.00

Weatherby Olympian

Gauge: 12, 20
Action: Box lock; top lever, break-open; selective automatic ejectors
Magazine: None
Barrel: Over and under double barrel; 26″ or 28″ full & modified; 26″ or 28″ modified & improved cylinder; 30″ full & modified; ventilated rib
Finish: Blued; checkered walnut pistol grip stock and fluted forearm; recoil pad
Approximate wt.: 7 to 8 lbs.
Comments: Made from the 1970's to early 1980's.
Estimated Value: Excellent: $700.00
Very good: $525.00

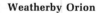

Weatherby Orion

Weatherby Orion Trap

Similar to the Orion in 12 gauge only; 30″ or 32″ full & improved modified or full & modified barrels; wide rib with center bead and ventilated rib between barrels; curved recoil pad; Monte Carlo or regular stock.

Estimated Value: New (retail): $899.95
Excellent: $675.00
Very good: $510.00

Weatherby Orion Skeet

Similar to the Orion with 26″ skeet choke barrels.
Estimated Value: New (retail): $859.95
Excellent: $645.00
Very good: $485.00

Weatherby Orion Field

Gauge: 12, 20
Action: Box lock; top lever, break-open; selective automatic ejectors; single selective trigger
Magazine: None
Barrel: Over and under double barrel; 26″ or 28″ modified & improved cylinder; 28″ or 30″ full & modified; ventilated rib; multi-choke in 1984
Finish: Blued; checkered walnut pistol grip stock and fluted forearm; rosewood cap at grip; recoil pad; engraved receiver; high lustre finish
Approximate wt.: 6½ to 7½ lbs.
Comments: Introduced in 1982.
Estimated Value: New (retail): $849.95
Excellent: $640.00
Very good: $480.00

Weatherby Athena

Weatherby Athena Trap

Similar to the Athena in 12 gauge only in 30″ or 32″ full & improved modified or full & modified barrels; wide rib with center bead sight; curved recoil pad; Monte Carlo stock.

Estimated Value:	New (retail):	$1,369.95
	Excellent:	$1,030.00
	Very good:	$ 770.00

Weatherby Athena Skeet

Similar to the Athena with 26″ skeet choke barrels.

Estimated Value:	New (retail):	$1,329.95
	Excellent:	$1,000.00
	Very good:	$ 750.00

Weatherby Athena Field

Gauge: 12, 20
Action: Box lock; top lever, break-open; selective automatic ejectors; single selective trigger
Magazine: None
Barrel: Over and under double barrel; 26″ or 28″ modified & improved cylinder; 28″ modified & full choke; ventilated rib on top and between barrels. Multi-choke in 1984.
Finish: Blued; special selected checkered walnut pistol grip stock and fluted forearm; high lustre finish; rosewood grip cap; recoil pad; silver grey engraved receiver
Approximate wt.: 7 to 8 lbs.
Comments: A high quality superposed shotgun introduced in 1982.

Estimated Value:	New (retail):	$1,349.95
	Excellent:	$1,015.00
	Very good:	$ 760.00

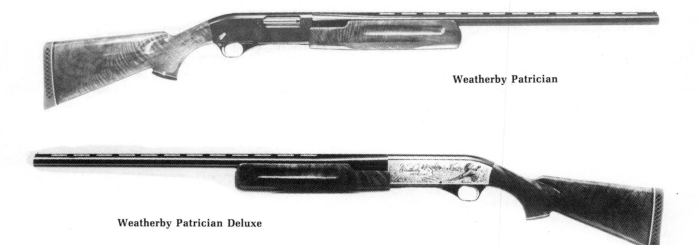

Weatherby Patrician

Weatherby Patrician Deluxe

Weatherby Patrician and Patrician II

Gauge: 12; Patrician II 12 gauge magnum
Action: Slide action; hammerless; side ejection
Magazine: Tubular
Barrel: 26″, 28″, 30″; variety of chokes; ventilated rib
Finish: Blued; checkered walnut pistol grip stock and grooved slide handle; recoil pad
Approximate wt.: 7½ lbs.
Comments: Made from the early 1970's to early 1980's. Add $20.00 for Trap.

Estimated Value:	Excellent:	$250.00
	Very good:	$190.00

Weatherby Patrician Deluxe

Similar to the Patrician with decorated satin silver receiver and higher quality wood.

Estimated Value:	Excellent:	$300.00
	Very good:	$225.00

Weatherby Ninety-Two, Ninety-Two IMC

Gauge: 12, regular or magnum
Action: Slide action; hammerless.
Magazine: 2-shot tubular, with plug.
Barrel: 26″ improved cylinder or skeet, 28″ modified or full, 30″ full; ventilated rib; multi-choke barrel on all after 1983.
Finish: Blued; checkered walnut, pistol grip stock and slide handle; high gloss finish; rosewood grip cap; etched receiver; recoil pad.
Approximate wt.: 7½ lbs.
Comments: Introduced in 1982. Trap model discontinued in 1983.
Estimated Value: New (retail): $339.95
Excellent: $300.00
Very good: $225.00

Weatherby Ninety-Two

Weatherby Ninety-Two Buckmaster

Similar to the Ninety-Two with a 22″ slug barrel and rifle sights.
Estimated Value: New (retail): $399.95
Excellent: $300.00
Very good: $225.00

Weatherby Centurion

Weatherby Centurion Deluxe

Similar to the Centurion with a decorated satin silver receiver and higher quality wood.
Estimated Value: Excellent: $350.00
Very good: $265.00

Weatherby Centurion and Centurion II

Gauge: 12; Centurion II 12 gauge magnum
Action: Semi-automatic, gas operated; hammerless
Magazine: Tubular
Barrel: 26″, 28″, 30″; variety of chokes; ventilated rib
Finish: Blued; checkered walnut pistol grip stock and grooved forearm; recoil pad
Approximate wt.: 7½ lbs.
Comments: Made from the early 1970's to early 1980's. Add $20.00 for Trap.
Estimated Value: Excellent: $300.00
Very good: $225.00

Weatherby Eighty-Two

Weatherby Eighty-Two Buckmaster

Similar to the Eighty-Two with 22″ slug barrel and rifle sights.
Estimated Value: New (retail): $469.95
Excellent: $350.00
Very good: $265.00

Weatherby Eighty-Two, Eighty-Two IMC

Gauge: 12, regular or magnum
Action: Gas operated, semi-automatic; hammerless
Magazine: 2-shot tubular with plug
Barrel: 26″ improved cylinder or skeet, 28″ modified or full, 39″ full; ventilated rib; "Multi-Choke" barrel on all after 1983.
Finish: Blued; checkered walnut, pistol grip stock and forearm; high gloss finish; rosewood grip cap; etched receiver; recoil pad.
Approximate wt.: 7½ lbs.
Comments: Introduced in 1982. Add $30.00 for Trap model, discontinued in 1983.
Estimated Value: New (retail): $469.95
Excellent: $350.00
Very good: $265.00

Western

Western Long Range

Gauge: 12, 16, 20, 410
Action: Box lock; top lever, break-open; hammerless; double or single trigger
Magazine: None
Barrel: Double barrel; 26″, 32″; modified & full choke
Finish: Blued; plain walnut, pistol grip stock and forearm
Approximate wt.: 7 lbs.
Comments: Made from the mid 1920's until the early 1940's by Western Arms Corp. which was later bought by Ithaca Arms Company. Add $25.00 for single trigger.
Estimated Value: Excellent: $300.00
Very good: $225.00

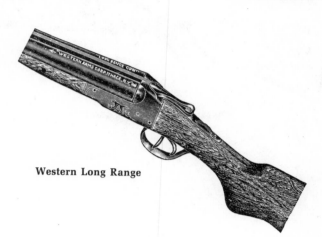

Western Long Range

Western Field

Western Field Model 100

Gauge: 12, 16, 20, 410
Action: Box lock; thumb sliding, break-open; hammerless; automatic ejectors; single shot
Magazine: None
Barrel: 26″-30″, full choke
Finish: Blued; wood semi-pistol grip stock and tapered forearm
Approximate wt.: 6¼ to 7 lbs.
Comments: Manufactured to the mid 1970's.
Estimated Value: Excellent: $60.00
Very good: $45.00

Western Field Model 100

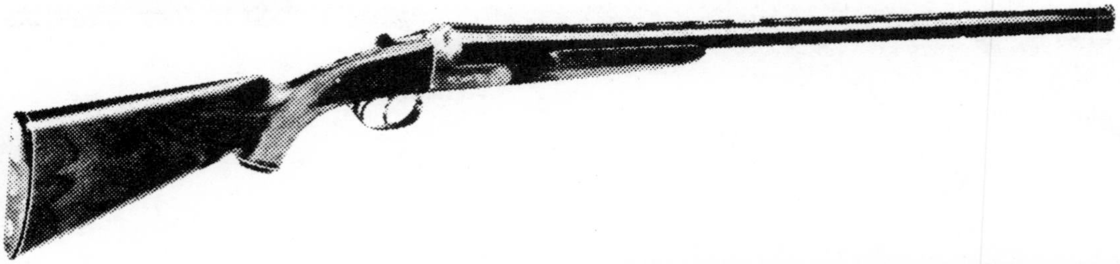

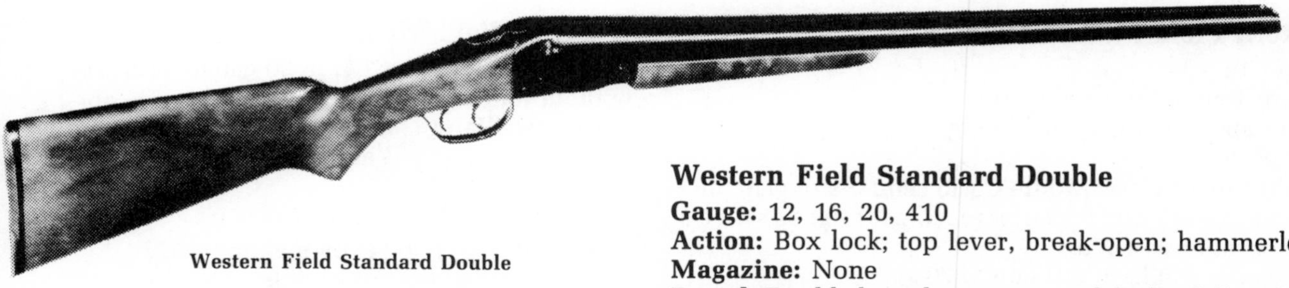

Western Field Standard Double

Western Field Standard Double

Gauge: 12, 16, 20, 410
Action: Box lock; top lever, break-open; hammerless
Magazine: None
Barrel: Double barrel; 26″-30″ modified & full or full & full chokes; ribbed barrels
Finish: Blued; wood semi-pistol grip stock and short tapered forearm
Approximate wt.: 6½ to 7 lbs.
Comments: Made to the mid 1970's.
Estimated Value: Excellent: $200.00
Very good: $150.00

Western Field Model 150C

Western Field Model 170

Western Field Model 172

Western Field Model 175

Western Field Model 150C
Gauge: 410
Action: Bolt action; repeating
Magazine: 3-shot; top loading
Barrel: 25″; full choke; 3″ chamber
Finish: Blued; wood Monte Carlo pistol grip one-piece
    stock and forearm
Approximate wt.: 5½lbs.
Comments: Manufactured to the early 1980's.
Estimated Value: **Excellent:**   **$75.00**
                  Very good: **$60.00**

Western Field Model 170
Gauge: 12
Action: Bolt action; repeating
Magazine: 3-shot detachable clip
Barrel: 28″
Finish: Blued; wood Monte Carlo semi-pistol grip one-
    piece stock and forearm; recoil pad; sights; swivels
Approximate wt.: 7 lbs.
Comments: Made to the late 1970's.
Estimated Value: **Excellent:**   **$80.00**
                  Very good: **$60.00**

Western Field Model 172
Similar to the Model 170 without sights or swivels; ad-
justable choke.
Estimated Value: **Excellent:**   **$70.00**
                  Very good: **$55.00**

Western Field Model 175
Similar to the Model 172 in 20 gauge with a 26″ barrel;
without adjustable choke.
Estimated Value: **Excellent:**   **$65.00**
                  Very good: **$55.00**

Western Field Bolt Action
Gauge: 12, 20, regular or magnum, 410
Action: bolt action; repeating
Magazine: 3-shot detachable box; 410 top loading
Barrel: 28″ full choke; 25″ in 410
Finish: Blued; smooth walnut finish hardwood one-piece
    pistol grip stock and forearm
Approximate wt.: 6½ lbs.
Comments: Add $10.00 for 12 gauge.
Estimated Value: **Excellent:**   **$75.00**
                  Very good: **$60.00**

Western Field Model 550

Western Field Model 550

Gauge: 12, 20, 410, regular or magnum
Action: Slide action; hammerless; repeating
Magazine: 4-shot magnum, 5-shot regular; tubular
Barrel: 26″ 410; 28″, 30″ 12 gauge; full or modified choke
Finish: Blued; smooth hardwood pistol grip stock with fluted comb, grooved slide handle
Approximate wt.: 6½ lbs.
Comments: Add $20.00 for ventilated rib and variable choke.
Estimated Value: Excellent: $125.00
　　　　　　　　　　Very good: $ 95.00

Western Field Model 550 Deluxe

Gauge: 12, 20, regular or magnum
Action: Slide action; hammerless; repeating
Magazine: 5-shot tubular; 4-shot in magnum
Barrel: 28″ with 3 interchangeable "Accu-choke" tubes; ventilated rib
Finish: Blued; checkered hardwood pistol grip stock and slide handle; chrome damascened finish on bolt; recoil pad; engraved receiver
Approximate wt.: 7¼ lbs.
Comments: Presently manufactured.
Estimated Value: Excellent: $180.00
　　　　　　　　　　Very good: $135.00

Winchester

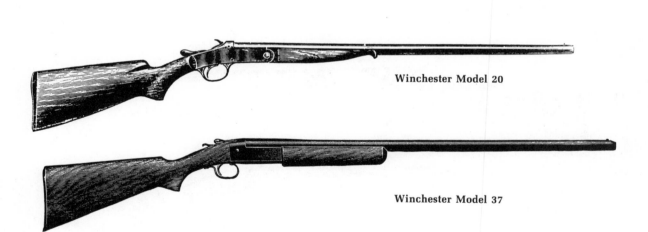

Winchester Model 20

Winchester Model 37

Winchester Model 20

Gauge: 410
Action: Top lever break-open; box lock; exposed hammer; single shot
Magazine: None
Barrel: 26″ full choke
Finish: Blued; plain or checkered wood pistol grip stock and lipped forearm
Approximate wt.: 6 lbs.
Comments: Made from about 1920 to 1925.
Estimated Value: Excellent: $250.00
　　　　　　　　　　Very good: $190.00

Winchester Model 37

Gauge: 12, 16, 20, 28, 410
Action: Top lever break-open; partial visible hammer; automatic ejector
Magazine: None
Barrel: 26″-32″; full choke, modified or cylinder bore
Finish: Blued; plain walnut semi-pistol grip stock and forearm
Approximate wt.: 6 lbs.
Comments: Made from the late 1930's to mid 1960's. Add $20.00 for 410 gauge.
Estimated Value: Excellent: $150.00
　　　　　　　　　　Very good: $120.00

Winchester Model 37A Youth

Winchester Model 37A

Winchester Model 370

Winchester Model 370

Gauge: 12, 16, 20, 28, 410
Action: Top lever break-open; box lock; exposed hammer; single shot; automatic ejector
Magazine: None
Barrel: 26″-32″ or 36″ full choke; modified in 20 gauge
Finish: Blued; plain wood semi-pistol grip stock and forearm
Approximate wt.: 5¼ to 6¼ lbs.
Comments: Made from the late 1960's to mid 1970's.
Estimated Value: Excellent: $65.00
Very good: $50.00

Winchester Model 37A

Similar to the Model 370 but also available in 36″ waterfowl barrel; has checkered stock, fluted forearm; engraved receiver; gold plated trigger. Manufactured to the late 1970's. Add $5.00 for 36″ barrel.
Estimated Value: Excellent: $75.00
Very good: $60.00

Winchester Model 37A Youth

Similar to the 37A with 26″ barrel.
Estimated Value: Excellent: $65.00
Very good: $50.00

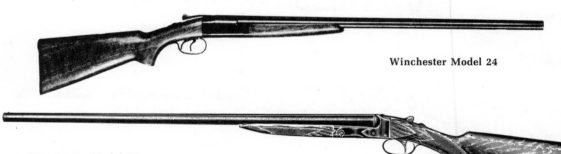

Winchester Model 24

Winchester Model 21

Winchester Model 21

Gauge: 12, 16, 20
Action: Box lock; top lever, break-open; hammerless
Magazine: None
Barrel: 26″-32″ double barrel; matted or ventilated rib; full, modified or cylinder bore
Finish: Checkered walnut, pistol grip stock and forearm
Approximate wt.: 7 lbs.
Comments: Made in this grade from 1930 to late 1950's. Fancier grades were produced. Prices here for Field grade. Still available as a custom order gun.
Estimated Value: Excellent: $2,000.00 - $6,500.00
Very good: $1,800.00 - $5,000.00

Winchester Model 24

Gauge: 12, 16, 20
Action: Box lock; top lever, break-open; hammerless; automatic ejectors; double triggers
Magazine: None
Barrel: Double barrel, 28″ cylinder bore & modified in 12 gauge; others modified & full choke; raised matted rib
Finish: Blued; plain or checkered walnut pistol grip stock and forearm
Approximate wt.: 7½ lbs.
Comments: Made from the late 1930's to the late 1950's.
Estimated Value: Excellent: $350.00
Very good: $265.00

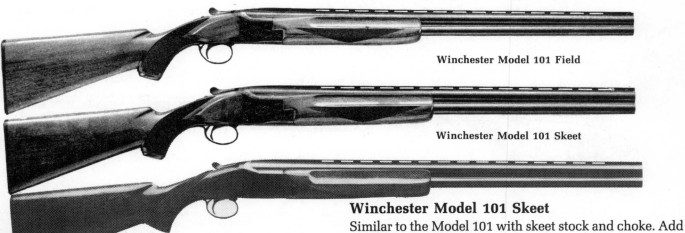

Winchester Model 23XTR Pigeon Grade

Winchester Model 23 Pigeon Grade Lightweight

Winchester Model 23 Pigeon Grade Lightweight

Similar to the Model 23 XTR Pigeon Grade with a straight grip stock; rubber butt pad; 25½″ ventilated rib barrels. Introduced in 1981. Add $40.00 for Winchoke.

Estimated Value:	New (retail):	$1,420.00
	Excellent:	$1,065.00
	Very good:	$ 800.00

Winchester Model 23 XTR Pigeon Grade

Gauge: 12, 20, regular or magnum
Action: Box lock; top lever, break-open; hammerless; selective automatic ejectors
Magazine: None
Barrel: Double barrel; 26″ improved cylinder & modified; 28″ modified & full choke; tapered ventilated rib. Winchoke after 1980.
Finish: Blued; checkered walnut semi-pistol grip stock and forearm; silver grey engraved receiver
Approximate wt.: 6½ to 7 lbs.
Comments: Made from the late 1970's.

Estimated Value:	New (retail):	$1,460.00
	Excellent:	$1,095.00
	Very good:	$ 820.00

Winchester Model 101 Field

Winchester Model 101 Skeet

Winchester Xpert Model 96

Winchester Model 101 Field

Gauge: 12, 20, 28, 410, regular or magnum 28, 410 discontinued in the late 1970's
Action: Box lock; top lever, break-open; hammerless; single trigger; automatic ejector
Magazine: None
Barrel: Over and under double barrel; 26″-30″, various chokes; ventilated rib
Finish: Blued; checkered walnut pistol grip stock and wide forearm; recoil pad on magnum; engraved receiver
Approximate wt.: 6½ to 7½ lbs.
Comments: Made from the mid 1960's to about 1980. Add $30.00 for 410 or 28 gauge; $10.00 for magnum.

| Estimated Value: | Excellent: | $950.00 |
| | Very good: | $710.00 |

Winchester Model 101 Skeet

Similar to the Model 101 with skeet stock and choke. Add $30.00 for 410 or 28 gauge.

| Estimated Value: | Excellent: | $1,000.00 |
| | Very good: | $ 750.00 |

Winchester Model 101 Trap

Similar to the Model 101 with regular or Monte Carlo stock; recoil pad; 30″-32 barrels; 12 gauge only.

| Estimated Value: | Excellent: | $1,000.00 |
| | Very good: | $ 750.00 |

Winchester Xpert Model 96

A lower cost version of the Model 101, lacking engraving as well as some of the internal and external extras. Produced in the late 1970's.

| Estimated Value: | Excellent: | $650.00 |
| | Very good: | $490.00 |

Winchester Xpert Model 96 Trap

Similar to the Xpert Model 96 with Monte Carlo stock and 30″ barrel.

| Estimated Value: | Excellent: | $675.00 |
| | Very good: | $500.00 |

Winchester Model 101 Lightweight Winchoke

Winchester Model 101 Waterfowl Winchoke

Winchester Model 101 Lightweight Winchoke

Similar to the Model 101 Field with interchangeable choke tube system; lighter weight; ventilated rib between barrels. Introduced in 1981. 12 or 20 gauge.

Estimated Value: New (retail): $1,225.00
                Excellent: $ 920.00
                Very good: $ 690.00

Winchester Model 101 Waterfowl Winchoke

Similar to the Model 101 Lightweight Winchoke in 12 gauge only; 32" ventilated rib barrels; interchangeable choke tube system; recoil pad. Introduced in 1981.

Estimated Value: New (retail): $1,225.00
                Excellent: $ 920.00
                Very good: $ 690.00

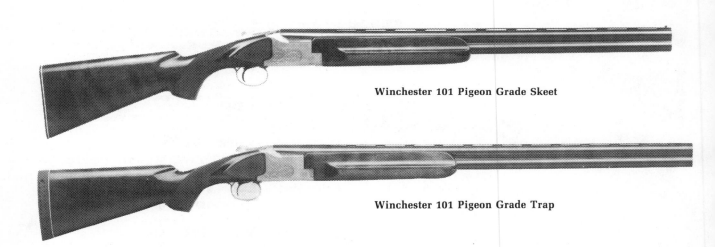

Winchester 101 Pigeon Grade Skeet

Winchester 101 Pigeon Grade Trap

Winchester 101 Pigeon Grade Skeet

Similar to the Pigeon Grade with 27" or 28" skeet choke barrels; front and center sighting beads; 410 or 28 gauge available.

Estimated Value: Excellent: $1,000.00
                Very good: $ 775.00

Winchester 101 Pigeon Grade Trap

Similar to the Pigeon Grade with a 30" or 32" barrel; recoil pad; regular or Monte Carlo stock.

Estimated Value: Excellent: $950.00
                Very good: $720.00

Winchester 101 Pigeon Grade

Gauge: 12, 20, regular or magnum
Action: Box lock; top lever, break-open; selective automatic ejectors; single selective trigger
Magazine: None
Barrel: Over and under double barrel; 26" improved cylinder & modified; 28" modified & full; ventilated rib
Finish: Blued; checkered walnut pistol grip stock and fluted forearm; silver grey engraved receiver; recoil pad on magnum
Approximate wt.: 7¼ lbs.
Comments: Made from the late 1970's to early 1980's.
Estimated Value: Excellent: $900.00
                Very good: $675.00

Winchester Pigeon Grade Lightweight

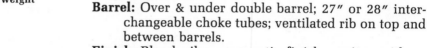

Winchester Pigeon Grade Featherweight

Winchester Model Pigeon Grade Lightweight

Gauge: 12, 20, 3″ chambers; 28 introduced in 1984
Action: Top lever, break-open
Magazine: None
Barrel: Over & under double barrel; 27″ or 28″ inter-changeable choke tubes; ventilated rib on top and between barrels.
Finish: Blued, silver grey satin finish receiver with et-ching of gamebirds and scroll work; checkered walnut rounded pistol grip stock and fluted forearm; recoil pad; straight stock available on 28 gauge.
Approximate wt.: 6½ to 7½ lbs.
Comments: Introduced in 1981.
Estimated Value: New (retail): $1,675.00
Excellent: $1,250.00
Very good: $ 940.00

Winchester Model Pigeon Grade Featherweight

Similar to the Pigeon Grade Lightweight with 25½″ bar-rels; improved cylinder & improved modified or improv-ed cylinder & modified; straight grip English style stock; rubber butt pad. Introduced in 1981.
Estimated Value: New (retail): $1,580.00
Excellent: $1,185.00
Very good: $ 890.00

Winchester Diamond Grade O/U Trap

Winchester Diamond Grade Single Barrel

Winchester Diamond Grade O/U Trap

Gauge: 12
Action: Top lever break-open
Magazine: None
Barrel: **Over and under double barrel;** 30″ or 32″ full choke top, interchangeable choke tube system bot-tom; ventilated rib on top and between barrels
Finish: Blued; silver grey satin finish on receiver with engraving; checkered walnut pistol grip stock and lipped forearm; ebony inlay in pistol grip; straight or Monte Carlo stock; recoil pad
Approximate wt.: 8¾ to 9 lbs.
Comments: Introduced in 1982.
Estimated Value: New (retail): $1,720.00
Excellent: $1,290.00
Very good: $ 975.00

Winchester Diamond Grade O/U Skeet

Similar to the Diamond Grade O/U Trap in 12, 20, 28 gauges and 410 bore; 27″ barrels. Introduced in 1982. Add $75.00 for Winchoke.
Estimated Value: New (retail): $1,720.00
Excellent: $1,290.00
Very good: $ 975.00

Winchester Diamond Grade Single Barrel

Similar to the Diamond Grade O/U Trap but with only one 32″ or 34″ barrel; interchangeable choke tube system; high ventilated rib. Introduced in 1982.
Estimated Value: New (retail): $1,820.00
Excellent: $1,365.00
Very good: $1,025.00

Winchester Diamond Grade Combination

Similar to the Diamond Grade O/U Trap with a set of 30″ or 32″ barrels and a 34″ high rib single barrel; lower barrel and single barrel use interchangeable choke tube system. Introduced in 1982.
Estimated Value: New (retail): $2,995.00
Excellent: $2,245.00
Very good: $1,685.00

Winchester Model 501 Grand European Skeet

Winchester Super Grade

Winchester Super Grade, Shotgun Rifle

Gauge: 12, 3″ chamber
Caliber: 30-06, 300 Win. mag; 243 Win.
Action: Top lever break-open
Magazine: None
Barrel: Over and under combination; 12 gauge shotgun barrel with interchangeable choke tube system over rifle barrel
Sights: Folding leaf rear, blade front
Finish: Blued; silver grey satin finish engraved receiver; checkered walnut Monte Carlo pistol grip stock and fluted forearm; recoil pad; swivels
Approximate wt.: 8½ lbs.
Comments: A limited production shotgun/rifle combination available in early 1980's.
Estimated Value: Excellent: $1,910.00
Very good: $1,435.00

Winchester Model 501 Grand European Trap

Gauge: 12
Action: Top lever break-open
Magazine: None
Barrel: Over and under double barrel; 30″ or 32″ improved modified & full choke; ventilated rib on top and between barrels
Finish: Blued; silver grey satin finish engraved receiver; checkered walnut pistol grip stock and fluted lipped forearm; regular or Monte Carlo stock; recoil pad
Approximate wt.: 8¼ to 8½ lbs.
Comments: A trap shotgun introduced in the early 1980's.
Estimated Value: New (retail): $1,720.00
Excellent: $1,290.00
Very good: $ 975.00

Winchester Model 501 Grand European Skeet

Similar to the Model 501 Grand European Trap with 27″ skeet choke barrels; weighs 6½ to 7½ lbs. Introduced in 1981. 12 or 20 gauge.
Estimated Value: New (retail): $1,720.00
Excellent: $1,290.00
Very good: $ 975.00

Winchester Model 1901

Winchester Model 36

Winchester Model 1901

Gauge: 10
Action: Lever action; repeating
Magazine: 4-shot tubular
Barrel: 30″, 32″ full choke
Finish: Blued; walnut, pistol grip stock and forearm
Approximate wt.: 8 to 9 lbs.
Comments: Made from 1901 to about 1920, an improved version of the Model 1887.
Estimated Value: Excellent: $550.00
Very good: $415.00

Winchester Model 36

Gauge: 9mm shot or ball cartridges
Action: Bolt action; single shot; rear cocking piece
Magazine: None
Barrel: 18″
Finish: Blued; straight grip one-piece stock and forearm
Approximate wt.: 3 lbs.
Comments: Made from the early to late 1920's.
Estimated Value: Excellent: $250.00
Very good: $200.00

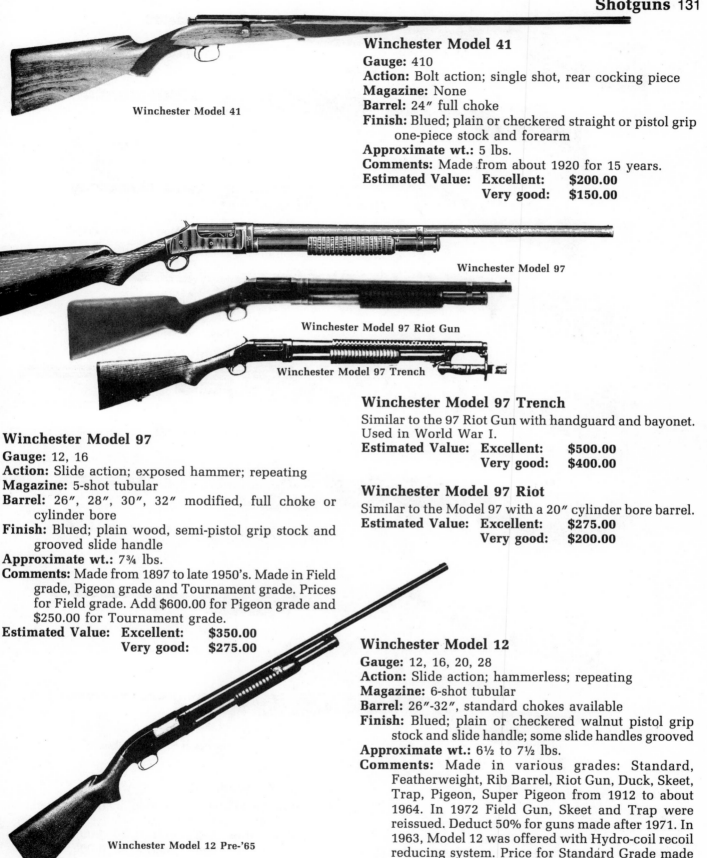

Winchester Model 41
Gauge: 410
Action: Bolt action; single shot, rear cocking piece
Magazine: None
Barrel: 24″ full choke
Finish: Blued; plain or checkered straight or pistol grip one-piece stock and forearm
Approximate wt.: 5 lbs.
Comments: Made from about 1920 for 15 years.
Estimated Value: Excellent: $200.00
**   Very good: $150.00**

Winchester Model 41

Winchester Model 97

Winchester Model 97 Riot Gun

Winchester Model 97 Trench

Winchester Model 97 Trench
Similar to the 97 Riot Gun with handguard and bayonet. Used in World War I.
Estimated Value: Excellent: $500.00
**   Very good: $400.00**

Winchester Model 97 Riot
Similar to the Model 97 with a 20″ cylinder bore barrel.
Estimated Value: Excellent: $275.00
**   Very good: $200.00**

Winchester Model 97
Gauge: 12, 16
Action: Slide action; exposed hammer; repeating
Magazine: 5-shot tubular
Barrel: 26″, 28″, 30″, 32″ modified, full choke or cylinder bore
Finish: Blued; plain wood, semi-pistol grip stock and grooved slide handle
Approximate wt.: 7¾ lbs.
Comments: Made from 1897 to late 1950's. Made in Field grade, Pigeon grade and Tournament grade. Prices for Field grade. Add $600.00 for Pigeon grade and $250.00 for Tournament grade.
Estimated Value: Excellent: $350.00
**   Very good: $275.00**

Winchester Model 12
Gauge: 12, 16, 20, 28
Action: Slide action; hammerless; repeating
Magazine: 6-shot tubular
Barrel: 26″-32″, standard chokes available
Finish: Blued; plain or checkered walnut pistol grip stock and slide handle; some slide handles grooved
Approximate wt.: 6½ to 7½ lbs.
Comments: Made in various grades: Standard, Featherweight, Rib Barrel, Riot Gun, Duck, Skeet, Trap, Pigeon, Super Pigeon from 1912 to about 1964. In 1972 Field Gun, Skeet and Trap were reissued. Deduct 50% for guns made after 1971. In 1963, Model 12 was offered with Hydro-coil recoil reducing system. Price for Standard Grade made before 1964. Add $50.00 for ventilated rib; $40.00 for raised matted rib; approximately 50% for Pigeon and approximately 120% for Super Pigeon grades. Deduct approximately 25% for Riot Gun.
Estimated Value: Excellent: $600.00
**   Very good: $450.00**

Winchester Model 12 Pre-'65

Winchester Model 12 Skeet Pre-'65

Winchester Model 12 Trap Pre-'65

Winchester Model 12 Duck Pre-'65

Winchester Model 12 Field After '72

Winchester Model 12 Super Pigeon After '72

Winchester Model 12 Trap After '72

Winchester Model 42

Winchester Model 42 Skeet

Winchester Model 42

Gauge: 410
Action: Slide action; hammerless; repeating
Magazine: 5-shot tubular and 6-shot tubular
Barrel: 26″, 28″ modified, full choke or cylinder bore
Finish: Blued; plain walnut pistol grip stock and grooved slide handle
Approximate wt.: 6 lbs.
Comments: Made from the mid 1930's to mid 1960's.
Estimated Value: Excellent: $650.00
Very good: $490.00

Winchester Model 42 Skeet

Similar to the Model 42 available in straight stock; has matted rib and skeet choke barrel.
Estimated Value: Excellent: $675.00
Very good: $510.00

Winchester Model 42 Deluxe

Similar to the Model 42 with higher quality finish; ventilated rib; select wood; checkering.
Estimated Value: Excellent: $800.00
Very good: $600.00

Winchester Model 25

Winchester Model 25 Riot Gun

Winchester Model 25
Gauge: 12
Action: Slide action; hammerless; repeating
Magazine: 4-shot tubular
Barrel: 26″, 28″; improved cylinder, modified or full chokes
Finish: Blued; plain walnut semi-pistol grip stock and grooved slide handle; sights
Approximate wt.: 7½ lbs.
Comments: Made from the late 1940's to mid 1950's.
Estimated Value: Excellent: $300.00
Very good: $225.00

Winchester Model 25 Riot Gun
Similar to the Model 25 with a 25″ cylinder bore barrel.
Estimated Value: Excellent: $260.00
Very good: $200.00

Winchester Model 1200

Winchester Model 1200 Deer

Winchester Model 1200 Skeet

Winchester Model 1200 Trap

Winchester Model 1200 Field
Gauge: 12, 16, 20, regular or magnum; 16 gauge dropped in mid 1970's
Action: Front lock; rotary bolt; slide action; repeating
Magazine: 4-shot tubular
Barrel: 26″-30″; various chokes or adjustable choke (Winchoke)
Finish: Blued; checkered walnut pistol grip stock and slide handle; recoil pad; alloy receiver
Approximate wt.: 6½ to 7½ lbs.
Comments: Made from the mid 1960's to the late 1970's. Add $15.00 for magnum; $5.00 for adjustable choke; $25.00 for ventilated rib.
Estimated Value: Excellent: $200.00
Very good: $150.00

Winchester Model 1200 Deer
Similar to the 1200 with 22″ barrel, rifle sights. Made from the mid 1960's to mid 1970's.
Estimated Value: Excellent: $210.00
Very good: $160.00

Winchester Model 1200 Skeet
Similar to 1200 except: 12 and 20 gauge on;y 26″ skeet choke; ventilated rib barrel. Made to the mid 1970's.
Estimated Value: Excellent: $230.00
Very good: $175.00

Winchester Model 1200 Trap
Similar to the 1200 with a 30″ full choke barrel; ventilated rib; regular or Monte Carlo stock. Made to the mid 1970's.
Estimated Value: Excellent: $235.00
Very good: $180.00

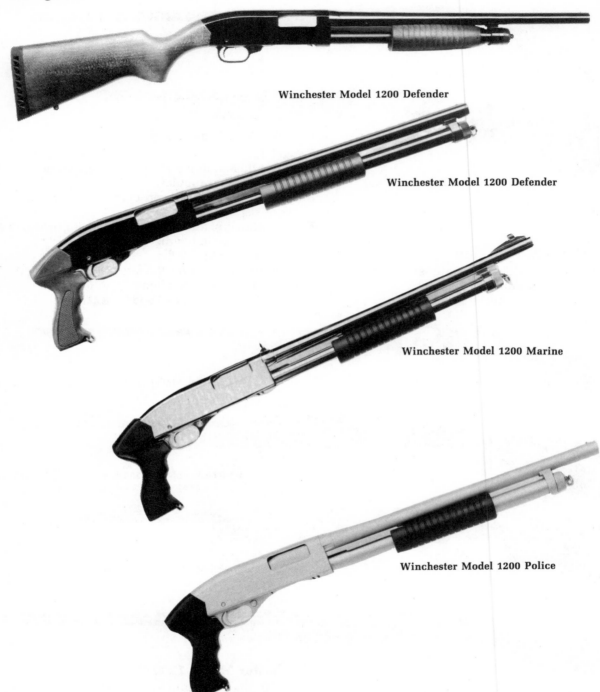

Winchester Model 1200 Defender

Winchester Model 1200 Defender

Winchester Model 1200 Marine

Winchester Model 1200 Police

Winchester Model 1200 Defender

Gauge: 12, regular and magnum
Action: Slide action front lock rotary bolt
Magazine: 6-shot tubular; 5-shot in magnum
Barrel: 18″ blue steel cylinder bore
Finish: Blued with plain wood semi-pistol grip stock and
grooved slide handle; pistol grip model made begin-
ning in 1984.
Approximate wt.: 6¾ lbs.; pistol grip model 5½ lbs.
Comments: Made from 1982 to present. Available with
rifle sights (add 7%). 20 gauge made in 1984 and
1985.
Estimated Value: New (retail): $240.95
Excellent: $180.00
Very good: $135.00

Winchester Model 1200 Police

Same as the Model 1200 Defender except: stainless steel
barrel and satin chrome finish on all other external metal
parts. Also made with shoulder stock or pistol grip (1984)
in 12 gauge only. Made from 1982 to 1986.
Estimated Value: Excellent: $265.00
Very good: $200.00

Winchester Model 1200 Marine

Same as the Model 1200 Police except: rifle sights stan-
dard. Made from 1982 to present.
Estimated Value: New (retail): $409.95
Excellent: $310.00
Very good: $230.00

Winchester Model 1300 XTR

Gauge: 12, 20, regular or magnum
Action: Slide action; hammerless; repeating
Magazine: 3-shot tubular
Barrel: 26″, 28″, 30″; improved cylinder, modified or full choke; ventilated rib available
Finish: Blued; checkered walnut pistol grip stock and slide handle
Approximate wt.: 6½ lbs.
Comments: Made from the late 1970's to early 1980's. Add $15.00 for ventilated rib.
Estimated Value: Excellent: $235.00
                                   Very good: $180.00

Winchester Model 1300XTR Deer Gun

Similar to the Model 1300XTR with a 22″ barrel, rifle sights; sling; recoil pad. 12 gauge only. Made from about 1980 to mid 1980's.
Estimated Value: Excellent: $270.00
                                   Very good: $200.00

Winchester Model 1300XTR Winchoke

Gauge: 12, 20 magnum
Action: Slide action, hammerless; repeating
Magazine: 4-shot tubular
Barrel: 28″; ventilated rib; Winchoke system (changeable choke tubes)
Finish: Blued; checkered walnut pistol grip stock and slide handle; recoil pad on 12 gauge
Approximate wt.: 7¼ lbs.
Comments: Made from early 1980's to present.
Estimated Value: New (retail): $360.95
                                   Excellent: $275.00
                                   Very good: $210.00

Winchester Model 1300 Featherweight

Similar to the Model 1300XTR Winchoke with a 22″ barrel; weighs 6½ lbs.
Estimated Value: New (retail): $342.95
                                   Excellent: $260.00
                                   Very good: $195.00

Winchester Model 1300 Waterfowl, Turkey

Similar to the Model 1300 Featherweight with sling swivels, 30″ barrel; 12 gauge only; weighs 7 lbs.
Estimated Value: New (retail): $360.95
                                   Excellent: $275.00
                                   Very good: $210.00

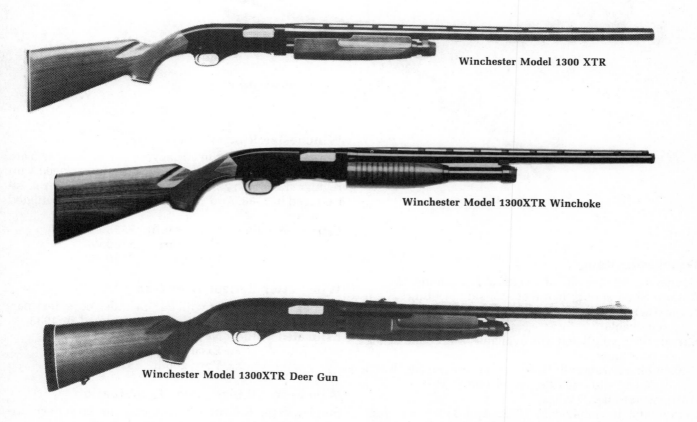

Winchester Model 1300 XTR

Winchester Model 1300XTR Winchoke

Winchester Model 1300XTR Deer Gun

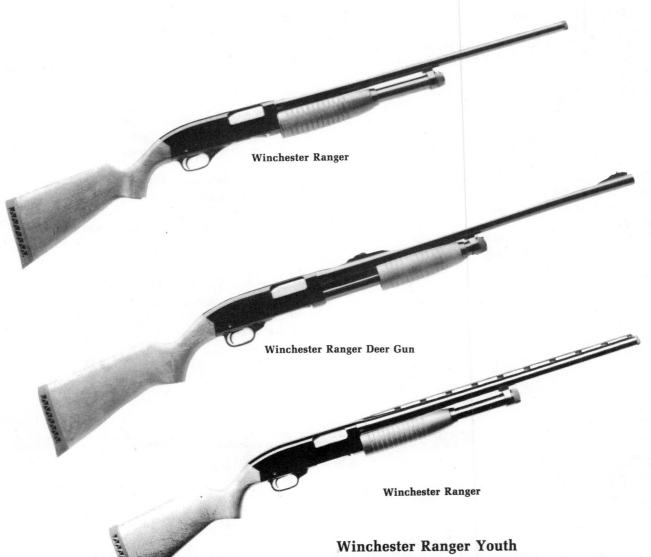

Winchester Ranger

Winchester Ranger Deer Gun

Winchester Ranger

Winchester Ranger

Gauge: 12, 20, regular or magnum interchangeably
Action: Slide action; hammerless; side ejecting
Magazine: 4-shot tubular; factory installed plug is removable
Barrel: 28″; ventilated rib available; interchangeable choke tubes
Finish: Blued; walnut-finished, semi-pistol grip stock and grooved slide handle; recoil pad
Approximate wt.: 7¼ lbs.
Comments: Introduced in 1982. Add $15.00 for ventilated rib; $30.00 for Winchoke and ventilated ribs.
Estimated Value: New (retail): $228.95
Excellent: $175.00
Very good: $130.00

Winchester Ranger Youth

Similar to the Ranger in 20 gauge; stock and forearm are modified for young shooters. Stock can be replaced with regular size stock; 22″ modified or Winchoke barrel. Introduced in 1983. Add 15% for Winchoke and ventilated rib barrel.
Estimated Value: New (retail): $235.95
Excellent: $180.00
Very good: $135.00

Winchester Ranger Deer Gun

Similar to the Ranger with 24″ cylinder bore deer barrel, rifle sights and recoil pad. Introduced in 1983.
Estimated Value: New (retail): $252.95
Excellent: $190.00
Very good: $140.00

Winchester Ranger Deer Combination

Similar to the Ranger with 24″ cylinder bore deer barrel and interchangeable 28″ Winchoke barrel.
Estimated Value: New (retail): $308.95
Excellent: $235.00
Very good: $175.00

Winchester Model 1911

Winchester Model 40 Skeet

Winchester Model 40

Gauge: 12
Action: Semi-automatic; hammerless
Magazine: 4-shot tubular
Barrel: 28″, 30″; modified or full choke
Finish: Blued; plain walnut pistol grip stock and forearm
Approximate wt.: 8 lbs.
Comments: Made in the early 1940's.
Estimated Value: **Excellent:** **$350.00**
                          Very good: **$265.00**

Winchester Model 40 Skeet

Similar to the Model 40 with a 24″ skeet barrel; checkering; "Cutts Compensator".
Estimated Value: **Excellent:** **$370.00**
                          Very good: **$285.00**

Winchester Model 1911

Gauge: 12
Action: Semi-automatic; hammerless
Magazine: 4-shot tubular
Barrel: 26″-32″; various chokes
Finish: Blued; plain or checkered semi-pistol grip stock and forearm
Approximate wt.: 8 lbs.
Comments: Made from 1911 to the mid 1920's.
Estimated Value: **Excellent:** **$450.00**
                          Very good: **$340.00**

Winchester Model 50

Winchester Model 50 Skeet

Winchester Model 59

Winchester Model 50

Gauge: 12, 20
Action: Semi-automatic; non-recoiling barrel; hammerless
Magazine: 2-shot tubular
Barrel: 26″-30″; variety of chokes
Finish: Blued; checkered walnut pistol grip stock and forearm
Approximate wt.: 7¾ lbs.
Comments: Made from the mid 1950's to early 1960's. Add $25.00 for ventilated rib.
Estimated Value: **Excellent:** **$300.00**
                          Very good: **$240.00**

Winchester Model 50 Skeet

Similar to the Model 50 with a skeet stock; 26″ skeet choke barrel; ventilated rib.
Estimated Value: **Excellent:** **$325.00**
                          Very good: **$250.00**

Winchester Model 50 Trap

Similar to the Model 50 except 12 gauge only; Monte Carlo stock; 30″ full choke; ventilated rib.
Estimated Value: **Excellent:** **$375.00**
                          Very good: **$280.00**

Winchester Model 59

Gauge: 12
Action: Semi-automatic; hammerless; non-recoiling barrel
Magazine: 2-shot tubular
Barrel: 26″-30″; variety of chokes; steel and glass fiber composition; interchangeable choke tubes available
Finish: Blued; checkered walnut pistol grip stock and forearm; alloy receiver
Approximate wt.: 6½ lbs.
Comments: Made from the late 1950's to mid 1960's.
Estimated Value: **Excellent:** **$300.00**
                          Very good: **$225.00**

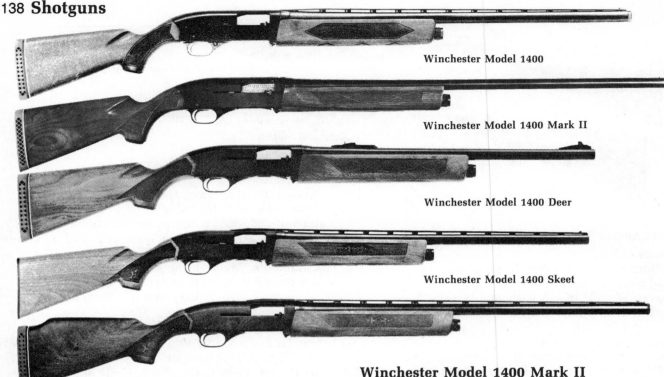

Winchester Model 1400

Winchester Model 1400 Mark II

Winchester Model 1400 Deer

Winchester Model 1400 Skeet

Winchester Model 1400 Trap

Winchester Model 1400, 1400 Winchoke

Gauge: 12, 16, 20
Action: Semi-automatic, gas operated
Magazine: 2-shot tubular
Barrel: 26″, 28″, 30″; variety of chokes or adjustable choke; all 1979 models have adjustable choke
Finish: Blued; checkered walnut pistol grip stock and forearm; recoil pad available; Cycolak stock available with recoil reduction system until late 1970's
Approximate wt.: 7½ lbs.
Comments: Made from the mid 1960's to late 1970's. Add $25.00 for ventilated rib or Cycolak stock and recoil reduction system.
Estimated Value: **Excellent:** $250.00
  Very good: $190.00

Winchester Model 1400 Mark II

Similar to the 1400 except lighter weight and with minor improvements. Introduced in the late 1960's.
Estimated Value: **Excellent:** $240.00
  Very good: $180.00

Winchester Model 1400 Deer Gun

Similar to the 1400 with a 22″ barrel for slugs and sights.
Estimated Value: **Excellent:** $260.00
  Very good: $200.00

Winchester Model 1400 Skeet

Similar to the 1400 in 12 or 20 gauge; 26″ barrel with ventilated rib. Add $25.00 for recoil reduction system.
Estimated Value: **Excellent:** $280.00
  Very good: $210.00

Winchester Model 1400 Trap

Similar to the 1400 in 12 gauge with a 30″ full choke, ventilated rib barrel. Available with Monte Carlo stock. Add $25.00 for recoil reduction system.
Estimated Value: **Excellent:** $290.00
  Very good: $215.00

Winchester Model 1500 XTR

Winchester Model 1500 XTR

Gauge: 12, 20, regular or magnum
Action: Semi-automatic, gas operated
Magazine: 3-shot tubular
Barrel: 26″, 28″, 30″; improved cylinder, modified or full choke; ventilated rib available
Finish: Blued; checkered walnut pistol grip stock and forearm; alloy receiver
Approximate wt.: 6½ to 7 lbs.
Comments: Made from late 1970's to early 1980's. Add $25.00 for ventilated rib.
Estimated Value: **Excellent:** $300.00
  Very good: $225.00

Winchester Model 1500 XTR Winchoke

Similar to the Model 1500XTR with removable choke tube system; 28″ barrel only; add $35.00 for ventilated rib. Made in early 1980's.
Estimated Value: **Excellent:** $320.00
  Very good: $240.00

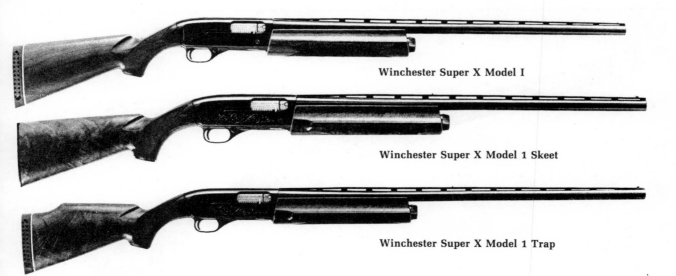

Winchester Super X Model I

Winchester Super X Model 1 Skeet

Winchester Super X Model 1 Trap

Winchester Super X Model 1, Super X Model 1 XTR
Gauge: 12
Action: Semi-automatic, gas operated
Magazine: 4-shot tubular
Barrel: 26″-30″; various chokes; ventilated rib
Finish: Blued; scroll engroved alloy receiver; checkered walnut pistol grip stock and forearm
Approximate wt.: 8¼ lbs.
Comments: Made from the mid 1970's to early 1980's.
Estimated Value: Excellent: $375.00
Very good: $285.00

Winchester Super X Model 1 Skeet
Similar to the Super X Model 1 with skeet stock; 26″ skeet choke; ventilated rib barrel.
Estimated Value: Excellent: $400.00
Very good: $300.00

Winchester Super X Model 1 Trap
Similar to the Super X Moidel 1 with regular or Monte Carlo stock; 30″ full choke barrel; recoil pad.
Estimated Value: Excellent: $425.00
Very good: $320.00

Winchester Ranger Semi-Automatic

Winchester Ranger Semi-Auto Deer
Similar to the Ranger Semi-Automatic with 24″ cylinder bore deer barrel, rifle sights. Introduced in 1984.
Estimated Value: New (retail): $308.95
Excellent: $235.00
Very good: $175.00

Winchester Ranger Semi-Auto Deer Combo
Similar to the Ranger Semi-Auto Deer with extra 28″ ventilated rib Winchoke barrel.
Estimated Value: New (retail): $342.95
Excellent: $260.00
Very good: $195.00

Winchester Ranger Semi-Automatic
Gauge: 12, 20 regular or magnum
Action: Gas operated semi-automatic
Magazine: 2-shot
Barrel: 28″ modified; Winchoke interchangeable tubes and ventilated rib
Finish: Blued; checkered hardwood semi-pistol grip stock and forearm
Approximate wt.: 7 lbs.
Comments: Introduced in 1983. Add $25.00 for ventilated rib and Winchoke.
Estimated Value: New (retail): $308.95
Excellent: $235.00
Very good: $175.00

Zoli

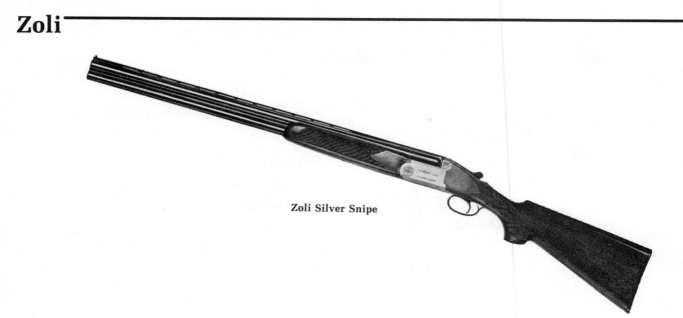

Zoli Silver Snipe

Zoli 300 Gray Eagle
Gauge: 12
Action: Box lock; top lever, break-open; hammerless
Magazine: None
Barrel: Over and under double barrel; 26″, 28″; ventilated rib; chrome lined; 3″ chambers
Finish: Blued; checkered walnut pistol grip stock and forearm
Approximate wt.: 7 lbs.
Comments: Manufactured in Italy
Estimated Value: **Excellent:** $440.00
                  Very good: $325.00

Zoli 302 Gray Eagle
Similar to the 300 in 20 gauge. Weight about 6¼ lbs.
Estimated Value: **Excellent:** $425.00
                  Very good: $320.00

Zoli Silver Snipe
Gauge: 12, 20
Action: Box lock; top lever, break-open; hammerless; single trigger
Magazine: None
Barrel: Over and under double barrel; 26″, 28″, 30″; ventilated rib; chrome lined
Finish: Blued; checkered walnut pistol grip stock and forearm; engraved.
Approximate wt.: 7 lbs.
Comments: Manufactured in Italy.
Estimated Value: **Excellent:** $400.00
                  Very good: $300.00

Zoli Golden Snipe
Similar to the Silver Snipe with automatic ejectors.
Estimated Value: **Excellent:** $450.00
                  Very good: $340.00

Rifles

Anschutz

Anschutz Model 64

Anschutz Model 64S

Anschutz Mark 12 Target

Anschutz Model 1407

Anschutz Model 64 & 64L Match

Caliber: 22 long rifle
Action: Bolt action; single shot
Magazine: None
Barrel: Blued 26″
Sights: None
Stock & Forearm: Match style; checkered walnut one-piece pistol grip stock and forearm; thumb rest; cheekpiece; adjustable butt plate; forward swivel
Approximate wt.: 7¾ lbs.
Comments: A match rifle made from about 1967 to the early 1980's. Add $10.00 for left hand action (64L).
Estimated Value: Excellent: $300.00
Very good: $225.00

Anschutz Model 64S & 64SL Match

Similar to Model 64 & 64L with special match sights. Add $20.00 for left hand version (64SL).
Estimated Value: Excellent: $325.00
Very good: $245.00

Anschutz Mark 12 Target

Similar to the Model 64 with a heavy barrel; non-adjustable butt plate; handstop; tapered stock and forearm. Introduced in the late 1970's.
Estimated Value: Excellent: $215.00
Very good: $160.00

Anschutz Model 1407, 1807, 1407L, 1807L

Caliber: 22 long rifle
Action: Bolt action; single shot
Magazine: None
Barrel: Blued; 26″
Sights: None
Stock & Forearm: Walnut one-piece pistol grip stock and wide forearm; thumb rest; cheekpiece; adjustable butt plate; forward swivel
Approximate wt.: 10 lbs.
Comments: A match rifle made from about 1967 to 1980's. Add $50.00 for left hand action (1407L), (1807L).
Estimated Value: Excellent: $530.00
Very good: $400.00

Anschutz Model 184

Caliber: 22 long rifle
Action: Bolt action; repeating
Magazine: 5-shot detachable clip
Barrel: Blued; 21½″
Sights: Folding leaf rear, hooded ramp front
Stock & Forearm: Checkered walnut Monte Carlo one-piece pistol grip stock and lipped forearm; swivels
Approximate wt.: 6 lbs.
Comments: Made from the mid 1960's to mid 1970's.
Estimated Value: Excellent: $200.00
Very good: $150.00

Anschutz Model 54

Anschutz Model 1432

Anschutz Model 153

Anschutz Model 1422D

Anschutz Model 54

Caliber: 22 long rifle
Action: Bolt action; repeating
Magazine: Detachable 5-shot clip or 10-shot clip
Barrel: Blued; 24″
Sights: Folding leaf rear, hooded ramp front
Stock & Forearm: Checkered walnut Monte Carlo one-piece pistol grip stock and lipped forearm
Approximate wt.: 6¾ lbs.
Comments: Made from the late 1960's to early 1980's.
Estimated Value: Excellent: $275.00
Very good: $210.00

Anschutz Model 54M

Similar to Model 54 in 22 Winchester magnum with a 4-shot clip.
Estimated Value: Excellent: $300.00
Very good: $275.00

Anschutz Model 1432, 1432D Custom

Caliber: 22 Hornet
Action: Bolt action; bottom load; repeating
Magazine: 5-shot clip
Barrel: Blued; 24″
Sights: Folding leaf rear, hooded ramp front
Stock & Forearm: Checkered walnut Monte Carlo one-piece pistol grip stock and lipped forearm; swivels
Approximate wt.: 6¾ lbs.
Comments: Currently manufactured as 1432D.
Estimated Value: New (retail): $764.00
Excellent: $570.00
Very good: $425.00

Anschutz Model 1422D, 1522D, 1532D, Custom

Similar to the Model 1432D Custom except in different calibers: 1422D is 22 long rifle; 1522D is 22 magnum; 1532D is 222 Remington; magazine will differ in some calibers.

Estimated Value:

	1422D	1522D	1532D
New (retail):	$693.00	$684.00	$764.00
Excellent:	$520.00	$510.00	$570.00
Very good:	$390.00	$385.00	$430.00

Anschutz Model 1422DCL, 1522DCL, 1432DCL, 1532DCL, Classic

Similar to the Custom models of this series except without deluxe features. Checkered walnut, one-piece pistol grip stock and tapered forearm.

Estimated Value:	1422DCL	1522DCL	1432DCL 1532DCL
New (retail):	$642.00	$646.00	$714.00
Excellent:	$480.00	$485.00	$535.00
Very good:	$360.00	$365.00	$400.00

Anschutz Model 141

Caliber: 22 long rifle, 22 magnum
Action: Bolt action; repeating
Magazine: Detachable 5-shot clip
Barrel: Blued; 24″
Sights: Folding leaf rear, hooded ramp front
Stock & Forearm: Checkered walnut Monte Carlo one-piece pistol grip stock and forearm
Approximate wt.: 6 lbs.
Comments: Made from the middle to late 1960's.
Estimated Value: Excellent: $240.00
Very good: $175.00

Anschutz Model 153

Similar to Model 141 with abruptly ended forearm trimmed in different wood. Made from the middle to late 1960's.
Estimated Value: Excellent: $230.00
Very good: $170.00

Anschutz Model 164

Anschutz Model 1418

Anschutz Model 64MS

Anschutz Model 164

Caliber: 22 long rifle
Action: Bolt action; repeating
Magazine: 5-shot clip or 10-shot clip
Barrel: Blued; 23″
Sights: Folding leaf rear, hooded ramp front
Stock & Forearm: Checkered walnut Monte Carlo one-piece pistol grip stock and lipped forearm
Approximate wt.: 6 lbs.
Comments: Made from the late 1960's to early 1980's.
Estimated Value: Excellent: $280.00
Very good: $210.00

Anschutz Model 164M

Similar to Model 164 in 22 Winchester magnum with a 4-shot clip.
Estimated Value: Excellent: $285.00
Very good: $215.00

Anschutz Model 1418, 1418D

Caliber: 22 long rifle
Action: Bolt action; repeating; double set or single set trigger
Magazine: 5-shot clip or 10-shot clip
Barrel: Blued; 19¾″
Sights: Folding leaf rear, hooded ramp front
Stock & Forearm: Checkered European Monte Carlo stock and full length forearm; cheekpiece; swivels
Approximate wt.: 5½ lbs.
Comments: Introduced in the late 1970's. Currently called 1418D.
Estimated Value: New (retail): $559.00
Excellent: $420.00
Very good: $315.00

Anschutz Model 1433D

Similar to the Model 1418D except in 22 Hornet caliber.
Estimated Value: New (retail): $875.00
Excellent: $660.00
Very good: $495.00

Anschutz Model 1518, 1518D

Similar to the Model 1418 except; in 22 WMR only; 4-shot clip magazine. Currently called 1518D.
Estimated Value: New (retail): $563.00
Excellent: $420.00
Very good: $315.00

Anschutz Model 1416D, 1516D

Similar to the Model 1418D, 1518D except regular length forearm, different stock with more defined pistol grip, 23″ barrel. Add 3% for magnum (1516D).
Estimated Value: New (retail): $393.00
Excellent: $295.00
Very good: $220.00

Anschutz Model 64MS

Caliber: 22 long rifle
Action: Bolt action; single shot; adjustable two-stage trigger
Magazine: None
Barrel: 21¾″ medium heavy
Sights: None; tapped for scope
Stock & Forearm: Silhouette-style one-piece stippled pistol grip stock and forearm
Approximate wt.: 8 lbs.
Comments: A silhouette-style rifle currently produced.
Estimated Value: New (retail): $477.50
Excellent: $350.00
Very good: $260.00

Anschutz Model 5148SMS

Similar to the Model 64MS with a 22″ barrel. Weighs 8½ lbs.
Estimated Value: New (retail): $804.00
Excellent: $600.00
Very good: $450.00

Anschutz Model 1411, 1811

Caliber: 22 long rifle
Action: Bolt action; single shot
Magazine: None
Barrel: 27½″ heavy
Sights: None; tapped for scope
Stock & Forearm: Select walnut one-piece Monte Carlo pistol grip stock and forearm; adjustable cheekpiece; hand rest swivel; adjustable butt plate
Approximate wt.: 12 lbs.
Comments: A match-style rifle.
Estimated Value: Excellent: $580.00
Very good: $435.00

Anschutz Model 520

Anschutz Mark 2000

Caliber: 22 long rifle
Action: Bolt action; hammerless; single shot
Magazine: None
Barrel: Blued; medium heavy 26"
Sights: None; sights can be purchased separately to fit
Stock & Forearm: Smooth hardwood one-piece semi-pistol grip stock and forearm
Approximate wt.: 8½ lbs.
Comments: A match rifle designed for young shooters. Made from the early 1980's to mid 1980's.
Estimated Value: Excellent: $160.00
Very good: $120.00

Anschutz Model 520 Sporter & Mark 525 Sporter

Caliber: 22 long rifle
Action: Semi-automatic
Magazine: 10-shot clip
Barrel: Blued 24"
Sights: Folding leaf rear, hooded ramp front
Stock & Forearm: Checkered walnut Monte Carlo semi-pistol grip stock and fluted forearm
Approximate wt.: 6½ lbs.
Comments: Introduced in the early 1980's; presently called Mark 525 Sporter.
Estimated Value: New (retail): $293.00
Excellent: $220.00
Very good: $165.00

Armalite

Armalite AR-7 Explorer

Armalite AR-7 Custom

Armalite AR-180 Sporter

Armalite AR-7 Explorer

Caliber: 22 long rifle
Action: Semi-automatic
Magazine: 8-shot clip
Barrel: 16" aluminum and steel lined
Sights: Peep rear, blade front
Stock & Forearm: Fiberglass pistol grip stock (no forearm); stock acts as case for gun when dismantled
Approximate wt.: 2¾ lbs.
Comments: A lightweight alloy rifle designed to float; breaks down to fit into stock. Made from the 1960's until the 1970's. After about 1973 marketed as Charter Arms AR-7.
Estimated Value: Excellent: $80.00
Very good: $60.00

Armalite AR-7 Custom

A sport version of the Explorer with a walnut Monte Carlo one-piece pistol grip stock and forearm. Slightly heavier.
Estimated Value: Excellent: $100.00
Very good: $ 75.00

Armalite AR-180 Sporter

Caliber: 223
Action: Semi-automatic gas opereated
Magazine: 5-shot detachable box
Barrel: Blued 18"
Sights: Adjustable rear and front; scope available
Stock & Forearm: Pistol grip; nylon folding stock; fiberglass forearm
Approximate wt.: 6½ lbs.
Comments: Made from the early 1970's to 1980's.
Estimated Value: Excellent: $520.00
Very good: $390.00

Browning

Browning B-78

Browning B-78 Round Barrel

Browning 78 Govt. 45-70

Browning 78

Caliber: 22-250, 6mm mag., 7mm mag., 25-06, 30-06
Action: Falling block, lever action; exposed hammer; single shot
Magazine: None
Barrel: Blued; 26″ round or octagon
Sights: None
Stock & Forearm: Checkered walnut Monte Carlo pistol grip stock and forearm
Approximate wt.: 7¾ to 8½ lbs.
Comments: A replica of John Browning's first patented rifle in 1878. Produced from the mid 1970's to early 1980's.
Estimated Value: Excellent: $355.00
                 Very good: $270.00

Browning 78 Govt. 45-70

Similar to 78 in Government 45-70 caliber with iron sights and straight grip stock, octagonal bull barrel. Discontinued in the early 1980's.
Estimated Value: Excellent: $375.00
                 Very good: $280.00

Browning T Bolt T-1

Browning T Bolt T-2

Browning T Bolt T-1

Caliber: 22 short, long, long rifle
Action: Bolt action; hammerless; side ejection; repeating; single shot conversion
Magazine: Removable 5-shot box
Barrel: Blued 22″
Sights: Peep rear, ramp front
Stock & Forearm: Walnut one-piece pistol grip stock and forearm
Approximate wt.: 6 lbs.
Comments: Made from the mid 1960's to the mid 1970's in Belgium.
Estimated Value: Excellent: $175.00
                 Very good: $130.00

Browning T Bolt T-2

A fancy version of the T Bolt T-1 with checkered stock and forearm.
Estimated Value: Excellent: $225.00
                 Very good: $170.00

Browning High Power Safari

Browning High Power Medallion

Browning High Power Medallion

A higher grade version of the Safari with more engraving and higher quality wood.

Estimated Value: Excellent: $975.00 - $1,200.00
Very good: $700.00 - $ 900.00

Browning High Power Olympian

Highest grade of High Power models with complete engraving and some gold inlay.

Estimated Value: Excellent: $1,500.00 - $2,500.00
Very good: $1,100.00 - $1,875.00

Browning High Power Safari

Caliber: 243, 270, 30-06, 308, 300 mag., 375 mag. in 1960; later in 264, 338, 222, 22-250, 243, 7mm mag.
Action: Mauser-type bolt action; repeating
Magazine: 3 or 5-shot, depending on caliber
Barrel: Blued 22″ or 24″
Sights: Adjustable sporting rear, hooded ramp front
Stock & Forearm: Checkered walnut Monte Carlo one-piece pistol grip stock and forearm; magnum calibers have recoil pad; swivels
Approximate wt.: 6 to 8 lbs.
Comments: Made from about 1960 through the mid 1970's. Short or medium action worth $25.00 less.
Estimated Value: Excellent: $775.00
Very good: $585.00

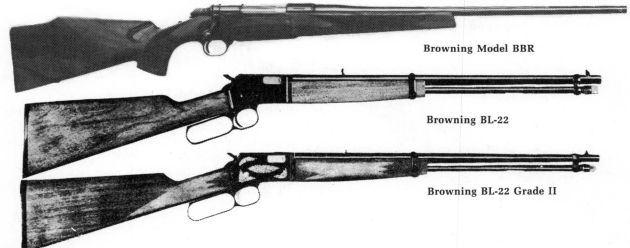

Browning Model BBR

Browning BL-22

Browning BL-22 Grade II

Browning BL-22

Caliber: 22 short, long, long rifle
Action: Lever action; short throw lever; exposed hammer
Magazine: Tubular; 15 long rifles; 17 longs; 22 shorts
Barrel: Blued 20″
Sights: Folding adjustable rear, bead front
Stock & Forearm: Plain walnut straight grip stock and forearm; barrel band
Approximate wt.: 5 lbs.
Comments: A small, lightweight 22 caliber rifle produced from 1970 to present.
Estimated Value: New (retail): $264.00
Excellent: $200.00
Very good: $150.00

Browning BL-22 Grade II

Similar to BL-22 with engraving; gold plated trigger; checkered stock and forearm.

Estimated Value: New (retail): $302.50
Excellent: $225.00
Very good: $170.00

Browning Model BBR, BBR Lightning Bolt

Caliber: 30-06 Sprg., 270 Win., 25-06 Rem., 7mm Rem. mag., 300 Win. mag.
Action: Bolt action; short throw; cocking indicator; repeating
Magazine: 4-shot; 3-shot in magnum; hinged floorplate, detachable box
Barrel: 24″ floating barrel, recessed muzzle
Sights: Nine; tapped for scope
Stock & Forearm: Checkered walnut Monte Carlo one-piece pistol grip stock and forearm; cheekpiece; low profile sling studs; recoil pad on magnum; stock and forearm changed slightly in 1982
Approximate wt.: 8 lbs.
Comments: A high powered hunting rifle introduced in the late 1970's. A limited edition (1,000) with engraved elk scenes was introduced in 1984.
Estimated Value: Excellent: $375.00
Very good: $280.00

Browning BLR

Browning Model 92

Browning BLR, '81 BLR

Caliber: 243, 308, 358; 22-250 Rem. (added in 1982); Added calibers 222, 223 Rem., 257 Roberts, 7mm-08 Rem. in mid 1980's
Action: Lever action; exposed hammer; repeating
Magazine: 4-shot removable box
Barrel: Blued 20″
Sights: Adjustable rear, hooded ramp front
Stock & Forearm: Checkered walnut straight grip stock and forearm; recoil pad; barrel band
Approximate wt.: 7 lbs.
Comments: A carbine produced from early 1970's to present.
Estimated Value: New (retail): $402.95
Excellent: $300.00
Very good: $225.00

Browning Model 92, B-92

Caliber: 44 magnum, 357 magnum (added 1982)
Action: Lever action; exposed three position hammer; repeating
Magazine: 11-shot tubular
Barrel: 20″ round
Sights: Adjustable cloverleaf rear, blade front
Stock & Forearm: Plain walnut, straight grip stock and forearm; barrel band
Approximate wt.: 5½ lbs.
Comments: An authentic remake of the 1892 Winchester designed by John Browning. Introduced in the late 1970's.
Estimated Value: New (retail): $341.50
Excellent: $255.00
Very good: $190.00

Browning Model 1895

Browning Model 1885

Caliber: 223 Rem., 22-250 Rem., 270 Win., 30-06 Springfield, 7mm Rem. magnum, 45-70 Gov't
Action: Falling block, lever action; single shot
Magazine: None, single shot
Barrel: 28″ octagon, blued
Sights: Drilled and tapped for scope; open sights on 45-70 model
Stock & Forearm: Checkered walnut, straight grip stock and lipped forearm; recoil pad
Approximate wt.: 8¾ lbs.
Comments: Introduced in 1985. Based on Browning's Winchester 1885.
Estimated Value: New (retail): $551.50
Excellent: $415.00
Very good: $310.00

Browning Model 1895

Caliber: 30-06 Springfield
Action: Lever action, exposed hammer, repeating
Magazine: 5 shot non-detachable box
Barrel: 24″
Sights: Buckhorn rear, beaded ramp front
Stock & Forearm: Walnut straight grip stock and lipped forearm; High Grade has checkered stock with engraved steel grey receiver
Approximate wt.: 8 lbs.
Comments: Introduced in 1984, this is a new version of John Browning's Model 1895 first produced by Winchester in 1896. Add 50% for High Grade.
Estimated Value: Excellent: $390.00
Very good: $290.00

Browning Model 1886

Caliber: 45-70 Gov't
Action: Lever action, repeating; exposed hammer
Magazine: 8-shot tubular, side-port load
Barrel: 26″ octagon
Sights: Open buckhorn
Stock & Forearm: Smooth walnut straight-grip stock and forearm; metal, crescent buttplate
Approximate wt.: 9¼ lbs.
Comments: Based on the Winchester Model 1886 designed by Browning. Introduced in 1986. Add 80% for High Grade.
Estimated Value: New (retail): $577.95
Excellent: $435.00
Very good: $325.00

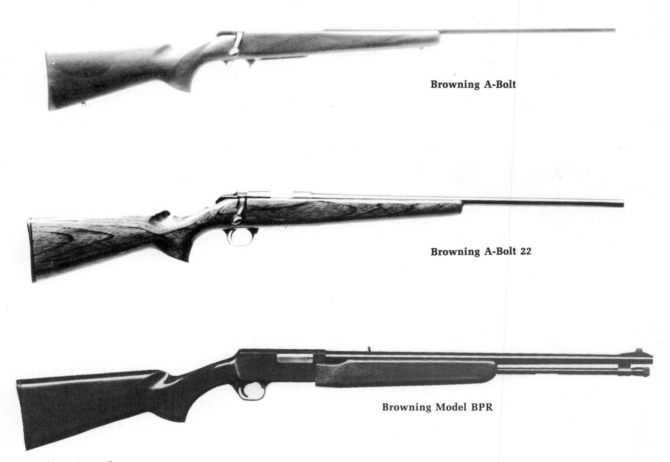

Browning A-Bolt

Browning A-Bolt 22

Browning Model BPR

Browning A-Bolt

Caliber: 22-250 Rem., 257 Roberts, 7mm-08 Rem., 25-06
Rem., 243 Win., 270 Win., 7mm Rem. magnum, 300
Win. magnum, 30-06 Springfield, 308 Win., 338
Win. magnum

Action: Bolt action, hammerless, repeating, short or long
action

Magazine: Hinged floorplate with detachable box 4-shot;
3-shot magnum

Barrel: 22″ or 24″ blued

Sights: None, drilled and tapped for scope mounts.
Hunter model available with iron sights

Stock & Forearm: Checkered walnut, one-piece pistol
grip stock and forearm; swivels; recoil pad on
magnum

Approximate wt.: 6½ to 7¼ lbs.

Comments: Introduced in 1985. Add 5% for sights.
Medallion has higher quality finish (add 20%).

Estimated Value: New (retail): $379.95
Excellent: $285.00
Very good: $215.00

Browning A-Bolt 22

Similar to the A-Bolt in 22 long rifle caliber; 5 or 15 shot
clip.

Estimated Value: New (retail): $299.95
Excellent: $225.00
Very good: $170.00

Browning Model BPR

Caliber: 22 long rifle; 22 Win. mag.

Action: Slide action; hammerless; repeating; slide release
on trigger guard

Magazine: 15-shot tubular; 11-shot on magnum

Barrel: 20¼″

Sights: Adjustable folding leaf rear, gold bead front

Stock & Forearm: Checkered walnut pistol grip stock
and slide handle

Approximate wt.: 6¼ lbs.

Comments: Made from the late 1970's to early 1980's.

Estimated Value: Excellent: $250.00
Very good: $960.00

Browning Model BPR Grade II

Similar to the BPR in magnum only; engraved squirrels
and rabbits on receiver.

Estimated Value: Excellent: $300.00
Very good: $230.00

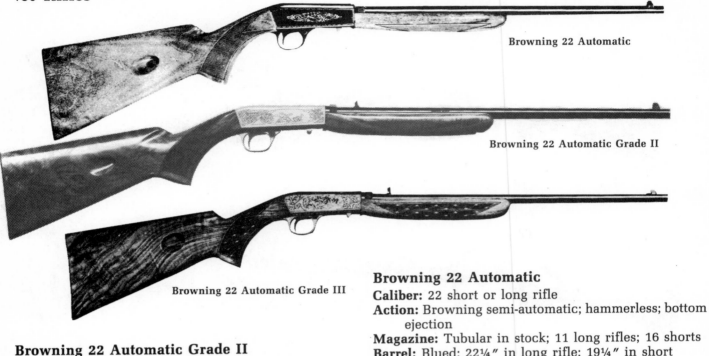

Browning 22 Automatic

Browning 22 Automatic Grade II

Browning 22 Automatic Grade III

Browning 22 Automatic Grade II

Similar to the 22 Automatic with chrome plated receiver and gold plated trigger. Receiver is engraved with squirrel scene. Discontinnued in mid 1980's.

Estimated Value: Excellent: $285.00
                      Very good: $215.00

Browning 22 Automatic Grade III

This is the same rifle as the Grade II except engraving is of bird dog and birds, high quality finish.

Estimated Value: Excellent: $610.00
                      Very good: $460.00

Browning 22 Automatic

Caliber: 22 short or long rifle
Action: Browning semi-automatic; hammerless; bottom ejection
Magazine: Tubular in stock; 11 long rifles; 16 shorts
Barrel: Blued; 22¼″ in long rifle; 19¼″ in short
Sights: Adjustable rear, dovetail bead front
Stock & Forearm: Hand checkered walnut pistol grip stock and forearm
Approximate wt.: 4¾ lbs.
Comments: This takedown model has been in production since the mid 1950's.
Estimated Value: New (retail): $295.50
                     Excellent: $220.00
                     Very good: $165.00

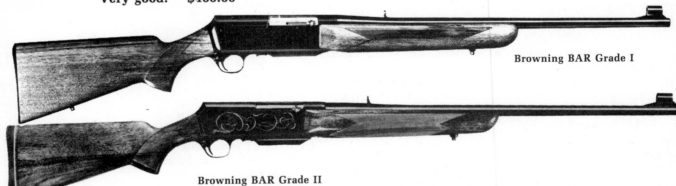

Browning BAR Grade I

Browning BAR Grade II

Browning BAR Grade II

Engraved version of BAR. Discontinued in the early 1970's.

Estimated Value: Excellent: $475.00
                      Very good: $375.00

Browning BAR Grade III

Similar to Grade I with elaborate engraving featuring antelope head. Discontinued early 1970's. Reintroduced in 1979 with rams and elk engravings. Add $60.00 for magnum. Discontinued in mid 1980's.

Estimated Value: Excellent: $ 825.00
                      Very good: $ 620.00

Browning BAR Grade I

Caliber: 243, 270, 308, 30-06, 7mm mag., 300 mag.
Action: Semi-automatic gas operated; side ejection; hammerless
Magazine: 4-shot removable box; 3-shot in magnum
Barrel: Blued 22″ or 24″
Sights: Folding rear, hooded ramp front
Stock & Forearm: Checkered walnut pistol grip stock and forearm
Approximate wt.: 7 to 8¼ lbs.
Comments: Made from the late 1960's to present. Add 10% for magnum calibers.
Estimated Value: New (retail): $552.00
                     Excellent: $415.00
                     Very good: $310.00

Browning BAR Grade IV

Browning Model BAR-22 Grade II

Browning BAR Grade IV

Similar to Grade I with elaborate engraving featuring two running antelope and running deer. Magnum has moose and elk engravings. Add 5% for magnum caliber. Still manufactured.

Estimated Value: New (retail): $1,670.00
Excellent: $1,250.00
Very good: $ 940.00

Browning BAR Grade V

Similar to other grades of BAR. This is the fanciest model. Discontinued in the early 1970's.

Estimated Value: Excellent: $2,500.00
Very good: $1,875.00

Browning Model BAR-22

Caliber: 22 long rifle
Action: Semi-automatic; blow back; hammerless; repeating
Magazine: 15-shot tubular
Barrel: 20″ reversed muzzle
Sights: Adjustable folding leaf rear, gold bead front
Stock & Forearm: Checkered walnut pistol grip stock and forearm; fluted comb
Approximate wt.: 5¾ lbs.
Comments: Produced in the late 1970's to mid 1980's.
Estimated Value: Excellent: $180.00
Very good: $140.00

Browning Model BAR-22 Grade II

Similar to the BAR-22 with engraved receiver, squirrels and rabbits.

Estimated Value: Excellent: $260.00
Very good: $195.00

BSA

BSA Model 12

Caliber: 22 long rifle
Action: Martini-type; single shot
Magazine: None
Barrel: 29″ blued
Sights: Match sights; some with open sights
Stock & Forearm: Checkered walnut straight grip stock and forearm; swivels
Approximate wt.: 9 lbs.
Comments: Made in England from about 1910 to 1930
Estimated Value: Excellent: $275.00
Very good: $200.00

BSA Model 12

BSA Model 13

Similar to Model 12 with a 25″ barrel. Weighs about 6 lbs.
Estimated Value: Excellent: $240.00
Very good: $185.00

BSA Model 13 Sporting

Similar to Model 13 in 22 Hornet caliber.
Estimated Value: Excellent: $300.00
Very good: $225.00

BSA Centurion

Similar to Model 15 with a special barrel guaranteed to produce accurate groups.
Estimated Value: Excellent: $360.00
Very good: $280.00

BSA Model 12/15

Similar to Model 12 and 15 in pre-war and post-war models. Made to about 1950.
Estimated Value: Excellent: $250.00
Very good: $190.00

BSA Model 15

Caliber: 22 long rifle
Action: Martini-type; single shot
Magazine: None
Barrel: Blued 29″
Sights: Special BSA match sights
Stock & Forearm: Walnut stock and forearm; cheekpiece; swivels
Approximate wt.: 9½ lbs.
Comments: A match rifle made in England from about 1915 to the early 1930's.
Estimated Value: Excellent: $325.00
Very good: $240.00

BSA Model 12/15

BSA Model 12/15 Heavy Barrel

Similar to Model 12/15 with heavy barrel. Weighs about 11 lbs.
Estimated Value: Excellent: $280.00
Very good: $210.00

BSA International - Light Pattern

BSA International Mark III

BSA International - Heavy Pattern

Caliber: 22 long rifle
Action: Martini-type; single shot
Magazine: None
Barrel: Blued 29″ heavy
Sights: Special Parker-Hale match sights
Stock & Forearm: Match style pistol grip stock with cheekpiece, wide forearm; hand stop; swivels
Approximate wt.: 13¾ lbs.
Comments: A target rifle made in England in the early 1950's.
Estimated Value: Excellent: $350.00
Very good: $260.00

BSA International - Light Pattern

Similar to Heavy Pattern but lighter weight with a 26″ barrel.
Estimated Value: Excellent: $325.00
Very good: $245.00

BSA International Mark II

Similar to Heavy and Light Patterns (choice of barrel). Stock and forearm changed slightly. Made from early to late 1950's.
Estimated Value: Excellent: $360.00
Very good: $270.00

BSA International Mark III

Similar to Heavy Pattern with: different stock and forearm; alloy frame; floating barrel. Made from the late 1950's to late 1960's.
Estimated Value: Excellent: $325.00
Very good: $250.00

BSA ISU

BSA Majestic Deluxe

BSA Majestic Deluxe

Caliber: 22 Hornet, 222, 243, 30-06, 308 Win., 7x57 mm
Action: Mauser-type bolt action; repeating
Magazine: 4-shot box
Barrel: Blued 22″
Sights: Folding leaf rear, hooded ramp front
Stock & Forearm: Checkered walnut Monte Carlo one-piece pistol grip stock and lipped forearm; swivels; cheekpiece; recoil pad
Approximate wt.: 7½ lbs.
Comments: Made in England from the early to mid 1960's
Estimated Value: Excellent: $275.00
Very good: $210.00

BSA Martini ISU

Caliber: 22 long rifle
Action: Martini-type; single shot
Magazine: None
Barrel: Blued 28″
Sights: Special Parker-Hale match sights
Stock & Forearm: Match style walnut pistol grip; adjustable butt plate
Approximate wt.: 10½ lbs.
Comments: A match rifle, made in England.
Estimated Value: Excellent: $500.00
Very good: $375.00

BSA Mark V

Similar to ISU with a heavy barrel. Weighs about 12½ lbs.
Estimated Value: Excellent: $525.00
Very good: $395.00

BSA Majestic Deluxe Featherweight

BSA Monarch Deluxe

BSA Deluxe Varmint

BSA Imperial

BSA CF-2

BSA Majestic Deluxe Featherweight

Similar to Deluxe with recoil reducer in barrel. Available in some magnum calibers.

Estimated Value: **Excellent:**   **$275.00**
            Very good: **$200.00**

BSA Monarch Deluxe

Similar to Majestic Deluxe with slight changes in stock and forearm and with a recoil pad. Made from mid 1960's to late 1970's.

Estimated Value: **Excellent:**   **$250.00**
            Very good: **$185.00**

BSA Deluxe Varmint

Similar to Monarch Deluxe with a heavier 24″ barrel.

Estimated Value: **Excellent:**   **$275.00**
            Very good: **$200.00**

BSA Imperial

Caliber: 22 Hornet, 222, 243, 257 Roberts, 270 Win., 7x57mm, 300 Savage, 30-06, 308 Win.

Action: Bolt action; repeating

Magazine: 4-shot box

Barrel: Blued 22″; recoil reducer

Sights: Open rear, ramp front

Stock & Forearm: Checkered walnut Monte Carlo one-piece pistol grip stock and lipped forearm; cheekpiece

Approximate wt.: 7 lbs.

Comments: Made in the early 1960's.

Estimated Value: **Excellent:**   **$280.00**
            Very good: **$210.00**

BSA CF-2

Caliber: 222 Rem., 22-250, 243 Win., 6.5x55, 7mm Mauser, 7x64, 270 Win., 308 Win., 30-06, 7mm Rem. mag., 300 Win. mag.

Action: Bolt action; repeating

Magazine: 4- or 5-shot box, 3-shot in magnum

Barrel: Blued 23½″; 24″ heavy barrel available in some calibers

Sights: Hooded ramp front, adjustable rear

Stock & Forearm: Checkered walnut Monte Carlo one-piece pistol grip stock and forearm; cheekpiece; contrasting fore-end tip and grip cap; swivels; recoil pad; European style has oil finish, American style has polyeurethane finish with white spacers.

Approximate wt.: 7½ to 8½ lbs.

Comments: Add 14% for European style; 8% for magnum calibers with heavy barrel.

Estimated Value: **New (retail):**   **$479.95**
                Excellent: **$360.00**
                Very good: **$270.00**

Carl Gustaf

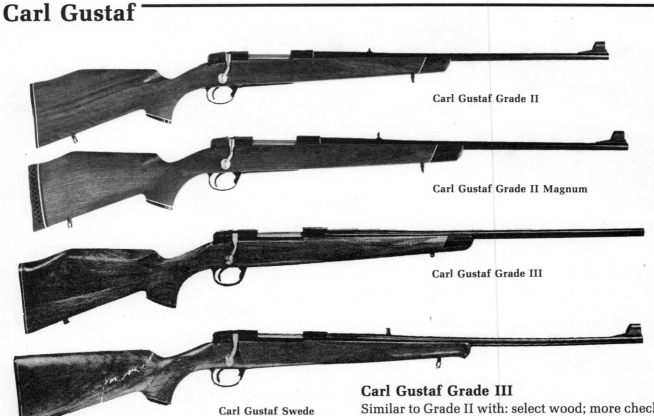

Carl Gustaf Grade II

Carl Gustaf Grade II Magnum

Carl Gustaf Grade III

Carl Gustaf Swede

Carl Gustaf Grade II

Caliber: 22-250, 243, 25-06, 270, 6.5x55, 30-06, 308
Action: Bolt action; repeating
Magazine: 5-shot staggered column
Barrel: Blued 23½"
Sights: Leaf rear, hooded ramp front
Stock & Forearm: Checkered walnut Monte Carlo one-piece pistol grip stock and forearm; swivels
Approximate wt.: 7 lbs.
Comments: Manufactured in Sweden.
Estimated Value: **Excellent:** $425.00
                Very good: $320.00

Carl Gustaf Grade II Magnum

Similar to Grade II except magnum calibers; recoil pad; 3-shot magazine.
Estimated Value: **Excellent:** $450.00
                Very good: $340.00

Carl Gustaf Grade III

Similar to Grade II with: select wood; more checkering; high quality finish; no sights.
Estimated Value: **Excellent:** $525.00
                Very good: $395.00

Carl Gustaf Grade III Magnum

Similar to Grade II Magnum with: select wood; more checkering; high quality finish; no sights.
Estimated Value: **Excellent:** $500.00
                Very good: $375.00

Carl Gustaf Swede

Similar to Grade II with lipped forearm but lacking the Monte Carlo comb.
Estimated Value: **Excellent:** $450.00
                Very good: $340.00

Carl Gustaf Swede Deluxe

Similar to Grade III with lipped forearm.
Estimated Value: **Excellent:** $450.00
                Very good: $340.00

Carl Gustaf Varmint-Target

Carl Gustaf Varmint-Target

Caliber: 22-250, 222, 243, 6.5x55
Action: Bolt action; repeating; large bolt knob
Magazine: 5-shot staggered column
Barrel: Blued 27"
Sights: None
Stock & Forearm: Plain walnut Monte Carlo one-piece pistol grip stock and forearm
Approximate wt.: 9½ lbs.
Comments: Manufactured in Sweden.
Estimated Value: **Excellent:** $500.00
                Very good: $375.00

Charles Daly

Charles Daly Hornet

Caliber: 22 Hornet
Action: Bolt action; double triggers
Magazine: 5-shot box
Barrel: 24″
Sights: Leaf rear, hooded ramp front
Stock & Forearm: Checkered walnut one-piece stock and forearm
Approximate wt.: 7¾ lbs.
Comments: Made during the 1930's. Also marked under the name Herold Rifle.
Estimated Value: Excellent: $900.00
                     Very good: $675.00

Charles Daly Hornet

Charter Arms

Charter Arms AR-7 Explorer

Caliber: 22 long rifle
Action: Semi-automatic
Magazine: 8-shot clip
Barrel: 16″ aluminum & steel lined, black or silvertone
Sights: Peep rear, blade front
Stock & Forearm: Fiberglass, pistol grip stock (no forearm); stock acts as case for gun when dismantled. Also available in silvertone or camouflage.
Approximate wt.: 2¾ lbs.
Comments: A lightweight alloy rifle designed to float and dismantle to fit into stock.

Charter Arms AR-7

Estimated Value: New (retail): $115.00
                     Excellent: $ 85.00
                     Very good: $ 65.00

Colt

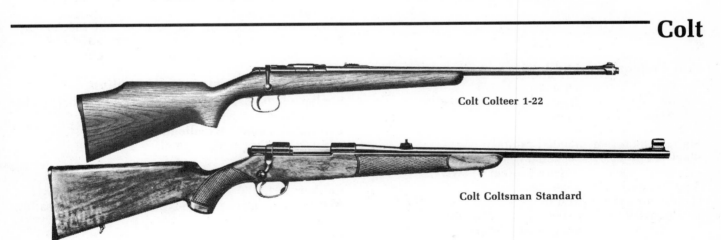

Colt Colteer 1-22

Colt Coltsman Standard

Colt Colteer 1-22

Caliber: 22 short, long, long rifle
Action: Bolt action; hammerless; single shot
Magazine: None
Barrel: Blued; 20″, 22″
Sights: Open rear, ramp front
Stock & Forearm: Plain walnut Monte Carlo pistol grip stock and forearm
Approximate wt.: 5 lbs.
Comments: Made for 10 years from about 1957.
Estimated Value: Excellent: $65.00
                     Very good: $50.00

Colt Coltsman Standard

Caliber: 300 H & H magnum, 30-06
Action: Mauser-type, bolt action; repeating
Magazine: 5-shot box
Barrel: Blued 22″
Sights: No rear, ramp front
Stock & Forearm: Checkered walnut one-piece pistol grip stock and tapered forearm; swivels
Approximate wt.: 7 lbs.
Comments: Made from about 1957 to the early 1960's.
Estimated Value: Excellent: $360.00
                     Very good: $270.00

Colt Coltsman Deluxe

Colt Coltsman Custom

Colt Coltsman Custom

Similar to the deluxe with: select wood; cheekpiece; engraving.

Estimated Value: Excellent: $470.00
Very good: $355.00

Colt Coltsman Deluxe

Similar to standard with: higher quality wood and finish; adjustable rear sight; Monte Carlo stock.

Estimated Value: Excellent: $400.00
Very good: $300.00

Colt Coltsman Sako Custom

Colt Coltsman Sako-Medium

Caliber: 243, 308 Win.
Action: Medium stroke, Sako-type bolt action; repeating
Magazine: 5-shot box
Barrel: Blued 24″
Sights: Folding leaf rear, hooded ramp front
Stock & Forearm: Checkered walnut Monte Carlo one-piece pistol grip stock and tapered forearm
Approximate wt.: 7 lbs.
Comments: Made from the early to mid 1960's.
Estimated Value: Excellent: $325.00
Very good: $245.00

Colt Coltsman Sako-Short

Caliber: 222, 222 magnum, 243, 308
Action: Short Sako-type bolt action; repeating
Magazine: 5-shot box
Barrel: Blued 22″
Sights: Open rear, hooded ramp front
Stock & Forearm: Checkered walnut Monte Carlo pistol grip stock and tapered forearm; swivels
Approximate wt.: 7 lbs.
Comments: Made from the late 1950's to mid 1960's.
Estimated Value: Excellent: $350.00
Very good: $260.00

Colt Coltsman Custom Sako-Medium

Similar to standard Sako-Medium with higher quality finish and recoil pad.

Estimated Value: Excellent: $390.00
Very good: $290.00

Colt Coltsman Sako-Long

Caliber: 264, 270 Win., 300 H&H, 30-06, 375 H&H
Action: Long stroke, Sako-type bolt action; repeating
Magazine: 5-shot box
Barrel: Blued 24″
Sights: Folding leaf rear, hooded ramp front
Stock & Forearm: Checkered walnut one-piece pistol grip stock and tapered forearm; swivels
Approximate wt.: 7 lbs.
Comments: Made from the early to mid 1960's.
Estimated Value: Excellent: $330.00
Very good: $250.00

Colt Coltsman Deluxe Sako-Short

Similar to Sako-Short with: adjustable rear sight; higher quality finish; in calibers 243, 308. Discontinued in the early 1960's.

Estimated Value: Excellent: $375.00
Very good: $285.00

Colt Coltsman Custom Sako-Short

Similar to Deluxe Sako-Short with: select wood; cheekpiece; engraving. Made until mid 1960's.

Estimated Value: Excellent: $450.00
Very good: $345.00

Colt Coltsman Custom Sako-Long

Similar to Sako-Long with: higher quality finish; recoil pad; Monte Carlo stock.

Estimated Value: Excellent: $400.00
Very good: $300.00

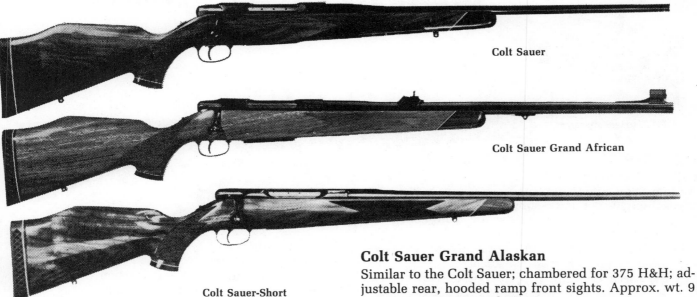

Colt Sauer

Colt Sauer Grand African

Colt Sauer-Short

Colt Sauer

Caliber: 25-06, 270, 30-06, 300 Win. mag., 7mm Rem. mag., 300 Weath. mag., 375 H&H mag., 458 Win. mag.
Action: Long stroke, Sauer-type bolt action; repeating
Magazine: 3-shot detachable box
Barrel: Blued 24″
Sights: None; tapped for scope
Stock & Forearm: Checkered walnut Monte Carlo one-piece pistol grip stock and tapered forearm; swivels; recoil pad
Approximate wt.: 7½ to 8 lbs.
Comments: Made from early 1970's to mid 1980's. Add $50.00 for magnum.
Estimated Value: Excellent: $ 945.00
Very good: $ 710.00

Colt Sauer Grand Alaskan

Similar to the Colt Sauer; chambered for 375 H&H; adjustable rear, hooded ramp front sights. Approx. wt. 9 lbs. Mid 1970's to mid 1980's.
Estimated Value: Excellent: $1,000.00
Very good: $ 750.00

Colt Sauer Grand African

Similar to Sauer with: higher quality finish; adjustable sights; 458 Win. calber only; 10 lbs. Mid 1970's to mid 1980's.
Estimated Value: Excellent: $1,050.00
Very good: $ 790.00

Colt Sauer-Sporting

Simiilar to Sauer with: short stroke action; chambered for 22-250, 243, 308 calibers. Made from mid 1970's to mid 1980's. Approx. wt. 7½ to 8½ lbs.
Estimated Value: Excellent: $ 945.00
Very good: $ 710.00

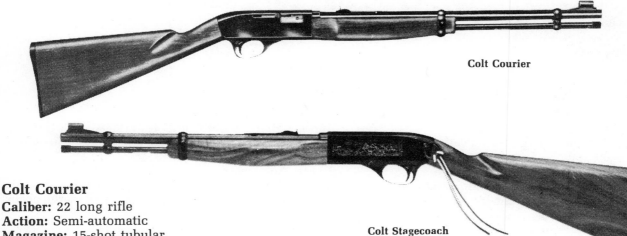

Colt Courier

Colt Stagecoach

Colt Courier

Caliber: 22 long rifle
Action: Semi-automatic
Magazine: 15-shot tubular
Barrel: Blued 19½″
Sights: Open rear, hooded ramp front
Stock & Forearm: Plain walnut straight grip stock and forearm; barrel band
Approximate wt.: 5 lbs.
Comments: Made from the mid 1960's to late 1970's.
Estimated Value: Excellent: $95.00
Very good: $70.00

Colt Stagecoach

Similar to the Courier with: engraving, 16½″ barrel; saddle ring with leather string. Made from mid 1960's to 1976.
Estimated Value: Excellent: $100.00
Very good: $ 75.00

Colt Lightning

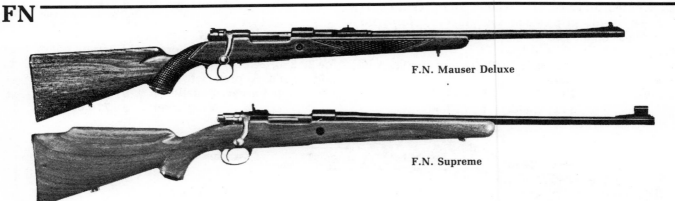

Colt AR-15

Caliber: 223; 9mm (1986)
Action: Semi-automatic
Magazine: 20-shot and 5-shot clips
Barrel: 20″ with flash supressor; 16″ with collapsible stock. Also heavy barrel available.
Sights: Adjustable rear, post front adjustable for elevation; 3X and 4X scopes available
Stock & Forearm: Pistol grip; fiberglass shoulder stock and handguard; swivels; carrying handle; collapsible stock available in both calibers
Approximate wt.: 6 to 8 lbs.
Comments: Made from the mid 1960's to present. Add 6% for collapsible stock; Add 14% for target sight & heavy barrel.
Estimated Value: New (retail): $706.50
                       Excellent: $530.00
                       Very good: $400.00

Colt AR-15

Colt Lightning

Caliber: 22 long rifle
Action: Slide action; exposed hammer; repeating
Magazine: Tubular: 15 longs, 16 shorts
Barrel: Blued 24″ round or octagon
Sights: Open rear, bead front
Stock & Forearm: Plain walnut straight grip stock and checkered slide handle
Approximate wt.: 5¾ lbs.
Comments: Made from the 1880's to about 1905.
Estimated Value: Excellent: $475.00
                       Very good: $350.00

FN

F.N. Mauser Deluxe

F.N. Supreme

F.N. Mauser Deluxe

Caliber: 220, 243, 244, 250-3000, 270, 7mm, 300, 308, 30-06
Action: Mauser-type bolt action; repeating
Magazine: 5-shot box
Barrel: Blued 24″
Sights: Adjustable rear, hooded ramp front
Stock & Forearm: Checkered one-piece pistol grip stock and forearm; swivels
Approximate wt.: 7½ to 8 lbs.
Comments: Made from World War II to the early 1960's.
Estimated Value: Excellent: $425.00
                       Very good: $320.00

F.N.M Mauser Deluxe Presentation

Similar to the Deluxe with Monte Carlo stock; engraving; select wood.
Estimated Value: Excellent: $675.00
                       Very good: $510.00

FN Supreme

Caliber: 243, 270, 7mm, 30-06, 308
Action: Mauser-type bolt action; repeating
Magazine: 5-shot box, 4-shot box in 308 or 243 calibers
Barrel: Blued 22″, 24″
Sights: Adjustable rear, hooded ramp front
Stock & Forearm: Checkered wood Monte Carlo one-piece pistol grip stock and tapered forearm; cheekpiece; swivels
Approximate wt.: 8 lbs.
Comments: Made from the late 1950's to the mid 1970's.
Estimated Value: Excellent: $500.00
                       Very good: $375.00

FN Supreme Magnum

Similar to the Supreme in magnum calibers and 3-shot box magazine.
Estimated Value: Excellent: $525.00
                       Very good: $395.00

Haenel

Haenel M-88

Similar to the Sporter with a box magazine.
Estimated Value: Excellent: $395.00
Very good: $300.00

Haenel Sporter M-88

Caliber: 7x57mm, 8x57mm, 9x57mm
Action: Mauser bolt action; double set trigger
Magazine: Detachable 5-shot clip
Barrel: 22″, 24″, half octagon barrel
Sights: Open rear, ramp front
Stock & Forearm: Checkered wood pistol grip stock and lipped forearm; swivels
Approximate wt.: 7¾ lbs.
Comments: A German sporting rifle, produced from about 1925 to 1940.
Estimated Value: Excellent: $465.00
Very good: $350.00

Harrington & Richardson

Harrington & Richardson 1873 Springfield Commemorative

Harrington & Richardson Little Big Horn Commemorative 174

Harrington & Richardson Cavalry 171 Deluxe Carbine

Harrington & Richardson 1873 Springfield Commemorative

Caliber: 45-70 Gov't
Action: Trap door; single shot
Magazine: None
Barrel: Blued 32″
Sights: Adjustable rear, blade front
Stock & Forearm: One-piece straight grip stock and full length forearm; barrel band; swivels
Approximate wt.: 8¾ lbs.
Comments: Manufactured to the late 1970's; replica of the 1873 U.S. Springfield Rifle.
Estimated Value: Excellent: $320.00
Very good: $235.00

Harrington & Richardson Little Big Horn Commemorative 174

Carbine version of the trap door Springfield, 22″ barrel; 7¼ lbs. Discontinued in 1984.
Estimated Value: Excellent: $275.00
Very good: $210.00

Harrington & Richardson Cavalry Carbine 171

Similar to the Little Big Horn with saddle ring.
Estimated Value: Excellent: $280.00
Very good: $210.00

Harrington & Richardson Cavalry 171 Deluxe

Similar to the Cavalry Carbine 171 with engraving.
Estimated Value: Excellent: $295.00
Very good: $220.00

Harrington & Richardson 158 Topper

Harrington & Richardson Mustang

Harrington & Richardson Model 157

Harrington & Richardson Shikari 155

Harrington & Richardson 158 Topper

Caliber: 22 Hornet, 30-30, 357 magnum, 44 magnum
Action: Box lock; top lever, break-open; exposed hammer; single shot
Magazine: None
Barrel: Blued 22″
Sights: Adjustable rear, ramp front
Stock & Forearm: Hardwood straight or semi-pistol grip stock and forearm; recoil pad
Approximate wt.: 5 lbs.
Comments: Made from the early 1960's to mid 1980's, magnum calibers added 1982.
Estimated Value: Excellent: $ 90.00
Very good: $ 65.00

Harrington & Richardson 158 C, 58 Topper, 258

Similar to the 158 with extra interchangeable 26″ 410 or 20 gauge shotgun barrel. Add 18% for nickel finish.
Estimated Value: Excellent: $150.00
Very good: $115.00

Harrington & Richardson Pioneer 765

Harrington & Richardson Mustang

Similar to the 158 with gold plated trigger and hammer; straight stock. Made in the 1960's.
Estimated Value: Excellent: $85.00
Very good: $65.00

Harrington & Richardson Model 157

Similar to the 158 with semi-pistol grip stock, full length forearm and swivels. Discontinued in 1984.
Estimated Value: Excellent: $95.00
Very good: $70.00

Harrington & Richardson Shikari 155

Caliber: 44 magnum, 45-70 Gov't.
Action: Single shot; exposed hammer
Magazine: None
Barrel: Blued 24″, 28″
Sights: Folding leaf rear, blade front
Stock & Forearm: Wood straight grip stock and forearm; barrel band
Approximate wt.: 7 to 7¼ lbs.
Comments: Manufactured to the early 1980's.
Estimated Value: Excellent: $90.00
Very good: $75.00

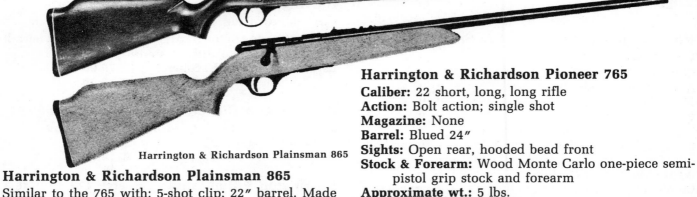

Harrington & Richardson Plainsman 865

Harrington & Richardson Plainsman 865

Similar to the 765 with: 5-shot clip; 22″ barrel. Made from about 1950 to 1986.
Estimated Value: Excellent: $ 80.00
Very good: $ 60.00

Harrington & Richardson Pioneer 765

Caliber: 22 short, long, long rifle
Action: Bolt action; single shot
Magazine: None
Barrel: Blued 24″
Sights: Open rear, hooded bead front
Stock & Forearm: Wood Monte Carlo one-piece semi-pistol grip stock and forearm
Approximate wt.: 5 lbs.
Comments: Made from the late 1940's to mid 1950's.
Estimated Value: Excellent: $50.00
Very good: $40.00

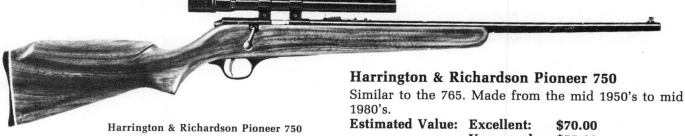

Harrington & Richardson Pioneer 750

Harrington & Richardson Pioneer 750

Similar to the 765. Made from the mid 1950's to mid 1980's.

Estimated Value: Excellent: $70.00
Very good: $55.00

Harrington & Richardson 866

Similar to the 865 with full length forearm. Made in early 1970's.

Estimated Value: Excellent: $75.00
Very good: $55.00

Harrington & Richardson Model 751

Similar to the 750 with full length forearm. Made from the early to mid 1970's.

Estimated Value: Excellent: $65.00
Very good: $50.00

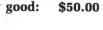

Harrington & Richardson Sahara 755

Harrington & Richardson Model 760

Harrington & Richardson Model 760

Similar to the 755 with short forearm. Discontinued in 1970.

Estimated Value: Excellent: $65.00
Very good: $50.00

Harrington & Richardson Medalist 450

Caliber: 22 long rifle
Action: Bolt action; repeating
Magazine: 5-shot detachable box
Barrel: Blued 26″
Sights: None
Stock & Forearm: Target style with pistol grip; swivels
Approximate wt.: 10½ lbs.
Comments: A target rifle made from the late 1940's to early 1960's.
Estimated Value: Excellent: $140.00
Very good: $110.00

Harrington & Richardson Medalist 451

Similar to the 450 with extension rear sight and Lyman front sight.

Estimated Value: Excellent: $145.00
Very good: $115.00

Harrington & Richardson Sahara 755

Caliber: 22 short, long, long rifle
Action: Blow back; hammerless; single shot; automatic ejector
Magazine: None
Barrel: Blued 22″
Sights: Open rear, military front
Stock & Forearm: Monte Carlo one-piece semi-pistol grip stock and full length forearm
Approximate wt.: 4 lbs.
Comments: Made from the early 1960's to early 1970's.
Estimated Value: Excellent: $75.00
Very good: $60.00

Harrington & Richardson Sportster 250

Caliber: 22 long rifle
Action: Bolt action; repeating
Magazine: 5-shot detachable box
Barrel: Blued 23″
Sights: Open rear, ramp front
Stock & Forearm: Wood one-piece semi-pistol grip stock and forearm
Approximate wt.: 6 lbs.
Comments: Made from the late 1940's to the early 1960's.
Estimated Value: Excellent: $65.00
Very good: $50.00

Harrington & Richardson 251

Similar to the 250 with a special Lyman rear sight.
Estimated Value: Excellent: $70.00
Very good: $55.00

Harrington & Richardson Fieldsman 852

Harrington & Richardson Fieldsman 852
Caliber: 22 short, long, long rifle
Action: Bolt action; repeating
Magazine: Tubular: 15 long rifles, 17 longs, 21 shorts
Barrel: Blued 24″
Sights: Open rear, bead front
Stock & Forearm: Plain wood one-piece semi-pistol grip stock and forearm
Approximate wt.: 5½ lbs.
Comments: Made in the early 1950's.
Estimated Value: Excellent: $70.00
Very good: $55.00

Harrington & Richardson Model 300

Harrington & Richardson Ultra 301

Harrington & Richardson Model 330

Harrington & Richardson Model 300
Caliber: 22-250 Rem., 243 Win., 270, 308, 30-06, 300 mag., 7mm mag.
Action: Mauser-type bolt action; repeating
Magazine: 5-shot box, 3-shot in magnum
Barrel: Blued 22″
Sights: Open rear, ramp front
Stock & Forearm: Checkered walnut Monte Carlo one-piece pistol grip stock and forearm; cheekpiece; recoil pad; swivels
Approximate wt.: 7¾ lbs.
Comments: Made from the mid 1960's to early 1980's.
Estimated Value: Excellent: $325.00
Very good: $245.00

Harrington & Richardson Ultra 301
Similar to the 300 with full length forearm and 18″ barrel; no swivels.
Estimated Value: Excellent: $400.00
Very good: $300.00

Harrington & Richardson Model 330
Similar to the Model 300 with less fancy finish. Discontinued in the early 1970's.
Estimated Value: Excellent: $290.00
Very good: $220.00

Harrington & Richardson Model 333
Similar to the Model 330 with no checkering or sights.
Estimated Value: Excellent: $240.00
Very good: $180.00

Harrington & Richardson
Ultra Wildcat 317

Harrington & Richardson 317 Presentation
Similar to the 317 with select wood, special basket-weave checkering.
Estimated Value: Excellent: $500.00
Very good: $375.00

Harrington & Richardson Ultra Wildcat 317
Caliber: 17 Rem., 222, 223 or 17/223 (Handload)
Action: Bolt action, Sako-type; repeating
Magazine: 6-shot box
Barrel: Blued 24″
Sights: None
Stock & Forearm: Wood Monte Carlo one-piece pistol grip stock and forearm; cheekpiece; recoil pad; swivels
Approximate wt.: 7¾ lbs.
Comments: Made from the mid 1960's to late 1970's.
Estimated Value: Excellent: $320.00
Very good: $240.00

Harrington & Richardson Ultra Medalist 370

Harrington & Richardson Model 340

Harrington & Richardson Model 340

Caliber: 243 Win., 270 Win., 30-06, 308 Win., 7mm Mauser (7x57)
Action: Bolt action; repeating; hinged floorplate; adjustable trigger
Magazine: 5-shot
Barrel: Blued 22″
Sights: None; drilled and tapped for sights or scope
Stock & Forearm: Checkered walnut one-piece pistol grip stock and forearm; cheekpiece; recoil pad
Approximate wt.: 7¼ lbs.
Comments: Introduced in 1981 in 30-06; other calibers added later. Discontinued in 1984.
Estimated Value: **Excellent:** $275.00
                Very good: $210.00

Harrington & Richardson Ultra Medalist 370

Caliber: 22-250, 243, 6mm
Action: Sako bolt action; repeating
Magazine: 4-shot box
Barrel: 24″ heavy
Sights: Open
Stock & Forearm: Monte Carlo one-piece pistol grip stock and forearm; cheekpiece; recoil pad; swivels
Approximate wt.: 9 lbs.
Comments: Made from the late 1960's to mid 1970's.
Estimated Value: **Excellent:** $350.00
                Very good: $260.00

Harrington & Richardson Model 5200 Sporter

Harrington & Richardson Model 5200 Match

Harrington & Richardson Model 5200 Match

Caliber: 22 long rifle
Action: Bolt action, single shot; adjustable trigger
Magazine: None
Barrel: 28″ heavy target weight, recessed muzzle
Sights: None; tapped for sights; scope bases included
Stock & Forearm: Smooth walnut one-piece match style stock and forearm; swivels and hand stop; rubber recoil pad
Approximate wt.: 11 lbs.
Comments: A moderately priced match rifle produced from 1981 to 1986.
Estimated Value: **Excellent:** $340.00
                Very good: $250.00

Harrington & Richardson Model 5200 Sporter

Caliber: 22 long rifle
Action: Bolt action; repeating
Magazine: 5-shot clip
Barrel: 24″ recessed muzzle
Sights: Adjustable receiver sight; hooded ramp front
Stock & Forearm: checkered walnut one-piece semi-pistol grip stock and forearm; rubber recoil pad
Approximate wt.: 6½ lbs.
Comments: A sporting version of the Model 5200 introduced in 1982. Discontinued 1983.
Estimated Value: **Excellent:** $300.00
                Very good: $225.00

Harrington & Richardson Model 422

Harrington & Richardson Model 749

Harrington & Richardson Reising 60

Harrington & Richardson General 65

Harrington & Richardson Leatherneck 165

Harrington & Richardson Model 422

Caliber: 22 short, long, long rifle
Action: Slide action; hammerless; repeating
Magazine: Tubular: 15 long rifles, 17 longs, 21 shorts
Barrel: Blued 24″
Sights: Open rear, ramp front
Stock & Forearm: Plain walnut semi-pistol grip stock and grooved slide handle
Approximate wt.: 6 lbs.
Comments: Made from the mid to late 1950's.
Estimated Value: Excellent: $100.00
Very good: $ 75.00

Harrington & Richardson Model 749

Caliber: 22 short, long, long rifle
Action: Slide action; exposed hammer; repeating
Magazine: Tubular: 18 shorts, 15 longs, 13 long rifles
Barrel: 19″ round, tapered
Sights: Open rear, blade front
Stock & Forearm: Plain hardwood pistol grip stock and tapered slide handle
Approximate wt.: 5 lbs.
Comments: Made in the early 1970's.
Estimated Value: Excellent: $80.00
Very good: $60.00

Harrington & Richardson Reising 60

Caliber: 45
Action: Semi-automatic
Magazine: 12 or 20-shot detachable box
Barrel: Blued 18¼″
Sights: Open rear, blade front
Stock & Forearm: Plain wood one-piece semi-pistol grip stock and forearm
Approximate wt.: 7¼ lbs.
Comments: Manufactured during World War II.
Estimated Value: Excellent: $425.00
Very good: $325.00

Harrington & Richardson General 65

Caliber: 22 long rifle
Action: Semi-automatic
Magazine: 10-shot detachable box
Barrel: Blued 23″
Sights: Peep rear, covered blade front
Stock & Forearm: Wood one-piece semi-pistol grip stock and forearm
Approximate wt.: 9 lbs.
Comments: Used as a Marine training rifle during World War II.
Estimated Value: Excellent: $275.00
Very good: $210.00

Harrington & Richardson Leatherneck 165

Lighter version of the 65 with ramp front sights. Made from World War II until the early 1960's.
Estimated Value: Excellent: $125.00
Very good: $100.00

Harrington & Richardson Reg'lar 265

Harrington & Richardson Targeteer Special 465

Harrington & Richardson Leatherneck 150

Harrington & Richardson Reg'lar 265
Similar to the 165 in bolt action with a 22″ barrel. Made from World War II until about 1950.
Estimated Value: **Excellent:** **$80.00**
Very good: **$60.00**

Harrington & Richardson Ace 365
Similar to the Model 265 except single shot. Made in the mid 1940's.
Estimated Value: **Excellent:** **$50.00**
Very good: **$35.00**

Harrington & Richardson Targeteer Special 465
Similar to the 265 with: 25″ barrel; swivels; slightly heavier. Made in the mid 1940's.
Estimated Value: **Excellent:** **$80.00**
Very good: **$60.00**

Harrington & Richardson Targeteer Jr.
A youth version of the 465 with: short stock; 5-shot magazine; 20″ barrel. Made from the late 1940's to early 1950's.
Estimated Value: **Excellent:** **$85.00**
Very good: **$65.00**

Harrington & Richardson Leatherneck 150
Caliber: 22 long rifle
Action: Semi-automatic; hammerless
Magazine: 5-shot detachable box
Barrel: Blued 22″
Sights: Open rear, ramp front
Stock & Forearm: Wood one-piece semi-pistol grip stock and forearm
Approximate wt.: 7 lbs.
Comments: Made from the late 1940's to early 1950's.
Estimated Value: **Excellent:** **$85.00**
Very good: **$70.00**

Harrington & Richardson Model 151
Similar to the 150 with a special peep rear sight.
Estimated Value: **Excellent:** **$90.00**
Very good: **$70.00**

Harrington & Richardson Model 308

Harrington & Richardson Model 308
Caliber: 264, 308
Action: Semi-automatic, gas operated
Magazine: 3-shot detachable box
Barrel: Blued 22″
Sights: Adjustable rear, bead front
Stock & Forearm: Checkered walnut Monte Carlo one-piece pistol grip stock and forearm; cheekpiece; swivels
Approximate wt.: 7 lbs.
Comments: Made from the mid 1960's to early 1970's.
Estimated Value: **Excellent:** **$275.00**
Very good: **$210.00**

Harrington & Richardson Lynx 800
Caliber: 22 long rifle
Action: Semi-automatic; hammerless
Magazine: 10-shot clip
Barrel: Blued 22″
Sights: Open rear, ramp front
Stock & Forearm: Walnut one-piece semi-pistol grip stock and forearm
Approximate wt.: 6 lbs.
Comments: Made from the late 1950's to about 1960.
Estimated Value: **Excellent:** **$75.00**
Very good: **$60.00**

Harrington & Richardson Model 360
Similar to the Model 308 except 243 caliber only.
Estimated Value: **Excellent:** **$270.00**
Very good: **$210.00**

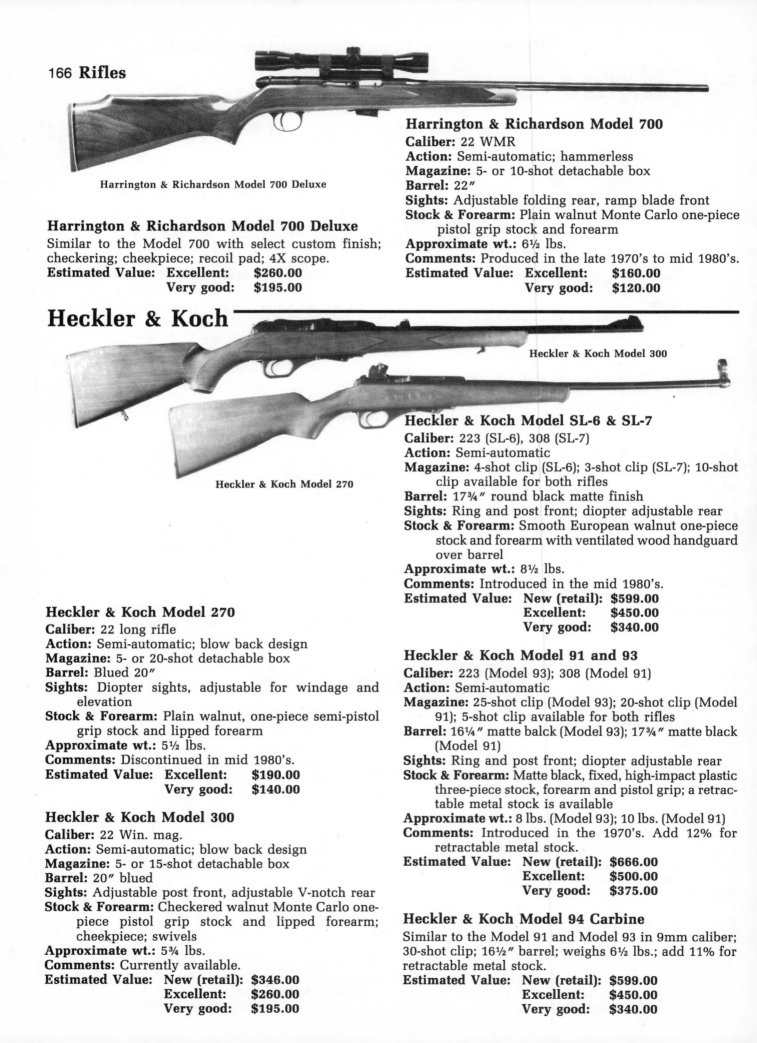

Harrington & Richardson Model 700 Deluxe

Harrington & Richardson Model 700 Deluxe

Similar to the Model 700 with select custom finish; checkering; cheekpiece; recoil pad; 4X scope.
Estimated Value: Excellent: $260.00
Very good: $195.00

Harrington & Richardson Model 700

Caliber: 22 WMR
Action: Semi-automatic; hammerless
Magazine: 5- or 10-shot detachable box
Barrel: 22″
Sights: Adjustable folding rear, ramp blade front
Stock & Forearm: Plain walnut Monte Carlo one-piece pistol grip stock and forearm
Approximate wt.: 6½ lbs.
Comments: Produced in the late 1970's to mid 1980's.
Estimated Value: Excellent: $160.00
Very good: $120.00

Heckler & Koch

Heckler & Koch Model 300

Heckler & Koch Model 270

Heckler & Koch Model 270

Caliber: 22 long rifle
Action: Semi-automatic; blow back design
Magazine: 5- or 20-shot detachable box
Barrel: Blued 20″
Sights: Diopter sights, adjustable for windage and elevation
Stock & Forearm: Plain walnut, one-piece semi-pistol grip stock and lipped forearm
Approximate wt.: 5½ lbs.
Comments: Discontinued in mid 1980's.
Estimated Value: Excellent: $190.00
Very good: $140.00

Heckler & Koch Model 300

Caliber: 22 Win. mag.
Action: Semi-automatic; blow back design
Magazine: 5- or 15-shot detachable box
Barrel: 20″ blued
Sights: Adjustable post front, adjustable V-notch rear
Stock & Forearm: Checkered walnut Monte Carlo one-piece pistol grip stock and lipped forearm; cheekpiece; swivels
Approximate wt.: 5¾ lbs.
Comments: Currently available.
Estimated Value: New (retail): $346.00
Excellent: $260.00
Very good: $195.00

Heckler & Koch Model SL-6 & SL-7

Caliber: 223 (SL-6), 308 (SL-7)
Action: Semi-automatic
Magazine: 4-shot clip (SL-6); 3-shot clip (SL-7); 10-shot clip available for both rifles
Barrel: 17¾″ round black matte finish
Sights: Ring and post front; diopter adjustable rear
Stock & Forearm: Smooth European walnut one-piece stock and forearm with ventilated wood handguard over barrel
Approximate wt.: 8½ lbs.
Comments: Introduced in the mid 1980's.
Estimated Value: New (retail): $599.00
Excellent: $450.00
Very good: $340.00

Heckler & Koch Model 91 and 93

Caliber: 223 (Model 93); 308 (Model 91)
Action: Semi-automatic
Magazine: 25-shot clip (Model 93); 20-shot clip (Model 91); 5-shot clip available for both rifles
Barrel: 16¼″ matte balck (Model 93); 17¾″ matte black (Model 91)
Sights: Ring and post front; diopter adjustable rear
Stock & Forearm: Matte black, fixed, high-impact plastic three-piece stock, forearm and pistol grip; a retractable metal stock is available
Approximate wt.: 8 lbs. (Model 93); 10 lbs. (Model 91)
Comments: Introduced in the 1970's. Add 12% for retractable metal stock.
Estimated Value: New (retail): $666.00
Excellent: $500.00
Very good: $375.00

Heckler & Koch Model 94 Carbine

Similar to the Model 91 and Model 93 in 9mm caliber; 30-shot clip; 16½″ barrel; weighs 6½ lbs.; add 11% for retractable metal stock.
Estimated Value: New (retail): $599.00
Excellent: $450.00
Very good: $340.00

Heckler & Koch Model 770

Heckler & Koch Model 940

Heckler & Koch Model 770

Similar to the Model 630 in 243 or 308 Win. calibers; 20″ barrel; weighs 8 lbs. 3-shot magazine.

Estimated Value: New (retail): $666.00
Excellent: $500.00
Very good: $375.00

Heckler & Koch Model 940

Similar to the Model 630 in 30-06 Springfield caliber; 22″ barrel; weighs 8¾ lbs. 3 shot magazine

Estimated Value: New (retail): $706.00
Excellent: $530.00
Very good: $395.00

Heckler & Koch Model 630

Caliber: 221, 222, 223, Rem., 22 Hornet
Action: Semi-automatic
Magazine: 4-shot box; 10-shot available
Barrel: 18″ blued
Sights: Adjustable post front, adjustable V-notch rear
Stock & Forearm: Checkered walnut, Monte Carlo pistol grip, one-piece stock and lipped forearm; cheekpiece; swivels.
Approximate wt.: 7 lbs.
Comments: Current available in 223 Remington caliber only.
Estimated Value: New (retail): $666.00
Excellent: $500.00
Very good: $375.00

High Standard

High Standard Flite King

High Standard Hi-Power

High Standard Hi-Power Deluxe

High Standard Flite King

Caliber: 22 short, long, long rifle
Action: Slide action; hammerless; repeating
Magazine: Tubular: 17 long rifle, 19 long, 24 short
Barrel: Blued 24″
Sights: Adjustable rear, post front
Stock & Forearm: Checkered walnut Monte Carlo pistol grip stock and grooved slide handle; early models have no checkering
Approximate wt.: 5½ lbs.
Comments: Made from about 1962 to late 1970's.
Estimated Value: Excellent: $100.00
Very good: $ 75.00

High Standard Hi-Power

Caliber: 270, 30-06
Action: Bolt action; Mauser-type; repeating
Magazine: 4-shot box
Barrel: Blued 22″
Sights: Folding leaf rear, ramp front
Stock & Forearm: Walnut one-piece semi-pistol grip stock and tapered forearm
Approximate wt.: 7 lb.
Comments: Made from the early to mid 1960's.
Estimated Value: Excellent: $240.00
Very good: $180.00

High Standard Hi-Power Deluxe

Similar to Hi-Power with a checkered Monte Carlo stock and swivels.
Estimated Value: Excellent: $270.00
Very good: $200.00

High Standard Early Sport King

High Standard Sport King Special

High Standard Sport King Carbine

High Standard Sport King Deluxe

High Standard Sport King

Caliber: 22 short, long, long rifle
Action: Semi-automatic
Magazine: Tubular: 15 long rifles, 17 longs, 21 shorts
Barrel: Blued 22¼"
Sights: Open rear, post front
Stock & Forearm: Checkered wood Monte Carlo one-piece pistol grip stock and forearm
Approximate wt.: 5½ lbs.
Comments: Sport King had no Monte Carlo stock before the mid 1970's; field model was made from about 1960 to the late 1970's.
Estimated Value: Excellent: $100.00
                    Very good: $ 75.00

High Standard Sport King Special

Similar to Sport King without checkering. Made from the early 1950's to mid 1960's.
Estimated Value: Excellent: $90.00
                    Very good: $65.00

High Standard Sport King Deluxe

Same specifications as Sport King. Made as Deluxe until mid 1970's.
Estimated Value: Excellent: $95.00
                    Very good: $75.00

High Standard Sport King Carbine

Carbine version of the Sport King. Straight stock; 18¼" barrel; smaller magazine; swivels. Made from the early 1960's to early 1970's.
Estimated Value: Excellent: $90.00
                    Very good: $65.00

Husqvarna

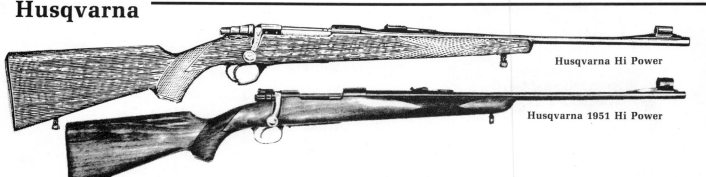

Husqvarna Hi Power

Husqvarna 1951 Hi Power

Husqvarna 1950 Hi Power

Similar to the Hi Power in 220, 270 and 30-06 calibers only. Made only in the early 1950's.
Estimated Value: Excellent: $260.00
                    Very good: $195.00

Husqvarna 1951 Hi Power

Similar to the Hi Power with a slightly higher stock. Made only in 1951.
Estimated Value: Excellent: $275.00
                    Very good: $210.00

Husqvarna Hi Power

Caliber: 220 Swift, 270, 30-06, 6.5x55, 8x57, 9.3x57
Action: Mauser-type bolt action; repeating
Magazine: 5-shot box
Barrel: Blued 23¾"
Sights: Open rear, hooded ramp front
Stock & Forearm: Checkered beech one-piece pistol grip stock and tapered forearm; swivels
Approximate wt.: 7¾ lbs.
Comments: Made from World War II to the late 1950's.
Estimated Value: Excellent: $250.00
                    Very good: $190.00

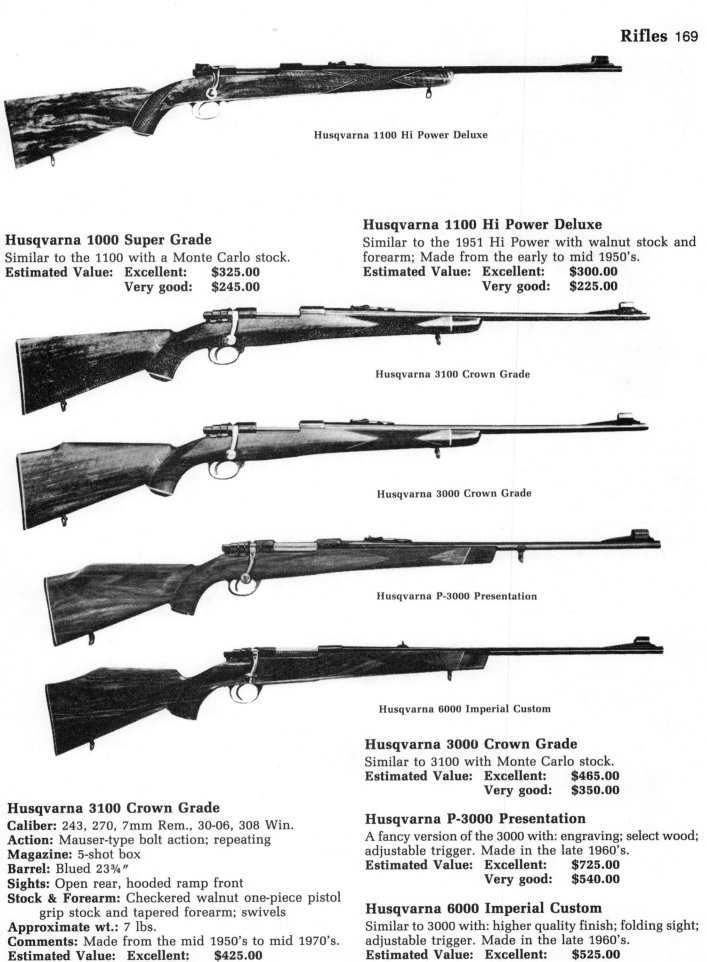

Husqvarna 1100 Hi Power Deluxe

Husqvarna 3100 Crown Grade

Husqvarna 3000 Crown Grade

Husqvarna P-3000 Presentation

Husqvarna 6000 Imperial Custom

Husqvarna 1000 Super Grade
Similar to the 1100 with a Monte Carlo stock.
Estimated Value: **Excellent:** **$325.00**
Very good: **$245.00**

Husqvarna 1100 Hi Power Deluxe
Similar to the 1951 Hi Power with walnut stock and forearm; Made from the early to mid 1950's.
Estimated Value: **Excellent:** **$300.00**
Very good: **$225.00**

Husqvarna 3000 Crown Grade
Similar to 3100 with Monte Carlo stock.
Estimated Value: **Excellent:** **$465.00**
Very good: **$350.00**

Husqvarna P-3000 Presentation
A fancy version of the 3000 with: engraving; select wood; adjustable trigger. Made in the late 1960's.
Estimated Value: **Excellent:** **$725.00**
Very good: **$540.00**

Husqvarna 6000 Imperial Custom
Similar to 3000 with: higher quality finish; folding sight; adjustable trigger. Made in the late 1960's.
Estimated Value: **Excellent:** **$525.00**
Very good: **$395.00**

Husqvarna 3100 Crown Grade
Caliber: 243, 270, 7mm Rem., 30-06, 308 Win.
Action: Mauser-type bolt action; repeating
Magazine: 5-shot box
Barrel: Blued 23¾"
Sights: Open rear, hooded ramp front
Stock & Forearm: Checkered walnut one-piece pistol grip stock and tapered forearm; swivels
Approximate wt.: 7 lbs.
Comments: Made from the mid 1950's to mid 1970's.
Estimated Value: **Excellent;** **$425.00**
Very good: **$320.00**

Husqvarna 4100 Lightweight

Husqvarna 4000 Lightweight

Husqvarna 456 Lightweight

Husqvarna 7000 Imperial Monte Carlo

Husqvarna 4100 Lightweight

Caliber: 243, 270, 7mm, 306, 308 Win.
Action: Mauser-type bolt action; repeating
Magazine: 5-shot box
Barrel: Blued 20½″
Sights: Open rear, hooded ramp front
Stock & Forearm: Checkered walnut one-piece pistol grip stock and tapered forearm
Approximate wt.: 6 lbs.
Comments: Made from the mid 1950's to mid 1970's.
Estimated Value: **Excellent:** **$400.00**
Very good: **$300.00**

Husqvarna 4000 Lightweight

Similar to 4100 with Monte Carlo stock and no rear sight.
Estimated Value: **Excellent:** **$420.00**
Very good: **$315.00**

Husqvarna 456 Lightweight

Similar to 4100 with full length stock and forearm. Made from about 1960 to 1970.
Estimated Value: **Excellent:** **$425.00**
Very good: **$320.00**

Husqvarna 7000 Imperial Monte Carlo

Similar to 4000 with: higher quality wood; lipped forearm; folding sight; adjustable trigger. Made in the late 1960's.
Estimated Value: **Excellent:** **$500.00**
Very good: **$375.00**

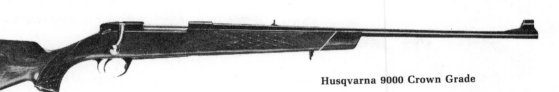

Husqvarna 9000 Crown Grade

Husqvarna 8000 Imperial Grade

Husqvarna 8000 Imperial Grade

Similar to 9000 with: select wood; engraving; no sights.
Estimated Value: **Excellent:** **$450.00**
Very good: **$350.00**

Husqvarna 9000 Crown Grade

Caliber: 270, 30-06, 7mm Remington mag., 300 Win. mag.
Action: Bolt action; repeating
Magazine: 5-shot box
Barrel: Blued 23¾″
Sights: Leaf rear, hooded ramp front
Stock & Forearm: Checkered walnut Monte Carlo one-piece pistol grip stock and forearm; swivels
Approximate wt.: 7¼ lbs.
Comments: Made in the early 1970's.
Estimated Value: **Excellent:** **$400.00**
Very good: **$300.00**

Husqvarna 610 Varmint

Husqvarna 610 Varmint

Caliber: 222
Action: Short stroke bolt action; repeating
Magazine: 4-shot detachable box
Barrel: Blued 24¾"
Sights: None; tapped for scope
Stock & Forearm: Checkered walnut Monte Carlo one-piece pistol grip stock and forearm; cheekpiece
Approximate wt.: 6½ lbs.
Comments: Made in the late 1960's.
Estimated Value: **Excellent:** **$375.00**
Very good: **$275.00**

Husqvarna 358 Magnum

Caliber: 358 Norma mag.
Action: Bolt action; repeating
Magazine: 3-shot box
Barrel: Blued 25½"
Sights: Folding leaf rear, hooded ramp front
Stock & Forearm: Checkered walnut Monte Carlo one-piece pistol grip stock and forearm; cheekpiece
Approximate wt.: 7¾ lbs.
Comments: Made in the late 1960's.
Estimated Value: **Excellent:** **$400.00**
Very good: **$300.00**

Ithaca

Ithaca Model LSA-55

Ithaca Model LSA-55 Deluxe

Ithaca Model LSA-65 Deluxe

Ithaca Model LSA-55

Caliber: 222, 22-250, 6mm, 243, 308
Action: Bolt action; repeating
Magazine: 3-shot detachable box
Barrel: Blued 22"
Sights: Iron; adjustable rear, hooded ramp front
Stock & Forearm: Monte Carlo one-piece pistol grip stock and tapered forearm
Approximate wt.: 6½ lbs.
Comments: Made from the early 1970's to late 1970's.
Estimated Value: **Excellent:** **$350.00**
Very good: **$260.00**

Ithaca Model LSA-55 Heavy Barrel

Similar to the LSA-55 except: cheekpiece; recoil pad; heavy barrel; weighs 8½ lbs.
Estimated Value: **Excellent:** **$375.00**
Very good: **$280.00**

Ithaca Model LSA-55 Deluxe

Similar to the LSA-55 except: checkering; recoil pad.
Estimated Value: **Excellent:** **$390.00**
Very good: **$295.00**

Ithaca Model LSA-65

Similar to Model LSA-55 in 25-06, 270, 30-06, with a 4-shot magazine; weighs 7 lbs.
Estimated Value: **Excellent:** **$375.00**
Very good: **$280.00**

Ithaca Model LSA-65 Deluxe

Similar to Model LSA-55 Deluxe in same calibers and weight as LSA-65.
Estimated Value: **Excellent:** **$400.00**
Very good: **$300.00**

Ithaca Model LSA-55 Turkey Gun

Ithaca Model 49 Saddlegun

Ithaca Model 49 Saddlegun

Caliber: 22 short, long, long rifle
Action: Lever action; exposed hammer; single shot
Magazine: None
Barrel: Blued 18″
Sights: Adjustable rear, bead front
Stock & Forearm: Plain wood straight grip stock and forearm; barrel band; recent model has checkering
Approximate wt.: 5½ lbs.
Comments: Made from about 1960 to late 1970's.
Estimated Value: Excellent: $50.00
Very good: $35.00

Ithaca Model LSA-55 Turkey Gun

Caliber: 222 under 12 gauge full choke
Action: Top lever break-open; exposed hammer
Magazine: None
Barrel: 24½″ rifle under full choke shotgun with matted rib
Sights: Folding rear, dovetail front
Stock & Forearm: Checkered walnut Monte Carlo pistol grip stock and forearm; cheekpiece; recoil pad; swivels
Approximate wt.: 7 lbs.
Comments: An over and under combination manufactured to the late 1970's.
Estimated Value: Excellent: $400.00
Very good: $300.00

Ithaca Model 49 Deluxe

Ithaca Model 49R

Ithaca Model 72 Saddlegun

Ithaca Model 49 Youth

Similar to Model 49 with an abbreviated stock for young shooters.
Estimated Value: Excellent: $45.00
Very good: $35.00

Ithaca Model 49 Magnum

Similar to Model 49 in 22 magnum rimfire.
Estimated Value: Excellent: $55.00
Very good: $40.00

Ithaca Model 49 Deluxe

Similar to Model 49 with checkered stock, gold hammer and trigger, and swivels. Discontinued in the mid 1970's when standard model was sold with checkering.
Estimated Value: Excellent: $60.00
Very good: $45.00

Ithaca Model 49 Presentation

Similar to Model 49 Deluxe with engraving and nameplate; calibers 22 short, long, long rifle or 22 magnum.
Estimated Value: Excellent: $100.00
Very good: $ 75.00

Ithaca Model 49R

Similar to Model 49 with 20″ barrel and 15-shot tubular magazine. Sold only in the late 1960's to early 1970's.
Estimated Value: Excellent: $80.00
Very good: $60.00

Ithaca Model 72 Saddlegun

Caliber: 22 long rifle
Action: Lever action; exposed hammer; repeating
Magazine: 15-shot tubular
Barrel: Blued 18½″
Sights: Adjustable rear, hooded ramp front
Stock & Forearm: Plain walnut straight grip stock and forearm; barrel band
Approximate wt.: 5½ lbs.
Comments: Made from the early to late 1970's.
Estimated Value: Excellent: $110.00
Very good: $ 80.00

Ithaca Model 72 Deluxe

Ithaca Model 72 Magnum

Similar to Model 72 in 22 magnum. Magazine holds 11 shots.

Estimated Value: Excellent: $120.00
Very good: $ 95.00

Ithaca Model 72 Deluxe

Similar to Model 72 except: brushed silver receiver; engraving; octagon barrel; blade front sight.

Estimated Value: Excellent: $130.00
Very good: $100.00

Ithaca Model X5-T

Ithaca Model X5-T

Similar to the X5-C with a 16-shot tubular magazine.

Estimated Value: Excellent: $100.00
Very good: $ 75.00

Ithaca Model X5-C

Caliber: 22 long rifle
Action: Semi-automatic; hammerless
Magazine: 7-shot clip
Barrel: Blued 22″
Sights: Open rear, Raybar front
Stock & Forearm: Wood one-piece semi-pistol grip stock and forearm
Approximate wt.: 6¼ lbs.
Comments: Made from the late 1950's to about 1965.
Estimated Value: Excellent: $90.00
Very good: $70.00

Iver Johnson

Iver Johnson Model 2X

Iver Johnson Lever Action

Caliber: 22 short, long, long rifle; 22 Win. magnum
Action: Lever action, side ejection; exposed hammer
Magazine: 21 shorts, 17 longs, 15 long rifles (mixed simultaneously); 12 magnum, tubular under barrel
Barrel: 18½″ round, blued
Sights: Hooded ramp front, adjustable rear
Stock & Forearm: Smooth hardwood stocka nd forearm, barrel band
Approximate wt.: 5¾ lbs.
Comments: Introduced in the mid 1980's. Add 7% for magnum.
Estimated Value: New (retail): $215.00
Excellent: $160.00
Very good: $120.00

Iver Johnson Model X

Caliber: 22 short, long, long rifle
Action: Bolt action; single shot
Magazine: None
Barrel: Blued 22″
Sights: Open rear, blade front
Stock & Forearm: Wood one-piece pistol grip stock and forearm
Approximate wt.: 4 lbs.
Comments: Made from the late 1920's to the early 1930's.
Estimated Value: Excellent: $50.00
Very good: $35.00

Iver Johnson Model 2X

Similar to the Model X with a 24″ barrel and improved stock. Made from about 1932 to the mid 1950's.

Estimated Value: Excellent: $55.00
Very good: $40.00

Iver Johnson Survival Carbine

Caliber: 30 carbine, 223 (5.7mm)
Action: Gas operated semi-automatic
Magazine: 5-, 15- or 30-shot detachable clip
Barrel: 18″ blued or stainless steel
Sights: Aperture rear, blade front with protective ears
Stock & Forearm: Hard plastic, one-piece pistol grip stock and forearm; metal handguard; folding stock available.
Approximate wt.: 5 lbs.
Comments: Produced from 1983 to 1986. Add 20% for folding stock; 25% for stainless steel finish.
Estimated Value: Excellent: $160.00
Very good: $120.00

Iver Johnson PM30G, Model M1, PM30

Caliber: 30 M1, 223 (discontinued 1985)
Action: Gas operated, semi-automatic
Magazine: 15-shot detachable clip; 5- or 30-shot available
Barrel: 18″ blued or stainless steel
Sights: Aperture rear, blade front with protective ears
Stock & Forearm: Wood, semi-pistol grip one-piece stock and forearm; slot in stock; metal ventilated or wood handguard
Approximate wt.: 6 lbs.
Comments: Made from about 1960 to late 1970's by Plainfield. Reintroduced in the late 1970's by Iver Johnson. Add 20% for stainless steel (discontinued 1985); add 7% for walnut.
Estimated Value: New (retail): $231.00
Excellent: $175.00
Very good: $130.00

Iver Johnson PM30S, Model M1 Sporter

Similar to the M1 Carbine with a wood hand guard and no slot in the stock. Discontinued in the early 1980's.
Estimated Value: Excellent: $175.00
Very good: $130.00

Johnson

Johnson Custom Deluxe Sporter

Similar to the MMJ with a Monte Carlo pistol grip stock and rear peep sight.
Estimated Value: Excellent: $240.00
Very good: $185.00

Johnson Folding Stock

Similar to the MMJ with a special metal folding shoulder stock.
Estimated Value: Excellent: $250.00
Very good: $190.00

Iver Johnson Trailblazer

Comments: 22 long rifle
Action: Semi-automatic, hammerless
Magazine: Clip
Barrel: 18½″ blued
Sights: Open rear, blade front
Stock & Forearm: Checkered walnut, one-piece Monte Carlo semi-pistol grip stock and forearm
Approximate wt.: 5 lbs.
Comments: Produced from 1984 to 1986.
Estimated Value: Excellent: $ 95.00
Very good: $ 75.00

Iver Johnson PM 30G

Iver Johnson PM30P, Commando or Paratrooper

Similar to the M1 Carbine with pistrol grip at rear and at forearm; telescoping wire shoulder stock. Add 20% for stainless steel.
Estimated Value: New (retail): $247.00
Excellent: $185.00
Very good: $135.00

Iver Johnson Model EW22 HBA, MHBA

Similar to the Model PM30 in 22 long rifle. Add 75% for magnum.
Estimated Value: New (retail): $183.00
Excellent: $135.00
Very good: $105.00

Iver Johnson Model 9MM

Similar to the Model PM30 in 9MM Parabellum with 16″ barrel and 20-shot magazine; weighs 5½ lbs.
Estimated Value: New (retail): $255.00
Excellent: $190.00
Very good: $145.00

Johnson MMJ Spitfire

Johnson MMJ Spitfire

Caliber: 223
Action: Semi-automatic
Magazine: 5-, 15-, 30-shot clip
Barrel: Blued 18″
Sights: Adjustable rear, ramp front
Stock & Forearm: Wood one-piece semi-pistol grip stock and forearm; wood hand guard
Approximate wt.: 5 lbs.
Comments: A conversion of the M1 carbine. Made in the mid 1960's.
Estimated Value: Excellent: $230.00
Very good: $175.00

Kimber

Kimber Model 82 M/S

Kimber Model 82

Kimber Model 82

Caliber: 22 long rifle, 22 Win. mag., 22 Hornet (after 1982)
Action: Bolt action; repeating
Magazine: 5-shot detachable box (10-shot available) in 22 long rifle; 3-shot in 22 Hornet; 4-shot in 22 Win. mag.
Barrel: 22½″ blued
Sights: None, drilled for scope; beaded ramp front and folding leaf rear available
Stock & Forearm: Checkered walnut, one-piece pistol grip stock and forearm (Classic); available with optional Monte Carlo stock and cheekpiece (Cascade); swivels.
Approximate wt.: 6½ lbs.
Comments: Produced from 1980 to 1986. Add 10% for Cascade model; 15% for .22 WMR; 25% for .22 Hornet; 90% for Super America model. Replaced by Model 82B.
Estimated Value: Excellent: $370.00
Very good: $280.00

Kimber Model 82 M/S

Similar to the Model 82 except single shot; 20½″ heavy barrel, adjustable target trigger; competition stock; 22 long rifle caliber only; this gun is designed for metallic silhouette shotting. Introduced in 1982.
Estimated Value: Excellent: $500.00
Very good: $375.00

Kimber Model 82B

Similar to the Model 82 with internal improvements. Introduced in 1986. Available in sporter or varmint barrel weight, left or right action. Add 12% for Cascade Model, 30% for Custom Classic, 100% for Brownell and 50% for Super America.
Estimated Value: New (retail): $750.00
Excellent: $560.00
Very good: $420.00

Kimber Model 84

Similar to the Model 82, introduced in 1984 in 223 Rem. caliber. Calibers added in 1986 were: 221 Fireball, 222 Rem. magnum, 17 Rem., 17 Match IV, 6x47, and 6x45. Add 12% for Cascade Model, 35% for Custom Classic and 50% for Super America.
Estimated Value: New (retail): $850.00
Excellent: $635.00
Very good: $475.00

Kleinguenther

Kleinguenther K-14

Kleinguenther MV 2130

Caliber: 243, 270, 30-06, 300 mag., 308, 7mm Rem.
Action: Mauser-type bolt action; repeating
Magazine: 2-shot box
Barrel: Blued 25″
Sights: None; drilled for scope
Stock & Forearm: Checkered walnut Monte Carlo one-piece pistol grip stock and tapered forearm; recoil pad
Approximate wt.: 7 lbs.
Comments: Made in the 1970's.
Estimated Value: Excellent: $475.00
Very good: $355.00

Kleinguenther K-14

Caliber: Same as MV 2130, also 25-06, 7x57, 375 H&H
Action: Bolt action
Magazine: Hidden clip, 3-shot
Barrel: Blued 24″, 26″
Sights: Open rear, ramp front
Stock & Forearm: Checkered walnut one-piece pistol grip stock and tapered forearm; recoil pad
Approximate wt.: 7¼ lbs.
Comments: Made in the 1970's.
Estimated Value: Excellent: $575.00
Very good: $430.00

Kleinguenther K-15 Insta-fire

Kleinguenther Model K-22

Caliber: 22 long rifle, 22 WMR
Action: Bolt action, repeating; adjustable trigger
Magazine: 5-shot hidden clip
Barrel: 21½″ chrome-poly steel
Sights: None; tapped for scope
Stock & Forearm: Checkered beechwood, Monte Carlo pistol grip one-piece stock and forearm; swivels; cheekpiece
Approximate wt.: 6½ lbs.
Comments: A rimfire rifle designed to be as accurate as the K-15. Introduced in 1984. Add 16% for magnum, 30% for deluxe, 133% for deluxe custom.
Estimated Value: New (retail): $299.00
Excellent: $225.00
Very good: $170.00

Kleinguenther K-15 Insta-fire

Caliber: 243, 25-06, 270, 30-06, 308 Win., 308 Norma mag., 300 Win. mag., 7mm Rem. mag., 375 H&H, 7x57, 270 mag., 300 Weath. mag., 257 Weath. mag.
Action: Bolt action; repeating; adjustable trigger
Magazine: 5-shot hidden clip; 3-shot in magnum
Barrel: 24″; 26″ in magnum
Sights: None; tapped for scope
Stock & Forearm: Checkered walnut Monte Carlo one-piece pistol grip stock and forearm; several shade choices; rosewood fore-end and cap; swivels; left or right hand model
Approximate wt.: 7½ lbs.
Comments: A high powered rifle that is advertised as "the world's most accurate hunting rifle." Engraving and select wood at additional cost. Add $50.00 for magnum; $50.00 for left hand model. Made from late 1970's.
Estimated Value: New (retail): $1,100.00
Excellent: $ 825.00
Very good: $ 620.00

Mannlicher

Mannlicher-Schoenauer 1905

Mannlicher-Schoenauer 1903

Caliber: 6.5 x 53mm
Action: Bolt action; repeating; double set trigger; "butter-knife" style bolt handle
Magazine: 5-shot rotary
Barrel: Blued 17¾″
Sights: Two leaf rear, ramp front
Stock & Forearm: Walnut semi-pistol grip stock and tapered, full-length forearm; swivels; cheekpiece
Approximate wt.: 6½ lbs.
Comments: Made from 1903 to World War II.
Estimated Value: Excellent: $775.00
Very good: $575.00

Mannlicher-Schoenauer 1905

Similar to 1903 with a 19¾″ barrel and in 9x56mm caliber.
Estimated Value: Excellent: $650.00
Very good: $490.00

Mannlicher-Schoenauer 1908

Similar to the 1903 with a 19¾″ barrel and in 7x57, and 8x56mm calibers.
Estimated Value: Excellent: $625.00
Very good: $470.00

Mannlicher-Schoenauer 1910

Similar to 1903 with 19¾″ barrel and in 9.5x57mm caliber.
Estimated Value: Excellent: $670.00
Very good: $500.00

Mannlicher-Schoenauer 1924

Similar to the 1903 with a 19¾″ barrel and in 30-06. Made from 1924 to World War II.
Estimated Value: Excellent: $800.00
Very good: $600.00

Mannlicher-Schoenauer High Velocity

Mannlicher-Schoenauer 1950 Sporter

Mannlicher-Schoenauer 1950 Carbine

Mannlicher-Schoenauer 1952 Sporter

Mannlicher-Schoenauer 1952 Carbine

Mannlicher-Schoenauer High Velocity

Caliber: 7x64, 30-06, 8x60, 9.3x62, 10.75x68
Action: Bolt action; repeating; "butter-knife" bolt handle
Magazine: 5-shot rotary
Barrel: Blued 23¾"
Sights: Three leaf rear, ramp front
Stock & Forearm: Checkered walnut one-piece pistol grip stock and tapered forearm; cheekpiece; swivels
Approximate wt.: 7½ lbs.
Comments: Made from the early 1920's to World War II.
Estimated Value: **Excellent:** $750.00
 Very good: $560.00

Mannlicher-Schoenauer 1950 Sporter

Caliber: 257, 270 Win., 30-06
Action: Bolt action; repeating; "butter-knife" bolt handle
Magazine: 5-shot rotary
Barrel: Blued 24"
Sights: Folding leaf rear, hooded ramp front
Stock & Forearm: Checkered walnut one-piece pistol grip stock and tapered forearm; cheekpiece; swivels
Approximate wt.: 7¼ lbs.
Comments: Made in the early 1950's.
Estimated Value: **Excellent:** $650.00
 Very good: $480.00

Mannlicher-Schoenauer 1950 Carbine

Similar to the Sporter with a 20" barrel and full length forearm.
Estimated Value: **Excellent:** $700.00
 Very good: $500.00

Mannlicher-Schoenauer 1950-6.5

Similar to the 1950 Carbine with 18" barrel and in 6.5x53mm caliber.
Estimated Value: **Excellent:** $675.00
 Very good: $505.00

Mannlicher-Schoenauer 1952 Sporter

Similar to 1950 Sporter with slight changes in stock and with slanted bolt handle. Made from about 1952 to 1956.
Estimated Value: **Excellent:** $660.00
 Very good: $500.00

Mannlicher-Schoenauer 1952 Carbine

Simialr to 1952 Sporter with a 20" barrel and full length forearm.
Estimated Value: **Excellent:** $680.00
 Very good: $510.00

Mannlicher-Schoenauer 1952-6.5

Similar to 1952 Carbine with 18" barrel and in 6.5x53mm caliber.
Estimated Value: **Excellent:** $650.00
 Very good: $490.00

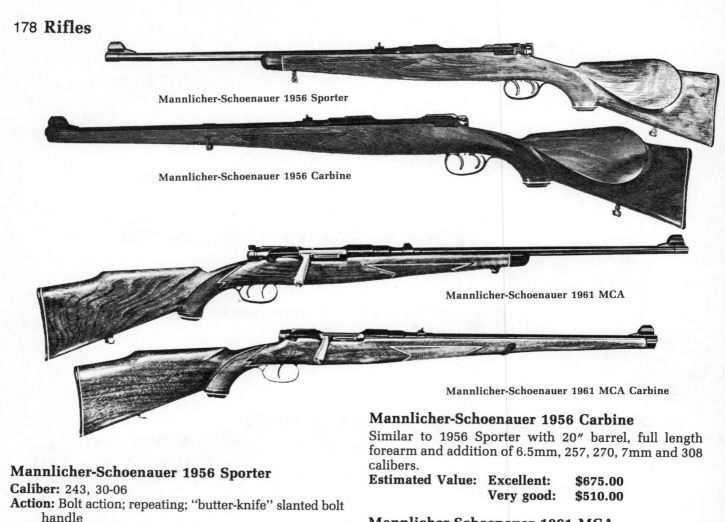

Mannlicher-Schoenauer 1956 Sporter

Mannlicher-Schoenauer 1956 Carbine

Mannlicher-Schoenauer 1961 MCA

Mannlicher-Schoenauer 1961 MCA Carbine

Mannlicher-Schoenauer 1956 Sporter

Caliber: 243, 30-06
Action: Bolt action; repeating; "butter-knife" slanted bolt handle
Magazine: 5-shot rotary
Barrel: Blued 22″
Sights: Folding leaf rear, hooded ramp front
Stock & Forearm: Checkered walnut pistol grip stock and forearm; high comb; cheekpiece; swivels
Approximate wt.: 7 lbs.
Comments: Made from the mid 1950's to about 1960.
Estimated Value: Excellent: $650.00
　　　　　　　　 Very good: $490.00

Mannlicher-Schoenauer 1956 Carbine

Similar to 1956 Sporter with 20″ barrel, full length forearm and addition of 6.5mm, 257, 270, 7mm and 308 calibers.
Estimated Value: Excellent: $675.00
　　　　　　　　 Very good: $510.00

Mannlicher-Schoenauer 1961 MCA

Similar to 1956 Sporter with Monte Carlo stock. Made from the early 1960's to early 1970's.
Estimated Value: Excellent: $660.00
　　　　　　　　 Very good: $500.00

Mannlicher-Schoenauer 1961 MCA Carbine

Similar to 1956 Carbine with Monte Carlo stock. Made from early 1960's to early 1970's.
Estimated Value: Excellent: $675.00
　　　　　　　　 Very good: $510.00

Steyr-Mannlicher Model SL

Steyr-Mannlicher Model SL

Caliber: 222 Rem., 222 magnum, 223, 5.6x50 magnum
Action: Bolt action; repeating
Magazine: 5-shot rotary
Barrel: 23½″ blued
Sights: Open rear, ramp front
Stock & Forearm: Checkered walnut, Monte Carlo pistol grip, one-piece stock and tapered forearm; recoil pad; cheekpiece; swivels
Approximate wt.: 5½ lbs.
Comments: Made from the mid 1960's to present; 5.6x50 no longer available.
Estimated Value: New (retail): $998.94
　　　　　　　　 Excellent: $750.00
　　　　　　　　 Very good: $560.00

Steyr-Mannlicher SL Carbine

Similar to the SL with a 20″ barrel and full length forearm.
Estimated Value: New (retail): $1,056.10
　　　　　　　　 Excellent: $ 790.00
　　　　　　　　 Very good: $ 600.00

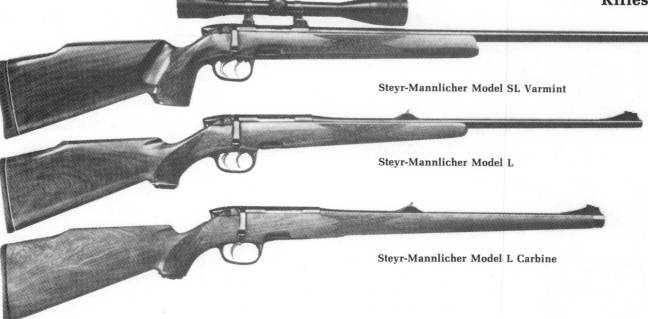

Steyr-Mannlicher Model SL Varmint

Steyr-Mannlicher Model L

Steyr-Mannlicher Model L Carbine

Steyr-Mannlicher Model SL Varmint

Similar to the Model SL with a varmint stock and 26″ heavy barrel.

Estimated Value:	New (retail):	$1,056.10
	Excellent:	$ 790.00
	Very good:	$ 600.00

Steyr-Mannlicher Model L Varmint

Similar to the Model L with a varmint stock and 26″ heavy barrel.

Estimated Value:	New (retail):	$1,056.10
	Excellent:	$ 790.00
	Very good:	$ 600.00

Steyr-Mannlicher Model L

Similar to the SL in 22-250, 5.6x57, 7mm, 243, 308.

Estimated Value:	New (retail):	$998.94
	Excellent:	$750.00
	Very good:	$560.00

Steyr-Mannlicher Model L Carbine

Similar to Model L with a 20″ barrel and full length forearm.

Estimated Value:	New (retail):	$1,056.10
	Excellent:	$ 790.00
	Very good:	$ 600.00

Steyr-Mannlicher Model M

Steyr-Mannlicher Model M Professional

Steyr-Mannlicher Model M Professional

Similar to the Model M with a parkerized metal finish and ABS Cycolac stock; 23½″ barrel only.

Estimated Value:	New (retail):	$897.82
	Excellent:	$670.00
	Very good:	$500.00

Steyr-Mannlicher Model M

Caliber: 6.5x55, 7x64, 270 Win., 30-06, 25-06 Rem.; 7x57, 9.3x62

Action: Bolt action; repeating

Magazine: 5-shot rotary

Barrel: Blued 20″ on full stock; 23½″ on half stock

Sights: Open rear, ramp front

Stock & Forearm: Checkered walnut Monte Carlo pistol grip stock; standard or full length forearm; cheekpiece; swivels; left hand model available

Approximate wt.: 6½ lbs.

Comments: Made from the mid 1970's to present. Add $220.00 for left hand model; $60.00 for full stock.

Estimated Value:	New (retail):	$998.94
	Excellent:	$750.00
	Very good:	$560.00

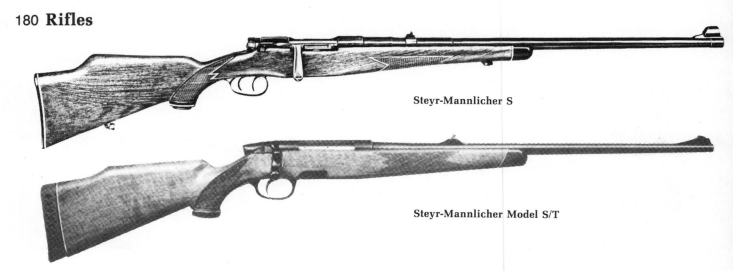

Steyr-Mannlicher S

Steyr-Mannlicher Model S/T

Steyr-Mannlicher S

Similar to Model M with 26″ barrel in magnum caliber, 7mm Rem., 257 Weath., 264 Win., 300 H&H, 388 Win., 375 H&H, and 458 Win. Half stock only; butt magazine optional. Add $50.00 for buttstock 4-shot magazine.

Estimated Value: New (retail): $1,258.00
Excellent: $ 945.00
Very good: $ 710.00

Steyr-Mannlicher S/T, Tropical

Similar to the Model S with a heavy barrel; 375 H&H mag. and 458 Win. mag. calibers. Add $50.00 for butt-stock magazine.

Estimated Value: New (retail): $1,332.27
Excellent: $1,000.00
Very good: $ 750.00

Mannlicher-Schoenauer M-72 LM Carbine

Steyr-Mannlicher ML 79 Luxus M

Caliber: 7x57, 7x64, 270 Win., 30-06 Springfield; others available on request
Action: Bolt action; short stroke; repeating
Magazine: 3-shot detachable, 6-shot available
Barrel: 23½″; 20″ on full stock model
Sights: Adjustable V-notch open rear, adjustable hooded ramp front
Stock & Forearm: Checkered European walnut Monte Carlo one-piece pistol grip stock and forearm; cheekpiece; swivels; full length stock available
Approximate wt.: 7 lbs.
Comments: Currently produced. Add $75.00 for full length stock or 6-shot magazine.
Estimated Value: New (retail): $1,298.41
Excellent: $ 975.00
Very good: $ 730.00

Mannlicher-Schoenauer M-72, M-72S

Caliber: 22-250, 5.6x57, 243, 6.5x57, 6mm, 7x57, 270
Action: Bolt action; repeating
Magazine: 5-shot rotary
Barrel: Blued 23½″
Sights: Open rear, ramp front
Stock & Forearm: Checkered walnut one-piece pistol grip stock and tapered forearm; cheekpiece; recoil pad; swivels
Approximate wt.: 7½ lbs.
Comments: Made from mid to late 1970's.
Estimated Value: Excellent: $780.00
Very good: $595.00

Mannlicher-Schoenauer M-72 LM Carbine

Similar to M-72 with a 20″ barrel and full length forearm.
Estimated Value: Excellent: $800.00
Very good: $600.00

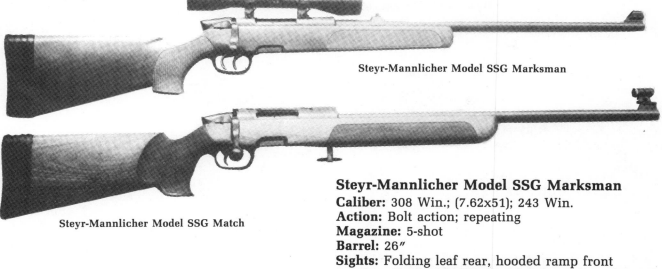

Steyr-Mannlicher Model SSG Marksman

Steyr-Mannlicher Model SSG Match

Steyr-Mannlicher Model SSG Marksman
Caliber: 308 Win.; (7.62x51); 243 Win.
Action: Bolt action; repeating
Magazine: 5-shot
Barrel: 26″
Sights: Folding leaf rear, hooded ramp front
Stock & Forearm: Checkered European walnut one-piece stock and forearm; recoil pad; ABS Cycolac stock available
Approximate wt.: 8½ lbs.
Comments: Currently produced. Deduct $185.00 for ABS Cycolac stock.
Estimated Value: New (retail): $1,180.00
Excellent: $ 885.00
Very good: $ 665.00

Steyr-Mannlicher Model SSG Match
A match rifle similar to the SSG Marksman with a heavy barrel; peep sight; stippled checkering; hand stop; weight: 11 lbs.; deduct $160.00 for ABS Cycolac stock.
Estimated Value: New (retail): $1,495.00
Excellent: $1,121.00
Very good: $ 840.00

Mark X

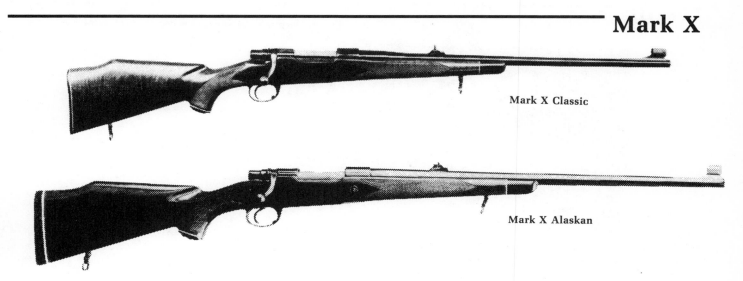

Mark X Classic

Mark X Alaskan

Mark X Alaskan
Caliber: 375 H & H, 458 Win. magnum
Action: Mauser-type bolt action; repeating; adjustable trigger
Magazine: 3-shot box with hinged floor plate
Barrel: 24″ blued
Sights: Adjustable rear; hooded ramp front
Stock & Forearm: Checkered, select walnut, Monte Carlo pistol grip, one-piece stock and forearm; recoil pad; swivels
Approximate wt.: 6 lbs.
Comments: Distributed by Interarms.
Estimated Value: Excellent: $345.00
Very good: $260.00

Mark X Classic
Caliber: 22-250, 25-06, 270, 308, 30-06, 7mm mag., 7x57, 300 mag.
Action: Bolt action; Mauser-type; repeating; adjustable trigger
Magazine: 3-shot box with hinged floor plate
Sights: None on some models; others adjustable rear, hooded ramp front
Stock & Forearm: Checkered walnut Monte Carlo one-piece pistol grip stock and forearm; swivels
Approximate wt.: 7½ lbs.
Comments: Add $15.00 for sights.
Estimated Value: Excellent: $275.00
Very good: $200.00

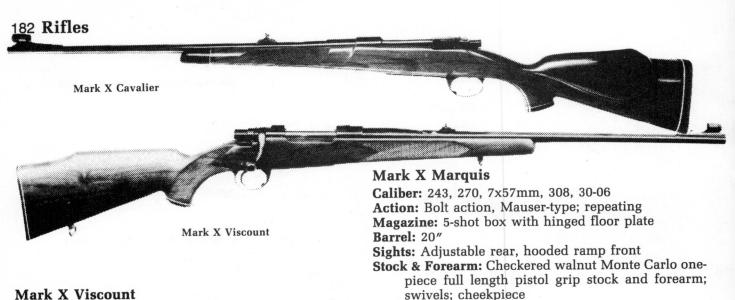

Mark X Cavalier

Mark X Viscount

Mark X Viscount

Similar to the Mark X except: special hammer forged, chrome vanadium steel barrel. Add $15.00 for sights.

Estimated Value: Excellent: $270.00
Very good: $195.00

Mark X Cavalier

Similar to the Mark X with fancier stock; cheekpiece; recoil pad. Add $15.00 for sights.

Estimated Value: Excellent: $320.00
Very good: $245.00

Mark X Marquis

Caliber: 243, 270, 7x57mm, 308, 30-06
Action: Bolt action, Mauser-type; repeating
Magazine: 5-shot box with hinged floor plate
Barrel: 20″
Sights: Adjustable rear, hooded ramp front
Stock & Forearm: Checkered walnut Monte Carlo one-piece full length pistol grip stock and forearm; swivels; cheekpiece
Approximate wt.: 7½ lbs.
Comments: Distributed by Interarms.
Estimated Value: Excellent: $325.00
Very good: $240.00

Mark X Continental

Similar to the Marquis with a "butter-knife" bolt handle and double set triggers.

Estimated Value: Excellent: $350.00
Very good: $270.00

Marlin

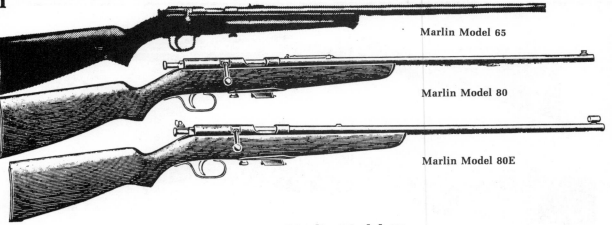

Marlin Model 65

Marlin Model 80

Marlin Model 80E

Marlin Model 80

Caliber: 22 short, long, long rifle
Action: Bolt action; takedown type; repeating
Magazine: 8-shot detachable box
Barrel: 24″
Sights: Open rear, bead front
Stock & Forearm: Plain pistol grip stock and forearm
Approximate wt.: 6¼ lbs.
Comments: Production began about 1934, continued until the mid 1940's.
Estimated Value: Excellent: $75.00
Very good: $60.00

Marlin Model 80E

Same rifle as Model 80 except hooded front sight and peep rear sight.

Estimated Value: Excellent: $80.00
Very good: $65.00

Marlin Model 65

Caliber: 22 short, long, long rifle
Action: Bolt action; single shot
Magazine: None
Barrel: 24″ round
Sights: Open rear, bead front
Stock & Forearm: Pistol grip stock and grooved forearm
Approximate wt.: 5 lbs.
Comments: This is a takedown rifle that was made between 1932 and 1935.
Estimated Value: Excellent: $50.00
Very good: $40.00

Marlin Model 65E

Same as Model 65 except hooded front sight and peep rear sight.

Estimated Value: Excellent: $55.00
Very good: $40.00

Marlin Model 80C

Marlin Model 80 DL

Marlin Glenfield Model 80 G

Marlin Model 81

Marlin Model 81 E

Marlin Model 81-DL

Marlin Glenfield Model 81 G

Marlin Model 80C

Basically the same gun as the Model 80 with slight improvements. Forearm is semi-beavertail. Production began in 1946, it was replaced by the 80 G in 1960.
Estimated Value: Excellent: **$70.00**
Very good: **$55.00**

Marlin Model 80 DL

Same rifle as Model 80-C except; swivels; hooded front sight; peep rear sight. Discontinued in 1965.
Estimated Value: Excellent: **$70.00**
Very good: **$55.00**

Marlin Glenfield Model 80 G

The same rifle as the Marlin Model 80 C. Discontinued about 1966.
Estimated Value: Excellent: **$60.00**
Very good: **$45.00**

Marlin Model 81 E

Same rifle as Model 82 except hooded front sight and peep rear sight.
Estimated Value: Excellent: **$80.00**
Very good: **$65.00**

Marlin Model 81 C

An improved Model 81; semi-beavertail forearm. It was produced from 1940 to 1970.
Estimated Value: Excellent: **$70.00**
Very good: **$55.00**

Marlin Model 81-DL

Same as Model 81 C except it has swivels; hooded front sight, peep rear sight.
Estimated Value: Excellent: **$80.00**
Very good: **$65.00**

Marlin Model 81

Caliber: 22 short, long, long rifle
Action: Bolt action; repeating
Magazine: Tubular under barrel: 24 shorts, 20 longs, 18 long rifles
Barrel: 24″
Sights: Open rear, bead front
Stock & Forearm: Plain pistol grip stock and forearm
Approximate wt.: 6¼ lbs.
Comments: This takedown model was produced from 1937 into the 1940's.
Estimated Value: Excellent: **$75.00**
Very good: **$60.00**

Marlin Glenfield Model 81 G

Basically the same as the Marlin Model 81 C. It was produced as the 81 G from about 1960 to 1965.
Estimated Value: Excellent: **$65.00**
Very good: **$50.00**

Marlin Model 100

Marlin Model 100 SB

Marlin Model 100S Tom Mix Special

Same as Model 100 except hooded front sight, peep rear sight. Discontinued in 1946.

Estimated Value: **Excellent:** **$100.00**
Very good: **$ 75.00**

Marlin Model 100 SB

Same as Model 100 except it is smooth bore to use with shot cartridges. Discontinued in 1941.

Estimated Value: **Excellent:** **$60.00**
Very good: **$45.00**

Marlin Model 100

Caliber: 22 short, long, long rifle
Action: Bolt action; single shot
Magazine: None
Barrel: 24″ round
Sights: Open rear, bead front
Stock & Forearm: Plain pistol grip stock and forearm
Approximate wt.: 4¾ lbs.
Comments: Takedown model was manufactured from 1936 to 1960. In 1960 it became the Model 100G or Glenfield and was replaced in the mid 1960's by the Glenfield 10.

Estimated Value: **Excellent:** **$50.00**
Very good: **$40.00**

Marlin Glenfield Model 100G

Marlin Model 101

Marlin Model 15Y (Little Buckaroo)

Marlin Glenfield Model 15

Marlin Glenfield Model 100G; Glenfield 10

Basically same as Marlin Model 10.
Estimated Value: **Excellent:** **$40.00**
Very good: **$30.00**

Marlin Model 101

Basically same as Model 100 except beavertail forearm. Weighs 5 lbs. Made from 1951 to late 1970's.
Estimated Value: **Excellent:** **$50.00**
Very good: **$40.00**

Marlin Model 101-DL

Same as Model 101 except hooded front sight, peep rear sight.
Estimated Value: **Excellent:** **$55.00**
Very good: **$45.00**

Marlin Glenfield Model 15, 15Y (Little Buckaroo)

Caliber: 22 short, long or long rifle
Action: Bolt action; single shot
Magazine: None
Barrel: 22″ round, 16¼″ on 15Y
Sights: Adjustable open rear, ramp front
Stock & Forearm: Checkered hardwood, Monte Carlo pistol grip one-piece stock and forearm
Approximate wt.: 5½ lbs., 4½ lbs. (15Y)
Comments: Introduced in the late 1970's. 15Y is for young shooters.

Estimated Value: **New (retail):** **$105.95**
Excellent: **$ 80.00**
Very good: **$ 60.00**

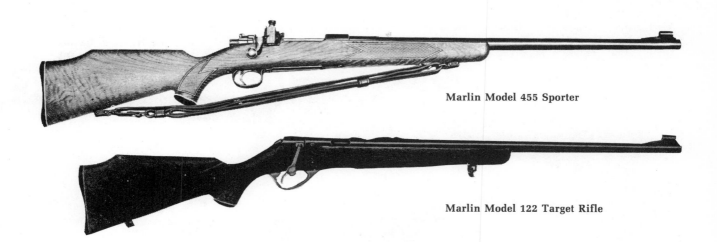

Marlin Model 322 Varmint

Marlin Model 422 Varmint King

Marlin Model 455 Sporter

Marlin Model 122 Target Rifle

Marlin Model 322 Varmint

Caliber: 222 Rem.
Action: Bolt action (Sako Short, Mauser); repeating
Magazine: 3-shot clip
Barrel: 24″
Sights: Peep sight rear, hooded ramp front
Stock & Forearm: Checkered hardwood stock and forearm
Approximate wt.: 7½ lbs.
Comments: Made for only 3 years beginning about 1954.
Estimated Value: Excellent: $265.00
Very good: $200.00

Marlin Model 422 Varmint King

Caliber: 222 Rem.
Action: Bolt action; repeating
Magazine: 3-shot detachable clip
Barrel: 24″ round
Sights: Peep sight rear, hooded ramp front
Stock & Forearm: Checkered Monte Carlo pistol grip stock and forearm
Approximate wt.: 7 lbs.
Comments: Replaced Model 322 about 1958 but was discontinued after one year.
Estimated Value: Excellent: $280.00
Very good: $210.00

Marlin Model 455 Sporter

Caliber: 270, 30-06, 308
Action: Bolt action, FN Mauser action with Sako trigger
Magazine: 5-shot box
Barrel: 24″ round, stainless steel
Sights: Receiver sight - Lyman 48, hooded ramp front
Stock & Forearm: Checkered wood Monte Carlo stock and forearm; cheekpiece
Approximate wt.: 8½ lbs.
Comments: Made from about 1957 to 1959.
Estimated Value: Excellent: $290.00
Very good: $220.00

Marlin Model 122 Target Rifle

Caliber: 22 short, long, long rifle
Action: Bolt action; single shot
Magazine: None
Barrel: 22″ round
Sights: Open rear, hooded ramp front
Stock & Forearm: Wood Monte Carlo pistol grip stock and forearm; swivels
Approximate wt.: 5 lbs.
Comments: Made from about 1961 to 1965.
Estimated Value: Excellent: $50.00
Very good: $40.00

Marlin Glenfield 20

Marlin Model 980

Marlin Model 980

Caliber: 22 Win. mag.
Action: Bolt action; repeating
Magazine: 8-shot clip
Barrel: Blued 24″ round
Sights: Open rear, hooded ramp front
Stock & Forearm: Monte Carlo one-piece stock and forearm; swivels
Approximate wt.: 6 lbs.
Comments: Made from about 1962 until 1970.
Estimated Value: Excellent: $80.00
                  Very good: $60.00

Marlin Glenfield 20, 25, 25M

Caliber: 22 short, long, long rifle; 22 mag. (25M)
Action: Bolt action, thumb safety
Magazine: 7-shot clip
Barrel: 22″ round, blued
Sights: Open rear, ramp front; some with scope
Stock & Forearm: Checkered walnut, semi-pistol grip stock and plain forearm; Model 25 has no checkering.
Approximate wt.: 5½ lbs.
Comments: Production on this model was from about 1966 to the early 1980's as Model 20; currently sold as Model 25. Add 15% for magnum (25M).
Estimated Value: New (retail): $108.95
                  Excellent: $ 80.00
                  Very good: $ 60.00

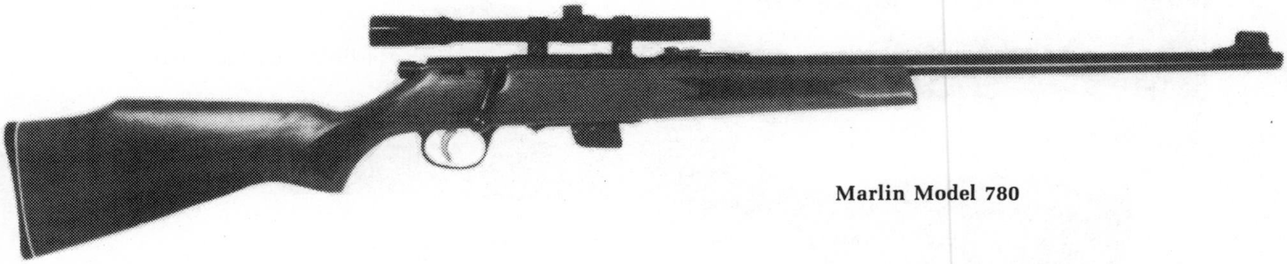

Marlin Model 780

Marlin Model 781

Marlin Model 780

Caliber: 22 short, long, long rifle
Action: Bolt action; repeating
Magazine: 7-shot clip
Barrel: Blued 22″
Sights: Adjustable rear, ramp front
Stock & Forearm: Checkered walnut Monte Carlo one-piece semi-pistol grip stock and forearm
Approximate wt.: 6 lbs.
Comments: Part of 700 series introduced about 1971.
Estimated Value: New (retail): $141.95
                  Excellent: $110.00
                  Very good: $ 85.00

Marlin Model 781

Same as Model 780 except tubular magazine; 25 shorts, 19 longs, 17 long rifles. Weighs 5½ lbs.
Estimated Value: New (retail): $147.95
                  Excellent: $110.00
                  Very good: $ 85.00

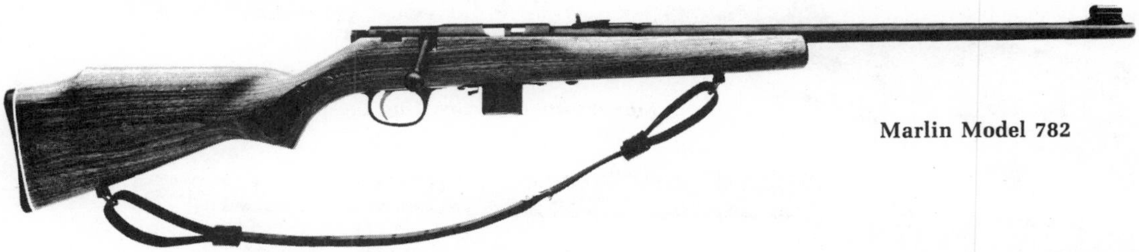

Marlin Model 782

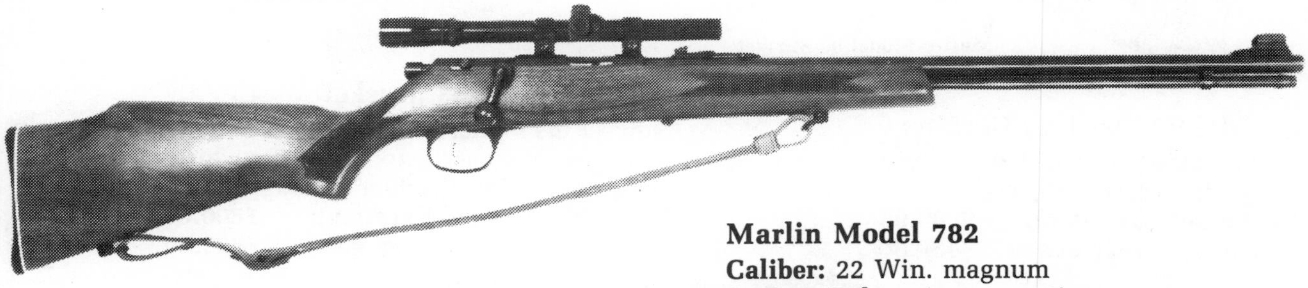

Marlin Model 783

Marlin Model 783

Same as Model 782 except 12-shot tubular magazine.
Estimated Value: New (retail): $161.95
Excellent: $120.00
Very good: $ 90.00

Marlin Model 782

Caliber: 22 Win. magnum
Action: Bolt action; repeating
Magazine: 7-shot clip
Barrel: 22″
Sights: Adjustable rear, ramp front
Stock & Forearm: Monte Carlo one-piece semi-pistol grip stock and forearm
Approximate wt.: 6 lbs.
Comments: Introduced in 1971 as one of the 700 series.
Estimated Value: New (retail): $155.95
Excellent: $115.00
Very good: $ 90.00

Marlin Model 92

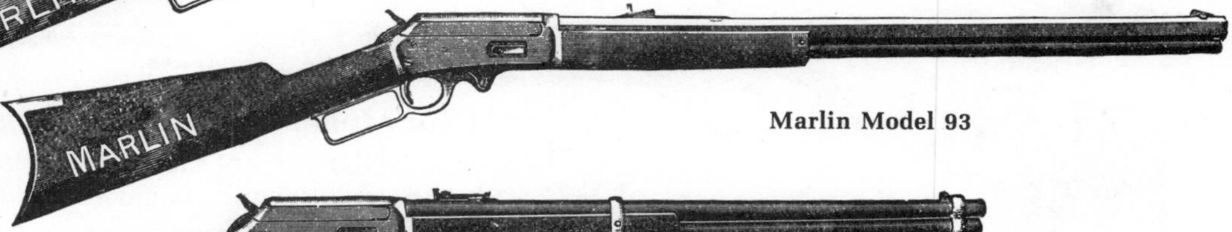

Marlin Model 93

Marlin Model 93 Carbine

Marlin Model 92

Caliber: 22 short, long, long rifle; 32 short or long, rim fire or center fire
Action: Lever action; exposed hammer
Magazine: 22 caliber: 25 shorts, 20 longs, 28 long rifles; 32 caliber: 17 shorts, 14 longs; tubular under barrel; 16″ barrel: 15 shorts, 12 longs, 10 long rifles
Barrel: 16″, 24″, 26″, 28″ round or octagon, blued
Sights: Open rear, blade front
Stock & Forearm: Plain walnut straight grip stock and forearm
Approximate wt.: 5 to 6 lbs.
Comments: Made from about 1892 to 1916. Also known as Model 1892.
Estimated Value: Excellent: $475.00
Very good: $350.00

Marlin Model 93

Caliber: 25-36 Marlin, 30-30, 32 special, 32-40, 38-55
Action: Lever action; exposed hammer; repeating
Magazine: 10-shot tubular; under barrel
Barrel: 26″-32″ round or octagon
Sights: Open rear, bead front
Stock & Forearm: Plain walnut straight grip stock and forearm
Approximate wt.: 7 to 8 lbs.
Comments: Manufactured from about 1893 until 1935. Produced in both takedown and solid frame models. Also known as Model 1893.
Estimated Value: Excellent: $600.00
Very good: $450.00

Marlin Model 93 Carbine

Basically same as the Model 93 except: produced in 30-30 and 32 special caliber only; standard carbine sights; 20″ round barrel; 7-shot magazine. Weighs between 6 and 7 lbs.
Estimated Value: Excellent: $650.00
Very good: $500.00

Marlin Model 93 Sporting Carbine

Marlin Model 93 Musket

Marlin Model 93 Sporting Carbine
Basically the same as Model 93 Carbine except the smaller magazine carries 5 shots.
Estimated Value: Excellent: $600.00
Very good: $450.00

Marlin Model 93 Musket
Same as the Model 93 except: 30″ standard barrel; equipped with a musket stock; military forearm; ramrod; angular bayonet. Production stopped about 1915.
Estimated Value: Excellent: $800.00
Very good: $600.00

Marlin Model 1894 (Current)

Marlin Model 1894C

Marlin Model 1895

Marlin Model 1895S

Marlin Model 1894C, 1894CS, 1894M
Similar to the current model 1894 except in 357 caliber; 18½″ barrel; 9-shot magazine. Introduced in 1979. 1894M is 22 WMRF.
Estimated Value: New (retail): $315.95
Excellent: $235.00
Very good: $175.00

Marlin Model 1895
Caliber: 33 WCF, 38-56, 40-65, 40-70, 40-82, 45-70
Action: Lever action; exposed hammer; repeating
Magazine: 9-shot tubular, under barrel
Barrel: 24″ octagon or round, blued
Sights: Open rear, bead front
Stock & Forearm: Walnut straight or pistol grip stock and forearm
Approximate wt.: 8 lbs.
Comments: Made in solid frame and takedown models from about 1895 to 1920.
Estimated Value: Excellent: $675.00
Very good: $520.00

Marlin Model 1894, 1894S
Caliber: 25-20, 32-20, 38-40, 44-40; current model 44 magnum (1970's to present)
Action: Lever action; exposed hammer; repeating
Magazine: 10-shot tubular, under barrel
Barrel: Round or octagon, 20″, 24″-32″; 20″ on current model
Sights: Open rear, bead front
Stock & Forearm: Plain walnut straight or pistol grip stock and forearm
Approximate wt.: 7 lbs.
Comments: Made from about 1894 to 1935 in both takedown and solid frame models. Reintroduced in the late 1970's in 44 magnum with 20″ barrel.

	Current	Early
Estimated Value: New (retail):	$315.95	
Excellent:	$235.00	$600.00
Very good:	$175.00	$450.00

Marlin Model 1895S, 1895SS
Similar to the Model 1895; introduced in the late 1970's; 45-70 gov't caliber; 22″ barrel; 4-shot magazine; swivels.
Estimated Value: New (retail): $339.95
Excellent: $255.00
Very good: $190.00

Marlin Model 1897

Marlin Model 36

Marlin Model 36 Sporting Carbine

Marlin Model 1897

Caliber: 22 short, long, long rifle
Action: Lever action; exposed hammer; repeating
Magazine: 25 shorts, 20 longs, 18 long rifles in full length; 16 shorts, 12 longs, 10 long rifles in half length; tubular under barrel
Barrel: Blued; 16", 24", 26", 28"
Sights: Open rear, bead front
Stock & Forearm: Plain walnut straight or pistol grip stock and forearm
Approximate wt.: 6 lbs.
Comments: Made from about 1897 to 1921.
Estimated Value: **Excellent:** $380.00
$\qquad$ **Very good:** $290.00

Marlin Model 36

Caliber: 30-30, 32 special
Action: Lever action; exposed hammer; repeating
Magazine: 6-shot tubular
Barrel: 20" round, blued
Sights: Open rear, bead front
Stock & Forearm: Pistol grip stock and semi-beavertail forearm; carbine barrel band
Approximate wt.: 6½ lbs.
Comments: Made from about 1936 to 1948.
Estimated Value: **Excellent:** $225.00
$\qquad$ **Very good:** $170.00

Marlin Model 36 Sporting Carbine

Same as Model 36A except weight is slightly less and barrel is 20".
Estimated Value: **Excellent:** $220.00
$\qquad$ **Very good:** $165.00

Marlin Model 36A

Marlin Model 36H-DL

Marlin Model 36A

Same as Model 36 carbine except: barrel is 24", ⅔ magazine; weighs slightly more; hooded front sight.
Estimated Value: **Excellent:** $230.00
$\qquad$ **Very good:** $175.00

Marlin Model 36H-DL

Same as Model 36A except stock are forearm are checkered and have swivels.
Estimated Value: **Excellent:** $250.00
$\qquad$ **Very good:** $190.00

Marlin Model 336C Carbine

Marlin Model 336 ER

Similar to the Model 336 C in 356 Winchester or 307 Winchester calibers; recoil pad, swivels and strap. Introduced in 1983.
Estimated Value: **New (retail):** $323.95
$\qquad$ **Excellent:** $245.00
$\qquad$ **Very good:** $180.00

Marlin Model 336C Carbine, 336CS

This is basically the same as the Model 36, with a round breech bolt and improved action. The 35 caliber Remington was introduced and the 32 Special stopped in 1963; 375 Winchester added in 1984. This gun has been produced since about 1948.
Estimated Value: **New (retail):** $295.95
$\qquad$ **Excellent:** $220.00
$\qquad$ **Very good:** $165.00

Marlin Model 336 T Texan Carbine

Marlin Model 336 Marauder

Marlin Model 336A

Marlin Model 336T Texan Carbine, 336TS

Same as Model 336C except stock is straight, 18½" barrel. It was never produced in 32 caliber, but was available from 1963 to 1967 in 44 magnum. Produced from 1953 to present.

Estimated Value: New (retail): $295.95
Excellent: $220.00
Very good: $165.00

Marlin Model 336 Marauder

Same as Model 336T except weight is slightly less and barrel is only 16¼". Produced from about 1963 to 1964.

Estimated Value: Excellent: $200.00
Very good: $150.00

Marlin Model 336A

Basically the same as Model 36A with a rounded breech bolt and improved action. Produced from about 1950 to 1963. Reintroduced in the 1970's; discontinued in early 1980's.

Estimated Value: Excellent: $200.00
Very good: $150.00

Marlin Model 336 A-DL

Marlin Model 336 Sporting Carbine

Marlin Model 336 Micro Groove Zipper

Marlin Model 336A-DL

Same as Model 336A except it has swivels and checkered stock and forearm.

Estimated Value: Excellent: $210.00
Very good: $160.00

Marlin Model 336 Sporting Carbine

Same as Model 336A except weight is slightly less and barrel is 20".

Estimated Value: Excellent: $190.00
Very good: $140.00

Marlin Model 336 Micro Groove Zipper

Caliber 219 Zipper; otherwise same rifle as Model 336A.

Estimated Value: Excellent: $250.00
Very good: $190.00

Marlin Model 336 Zane Gray Century

Same basic rifle as Model 336A except: 22" barrel is octagon; brass fore-end cap; brass buttplate and medallion in receiver. Only 10,000 were produced in 1972.

Estimated Value: Excellent: $220.00
Very good: $160.00

Marlin Model 336 Zane Grey Century

Marlin Model 39

Marlin Model 39A

Marlin Model 39A Mountie

Marlin Model 39M

Marlin Model 39M Golden Mountie

Marlin Model 39

Caliber: 22 short, long, long rifle
Action: Lever action; exposed hammer; repeating; take-down type
Magazine: 25 shorts, 20 longs, 18 long rifles; tubular under barrel
Barrel: 24″ octagon
Sights: Bead front, open adjustable rear
Stock & Forearm: Plain pistol grip stock and forearm
Approximate wt.: 6½ lbs.
Comments: Made from about 1938 to 1958.
Estimated Value: Excellent: $260.00
Very good: $190.00

Marlin Model 39A

Same as Model 39 except: round barrel; heavier stock; semi-beavertail forearm; weight 6½ lbs. Began production about 1938 and was discontinued in 1957. Replaced by Golden 39A.
Estimated Value: Excellent: $175.00
Very good: $130.00

Marlin Model 39M

Similar to 39A with 20″ barrel; less capacity in magazine; straight grip stock.
Estimated Value: Excellent: $160.00
Very good: $120.00

Marlin Model 39A Mountie

Same as the Model 39 except: straight grip, lighter stock with trim forearm; weight is 6 to 6½ lbs.; 20″ barrel; produced from 1950's to 1960.
Estimated Value: Excellent: $150.00
Very good: $115.00

Marlin Model 39M Golden Mountie

Same gun as Model 39A Mountie except: gold plated trigger; 20″ barrel; weight 6 lbs.; magazine capacity 21 shorts, 16 longs or 15 long rifles. Produced from 1950's to present.
Estimated Value: New (retail): $281.95
Excellent: $210.00
Very good: $160.00

Marlin Model Golden 39A

Caliber: 22 short, long, long rifle
Action: Lever-action; exposed hammer; takedown type; gold plated trigger
Magazine: 26 shorts, 21 long rifles; tubular under barrel
Barrel: 24″ micro-groove round barrel
Sights: Bead front with removable hood; adjustable folding semi-buckhorn rear
Stock & Forearm: Walnut plain pistol grip stock and forearm; steel cap on end
Approximate wt.: 6¾ lbs.
Comments: Made from about 1960 to date; equipped with sling swivels.
Estimated Value: New (retail): $281.95
Excellent: $210.00
Very good: $160.00

Marlin 39A Article II

A commemorative model of the Model 39A produced for the NRA Centennial in 1971. It has these special features: 24″ octagon barrel; walnut pistol grip stock and forearm; brass inlays as in Model 39 Century LTD.
Estimated Value: Excellent: $225.00
Very good: $170.00

Marlin Model 39M Article II Carbine

Same gun as 39A Article II rifle except: straight grip stock; square lever; 20″ octagon barrel; magazine capacity 21 shorts, 16 longs, 15 long rifles.
Estimated Value: Excellent: $230.00
Very good: $175.00

Marlin 39 Century LTD.

A commemorative model based on Model 39A. Made for the Marlin Centennial in 1970, it has these special features: square lever; 20″ octagon barrel; brass inlaid receiver; nameplate in stock and brass buttplate; walnut straight stock and forearm.
Estimated Value: Excellent: $235.00
Very good: $180.00

Marlin Model 444, 444S, 444SS

Caliber: 444 Marlin
Action: Action-lever; repeating
Magazine: 4-shot tubular under barrel
Barrel: Blued; 22″ micro-groove
Sights: Folding open rear, hooded ramp front
Stock & Forearm: Monte Carlo straight or pistol grip stock; carbine-type forearm; barrel band; swivels
Approximate wt.: 7½ lbs.
Comments: Made from about 1965 to present. Currently called 444SS.
Estimated Value: New (retail): $339.95
Excellent: $255.00
Very good: $190.00

Marlin Model Golden 39A

Marlin Model 39 Century LTD

Marlin 39A Article II

Marlin Model 39M Article II Carbine

Marlin Model 444

Marlin Glenfield Model 30

Caliber: 30-30 Win.
Action: Lever-action; repeating
Magazine: 6-shot tubular
Barrel: Blued; 20″ round
Sights: Adjustable rear, bead front
Stock & Forearm: Walnut, plain or checkered; semi-pistol grip stock and forearm
Approximate wt.: 7 lbs.
Comments: Made from about 1966 to the late 1970's.
Estimated Value: Excellent: $180.00
Very good: $135.00

Marlin Glenfield Model 30 GT

Similar to the Glenfield 30 with a straight grip stock and 18½″ barrel. Made from the late 1970's to early 1980's.
Estimated Value: Excellent: $175.00
Very good: $130.00

Marlin Glenfield Model 30A, Marlin 30AS

Similar to the Glenfield 30. Made from the late 1970's to present. Plain stock on the 30AS.
Estimated Value: New (retail): $282.95
Excellent: $210.00
Very good: $160.00

Marlin Model 375

Caliber: 375 Win.
Action: Lever-action; side ejection; repeating
Magazine: 5-shot tubular
Barrel: 20″ round
Sights: Adjustable semi-buckhorn rear, ramp front with brass bead
Stock & Forearm: Plain walnut pistol grip stock and forearm with fluted comb; swivels
Approximate wt.: 6¾ lbs.
Comments: Produced from 1980 to mid 1980's.
Estimated Value: Excellent: $230.00
Very good: $170.00

Marlin Glenfield Model 30

Marlin Model 375

Marlin Model 57

Marlin Model 57

Caliber: 22 short, long, long rifle
Action: Lever-action; repeating
Magazine: Tubular under barrel; 19 long rifles, 21 longs, 27 shorts
Barrel: Blued; 22″ round
Sights: Open rear, hooded ramp front
Stock & Forearm: Plain Monte Carlo pistol grip stock and forearm
Approximate wt.: 6¼ lbs.
Comments: Made from about 1959 to 1965.
Estimated Value: Excellent: $125.00
Very good: $ 95.00

Marlin Model 56 Levermatic

Caliber: 22 short, long, long rifle
Action: Lever-action; repeating
Magazine: 8-shot clip
Barrel: Blued; 22″ round
Sights: Open rear, hooded ramp front
Stock & Forearm: Monte Carlo pistol grip stock and forearm
Approximate wt.: 5¾ lbs.
Comments: Similar to Model 57, produced from about 1955 to 1965.
Estimated Value: Excellent: $110.00
Very good: $ 85.00

Marlin Model 57M Levermatic

Caliber: 22 Win. mag.
Action: Lever-action; repeating
Magazine: 15-shot tubular; under barrel
Barrel: 24″ round
Sights: Open rear, hooded ramp front
Stock & Forearm: Monte Carlo pistol grip stock and forearm
Approximate wt.: 6¼ lbs.
Comments: Similar to Model 57; produced from about 1960 to 1969.
Estimated Value: Excellent: $120.00
Very good: $ 90.00

Marlin Model 62 Levermatic

Caliber: 256 mag. (1963 to 1966); 30 carbine (1966-1969)
Action: Lever-action; repeating
Magazine: 4-shot clip
Barrel: Blued; 23″ round
Sights: Open rear; hooded ramp front
Stock & Forearm: Monte Carlo pistol grip stock and forearm
Approximate wt.: 7 lbs.
Comments: Made from about 1963 to 1969.
Estimated Value: Excellent: $150.00
Very good: $110.00

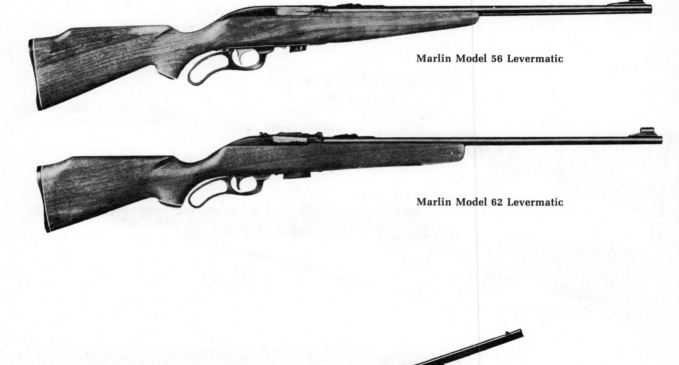

Marlin Model 56 Levermatic

Marlin Model 62 Levermatic

Marlin Model 18 Baby Slide Action

Marlin Model 18 Baby Slide Action

Caliber: 22 short, long, long rifle
Action: Slide action; exposed hammer; repeating
Magazine: Tubular under barrel; 15 shorts, 12 longs, 10 long rifles
Barrel: Blued; 20″ round or octagon
Sights: Open rear, bead front
Stock & Forearm: Plain walnut straight grip stock and slide handle
Approximate wt.: 3½ to 4 lbs.
Comments: Production began on this model about 1906 but was discontinued three years later.
Estimated Value: Excellent: $275.00
Very good: $210.00

Marlin Model 20

Marlin Model 29

Marlin Model 20 or 20 S

Caliber: 22 short, long, long rifle
Action: Slide action; exposed hammer; repeating
Magazine: 25 shorts, 20 longs, 18 long rifles in full length; 15 shorts, 12 longs, 10 long rifles in half length; tubular, under barrel
Barrel: Blued; 24″ octagon
Sights: Open rear, bead front
Stock & Forearm: Plain walnut straight grip stock and grooves slide handle
Approximate wt.: 5 lbs.
Comments: This rifle was produced from about 1907 in takedown model and known as Model 20 S after 1920. Discontinued about 1922.
Estimated Value: **Excellent:** $280.00
Very good: $215.00

Marlin Model 29

Similar to Model 20 except: round 23″ barrel; weighs about 5¾ lbs.; magazine available in half length only; produced from about 1913 to 1916.
Estimated Value: **Excellent:** $290.00
Very good: $225.00

Marlin Model 25

Marlin Model 27

Marlin Model 27 S

Marlin Model 25

Caliber: 22 short and 22 CB caps only
Action: Slide action; exposed hammer; repeating
Magazine: 15-shot tubular, under barrel
Barrel: Blued; 23″ octagon
Sights: Open rear, bead front
Stock & Forearm: Plain walnut straight grip stock and slide handle
Approximate wt.: 4 lbs.
Comments: Production on this takedown model began in 1909 and was stopped one year later.
Estimated Value: **Excellent:** $285.00
Very good: $220.00

Marlin Model 27

Caliber: 25-20, 32-20
Action: Slide action; exposed hammer; repeating
Magazine: 6-shot, ⅔ tubular, under barrel
Barrel: Blued; 24″ octagon
Sights: Open rear, bead front
Stock & Forearm: Plain walnut straight grip stock and grooved slide handle
Approximate wt.: 5¾ lbs.
Comments: This takedown model was produced from about 1910 to 1915.
Estimated Value: **Excellent:** $290.00
Very good: $225.00

Marlin Model 27 S

Same as the Model 27 except: caliber 25 Stevens RF; round barrel; produced from about 1920 to 1932.
Estimated Value: **Excellent:** $250.00
Very good: $190.00

Marlin Model 32

Caliber: 22 short, long, long rifle
Action: Slide action; concealed hammer; repeating
Magazine: 25 shorts, 20 longs, 18 long rifles in full length; 15 shorts, 12 longs, 10 long rifles in ⅔ length; tubular, under barrel
Barrel: Blued; 24″ octagon
Sights: Open rear, bead front
Stock & Forearm: Walnut pistol grip stock and grooved slide handle
Approximate wt.: 5½ lbs.
Comments: Takedown model produced from about 1914 for one year.
Estimated Value: **Excellent:**   **$300.00**
                  Very good: **$225.00**

Marlin Model 38

Caliber: 22 short, long, long rifle
Action: Slide action; concealed hammer; repeating
Magazine: 15 shorts, 12 longs, 10 long rifles, ⅔ tubular, under barrel
Barrel: Blued; 24″, octagon or round
Sights: Open rear, bead front
Stock & Forearm: Plain pistol grip stock and grooved slide handle
Approximate wt.: 5½ lbs.
Comments: Production began about 1921 on this takedown model and was discontinued about 1930.
Estimated Value: **Excellent:**   **$285.00**
                  Very good: **$215.00**

Marlin Model 32

Marlin Model 38

Marlin Model 37

Marlin Model 47

Marlin Model 47

Basically same as Model 37, used as a bonus give-away with purchase of Marlin Stocks. Discontinued in 1931 after six years production.
Estimated Value: **Excellent:**   **$400.00**
                  Very good: **$300.00**

Marlin Model 37

Caliber: 22 short, long, long rifle
Action: Slide action; exposed hammer; repeating
Magazine: 25 shorts, 20 longs, 18 long rifles; tubular, under barrel
Barrel: 24″ round
Sights: Open rear, bead front
Stock & Forearm: Walnut pistol grip stock and forearm
Approximate wt.: 5 lbs.
Comments: This rifle was produced from about 1923 until 1933; takedown model.
Estimated Value: **Excellent:**   **$250.00**
                  Very good: **$190.00**

Marlin Model 50

Marlin Model A-1

Marlin Model A-1E

Marlin Model A-1

Caliber: 22 long rifle
Action: Semi-automatic; repeating
Magazine: 6-shot detachable box
Barrel: Blued 24″
Sights: Open rear, bead front
Stock & Forearm: Plain pistol grip stock and forearm
Approximate wt.: 6 lbs.
Comments: Takedown model made from about 1935 to 1946.
Estimated Value: **Excellent:**   **$90.00**
                       Very good: **$70.00**

Marlin Model A-1E

Same as Model A-1 except hooded front sight; peep rear sight.
Estimated Value: **Excellent:**   **$95.00**
                       Very good: **$75.00**

Model A-1C

An improved Model A-1; semi-beavertail forearm. Produced from about 1940 for six years.
Estimated Value: **Excellent:**   **$90.00**
                       Very good: **$70.00**

Marlin Model A-1DL

Same as A-1C except; swivels; hooded front sight; peep rear sight.
Estimated Value: **Excellent:**   **$95.00**
                       Very good: **$75.00**

Marlin Model 50

Caliber: 22 long rifle
Action: Semi-automatic; takedown model; repeating
Magazine: 6-shot detachable box
Barrel: Blued 24″ round
Sights: Open rear, bead front
Stock & Forearm: Plain pistol grip stock and grooved forearm
Approximate wt.: 6 lbs.
Comments: Production began about 1931 and ended three years later.
Estimated Value: **Excellent:**   **$85.00**
                       Very good: **$65.00**

Marlin Model 50 E

Same as Model 50 except hooded front sight and peep rear sight.
Estimated Value: **Excellent:**   **$90.00**
                       Very good: **$70.00**

Marlin Model 88-C

Caliber: 22 long rifle
Action: Semi-automatic
Magazine: 14-shot tubular, in stock
Barrel: Blued 24″ round
Sights: Open rear, hooded front
Stock & Forearm: Pistol grip stock and forearm
Approximate wt.: 6¾ lbs.
Comments: A takedown model produced from about 1947 to 1956.
Estimated Value: **Excellent:** **$80.00**
Very good: **$60.00**

Marlin Model 88 DL

Same as Model 88-C except checkered stock, swivels and peep sight on receiver. Produced for three years beginning about 1953.
Estimated Value: **Excellent:** **$85.00**
Very good: **$65.00**

Marlin Model 89-C

Same as Model 88-C except magazine is 7 or 12-shot clip and it has a tapered forearm. Produced from about 1950 to 1961.
Estimated Value: **Excellent:** **$75.00**
Very good: **$55.00**

Marlin Model 89-DL

Same rifle as Model 89-C except it has swivels and peep sight on receiver.
Estimated Value: **Excellent:** **$80.00**
Very good: **$60.00**

Marlin Model 98

Caliber: 22 long rifle
Action: Semi-automatic
Magazine: 15-shot tubular
Barrel: Blued 22″ round
Sights: Open rear, hooded ramp front
Stock & Forearm: Walnut Monte Carlo with cheekpiece
Approximate wt.: 6¾ lbs.
Comments: A solid frame rifle produced from about 1950 to 1959.
Estimated Value: **Excellent:** **$85.00**
Very good: **$65.00**

Marlin Model 99

Caliber: 22 long rifle
Action: Semi-automatic
Magazine: 18-shot tubular
Barrel: Blued 22″ round
Sights: Open rear, hooded ramp front
Stock & Forearm: Plain pistol grip stock and forearm
Approximate wt.: 5½ lbs.
Comments: Made from about 1959 until 1961.
Estimated Value: **Excellent:** **$75.00**
Very good: **$55.00**

Marlin Model 88-C

Marlin Model 88 DL

Marlin Model 89-C

Marlin Model 98

Marlin Model 99C

Marlin Model 99DL

Marlin Glenfield Model 99G

Marlin Model 989

Marlin Glenfield Model 989G

Marlin Model 99C

Same as Model 99 except Monte Carlo stock (some are checkered); gold plated trigger; grooved receiver. Produced from 1962 to late 1970's.

Estimated Value: **Excellent:** **$70.00**
Very good: **$55.00**

Marlin Model 99DL

Same as Model 99C except it has swivels and jeweled breech bolt. Made for five years beginning about 1960.

Estimated Value: **Excellent:** **$80.00**
Very good: **$65.00**

Marlin Glenfield Model 99G

Basically the same as Model 99 with a plain stock. Produced from about 1963 to 1965.

Estimated Value: **Excellent:** **$60.00**
Very good: **$45.00**

Marlin Model 989

Caliber: 22 long rifle only
Action: Semi-automatic
Magazine: 7-shot clip
Barrel: Blued 22″ round
Sights: Open rear, hooded ramp front
Stock & Forearm: Monte Carlo pistol grip stock and forearm
Approximate wt.: 5½ lbs.
Comments: Produced for four years beginning in 1962.

Estimated Value: **Excellent:** **$75.00**
Very good: **$55.00**

Marlin Glenfield Model 989G

Basically same as Marlin Model 989 except plain stock and bead front sight. Produced from about 1962 to 1964.

Estimated Value: **Excellent:** **$60.00**
Very good: **$45.00**

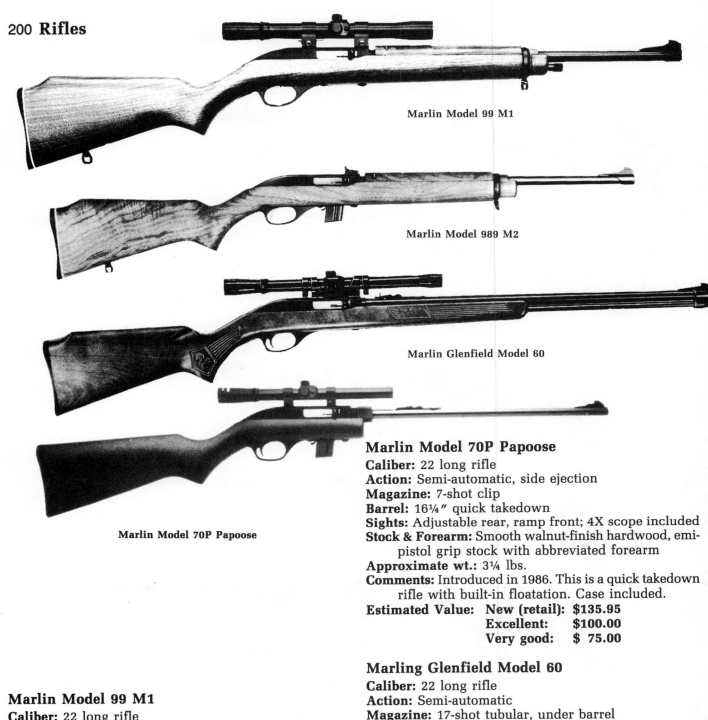

Marlin Model 99 M1

Marlin Model 989 M2

Marlin Glenfield Model 60

Marlin Model 70P Papoose

Marlin Model 70P Papoose

Caliber: 22 long rifle
Action: Semi-automatic, side ejection
Magazine: 7-shot clip
Barrel: 16¼" quick takedown
Sights: Adjustable rear, ramp front; 4X scope included
Stock & Forearm: Smooth walnut-finish hardwood, semi-pistol grip stock with abbreviated forearm
Approximate wt.: 3¼ lbs.
Comments: Introduced in 1986. This is a quick takedown rifle with built-in floatation. Case included.
Estimated Value: New (retail): $135.95
          Excellent: $100.00
          Very good: $ 75.00

Marling Glenfield Model 60

Caliber: 22 long rifle
Action: Semi-automatic
Magazine: 17-shot tubular, under barrel
Barrel: Blued 22" round
Sights: Open rear, ramp front; some with scope
Stock & Forearm: Checkered or smooth hardwood semi-pistol grip stock and forearm; or Monte Carlo.
Approximate wt.: 5½ lbs.
Comments: In production since about 1966. Price includes scope.
Estimated Value: New (retail): $109.95
          Excellent: $ 85.00
          Very good: $ 65.00

Marlin Model 99 M1

Caliber: 22 long rifle
Action: Semi-automatic
Magazine: 9-shot tubular
Barrel: Blued 18" micro-groove
Sights: Open rear, ramp front (military)
Stock & Forearm: Carbine stock, hand guard and barrel band; swivels
Approximate wt.: 4½ lbs.
Comments: Styled after the U.S. 30 M1 Carbine; in production from about 1966 to the late 1970's.
Estimated Value: Excellent: $75.00
          Very good: $60.00

Marlin Model 989 M2

Same rifle as the Model 99 M1 except it has a 7-shot clip magazine.
Estimated Value: Excellent: $80.00
          Very good: $65.00

Marlin Model 75C

Similar to the Model 60 except: 13-shot magazine, 18" barrel.
Estimated Value: New (retail): $109.95
          Excellent: $ 80.00
          Very good: $ 60.00

Marlin Model 49

Marlin Model 49 DL

Marlin Glenfield Model 70

Marlin Glenfield Model 70 Carbine

Caliber: 22 long rifle
Action: Semi-automatic
Magazine: 7-shot clip
Barrel: Blued 18″ round
Sights: Open rear, ramp front
Stock & Forearm: Checkered walnut Monte Carlo stock and plain forearm; barrel band; swivels
Approximate wt.: 5½ lbs.
Comments: Production from about 1966 to present.
Estimated Value: New (retail): $109.95
    Excellent: $ 85.00
    Very good: $ 65.00

Marlin Model 49

Caliber: 22 long rifle
Action: Semi-automatic
Magazine: 18-shot tubular
Barrel: Blued 22″ round
Sights: Adjustable open rear, ramp front
Stock & Forearm: Monte Carlo pistol grip stock and forearm
Approximate wt.: 5½ lbs.
Comments: Made in the late 1960's and 1970's.
Estimated Value: Excellent: $70.00
    Very good: $55.00

Marlin Model 49 DL

Same as the Model 49 except checkered stock and forearm and gold plated trigger. Production began about 1971; ended in late 1970's.
Estimated Value: Excellent: $75.00
    Very good: $60.00

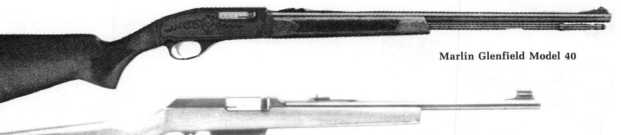

Marlin Glenfield Model 40

Marlin Model 9 Camp Carbine

Marlin Model 9 Camp Carbine

Caliber: 9mm
Action: Semi-automatic; manual bolt hold-open, automatic last-shot bolt hold-open
Magazine: 12-shot clip; 20-shot clip available
Barrel: 16½″ round, blued
Sights: Adjustable rear, ramp front with brass head forearm
Approximate wt.: 6¾ lbs.
Comments: Introduced in 1985.
Estimated Value: New (retail): $259.95
    Excellent: $195.00
    Very good: $145.00

Marlin Glenfield Model 40

Caliber: 22 long rifle
Action: Semi-automatic; hammerless; side ejection; repeating
Magazine: 18-shot tubular
Barrel: 22″
Sights: Adjustable open rear, ramp front
Stock & Forearm: Checkered hardwood Monte Carlo semi-pistol grip stock and forearm
Approximate wt.: 5½ lbs.
Comments: Produce in the late 1970's.
Estimated Value: Excellent: $70.00
    Very good: $55.00

Marlin Model 45

Similar to the Model 9 in 45ACP caliber; 7-shot clip. Introduced in 1986.
Estimated Value: New (retail): $259.95
    Excellent: $195.00
    Very good: $145.00

Marlin Model 990

Marlin Model 995

Marlin Model 990
Caliber: 22 long rifle
Action: Semi-automatic; repeating; side ejection
Magazine: 18-shot tubular
Barrel: 22″ round
Sights: Adjustable folding semi-buckhorn rear, ramp front with brass bead
Stock & Forearm: Checkered walnut Monte Carlo one-piece pistol grip stock and forearm
Approximate wt.: 5½ lbs.
Comments: Introduced in the late 1970's.
Estimated Value: New (retail): $147.95
Excellent: $105.00
Very good: $ 80.00

Marlin Model 995
Similar to the Model 990 with a 7-shot clip magazine and 18″ barrel.
Estimated Value: New (retail): $137.95
Excellent: $105.00
Very good: $ 80.00

Mauser

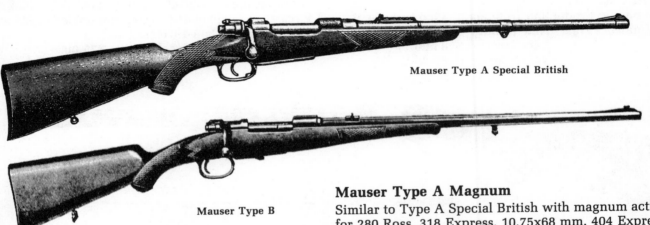

Mauser Type A Special British

Mauser Type B

Mauser Type A Special British
Caliber: 30-06, 7x57, 8x60, 9x57, 9.3x62 mm
Action: Bolt action; repeating
Magazine: 5-shot box
Barrel: Blued 23½″, octagon or round
Sights: Express rear, hooded ramp front
Stock & Forearm: Checkered walnut one-piece pistol grip stock and tapered forearm; swivels
Approximate wt.: 7¼ lbs.
Comments: Made from about 1910 to 1938.
Estimated Value: Excellent: $650.00
Very good: $500.00

Mauser Type A Short Model
Similar to Type A Special British with 21½″ barrel and a short action.
Estimated Value: Excellent: $625.00
Very good: $480.00

Mauser Type A Magnum
Similar to Type A Special British with magnum action for 280 Ross, 318 Express, 10.75x68 mm, 404 Express.
Estimated Value: Excellent: $700.00
Very good: $540.00

Mauser Type B
Caliber: 30-06, 7x57, 8x57, 8x60, 9.3x62, 10.75x68
Action: Bolt action; repeating
Magazine: 5-shot box
Barrel: Blued 23½″
Sights: Leaf rear, ramp front
Stock & Forearm: Checkered walnut one-piece pistol grip stock and lipped forearm; swivels
Approximate wt.: 7½ lbs.
Comments: Made from about 1910 to 1940.
Estimated Value: Excellent: $625.00
Very good: $470.00

Mauser Type K
Similar to Type B with 21½″ barrel and short action.
Estimated Value: Excellent: $600.00
Very good: $450.00

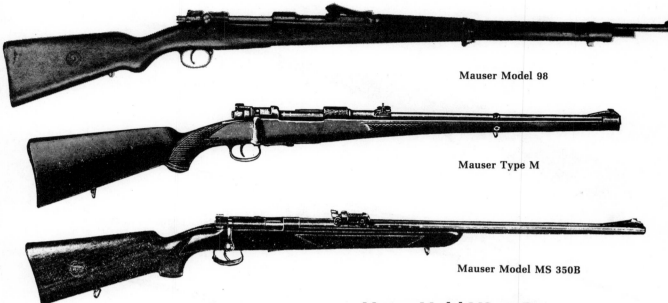

Mauser Model 98

Mauser Type M

Mauser Model MS 350B

Mauser Model 98

Caliber: 7mm, 7.9mm
Action: Bolt action; repeating
Magazine: 5-shot box
Barrel: Blued 23½″
Sights: Adjustable rear, blade front
Stock & Forearm: Walnut one-piece semi-pistol grip stock and fluted forearm; barrel band
Approximate wt.: 7½ lbs.
Comments: Made from about 1920 to 1938.
Estimated Value: Excellent: $525.00
Very good: $390.00

Mauser Type M

Caliber: 30-06, 6.5x54, 7x57, 8x52, 8x60, 9x57
Action: Bolt action; repeating
Magazine: 5-shot box
Barrel: Blued 19¾″
Sights: 3 leaf rear, ramp front
Stock & Forearm: Checkered walnut one-piece pistol grip stock and full-length forearm; swivels
Approximate wt.: 6½ lbs.
Comments: Made from about 1910 to 1940.
Estimated Value: Excellent: $650.00
Very good: $490.00

Mauser Type S

Caliber: 6.5x54, 7x57, 8x51, 8x60, 9x57
Action: Bolt action; repeating
Magazine: 5-shot box
Barrel: Blued 19¾″
Sights: 3 leaf rear, ramp front
Stock & Forearm: Checkered walnut one-piece pistol grip stock and lipped full-length forearm; swivels
Approximate wt.: 6½ lbs.
Comments: Made from from about 1910 to 1940.
Estimated Value: Excellent: $600.00
Very good: $450.00

Mauser Model MS 350B

Caliber: 22 long rifle
Action: Bolt action; repeating
Magazine: 5-shot box
Barrel: Blued 27½″
Sights: Micrometer rear, ramp front
Stock & Forearm: Match-type; checkered pistol grip; swivels
Approximate wt.: 8 lbs.
Comments: Made from the mid 1920's to mid 1930's.
Estimated Value: Excellent: $500.00
Very good: $375.00

Mauser Model ES 350

Similar to MS 350B with different sights and 26¾″ barrel. Made from the mid to late 1930's. Single shot.
Estimated Value: Excellent: $450.00
Very good: $340.00

Mauser Model ES 350B

Similar to MS 350B in single shot. Target sights.
Estimated Value: Excellent: $400.00
Very good: $300.00

Mauser Model ES 340

Caliber: 22 long rifle
Action: Bolt action; single shot
Magazine: None
Barrel: Blued 25½″
Sights: Tangent curve rear, ramp front
Stock & Forearm: Checkered walnut one-piece pistol grip stock and forearm; swivels
Approximate wt.: 6½ lbs.
Comments: Made from the early 1920's to mid 1930's.
Estimated Value: Excellent: $300.00
Very good: $225.00

Mauser Model ES 340B

Similar to the ES 340 with a 26¾″ barrel. Made from the mid to late 1930's.
Estimated Value: Excellent: $320.00
Very good: $240.00

Mauser Model MS 420

Mauser Model MS 420B

Mauser Model MM 410

Mauser Model EL 320

Similar to ES 340 with a 23½″ barrel, adjustable rear sight and bead front sight. Made from the late 1920's to mid 1930's.

| Estimated Value: | Excellent: | $330.00 |
| | Very good: | $250.00 |

Mauser Model MS 420

Caliber: 22 long rifle
Action: Bolt action; repeating
Magazine: 5-shot detachable box
Barrel: Blued 25½″
Sights: Tangent curve rear, ramp front
Stock & Forearm: Checkered walnut one-piece pistol grip stock and forearm; swivels
Approximate wt.: 6½ lbs.
Comments: Made from the mid 1920's to mid 1930's.

| Estimated Value: | Excellent: | $350.00 |
| | Very good: | $260.00 |

Mauser Model MS 420B

Similar to MS 420 with better wood. Made from the mid to late 1930's.

| Estimated Value: | Excellent: | $450.00 |
| | Very good: | $340.00 |

Mauser Model MM 410

Caliber: 22 long rifle
Action: Bolt action; repeating
Magazine: 5-shot detachable box
Barrel: Blued 23½″
Sights: Tangent curve rear, ramp front
Stock & Forearm: Checkered one-piece pistol grip stock and forearm; swivels
Approximate wt.: 6½ lbs.
Comments: Made from the mid 1920's to mid 1930's.

| Estimated Value: | Excellent: | $350.00 |
| | Very good: | $260.00 |

Mauser Model MM 410 B

Similar to MM 410 except lighter weight model. Made from mid to late 1930's.

| Estimated Value: | Excellent: | $400.00 |
| | Very good: | $300.00 |

Mauser Model DSM 34

Similar to the 98 in appearance, in 22 long rifle with a 26″ barrel. Made from the mid 1930's to late 1930's. Single shot.

| Estimated Value: | Excellent: | $425.00 |
| | Very good: | $320.00 |

Mauser Model KKW

Similar to DSM 34. Made from the mid to late 1930's.

| Estimated Value: | Excellent: | $400.00 |
| | Very good: | $300.00 |

Mauser Model 2000

Mauser 660 Safari

Mauser 3000

Mauser Varminter 10

Mauser Model 2000

Caliber: 270 Win., 308 Win., 30-06
Action: Bolt action; repeating; adjustable trigger
Magazine: 5-shot box; hinged floor plate
Barrel: 24″ Krupp steel
Sights: Folding leaf rear, hooded ramp front
Stock & Forearm: Checkered walnut Monte Carlo one-piece pistol grip stock and forearm; swivels; cheekpiece
Approximate wt.: 7½ lbs.
Comments: Made from the late 1960's to early 1970's.
Estimated Value: **Excellent:** $350.00
 Very good: $260.00

Mauser Model 660

Caliber: 243, 25-06, 270, 308, 30-06, 7x57, 7mm
Action: Short bolt action; repeating
Magazine: 5-shot box
Barrel: Blued 24″
Sights: None
Stock & Forearm: Checkered walnut Monte Carlo one-piece pistol grip stock and forearm; swivels; recoil pad
Approximate wt.: 7 lbs.
Comments: Made in the early 1970's.
Estimated Value: **Excellent:** $650.00
 Very good: $490.00

Mauser Model 660 Safari

Similar to 660 except: magnum calibers; 28″ barrel; express rear sight and ramp front sight; calibers 458 Win., 375 H&H, 338 Win., and 7mm Rem.; approximate weight 9 lbs.
Estimated Value: **Excellent:** $700.00
 Very good: $525.00

Mauser Model 3000

Caliber: 243, 270, 30-06, 308, 375 mag., 7mm mag.
Action: Bolt action; repeating
Magazine: 5-shot box
Barrel: 22″, 26″ magnum
Sights: None
Stock & Forearm: Checkered walnut Monte Carlo one-piece pistol grip stock and forearm; recoil pad; swivels
Approximate wt.: 7 lbs.
Comments: Made from the early 1970's to present. No longer available in the U.S.
Estimated Value: **Excellent:** $400.00
 Very good: $300.00

Mauser Varminter 10

Caliber: 22-250
Action: Bolt action; repeating
Magazine: 5-shot box
Barrel: Blued 24″, heavy
Sights: None
Stock & Forearm: Checkered walnut Monte Carlo one-piece pistol grip stock and forearm
Approximate wt.: 8 lbs.
Comments: Made from early 1970's to present. No longer available in U.S.
Estimated Value: **Excellent:** $375.00
 Very good: $280.00

Mauser Model 66S

Caliber: 243, 6.5x57, 270, 7x64, 30-06, 308, 5.6x61 V.H. mag., 6.5x68 mag., 7mm Rem. mag., 7mm V.H. mag., 8x68S mag., 300 Win. mag., 300 Weath. mag., 9.3x62 mag., 9.3x64 mag.
Action: Mauser telescopic short bolt action; repeating
Magazine: 5-shot box
Barrel: Blued 21″, 24″, 26″; interchangeable barrels available
Sights: Adjustable rear, hooded ramp front
Stock & Forearm: Select European walnut, checkered Monte Carlo one-piece pistol grip stock and forearm; rosewood tip at fore-end and pistol grip; recoil pad; swivels; full length forearm available
Approximate wt.: 7 lbs.
Comments: Add $100.00 for 21″ or 26″ barrel or full length forearm.
Estimated Value: New (retail): $1,250.00
Excellent: $ 940.00
Very good: $ 710.00

Mauser Model 66SM

Similar to the Model 66S with lipped forearm (no rosewood grip) and internal alterations. Add $100.00 for 21″ or 26″ barrel or full length forearm.
Estimated Value: New (retail): $1,545.00
Excellent: $1,160.00
Very good: $ 870.00

Mauser Model 66SL

Similar to the Model 66SM with select walnut stock and forearm. Add $1,000.00 for Diplomat Model with custom engraving.
Estimated Value: New (retail): $1,822.00
Excellent: $1,370.00
Very good: $1,025.00

Mauser Model 66S Big Game

Similar to the Model 66S in 375 H&H or 458 Win. magnum caliber; 26″ barrel; fold down rear sight; weight about 10 lbs.
Estimated Value: New (retail): $1,597.00
Excellent: $1,200.00
Very good: $ 900.00

Mauser Model 77

Caliber: 243 Win., 270 Win., 308 Win., 30-06, 6.5x57, 7x64, 7mm Rem. mag., 6.5x68 mag., 300 Win. mag., 9.3x62 mag., 8x68S mag.
Action: Mauser short bolt action; repeating
Magazine: 3-shot clip
Barrel: Blued; 20″, 24″, 26″
Sights: Adjustable rear, hooded ramp front
Stock & Forearm: Checkered walnut one-piece pistol grip stock and lipped forearm; full length forearm available; recoil pad; swivels
Approximate wt.: 7½ lbs.
Comments: Introduced in the early 1980's. Add $100.00 for 20″ or 26″ barrel or full length forearm.
Estimated Value: New (retail): $1,220.00
Excellent: $ 915.00
Very good: $ 685.00

Mauser Model 77 DJV Sportsman

Similar to the Model 77 with stippled stock and forearm; no sights.
Estimated Value: New (retail): $1,530.00
Excellent: $1,150.00
Very good: $ 860.00

Mauser Model 77 Big Game

Similar to the Model 77 in 375 H&H magnum caliber; 26″ barrel.
Estimated Value: New (retail): $1,427.00
Excellent: $1,070.00
Very good: $ 800.00

Military, Argentine

Argentine M 1891 Mauser

Argentine Model 1891 Mauser

Caliber: 7x65mm rimless
Action: Manually-operated bolt action; straight bolt handle
Magazine: 5-shot single column box
Barrel: 29″ round barrel; cleaning rod in forearm
Sights: Barley corn front; rear adjustable for elevation
Stock & Forearm: Military-type one-piece straight grip stock and full forearm; bayonet lug; two barrel bands
Approximate wt.: 8½ lbs.
Comments: Similar to 7.65mm M1890 Turkish Mauser; obsolete.
Estimated Value: Very good: $125.00
Good: $ 90.00

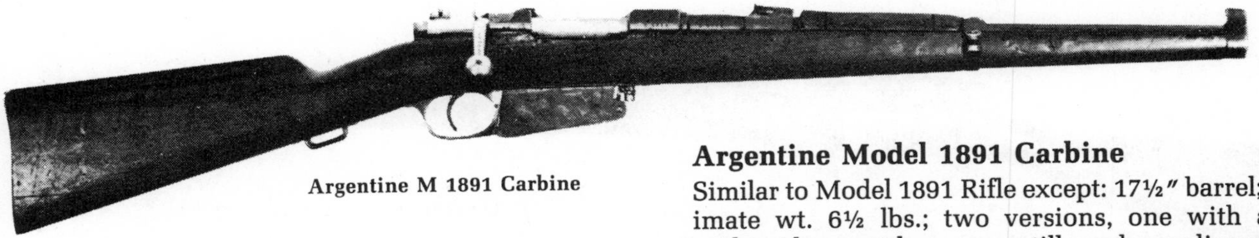

Argentine M 1891 Carbine

Argentine Model 1891 Carbine
Similar to Model 1891 Rifle except: 17½″ barrel; approximate wt. 6½ lbs.; two versions, one with and one without bayonet lug; some still used as police weapons.
Estimated Value: Excellent: $120.00
Very good: $ 90.00

Argentine M 1909 Mauser

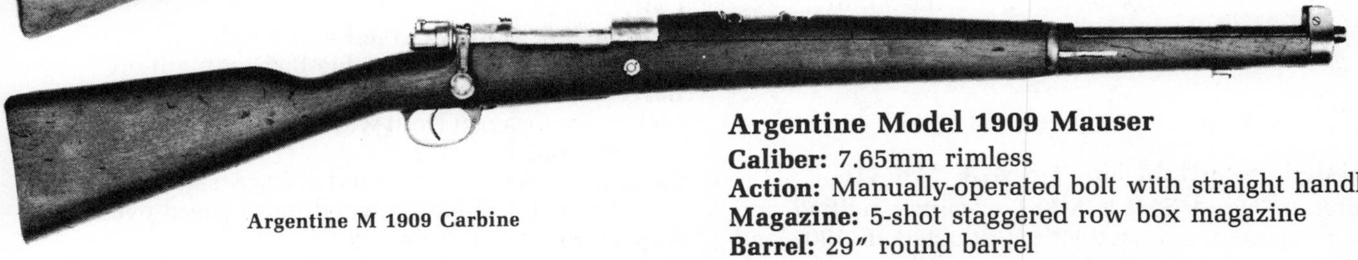

Argentine M 1909 Carbine

Argentine Model 1909 Mauser
Caliber: 7.65mm rimless
Action: Manually-operated bolt with straight handle
Magazine: 5-shot staggered row box magazine
Barrel: 29″ round barrel
Sights: Barley corn, tangent leaf rear
Stock & Forearm: Military-type one-piece semi-pistol grip stock and full forearm; two barrel bands; cleaning rod in forearm
Approximate wt.: 9 lbs.
Comments: A slight modification of the German Gewehr 98; obsolete.
Estimated Value: Excellent: $150.00
Very good: $115.00

Argentine Model 1909 Carbine
Similar to Model 1909 Rifle except: 17½″ barrel; approximate wt. 6½ lbs.; with and without bayonet lugs.
Estimated Value: Excellent: $145.00
Very good: $110.00

Military, British

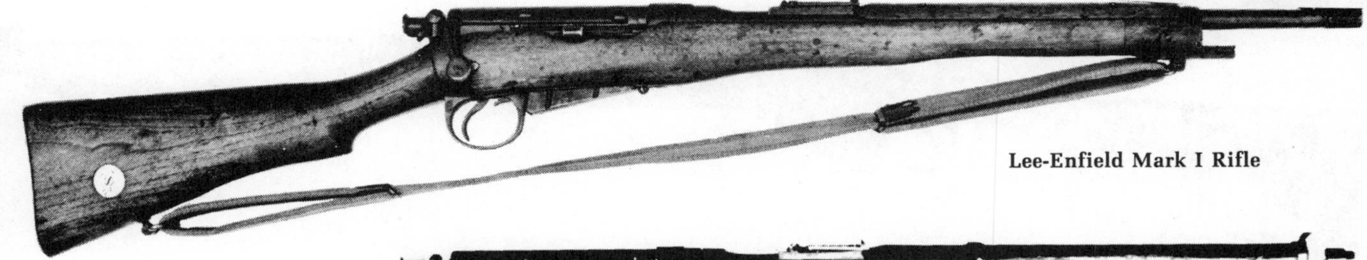

Lee-Enfield Mark I Rifle

Lee-Enfield Mark I Carbine

British Lee-Enfield Mark I
Caliber: 303
Action: Bolt action; repeating; bolt handle curved downward
Magazine: 10-shot detachable box with cut-off
Barrel: 30″
Sights: Barley corn front, vertical leaf rear
Stock & Forearm: Plain military-type stock and forearm
Approximate wt.: 9¼ lbs.
Comments: Adopted by British Army about 1899.
Estimated Value: Excellent: $130.00
Very good: $100.00

British Lee-Enfield Mark I Carbine
Similar to Lee-Enfield Mark I Rifle except 21″ barrel.
Estimated Value: Excellent: $135.00
Very good: $105.00

Lee-Enfield No. 1 SMLE MK1

Lee-Enfield No. 1 SMLE MK III

(Pattern 14)
No. 3 MK 1

British Lee-Enfield No. 4 MKI

British Lee-Enfield No. 1 SMLE MK III

Similar to No. 1 SMLE MK I except: modified and simplified for mass production; adopted in 1907 and modified again in 1918.

Estimated Value: Very good: $150.00
Good: $110.00

British Lee-Enfield No. 1 SMLE MK1

Caliber: 303
Action: Bolt action; curved volt handle
Magazine: 10-shot detachable box with cut-off
Barrel: 25¼″
Sights: Barley corn front with protective earns; tangent leaf rear
Stock & Forearm: Plain wood military stock to the muzzle with full length wood hand guard over barrel
Approximate wt.: 8 lbs.
Comments: Adopted about 1902 by British Army.
Estimated Value: Excellent: $160.00
Very good: $120.00

British (Pattern 14) No. 3 MK 1

Caliber: 303
Action: Bolt action; modified Mauser-type action; cocked as bolt is moved foreward
Magazine: 5-shot non-removable box
Barrel: 26″
Sights: Blade front with protective ears, vertical leaf with aperture rear
Stock & Forearm: Plain military stock with wood hand guard over barrel
Approximate wt.: 9 lbs.
Comments: Made in U.S.A. during World War I for the British Army.
Estimated Value: Excellent: $140.00
Very good: $110.00

British Lee-Enfield No. 4 MK1

Caliber: 303
Action: Bolt action
Magazine: 10-shot detachable box
Barrel: 25″
Sights: Blade front with protective ears, vertical leaf with aperture rear
Stock & Forearm: Plain military stock with wood hand guard over barrel
Approximate wt.: 8¾ lbs.
Comments: First produced about 1931 and was redesigned for mass production in 1939 by utilizing stamped parts and other short cuts.
Estimated Value: Excellent: $135.00
Very good: $100.00

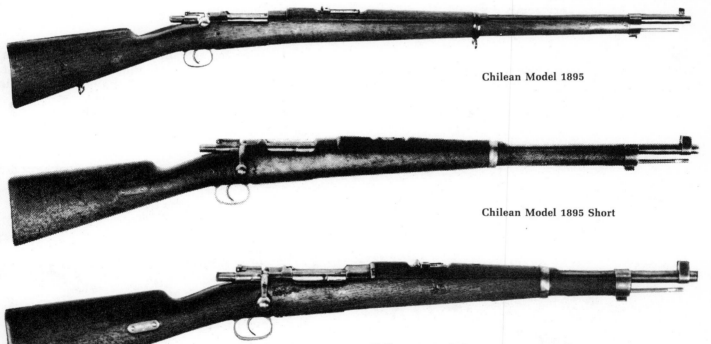

**Jungle Carbine
No. 5 MK 1**

British Jungle Carbine No. 5 MK1

Caliber: 303
Action: Bolt action
Magazine: 10-shot detachable box
Barrel: 18¾"
Sights: Blade front with protective ears; verticle leaf rear with aperture
Stock & Forearm: Military-type one-piece stock and forearm; wood hand guard over barrel; one barrel band
Approximate wt.: 7 lbs.
Comments: Made during World War II for jungle fighting.
Estimated Value: **Excellent:** $180.00
Very good: $145.00

Military, Chilean

Chilean Model 1895

Chilean Model 1895 Short

Chilean Model 1895 Carbine

Chilean Model 1895 Short

Similar to Model 1895 Rifle except: 22" barrel; approximate wt. 8½ lbs.
Estimated Value: **Excellent:** $100.00
Very good: $ 75.00

Chilean Model 1895 Carbine

Similar to Model 1895 Rifle except: 18¼" barrel; approximate wt. 7½ lbs.
Estimated Value: **Excellent:** $100.00
Very good: $ 80.00

Chilean Model 1895

Caliber: 7mm
Action: Bolt action; straight or turned bolt handle; similar to the Spanish Model 1893 Mauser
Magazine: 5-shot staggered non-detachable box
Barrel: 29"
Sights: Barley corn front; leaf rear
Stock & Forearm: Plain military-type stock with wood hand guard over barrel
Approximate wt.: 9 lbs.
Comments: Since Chile's adoption of the FN rifle, quantitites of the Chileas Mausers have been purchased by U.S.A. arms dealers.
Estimated Value: **Excellent:** $110.00
Very good: $ 80.00

German Model 1888 (GEW 88)

German Model 1888 Carbine

German Model 1888 Carbine

Similar to the Model 1888 Rifle except: 18″ barrel; approximate wt. 6¾ lbs.; full length stock to muzzle; curved flattened top bolt handle.

Estimated Value: Very good: $95.00
Good: $70.00

German Model 1891

Similar to Model 1888 Carbine except: stacking hook under forearm and although it is called a rifle, it has an 18″ barrel like the carbines.

Estimated Value: Excellent: $100.00
Very good: $ 75.00

German Model 1888 (GEW 88)

Caliber: 7.92mm
Action: Bolt action; straight bolt handle
Magazine: 5-shot in line non-detachable box
Barrel: 29″
Sights: Barley corn front; leaves with "v" notches rear
Stock & Forearm: Plain, straight grip military stock; no hand guard but uses a metal barrel jacket that covers barrel to muzzle
Approximate wt.: 8¾ lbs.
Comments: This arm is sometimes called a Mauser or Mannlicher but actually it is neither; it combines the magazine of the Mannlicher with the bolt features of the Mauser 1871/84; it is unsafe to use with the modern 7.92mm cartridge.

Estimated Value: Very good: $ 95.00
Good: $ 70.00

German Gewehr 98 (GEW 98)

German Model 98 (Kar 98) Carbine

German Model 98 (Kar 98) Carbine

Similar to Model Gewehr 98 Rifle except: 17″ barrel; approximate wt. 7½ lbs.; full stock to muzzle; section of forearm from barrel band to muzzle tapered to much smaller size than rest of forearm; curved bolt handle.

Estimated Value: Excellent: $150.00
Very good: $125.00

German Gewehr 98 (GEW 98)

Caliber: 7.92mm
Action: Bolt action; straight or curved bolt handle
Magazine: 5-shot staggered non-detachable box; also during World War II, 20 and 25-shot magazines
Barrel: 29″
Sights: Barley corn front, tangent bridge type or tangent leaf "v" rear
Stock & Forearm: Plain military semi-pistol grip stock and forearm; wood hand guard
Approximate wt.: 9 lbs.
Comments: This was one of the principle rifles of the German Army in World War I; it also appeared in a caliber 22 training rifle in World War I by fitting a liner in the barrel.

Estimated Value: Very good: $160.00
Good: $120.00

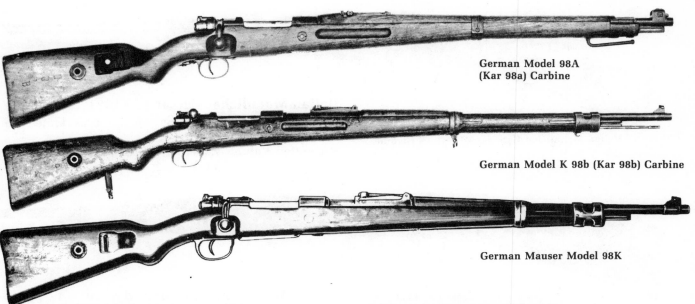

German Model 98A
(Kar 98a) Carbine

German Model K 98b (Kar 98b) Carbine

German Mauser Model 98K

German Model 98A (Kar 98a) Carbine

Similar to Model Gewehr 98 Rifle except: 24″ barrel; appeared in 1904 and made in tremendous quantities until 1918; used in World War I and had limited use in World War II; cut out in stock below bolt handle; curved bolt handle; grip grooves on forearm; stacking hook.

Estimated Value: Very good: $165.00
                  Good: $125.00

German Model K 98b (Kar 98b) Carbine

Although designed as a carbine, it is same length and is similar to Gewehr 98 Rifle except: turned down bolt; grip grooved forearm; these were used in the 1920's and early in World War II.

Estimated Value: Very good: $145.00
                  Good: $110.00

German Mauser Model 98K

Caliber: 7.92mm
Action: Bolt action; turned down bolt handle
Magazine: 5-shot staggered row non-detachable box
Barrel: 24″
Sights: Barley corn open or hooded front, tangent rear with "v" notch
Stock & Forearm: Plain military semi-pistol grip stock and forearm; wood hand guard; cut out in stock under bolt handle
Approximate wt.: 8¾ lbs.
Comments: The standard infantry rifle during World War II; widely fluctuating prices on these rifles because some have special unit markings which affect their values.
Estimated Value: Very good: $150.00 - $500.00
                  Good: $120.00 - $400.00

Military, Italian

Italian Mannlicher Carcano M 1891

Mannlicher Carcano M 1891 Carbine

Italian Mannlicher Carcano M 1891 Carbine

Generally the same specifications as M 1891 Military rifle except: 18″ barrel; bent bolt handle; folding bayonet permanently attached; approximate wt. 7 lbs.

Estimated Value: Very good: $95.00
                  Good: $65.00

Italian Mannlicher Carcano M 1891

Caliber: 6.5mm
Action: Bolt action; straight bolt handle; a modified Mauser-type action
Magazine: 6-shot in line non-detachable box
Barrel: 30½″
Sights: Barley corn front, tangent with "v" notch graduated from 500 to 2000 meters
Stock & Forearm: Plain straight grip military stock with wood hand guard over barrel
Approximate wt.: 8¾ lbs.
Comments: Uses knife-type bayonet.
Estimated Value: Very good: $90.00
                  Good: $60.00

Italian Mannlicher Carcano M 1891 TS Carbine

Italian Mannlicher Carcano M 1891 TS Carbine

Similar to M 1891 Carbine except: uses knife-type removable bayonet.

Estimated Value: Excellent: $95.00
Very good: $60.00

Mannlicher Carcano M 1938

Italian Mannlicher Carcano M 1938 Carbine

Similar to M 1938 Military Rifle except: 18″ barrel; folding bayonet permanently attached.

Estimated Value: Excellent: $95.00
Very good: $70.00

Italian Mannlicher Carcano M 1938 TS Carbine

Same as M 1938 Carbine except: detachable knife-type bayonet.

Estimated Value: Excellent: $90.00
Very good: $65.00

Italian Mannlicher Carcano M 1938

Caliber: 7.35mm, 6.5mm
Action: Bolt action; bent bolt handle
Magazine: 6-shot in line, non-detachable box
Barrel: 21″
Sights: Barley corn front, adjustable rear
Stock & Forearm: Plain straight grip military stock; wood hand guard over barrel
Approximate wt.: 7½ lbs.
Comments: First of the Italian rifles chambered for the 7.35mm cartridge; in 1940 the 7.35mm caliber was dropped; this is the type rifle used to assassinate President John F. Kennedy in 1963; it was a 6.5mm made in 1940 and sold in U.S.A. as Army surplus.
Estimated Value: Excellent: $100.00
Very good: $ 70.00

Military, Japanese

Japanese Type 38 Arisaka

Japanese Type 38 Arisaka Carbine

Japanese Type 38 Arisaka Carbine

Similar to Type 38 Arisaka Rifle except: 20″ barrel; folding bayonet; approximate wt. 7¼ lbs.; some were converted for paratrooper use by the fitting of a hinged butt stock.

Estimated Value:

	Carbine	Paratrooper Carbine
Very good:	$150.00	$180.00
Good:	$110.00	$135.00

Japanese Type 38 Arisaka

Caliber: 6.5mm Japanese
Action: Bolt action; straight bolt handle
Magazine: 5-shot box magazine with floor plate
Barrel: 31½″ round
Sights: Barley corn front with protecting ears, rear sight adjustable for elevation
Stock & Forearm: Military finish; plain wood one-piece full stock; semi-pistol grip; steel buttplate; cleaning rod under barrel; wood hand guard on top of barrel; two steel barrel bands with bayonet lug on front band
Approximate wt.: 9¼ lbs.
Comments: Adopted by Japanese Military in 1905, the 38th year of the Meiji reign.
Estimated Value: Very good: $160.00
Good: $120.00

Japanese Type 97 Sniper

Japanese Type 44 Cavalry Carbine

Japanese Type 99 Service

Japanese Type 99 Takedown

Japanese Type 99 Sniper

Japanese Type 97 Sniper

Similar to Type 38 Arisaka Rifle except: a snipers version adopted in 1937 with a 2.5 power scope; approximate wt. with scope: 11 lbs. Priced for rifle with scope.

Estimated Value: Very good: $275.00
Good: $220.00

Japanese Type 44 Cavalry Carbine

Similar to Type 38 Arisaka carbine except: heavier weight, about 9 lbs.; adopted by Japanese Military in 1911, the 44th year of the Meiji reign; permanently attached folding bayonet.

Estimated Value: Excellent: $150.00
Very good: $110.00

Japanese Type 99 Takedown

Similar to Type 99 Service Rifle except it has a 25″ barrel only. A takedown model, it has a screw-in key that serves as a locking pin. When key is removed, the barrel can be unscrewed from the receiver; however, the takedown arrangement was unsatisfactory because it weakened the receiver and affected the accuracy.

Estimated Value: Excellent: $175.00
Very good: $130.00

Japanese Type 99 Sniper

Similar to Type 99 Service Rifle except: adopted in 1942 and equiped with a 4X scope; 25½″ barrel only. Prices include matching number and scope mounted.

Estimated Value: Excellent: $300.00
Very good: $250.00

Japanese Type 99 Service

Caliber: 7.7mm Japanese
Action: Bolt action
Magazine: 5-shot magazine, non-detachable
Barrel: 25½″ or 31½″ round
Sights: Fixed front, adjustable or fixed rear
Stock & Forearm: Military finish; plain wood, one-piece full stock; semi-pistol grip; steel buttplate; cleaning rod under barrel; some had bipod attached under forearm; wood hand guard on top of barrel; two steel barrel bands with bayonet lug on front band
Approximate wt.: 8½ to 9 lbs.
Comments: Some of the last rifles made were of poor quality and unsafe to shoot with heavy load cartridges. Adopted by Japanese Military in 1939, which was Japanese year of 2599.
Estimated Value: Very good: $140.00
Good: $100.00

Military, Mexican

Mexican Model 1895 Mauser Military

Mexican Model 1902

Mexican Arisaka (Japanese Type 38 Rifle)

Mexican Model 1936

Mexican Model 1954

Mexican Model 1895 Mauser

Almost identical to the Spanish 1893 Military Rifle in caliber 7mm. See Spanish Model 1893 for description.
Estimated Value: Very good: **$90.00**
Good: **$60.00**

Mexican Models 1902 and 1912 Mauser

Almost identical to the Model 1895 Mauser Military Rifle except that the actions were almost the same as Model 98 7.92 mm German rifle except in 7mm caliber.
Estimated Value: Very good: **$95.00**
Good: **$65.00**

Mexican Arisaka (Japanese Type 38 Rifle)

Between 1910 and 1920, Mexico procured arms from many companies. The Arisaka Rifle was purchased from Japan in caliber 7mm and had the Mexican escutcheon stamped on the receiver.
Estimated Value: Excellent: **$150.00**
Very good: **$110.00**

Mexican Model 1936

Caliber: 7mm
Action: Bolt action; curved bolt handle; Mauser short-type action
Magazine: 5-shot staggered row, non-detachable box
Barrel: 20″
Sights: Hooded barley corn front; tangent rear with "V" notch
Stock & Forearm: Plain semi-pistol grip stock with grip grooves in forearm; wood hand guard
Approximate wt.: 8½ lbs.
Comments: A very well made arm of Mexican manufacture; resembles the U.S. Springfield M 1903 - A-1 in appearance.
Estimated Value: Excellent: **$160.00**
Very good: **$120.00**

Mexican Model 1954

Caliber: 30-06
Action: Bolt action; curved bolt handle
Magazine: 5-shot staggered row, non-detachable box
Barrel: 24″
Sights: Hooded barley corn front; ramp type aperture rear
Stock & Forearm: Plain semi-pistol grip military stock and wood hand guard; stock is made of laminated plywood
Approximate wt.: 9 lbs.
Comments: This rifle is patterned after the U.S. Springfield M 1903 - A3 Military Rifle.
Estimated Value: Very good: **$175.00**
Good: **$130.00**

Military, Russian

Russian Moisin-Nagant M 1891

Caliber: 7.62 mm
Action: Bolt action; straight bolt; hexagonal receiver
Magazine: 5-shot box with hinged floor plate
Barrel: 31½″
Sights: Blade front, leaf rear
Stock & Forearm: Plain straight grip, military stock and gripped grooved forearm; early models had no hand guard and used swivels for attaching sling; later models (beginning about 1908) used sling slots and had wood hand guard
Approximate wt.: 9¾ lbs.
Comments: Adopted in 1891 by Imperial Russia.
Estimated Value: Very good: $90.00
Good: $60.00

Russian M 1910 Carbine

Caliber: 7.62mm
Action: Bolt action; straight bolt handle; hexagonal receiver
Magazine: 5-shot box with floor plate
Barrel: 20″
Sights: Blade front, leaf type rear adjustable for elevation
Stock & Forearm: Plain straight grip military stock; sling slots in stock and forearm; wood hand guard and grip grooved forearm
Approximate wt.: 7½ lbs.
Comments: This carbine does not accept a bayonet.
Estimated Value: Very good: $100.00
Good: $ 75.00

Russian Moisin-Nagant M 1891

Russian M-1910 Carbine

Russian M-1938 Carbine

Russian Tokarev M 1938

Russian M1938 Carbine

This carbine replaced by M1910 and is very similar except: it has a round receiver; hooded front sight and tangent type rear graduated from 100 to 1000 meters; no bayonet attachment.
Estimated Value: Very good: $95.00
Good: $70.00

Russian Tokarev M 1938

Caliber: 7.62mm
Action: Semi-automatic; gas operated
Magazine: 10-shot removable box
Barrel: 25″
Sights: Hooded post front, tangent rear
Stock & Forearm: Plain semi-pistol grip two-piece stock and forearm; cleaning rod on right side of forearm; sling swivels
Approximate wt.: 8¾ lbs.
Comments: The first of the Tokarev series; wasn't very successful and was replaced by the Tokarev M 1940.
Estimated Value: Very good: $180.00
Good: $135.00

Russian Tokarev M 1940

Russian M 1944 Carbine

Russian Tokarev M 1940

Similar to Tokarev M 1938 except: improved version; cleaning rod in forearm under barrel; 24½″ baarrel.
Estimated Value: Very good: $190.00
Good: $140.00

Russian M 1944 Military Carbine

Similar to the M 1938 except: introduced during World War II; permanently fixed bayonet which folds along the right side of the stock; barrel length 20½″.
Estimated Value: Excellent: $175.00
Very good: $120.00

Military, Spanish

Spanish Model 1893 Military

Spanish Model 1893 Short

Spanish Model 1895 Carbine

Spanish Model 1893

Caliber: 7mm
Action: Bolt action; straight bolt handle
Magazine: 5-shot staggered row non-detachable
Barrel: 30″
Sights: Barley corn front, leaf rear
Stock & Forearm: Plain straight grip military stock with wood hand guard over barrel
Approximate wt.: 9 lbs.
Comments: A number of variations in the Model 1893 were made; it was the principal rifle used in the Spanish-American War.
Estimated Value: Very good: $80.00
Good: $55.00

Spanish Model 1893 Short

Similar to the M 1893 Rifle except: 22″ barrel; approximate wt. 8½ lbs.; curved bolt handle.
Estimated Value: Very good: $75.00
Good: $50.00

Spanish Model 1895 Carbine

Similar to M 1893 Rifle except: 18″ barrel; full stock to muzzle; barley corn front sight with protective ears; approximate wt. 7½ lbs.
Estimated Value: Very good: $85.00
Good: $60.00

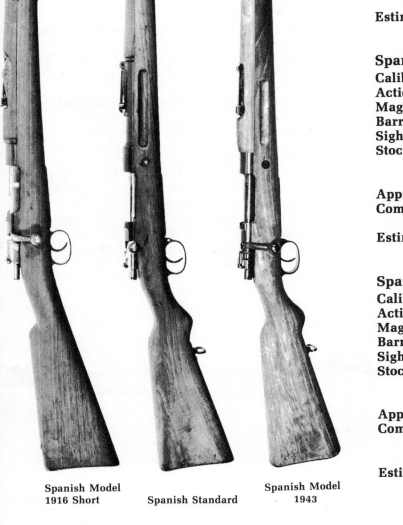

Spanish Model 1916 Short
Caliber: 7mm
Action: Bolt action; bolt handle curved down
Magazine: 5-shot staggered row, non-detachable box
Barrel: 24″
Sights: Barley corn front with ears, tangent rear
Stock & Forearm: Plain military stock and wood hand guard
Approximate wt.: 8½ lbs.
Comments: Made in large quantities during Spanish Civil War; later many were convered to caliber 7.62mm NATO.
Estimated Value: Very good: $95.00
                      Good: $70.00

Spanish Standard Model Mauser
Caliber: 7.92mm
Action: Bolt action; straight bolt handle
Magazine: 5-shot staggered row, non-detachable box
Barrel: 24″
Sights: Barley corn front, tangent rear
Stock & Forearm: Plain military semi-pistol grip stock and forearm grooved for finger grip; wood hand guard
Approximate wt.: 9 lbs.
Comments: Procured in large quantities from other countries during the Spanish Civil War.
Estimated Value: Very good: $90.00
                      Good: $65.00

Spanish Model 1943
Caliber: 7.92mm
Action: Bolt action; curved bolt handle
Magazine: 5-shot staggered row, non-detachable box
Barrel: 24″
Sights: Barley corn front, tangent rear
Stock & Forearm: Plain military semi-pistol grip stock and forearm grooved for finger grip; wood hand guard
Approximate wt.: 9 lbs.
Comments: Adopted in 1943 and continued to mid 1950's; this is a modified copy of the German 7.92mm Kar 98K.
Estimated Value: Very good: $150.00
                      Good: $110.00

Spanish Model
1916 Short   Spanish Standard   Spanish Model
1943

Military, U.S.

U.S. M 1903 Springfield

U.S. M 1903 Springfield

Caliber: 30-06
Action: Bolt action; repeating; cocked as bolt handle is rotated clockwise to close and lock; knob at rear protrudes when piece is cocked; manual thumb safety at rear of bolt; turned down bolt handle; action is basically a modification of the Mauser Model 98
Magazine: 5-shot staggered row, non-detachable box magazine
Barrel: 24″
Sights: Blade front, leaf with aperture and notched battle rear
Stock & Forearm: Plain straight one-piece stock and forearm; wood hand guard over barrel; a cleaning rod-type bayonet contained in the forearm under barrel
Approximate wt.: 8¾ lbs.
Comments: Adopted by U.S. 1903; made by Springfield and Rock Island.
Estimated Value: Very good: $275.00
                  Good: $210.00

U.S. M 1903 - A1 Springfield

Basically the same as M 1903 Military rifle except: pistol grip stock; checkered buttplate and serrated trigger; adopted in 1929; and made until 1939 by Springfield Armory - last serial number was about 1,532,878; in 1942 Remington Arms Co. made about 348,000 with a few minor modifications before the M 1903 A3 was adopted; serial numbers from 3,000,001 to 3,348,085.
Estimated Value: Very good: $300.00
                  Good: $225.00

U.S. M 1903 - A3 Springfield

Generally the same as the U.S. M 1903 - A1 except: many parts are stamped sheet metal and other modifications to lower cost and increase production; straight or pistol grip stock; made during World War II under emergency conditions.
Estimated Value: Very good: $200.00
                  Good: $150.00

U.S. M 1917 Enfield

Caliber: 30-06
Action: Bolt action; repeating; cocked as bolt is moved forward; bolt handle is crooked rear-ward; modified Mauser-type action
Magazine: 5-shot staggered row, non-detachable box type
Barrel: 26″
Sights: Blade front with protecting ears, leaf with aperture rear
Stock & Forearm: Plain one-piece semi-pistol grip stock and forearm; wood hand guard over barrel
Approximate wt.: 8¼ lbs.
Comments: This gun was developed from the British P-13 and P-14 system as an emergency arm for U.S. in World War I. Made from about 1917 to 1918. Also manufactured in the U.S. for Great Britain in caliber 303 in 1917.
Estimated Value: Very good: $200.00
                  Good: $150.00

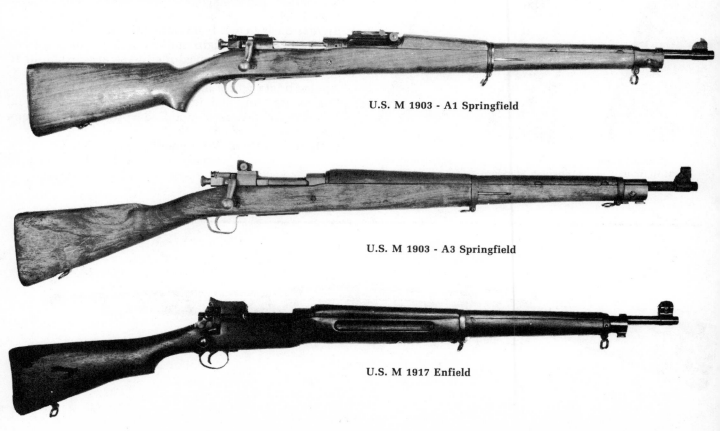

U.S. M 1903 - A1 Springfield

U.S. M 1903 - A3 Springfield

U.S. M 1917 Enfield

U.S. M1

U.S. Garand 30 Caliber M1

Johnson M 1941

U.S. Garand M1 Rifle

Caliber: 30-06
Action: Semi-automatic; gas operated
Magazine: 8-shot staggered row, non-detachable box
Barrel: 24″
Sights: Blade front with protective ears, aperture rear or flip-over type rear
Stock & Forearm: One-piece stock and forearm; wood hand guard over top of barrel
Approximate wt.: 9½ lbs.
Comments: Produced by Winchester and Springfield during World War II. Additional M1's produced after World War II by International Harvester and Harrington & Richardson. Add $150.00 for Winchester.
Estimated Value: Very good: $700.00
Good: $525.00

U.S. M1 Carbine

Caliber: 30 M1 Carbine
Action: Semi-automatic; gas operated
Magazine: 15- or 30-shot staggered row, detachable box
Barrel: 18″
Sights: Blade front with protective ears; aperture rear or flip-down rear
Stock & Forearm: One-piece wood stock and forearm; wood hand guard on top of barrel
Approximate wt.: 5½ lbs.
Comments: Developed during World War II to replace the sidearms used by non-commissioned officers, special troops and company grade officers.
Estimated Value: Very good: $375.00
Good: $280.00

U.S. M1 A1 Carbine

Same general specifications as U.S. M1 Carbine except: folding metal stock; 25″ overall length when folded; approximate wt. 6¼ lbs.
Estimated Value: Very good: $550.00
Good: $410.00

Johnson M 1941

Caliber: 30-06
Action: Semi-automatic; recoil action; hesitation-locked breech; barrel partially recoils to begin unlocking phase; manual safety in front of trigger guard
Magazine: 10-shot rotary type; a vertical feed magazine was also made
Barrel: 22″
Sights: Post front with protective ears, aperture rear
Stock & Forearm: Plain wood semi-pistol grip stock and forearm; metal hand guard over barrel above forearm
Approximate wt.: 9½ lbs.
Comments: The Johnson was thought to be superior to the M1 but a series of tests and demonstrations in 1939 and 1940 indicated otherwise; used by U.S. Marines for a limited period in World War II and by the Dutch in the East Indies; many rebarreled in other calibers after World War II.
Estimated Value: Very good: $600.00
Good: $450.00

Mossberg

Mossberg Model 35

Mossberg Model B

Caliber: 22 short, long, long rifle
Action: Bolt action; single shot
Magazine: None
Barrel: Blued 22″
Sights: Open rear, bead front
Stock & Forearm: Plain wood semi-pistol grip stock and forearm
Approximate wt.: 5 lbs.
Comments: Made in the early 1930's.
Estimated Value: Excellent: $60.00
Very good: $45.00

Mossberg Model R

Caliber: 22 short, long, long rifle
Action: Bolt action; repeating
Magazine: Tubular; 14 long rifles, 16 longs, 20 shorts
Barrel: Blued 24″
Sights: Open rear, bead front
Stock & Forearm: Walnut semi-pistol grip stock and forearm
Approximate wt.: 5 lbs.
Comments: Made in the early 1930's.
Estimated Value: Excellent: $70.00
Very good: $55.00

Mossberg Model 10

Caliber: 22 short, long, long rifle
Action: Bolt action; single shot
Magazine: None
Barrel: Blued 22″
Sights: Open rear, bead front
Stock & Forearm: Walnut semi-pistol grip stock and forearm; swivels
Approximate wt.: 4 lbs.
Comments: Made from the early to mid 1930's. Takedown type.
Estimated Value: Excellent: $60.00
Very good: $45.00

Mossberg Model 20

Similar to the Model 10 with a 24″ barrel and grooved forearm.
Estimated Value: Excellent: $60.00
Very good: $45.00

Mossberg Model 30

Similar to the Model 20 with peep rear sight and hooded ramp front sight.
Estimated Value: Excellent: $65.00
Very good: $50.00

Mossberg Model 40

Similar to the Model 30 with tubular magazine that holds 16 long rifles, 18 longs, 22 shorts; bolt action; repeating.
Estimated Value: Excellent: $70.00
Very good: $55.00·

Mossberg Model M

Caliber: 22 short, long, long rifle
Action: Bolt action; single shot; cocking piece
Magazine: None
Barrel: 20″ round
Sights: Open rear, blade front
Stock & Forearm: Plain one-piece semi-pistol grip stock and tapered forearm
Approximate wt.: 4½ lbs.
Comments: A small boys' rifle made in the early 1930's.
Estimated Value: Excellent: $65.00
Very good: $50.00

Mossberg Model 14

Caliber: 22 short, long, long rifle
Action: Bolt action; single shot
Magazine: None
Barrel: Blued 24″
Sights: Peep rear, hooded ramp front
Stock & Forearm: Plain one-piece semi-pistol grip stock and forearm; swivels
Approximate wt.: 5½ lbs.
Comments: Made in the mid 1930's.
Estimated Value: Excellent: $60.00
Very good: $45.00

Mossberg Model 34

Similar to the Model 14, made in the mid 1930's.
Estimated Value: Excellent: $60.00
Very good: $45.00

Mossberg Model 35

Caliber: 22 long rifle
Action: Bolt action; single shot
Magazine: None
Barrel: Blued, 26″ heavy
Sights: Micrometer rear, hooded ramp front
Stock & Forearm: Plain walnut one-piece semi-pistol grip stock and forearm; cheekpiece; swivels
Approximate wt.: 8¼ lbs.
Comments: Made in the mid 1930's.
Estimated Value: Excellent: $100.00
Very good: $ 75.00

Mossberg Model 35A

Similar to the Model 35; target stock and sights. Made in the late 1930's.
Estimated Value: Excellent: $90.00
Very good: $70.00

Mossberg Model 35A-LS

Similar to the 35A with special Lyman sights.
Estimated Value: Excellent: $110.00
Very good: $ 80.00

Mossberg Model 42B

Mossberg Model 42A, L42A

Mossberg Model 42C

Mossberg Model 43, L43

Mossberg Model 42

Caliber: 22 short, long, long rifle
Action: Bolt action; repeating
Magazine: 7-shot detachable box
Barrel: Blued 24″
Sights: Open rear, receiver peep, hooded ramp front
Stock & Forearm: Plain walnut one-piece semi-pistol grip stock and forearm; swivels
Approximate wt.: 5 lbs.
Comments: Made in the mid 1930's; takedown model.
Estimated Value: Excellent: $70.00
  Very good: $50.00

Mossberg Model 42A, L42A

Similar to the Model 42 but higher quality. L42A is left hand action. Made in the late 1930's.
Estimated Value: Excellent: $75.00
  Very good: $55.00

Mossberg Model 42B

An improved version of the Model 42A with micrometer peep sight and 5-shot magazine. Made from the late 1930's to early 1940's.
Estimated Value: Excellent: $80.00
  Very good: $60.00

Mossberg Model 42C

Similar to the Model 42B without the peep sight.
Estimated Value: Excellent: $75.00
  Very good: $55.00

Mossberg Model 42M

More modern version of the Model 42 with a 23″ barrel; full length; two-piece stock and forearm; cheekpiece; 7-shot magazine. Made from the early 1940's to early 1950's.
Estimated Value: Excellent: $75.00
  Very good: $55.00

Mossberg Model 42MB

Similar to the Model 42. Used as military training rifle in Great Britain in World War II; full stock.
Estimated Value: Excellent: $125.00
  Very good: $ 90.00

Mossberg Model 43, L43

Caliber: 22 long rifle
Action: Bolt action; repeating
Magazine: 7-shot detachable box
Barrel: Blued 26″
Sights: Special Lyman sights
Stock & Forearm: Walnut one-piece semi-pistol grip stock and forearm; cheekpiece; swivels
Approximate wt.: 8¼ lbs.
Comments: Made in the late 1930's. L43 is left hand action.
Estimated Value: Excellent: $100.00
  Very good: $ 75.00

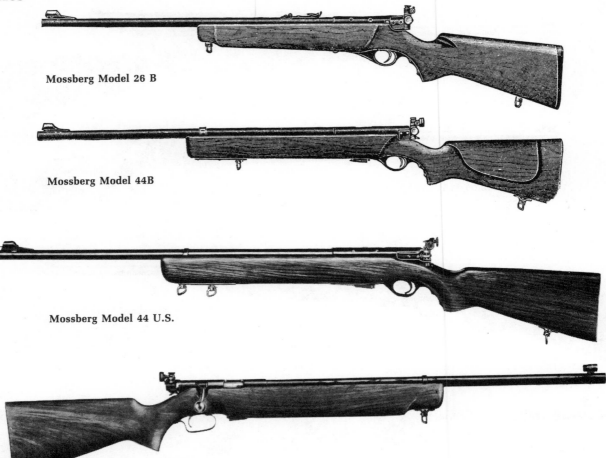

Mossberg Model 26 B

Mossberg Model 44B

Mossberg Model 44 U.S.

Mossberg Model 43B

Mossberg Model 26B

Caliber: 22 short, long, long rifle
Action: Bolt action; single shot
Magazine: None
Barrel: Blued 26″
Sights: Micrometer rear, hooded ramp front
Stock & Forearm: Plain one-piece semi-pistol grip stock and forearm; swivels
Approximate wt.: 5½ lbs.
Comments: Made in the late 1930's.
Estimated Value: Excellent: $75.00
  Very good: $55.00

Mossberg Model 26C

Similar to the 26B without swivels or peep sight.
Estimated Value: Excellent: $60.00
  Very good: $45.00

Mossberg Model 44

Caliber: 22 short, long, long rifle
Action: Bolt action; repeating
Magazine: Tubular; 16 long rifles, 18 longs, 22 shorts
Barrel: Blued 24″
Sights: Peep rear, hooded ramp front
Stock & Forearm: Plain walnut one-piece semi-pistol grip stock and forearm; swivels
Approximate wt.: 6 lbs.
Comments: Made in the mid 1930's.
Estimated Value: Excellent: $75.00
  Very good: $60.00

Mossberg Model 44B

Caliber: 22 long rifle
Action: Bolt action; repeating
Magazine: 7-shot detachable box
Barrel: 26″ heavy barrel
Sights: Micrometer receiver, hooded front
Stock & Forearm: Plain one-piece semi-pistol grip stock and forearm; swivels; cheekpiece
Approximate wt.: 8 lbs.
Comments: Made from the late 1930's to early 1940's.
Estimated Value: Excellent: $80.00
  Very good: $60.00

Mossberg Model 35B

Single shot version of the Model 44B. Made in the late 1930's.
Estimated Value: Excellent: $75.00
  Very good: $50.00

Mossberg Model 43B

Similar to the 44B with special Lyman sights.
Estimated Value: Excellent: $85.00
  Very good: $65.00

Mossberg Model 44 U.S.

Improved version of the Model 44B. Made in the late 1930's.
Estimated Value: Excellent: $120.00
  Very good: $ 90.00

Mossberg Model 45

Mossberg Model 45A, L45A

Mossberg Model 45B

Mossberg Model 46

Mossberg Model 25

Caliber: 22 short, long, long rifle
Action: Bolt action; single shot
Magazine: None
Barrel: Blued 24″
Sights: Peep rear, hooded ramp front
Stock & Forearm: Plain walnut one-piece pistol grip stock and forearm; swivels
Approximate wt.: 5 lbs.
Comments: Made in the mid 1930's.
Estimated Value: Excellent: $65.00
Very good: $50.00

Mossberg Model 25A

Similar to the Model 25 with higher quality finish and better wood. Made in the late 1930's.
Estimated Value: Excellent: $70.00
Very good: $55.00

Mossberg Model 45

Caliber: 22 short, long, long rifle
Action: Bolt action; repeating
Magazine: Tubular; 15 long rifles, 18 longs, 22 shorts
Barrel: Blued 24″
Sights: Peep rear, hooded ramp front
Stock & Forearm: Plain one-piece semi-pistol grip stock and forearm; swivels
Approximate wt.: 6¾ lbs.
Comments: Made in the mid 1930's.
Estimated Value: Excellent: $75.00
Very good: $60.00

Mossberg Model 45C

Similar to the Model 45 without sights.
Estimated Value: Excellent: $70.00
Very good: $55.00

Mossberg Model 45A, L45A

Improved version of the Model 45, made in the late 1930's. L45A is left hand action.
Estimated Value: Excellent: $80.00
Very good: $65.00

Mossberg Model 45AC

Similar to the Model 45A without sights.
Estimated Value: Excellent: $70.00
Very good: $55.00

Mossberg Model 45B

Similar to the Model 45A with open rear sight. Made in the late 1930's.
Estimated Value: Excellent: $75.00
Very good: $60.00

Mossberg Model 46

Caliber: 22 short, long, long rifle
Action: Bolt action; repeating
Magazine: Tubular; 15 long rifles, 18 longs, 22 shorts
Barrel: Blued 26″
Sights: Micrometer rear, hooded ramp front
Stock & Forearm: Plain one-piece semi-pistol grip stock and forearm; cheekpiece; swivels
Approximate wt.: 7½ lbs.
Comments: Made in the mid 1930's.
Estimated Value: Excellent: $80.00
Very good: $60.00

Mossberg Model 46C

A heavy barrel version of the Model 46.
Estimated Value: **Excellent:** **$85.00**
Very good: **$65.00**

Mossberg Model 46A

An improved version of the Model 46 made in the late 1930's.
Estimated Value: **Excellent:** **$85.00**
Very good: **$60.00**

Mossberg Model 46 AC

Similar to the 46A with open rear sight.
Estimated Value: **Excellent:** **$75.00**
Very good: **$60.00**

Mossberg Model 46A-LS, L46A-LS

Similar to the Model 46A with special Lyman sights. L46A-LS is left hand action.
Estimated Value: **Excellent:** **$90.00**
Very good: **$70.00**

Mossberg Model 46B

Similar to the Model 46A with open rear sight and receiver peep sight. Made in the late 1930's.
Estimated Value: **Excellent:** **$80.00**
Very good: **$60.00**

Mossberg Model 46BT

A heavy barrel version of the Model 46B.
Estimated Value: **Excellent:** **$90.00**
Very good: **$65.00**

Mossberg Model 46M

Similar to the Model 46 with full length two-piece forearm. Made about 1940 to the early 1950's.
Estimated Value: **Excellent:** **$85.00**
Very good: **$60.00**

Mossberg Model 346K

Caliber: 22 short, long, long rifle
Action: Bolt action; repeating
Magazine: Tubular; 20 long rifles, 23 longs, 30 shorts
Barrel: Blued 26″
Sights: Micrometer rear, hooded front
Stock & Forearm: Plain Monte Carlo one-piece pistol grip stock and lipped forearm; cheekpiece; swivels
Approximate wt.: 7 lbs.
Comments: Made from the late 1940's to mid 1950's.
Estimated Value: **Excellent:** **$80.00**
Very good: **$55.00**

Mossberg Model L46A-LS

Mossberg Model 46B

Mossberg Model 46 BT

Mossberg Model 46M

Mossberg Model 346K

Mossberg Model 346 B

Mossberg Model 320K

Mossberg Model 340K

Mossberg Model 340B

Mossberg Model 320 B

Mossberg Model 340M Carbine

Mossberg Model 346 B
Similar to the Model 346K with peep rear sight and hooded ramp front sight.
Estimated Value: **Excellent:** **$75.00**
              Very good: **$55.00**

Mossberg Model 320K
Single shot version of the Model 346K. Weighs about 5¾ lbs. Discontinued about 1960.
Estimated Value: **Excellent:** **$60.00**
              Very good: **$45.00**

Mossberg Model 340K
Similar to the Model 346K with 7-shot clip magazine.
Estimated Value: **Excellent:** **$70.00**
              Very good: **$50.00**

Mossberg Model 340B
Similar to the 346B with 7-shot clip magazine.
Estimated Value: **Excellent:** **$70.00**
              Very good: **$55.00**

Mossberg Model 320 B
Similar to the 340K in single shot. Made from about 1960 for 11 years.
Estimated Value: **Excellent:** **$65.00**
              Very good: **$50.00**

Mossberg Model 340M Carbine
Similar to the Model 340K with full length forearm and 18″ barrel. Made in the early 1970's.
Estimated Value: **Excellent:** **$90.00**
              Very good: **$65.00**

Mossberg Model 342K

Mossberg Model 144

Mossberg Model 146B

Mossberg Model 342K

Similar to the 340K with 18″ barrel; hinged forearm for forward grip; side mounted swivels. Made to the mid 1970's.

Estimated Value: Excellent: $75.00
Very good: $60.00

Mossberg Model 144

Caliber: 22 long rifle
Action: Bolt action; repeating
Magazine: 7-shot clip
Barrel: Blued 26″, heavy
Sights: Micrometer receiver, hooded front
Stock & Forearm: Walnut one-piece semi-pistol grip stock and forearm; hand rest; swivels
Approximate wt.: 8 lbs.
Comments: Made from the late 1940's to mid 1980's.
Estimated Value: Excellent: $180.00
Very good: $135.00

Mossberg Model 146B

Caliber: 22 short, long, long rifle
Action: Bolt action; repeating
Magazine: Tubular; 20 long rifles, 23 longs, 30 shorts
Barrel: Blued 26″
Sights: Micrometer rear, hooded front
Stock & Forearm: Plain Monte Carlo one-piece pistol grip stock and lipped forearm; cheekpiece; swivels
Approximate wt.: 7 lbs.
Comments: Made from the late 1940's to mid 1950's.
Estimated Value: Excellent: $90.00
Very good: $70.00

Mossberg Model 140K

Mossberg Model 140B

Mossberg Model 140K

Caliber: 22 short, long, long rifle
Action: Bolt action; repeating
Magazine: 7-shot clip
Barrel: Blued 24½″
Sights: Open rear, bead front
Stock & Forearm: Walnut Monte Carlo one-piece pistol grip stock and forearm; cheekpiece; swivels
Approximate wt.: 5¾ lbs.
Comments: Made in the mid 1950's.
Estimated Value: Excellent: $70.00
Very good: $55.00

Mossberg Model 140B

Similar to the 140 K with hooded ramp front sight, peep rear sight.
Estimated Value: Excellent: $75.00
Very good: $60.00

Mossberg Model 640k Chuckster

Mossberg Model 620K

Mossberg Model 321K

Mossberg Model 341

Mossberg Model 353

Mossberg Model 640K Chuckster

Caliber: 22 magnum
Action: Bolt action; repeating
Magazine: 5-shot box
Barrel: Blued 24″
Sights: Open rear, bead front; adjustable
Stock & Forearm: Checkered walnut Monte Carlo one-piece pistol grip stock and forearm; swivels
Approximate wt.: 6 lbs.
Comments: Made from about 1960 to mid 1980's.
Estimated Value: Excellent: $110.00
  Very good: $ 80.00

Mossberg Model 620K

Similar to the 640K in single shot. Discontinued in mid 1970's.
Estimated Value: Excellent: $75.00
  Very good: $60.00

Mossberg Model 321K

Caliber: 22 short, long, long rifle
Action: Bolt action; single shot
Magazine: None
Barrel: Blued 24″
Sights: Open rear, ramp front
Stock & Forearm: Checkered Monte Carlo one-piece pistol grip stock and forearm
Approximate wt.: 6½ lbs.
Comments: Made from the early 1970's to early 1980's.
Estimated Value: Excellent: $60.00
  Very good: $45.00

Mossberg Model 341

Similar to the 321K with: 7-shot clip magazine; swivels; bolt action; repeating; adjustable sights.
Estimated Value: Excellent: $ 80.00
  Very good: $ 60.00

Mossberg Model 353

Similar to the 321K except: semi-automatic; hinged grip forearm (tenite); 18″ barrel; 7-shot clip magazine; 22 long rifle only; adjustable sight.
Estimated Value: Excellent: $ 90.00
  Very good: $ 70.00

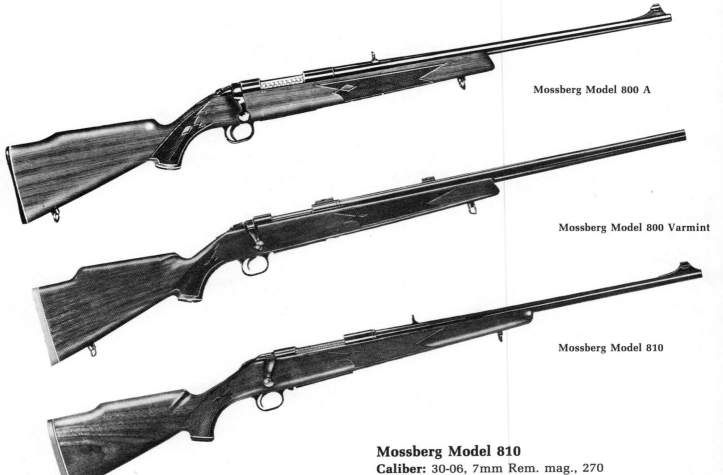

Mossberg Model 800 A

Mossberg Model 800 Varmint

Mossberg Model 810

Mossberg Model 800 A

Caliber: 308, 243, 22-250
Action: Bolt action; repeating
Magazine: 4-shot box
Barrel: Blued 22″
Sights: Leaf rear, ramp front
Stock & Forearm: Checkered wood Monte Carlo one-piece pistol grip stock and forearm; swivels
Approximate wt.: 6½ lbs.
Comments: Discontinued in the late 1970's.
Estimated Value: **Excellent:** **$200.00**
Very good: **$150.00**

Mossberg Model 800 Varmint

Similar to the 800A with a 24″ barrel and scope mounts. In 243 and 22-250 calibers.
Estimated Value: **Excellent:** **$210.00**
Very good: **$160.00**

Mossberg Model 800 Target

Similar to the 800A with scope mounts and scope in 308, 243, 22-250 calibers.
Estimated Value: **Excellent:** **$250.00**
Very good: **$190.00**

Mossberg Model 810

Caliber: 30-06, 7mm Rem. mag., 270
Action: Bolt action; repeating
Magazine: 4-shot detachable box
Barrel: Blued 22″
Sights: Leaf rear, ramp front
Stock & Forearm: Checkered Monte Carlo one-piece pistol grip stock and forearm; swivels; recoil pad
Approximate wt.: 7½ to 8 lbs.
Comments: Add $15.00 for 7mm Rem. magnum. Discontinued in the late 1970's.
Estimated Value: **Excellent:** **$220.00**
Very good: **$165.00**

Mossberg Model RM-7A

Caliber: 30-06
Action: Bolt action; repeating; hammerless
Magazine: 4-shot rotary
Barrel: 22″ round
Sights: Adjustable folding leaf rear, ramp front
Stock & Forearm: Checkered walnut one-piece pistol grip stock and forearm; fluted comb; recoil pad
Approximate wt.: 7½ lbs.
Comments: Made in the late 1970's.
Estimated Value: **Excellent:** **$215.00**
Very good: **$160.00**

Mossberg Model RM-7B

Similar to the Model RM-7A; 7mm Rem. magnum caliber, 3-shot magazine, 24″ barrel.
Estimated Value: **Excellent:** **$225.00**
Very good: **$170.00**

Mossberg Model 1500 Mountaineer

Mossberg Model 1700 Classic Hunter L/S

Mossberg Model 1500 Varmint

Mossberg Model 1500 Varmint

Similar to the Model 1500 with a 24″ heavy barrel in 223, 22-250 or 308 caliber; Monte Carlo stock; available in blued or Parkerized finish (add $10.00).

Estimated Value: New (retail): $424.95
Excellent: $320.00
Very good: $240.00

Mossberg Model 1550 Mountaineer

Similar to the Model 1500 with removable magazine, 22″ barrel, in 243, 270 and 30-06 calibers; add $20.00 for sights.

Estimated Value: New (retail): $362.95
Excellent: $270.00
Very good: $200.00

Mossberg Model 1700 Classic Hunter L/S

Similar to the Model 1500 with 22″ barrel, lipped forearm, pistol grip cap and recoil pad, in calibers: 243, 270 and 30-06.

Estimated Value: New (retail): $453.95
Excellent: $340.00
Very good: $255.00

Mossberg Model 1500 Mountaineer

Caliber: 223, 22-250, 243, 270, 308, 30-06, 7mm magnum, 300 Win. magnum, 338 Win. magnum

Action: Bolt action, hammerless; repeating

Magazine: 5 or 6-shot box

Barrel: 22″ or 24″

Sights: Available without or with adjustable rear, hooded ramp front

Stock & Forearm: Checkered walnut one-piece pistol grip stock and forearm; recoil pad on magnum

Approximate wt.: 7¾ lbs.

Comments: Introduced by Mossberg in 1985. Add $15.00 for magnum, $20.00 for sights.

Estimated Value: New (retail): $341.95
Excellent: $255.00
Very good: $190.00

Mossberg Model L

Mossberg Model 400 Palomino

Mossberg Model 402

Mossberg Model 472 PCA

Mossberg Model 472, SCA

Mossberg Model L
Caliber: 22 short, long, long rifle
Action: Lever-action, falling block; single shot
Magazine: None
Barrel: Blued 24″
Sights: Open rear, bead front
Stock & Forearm: Plain walnut semi-pistol grip stock and small forearm
Approximate wt.: 5 lbs.
Comments: Made from the late 1920's to early 1930's.
Estimated Value: Excellent: $210.00
Very good: $160.00

Mossberg Model 400 Palomino
Caliber: 22 short, long, long rifle
Action: Lever-action; hammerless; repeating
Magazine: Tubular; 15 long rifles, 17 longs, 20 shorts
Barrel: Blued 24″
Sights: Adjustable open rear, bead front
Stock & Forearm: Checkered walnut Monte Carlo pistol grip stock and forearm; barrel bands; swivels
Approximate wt.: 4¾ lbs.
Comments: Made in the early 1960's.
Estimated Value: Excellent: $80.00
Very good: $60.00

Mossberg Model 402
Similar to the Model 400 with smaller capacity magazine. Discontinued in the early 1970's.
Estimated Value: Excellent: $75.00
Very good: $55.00

Mossberg Model 472 PCA, SCA, 479 PCA, SCA
Caliber: 30-30, 35 Rem.
Action: Lever-action; exposed hammer; repeating
Magazine: 6-shot tubular
Barrel: Blued 20″
Sights: Adjustable rear, ramp front
Stock & Forearm: Plain pistol grip stock and forearm; barrel band; swivels; or straight grip stock (SCA)
Approximate wt.: 7½ lbs.
Comments: Sold first as the 472 Series, then 479 Series.
Estimated Value: Excellent: $150.00
Very good: $110.00

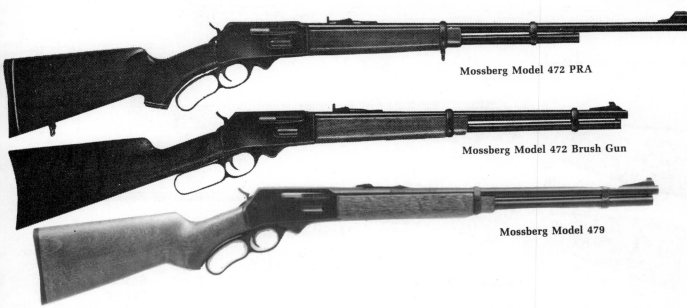

Mossberg Model 472 PRA

Mossberg Model 472 Brush Gun

Mossberg Model 479

Mossberg Model 472 Brush Gun
Similar to the Model 472 PCA with 18″ barrel; straight stock; 5-shot magazine.
Estimated Value: Excellent: $160.00
Very good: $120.00

Mossberg Model 479
Caliber: 30-30 Win.
Action: Lever action, exposed hammer, repeating
Magazine: 5-shot tubular
Barrel: 20″
Sights: Adjustable open rear, beaded ramp front; drilled and tapped for scope
Stock & Forearm: Hardwood semi-pistol grip stock and forearm; barrel band
Approximate wt.: 6¾ lb.
Comments: Produced from the early 1980's to mid 1980's.
Estimated Value: Excellent: $200.00
Very good: $150.00

Mossberg Model 472 PRA, SBA
Similar to the 472 PCA with 24″ barrel; hooded front sight. Discontinued in the late 1970's.
Estimated Value: Excellent: $155.00
Very good: $115.00

Mossberg Model K
Caliber: 22 short, long, long rifle
Action: Slide action; hammerless; repeating
Magazine: Tubular; 14 long rifles, 16 longs, 20 shorts
Barrel: Blued 22″
Sights: Open rear, bead front
Stock & Forearm: Plain walnut straight grip stock and grooved slide handle
Approximate wt.: 5 lbs.
Comments: Made from the early 1920's to early 1930's; takedown model.
Estimated Value: Excellent: $90.00
Very good: $70.00

Mossberg Model 50

Mossberg Model 50
Caliber: 22 long rifle
Action: Semi-automatic; hammerless
Magazine: 15-shot tubular in stock
Barrel: Blued 24″
Sights: Open rear, hooded ramp front
Stock & Forearm: Walnut one-piece semi-pistol grip stock and forearm
Approximate wt.: 7 lbs.
Comments: Made from the late 1930's to early 1940's.
Estimated Value: Excellent: $75.00
Very good: $60.00

Mossberg Model 51

Mossberg Model 51
Similar to the Model 50 with receiver peep sight; swivels; cheekpiece. Made in the late 1930's.
Estimated Value: Excellent: $80.00
Very good: $65.00

Mossberg Model 51M

Mossberg Model 151M

Mossberg Model 151 K

Mossberg Model 152

Mossberg Model 152K

Mossberg Model 142

Mossberg Model 151M

Improved version of the Model 51M with easy takedown features. Made from the mid 1940's to late 1950's.

Estimated Value: **Excellent:** **$85.00**
Very good: **$65.00**

Mossberg Model 51M

Similar to the Model 51 with full length, two-piece forearm and 20″ barrel. Made from the late 1930's to mid 1940's.

Estimated Value: **Excellent:** **$80.00**
Very good: **$65.00**

Mossberg Model 151K

Similar to the 151M with Monte Carlo stock; standard length lipped forearm; 24″ barrel; no peep sight or swivels.

Estimated Value: **Excellent:** **$80.00**
Very good: **$60.00**

Mossberg Model 152

Caliber: 22 long rifle
Action: Semi-automatic
Magazine: 7-shot detachable box
Barrel: Blued 18″
Sights: Peep rear, military front
Stock & Forearm: Plain one-piece semi-pistol grip stock and hinged forearm for forward grip; side mounted swivels
Approximate wt.: 5 lbs.
Comments: Made from the late 1940's to late 1950's.
Estimated Value: **Excellent:** **$80.00**
Very good: **$65.00**

Mossberg Model 152K

Similar to the Model 152 with open rear sight; shorter barrel.

Estimated Value: **Excellent:** **$85.00**
Very good: **$70.00**

Mossberg Model 142

Similar to the Model 152 in bolt action; available in short, long or long rifle; with peep sight.

Estimated Value: **Excellent:** **$75.00**
Very good: **$60.00**

Mossberg Model 142K

Similar to the Model 142 with open rear sight.

Estimated Value: **Excellent:** **$70.00**
Very good: **$55.00**

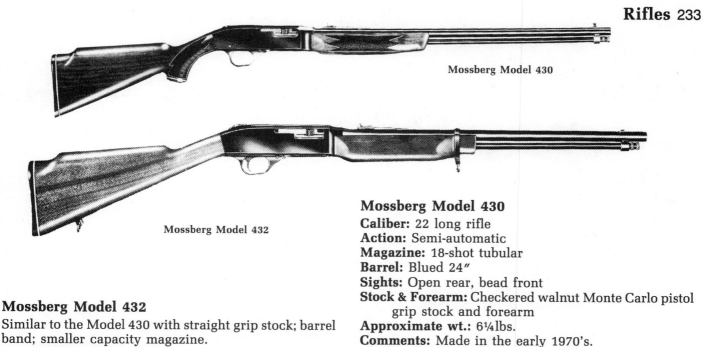

Mossberg Model 430

Mossberg Model 432

Mossberg Model 432

Similar to the Model 430 with straight grip stock; barrel band; smaller capacity magazine.
Estimated Value: **Excellent:** $75.00
Very good: $60.00

Mossberg Model 430

Caliber: 22 long rifle
Action: Semi-automatic
Magazine: 18-shot tubular
Barrel: Blued 24″
Sights: Open rear, bead front
Stock & Forearm: Checkered walnut Monte Carlo pistol grip stock and forearm
Approximate wt.: 6¼lbs.
Comments: Made in the early 1970's.
Estimated Value: **Excellent:** $80.00
Very good: $60.00

Mossberg Model 351 C (Carbine)

Mossberg Model 351K

Mossberg Model 350K

Mossberg Model 351 C (Carbine)

Similar to the 351K with 18½″ barrel; barrel bands; swivels.
Estimated Value: **Excellent:** $75.00
Very good: $60.00

Mossberg Model 351K

Caliber: 22 long rifle
Action: Semi-automatic
Magazine: 15-shot tubular, in stock
Barrel: Blued 24″
Sights: Open rear, bead front
Stock & Forearm: Walnut Monte Carlo one-piece semi-pistol grip stock and forearm
Approximate wt.: 6 lbs.
Comments: Made from about 1960 to 1970.
Estimated Value: **Excellent:** $80.00
Very good: $65.00

Mossberg Model 350K

Caliber: 22 long rifle
Action: Semi-automatic
Magazine: 7-shot clip
Barrel: Blued 23½″
Sights: Open rear, bead front
Stock & Forearm: Walnut Monte Carlo one-piece semi-pistol grip stock and forearm
Approximate wt.: 6 lbs.
Comments: Made from the late 1950's to early 1970's.
Estimated Value: **Excellent:** $75.00
Very good: $60.00

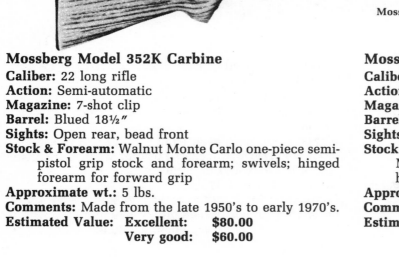

Mossberg Model 377 Plinkster

Mossberg Model 352K Carbine

Mossberg Model 352K Carbine

Caliber: 22 long rifle
Action: Semi-automatic
Magazine: 7-shot clip
Barrel: Blued 18½″
Sights: Open rear, bead front
Stock & Forearm: Walnut Monte Carlo one-piece semi-pistol grip stock and forearm; swivels; hinged forearm for forward grip
Approximate wt.: 5 lbs.
Comments: Made from the late 1950's to early 1970's.
Estimated Value: Excellent: $80.00
Very good: $60.00

Mossberg Model 377 Plinkster

Caliber: 22 long rifle
Action: Semi-automatic; hammerless
Magazine: 15-shot tubular; stock load
Barrel: 20″ round
Sights: None; 4X scope standard
Stock & Forearm: Molded structural foam; one-piece Monte Carlo pistol grip stock and forearm; thumb hole; cheekpiece
Approximate wt.: 6¼ lbs.
Comments: Produced from the late 1970's to mid 1980's.
Estimated Value: Excellent: $ 85.00
Very good: $ 65.00

Musketeer

Musketeer Mauser

Musketeer Mauser

Caliber: 243, 25-06, 270, 264 mag., 308, 30-06, 7mm mag., 300 mag.
Action: FN Mauser bolt action
Magazine: 5-shot, 3-shot magnum
Barrel: Blued 24″
Sights: Leaf rear, hooded ramp front
Stock & Forearm: Checkered walnut Monte Carlo one-piece pistol grip stock and forearm
Approximate wt.: 7¼ lbs.
Comments: Made from the 1960's to the early 1970's.
Estimated Value: Excellent: $300.00
Very good: $225.00

Musketeer Carbine

Same as Musketeer Mauser except shorter barrel.
Estimated Value: Excellent: $275.00
Very good: $210.00

New Haven

New Haven Model 453 T

New Haven Model 453T

Caliber: 22 short, long, long rifle
Action: Semi-automatic; hammerless
Magazine: 7-shot clip
Barrel: Blued 18″
Sights: Open rear, bead front
Stock & Forearm: Plain one-piece Monte Carlo pistol grip stock and forearm
Approximate wt.: 5½ lbs.
Comments: Introduced in the late 1970's.
Estimated Value: Excellent: $75.00
Very good: $55.00

New Haven Model 453 TS

Similar to the Model 453T with a 4X scope.
Estimated Value: Excellent: $80.00
Very good: $60.00

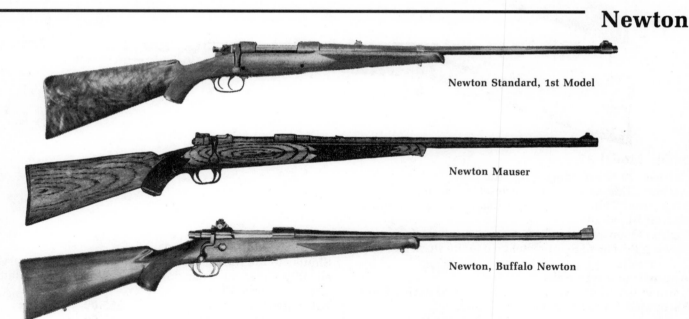

New Haven Model 740T

New Haven Model 679

Caliber: 30-30 Win.
Action: Lever-action; exposed hammer; repeating
Magazine: 6-shot tubular
Barrel: Blued 20″
Sights: Open rear, ramp front
Stock & Forearm: Plain birch semi-pistol grip stock and forearm; barrel band
Approximate wt.: 6¾ lbs.
Comments: Made from the late 1970's to early 1980's.
Estimated Value: **Excellent:**   **$140.00**
          Very good: **$105.00**

New Haven Model 740T

Caliber: 22 Win. mag.
Action: Bolt action; hammerless; repeating
Magazine: 5-shot clip
Barrel: Blued 26″
Sights: Open rear, blade front
Stock & Forearm: Plain birch one-piece Monte Carlo pistol grip stock and forearm
Approximate wt.: 6½ lbs.
Comments: Introduced in the late 1970's.
Estimated Value: **Excellent:**   **$85.00**
          Very good: **$65.00**

New Haven Model 740TS

Similar to the Model 740T with 4X scope.
Estimated Value: **Excellent:**   **$90.00**
          Very good: **$65.00**

Newton

Newton Standard, 1st Model

Newton Mauser

Newton, Buffalo Newton

Newton Standard, 1st Model

Caliber: 22, 256, 280, 30-06, 30 Newton, 35 Newton
Action: Bolt action; double set trigger
Magazine: 5-shot box
Barrel: Blued 24″
Sights: Open rear, ramp front
Stock & Forearm: Checkered wood pistol grip stock and forearm
Approximate wt.: 7½ lbs.
Comments: Made for a short time before World War I.
Estimated Value: **Excellent:**   **$600.00**
          Very good: **$450.00**

Newton Standard, 2nd Model

Very similar to 1st Model with improved action. Made to about 1920's.
Estimated Value: **Excellent:**   **$650.00**
          Very good: **$490.00**

Newton, Buffalo Newton

Similar to the 2nd Model made from the early 1920's to early 1930's.
Estimated Value: **Excellent:**   **$575.00**
          Very good: **$430.00**

Newton Mauser

Caliber: 256
Action: Mauser-type bolt action; reversed double set trigger
Magazine: 5-shot box
Barrel: Blued 24″
Sights: Open rear, ramp front
Stock & Forearm: Checkered wood pistol grip stock and forearm
Approximate wt.: 7 lbs.
Comments: Made in the early 1920's.
Estimated Value: **Excellent:**   **$550.00**
          Very good: **$415.00**

Noble

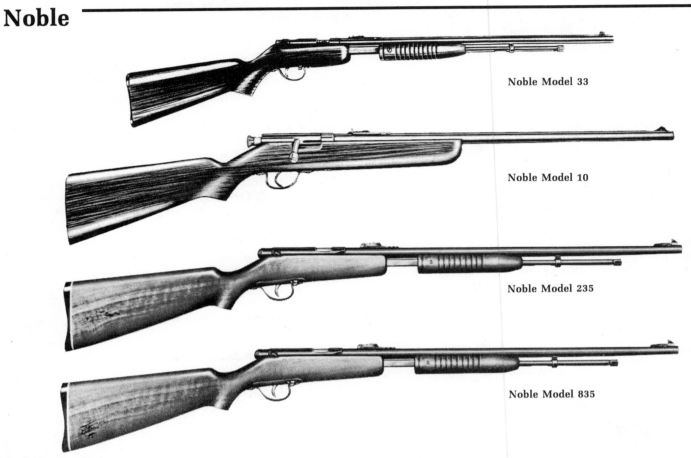

Noble Model 33

Noble Model 10

Noble Model 235

Noble Model 835

Noble Model 33
Caliber: 22 short, long, long rifle
Action: Slide action; hammerless; repeating
Magazine: Tubular; 15 long rifles, 17 longs, 21 shorts
Barrel: Blued 24″
Sights: Open rear, blade front
Stock & Forearm: Semi-pistol grip tenite stock and slide
    handle
Approximate wt.: 6 lbs.
Comments: Made from the late 1940's to early 1950's.
Estimated Value: **Excellent:**   **$80.00**
                  Very good: **$60.00**

Noble Model 33A
Similar to the Model 33 with a wood stock and grooved slide handle. Made until the mid 1950's.
Estimated Value: **Excellent:**   **$85.00**
                  Very good: **$65.00**

Noble Model 10
Caliber: 22 short, long, long rifle
Action: Bolt action; single shot
Magazine: None
Barrel: Blued 24″
Sights: Open rear, bead front
Stock & Forearm: Walnut one-piece semi-pistol grip
    stock and forearm
Approximate wt.: 4 lbs.
Comments: Made from the middle to late 1950's.
Estimated Value: **Excellent:**   **$50.00**
                  Very good: **$40.00**

Noble Model 20
Similar to the Model 10 with: 22″ barrel; slightly curved buttplate; manual cocking device. Made from the late 1950's to early 1960's.
Estimated Value: **Excellent:**   **$55.00**
                  Very good: **$45.00**

Noble Model 235
Caliber: 22 short, long, long rifle
Action: Slide action; hammerless; repeating
Magazine: Tubular; 15 long rifles, 17 longs, 21 shorts
Barrel: Blued 24″
Sights: Open rear, ramp front
Stock & Forearm: Wood semi-pistol grip stock and
    grooved slide handle
Approximate wt.: 5½ lbs.
Comments: Made from the early 1950's to the early
    1970's.
Estimated Value: **Excellent:**   **$75.00**
                  Very good: **$60.00**

Noble Model 835
Similar to the Model 235. Made in the early 1970's.
Estimated Value: **Excellent:**   **$70.00**
                  Very good: **$55.00**

Noble Model 222

Noble Model 275

Noble Model 875

Noble Model 285

Noble Model 222

Caliber: 22 short, long, long rifle
Action: Bolt action; single shot; manual cocking
Magazine: None
Barrel: Blued 22"
Sights: Peep or V notch rear, ramp front
Stock & Forearm: Wood one-piece semi-pistol grip stock and forearm
Approximate wt.: 5 lbs.
Comments: Made from the late 1950's to early 1970's.
Estimated Value: Excellent: $50.00
Very good: $40.00

Noble Model 275 and 875

Caliber: 22 short, long, long rifle
Action: Lever-action; hammerless; repeating
Magazine: Tubular; 15 long rifles, 17 longs, 21 shorts
Barrel: Blued 24"
Sights: Open rear, ramp front
Stock & Forearm: Wood one-piece semi-pistol grip stock and forearm
Approximate wt.: 5½ lbs.
Comments: Made from the late 1950's to early 1970's (Model 275); early to mid 1970's (Model 875).
Estimated Value: Excellent: $75.00
Very good: $60.00

Noble Model 285 and 885

Caliber: 22 long rifle
Action: Semi-automatic
Magazine: 15-shot tubular
Barrel: Blued 22"
Sights: Open adjustaable rear, blade front
Stock & Forearm: Wood one-piece semi-pistol grip stock and forearm
Approximate wt.: 5½ lbs.
Comments: Made from the early to mid 1970's.
Estimated Value: Excellent: $80.00
Very good: $65.00

Pedersen

Pedersen Model 3500

Pedersen Model 3000

Pedersen Model 4700

Pedersen Model 3500

Caliber: 7mm mag., 270, 30-06
Action: Bolt action; adjustable trigger
Magazine: 3-shot box
Barrel: Blued 22″, 24″
Sights: None
Stock & Forearm: Checkered walnut pistol grip stock and forearm
Approximate wt.: 6¾ lbs.
Comments: Made during the 1970's.
Estimated Value: **Excellent:**   **$300.00**
                              Very good: **$220.00**

Pedersen Model 3500 A

Same as the 3500 with a better finish; select walnut; cheek piece; sights.
Estimated Value: **Excellent:**   **$375.00**
                              Very good: **$280.00**

Pedersen Model 3000

Caliber: 270, 30-06, 7mm mag.
Action: Mossberg-type bolt action; adjustable trigger
Magazine: 3-shot box
Barrel: Blued 22″, 24″
Sights: None
Stock & Forearm: Checkered walnut one-piece pistol grip stock and forearm; cheekpiece; swivels
Action: 6¾ lbs.
Comments: Made in three grades during the 1970's.
Estimated Value:

	Grade I	Grade II	Grade III
Excellent:	$800.00	$650.00	$500.00
Very good:	$600.00	$485.00	$375.00

Pedersen Model 4700

Caliber: 30-30, 35 Rem.
Action: Lever-action; exposed hammer; repeating
Magazine: 5-shot tubular
Barrel: Blued 24″
Sights: Open rear, hooded ramp front
Stock & Forearm: Walnut pistol grip stock and short forearm; barrel band; swivels
Approximate wt.: 7½ lbs.
Comments: Made during the 1970's.
Estimated Value: **Excellent:**   **$250.00**
                              Very good: **$175.00**

Plainfield

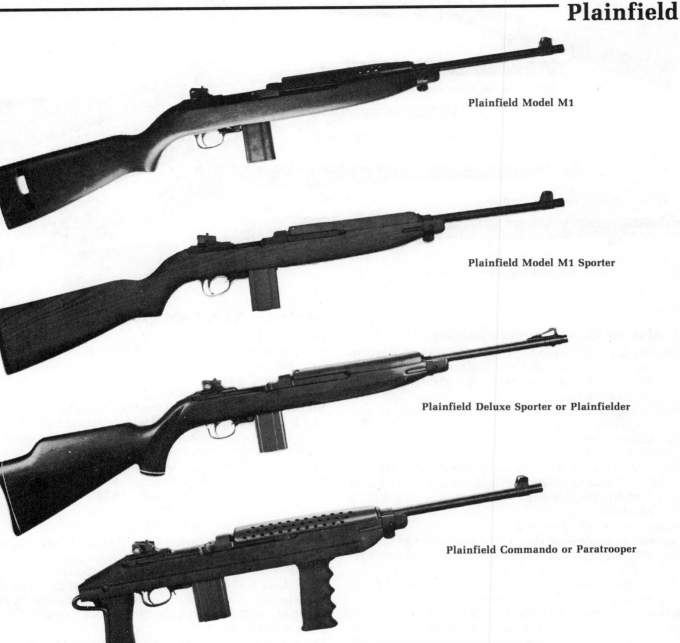

Plainfield Model M1

Plainfield Model M1 Sporter

Plainfield Deluxe Sporter or Plainfielder

Plainfield Commando or Paratrooper

Plainfield Model M1

Caliber: 30 M1, 223 (5.7mm)
Action: Semi-automatic, gas operated
Magazine: 15-shot detachable clip
Barrel: Blued or stainless steel 18″
Sights: Open adjustable rear, gold beaded ramp front
Stock & Forearm: Wood one-piece semi-pistol grip stock and forearm; slot in stock; metal ventilated hand guard
Approximate wt.: 6 lbs.
Comments: Made from about 1960 to late 1970's. Reintroduced in the late 1970's by Iver Johnson. See Iver Johnson; add 30% for stainless steel.
Estimated Value: **Excellent:** **$175.00**
                   Very good: **$130.00**

Plainfield Model M1 Sporter

Similar to the M1 Carbine with a wood hand guard and no slot in the stock. See Iver Johnson.
Estimated Value: **Excellent:** **$185.00**
                   Very good: **$135.00**

Plainfield Deluxe Sporter or Plainfielder

Similar to the Sporter with a checkered walnut Monte Carlo pistol grip stock and forearm.
Estimated Value: **Excellent:** **$175.00**
                   Very good: **$130.00**

Plainfield Commando or Paratrooper

Similar to the M1 Carbine with pistol grip at rear and at forearm; telescoping wire shoulder stock. Add 30% for stainless steel. See Iver Johnson.
Estimated Value: **Excellent:** **$210.00**
                   Very good: **$160.00**

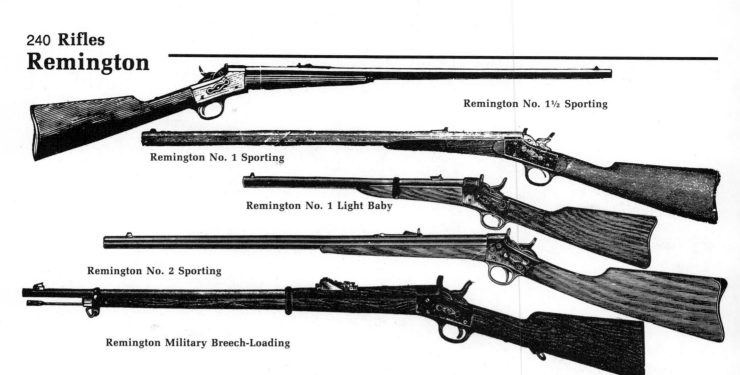

Remington No. 1½ Sporting

Remington No. 1 Sporting

Remington No. 1 Light Baby

Remington No. 2 Sporting

Remington Military Breech-Loading

Remington Military Breech-Loading

Caliber: C.F. 43 Spanish, 43 Egyptian, 50-70 Government, 58 Berdan. Early models used rim fire cartridges. Models for center fire cartridges produced after 1872.

Action: Single shot; rolling block with single trigger; visible hammer

Magazine: None

Barrel: 30″ to 36″ round

Sights: Military (post front and folding leaf rear)

Stock & Forearm: Plain walnut straight stock and forearm; long forearm with ram rod; steel buttplate on stock

Approximate wt.: 8 to 11 lbs.

Comments: Made from about 1867 to 1902 (large number sold to Egypt, France and Spain) and sold commercially in U.S.A. Some are unmarked; some have Arabic marked barrels and some marked Remington's, caliber not marked.

Estimated Value: Excellent: $175.00
Very good: $130.00

Remington No. 1 Sporting

Caliber: Early guns for rim fire 50-70, 44 long and extra long or 46 long and extra long. After 1872 made for centerfire 40-50, 40-70, 44-77, 45-70, or 45 sporting cartridge.

Action: Single shot; rolling block with single trigger; visible hammer

Magazine: None

Barrel: 28″ or 30″ tapered octagon

Sights: Sporting front, folding leaf rear

Stock & Forearm: Plain walnut straight grip stock with flanged-top steel buttplate and short plain walnut forearm with thin roundfront

Approximate wt.: 8½ to 12 lbs.

Comments: Made from about 1868 to 1902. Caliber marked on barrel.

Estimated Value: Excellent: $350.00
Very good: $260.00

Remington No. 1 Light Baby Carbine

Caliber: 44-40

Action: Single-shot; rolling block with single trigger; visible hammer

Magazine: None

Barrel: 20″, light round

Sights: Pointed post front, military folding leaf rear

Stock & Forearm: Plain oiled walnut straight stock with metal buttplate and short forearm; barrel band

Approximate wt.: 5¾ lbs.

Comments: Made from about 1892 to 1902.

Estimated Value: Excellent: $400.00
Very good: $300.00

Remington No. 1½ Sporting

Similar to No. 1 Sporting Rifle except: lighter action, stocks and smaller caliber barrels; approximate wt. 5½ to 7 lbs.; made in following pistol calibers: rim fire 22 short, long and extra long; 25 Stevens and 25 longs; 32 or 38 long and extra long; center fire Winchester 32-20; 38-40; or 44-40; barrel lengths 24″, 26″, 28″, or 30″. Made from about 1869 to 1902.

Estimated Value: Excellent: $300.00
Very good: $225.00

Remington No. 2 Sporting

Caliber: Early models were for rim fire 22, 25, 32 or 38. Later models for center fire 22, 25-21, 25-25, 25-20, 32 long, 38 long or 38-40

Action: Single-shot; rolling block; single trigger

Magazine: None

Barrel: 24″ to 30″ light weight; octagon

Sights: Bead front sight, sporting rear with elevation adjustment

Stock & Forearm: Plain oil-finish walnut, straight stock and forearm with lip at front

Approximate wt.: 5 to 6 lbs.

Comments: Made from about 1873 to 1902; caliber stamped under barrel at forearm.

Estimated Value: Excellent: $325.00
Very good: $240.00

Remington No. 5 1897 Model Military

Remington No. 5 1897 Carbine

Caliber: 7mm

Action: Single shot; rolling block; ornance steel; smokeless powder action with case hardened steel frame; visible hammer

Magazine: None

Barrel: 20″ round, smokeless steel barrel

Sights: Post front, military rear

Stock & Forearm: Plain straight grip, oiled walnut, two-piece stock and forearm; steel buttplate; short forearm; barrel band; hand guard on top of barrel

Approximate wt.: 5 lbs.

Comments: Made from about 1897 to 1906.

Estimated Value: Excellent: $275.00
Very good: $210.00

Remington No. 5 1897 Model Military

Caliber: 7mm to 30 Government

Action: Single-shot; rolling block; smokeless powder action with case hardened frame; visible hammer

Magazine: None

Barrel: 30″ light round tapered barrel

Sights: Post front, folding leaf rear

Stock & Forearm: Plain straight stock, oiled walnut, two-piece, full stock with steel buttplate and capped forearm; ramrod under forearm; two barrel bands; hand guard on top of barrel

Approximate wt.: 8½ lbs.

Comments: Made from about 1897 to 1906.

Estimated Value: Excellent: $300.00
Very good: $225.00

Remington-Hepburn No. 3 Sporting

Remington No. 4 New Model

Remington-Hepburn No. 3 Sporting

Caliber: Center fire 22, 25-20, 25-25, 32, 32-10, 32-20, 32-40, 38, 38-40, 38-50, 38-55, 40-60, 40-65, 40-82, 45-70 Government or 45-90. Also made by order for 40-50, 40-70, 40-90 or 44-77 bottle neck Remington, 45-90, 45-105 or 50-90 Sharps and 50-70 Government.

Action: Hepburn drop block; side-lever opens and closes action; single-shot with low visible hammer; early models with single trigger; later models with single or double set triggers

Magazine: None

Barrel: 28″ to 32″ round, octagon or half octagon

Sights: Blade front; sporting rear adjustable for elevation

Stock & Forearm: Plain straight grip or checkered pistol grip, oiled wood stock with steel buttplate and matching short forearm with lipped front

Approximate wt.: 8 to 12 lbs.

Comments: Made from about 1880 to 1906.

Estimated Value: Excellent: $450.00
Very good: $335.00

Remington No. 4 New Model

Caliber: Rim fire only in 22 short, long and long rifle, 25 Stevens or 32 long

Action: Single-shot; rolling block; light short action with automatic shell ejector; visible hammer

Magazine: None

Barrel: 22½″ light octagon in 22 and 25 caliber; 24″ in 32 caliber; round barrel after about 1931

Sights: Bead front, plain "V" notch rear

Stock & Forearm: Plain varnished, two-piece straight grip stock and forearm; short round front forearm

Approximate wt.: 4¼ lbs.

Comments: Made from about 1891 to 1934.

Estimated Value: Excellent: $200.00
Very good: $150.00

Remington No. 4 S Boy Scout

Remington No. 5 Rolling-Block

Remington No. 6

Remington No. 7 Target

Remington No. 4 S Boy Scout or Military Model

Caliber: 22 short only until 1915; then chambered for 22 short or 22 long

Action: Single-shot; case hardened No. 4 rolling-block action; visible hammer

Magazine: None

Barrel: 28″ medium, round barrel

Sights: Blade front; open "v" notch rear adjustable for elevation

Stock & Forearm: Musket-style, oiled walnut, one-piece, full-length stock and forearm with steel buttplate and one barrel band; bayonet lug below barrel near muzzle; hand guard on top of barrel

Approximate wt.: 5 lbs.

Comments: Called Boy Scout model from 1913 to 1915 then renamed Military Model. Produced from about 1913 to 1932.

Estimated Value: Excellent: $360.00
Very good: $270.00

Remington No. 5 Rolling-Block

Caliber: 7mm Mauser, 30-30 or 30-40 Krag

Action: New Ordnance steel, single-shot; rolling block; smokeless powder action with case hardened frame

Magazine: None

Barrel: 28″-30″ light steel round barrel

Sights: Blade front, Rocky Mountain rear

Stock & Forearm: Plain varnished walnut, two-piece straight grip stock and forearm; steel buttplate on stock; forearm lipped at front

Approximate wt.: 7¼ lbs.

Comments: Made from about 1896 to 1906.

Estimated Value: Excellent: $300.00
Very good: $225.00

Remington No. 6

Caliber: 22 short, long, long rifle, 32 short and long RF

Action: Single-shot; rolling-block; visible hammer; takedown model

Magazine: None

Barrel: 20″ round tapered barrel

Sights: Bead front; open rear; also tang peep sight available

Stock & Forearm: Plain varnished walnut straight grip stock and forearm; steel buttplate

Approximate wt.: 4 lbs.

Comments: Made from about 1902 to 1934.

Estimated Value: Excellent: $180.00
Very good: $135.00

Remington No. 7 Target

Caliber: 22 long rifle, 32 MRF or 25 Stevens RF

Action: Single-action; rolling block; visible hammer

Magazine: None

Barrel: 24″, 26″, 28″; half-octagon barrel

Sights: Bead front, adjustable dovetail rear

Stock & Forearm: Varnished checkered walnut pistol grip stock and forearm; capped pistol grip; rubber buttplate; lipped forearm

Approximate wt.: 7 lbs.

Comments: Made from about 1904 to 1906.

Estimated Value: Excellent: $700.00
Very good: $520.00

Remington-Lee Sporting

Remington-Lee Military

Remington-Lee Military Carbine

Remington-Lee Sporting

Caliber: 6mm U.S. Navy, 30-30 Sporting, 30-40 U.S. Government, 7mm Mauser, or 7.65mm Mauser

Action: Improved smokeless powder, bolt action; repeating

Magazine: 5-shot removable box

Barrel: 24″ to 28″ round smokeless steel barrel

Sights: Bead or blade front, open rear adjustable for elevation

Stock & Forearm: Checkered walnut one-piece semi-pistol grip stock and forearm; forearm grooved on each side with lip at front

Approximate wt.: 6¾ lbs.

Comments: Some were produced with deluxe grand walnut stock, half-octagon barrel and Lyman sights. Made from about 1897 to 1906. Prices are for standard grade.

Estimated Value: **Excellent:**   **$325.00**
                Very good: **$245.00**

Remington-Lee Military

Caliber: 30-40 Krag, 303 British, 6mm Lee Navy, 7mm Mauser or 7.65mm Mauser

Action: Improved smokeless powder, bolt action; repeating, rimless cartridges

Magazine: 5-shot removable box

Barrel: 29″ round smokeless steel barrel

Sights: Post front; folding leaf rear

Stock & Forearm: Plain walnut one-piece straight grip stock and long forearm; cleaning rod; barrel bands; wood hand guard on top of barrel

Approximate wt.: 8½ lbs.

Comments: Made from about 1897 to 1902.

Estimated Value: **Excellent:**   **$300.00**
                Very good: **$225.00**

Remington-Lee Military Carbine

Similar to Remington-Lee rifle except: 20″ barrel; one barrel band; approximate wt. 6½ lbs.

Estimated Value: **Excellent:**   **$325.00**
                Very good: **$245.00**

Remington Model 1907-15

Caliber: 8mm Lebel

Action: Smokeless powder bolt action; repeating; self-cocking striker with knurled top for uncocking and manual cocking

Magazine: 5-shot box

Barrel: 26″ to 31″ round with 4 groove rifling

Sights: Ivory bead dovetail front, folding leaf rear

Stock & Forearm: Plain varnished walnut one-piece stock and long forearm; barrel bands; cleaning rod in forearm under barrel

Approximate wt.: 8 to 9 lbs.

Comments: Made from about 1907 to 1915; left side of action marked "Remington MLE 1907-15"; right side of barrel near action marked "RAC 1907-15".

Estimated Value: **Excellent:**   **$200.00**
                Very good: **$150.00**

Remington Model 1907-15 Carbine

Same as Remington Model 1907-15 repeating rifle except: 22″ barrel; no barrel bands; short forearm; approximate wt. 6½ lbs.

Estimated Value: **Excellent:**   **$190.00**
                Very good: **$145.00**

Remington, Enfield Pattern, 1914 Military

Caliber: 303 British (rimmed)
Action: British smokeless powder bolt action; repeating; self-cocking on down stroke of bolt handle
Magazine: 5-shot box
Barrel: 26″ round tapered barrel
Sights: Protected post front; protected folding leaf rear
Stock & Forearm: Oil finished walnut, one-piece stock and forearm; wood hand guard on top of barrel; modified pistol grip stock; full length forearm with two barrel bands
Approximate wt.: 10 lbs.
Comments: Made afrom about 1915 to 1916 for the British Army; Serial No. on action and bolt, "R" preceeding action serial no.; approximately 600,000 produced.
Estimated Value: Excellent: $265.00
 Very good: $195.00

Remington, Enfield U.S. Model 1917 Military

Caliber: 30-06 Government, rimless
Action: Smokeless powder bolt action; repeating; self-cocking on down stroke of bolt handle; actions made with interchangeable parts
Magazine: 5-shot box
Barrel: 26″ round tapered
Sights: Protected post front, protected folding leaf rear
Stock & Forearm: Plain one-piece walnut stock and forearm; wood hand guard over barrel; modified pistol grip stock; full length forearm with finger grooves and two barrel bands; equipped with sling loops and bayonet lug
Approximate wt.: 10 lbs.
Comments: Made from about 1917 to 1918. Marked "Model of 1917", Remington and serial no. on bridge.
Estimated Value: Excellent: $270.00
 Very good: $200.00

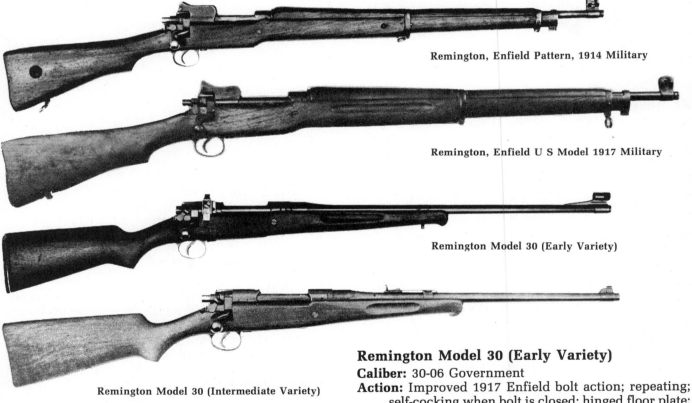

Remington, Enfield Pattern, 1914 Military

Remington, Enfield U S Model 1917 Military

Remington Model 30 (Early Variety)

Remington Model 30 (Intermediate Variety)

Remington Model 30 (Intermediate Variety)

Same as Model 30 (Early Variety) rifle except: calibers 30-06 Government, 25, 30, 32 and 35 Remington and 7mm Mauser; 22″ barrel length; also made in 20″ barrel carbine. Made from about 1926 to 1930. Approximate wt. 7 lbs.
Estimated Value: Excellent: $285.00
 Very good: $210.00

Remington Model 30 (Early Variety)

Caliber: 30-06 Government
Action: Improved 1917 Enfield bolt action; repeating; self-cocking when bolt is closed; hinged floor plate; side-safety
Magazine: 5-shot box
Barrel: 24″ light round
Sights: Slip-on band front sight, adjustable rear sight
Stock & Forearm: Plain varnished walnut, one-piece pistol grip stock and forearm; steel buttplate; grooved forearm with lipped front tip
Approximate wt.: 8 lbs.
Comments: Made from about 1921 to 1926; approximately 8,500 produced; marked "Remington Arms Co. Inc., Remington Ilion Works, Ilion, N.Y. Made in U.S.A."
Estimated Value: Excellent: $300.00
 Very good: $225.00

Remington Model 30 Express

Remington Model 33

Remington Model 34

Remington Model 30 Express

Caliber: 25, 30, 32 or 35 Remington, 30-06 Government, 7mm Mauser until 1936. After 1936 caliber 257 Roberts and 30-06 Government only
Action: Bolt action; repeating; self-cocking; thumb safety
Magazine: 5-shot box
Barrel: 22″ or 24″ round barrel
Sights: Bead front, adjustable open rear
Stock & Forearm: Plain or checkered walnut pistol grip one-piece stock and forearm; early models have grooved forearm with lipped tip
Approximate wt.: 7½ lbs.
Comments: Made from about 1921 to 1940.
Estimated Value: **Excellent:** $285.00
 Very good: $215.00

Remington Model 30R Carbine

Same as Model 30 Express Rifle except: 20″ barrel; plain walnut one-piece stock and forearm; approximate wt. 7 lbs.
Estimated Value: **Excellent:** $275.00
 Very good: $210.00

Remington Model 30S Sporting

Similar to Model 30 Express Rifle except: caliber 257 Roberts, 7mm Mauser or 30-06; approximate wt. 8 lbs.; rear peep sight; special grade high comb stock; produced from about 1930 to 1940; 24″ barrel.
Estimated Value: **Excellent:** $330.00
 Very good: $250.00

Remington Model 33

Caliber: 22 short, long, long rifle
Action: Single-shot; bolt action; takedown model; exposed knurled cocking-piece
Magazine: None
Barrel: 24″ round
Sights: Bead front, open rear, adjustable for elevation
Stock & Forearm: Plain varnished walnut one-piece pistol grip stock and forearm
Approximate wt.: 4 lbs.
Comments: Made from about 1931 to 1936; finger grooves added to forearm in 1934.
Estimated Value: **Excellent:** $75.00
 Very good: $55.00

Remington Model 33 NRA Junior Target

Same as Model 33 except: post front sight; reep rear sight; equipped with 1″ leather sling; swivels; approximate wt. 4½ lbs.
Estimated Value: **Excellent:** $85.00
 Very good: $65.00

Remington Model 34

Caliber: 22 short, long, long rifle
Action: Bolt action; repeating; takedown model; self-cocking; thumb safety
Magazine: Tubular under barrel; 22 shorts, 17 longs, 15 long rifles
Barrel: 24″ round
Sights: Bead front, adjustable open rear
Stock & Forearm: Plain wood, one-piece pistol grip stock and grooved forearm
Approximate wt.: 5½ lbs.
Comments: Made from about 1933 to 1935; also produced in Model 34 NRA target model with peep rear sight and sling swivels.
Estimated Value: **Excellent:** $125.00
 Very good: $ 90.00

Remington Model 41

Caliber: 22 short, long, long rifle, 22 WRF
Action: Bolt action; single-shot; takedown model; exposed knurled cocking-piece
Magazine: None
Barrel: 27″ round
Sights: Bead or hooded ramp front sight, open rear adjustable for elevation or peep rear sight
Stock & Forearm: Plain one-piece pistol grip stock and forearm; hard rubber buttplate
Approximate wt.: 5 lbs.
Comments: Made from about 1936 to 1940 in following models:
    41 A - "Standard" model with open sights;
    41 P - "Target" model with target sights;
    41 AS - "Special" model chambered for 22 WRF;
    41 SB - "Smoothbore" model; no rifling, chambered for 22 LR shot shell only.
Estimated Value: Excellent: $85.00
                  Very good: $65.00

Remington Model 341 Sportsmaster

Caliber: 22 short, long, long rifle
Action: Bolt action; repeating; takedown model; self-cocking; thumb safety
Magazine: Tubular under barrel; 22 shorts, 17 longs, 15 long rifles
Barrel: 27″ round
Sights: Bead front, open rear adjustable for elevation
Stock & Forearm: Plain wood one-piece pistol grip stock and forearm
Approximate wt.: 6 lbs.
Comments: Made from about 1935 to 1940. Also made in Model 341 P, which has hooded front sight and peep rear sight.
Estimated Value: Excellent: $90.00
                  Very good: $70.00

Remington Model 341 S Sportsmaster

Same as Model 341 except: smooth bore for 22 shot cartridges.
Estimated Value: 'Excellent: $75.00
                  Very good: $60.00

Remington Model 37 Rangemaster

Caliber: 22 long rifle
Action: Bolt action; repeating self-cocking; thumb safety; adjustable trigger
Magazine: 5-shot clip and single-shot adapter
Barrel: 28″ heavy, semi-floating target barrel
Sights: Target sights; drilled for scope mount
Stock & Forearm: Lacquer finished heavy target, one-piece walnut stock and forearm; high flute comb stock with plain pistol grip and steel buttplate; early models had rounded beavertail forearm with one barrel band; barrel band dropped in 1938 and forearm modified
Approximate wt.: 12 lbs.
Comments: Made from about 1937 to 1940.
Estimated Value: Excellent: $350.00
                  Very good: $265.00

Remington Model 37 (1940 Model)

Similar to Model 37 rifle except: improved trigger mechanism; re-designed stock; wide beavertail forearm; produced from about 1940 to 1955.
Estimated Value: Excellent: $360.00
                  Very good: $275.00

Remington Model 41

Remington Model 341

Remington Model 37

Remington Model 37 (1940 Model)

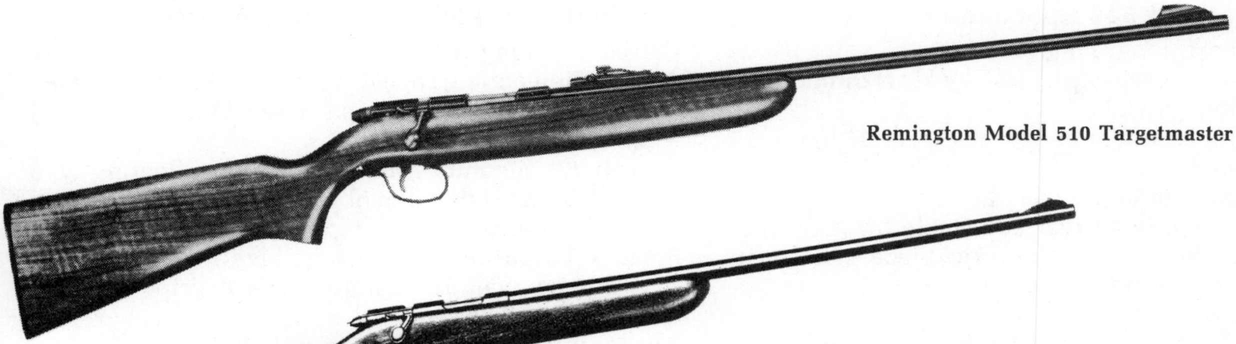

Remington Model 510 Targetmaster

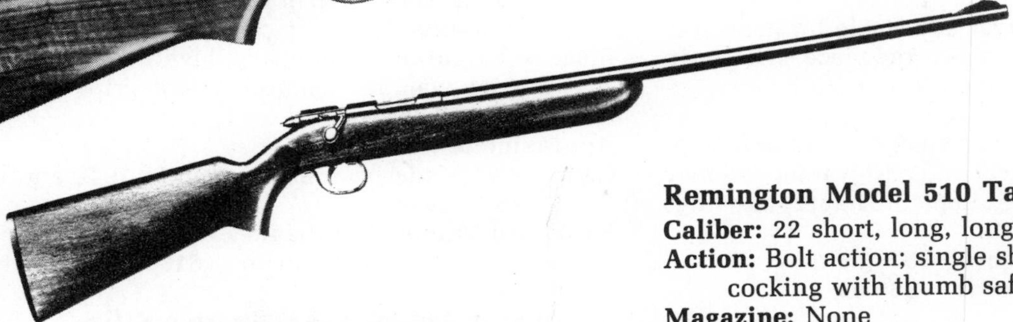

Remington Model 510 C Carbine

Remington Model 510 Targetmaster
Caliber: 22 short, long, long rifle
Action: Bolt action; single shot; takedown model; self-cocking with thumb safety and cocking indicator
Magazine: None
Barrel: 25″ light round
Sights: Sporting or target sights
Stock & Forearm: Plain walnut one-piece pistol grip stock and forearm
Approximate wt.: 5 lbs.
Comments: Made from about 1939 to 1962 in three models: 510 A Standard model; 510 P with peep sights; and 510 SB, a smooth-bore chambered for 22 shot shells; minor changes in manufacture, in markings and in stocks for the pre-World War II and post-World War II models.
Estimated Value: **Excellent:**   **$80.00**
                      Very good: **$60.00**

Remington Model 510 C Carbine
Same as Model 510 A single shot rifle except: 21″ barrel and approximate wt. of 5½ lbs. Made from about 1961 to 1962.
Estimated Value: **Excellent:**   **$70.00**
                      Very good: **$50.00**

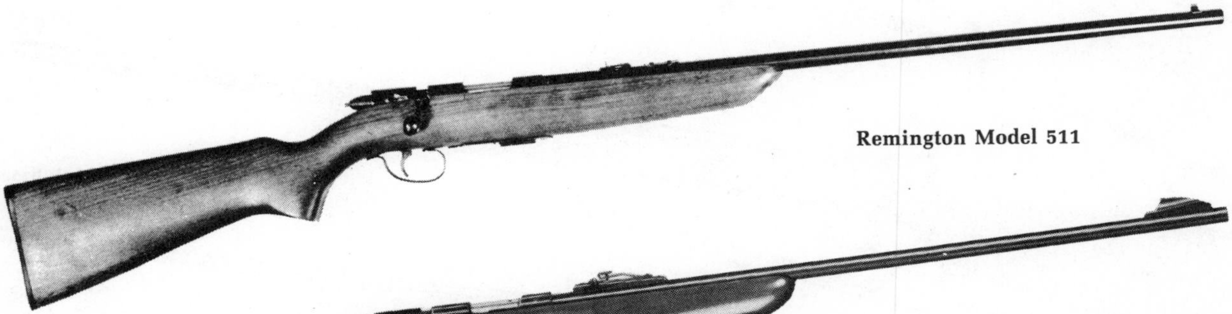

Remington Model 511

Remington Model 511 SB

Remington Model 511 Scoremaster
Caliber: 22 short, long, long rifle
Action: Bolt action; repeating; self-cocking; thumb safety; cocking indicator; takedown model
Magazine: 6-shot clip; also 10-shot clip after 1952
Barrel: 25″ light round
Sights: Open sporting sights
Stock & Forearm: Plain wood, one-piece pistol grip stock and forearm
Approximate wt.: 5¾ lbs.
Comments: Made from about 1939 to 1962 with production stopped during World War II; made in pre-war and post-war models. Add $10.00 fpr pre-1942.
Estimated Value: **Excellent:**   **$95.00**
                      Very good: **$70.00**

Remington Model 511 SB
Same as Model 511 Scoremaster Rifle except: smooth bore for using 22 shot cartridges.
Estimated Value: **Excellent:**   **$80.00**
                      Very good: **$60.00**

Remington Model 512 Sportmaster

Caliber: 22 short, long, long rifle
Action: Bolt action; repeating; self-cocking; thumb safety; cocking indicator
Magazine: Tubular under barrel; 22 shorts, 17 longs, 15 long rifles
Barrel: 25″ light round
Sights: Bead front, open rear adjustable for elevation
Stock & Forearm: Plain walnut one-piece pistol grip stock and forearm; composition buttplate
Approximate wt.: 5½ lbs.
Comments: Made from about 1940 to 1942 and from 1946 to 1962; the pre-war and post-war models may have minor differences in manufacture, markings and stocks.

Estimated Value: Excellent: $75.00
Very good: $60.00

Remington Model 512 SB

Same as Model 512 Sportmaster except smooth bore for 22 shot cartridges.

Estimated Value: Excellent: $70.00
Very good: $55.00

Remington Model 513 T Matchmaster

Caliber: 22 long rifle
Action: Bolt action; repeating; self-cocking; side safety; cocking indicator; adjustable trigger
Magazine: 6-shot clip
Barrel: 27″ medium round barrel; semi-floating type
Sights: Target sights; top of receiver grooved for scope mount after 1954
Stock & Forearm: Plain, heavy, high fluted comb; lacquered walnut one-piece pistol grip stock and beavertail forearm
Approximate wt.: 9 lbs.
Comments: Made from about 1940 to 1942 and from 1945 to 1968.

Estimated Value: Excellent: $180.00
Very good: $135.00

Remington Model 513 S Sporter Rifle

Similar to Model 513 T Matchmaster except: lighter sporting checkered walnut one-piece stock and forearm; approximate wt. 6¾ lbs.; ramp front sight and adjustable open rear sight; produced from about 1940 to 1958.

Estimated Value: Excellent: $175.00
Very good: $130.00

Remington Model 512 Sportmaster

Remington Model 512 SB

Remington Model 513 T Matchmaster

Remington Model 514

Remington Model 514

Caliber: 22 short, long, long rifle
Action: Bolt action; single-shot; takedown model; self-cocking
Magazine: None
Barrel: 21″ (514 BR) or 24″ light round
Sights: Sporting or target sights
Stock & Forearm: Plain walnut one-piece pistol grip stock and forearm
Approximate wt.: 4¼ lbs.
Comments: Made from about 1948 to 1972 in three models: 514 Standard Model; 514 P had target sights (peep rear sight); 514 BR Boys Rifle had 1″ shorter stock and 21″ barrel.

Estimated Value: Excellent: $55.00
Very good: $45.00

Remington Model 720

Remington Model 721

Remington Model 720

Caliber: 257 Roberts, 270 Win., 30-06 Government
Action: Bolt action; repeating; self-cocking; side-safety
Magazine: 5-shot box; removable floor plate
Barrel: 20″, 22″, or 24″ round
Sights: Ramp front, adjustable open rear sights
Stock & Forearm: Checkered walnut one-piece pistol grip stock and forearm
Approximate wt.: 8 lbs.
Comments: Made from about 1941 to 1946.
Estimated Value: Excellent: $275.00
                     Very good: $210.00

Remington Model 721

Caliber: 270, 30-06 or 300 mag.; after 1959, 280 Rem.
Action: Bolt action; repeating; self-cocking; side safety; adjustable trigger
Magazine: 4-shot box with fixed floor plate; 3-shot in 300 magnum
Barrel: 24″ or 26″ round
Sights: Ramp front, sporting rear with step elevator
Stock & Forearm: Checkered walnut or plain one-piece pistol grip stock and forearm; aluminum shotgun buttplate
Approximate wt.: 8 lbs.
Comments: Made from about 1948 to 1958 in six grades: standard grade made from 1948 to 1961. Prices are for standard grade.
Estimated Value: Excellent: $180.00
                     Very good: $135.00

Remington Model 521

Remington Model 722

Remington Model 521 TL Target

Caliber: 22 long rifle
Action: Bolt action; repeating; self-cocking; thumb safety; cocking indicator
Magazine: 5- or 10-shot clip
Barrel: 25″ medium weight round barrel
Sights: Post front, Lyman #57 receiver sight (peep sight)
Stock & Forearm: Heavy target one-piece pistol grip stock and beavertail forearm; varnished or oil finished; rubber buttplate
Approximate wt.: 6½ lbs.
Comments: Made from about 1948 to 1968; a low-cost rifle intended for junior target shooter.
Estimated Value: Excellent: $100.00
                     Very good: $ 75.00

Remington Model 722

Caliber: 257 Roberts or 300 Savage; in 1950 222 Rem.; in 1956 308 Win. and 244 Rem.; in 1958 222 Rem. mag.; in 1960 243 Win.
Action: Bolt action; repeating; self-cocking; side-safety; fixed floor plate; adjustable trigger
Magazine: 4-shot box; 5-shot in 222 magnum
Barrel: 22″ or 24″ round
Sights: Ramp bead front, open adjustable rear
Stock & Forearm: Checkered or plain varnished walnut one-piece pistol grip stock and forearm; after 1950 option of high-comb stock and tapered forearm
Approximate wt.: 7 to 8½ lbs.
Comments: Made from about 1948 to 1958 in seven grades; standard grade made from about 1948 to 1961.
Estimated Value: Excellent: $200.00
                     Very good: $150.00

Remington Model 725 (Early)

Caliber: 270, 280, 30-06
Action: Bolt action; repeating; self-cocking; thumb safety
Magazine: 4-shot box
Barrel: 22″ round
Sights: Adjustable open rear, hooded ramp front
Stock & Forearm: Checkered walnut Monte Carlo one-piece pistol grip stock and forearm; capped grip stock with shotgun buttplate and sling loops
Approximate wt.: 7½ lbs.
Comments: Made from about 1958 to 1959.
Estimated Value: **Excellent:** **$275.00**
  Very good: **$210.00**

Remington Model 725 (Late)

Same as Model 725 (Early) Rifle except: also in calibers 243 Win.; 244 Rem.; or 222 Rem.; 24″ barrel in 222 Rem. and aluminum buttplate on all calibers. Made from about 1960 to 1961 in three grades. Prices are for standard grade.
Estimated Value: **Excellent:** **$325.00**
  Very good: **$245.00**

Remington Model 725 Magnum

Caliber: 375 or 458 Win. magnum
Action: Bolt action; repeating; self-cocking; thumb safety
Magazine: 3-shot box
Barrel: 26″ heavy round barrel with muzzle brake
Sights: Ramp front, deluxe adjustable rear
Stock & Forearm: Fancy reinforced, checkered walnut Monte Carlo one-piece pistol grip stock and forearm; stock with cap and rubber recoil pad; black forearm tip; quick detachable leather sling
Approximate wt.: 9 lbs.
Comments: Made from about 1960 to 1961 in three grades. Prices are for ADL grade.
Estimated Value: **Excellent:** **$500.00**
  Very good: **$375.00**

Remington Model 725 (Early)

Remington Model 725 (Late)

Remington Model 725 Magnum

Remington Model 10 Nylon

Remington Model 10 Nylon Carbine

Caliber: 22 short, long, long rifle
Action: Bolt action; self-cocking striker with indicator; single-shot; slide safety
Magazine: None
Barrel: 19½″ round
Sights: Ramp front; adjustable open rear
Stock & Forearm: Nylon checkered one-piece pistol grip stock and forearm; shotgun buttplate
Approximate wt.: 4 lbs.
Comments: Made from about 1963 to 1964.
Estimated Value: **Excellent:** **$50.00**
  Very good: **$40.00**

Remington Model 10 SB

Same as Model 10 except: smooth bore; chambered for 22 shot shells.
Estimated Value: **Excellent:** **$45.00**
  Very good: **$35.00**

Remington Nylon 11

Remington Nylon 12

Remington Nylon 11

Caliber: 22 short, long, long rifle
Action: Bolt action; repeating; self-cocking; cocking indicator
Magazine: 6- or 10-shot clip
Barrel: 19½″ round
Sights: Ramp front, adjustable open rear
Stock & Forearm: Polished brown nylon one-piece stock, forearm and handguard over barrel; checkered, capped, pistol grip stock with shot gun buttplate; checkered forearm with blunt reversed cap; white liners and two white diamond inlays on each side
Approximate wt.: 4½ lbs.
Comments: Made from about 1962 to 1964.
Estimated Value: Excellent: $85.00
Very good: $65.00

Remington Nylon 12

Similar to Remington Nylon 11 Rifle except: tubular magazine under barrel holds 14 to 21 shots.
Estimated Value: Excellent: $90.00
Very good: $70.00

Remington Model 600

Remington Model 600 Magnum

Remington Model 660

Remington Model 600

Caliber: 6mm Rem., 222 Rem., 243 Win., 308 Win., 35 Rem.
Action: Bolt action; repeating
Magazine: 5-shot box
Barrel: 18½″; ventilated rib
Sights: Open rear, bead front
Stock & Forearm: Checkered walnut Monte Carlo one-piece pistol grip stock and forearm
Approximate wt.: 6 lbs.
Comments: A carbine style rifle made in the mid 1960's.
Estimated Value: Excellent: $200.00
Very good: $150.00

Remington Model 600 Magnum

Similar to the Model 600 in magnum calibers; 4-shot magazine; walnut and beechwood stock; swivels; recoil pad.
Estimated Value: Excellent: $225.00
Very good: $170.00

Remington Model 660

Similar to the Model 600; 20″ barrel without rib; beaded front sight; made in the late 1960's and early 1970's.
Estimated Value: Excellent: $175.00
Very good: $130.00

Remington Model 660 Magnum

Similar to the Model 600 Magnum; 20″ barrel without rib; beaded front sight; made in the late 1960's to early 1970's.
Estimated Value: Excellent: $195.00
Very good: $145.00

Remington Model 580

Caliber: 22 short, long, long rifle
Action: Bolt action; single-shot; self-cocking striker
Magazine: None
Barrel: 24″ round
Sights: Bead front; adjustable open rear
Stock & Forearm: Plain wood Monte Carlo one-piece pistol grip stock and forearm; plastic shotgun buttplate
Approximate wt.: 5 lbs.
Comments: Made from about 1967 to late 1970's; also available in Boys' model with shorter stock for young shooters.
Estimated Value: Excellent: $65.00
Very good: $50.00

Remington Model 580 SB

Same as Model 580 except: smooth bore for 22 long rifle shot shell only.
Estimated Value: Excellent: $60.00
Very good: $45.00

Remington Model 581 and 581-S

Caliber: 22 short, long, long rifle
Action: Bolt action; repeating; self-cocking; thumb safety
Magazine: 5-shot clip; single shot adapter
Barrel: 24″ round
Sights: Bead front, adjustable open rear sight
Stock & Forearm: Plain wood Monte Carlo one-piece pistol grip stock and forearm
Approximate wt.: 5¼ lbs.
Comments: Made from about 1967 to 1983; reintroduced in 1986 as "Sportsman" 581-S.
Estimated Value: New (retail): $221.95
Excellent: $165.00
Very good: $125.00

Remington Model 582

Same as Model 581 except: 14 to 20 shot tubular magazine under barrel. Add $13.00 for swivels and sling.
Estimated Value: Excellent: $140.00
Very good: $110.00

Remington Model 580

Remington Model 580 SB

Remington Model 581

Remington Model 582

Remington Model 788

Remington Model 788

Caliber: 222, 22-250, 223 Rem., 6mm Rem., 243 Win., 308 Win.; 7mm-08 Rem. added 1980
Action: Bolt action; repeating; self-cocking; thumb safety
Magazine: 5-shot clip in 222; 4-shot clip in other calibers
Barrel: 24″ round tapered barrel in calibers 222, 22-250 and 223 Rem.; 22″ barrel in other calibers; 18½″ barrel available 1980
Sights: Blade front, adjustable rear
Stock & Forearm: Monte Carlo one-piece pistol grip stock and forearm; current model has fluted comb and wider pistol grip and forearm; swivels available
Approximate wt.: 7½ lbs.
Comments: Made from about 1967 to 1983. Add $5.00 for left hand action, $50.00 for scope.
Estimated Value: Excellent: $225.00
Very good: $170.00

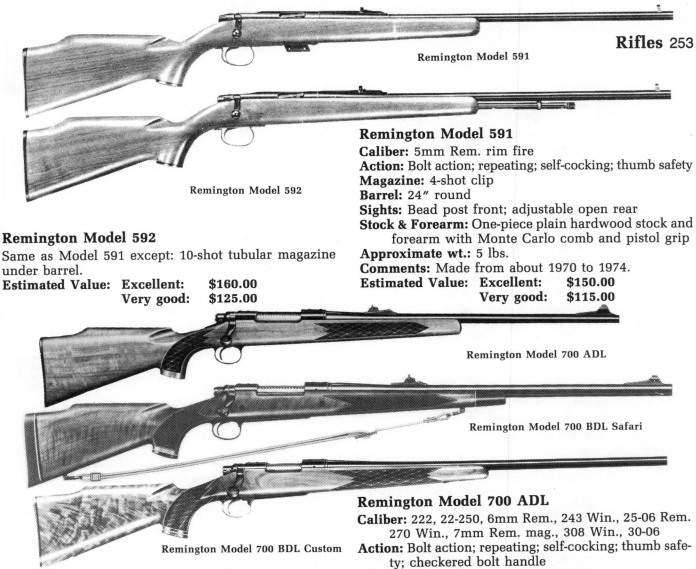

Remington Model 591

Remington Model 592

Remington Model 700 ADL

Remington Model 700 BDL Safari

Remington Model 700 BDL Custom

Remington Model 591

Caliber: 5mm Rem. rim fire
Action: Bolt action; repeating; self-cocking; thumb safety
Magazine: 4-shot clip
Barrel: 24″ round
Sights: Bead post front; adjustable open rear
Stock & Forearm: One-piece plain hardwood stock and forearm with Monte Carlo comb and pistol grip
Approximate wt.: 5 lbs.
Comments: Made from about 1970 to 1974.
Estimated Value: Excellent: $150.00
Very good: $115.00

Remington Model 592

Same as Model 591 except: 10-shot tubular magazine under barrel.
Estimated Value: Excellent: $160.00
Very good: $125.00

Remington Model 700 ADL

Caliber: 222, 22-250, 6mm Rem., 243 Win., 25-06 Rem. 270 Win., 7mm Rem. mag., 308 Win., 30-06
Action: Bolt action; repeating; self-cocking; thumb safety; checkered bolt handle
Magazine: 4- to 6-shot box magazine
Barrel: 22″ or 24″ round tapered barrel
Sights: Ramp front; adjustable, notched, removable rear
Stock & Forearm: Checkered walnut Monte Carlo pistol grip, one-piece stock and forearm; shotgun buttplate
Approximate wt.: 7½ lbs.
Comments: Produced from about 1962 to present. Add $20.00 for magnum or swivels and sling.
Estimated Value: New (retail): $439.95
Excellent: $330.00
Very good: $250.00

Remington Model 700 BDL Safari

Similar to 700 BDL in 375 H&H magnum and 458 Win. magnum; recoil pad. 8mm Rem. magnum caliber added in 1986.
Estimated Value: New (retail): $851.95
Excellent: $640.00
Very good: $480.00

Remington Model 700 BDL Varmint Special

Similar to 700 BDL with heavy barrel in 222 Rem., 22-250 Rem., 223 Rem., 6mm Rem., 243 Win., 25-06 Rem., 7mm-08, 308 Win.
Estimated Value: New (retail): $551.95
Excellent: $415.00
Very good: $310.00

Remington Model 700 BDL Classic

Similar to 700 BDL with stock styling changes; calibers 22-250 Rem., 6mm Rem., 243 Win., 270 Win., 30-06. Add $20.00 for magnum. A limited number available in 1981 in 7mm magnum; 1982, 257 Roberts; 1983, 300 H & H magnum; 1984, 250 Savage; 1985, 350 Rem. magnum; 1986, 264 Win. magnum.
Estimated Value: New (retail): $492.95
Excellent: $370.00
Very good: $280.00

Remington Model 700 BDL Custom

Similar to Model 700 BDL except: custom deluxe grade with black forearm end; sling strap; additional calibers: 17 Rem., 223 Rem., 264 Win. magnum, 300 Win. magnum.
Estimated Value: New (retail): $519.95
Excellent: $390.00
Very good: $295.00

Remington Model 700 "Mountain Rifle"

Similar to 700 BDL except: 270 Win., 280 Rem. and 30-06 caliber; approx. wt. 7 lbs.; 4-shot magazine; no sights; introduced in 1986.
Estimated Value: New (retail): $527.95
Excellent: $395.00
Very good: $295.00

Remington Model 7

Remington Sportsman 78

Remington Model 40 X Target

Remington Model 40XR

Remington Model 40XB

Remington Model 40XBBR

Remington Sportsman 78

Similar to the Model 700 with lesser quality finish; hardwood with no checkering; 22″ barrel; 270 Win. and 30-06 calibers. Introduced in 1984. 243 and 308 calibers added in 1985; 223 caliber added in 1986.

Estimated Value: New (retail): $361.95
Excellent: $270.00
Very good: $200.00

Remington Model 7

Caliber: 222 Rem., 223 Rem., 243 Win., 6mm Rem., 7mm-08 Rem., 308 Win.
Action: Bolt action; repeating
Magazine: 4- or 5-shot box with steel floor plate
Barrel: 18½″ tapered
Sights: Adjustable U-notch rear on inclined ramp, beaded ramp front
Stock & Forearm: Checkered walnut one-piece pistol grip stock and slightly lipped forearm; recoil pad, swivels
Approximate wt.: 6¼ lbs.
Comments: Introduced in 1983. 222 caliber discontinued in 1985.
Estimated Value: New (retail): $505.95
Excellent: $380.00
Very good: $285.00

Remington Model 40 X Target

Caliber: 22 long rifle in 1960; 222 Rem. in 1961; 308, 30-06; others on special order
Action: Bolt action; single-shot; self-cocking; thumb safety; adjustable trigger
Magazine: None
Barrel: 28″ standard or heavy round barrel with bedding device in forearm
Sights: Removable target sights, scope block on barrel
Stock & Forearm: Oiled, plain, heavy target one-piece pistol grip stock and blade front; rubber shotgun buttplate; high fluted comb stock
Approximate wt.: 11 to 12 lbs.
Comments: Made from about 1956 to 1963. Replaced by Model 40 XB match rifle in 1964 to 1975.
Estimated Value: Excellent: $325.00
Very good: $245.00

Remington Model 40XR

A target rifle similar to the Model 40X Target with widened stock and forearm; adjustable buttplate; hand stop; introduced in the late 1970's. 22 long rifle only.
Estimated Value: New (retail): $786.95
Excellent: $590.00
Very good: $440.00

Remington Model 40XB Rangemaster

Similar to the Model 40X target with a stainless steel barrel. Available in calibers 222 Rem., 22-250 Rem., 243 Win., 6mm Rem., 25-06 Rem., 7mm Rem. magnum, 7.62mm NATO, 30-06, 30-338, 300 Win. magnum; add $50.00 for repeating model. Currently produced.
Estimated Value: New (retail): $991.95
Excellent: $745.00
Very good: $560.00

Remington Model 40XBBR

Similar to the Model 40XB Rangemaster with a 20″ or 24″ barrel. Currently produced.
Estimated Value: New (retail): $1,045.95
Excellent: $ 785.00
Very good: $ 590.00

Remington Model 540-X

Remington Model 540XR

Remington Model 541 S

Remington Model 540-X, 540 XR

Caliber: 22 long rifle
Action: Bolt action; single-shot; self-cocking striker; slide safety; adjustable match trigger
Magazine: None
Barrel: 26″ heavy target barrel
Sights: Receiver drilled and tapped for scope mount; sights optional equipment
Stock & Forearm: Full pistol grip, heavy wood one-piece stock and forearm; thumb-grooved stock with 4-way adjustable buttplate rail
Approximate wt.: 8¾ lbs.
Comments: Made from about 1970 to 1983. A heavy rifle designed for bench shooting.
Estimated Value: Excellent: $255.00
                   Very good: $190.00

Remington Model 541 S Custom and 541-T

Caliber: 22 short, long and long rifle
Action: Bolt action; repeating; self-cocking; thumb safety
Magazine: 5-shot clip
Barrel: 24″
Sights: None; barrel and receiver are drilled for a wide variety of optional scopes or sights
Stock & Forearm: One-piece checkered pistol grip stock and forearm
Approximate wt.: 5½ lbs.
Comments: Designed after the Remington Model 540 X Target Rifle; made from about 1972 to 1983. Reintroduced in 1986 as Model 541-T.
Estimated Value: New (retail): $406.95
                   Excellent: $305.00
                   Very good: $225.00

Remington Nylon 76

Remington Nylon 76

Caliber: 22 long rifle
Action: Lever-action; repeating; side ejection; lever under stock operates sliding bolt which ejects empty case, chambers cartridge from magazine and cocks concealed striker; safety located on top of stock behind receiver
Magazine: 14-shot tubular magazine in stock
Barrel: 19½″ round
Sights: Blade front, open rear sight
Stock & Forearm: Checkered nylon two-piece stock and forearm; pistol grip stock; forearm lipped at tip with nylon hand guard over barrel
Approximate wt.: 4½ lbs.
Comments: Made from about 1962 to 1964; the only lever action repeater made by Remington Arms Co.
Estimated Value: Excellent: $150.00
                   Very good: $115.00

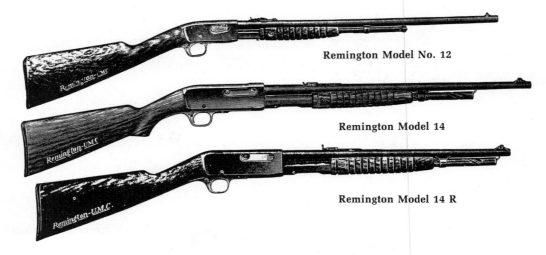

Remington Model No. 12

Remington Model 14

Remington Model 14 R

Remington Model 14

Caliber: 25, 30, 32, 35 Rem.
Action: Slide action; hammerless; takedown model
Magazine: 5-shot tubular, under barrel
Barrel: 22″ round
Sights: Bead front, adjustable rear
Stock & Forearm: Plain or checkered walnut pistol grip stock and grooved or checkered forearm
Approximate wt.: 7 lbs.
Comments: Made from about 1912 to 1935 in four grades; higher grades had checkering and engraving. Prices are for (plain) standard grade.
Estimated Value: **Excellent:** $250.00
  Very good: $190.00

Remington Model 14½

Similar to Model 14 rifle except: caliber 38-40 and 44-40 only; 22½″ barrel; 11-shot magazine; discontinued about 1925; standard grade only.
Estimated Value: **Excellent:** $300.00
  Very good: $225.00

Remington Model 14 R Carbine

Same as Model 14 rifle except: 18½″ barrel; straight grip stock; approximate wt. 6 lbs.; standard grade only.
Estimated Value: **Excellent:** $200.00
  Very good: $150.00

Remington Model 14½ Carbine

Same as Model 14½ rifle except 18½″ barrel and 9-shot magazine.
Estimated Value: **Excellent:** $310.00
  Very good: $235.00

Remington Model No. 12

Caliber: 22 short, long, long rifle
Action: Slide action; hammerless; takedown model
Magazine: 10- to 15-shot tubular, under barrel
Barrel: 22″ or 24″ round or octagon
Sights: Bead front, rear adjustable for elevation
Stock & Forearm: Plain or engraved; varnished plain or checkered, straight or pistol grip, walnut stock with rubber or steel buttplate; forearm grooved or checkered walnut
Approximate wt.: 5½ lbs.
Comments: Made from about 1909 to 1936 in four grades; higher grades had checkering and engraving. Prices are for (plain) standard grade.
Estimated Value: **Excellent:** $175.00
  Very good: $130.00

Remington Model 25

Remington Model 25 R Carbine

Same as Model 25 Rifle except: 18½″ barrel; straight grip stock; 6-shot magazine; approximate wt. 4½ lbs.; standard grade only.
Estimated Value: **Excellent:** $260.00
  Very good: $200.00

Remington Model 25

Caliber: 25-20, 32-20
Action: Slide action; hammerless; takedown model
Magazine: 10-shot tubular, under barrel
Barrel: 24″
Sights: Bead front, open rear
Stock & Forearm: Checkered or plain walnut pistol grip stock and grooved or checkered slide handle
Approximate wt.: 6 lbs.
Comments: Made from about 1923 to 1936 in four grades; higher grades had checkering and engraving. Prices are for (plain) standard grade.
Estimated Value: **Excellent:** $250.00
  Very good: $190.00

Remington Model 141 Gamemaster

Remington Model 121 Fieldmaster

Remington Model 121 Fieldmaster

Caliber: 22 short, long, long rifle
Action: Slide action; hammerless; takedown model
Magazine: Tubular, under barrel; 20 shorts, 15 longs, 14 long rifles
Barrel: 24″ round
Sights: Bead front, adjustable rear
Stock & Forearm: Checkered or plain walnut pistol grip stock and grooved or checkered semi-beavertail slide handle
Approximate wt.: 6 lbs.
Comments: Made from about 1936 to 1942 and from 1946 to 1955 in four grades; higher grades checkered and engraved. Prices are for (plain) standard grade.
Estimated Value: Excellent: $225.00
                      Very good: $170.00

Remington Model 141 Gamemaster

Caliber: 30, 32 and 35 Rem.
Action: Slide action; hammerless; takedown model
Magazine: 5-shot tubular, under barrel
Barrel: 24″ round
Sights: Ramp front, adjustable rear
Stock & Forearm: Checkered or plain walnut pistol grip stock and grooved or checkered semi-beavertail slide handle
Approximate wt.: 7 lbs.
Comments: Made from about 1936 to 1942 and from 1946 to 1950 in four grades; higher grades had checkered pistol grip stock and forearm and engraving. Prices are for (plain) standard grade.
Estimated Value: Excellent: $300.00
                      Very good: $225.00

Remington 141 R Carbine

Same as Model 141 A rifle except: 18½″ barrel; approximate wt. 5½ lbs.; standard grade only.
Estimated Value: Excellent: $290.00
                      Very good: $215.00

Remington Model 121 SB

Same as Model 121 except smooth bore barrel for 22 shot cartridges.
Estimated Value: Excellent: $220.00
                      Very good: $165.00

Remington Model 121 S

Similar to Model 121 except: caliber 22 Rem. special only; 12-shot magazine; standard grade.
Estimated Value: Excellent: $200.00
                      Very good: $150.00

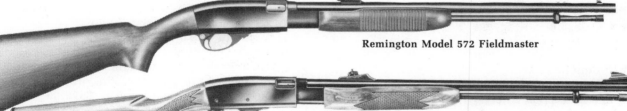

Remington Model 572 Fieldmaster

Remington Model 572 BDL

Remington Model 572 SB

Same as Model 572 rifle except: smooth bore for 22 shot cartridges; standard grade only.
Estimated Value: Excellent: $130.00
                      Very good: $100.00

Remington 572 BDL Fieldmaster

Deluxe version of the 572A Fieldmaster. Currently produced. Add $17.00 for swivels and sling.
Estimated Value: New (retail): $239.95
                      Excellent: $180.00
                      Very good: $135.00

Remington Model 572 A Fieldmaster

Caliber: 22 short, long, long rifle
Action: Slide action; hammerless; solid frame; side ejection
Magazine: 14- to 20-shot tubular, under barrel
Barrel: 21″ and 24″ round tapered
Sights: Bead front, adjustable open rear
Stock & Forearm: Checkered or plain walnut pistol grip stock and grooved or checkered slide handle
Approximate wt.: 5½ lbs.
Comments: Made from about 1955 to present; add $17.00 for sling and swivels.
Estimated Value: New (retail): $212.95
                      Excellent: $160.00
                      Very good: $120.00

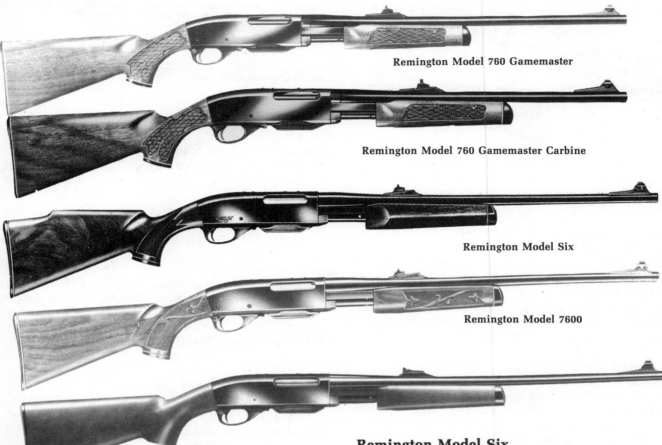

Remington Model 760 Gamemaster

Remington Model 760 Gamemaster Carbine

Remington Model Six

Remington Model 7600

Remington Sportsman 76

Remington Model 760 Gamemaster, 760 Carbine

Caliber: 30-06, 308, 300 Savage, 35 Rem., 280, 270 Win., 257 Roberts, 244 Rem., 243 Win., 6mm Rem., 223 and 222; presently made in calibers 30-06, 308 Win., 270 Rem., 243 Win., and 6mm Rem.

Action: Slide action; hammerless; side ejection; solid frame; cross-bolt safety

Magazine: 4-shot box

Barrel: 22″ round tapered; 18½″ on carbine

Sights: Ramp bead front, adjustable open rear

Stock & Forearm: Checkered or plain walnut pistol grip stock and grooved checkered semi-beavertail slide handle

Approximate wt.: 7½ lbs.

Comments: Made from about 1952 to about 1980; carbine from 1960 to 1969 in 270 or 280 caliber; 1962 to about 1980 in 30-06 and 308 Win.

Estimated Value: Excellent: $300.00
Very good: $225.00

Remington Model 760 BDL Gamemaster

Similar to Model 760 with basketweave checkering, Monte Carlo stock; available in 30-06, 270, 308.
Estimated Value: Excellent: $310.00
Very good: $230.00

Remington Model Six

Caliber: 6mm Rem., 243 Win., 270 Win., 30-06, 308 Win.

Action: Slide action; hammerless; repeating

Magazine: 4-shot clip

Barrel: Blued 22″

Sights: Blade ramp front, adjustable sliding ramp rear

Stock & Forearm: Checkered walnut Monte Carlo pistol grip stock and slide handle; black grip cap and fore-end tip; recessed finger groove in slide handle; cheekpiece; high gloss finish

Approximate wt.: 7½ lbs.

Comments: Introduced in 1981 to replace the Model 760. Custom grades are available at increased prices. Calibers 6mm and 308 Win. dropped in 1985.

Estimated Value: New (retail): $532.95
Excellent: $400.00
Very good: $300.00

Remington Model 7600

Similar to the Model Six. No Monte Carlo stock or cheekpiece; design checkering. Caliber 6mm dropped in 1985.

Estimated Value: New (retail): $458.95
Excellent: $345.00
Very good: $260.00

Remington Sportsman 76

Similar to the Model 7600 with lesser quality finish; hardwood with no checkering; 22″ barrel; 30-06 caliber only. Introduced in 1984.

Estimated Value: New (retail): $379.95
Excellent: $285.00
Very good: $215.00

Remington Model No. 8

Remington Model No. 16

Remington Model No. 16

Caliber: 22 Rem. automatic

Action: Semi-automatic; hammerless; solid breech; sliding bolt; side ejection; takedown model

Magazine: 15-shot tubular, in stock

Barrel: 22″ round

Sights: Bead front, adjustable notch sporting rear

Stock & Forearm: Plain or engraved; varnished, plain or checkered, straight grip, two-piece walnut stock and forearm; steel buttplate and blunt lip on forearm

Approximate wt.: 5¾ lbs.

Comments: Made from about 1914 to 1928 in four grades, A, C, D and F. Prices for standard grade.

Estimated Value: **Excellent:** **$220.00**
 Very good: **$165.00**

Remington Model No. 8

Caliber: 25, 30, 32 or 35 Rem.

Action: Semi-automatic; top ejection; for smokeless powder; takedown model; solid breech and sliding barrel type

Magazine: 5-shot detachable box

Barrel: 22″ round

Sights: Bead front, open rear

Stock & Forearm: Plain or engraved; varnished, plain or checkered, two-piece walnut straight grip stock and forearm; rubber or steel buttplate and lipped forearm

Approximate wt.: 7¾ lbs.

Comments: Made from about 1906 to 1936 in five grades, A, C, D, E and F; jacket marked "Manufactured by the Remington Arms Co. Ilion, N.Y., U.S.A." "Browning's Patent's Oct. 8, 1900. Oct. 15, 1900. July 2, 1902." Prices for standard grade.

Estimated Value: **Excellent:** **$280.00**
 Very good: **$210.00**

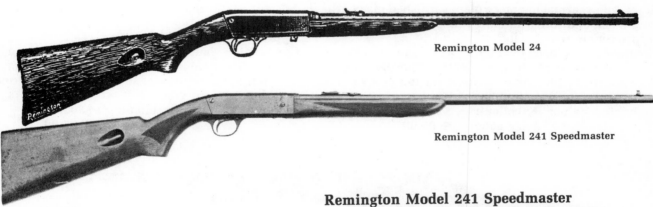

Remington Model 24

Remington Model 241 Speedmaster

Remington Model 24

Caliber: 22 long rifle only or 22 short only

Action: Semi-automatic; hammerless; solid breech; sliding bolt; bottom ejection

Magazine: 15-shot stock tube in 22 short and 10-shot in 22 long rifle

Barrel: 19″ round

Sights: Bead front, adjustable rear

Stock & Forearm: Plain or engraved; varnished, plain or checkered, two-piece walnut semi-pistol grip stock and forearm; steel buttplate with lipped forearm

Approximate wt.: 4¾ lbs.

Comments: Made from about 1922 to 1935 in five grades, A, C, D, E and F. Prices for standard grade.

Estimated Value: **Excellent:** **$200.00**
 Very good: **$150.00**

Remington Model 241 Speedmaster

Caliber: 22 long rifle only or 22 short only

Action: Semi-automatic; hammerless; solid breech; bottom ejection; takedown type; sliding bolt action; thumb safety

Magazine: 15-shot in 22 short; 10-shot in 22 long rifle; tubular in stock

Barrel: 24″ round

Sights: Bead front, notched rear adjustable for elevation

Stock & Forearm: Plain or engraved; varnished walnut, plain or checkered, two-piece pistol grip stock and forearm; semi-beavertail

Approximate wt.: 6 lbs.

Comments: Improved version of Model 24; produced from about 1935 to 1951 in five grades, A, B, D, E and F. Prices for standard grade.

Estimated Value: **Excellent:** **$220.00**
 Very good: **$170.00**

Remington Model 81 Woodsmaster

Remington Model 550 A

Remington Model 550-2G Gallery

Remington Model 550 A

Caliber: 22 short, long, long rifle
Action: Semi-automatic; hammerless; side ejection; solid breech; sliding bolt; floating power piston which permits using 22 short, long or long rifle interchangeably and still function as semi-automatic; takedown type with thumb safety
Magazine: 20-shot in 22 short; 15-shot in 22 long rifle
Barrel: 24″ round
Sights: Dovetail bead front, notched rear adjustable for elevation
Stock & Forearm: One-piece plain varnished pistol grip stock and forearm; hard rubber buttplate
Approximate wt.: 6½ lbs.
Comments: Replaced the Model 241 because it was less expensive to produce. Made from bout 1941 to 1942 and from 1946 to 1970. Receiver top grooved for telescope sight mounts.
Estimated Value: Excellent: $125.00
Very good: $ 95.00

Remington Model 550-2G Gallery

Similar to Model 550 A except chambered for 22 short caliber only.
Estimated Value: Excellent: $100.00
Very good: $ 75.00

Remington Model 81 Woodsmaster

Caliber: From 1936 to 1942, 25, 30, 32, 35 Rem.; from 1946 to 1950, 30, 32, 35, 300 Savage
Action: Semi-automatic; top ejection; takedown model; solid breech; sliding barrel type
Magazine: 5-shot detachable box
Barrel: 22″ round
Sights: Bead front, sporting rear with notched elevator
Stock & Forearm: Plain or engraved; varnished walnut, plain or checkered two-piece pistol grip stock and forearm; rubber buttplate and semi-beavertail style forearm
Approximate wt.: 7¾ lbs.
Comments: Made from about 1936 to 1942 and from 1946 to 1950 in five grades, A, B, D, E, and F. An improved version of the Model No. 8. Prices are for standard grade.
Estimated Value: Excellent: $300.00
Very good: $225.00

Remington Model 740 A

Remington Model 740 ADL Deluxe Grade

Same as Model 740 A except: deluxe checkered stock and forearm; also grip cap and sling swivels.
Estimated Value: Excellent: $260.00
Very good: $200.00

Remington Model 740 BDL Special Grade

Same as Model 740 ADL Deluxe Grade except: stock and forearm have deluxe finish on select wood.
Estimated Value: Excellent: $300.00
Very good: $225.00

Remington Model 740 A Woodsmaster

Caliber: 30-06 or 308
Action: Semi-automatic; gas operated; side ejection; hammerless
Magazine: 4-shot detachable box
Barrel: 22″ round
Sights: Ramp front, open rear adjustable for elevation
Stock & Forearm: Plain pistol grip stock and forearm; semi-beavertail forearm with finger grooves
Approximate wt.: 7½ lbs.
Comments: Made from about 1950 to 1960.
Estimated Value: Excellent: $250.00
Very good: $190.00

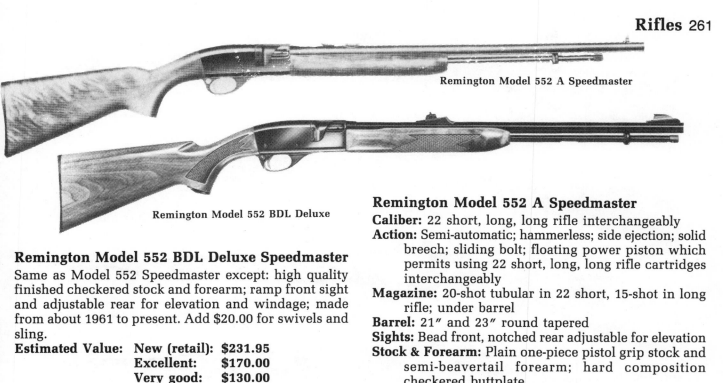

Remington Model 552 A Speedmaster

Remington Model 552 BDL Deluxe

Remington Model 552 BDL Deluxe Speedmaster

Same as Model 552 Speedmaster except: high quality finished checkered stock and forearm; ramp front sight and adjustable rear for elevation and windage; made from about 1961 to present. Add $20.00 for swivels and sling.

Estimated Value:	New (retail):	$231.95
	Excellent:	$170.00
	Very good:	$130.00

Remington Model 552 GS Gallery Special

Same as Model 552 Speedmaster except caliber 22 short only.

| Estimated Value: | Excellent: | $125.00 |
| | Very good: | $100.00 |

Remington Model 552 A Speedmaster

Caliber: 22 short, long, long rifle interchangeably
Action: Semi-automatic; hammerless; side ejection; solid breech; sliding bolt; floating power piston which permits using 22 short, long, long rifle cartridges interchangeably
Magazine: 20-shot tubular in 22 short, 15-shot in long rifle; under barrel
Barrel: 21″ and 23″ round tapered
Sights: Bead front, notched rear adjustable for elevation
Stock & Forearm: Plain one-piece pistol grip stock and semi-beavertail forearm; hard composition checkered buttplate
Approximate wt.: 5¾ lbs.
Comments: Made from about 1958 to present. Add $20.00 for swivels and sling.

Estimated Value:	New (retail): $202.95
	Excellent:	$150.00
	Very good:	$115.00

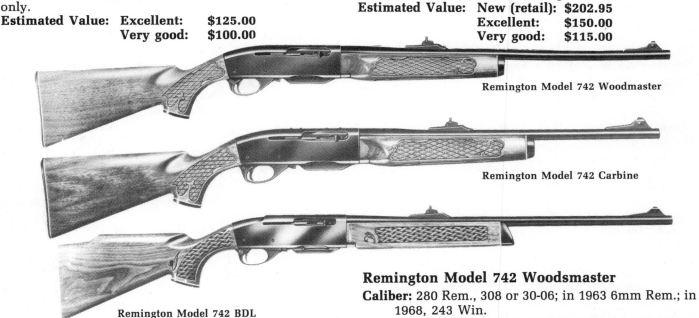

Remington Model 742 Woodmaster

Remington Model 742 Carbine

Remington Model 742 BDL

Remington Model 742 Woodsmaster Carbine

Same as Model 742 Woodsmaster Rifle except: 18½″ barrel; approximate wt. 6½ lbs.; calibers 280, 30-06 or 308 only.

| Estimated Value: | Excellent: | $290.00 |
| | Very good: | $220.00 |

Remington Model 742 BDL Woodsmaster

Same as Model 742 Woodsmaster Rifle except: calibers 30-06 or 308 only; left or right hand models; checkered Monte Carlo stock; black tipped forearm.

| Estimated Value: | Excellent: | $320.00 |
| | Very good: | $240.00 |

Remington Model 742 Woodsmaster

Caliber: 280 Rem., 308 or 30-06; in 1963 6mm Rem.; in 1968, 243 Win.
Action: Semi-automatic; hammerless; side ejection; gas operated sliding bolt
Magazine: 4-shot detachable box
Barrel: 22″ round tapered
Sights: Gold bead front, step adjustable rear with windage adjustment
Stock & Forearm: Plain or checkered and standard or deluxe finish two-piece walnut stock and semi-beavertail forearm; aluminum buttplate
Approximate wt.: 7½ lbs.
Comments: Manufactured from about 1960 to about 1980; in 1969 Remington advertised many fancy grades. Prices are for standard grade.

| Estimated Value: | Excellent: | $300.00 |
| | Very good: | $225.00 |

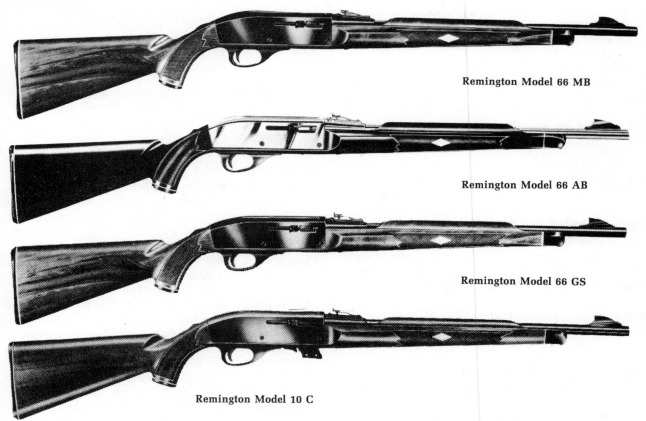

Remington Model 66 MB

Remington Model 66 AB

Remington Model 66 GS

Remington Model 10 C

Remington Model 66 MB and 66 SG

Caliber: 22 long rifle
Action: Semi-automatic; side ejection; solid breech; sliding bolt
Magazine: 14-shot tubular in stock
Barrel: 20″ round
Sights: Blade front; rear sight adjustable for windage and elevation
Stock & Forearm: Du-Pont "Zytel" nylon, brown one-piece receiver, stock and forearm; checkered pistol grip stock and lipped forearm which covers top of barrel
Approximate wt.: 4 lbs.
Comments: Made from about 1959 to present; based on a design concept in which the stock, receiver and forearm are made in one piece; Model 66 SG - Seneca Green discontinued.
Estimated Value: New (retail): $146.95
Excellent: $110.00
Very good: $ 85.00

Remington Model 66 AB, 66 BD

Same as Remington Model 66 MB except: black stock and forearm with chrome plated barrel and receiver covers; made from about 1962. AB discontinued in 1984. BD has black receiver.
Estimated Value: New (retail): $146.95
Excellent: $110.00
Very good: $ 85.00

Remington Model 66 GS

Similar to the Model 66 MB except: chambered for 22 short only (Gallery Special). Made from about 1963 to about 1980.
Estimated Value: Excellent: $95.00
Very good: $70.00

Remington Model 10 C

Same as Remington Model 66 MB except: 10-shot removable box magazine. Produced from about 1970 to late 1970's.
Estimated Value: Excellent: $100.00
Very good: $ 75.00

Remington Bicentennial Model 66

Same as Remington Model 66 MB except: limited number of selected rifles produced in 1976 to commemorate 200 years of nation's history; eagle inscribed on left side of receiver.
Estimated Value: Excellent: $125.00
Very good: $ 95.00

Remington Bicentennial Model 66

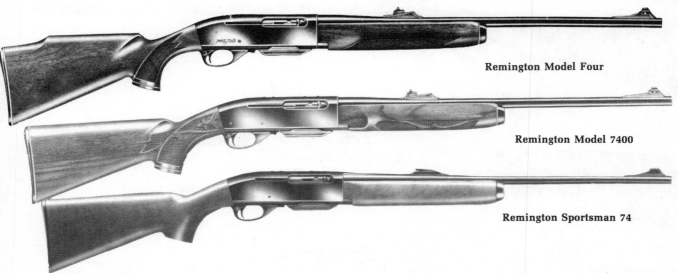

Remington Model Four

Remington Model 7400

Remington Sportsman 74

Remington Model Four

Caliber: 6mm Rem., 243 Win., 270 Win., 280 Rem. (7mm Express Rem.); 30-06, 308 Win.

Action: Semi-automatic; side ejection; gas operated

Magazine: 4-shot clip

Barrel: Blued 22″

Sights: Blade ramp front, adjustable sliding ramp rear

Stock & Forearm: Checkered walnut Monte Carlo pistol grip stock and forearm; black grip cap and fore-end tip; recessed finger groove in forearm; cheekpiece; high gloss finish

Approximate wt.: 7½ lbs.

Comments: Introduced in 1981 to replace the Model 742. Custom grades are available at increased prices. Calibers 6mm and 308 Win. dropped in 1985.

Estimated Value: New (retail): $579.95
Excellent: $430.00
Very good: $320.00

Remington Model 7400

Similar to the Model Four except: no Monte Carlo stock; design checkering.

Estimated Value: New (retail): $505.95
Excellent: $380.00
Very good: $285.00

Remington Sportsman 74

Similar to the Model 7400 with lesser quality finish; hardwood with no checkering: 22″ barrel; 30-06 caliber only. Introduced in 1984.

Estimated Value: New (retail): 425.95
Excellent: $320.00
Very good: $240.00

Ruger

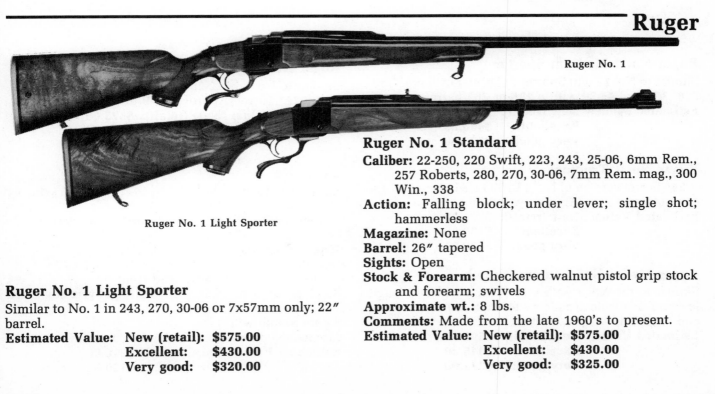

Ruger No. 1

Ruger No. 1 Light Sporter

Ruger No. 1 Light Sporter

Similar to No. 1 in 243, 270, 30-06 or 7x57mm only; 22″ barrel.

Estimated Value: New (retail): $575.00
Excellent: $430.00
Very good: $320.00

Ruger No. 1 Standard

Caliber: 22-250, 220 Swift, 223, 243, 25-06, 6mm Rem., 257 Roberts, 280, 270, 30-06, 7mm Rem. mag., 300 Win., 338

Action: Falling block; under lever; single shot; hammerless

Magazine: None

Barrel: 26″ tapered

Sights: Open

Stock & Forearm: Checkered walnut pistol grip stock and forearm; swivels

Approximate wt.: 8 lbs.

Comments: Made from the late 1960's to present.

Estimated Value: New (retail): $575.00
Excellent: $430.00
Very good: $325.00

Ruger No. 1 Medium Sporter

Ruger No. 1 Tropical

Ruger Model No. 1 International

Ruger No. 1 Special Varminter

Ruger No. 3

Ruger No. 1 Medium Sporter

Similar to No. 1 Light Sporter in heavier calibers, 7mm, 338, 300 and 45-70 with a 22" or 26" barrel.

Estimated Value: New (retail): $575.00
Excellent: $430.00
Very good: $320.00

Ruger No. 1 Tropical

A 24" barrel version of No. 1 in 375 H&H magnum and 458 magnum only. Approx. wt. 8½ lbs.

Estimated Value: New (retail): $575.00
Excellent: $430.00
Very good: $320.00

Ruger Model No. 1 International

Similar to the No. 1 with a 20" barrel with full length forearm; available in calibers 243 Win., 30-06, 270 Win., and 7x57mm; weighs 7¼ lbs.

Estimated Value: New (retail): $595.00
Excellent: $445.00
Very good: $335.00

Ruger No. 1 Special Varminter

Similar to No. 1 in 22-250, 220 Swift, 223, 25-06, 6mm; heavy 24" barrel. Approx. wt. 9 lbs.

Estimated Value: New (retail): $575.00
Excellent: $430.00
Very good: $320.00

Ruger No. 3

Caliber: 22 Hornet, 30-40 Krag, 45-70, 223, 375 Win., 44 mag.
Action: Falling block, under lever; hammerless; single shot
Magazine: None
Barrel: Blued 22"
Sights: Folding leaf rear, bead front
Stock & Forearm: Plain walnut straight grip stock and forearm; barrel band
Approximate wt.: 6 lbs.
Comments: Made from the late 1960's to mid 1980's.
Estimated Value: Excellent: $210.00
Very good: $160.00

Ruger Model 77

Ruger 77 Round Top

Ruger 77 International

Ruger 77 Varmint

Ruger 77 Round Top, M-77ST
Similar to Model 77 with round top receiver and open sights. Made from early 1970's to early 1980's.
Estimated Value: **Excellent:** $295.00
Very good: $220.00

Ruger Model 77 International, M-77RSI
Similar to the Model 77 with 18½″ barrel and full length Mannlicher-type forearm; 22-250, 250-3000, 243, 308, 270 and 30-06 calibers; no sights, integral scope mounts. Introduced in 1982.
Estimated Value: **New (retail):** $480.00
Excellent: $360.00
Very good: $270.00

Ruger Model 77, 77R, 77RS, 77RS Tropical
Caliber: 220 Swift, 22-250, 25-06, 243 Win., 250-3000, 257, 6mm, 270 Win., 7mm Rem. mag., 7x57mm, 300 mag., 30-06, 338 mag., 458 Win. mag. (Tropical)
Action: Bolt action; repeating; either short or magnum action
Magazine: 5-shot box with hinged floor plate; 4-shot in magnum calibers
Barrel: 22″ or 24″ blued
Sights: Adjustable leaf rear, beaded ramp front; nor no sights, integral scope mounts
Stock & Forearm: Checkered walnut, pistol grip, one-piece stock and tapered forearm; recoil pad; swivels
Approximate wt.: 6¾ lbs., 7 lbs., 8¾ lbs.
Comments: Made from the late 1960's to present. Add 29% for 458 magnum (Tropical); add 8% for sights.
Estimated Value: **New (retail):** $440.00
Excellent: $330.00
Very good: $250.00

Ruger 77V Varmint, M-77 Varmint
Similar to Model 77 in 22-250, 220 Swift, 243, 6mm, 308 or 25-06 calibers; 24″ or 26″ tapered barrel; no sights. Made from early 1970's to present. Approx. wt. 9 lbs.
Estimated Value: **New (retail):** $440.00
Excellent: $330.00
Very good: $250.00

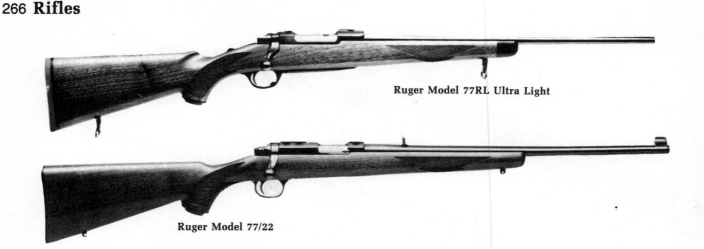

Ruger Model 77RL Ultra Light

Ruger Model 77/22

Ruger Model 77RL Ultra Light

Similar to the Model 77R with 20″ barrel; weighs 6 lbs. Introduced in 1984. Caliber 22-250, 243, 270, 250-3000, 257, 30-06 and 308

Estimated Value: New (retail): **$455.00**
Excellent: **$340.00**
Very good: **$255.00**

Ruger Model 77/22

Similar to the Model 77R in 22 long rifle caliber; 10-shot rotary magazine; 20″ barrel; weighs 5¾ lbs. Introduced in 1984.

Estimated Value: New (retail): **$364.50**
Excellent: **$275.00**
Very good: **$205.00**

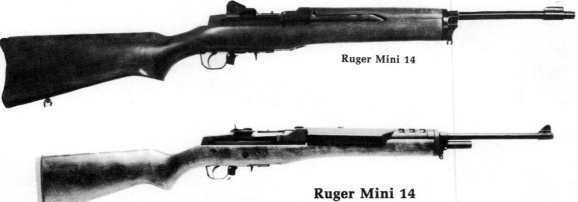

Ruger Mini 14

Ruger Model XGI

Ruger Model XGI

Caliber: 243 or 308
Action: Gas operated, semi-automatic, based on the Garand system used in the U.S. M1 and M14 military rifles
Magazine: 5-shot staggered column, detachable box
Barrel: 20″ blued with handguard cover
Sights: Ramp front and adjustable folding peep rear
Stock & Forearm: Plain, one-piece American hardwood, reinforced with steel liners
Approximate wt.: 8 lbs.
Comments: Introduced in 1986. Similar to the Ruger Mini 14 rifles.

Estimated Value: New (retail): **$425.00**
Excellent: **$320.00**
Very good: **$240.00**

Ruger Mini 14

Caliber: 223 Commercial or Military
Action: Semi-automatic, gas operated
Magazine: 5-shot detachable box; 10- and 20-shot available
Barrel: Blued 18½″; also stainless steel in 1980
Sights: Adjustable rear, bed front
Stock & Forearm: Plain walnut, semi-pistol grip, one piece stock and forearm; handguard over barrel; folding stock and pistol grip available after mid 1980's.
Approximate wt.: 6½ lbs.
Comments: Made from 1974 to present. Add 9½% for stainless steel finish; 19% for folding stock.

Estimated Value: New (retail): **$390.00**
Excellent: **$290.00**
Very good: **$220.00**

Ruger Mini 14/5-R, Ranch Rifle

Similar to the Mini 14 with internal improvements and integral scope mounts. Introduced in 1982; Add 9½% for stainless steel. Add 14% for folding stock.
Estimated Value: New (retail): **$420.00**
Excellent: **$315.00**
Very good: **$235.00**

Ruger Model 10/22

Ruger Model 10/22 Sporter

Ruger Model 10/22 International

Ruger Model 10/22
Caliber: 22 long rifle
Action: Semi-automatic
Magazine: 10-shot detachable rotary
Barrel: Blued 18½"
Sights: Adjustable leaf rear, bead front
Stock & Forearm: Plain walnut one-piece semi-pistol grip stock and forearm; barrel band
Approximate wt.: 5 lbs.
Comments: Made from about 1964 to present.
Estimated Value: New (retail): $176.00
Excellent: $130.00
Very good: $100.00

Ruger Model 10/22, Deluxe Sporter
Similar to the Model 10/22 with: Monte Carlo or regular checkered stock; fluted bandless forearm; swivels.
Estimated Value: New (retail): $222.00
Excellent: $165.00
Very good: $125.00

Ruger Model 10/22 International
Similar to Model 10/22 with full length stock and swivels. Made to early 1970's.
Estimated Value: Excellent: $140.00
Very good: $110.00

Ruger Model 44

Ruger Model 44 RS Deluxe

Ruger Model 44
Caliber: 44 magnum
Action: Semi-automatic, gas operated
Magazine: 4-shot tubular
Barrel: Blued 18½"
Sights: Leaf rear, bead front
Stock & Forearm: Plain walnut one-piece semi-pistol grip stock and forearm; barrel band
Approximate wt.: 5¾ lbs.
Comments: Made from about 1960 to mid 1980's.
Estimated Value: Excellent: $270.00
Very good: $200.00

Ruger Model 44 RS Deluxe
Similar to Model 44 with peep sight and swivels.
Estimated Value: Excellent: $280.00
Very good: $210.00

Ruger Model 44 Sporter

Ruger Model 44 International

Sako Finsport 2700

Sako Vixen Sporter

Sako Vixen Mannlicher

Ruger Model 44 Sporter
Similar to Model 44 with Monte Carlo stock, fluted forearm and swivels. Made to early 1970's.
Estimated Value: Excellent: $260.00
              Very good: $195.00

Ruger Model 44 International
Similar to Model 44 with a full length stock and swivels. Made to early 1970's.
Estimated Value: Excellent: $275.00
              Very good: $210.00

Sako

Sako Finsport 2700
Caliber: 270 Win., 30-06, 7mm Rem. mag., 338 Win. mag.
Action: Long throw bolt action; adjustable trigger
Magazine: 5-shot
Barrel: 23½″ blued
Sights: None
Stock & Forearm: Checkered walnut, Monte Carlo pistol grip, one-piece stock and forearm; recoil pad; swivels
Approximate wt.: 6½ lbs.
Comments: Introduced in 1983.
Estimated Value: New (retail): $909.95
              Excellent: $680.00
              Very good: $510.00

Sako Vixen Sporter
Caliber: 218 Bee, 22 Hornet, 222, 222 mag., 223
Action: Bolt action, short stroke, Mauser-type
Magazine: 5-shot
Barrel: Blued 23½″
Sights: Open rear, hooded ramp front
Approximate wt.: 6½ lbs.
Comments: Made from World War II to the early 1970's. Vixen, Forester and Finnbear became M74 Short, Medium and Long actions.
Estimated Value: Excellent: $420.00
              Very good: $315.00

Sako Vixen Mannlicher
Similar to Sporter with a full length stock; 20″ barrel; barrel band.
Estimated Value: Excellent: $450.00
              Very good: $340.00

Sako Vixen Heavy Barrel

Sako Forester Sporter

Sako Forester Mannlicher

Sako Forester Heavy Barrel

Sako Finnbear

Sako Finnbear Mannlicher

Sako Vixen Heavy Barrel

Similar to Sporter with heavy barrel and in larger calibers only.

Estimated Value: **Excellent:**   **$450.00**
                         Very good: **$340.00**

Sako Forester Sporter

Similar to Vixen Sporter with medium action and in 22-250, 243 and 308 calibers. Made from the late 1950's to early 1970's.

Estimated Value: **Excellent:**   **$430.00**
                         Very good: **$320.00**

Sako Forester Mannlicher

Similar to Forester Sporter with full length stock; 20″ barrel; barrel band.

Estimated Value: **Excellent:**   **$460.00**
                         Very good: **$350.00**

Sako Forester Heavy Barrel

Similar to Forester with a heavy 24″ barrel.

Estimated Value: **Excellent:**   **$475.00**
                         Very good: **$360.00**

Sako Finnbear

Similar to Vixen with: long action; recoil pad; 25-06, 264 magnum, 270, 30-06, 300 magnum, 7mm magnum; 375 H&H. Made from the early 1960's to the early 1970's.

Estimated Value: **Excellent:**   **$480.00**
                         Very good: **$360.00**

Sako Finnbear Mannlicher

Similar to Finnbear with: full length stock; 20″ barrel; barrel band.

Estimated Value: **Excellent:**   **$500.00**
                         Very good: **$375.00**

270 Rifles

Sako Model 74 Super Sporter

Sako Model 74 Super Sporter Heavy Barrel

Sako Model 74 Deluxe Sporter

Sako Mauser

Sako Model A11 Standard

Sako Model 74 Super Sporter

Similar to Vixen, Forester and Finnbear in short action, medium action and long action; 23″ or 24″ barrel. Made in 1970's.

Estimated Value: Excellent: **$420.00**
                     Very good: **$315.00**

Sako Model 74 Super Sporter Heavy Barrel

Similar to Model 74 Super Sporter in short, medium or long action and heavy barrel.

Estimated Value: Excellent: **$450.00**
                     Very good: **$340.00**

Sako Model 74 Deluxe Sporter

Similar to Model 74 Super Sporter with recoil pad, select wood and high quality finish. Add $25.00 for magnum.

Estimated Value: Excellent: **$525.00**
                     Very good: **$400.00**

Sako Mauser

Caliber: 270, 30-06
Action: FN Mauser bolt action; repeating
Magazine: 5-shot box
Barrel: Blued 24″
Sights: Leaf rear, hooded ramp front
Stock & Forearm: Checkered walnut Monte Carlo one-piece pistol grip stock and tapered forearm; swivels
Approximate wt.: 7½ lbs.
Comments: Made from World War II to about 1960.
Estimated Value: Excellent: **$450.00**
                     Very good: **$340.00**

Sako Mauser Magnum

Similar to Sako Mauser in magnum calibers 300 H&H and 375 H&H; recoil pad.

Estimated Value: Excellent: **$500.00**
                     Very good: **$375.00**

Sako Model A1 Standard

Caliber: 17 Rem., 222 Rem., 223 Rem.
Action: Bolt action; repeating; short-throw
Magazine: 5-shot
Barrel: 23½″
Sights: None
Stock & Forearm: Checkered walnut Monte Carlo one-piece pistol grip stock and forearm; swivels
Approximate wt.: 6½ lbs.
Comments: Currently available. Add $25.00 for 17 Rem. caliber.
Estimated Value: New (retail): **$763.95**
                     Excellent: **$570.00**
                     Very good: **$425.00**

Sako Model A11 Standard

Similar to the A1 Standard with a medium throw action and in 220 Swift, 22-250 Rem., 243 Win., 308 Win. calibers.

Estimated Value: New (retail): **$763.95**
                     Excellent: **$570.00**
                     Very good: **$425.00**

Sako Model A1 Deluxe

Sako Varmint

Sako Carbine

Sako Model A111 Standard

Similar to the Model A1 Standard with a long throw action; 25-06 Rem., 270 Win., 30-06, 7mm Rem. magnum, 300 Win. magnum, 338 Win. magnum, 375 H & H magnum; recoil pad. Add $25.00-$40.00 for magnum.
Estimated Value: New (retail): $779.95
Excellent: $580.00
Very good: $435.00

Sako Model A1 Deluxe

A deluxe version of the A1; recoil pad.
Estimated Value: New (retail): $1,041.95
Excellent: $ 780.00
Very good: $ 585.00

Sako Model A11 Deluxe

Similar to the Model A11 with deluxe features; recoil pad.
Estimated Value: New (retail): $1,041.95
Excellent: $ 780.00
Very good: $ 585.00

Sako Model A111 Deluxe

Similar to the Model A111 with deluxe features. Add $25.00 for magnum.
Estimated Value: New (retail): $1,041.95
Excellent: $ 780.00
Very good: $ 585.00

Sako Varmint

Similar to the Models A1, A11 and A111 with heavy varmint barrel.
Estimated Value: New (retail): $919.95
Excellent: $690.00
Very good: $515.00

Sako Carbine

Similar to the Models A1, A11 and A111 with a 20″ barrel and full length forearm. Add $50.00 for 375 H & H.
Estimated Value: New (retail): $866.95
Excellent: $650.00
Very good: $485.00

Sako Classic Grade

Sako Safari Grade

Sako Classic Grade

Similar to the A111 and A11 with styling changes in 243 Win., 270 Win., 30-06, 7mm Rem. magnum; select American walnut stock.
Estimated Value: New (retail): $953.95
Excellent: $715.00
Very good: $535.00

Sako Safari Grade

Similar to the A111 with extended magazine, barrel band swivels, select French walnut stock; choice of satin or matte blue finish; calibers 300 Win. magnum, 338 Win. magnum, 375 H&H magnum.
Estimated Value: New (retail): $2,095.95
Excellent: $1,570.00
Very good: $1,175.00

Sako Finnwolf Sporter

Sako Model 78

Caliber: 22 long rifle, 22 Win. magnum, 22 Hornet
Action: Bolt action; repeating
Magazine: 5-shot; 4-shot in magnum
Barrel: 22½″; heavy barrel available
Sights: Folding leaf rear, hooded ramp front
Stock & Forearm: One-piece checkered walnut Monte Carlo pistol grip stock and forearm; swivels
Approximate wt.: 6¾ lbs.
Comments: Made from the late 1970's. Add $25.00 for 22 Hornet.
Estimated Value: New (retail): $603.95
Excellent: $450.00
Very good: $340.00

Sako Finnwolf Sporter

Caliber: 243, 308
Action: Lever-action; hammerless; repeating
Magazine: 4-shot clip
Barrel: Blued 23″
Sights: No rear, hooded ramp front
Stock & Forearm: Checkered walnut Monte Carlo one-piece pistol grip stock and tapered forearm; swivels
Approximate wt.: 7 lbs.
Comments: Made from the mid 1960's to early 1970's.
Estimated Value: Excellent: $460.00
Very good: $350.00

Sako Finnwolf Deluxe Sporter

Same as Finnwolf with select wood.
Estimated Value: Excellent: $475.00
Very good: $360.00

Savage

Savage Model 1904

Savage Model 1905

Savage Model 1911 Target

Savage Model 1905

Caliber: 22 short, long, long rifle
Action: Bolt action; single shot
Magazine: None
Barrel: 22″
Sights: Open rear, bead front
Stock & Forearm: Plain one-piece straight grip stock and forearm
Approximate wt.: 5 lbs.
Comments: A lightweight takedown boy's rifle produced until about 1917.
Estimated Value: Excellent: $95.00
Very good: $75.00

Savage Model 1904

Caliber: 22 short, long, long rifle
Action: Bolt action; single shot
Magazine: None
Barrel: 18″
Sights: Open rear, bead front
Stock & Forearm: Straight wood one-piece stock and forearm
Approximate wt.: 3 lbs.
Comments: This is a boy's lightweight takedown rifle produced from 1904 to 1917.
Estimated Value: Excellent: $90.00
Very good: $65.00

Savage Model 1911 Target

Caliber: 22 short
Action: Bolt action; single shot
Magazine: None
Barrel: 20″
Sights: Adjustable rear, bead front
Stock & Forearm: Walnut one-piece straight grip stock and forearm
Approximate wt.: 4 lbs.
Comments: Made from from 1911 to 1916.
Estimated Value: Excellent: $100.00
Very good: $ 75.00

Savage Model 19

Savage Model 19, 19L Target

Caliber: 22 long rifle
Action: Bolt action; repeating; speed lock
Magazine: 5-shot detachable box
Barrel: 25″
Sights: Extension rear, hooded front
Stock & Forearm: Walnut pistol grip stock and beaver-tail forearm; swivels
Approximate wt.: 7½ lbs.
Comments: Made from 1933 to the mid 1940's. The model 19L has special Lyman receiver and front sights; add $10.00-$15.00.
Estimated Value: **Excellent:** $200.00
Very good: $150.00

Savage Model 19M

This is the same rifle as the Model 19 except it has a heavier 28″ barrel. Approximate wt is 9¼ lbs.
Estimated Value: **Excellent:** $210.00
Very good: $160.00

Savage Model 19H Hornet

Same as Model 19 except loading port, bolt mechanism and magazine are like Model 23-D.
Estimated Value: **Excellent:** $270.00
Very good: $200.00

Savage Model 19 NRA

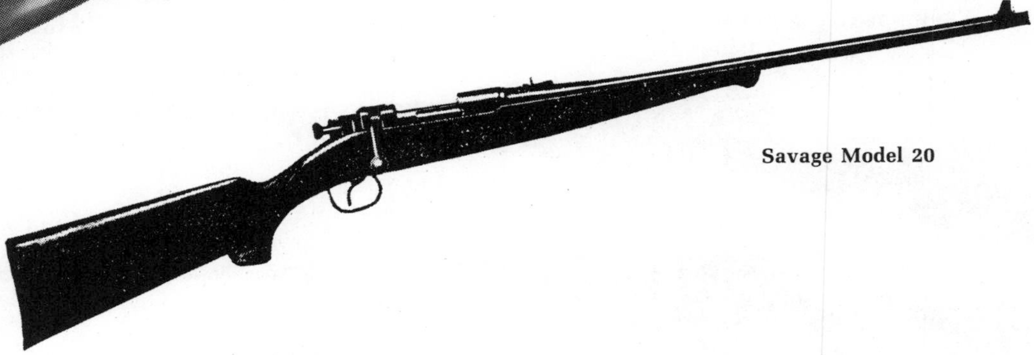

Savage Model 20

Savage Model 19 NRA Match Rifle

Caliber: 22 long rifle
Action: Bolt action; repeating
Magazine: 5-shot detachable box
Barrel: 25″
Sights: Adjustable peep rear, blade front
Stock & Forearm: Wood full military pistol grip stock and forearm
Approximate wt.: 7 lbs.
Comments: Made from 1919 until 1932.
Estimated Value: **Excellent:** $190.00
Very good: $140.00

Savage Model 20

Caliber: 300 Savage, 250-3000
Action: Bolt action; repeating
Magazine: 5-shot
Barrel: 22″ in 250 caliber; 24″ in 300 caliber
Sights: Open rear, bead front; in 1926, rear peep sight
Stock & Forearm: Checkered walnut pistol grip stock and forearm; in 1926 cut to semi-pistol grip
Approximate wt.: 5¾ to 7 lbs.
Comments: Made from from 1920 through 1929.
Estimated Value: **Excellent:** $275.00
Very good: $210.00

Savage Model 23A Sporter

Savage Model 23 AA

Savage Model 23 B

Savage Model 3

Savage Model 3, 3S, 3ST

Caliber: 22 short, long, long rifle
Action: Bolt action; single shot
Magazine: None
Barrel: 26″ before World War II, 24″ after
Sights: Open rear, bead front; 3S and 3ST have peep rear and hooded front
Stock & Forearm: One-piece walnut semi-pistol grip stock and forearm; 3ST has swivels
Approximate wt.: 4 to 5 lbs.
Comments: A takedown model produced from 1933 until the early 1950's. The 3ST was discontinued before World War II.
Estimated Value: Excellent: $75.00
  Very good: $60.00

Savage Model 23A Sporter, 23 AA, 23 B, 23 C, 23 D

Caliber: 22 long rifle (Model 23A, 23AA); from 1933 to 1947 in 22 Hornet (Model 23D); 25-20 (Model 23B); 32-20 (Model 23C)
Action: Bolt action; from 1933-1942 (Model 23AA) speed lock
Magazine: 5-shot detachable box
Barrel: 23″; 25″ from 1933 till 1942 on Model 23B
Sights: Open rear, bead or blade front
Stock & Forearm: Plain walnut semi-pistol grip stock and forearm
Approximate wt.: 6 to 6½ lbs.
Comments: Produced: 23A from 1923-1933; Model 23AA with improved lock, 1933-1942; Model 23B, 1933-1942; Model 23C, 23D, 1933-1947.
Estimated Value: Excellent: $175.00
  Very good: $130.00

Savage Model 40

Savage Model 45

Savage Model 45

This is a special grade version of the Model 40. It has a checkered stock and forearm and a special receiver sight. Discontinued in 1940.
Estimated Value: Excellent: $300.00
  Very good: $225.00

Savage Model 40

Caliber: 250-3000, 300 Savage, 30-30, 30-06
Action: Bolt action; repeating
Magazine: 4-shot detachable box
Barrel: 22″ for caliber 250-3000 and 30-30; 24″ for other models
Sights: Open rear, ramp front
Stock & Forearm: Plain walnut pistol grip stock and lipped forearm after 1936; checkered stock after 1940
Approximate wt.: 7½ lbs.
Comments: Made from 1928 until World War II.
Estimated Value: Excellent: $275.00
  Very good: $200.00

Savage Model 4

Savage Model 4S

Savage Model 4M

Savage Model 5

Savage Model 5S

Savage Model 4, 4s, 4M

Caliber: 22 short, long, long rifle; 4M chambered for 22 mag.

Action: Bolt action; repeating

Magazine: 5-shot detachable box

Barrel: 24″

Sights: Open rear, bead front; 4S has peep rear and hooded front

Stock & Forearm: Checkered walnut pistol grip stock and grooved forearm on pre-World War II models; plain on post-World War II models.

Approximate wt.: 5½ lbs.

Comments: The Model 4 and 4S were produced from 1933 until the mid 1960's. 4M was made during the early to mid 1960's. Add $10.00 for model 4M.

Estimated Value: **Excellent:** **$90.00**
Very good: **$65.00**

Savage Model 5, 5S

Similar to the Model 4 except the magazine is tubular and the gun weighs about 6 lbs. The Model 5S has peep rear and hooded front sight. They were produced from the mid 1930's until 1961; caliber 22 short, long and long rifle. Add $10.00 for Model 5S.

Estimated Value: **Excellent:** **$95.00**
Very good: **$70.00**

Savage Model 219

Savage Model 219L

Savage Model 221 Utility Gun

Savage Model 219, 219L

Caliber: 22 Hornet, 25-20, 32-20, 30-30
Action: Hammerless; single shot; automatic ejector; shotgun style, top break lever; 219L has side lever
Magazine: Single shot
Barrel: 26″
Sights: Open rear, bead front
Stock & Forearm: Plain walnut pistol grip stock and forearm
Approximate wt.: 6 lbs.
Comments: A takedown model made from 1938 to 1965 was Model 219; from 1965 for two years with side lever, as 219L.
Estimated Value: Excellent: $100.00
Very good: $ 75.00

Savage Model 221 Utility Gun

Same rifle as the Model 219 except it was offered in 30-30 only with an interchangeable 12 gauge 30″ shotgun barrel. Prices include the 12 gauge interchangeable shotgun barrel.
Estimated Value: Excellent: $120.00
Very good: $ 90.00

Savage Model 222

Same as Model 221 except shotgun barrel is 16 gauge; 28″.
Estimated Value: Excellent: $110.00
Very good: $ 85.00

Savage Model 223

Same as Model 221 except shotgun barrel is 20 gauge, 28″.
Estimated Value: Excellent: $110.00
Very good: $ 85.00

Savage Model 227

Same as Model 221 except it is 22 Hornet and the shotgun barrel is 20 gauge, 30″.
Estimated Value: Excellent: $120.00
Very good: $ 95.00

Savage Model 228

Same as Model 227 except shotgun barrel is 16 gauge, 28″.
Estimated Value: Excellent: $120.00
Very good: $ 95.00

Savage Model 229

Same as Model 227 except shotgun barrel is 20 gauge, 28″.
Estimated Value: Excellent: $120.00
Very good: $ 95.00

Savage Model 110 Sporter

Savage Model 110 MC and MCL

Same as 110 Sporter except: 22-250 caliber added. 24″. A Monte Carlo stock was also included. The MCL is the same in left-hand action, add $10.00. Made from the late 1950's to about 1969.
Estimated Value: Excellent: $245.00
Very good: $180.00

Savage Model 110 Sporter

Caliber: 243, 270, 308, 30-06
Action: Bolt action; repeating
Magazine: 4-shot staggered box
Barrel: 22″
Sights: Open rear, ramp front
Stock & Forearm: Checkered walnut pistol grip stock and forearm
Approximate wt.: 6¾ lbs.
Comments: Made from 1958 until the early 1960's when it was replaced by 110E.
Estimated Value: Excellent: $200.00
Very good: $150.00

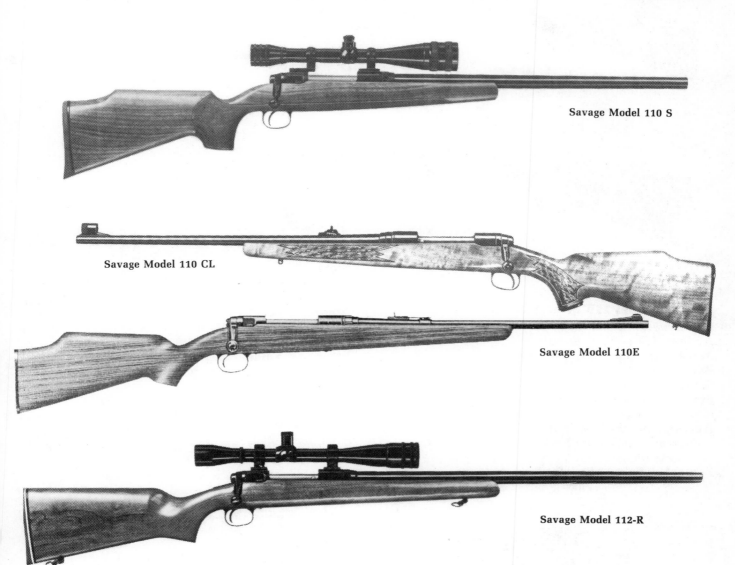

Savage Model 110 S

Savage Model 110 CL

Savage Model 110E

Savage Model 112-R

Savage Model 110C, 110CL

Caliber: 22-250, 243, 25-06, 270, 308, 30-06, 7mm Rem.
  mag., 300 Win. mag.
Action: Bolt action; repeating
Magazine: 4-shot clip, 3-shot clip in magnum calibers
Barrel: 22″ and 24″
Sights: Open rear, ramp front
Stock & Forearm: Checkered walnut Monte Carlo stock
  and forearm; magnum has recoil pad
Approximate wt.: 6¾ to 8 lbs.
Comments: This rifle has been in production since 1966.
  Discontinued 1986. Add $20.00 for left hand model
  (110CL).
Estimated Value: Excellent: $300.00
              Very good: $225.00

Savage Model 110S

Similar to the Model 110C with heavy barrel; no sights;
stippled checkering; recoil pad; 7mm/08 and 308 calibers;
introduced in the late 1970's to mid 1980's.
Estimated Value: Excellent: $275.00
              Very good: $200.00

Savage Model 112-R

A varmint rifle similar to the Model 110C; plain walnut
one-piece semi-pistol grip stock and forearm; swivels;
recoil pad; no sights; 22-250; 25-06 calibers; made from
about 1979 to early 1980's.
Estimated Value: Excellent: $210.00
              Very good: $160.00

Savage Model 110E, 110EL (Early)

Caliber: 243 Win., 7mm Rem. mag., 30-06
Action: Bolt action; repeating
Magazine: 4-shot staggered box; 3-shot in magnum
Barrel: Blued 20″; stainless steel in magnum
Sights: Open rear, ramp front
Stock & Forearm: One-piece checkered or plain walnut
  Monte Carlo stock and forearm; magnum has recoil
  pad
Approximate wt.: 6¾ to 7¾ lbs.
Comments: Made from 1963 to late 1970's. A later model
  was also designated 110E. Add $20.00 for left hand
  model (110EL).
Estimated Value: Excellent: $225.00
              Very good: $170.00

Savage Model 110 M

Savage Model 110P

Savage 110PE

Savage Model 110 M and 110 ML

Caliber: 7mm Rem. mag., 264, 300, 338 Win.
Action: Bolt action; repeating
Magazine: 4-shot box, staggered
Barrel: 24″
Sights: Open rear, ramp front
Stock & Forearm: Walnut Monte Carlo pistol grip stock and forearm; recoil pad
Approximate wt.: 7½ to 8 lbs.
Comments: Made from 1963 to 1969; 110 ML is the same in left-hand action, add $10.00.
Estimated Value: **Excellent:** $250.00
Very good: $190.00

Savage Model 110P Premier and 110PL

Caliber: 243 Win., 7mm Rem. mag., 30-06
Action: Bolt action; repeating
Magazine: 4-shot box, staggered; 3-shot in magnum
Barrel: Blued 22″; 24″ stainless steel in magnum
Sights: Open rear folding leaf, ramp front
Stock & Forearm: Walnut and rosewood Monte Carlo stock and forearm; swivels; magnum has recoil pad
Approximate wt.: 7 to 8 lbs.
Comments: Made from mid 1960's until 1970; 110PL is left-hand action. Add $15.00 for magnum.
Estimated Value: **Excellent:** $360.00
Very good: $270.00

Savage 110PE Presentation, 110PEL

Same as Models 110P and 110PL except receiver, floor plate and trigger guard are engraved. It was produced for two years beginning in 1968. Add $15.00 for magnum.
Estimated Value: **Excellent:** $575.00
Very good: $430.00

Savage Model 110E, 110ES

Savage Model 110-D, 110-DL

Caliber: 223, 243, 270, 30-06, 7mm Rem. magnum, 338 Win. magnum
Action: Bolt action; repeting
Magazine: 4-shot internal box; 3-shot for magnums
Barrel: 22″ blue; 24″ for magnums
Sights: Hooded ramp front, adjustable rear
Stock & Forearm: Select walnut, checkered semi-pistol grip, Monte Carlo, one piece stock and forearm
Approximate wt.: 6¾ lbs.; 7 lbs. in magnum
Comments: Introduced in 1986. Model 110-DL is left hand model not available in 338 Win. magnum. Add 14% for Model 110-DL. Add 18% for magnum calibers.
Estimated Value: **New (retail):** $369.00
Excellent: $275.00
Very good: $210.00

Savage Model 110E, 110ES (Late)

Caliber: 22-250, 223, 243, 308 Win., 270, 30-06, 7mm Rem. magnum
Action: Bolt action; repeating
Magazine: 4-shot box, internal
Barrel: Blued 22″; 24″ in 7mm magnum
Sights: Removable ramp front, removable adjustable rear; 110ES has 4X scope
Stock & Forearm: Checkered hardwood Monte Carlo one-piece semi-pistol grip stock and forearm
Approximate wt.: 7 lbs.
Comments: Merchandised from late 1970's to 1981 as Stevens, and 1982 to present as Savage. Add $75.00 for scope (110ES).
Estimated Value: **New (retail):** $289.00
Excellent: $215.00
Very good: $165.00

Savage Model 110V

Similar to late Model 110E except: 22-250 or 223 caliber. No sights; a heavy 26″ barrel with swell pistol grip and stippling; recoil pad. Introduced in the mid 1980's. Approx. wt. 9 lbs.
Estimated Value: **New (retail):** $385.00
Excellent: $290.00
Very good: $220.00

Savage Model 111

Caliber: 7mm (7x57), 243, 270, 30-06, 7mm magnum
Action: Bolt action; repeating
Magazine: 4-shot box; 3-shot box in magnum
Barrel: 24″
Sights: Adjustable removable rear, removable hooded ramp front
Stock & Forearm: Checkered walnut Monte Carlo one-piece pistol grip stock and forearm; swivels
Approximate wt.: 6¾ lbs.
Comments: A deluxe high powered rifle made from the mid to late 1970's. Add $10.00 for magnum.
Estimated Value: Excellent: $265.00
Very good: $200.00

Savage Model 112V

Caliber: 222, 223, 22-250, 220 Swift, 25-06, 243
Action: Bolt action; single shot; hammerless
Magazine: None
Barrel: 26″ chrome-moly steel; tapered
Sights: None
Stock & Forearm: Checkered walnut one-piece pistol grip stock and forearm; fluted comb; swivels
Approximate wt.: 9¼ lbs.
Comments: A varmint rifle made in the mid to late 1970's.
Estimated Value: Excellent: $250.00
Very good: $190.00

Savage Model 840

Caliber: 222 Rem.
Action: Bolt action; repeating; bolt cocks on opening stroke
Magazine: 4-shot detachable clip
Barrel: 24″ tapered medium weight steel barrel
Sights: Ramp front with gold bead; sporting rear with step elevator
Stock & Forearm: Plain one-piece hardwood stock and forearm, pistol grip; fluted comb
Approximate wt.: 6¾ lbs.
Comments: Made in the mid 1970's.
Estimated Value: Excellent: $120.00
Very good: $ 90.00

Savage Model 840-T

Same as the Model 840 with a 4X scope.
Estimated Value: Excellent: $135.00
Very good: $100.00

Savage Model 111

Savage Model 112V

Savage Model 340

Savage Model 340C Carbine

Savage Model 340S

Same as Model 340 except sights are peep rear, hooded front. It was produced from about 1955 to 1960.
Estimated Value: Excellent: $185.00
Very good: $135.00

Savage Model 340C Carbine

Same as Model 340 in caliber 30-30. The barrel is slightly over 18″. Produced in the 1950's. Peep sight, checkered stock and sling swivels.
Estimated Value: Excellent: $180.00
Very good: $135.00

Savage Model 340

Caliber: 22 Hornet, 222 Rem., 223 Rem., 30-30
Action: Bolt action; repeating
Magazine: 4-shot clip in 22 Hornet and 222 Rem.; 3-shot clip in 30-30
Barrel: 20″, 22″, 24″
Sights: Open rear, ramp front; hooded ramp after 1980
Stock & Forearm: Plain walnut pistol grip stock and forearm; checkered after 1965
Approximate wt.: 6 to 7 lbs.
Comments: Made from 1950 to 1986; before 1950 this model was manufactured as a Stevens.
Estimated Value: Excellent: $175.00
Very good: $130.00

Savage Model 65-M

Savage Fox Model FB-1

Savage Model 65-M

Caliber: 22 magnum
Action: Bolt action; repeating
Magazine: 5-shot clip
Barrel: Blued 22″
Sights: Open rear, ramp front
Stock & Forearm: Checkered walnut one-piece semi-pistol grip stock and forearm
Approximate wt.: 5¾ lbs.
Comments: Made in the late 1970's.
Estimated Value: Excellent: $75.00
Very good: $60.00

Savage Fox Model FB-1

Caliber: 22 short, long, long rifle
Action: Bolt action; repeating
Magazine: 5-shot detachable clip
Barrel: Blued 24″
Sights: Adjustable leaf rear, hooded ramp front; drilled and tapped for scope
Stock & Forearm: Checkered walnut Monte Carlo one-piece semi-pistol grip stock and forearm; cheekpiece; swivels; rosewood fore-end tip and grip cap
Approximate wt.: 6½ lbs.
Comments: Introduced in 1981, discontinued in 1982.
Estimated Value: Excellent: $200.00
Very good: $150.00

Savage Model 982DL

Savage Model 982 MDL

Savage Model 982DL

Caliber: 22 short, long, long rifle
Action: Bolt action; repeating
Magazine: 5-shot clip, push button release
Barrel: Blued 22″
Sights: Ramp front, folding leaf rear
Stock & Forearm: Checkered walnut one-piece Monte Carlo semi-pistol grip stock and forearm
Approximate wt.: 6 lbs.
Comments: Introduced in 1981, discontinued in 1982.
Estimated Value: Excellent: $95.00
Very good: $70.00

Savage Model 982 MDL

Caliber: 22 magnum
Action: Bolt action; repeating
Magazine: 5-shot detachable clip
Barrel: Blued 22″
Sights: Ramp front, folding leaf rear; grooved for scope
Stock & Forearm: Checkered walnut Monte Carlo one-piece semi-pistol grip stock and forearm
Approximate wt.: 6 lbs.
Comments: Introduced in 1981, discontinued in 1982.
Estimated Value: Excellent: $100.00
Very good: $ 75.00

Savage Model 1899 (99)

Savage Model 1899 Military

Savage Model 99A

Savage Model 99H Carbine

Savage Model 99E Carbine

Savage Model 99E

Savage Model 1899 (99)

Caliber: 303 Savage, 25-35, 32-40, 38-55
Action: Lever-action; hammerless
Magazine: 5-shot rotary
Barrel: 20″, 22″, 26″; round, half octagon or octagon
Sights: Adjustable rear, dovetail; open sporting front
Stock & Forearm: Walnut straight grip stock and tapered forearm
Approximate wt.: 7½ lbs.
Comments: The backbone of the Savage line which has been manufactured in many variations over the years. It was produced from 1899 to 1922.
Estimated Value: Excellent: $250.00
Very good: $190.00

Savage Model 99B

Takedown version of Model 99A; produced from about 1922 to 1937.
Estimated Value: Excellent: $250.00
Very good: $190.00

Savage Model 99H Carbine

Basically the same as 99A with: addition of 250-3000 caliber; short barrel; carbine stock and forearm; barrel bands. Produced from 1932 to 1941.
Estimated Value: Excellent: $275.00
Very good: $205.00

Savage Model 1899 Military

Same as the Model 99 except: barrel is 28″; bayonet; stock is musket style; sights are military. Produced from about 1899 to 1907; caliber 30-30 Win.
Estimated Value: Excellent: $400.00
Very good: $300.00

Savage Model 99A

Basically the same as Model 1899 in solid frame and in calibers 300 Savage, 303 Savage and 30-30. It was produced from 1922 to 1984. Later models in calibers 243, 308, 250 Savage, and 375.
Estimated Value: Excellent: $260.00
Very good: $195.00

Savage Model 99E

Similar to the Model 99A in 22 Hi Power, 250-3000, 30-30, 300 Savage, 303 Savage; 22″ or 24″ barrel. Unlipped tapered forearm.
Estimated Value: Excellent: $240.00
Very good: $180.00

Savage Model 99E Carbine

Similar to Model 99H in 243 Win., 250 Savage, 300 Savage, 308 Win., calibers only. Checkered walnut stock and tapered forearm without barrel band. Production began in 1961. Monte Carlo stock after 1982. Discontinued in 1985.
Estimated Value: Excellent: $260.00
Very good: $195.00

Savage Model 99F

Savage Model 99CD

Savage Model 99K

Savage Model 99EG

Savage Model 99R

Savage Model 99 RS

Savage Model 99EG

This is the Model G produced after World War II, from 1955 to 1961.

Estimated Value: Excellent: **$225.00**
                   Very good: **$170.00**

Savage Model 99 CD

A solid frame version of Model 99F with a checkered pistol grip stock and forearm. In production from 1955 to about 1980; 4-shot detachable box magazine.

Estimated Value: Excellent: **$260.00**
                   Very good: **$195.00**

Savage Model 99G

A takedown version of the Model 99E with a checkered walnut pistol grip stock and forearm. Discontinued in 1940.

Estimated Value: Excellent: **$275.00**
                   Very good: **$200.00**

Savage Model 99K

A fancy Model 99G with deluxe stock and light engraving. Rear sight is peep and there is a folding middle sight. It was discontinued in 1940's.

Estimated Value: Excellent: **$800.00**
                   Very good: **$600.00**

Savage Model 99F

This is a lightweight takedown version of the Model 99E, produced until about 1940. Production resumed about 1955 to 1972 in caliber 243, 300 and 308. Add $100.00 for pre-1940.

Estimated Value: Excellent: **$240.00**
                   Very good: **$180.00**

Savage Model 99R

Similar to other Model 99's. Production stopped in 1940. It was resumed from 1955 to 1961 in 24" barrel only with swivel attachments in a variety of calibers. Add $100.00 for pre-World War II models.

Estimated Value: Excellent: **$235.00**
                   Very good: **$175.00**

Savage Model 99RS

The same rifle as Model 99 except those before World War II have rear peep sight and folding middle sight. Those made after the war have a special receiver sight. Discontinued in 1961; solid frame. Add $100.00 for pre-World War II models.

Estimated Value: Excellent: **$240.00**
                   Very good: **$180.00**

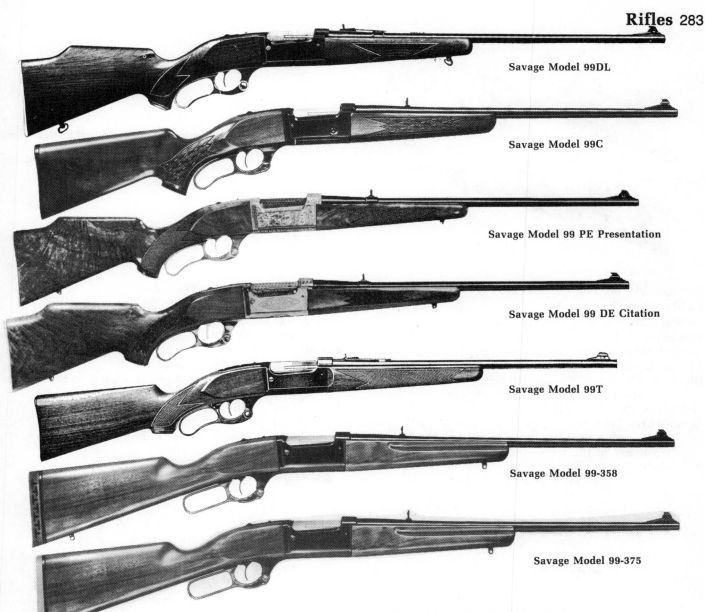

Savage Model 99DL

Savage Model 99C

Savage Model 99 PE Presentation

Savage Model 99 DE Citation

Savage Model 99T

Savage Model 99-358

Savage Model 99-375

Savage Model 99 DL

This is a late Model 99, in production from about 1960 to mid 1970's. Basically the same as Model 99F with a Monte Carlo stock and swivels.

| Estimated Value: | Excellent: | $250.00 |
| | Very good: | $190.00 |

Savage Model 99C

Currently in production. Model 99C is much like the Model 99F except it has a 3-or 4-shot detachable clip magazine. It has been in production since 1965; calibers: 22-250, 243, 308, 7mm/08. Monte Carlo stock after 1982.

Estimated Value:	New (retail):	$469.95
	Excellent:	$350.00
	Very good:	$260.00

Savage Model 99 PE Presentation

Much like the Model 99DL except engraved receiver, hand checkered Monte Carlo stock and forearm. Produced from 1968 to 1970.

| Estimated Value: | Excellent: | $650.00 |
| | Very good: | $480.00 |

Savage Model 99 DE Citation

A less elaborate example of the Model 99 PE. Produced from 1968 to 1970.

| Estimated Value: | Excellent: | $400.00 |
| | Very good: | $300.00 |

Savage Model 99T

Basically the same as the other Model 99's. It is a solid frame with a checkered walnut pistol grip stock and forearm. Produced until 1940.

| Estimated Value: | Excellent: | $320.00 |
| | Very good: | $240.00 |

Savage Model 99-358

Similar to the Model 99A in 358 caliber; forearm rounded; swivels; recoil pad.

| Estimated Value: | Excellent: | $275.00 |
| | Very good: | $210.00 |

Savage Model 99-375

Similar to the Model 99-358 in 375 Win. caliber.

| Estimated Value: | Excellent: | $280.00 |
| | Very good: | $215.00 |

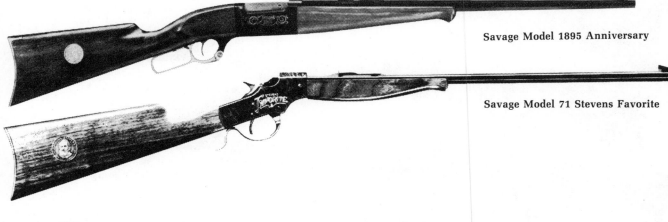

Savage Model 1895 Anniversary

Savage Model 71 Stevens Favorite

Savage Model 1895 Anniversary

Caliber: 308 Win.
Action: Lever-action; hammerless
Magazine: 5-shot rotary
Barrel: 24″ octagon
Sights: Open rear, blade front (brass)
Stock & Forearm: Walnut straight grip with brass medallion inlaid and brass buttplate
Approximate wt.: 7½ lbs.
Comments: Less than 10,000 of this limited commemorative were produced in 1970 on the 75th anniversary of the rifle.
Estimated Value: Excellent: $350.00
Very good: $260.00

Savage Model 71 Stevens Favorite

Caliber: 22 long rifle
Action: Lever-action; exposed hammer; falling block
Magazine: Single shot
Barrel: 22″ octagon
Sights: Open rear, blade front
Stock & Forearm: Plain walnut, straight grip stock and lipped forearm; brass medallion in stock
Approximate wt.: 4½ lbs.
Comments: This commemorative is a replica of the Stevens Favorite issued to honor Joshua Stevens; 15,000 produced in 1971.
Estimated Value: Excellent: $135.00
Very good: $110.00

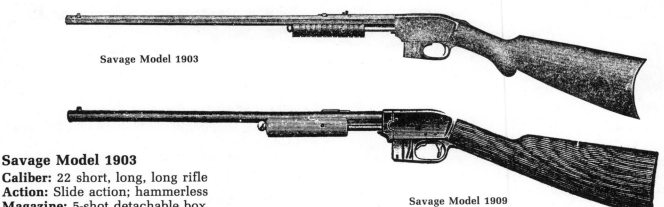

Savage Model 1903

Savage Model 1909

Savage Model 1903

Caliber: 22 short, long, long rifle
Action: Slide action; hammerless
Magazine: 5-shot detachable box
Barrel: 24″ octagon
Sights: Open rear, bead front
Stock & Forearm: Checkered walnut pistol grip stock and grooved slide handle
Approximate wt.: 5 lbs.
Comments: This takedown model was produced from 1903 to 1922.
Estimated Value: Excellent: $150.00
Very good: $115.00

Savage Model 1909

A lighter version of the Model 1903 with a straight stock and forearm and a round 20″ barrel. Discontinued about 1915.
Estimated Value: Excellent: $140.00
Very good: $100.00

Savage Model 1914

Caliber: 22 short, long, long rifle
Action: Slide action; hammerless
Magazine: Tubular; 20 shorts, 17 longs, 15 long rifles
Barrel: 24″ octagon or half octagon
Sights: Open rear, bead front
Stock & Forearm: Plain wood pistol grip stock and grooved slide handle
Approximate wt.: 5¾ lbs.
Comments: A takedown rifle produced until 1924.
Estimated Value: Excellent: $160.00
Very good: $115.00

Savage Model 25

Savage Model 29

Savage Model 170-C

Savage Model 6

Savage Model 6S

Savage Model 29

Very similar to the Model 25 except pre-war models were checkered; barrel is round on post-war models. Made from 1929 until the late 1960's. Add $50.00 for pre-World War II models with octagon barrel.

Estimated Value: Excellent: $140.00
Very good: $105.00

Savage Model 25

Caliber: 22 short, long, long rifle
Action: Slide action; hammerless
Magazine: Tubular; 20 shorts, 17 longs, 15 long rifles
Barrel: 24″ octagon
Sights: Open rear, blade front
Stock & Forearm: Walnut pistol grip stock and grooved slide handle
Approximate wt.: 5¾ lbs.
Comments: A takedown model produced from the mid 1920's until 1929.

Estimated Value: Excellent: $160.00
Very good: $115.00

Savage Model 170

Caliber: 30-30, 35
Action: Slide action; hammerless; repeating
Magazine: 3-shot tubular
Barrel: Blued 22″
Sights: Ramp front, folding leaf rear; hooded ramp after 1980
Stock & Forearm: Checkered walnut Monte Carlo semi-pistol grip stock and fluted slide handle; swivels
Approximate wt.: 6¾ lbs.
Comments: Made from the late 1970's to early 1980's.
Estimated Value: Excellent: $160.00
Very good: $120.00

Savage Model 170-C

A carbine version of the Model 170; not available with a Monte Carlo stock; 18½″ barrel; not available in 35 caliber.

Estimated Value: Excellent: $150.00
Very good: $115.00

Savage Model 1912

Caliber: 22 long rifle
Action: Semi-automatic; hammerless
Magazine: 7-shot detachable box
Barrel: 20″ half-octagon
Sights: Open rear, bead front
Stock & Forearm: Plain wood straight grip stock and forearm
Approximate wt.: 4½ lbs.
Comments: This takedown was Savage's first semi-automatic; discontinued in 1916.
Estimated Value: Excellent: $200.00
Very good: $150.00

Savage Model 6, 6S

Caliber: 22 short, long, long rifle
Action: Semi-automatic
Magazine: Tubular; 21 shorts, 17 longs, 15 long rifles
Barrel: 24″
Sights: Open rear, bead front; 6S has peep rear, hooded front
Stock & Forearm: Checkered walnut pistol grip before World War II; plain walnut pistol grip after the war
Approximate wt.: 6 lbs.
Comments: A takedown model manufactured from 1938 until late 1960's.
Estimated Value: Excellent: $90.00
Very good: $70.00

Savage Model 7

Savage Model 7S

Savage Model 80

Savage Model 980DL

Savage Model 7, 7S

Basically the same as Model 6 and 6S except they are equipped with a 5-shot detachable box magazine. Produced from the late 1930's until the early 1950's.

Estimated Value: Excellent: $90.00
Very good: $70.00

Savage Model 980DL

Caliber: 22 long rifle
Action: Semi-automatic
Magazine: 15-shot tubular
Barrel: Blued 20″
Sights: Hooded ramp front, folding leaf adjustable rear
Stock & Forearm: Checkered walnut one-piece Monte Carlo semi-pistol grip stock and forearm
Approximate wt.: 6 lbs.
Comments: Produced from 1981 to 1984.
Estimated Value: Excellent: $110.00
Very good: $ 85.00

Savage Model 80

Caliber: 22 long rifle
Action: Semi-automatic
Magazine: 15-shot tubular
Barrel: Blued 20″
Sights: Open rear, blade front
Stock & Forearm: Checkered walnut one-piece Monte Carlo pistol grip stock and forearm
Approximate wt.: 6 lbs.
Comments: Made from the mid to late 1970's. Due to a possible safety malfunction, certain models were recalled in 1982 and inspected by Stevens at no cost to the owner. Serial numbers that were recalled were B256621 or higher; C000001 or higher; D000001 or higher.
Estimated Value: Excellent: $75.00
Very good: $55.00

Sears

Sears Model 53

Caliber: 243, 30-06
Action: Bolt action; repeating; hammerless
Magazine: 5-shot tubular
Barrel: Blued 24″
Sights: Folding rear, ramp front
Stock & Forearm: Checkered walnut Monte Carlo one-piece pistol grip stock and tapered forearm; swivels
Approximate wt.: 6¾ lbs.
Comments: Made until mid 1970's.
Estimated Value: Excellent: $150.00
Very good: $110.00

Sears Ted Williams Model 53 A

Same as Model 53 in 30-06 caliber only; 22″ barrel.
Estimated Value: Excellent: $145.00
Very good: $105.00

Sears Ted Williams Model 73

Same as Ted Williams 53 with select wood and fancy finish.
Estimated Value: Excellent: $175.00
Very good: $130.00

Sears Model 1

Sears Model 2

Sears Model 1

Similar to Model 2 but single shot version, no Monte Carlo stock.

Estimated Value: **Excellent:** $40.00
Very good: $30.00

Sears Model 2200 Semi-Automatic

Caliber: 22 long rifle
Action: Semi-automatic; hammerless; side ejection
Magazine: 15-shot tubular
Barrel: Blued 20″ round
Sights: Sporting front, rear adjustable for elevation; receiver grooved for scope
Stock & Forearm: Checkered walnut-finish hardwood one-piece pistol grip stock and forearm
Approximate wt.: 5½ lbs.
Comments: Add $10.00 for scope. Due to a possible safety malfunction, certain models were recalled in 1982 and inspected by Stevens at no cost to the owner. Serial numbers recalled were B256621 or higher; C000001 or higher; D000001 or higher.
Estimated Value: **Excellent:** $60.00
Very good: $50.00

Sears Model 2

Caliber: 22 short, long, long rifle
Action: Bolt action; repeating; hammerless
Magazine: 6-shot clip
Barrel: Blued 20″
Sights: Open rear, bead front
Stock & Forearm: Wood Monte Carlo one-piece semi-pistol grip stock and tapered forearm
Approximate wt.: 5 lbs.
Comments: Manufactured in the 1970's.
Estimated Value: **Excellent:** $60.00
Very good: $50.00

Sears Model 2200, Bolt Action

Same as the Model 2200 Semi-Automatic except: bolt action repeater; 5-shot box magazine; 22 short, long or long rifle caliber.
Estimated Value: **Excellent:** $55.00
Very good: $45.00

Sears Model 2200 Lever Action

Caliber: 22 short, long, long rifle
Action: Lever-action; single shot; exposed hammer
Magazine: None
Barrel: Blued 18½″ round
Sights: Sporting front, rear adjustable for elevation
Stock & Forearm: Smooth two-piece hardwood straight grip stock and forearm
Approximate wt.: 5½ lbs.
Comments: Manufactured to the mid 1980's.
Estimated Value: **Excellent:** $50.00
Very good: $40.00

Sears Ted Williams Model 100

Sears Ted Williams Model 100

Caliber: 30-30 Win.
Action: Lever-action; exposed hammer; repeating
Magazine: 6-shot tubular
Barrel: Blued 20″
Sights: Open rear, blade front
Stock & Forearm: Walnut straight grip stock and forearm
Approximate wt.: 6½ lbs.
Comments: Made for Sears by Winchester.
Estimated Value: **Excellent:** $130.00
Very good: $100.00

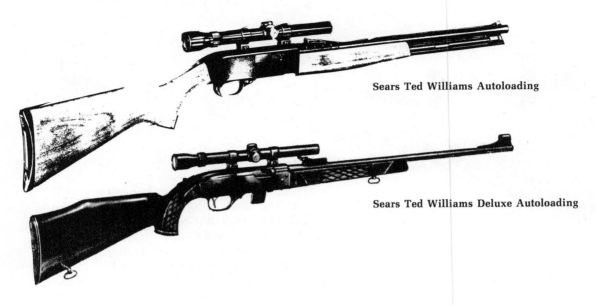

Sears Ted Williams Autoloading

Sears Ted Williams Deluxe Autoloading

Sears Ted Williams Autoloading

Caliber: 22 short, long, long rifle
Action: Semi-automatic; hammerless; side ejection
Magazine: Tubular; 15 long rifles, 17 longs, 21 shorts
Barrel: Blued 20½″
Sights: None, scope
Stock & Forearm: Wood semi-pistol grip stock and forearm
Approximate wt.: 5 lbs.
Comments: Manufactured in the 1970's.
Estimated Value: Excellent: $65.00
Very good: $55.00

Sears Ted Williams Deluxe Autoloading

Caliber: 22 short, long, long rifle
Action: Semi-automatic; hammerless; side ejection
Magazine: 5-shot clip
Barrel: Blued 20″
Sights: Rear tangent, hooded ramp front
Stock & Forearm: Checkered walnut Monte Carlo one-piece pistol grip stock and tapered forearm; swivels
Approximate wt.: 6 lbs.
Comments: Manufactured in the 1970's.
Estimated Value: Excellent: $70.00
Very good: $60.00

Sedgley

Sedgley Springfield Sporter

Sedgley Springfield Sporter

Caliber: 218 Bee, 220 Swift, 22 Hornet, 22-4000, 25-35, 250-3000, 257 Roberts, 270 Win., 7mm, 30-06
Action: Bolt action; Springfield-type (1903)
Magazine: 5-shot box
Barrel: 24″
Sights: Lyman rear, hooded ramp front
Stock & Forearm: Checkered walnut one-piece pistol grip stock and lipped forearm; swivels
Approximate wt.: 7½ lbs.
Comments: Manufactured in left and right hand action from the late 1920's to World War II.
Estimated Value: Excellent: $480.00
Very good: $360.00

Sedgley Mannlicher

Similar to the Sporter with a full length forearm; 20″ barrel.
Estimated Value: Excellent: $525.00
Very good: $395.00

Smith & Wesson

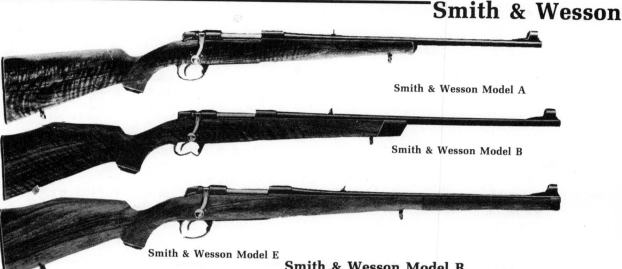

Smith & Wesson Model A

Smith & Wesson Model B

Smith & Wesson Model E

Smith & Wesson Model A

Caliber: 22-250, 243, 270, 308, 30-06, 7mm mag., 300 mag.
Action: Bolt action; repeating; adjustable trigger
Magazine: 5-shot box
Barrel: Blued 23¾" tapered
Sights: Folding rear, hooded ramp front with silver bead
Stock & Forearm: Checkered walnut Monte Carlo one-piece pistol grip stock and tapered forearm
Approximate wt.: 7 lbs.
Comments: Made only in the early 1970's.
Estimated Value: Excellent: $290.00
Very good: $220.00

Smith & Wesson Model B

A 20" barrel version of the Model A; not available in 22-250 or magnum; Monte Carlo stock.
Estimated Value: Excellent: $250.00
Very good: $190.00

Smith & Wesson Model C

Same as Model B except straight grip stock.
Estimated Value: Excellent: $240.00
Very good: $180.00

Smith & Wesson Model D

Same as Model C with full length forearm.
Estimated Value: Excellent: $300.00
Very good: $225.00

Smith & Wesson Model E

Same as Model B with full length forearm.
Estimated Value: Excellent: $325.00
Very good: $245.00

Smith & Wesson Model 1500

Smith & Wesson Model 1700LS Classic Hunter

Similar to the Model 1500 except light weight with lipped forearm, removable 5-shot magazine with floor plate; available in calibers 243 Win., 270 Win., and 30-06. Introduced in 1984.
Estimated Value: Excellent: $370.00
Very good: $280.00

Smith & Wesson Model 1500 Deluxe Varmint

Similar to the Model 1500 with a 22" heavy barrel, adjustable trigger; 222 Rem., 22-250 Rem., and 223 Rem. calibers. Produced from 1982 to 1985. Add 3% for Parkerized finish.
Estimated Value: Excellent: $340.00
Very good: $260.00

Smith & Wesson Model 1500, 1500 Mountaineer

Caliber: 30-06, 270 Win., 243 Win., 25-06 Rem., 7mm Rem. mag., 300 Win. mag.; 222 Rem.; 223 Rem. and 308 Win. added in 1982
Action: Bolt action; hammerless; repeating
Magazine: 5-shot box
Barrel: 23½"
Sights: Folding leaf rear, hooded ramp front or no sights
Stock & Forearm: Checkered walnut pistol grip, one-piece stock and forearm; swivels; recoil pad on magnum
Approximate wt.: 7 lbs.
Comments: Discontinued 1985. Add 4% for magnum; 19% for Deluxe Model; 7% for sights.
Estimated Value: Excellent: $270.00
Very good: $200.00

Standard

Standard Model M
A slide action version of the Standard G.
Estimated Value: Excellent: $250.00
Very good: $190.00

Standard Model G
Caliber: 25-35, 30-30, 25 Rem., 30 Rem., 35 Rem.
Action: Semi-automatic; gas operated; hammerless; can also be operated as slide action
Magazine: 4- or 5-shot tubular
Barrel: Blued 22"
Sights: Bead front, open rear
Stock & Forearm: Wood straight grip stock and slide handle
Approximate wt.: 7¾ lbs.
Comments: Made in the early 1900's, the Standard G was one of the first gas operated auto-loaders available.
Estimated Value: Excellent: $340.00
Very good: $250.00

Stevens

Stevens Model No. 14½ Little Scout

Stevens Model No. 14 Little Scout
Caliber: 22 long rifle
Action: Pivoted block; exposed hammer; single shot
Magazine: None
Barrel: 18", round
Sights: Flat front, open rear
Stock & Forearm: Plain walnut one-piece straight grip stock and forearm
Approximate wt.: 2½ lbs.
Comments: Made from 1904 to about 1912 when it was replaced by Model 14½.
Estimated Value: Excellent: $160.00
Very good: $120.00

Stevens Model No. 14½ Little Scout
Very similar to Model No. 14 except rolling block action and separated, short forearm. Produced from 1912 to World War II.
Estimated Value: Excellent: $150.00
Very good: $115.00

Stevens Model No. 16 Crack Shot

Stevens Model No. 16 Crack Shot
Caliber: 22 long rifle; 32 short
Action: Falling block; single shot; exposed hammer; lever action
Magazine: None
Barrel: 20" round
Sights: Open rear, blade front
Stock & Forearm: Plain walnut straight grip stock with slightly lipped forearm
Approximate wt.: 3¾ lbs.
Comments: Produced from the turn of the century until 1912 when it was replaced by the Model No. 26.
Estimated Value: Excellent: $250.00
Very good: $200.00

Stevens Model No. 16½ Crack Shot
Same as No. 16 except it is smooth bore for shot cartridges. Produced from 1907 to 1912.
Estimated Value: Excellent: $240.00
Very good: $190.00

Stevens Tip Up Model No. 2

Stevens Tip Up Model No. 13 Ladies

Stevens Tip Up Model No. 15

Stevens Tip Up Models No. 2, 5, 6, 7, 8, 9, 11 Ladies and 13 Ladies

Caliber: RF 22 long rifles, 25 Stevens, 32 long (in #11)
Action: Single shot, tip up; exposed hammer
Magazine: None
Barrel: 24″ octagon for #2; 28″ half octagon optional on #7, all others 24″ half octagon
Sights: Beach combination front, open rear; peep on #5,#7 and #13; blade front, open rear on #2; open on #11
Stock & Forearm: Walnut straight stock and forearm; no forearm on #2 and #5
Approximate wt.: 5½ to 6½ lbs.
Comments: This series replaced the 1888 and was produced until it was replaced in 1902 by a line of falling block rifles.
Estimated Value: Excellent: $250.00
                Very good: $190.00

Stevens Model No. 15 Maynard Jr.

Caliber: 22 long rifle or short
Action: Lever-action; tip up; exposed hammer
Magazine: None
Barrel: 18″ part octagon
Sights: Open rear, blade front
Stock & Forearm: Plain walnut, straight stock and short forearm
Approximate wt.: 2¾ lbs.
Comments: This small rifle was made to compete with cheap imports. Produced from 1901 to 1910.
Estimated Value: Excellent: $140.00
                Very good: $110.00

Stevens Model No. 15½ Maynard Jr.

This is the same as the No. 15 except it is smooth bore for 22 long rifle shot cartridges.
Estimated Value: Excellent: $135.00
                Very good: $100.00

Stevens Model No. 17 Favorite

Stevens Models No. 27 Favorite

Stevens Model No. 18

Stevens Models No. 17 and 27 Favorite

Caliber: 22 long rifle, 25 RF, 32 RF
Action: Lever-action; single shot; exposed hammer
Magazine: None
Barrel: 24″ round (octagon barrel on Model 27); other lengths available as option
Sights: Open rear, Rocky Mountain front
Stock & Forearm: Plain walnut straight grip stock, short tapered forearm
Approximate wt.: 4 to 5 lbs.
Comments: Takedown model produced from the 1890's until the mid 1930's.
Estimated Value: Excellent: $150.00
                Very good: $120.00

Stevens Models No. 18 & 28 Favorite

Same as the Model No. 17 except it has a Beach combination front sight, Vernier peep rear sight and leaf middle sight. Model 28 has octagon barrel.
Estimated Value: Excellent: $160.00
                Very good: $130.00

Stevens Model No. 20 Favorite

Stevens Model No. 44 Ideal

Stevens Model No. 49

Stevens Model No. 51

Stevens Model No. 52

Stevens Models No. 19 & 29 Favorite

Same as the Model No. 17 except is has Lyman front sight, leaf middle sight and Lyman combination rear sight. Model 29 has octagon barrel.

Estimated Value: Excellent: $180.00
Very good: $145.00

Stevens Model No. 20 Favorite

Same as the Model No. 17 except the barrel is smooth bore for 22 RF and 32 RF shot cartridges.

Estimated Value: Excellent: $160.00
Very good: $120.00

Stevens Model No. 44 Ideal

Caliber: 22 long rifle; 25 RF, 25-20 SS, 32-20, 32-40, 38-55, 44-40

Action: Lever-action; rolling block; exposed hammer; single shot

Magazine: None

Barrel: 24″ or 26″ round, octagon or half-octagon

Sights: Open rear, Rocky Mountain front

Stock & Forearm: Plain walnut, straight grip

Approximate wt.: 7 lbs.

Comments: Produced from the late 1890's until the early 1930's; a takedown model.

Estimated Value: Excellent: $325.00
Very good: $250.00

Steven Model No. 44½ Ideal

Same as the Model 44 except it has a falling block action. Discontinued in 1916.

Estimated Value: Excellent: $425.00
Very good: $320.00

Stevens Model No. 45 to 54

These rifles are structurally the same as the Model 44. They differ in engraving and finishes and are generally fancy models that bring extremely high prices. They were produced until World War I; target sights and stocks.

Estimated Value: Excellent: $550.00 - $1,000.00
Very good: $415.00 - $ 750.00

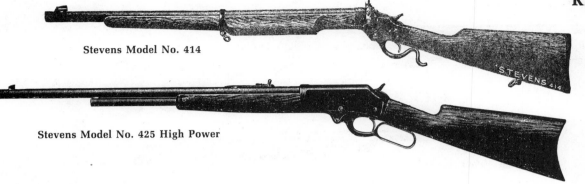

Stevens Model No. 414

Stevens Model No. 425 High Power

Stevens Model No. 414 Armory

Caliber: 22 long rifle or 22 short only
Action: Lever-action; exposed hammer; rolling block
Magazine: None
Barrel: 26″ heavy round
Sights: Rocky Mountain front, adjustable receiver rear
Stock & Forearm: Plain walnut straight grip, military stock and forearms; bands; swivels
Approximate wt.: 8 lbs.
Comments: Made from 1912 until just before World War I.
Estimated Value: Excellent: $350.00
 Very good: $260.00

Stevens Model No. 425 High Power

Caliber: Rimless Rem. 25, 30, 32, 35; smokeless flatnose
Action: Lever-action; exposed hammer; single extractor
Magazine: 5-shot tubular, under barrel
Barrel: 22″ round
Sights: Post front, adjustable sporting rear
Stock & Forearm: Plain walnut straight grip stock and forearm
Approximate wt.: 7 lbs.
Comments: Made for about five years beginning in 1911.
Estimated Value: Excellent: $215.00
 Very good: $160.00

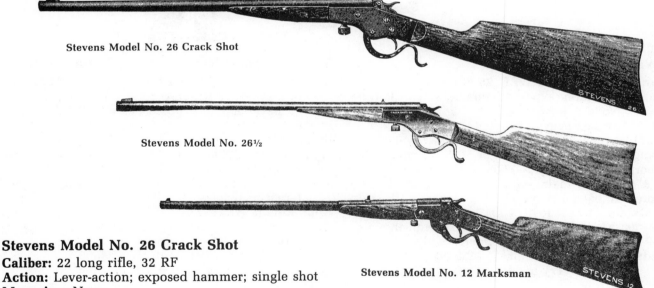

Stevens Model No. 26 Crack Shot

Stevens Model No. 26½

Stevens Model No. 12 Marksman

Stevens Model No. 26 Crack Shot

Caliber: 22 long rifle, 32 RF
Action: Lever-action; exposed hammer; single shot
Magazine: None
Barrel: 18″, 22″
Sights: Open rear, blade front
Stock & Forearm: Plain walnut straight grip stock and tapered forearm
Approximate wt.: 3¼ to 3½ lbs.
Comments: Takedown rifle produced from 1913 until just prior to World War II.
Estimated Value: Excellent: $150.00
 Very good: $120.00

Stevens Model No. 26½

Same as the No. 26 except it is smooth bore for shot cartridges.
Estimated Value: Excellent: $140.00
 Very good: $110.00

Stevens Model No. 12 Marksman

Caliber: 22 long rifle, 25 RF, 32 RF
Action: Lever action; tip up; exposed hammer; single shot
Magazine: None, single shot
Barrel: 20″, round
Sights: Bead front, open rear
Stock & Forearm: Plain walnut, straight grip stock and short tapered forearm
Approximate wt.: 4 lbs.
Comments: Replaced the Maynard Jr. Made from 1912 until just before World War II.
Estimated Value: Excellent: $130.00
 Very good: $100.00

Stevens Model No. 417½

Stevens Model No. 417

Stevens Model No. 417-1

Stevens Model No. 417-2

Stevens Model No. 418

Stevens Model No. 418½

Stevens Models No. 417, 417½, 417-1, 417-2, 417-3 Walnut Hill

Caliber: 22 long rifle, 22 WRF, 25 Stevens
Action: Lever-action; exposed hammer; single shot
Magazine: None
Barrel: 28″ or 29″ heavy
Sights: 417: Lyman 52L extension rear; 417½: Lyman 144 tang peep and folding center; 417-1: Lyman 48L rear; 417-2: 144 rear; 417-3: no sights
Stock & Forearm: Plain walnut pistol grip stock and forearm; bands, swivels
Approximate wt.: 8¼ to 10½ lbs.
Comments: Made from the early 1930's until the late 1940's. Models differ only in sights.
Estimated Value: Excellent: $450.00
                      Very good: $340.00

Stevens Models No. 418, 418½ Walnut Hill

Caliber: 418: 22 long rifle, 22 short only; 418½: 22 WRF or 25 Stevens RF only
Action: Lever-action; exposed hammer; single shot
Magazine: None
Barrel: 26″
Sights: Lyman 144 tang peep, blade front; 418½: Lyman 2A tang peep, bead front
Stock & Forearm: Plain walnut pistol grip stock and forearm; swivels
Approximate wt.: 6½ lbs.
Comments: Made from the early 1930's to just before World War II.
Estimated Value: Excellent: $300.00
                      Very good: $225.00

Stevens Model No. 72 Crackshot

Stevens Model No. 72 Crackshot

Caliber: 22 short, long, long rifle
Action: Lever-action, falling block; single shot
Magazine: None
Barrel: 22″ octagon
Sights: Sporting front, open rear
Stock & Forearm: Plain walnut straight grip stock and tapered forearm; case hardened receiver
Approximate wt.: 4½ lbs.
Comments: Made from early 1970's to present.
Estimated Value: New (retail): $144.39
                      Excellent: $110.00
                      Very good: $ 80.00

Stevens Model No. 89

Stevens Model No. 65

Stevens - Springfield Model No. 51 Reliance

Stevens - Springfield Model No. 52 Challenge

Stevens - Springfield Model No. 53 Springfield Jr.

Stevens Model No. 89

Caliber: 22 short, long, long rifle
Action: Lever-action; exposed hammer; single shot; automatic ejection
Magazine: None
Barrel: 18½″
Sights: Sporting front, open rear
Stock & Forearm: Straight walnut stock and forearm with carbine band
Approximate wt.: 5 lbs.
Comments: Produced from mid 1970's to mid 1980's.
Estimated Value: Excellent: $60.00
Very good: $45.00

Stevens Model No. 65 Little Krag

Caliber: 22 short, long, long rifle
Action: Bolt action; single shot
Magazine: None
Barrel: 20″, round
Sights: Bead front, fixed peep or open rear
Stock & Forearm: Plain walnut one-piece straight grip stock and forearm
Approximate wt.: 3¼ lbs.
Comments: This small 22 rifle was produced from 1903 until about 1910.
Estimated Value: Excellent: $125.00
Very good: $ 95.00

Stevens - Springfield Model No. 52 Challenge

Caliber: 22 short, long, long rifle
Action: Bolt action; single shot
Magazine: None
Barrel: 22″, round
Sights: Bead front, adjustable sporting rear
Stock & Forearm: Plain walnut one-piece pistol grip stock and forearm
Approximate wt.: 3½ lbs.
Comments: Takedown, produced from early 1930's to just before World War II.
Estimated Value: Excellent: $60.00
Very good: $50.00

Stevens - Springfield Model No. 51 Reliance

Caliber: 22 short, long, long rifle
Action: Bolt action; single shot
Magazine: None
Barrel: 20″, round
Sights: Open rear, blade front
Stock & Forearm: Plain walnut one-piece straight grip stock and forearm
Approximate wt.: 3 lbs.
Comments: Takedown, made from 1930 for about five years.
Estimated Value: Excellent: $75.00
Very good: $55.00

Stevens - Springfield Model No. 53 Springfield Jr.

Caliber: 22 short, long, long rifle
Action: Bolt action; single shot
Magazine: None
Barrel: 24″
Sights: Bead front, adjustable sporting rear
Stock & Forearm: Plain walnut semi-pistol grip stock and forearm
Approximate wt.: 4½ lbs.
Comments: Takedown produced from 1930 until shortly after World War II.
Estimated Value: Excellent: $55.00
Very good: $45.00

Stevens Model No. 419 Junior Target

Stevens Model No. 053 Buckhorn

Stevens Model No. 419 Junior Target

Caliber: 22 short, long, long rifle
Action: Bolt action; single shot
Magazine: None
Barrel: 26″
Sights: Blade front, peep rear
Stock & Forearm: Plain walnut pistol grip stock with grooved forearm; swivels
Approximate wt.: 5½ lbs.
Comments: Made from 1932 until 1936.
Estimated Value: Excellent: $80.00
Very good: $65.00

Stevens Model No. 53, 053 Buckhorn

Caliber: 22 short, long, long rifle
Action: Bolt action; single shot
Magazine: None
Barrel: 24″
Sights: 053: hooded ramp front, open middle peep receiver; 53: open rear, bead front
Stock & Forearm: Plain walnut pistol grip stock and forearm
Approximate wt.: 5½ lbs.
Comments: A takedown rifle made from the mid 1930's until the late 1940's.
Estimated Value: Excellent: $60.00
Very good: $45.00

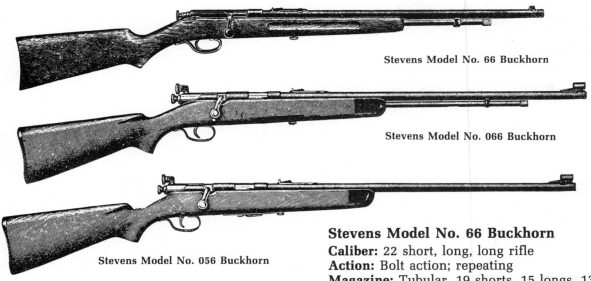

Stevens Model No. 66 Buckhorn

Stevens Model No. 066 Buckhorn

Stevens Model No. 056 Buckhorn

Stevens Model No. 56 and 056 Buckhorn

Caliber: 22 short, long, long rifle
Action: Bolt action; repeating
Magazine: 5-shot clip
Barrel: 24″
Sights: 56: bead front, open rear; 056: hooded ramp front, open middle receiver peep
Stock & Forearm: Plain walnut pistol grip stock and black tipped forearm
Approximate wt.: 6 lbs.
Comments: Takedown made from mid 1930's to late 1940's.
Estimated Value: Excellent: $70.00
Very good: $55.00

Stevens Model No. 66 Buckhorn

Caliber: 22 short, long, long rifle
Action: Bolt action; repeating
Magazine: Tubular, 19 shorts, 15 longs, 13 long rifles
Barrel: 24″
Sights: Open rear, bead front
Stock & Forearm: Plain walnut semi-pistol grip stock and forearm
Approximate wt.: 5 lbs.
Comments: A takedown rifle made from the 1920's until after World War I.
Estimated Value: Excellent: $75.00
Very good: $60.00

Stevens Model No. 066 Buckhorn

Same as the Model No. 66 except: hooded ramp front sight; open middle sight; receiver peep sight. Made from mid 1930's until late 1940's.
Estimated Value: Excellent: $75.00
Very good: $60.00

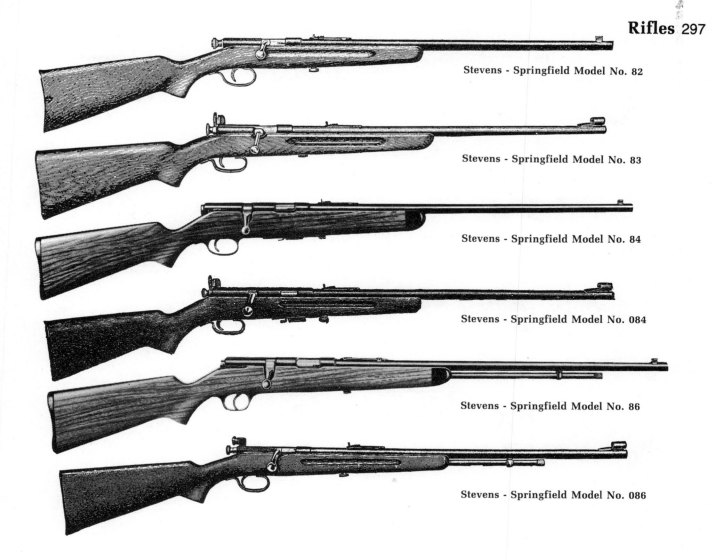

Stevens - Springfield Model No. 82

Stevens - Springfield Model No. 83

Stevens - Springfield Model No. 84

Stevens - Springfield Model No. 084

Stevens - Springfield Model No. 86

Stevens - Springfield Model No. 086

Stevens - Springfield Model No. 82
Caliber: 22
Action: Bolt action; single shot
Magazine: None
Barrel: 22″
Sights: Open rear, bead front
Stock & Forearm: Plain walnut pistol grip stock, groove in forearm
Approximate wt.: 4 lbs.
Comments: Takedown made from middle 1930's until 1940.
Estimated Value: Excellent: $55.00
   Very good: $40.00

Stevens - Springfield Model No. 83
Caliber: 22 short, long, long rifle, 22 WRF, 25 Stevens RF
Action: Bolt action; single shot
Magazine: None
Barrel: 24″
Sights: Peep rear, open middle, hooded ramp front
Stock & Forearm: Plain walnut pistol grip stock with groove in forearm
Approximate wt.: 4½ lbs.
Comments: Takedown made from the middle 1930's until 1940.
Estimated Value: Excellent: $60.00
   Very good: $45.00

Stevens - Springfield Models No. 84 and 084
(Stevens Model No. 84 after 1948)
Caliber: 22 short, long, long rifle
Action: Bolt action; repeating
Magazine: 5-shot clip
Barrel: 24″
Sights: 84: bead front, open rear; 84 Stevens or 084 peep rear and hooded ramp front
Stock & Forearm: Plain walnut pistol grip stock and forearm; black tip on forearm of Model 84
Approximate wt.: 6 lbs.
Comments: Takedown made from early 1940 until the mid 1960's.
Estimated Value: Excellent: $70.00
   Very good: $55.00

Stevens - Springfield Model No. 86, 086
(Stevens Model No. 86 after 1948)
Model 86 is same as Model 84 except it has a tubular magazine that holds 21 shorts, 17 longs, 15 long rifles. Made from mid 1930's until mid 1960's. Model 86 Stevens or 086 Stevens is same as 084 or 84 Stevens except it has tubular magazine.
Estimated Value: Excellent: $80.00
   Very good: $65.00

Stevens Model No. 416

Stevens - Springfield Model No. 15

Stevens - Springfield Model No. 15Y

Stevens Model No. 322

Stevens Model No. 416

Caliber: 22 long rifle
Action: Bolt action; repeating
Magazine: 5-shot clip
Barrel: 26″ heavy
Sights: Receiver peep, hooded ramp front
Stock & Forearm: Plain walnut pistol grip stock and forearm
Approximate wt.: 9½ lbs.
Comments: Made from the late 1930's to late 1940's.
Estimated Value: **Excellent:** $160.00
 Very good: $120.00

Stevens - Springfield Model No. 15,
Stevens 15, 15Y

Caliber: 22 short, long, long rifle
Action: Bolt action; single shot
Magazine: None
Barrel: Stevens-Springfield: 22″; Stevens 15, 24″; Stevens 15Y, 21″
Sights: Open rear, bead front
Stock & Forearm: Plain walnut pistol grip, 15Y; short butt stock, black tipped forearm
Approximate wt.: 4 to 5 lbs.
Comments: Manufactured: Stevens-Springfield 25, late 1930's to late 1940's; Stevens 15, late 1940's to mid 1960's; Stevens 15Y, late 1950's to mid 1960's.
Estimated Value: **Excellent:** $50.00
 Very good: $35.00

Stevens Model No. 322, 322S

Caliber: 22 Hornet
Action: Bolt action; repeating
Magazine: 5-shot clip
Barrel: 21″
Sights: Ramp front, open rear; 322S has peep rear
Stock & Forearm: Plain walnut pistol grip stock and forearm
Approximate wt.: 6¾ lbs.
Comments: Made from late 1940's to early 1950's.
Estimated Value: **Excellent:** $125.00
 Very good: $100.00

Sevens Model No. 325, 325S

Caliber: 30-30
Action: Bolt action; repeating
Magazine: 3-shot clip
Barrel: 21″
Sights: Open rear, bead front; 325S peep rear
Stock & Forearm: Plain walnut pistol grip stock and forearm
Approximate wt.: 6¾ lbs.
Comments: Made from late 1940's to early 1950's.
Estimated Value: **Excellent:** $100.00
 Very good: $75.00

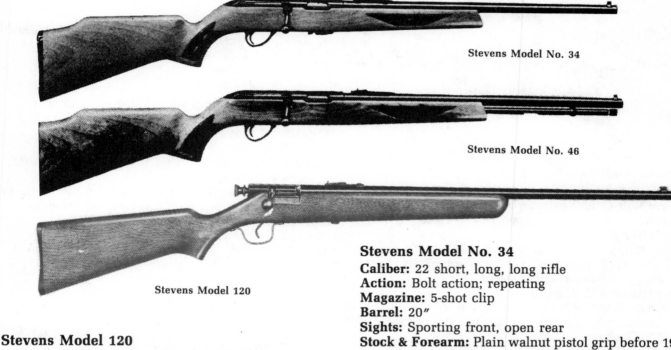

Stevens Model No. 34

Stevens Model No. 46

Stevens Model 120

Stevens Model 120

Caliber: 22 short, long, long rifle
Action: Bolt action; single shot; cocking piece
Magazine: None
Barrel: Blued 24″
Sights: Blade front, elevator open rear
Stock & Forearm: Plain hardwood one-piece semi-pistol grip stock and forearm
Approximate wt.: 5 lbs.
Comments: Produced in the late 1970's.
Estimated Value: Excellent: $55.00
                              Very good: $45.00

Stevens Model No. 34

Caliber: 22 short, long, long rifle
Action: Bolt action; repeating
Magazine: 5-shot clip
Barrel: 20″
Sights: Sporting front, open rear
Stock & Forearm: Plain walnut pistol grip before 1969; checkered Monte Carlo after 1969
Approximate wt.: 5½ lbs.
Comments: Made from mid 1960's to early 1980's.
Estimated Value: Excellent: $65.00
                              Very good: $55.00

Stevens Model No. 46

Similar to Model 34 except with tubular magazine. Discontinued in late 1960's.
Estimated Value: Excellent: $70.00
                              Very good: $60.00

Stevens Model 246

Stevens Model No. 73

Stevens Model 246

Caliber: 22 short, long, long rifle
Action: Bolt action; repeating
Magazine: Tubular, 22 shorts, 17 longs, 15 long rifles
Barrel: Blued 20″
Sights: Blade front, elevator open rear
Stock & Forearm: Checkered hardwood one-piece semi-pistol grip stock and forearm
Approximate wt.: 5 lbs.
Comments: Produced in the late 1970's.
Estimated Value: Excellent: $75.00
                              Very good: $60.00

Stevens Model No. 73, 73Y

Caliber: 22 short, long, long rifle
Action: Bolt action; single shot
Magazine: None
Barrel: 20″ on 73; 18″ on 73Y
Sights: Sporting front, open rear
Stock & Forearm: Plain walnut pistol grip; short stock on 73Y
Approximate wt.: 73 - 4¾ lbs.; 73Y - 4½ lbs.
Comments: Made from 1965 to early 1980's.
Estimated Value: Excellent: $55.00
                              Very good: $45.00

Stevens Model 110 E

Stevens Model 35, 35M

Stevens Model 110E, 110ES

Caliber: 243, 30-06, 308
Action: Bolt action; hammerless; repeating
Magazine: 4-shot box, internal
Barrel: Blued 22″
Sights: Ramp front, open rear; 110ES has 4X scope; checkered hardwood one-piece Monte Carlo semi-pistol grip stock and forearm
Approximate wt.: 7 lbs.
Comments: Made from the late 1970's to 1981 as Stevens. Merchandised in 1982 as Savage. Add $20.00 for 110ES scope.
Estimated Value: Excellent: $200.00
Very good: $150.00

Stevens Model 35, 35M

Caliber: 22 short, long, long rifle; 35M is 22 mag.
Action: Bolt action; repeating
Magazine: 4-shot detachable clip
Barrel: Blued 22″
Sights: Ramp front, sporting rear with step elevator; grooved for scope
Stock & Forearm: Checkered hardwood Monte Carlo one-piece semi-pistol grip stock and forearm
Approximate wt.: 4¾ lbs.
Comments: Produced from 1982 to 1985.
Estimated Value: Excellent: $75.00
Very good: $55.00

Stevens Model 982

Stevens Model 36

Stevens Model 125

Stevens Model 125

Caliber: 22 short, long, long rifle
Action: Bolt action; single shot; thumb pull hammer
Magazine: None
Barrel: Blued 22″
Sights: Sporting front, open rear with elevator
Stock & Forearm: Checkered hardwood one-piece semi-pistol grip stock and forearm
Approximate wt.: 5 lbs.
Comments: Discontinued in mid 1980's.
Estimated Value: Excellent: $50.00
Very good: $40.00

Stevens Model 125Y

A youth version of the Model 125 with shorter stock. Discontinued in the early 1980's.
Estimated Value: Excellent: $50.00
Very good: $40.00

Stevens Model 982

Caliber: 22 short, long, long rifle
Action: Bolt action; repeating
Magazine: 5-shot detachable clip; 10-shot available
Barrel: Blued 22″
Sights: Ramp front, open rear with elevator
Stock & Forearm: Checkered hardwood one-piece Monte Carlo semi-pistol grip stock and forearm
Approximate wt.: 5¾ lbs.
Comments: Advertised in 1981 only.
Estimated Value: Excellent: $80.00
Very good: $65.00

Stevens Model 36

Caliber: 22 short, long, long rifle
Action: Bolt action; hammerless, single shot
Magazine: None, single shot
Barrel: 22″
Sights: Open rear, blade front
Stock & Forearm: Hardwood, one-piece semi-pistol grip stock & forearm
Approximate wt.: 5 lbs.
Comments: Introduced in 1984 and advertised as a good choice for a first rifle. Discontinued in 1985.
Estimated Value: Excellent: $70.00
Very good: $50.00

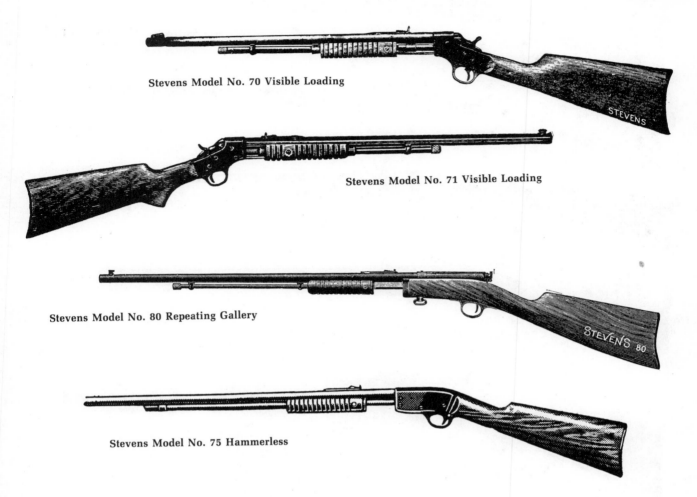

Stevens Model No. 70 Visible Loading

Stevens Model No. 71 Visible Loading

Stevens Model No. 80 Repeating Gallery

Stevens Model No. 75 Hammerless

Stevens Model No. 70 Visible Loading

Caliber: 22 short, long, long rifle
Action: Slide action; exposed hammer
Magazine: Tubular; 11 long rifles, 13 longs, 15 shorts
Barrel: 20″, 22″; round
Sights: Open rear, bead front
Stock & Forearm: Plain walnut straight grip stock and grooved slide handle
Approximate wt.: 4½ lbs.
Comments: Made from 1907 until the early 1930's.
Estimated Value: Excellent: $200.00
　　　　　　　　　Very good: $150.00

Stevens Model No. 71 Visible Loading

Caliber: 22 short, long, long rifle
Action: Slide action; exposed hammer
Magazine: Tubular; 15 shorts, 13 longs, 11 long rifles
Barrel: 24″ octagon
Sights: Bead front, adjustable flat-top sporting rear
Stock & Forearm: Plain walnut pistol grip stock and grooved slide handle
Approximate wt.: 5 lbs.
Comments: This replaced the No. 70; discontinued prior to World War II.
Estimated Value: Excellent: $195.00
　　　　　　　　　Very good: $150.00

Stevens Model No. 75 Hammerless

Caliber: 22 short, long, long rifle
Action: Slide action; hammerless; side ejection
Magazine: Tubular, 20 shorts, 17 longs, 15 long rifles
Barrel: 24″
Sights: Bead front, adjustable rear
Stock & Forearm: Plain walnut, straight grip stock and grooved slide handle
Approximate wt.: 5¼ lbs.
Comments: Made from the early 1930's until World War II.
Estimated Value: Excellent: $200.00
　　　　　　　　　Very good: $150.00

Stevens Model No. 80 Repeating Gallery

Caliber: 22 short
Action: Slide action; hammerless
Magazine: 16-shot tubular
Barrel: 24″ round
Sights: Open rear, bead front
Stock & Forearm: Plain walnut straight grip stock and grooved forearm
Approximate wt.: 5¼ lbs.
Comments: Takedown made for about five years beginning in 1906.
Estimated Value: Excellent: $225.00
　　　　　　　　　Very good: $165.00

Stevens - Springfield Model No. 85

Stevens - Springfield Model No. 87

Stevens Model No. 57

Stevens Model No. 76

Stevens Model No. 987, 987T

Stevens - Springfield Model No. 85, 085
(Stevens Model No. 85 after 1948)

Caliber: 22 long rifle
Action: Semi-automatic; repeating
Magazine: 5-shot clip
Barrel: 24″
Sights: Open rear, bead front on 85; hooded ramp front and peep rear on 085 and 85 Stevens
Stock & Forearm: Plain walnut pistol grip stock and forearm; 85 has black tipped forearm
Approximate wt.: 6 lbs.
Comments: Produced from the late 1930's until after World War II.

Estimated Value:	Excellent:	$80.00
	Very good:	$60.00

Stevens - Springfield Model No. 87, 087
(Stevens Model 87 after 1948)

Same as the No. 85, 085 except it has a 15-shot tubular magazine.

Estimated Value:	Excellent:	$85.00
	Very good:	$65.00

Stevens Model No. 87 K Scout

Carbine version of Model No. 87; 20″ barrel; produced until 1969.

Estimated Value:	Excellent:	$75.00
	Very good:	$55.00

Stevens Model 987, 987T

Caliber: 22 long rifle
Action: Semi-automatic
Magazine: 14-shot tubular
Barrel: 20″ blued
Sights: Ramp front, open rear with elevator; 987T has 4X scope
Stock & Forearm: Checkered hardwood, one-piece semi-pistol grip Monte Carlo stock and forearm
Approximate wt.: 6 lbs.
Comments: Introduced in 1981. Add $10.00 for scope (987T).

Estimated Value:	New (retail):	$106.50
	Excellent:	$ 80.00
	Very good:	$ 60.00

Stevens Model No. 57, 057

Caliber: 22 long rifle
Action: Semi-automatic; repeating
Magazine: 5-shot clip
Barrel: 24″
Sights: Open rear, bead front on 57; hooded ramp front, open middle, receiver peep on 057
Stock & Forearm: Plain walnut pistol grip stock and forearm; black tipped forearm on 57
Approximate wt.: 6 lbs.
Comments: Made from late 1930's to late 1940's.

Estimated Value:	Excellent:	$80.00
	Very good:	$60.00

Stevens Model No. 76, 076

Same as 057 and 57 except with 15-shot tubular magazine.

Estimated Value:	Excellent:	$85.00
	Very good:	$65.00

Stevens Model No. 887-T

Stevens Model 887

Caliber: 22 long rifle
Action: Semi-automatic
Magazine: 15-shot tubular
Barrel: Blued 20″
Sights: Blade front, elevator open rear
Stock & Forearm: Checkered hardwood, one-piece semi-pistol grip stock and forearm
Approximate wt.: 6 lbs.
Comments: Produced in the late 1970's. Due to a possible safety malfunction, certain models were recalled in 1982 and inspected by Stevens at no cost to the owner. Serial numbers recalled were B256621 or higher; C000001 or higher; D000001 or higher.
Estimated Value: Excellent: $70.00
                 Very good: $55.00

Stevens Model 887-T

Similar to the Model 887 with a 4X scope. Due to a possible safety malfunction, certain models were recalled in 1982 and inspected by Stevens at no cost to the owner. Serial numbers recalled were B256621 or higher; C000001 or higher; D000001 or higher.
Estimated Value: Excellent: $75.00
                 Very good: $60.00

Thompson Center

Thompson Center Model TCR 83 Aristocrat

Thompson Center Contender Carbine

Thompson Center Model TCR '83 Hunter

Caliber: 22 Hornet, 222 Rem., 223 Rem., 22-250 Rem., 243 Win., 270 Win., 7mm Rem. magnum, 308 Win., 30-06 Springfield; caliber can be selected by replacing different caliber barrel
Action: Top lever, break-open; single shot; hammerless
Magazine: None
Barrel: 23″ interchangeable to select caliber
Sights: Ramp front, folding leaf rear
Stock & Forearm: Checkered walnut semi-pistol grip stock and grooved forearm; cheekpiece; recoil pad
Approximate wt.: 6¾ lbs.
Comments: Introduced in 1983 by a company well known for black powder firearms and single shot pistols. Add 30% for each additional barrel.
Estimated Value: New (retail): $435.00
                 Excellent: $325.00
                 Very good: $245.00

Thompson Center Contender Carbine

Caliber: 22 long rifle, 22 Hornet, 222 Rem., 7mm TCU, 7x30 Waters, 30-30 Win., 357 Win. magnum
Action: single shot, frame accomodates any caliber interchangeable barrel, hammer adjusts
Magazine: None, single shot
Barrel: 21″ interchangeable for caliber
Sights: Adjustable; tapped for scope mounts
Stock & Forearm: Checkered walnut, pistol grip stock and grooved forearm; recoil pad
Approximate wt.: lbs.
Comments: A shooting system introduced in 1986. Based on the design of the popular Contender handgun. Add 35% for each additional barrel.
Estimated Value: New (retail): $345.00
                 Excellent: $260.00
                 Very good: $195.00

Thompson Center Model TCR 83 Arstocrat

Similar to the Hunter with checkered forearm and stainless steel, adjustable double set triggers.
Estimated Value: New (retail): $475.00
                 Excellent: $355.00
                 Very good: $265.00

Universal 440 Vulcan

Universal M1 or 1000

Universal M1 or 1000 Deluxe

Universal 1020

Universal Ferret

Universal M1 or 1000, 1003

Similar to the U.S. M1 Carbine with a 5-shot detachable clip. Made in 30 caliber from the mid 1960's to present. Add $50.00 for scope and detachable mount. See also Iver Johnson.

Estimated Value: New (retail): $218.00
Excellent: $165.00
Very good: $120.00

Universal 1020, 1020 TB, 1020 TCO, 1030

Similar to the 1000 with a Monte Carlo stock and a water resistant teflon finish in green, blue, tan, black or gray. Currently produced as 1020 TB (black) and 1020 TCO (green), 1030 (gray).

Estimated Value: Excellent: $200.00
Very good: $150.00

Universal 440 Vulcan

Caliber: 44 magnum
Action: Slide action; hammerless; repeating
Magazine: 5-shot clip
Barrel: 18¼" carbine
Sights: Adjustable rear, ramp front with gold bead
Stock & Forearm: Walnut semi-pistol grip stock and slide handle
Approximate wt.: 6 lbs.
Comments: Made from the mid 1960's to early 1970's.
Estimated Value: Excellent: $200.00
Very good: $150.00

Universal M1 or 1000 Deluxe, 1005 SB, 1010N, 1015G, 1011

Same as the 1000 with a Monte Carlo stock; also available in nickel, gold plate or chrome.

Estimated Value:

	1005SB Blue	1010N Nickel	1015G Gold	1011 Chrome
Excellent:	$160.00	$170.00	$210.00	$170.00
Very good:	$125.00	$140.00	$175.00	$140.00

Universal Ferret

Similar to the M1 with a Monte Carlo stock, no sights, and in 256 caliber.

Estimated Value: Excellent: $175.00
Very good: $130.00

Universal Model 1035, 1040, 1045

Similar to the Model 1020 with a military stock.
Estimated Value: Excellent: $190.00
Very good: $140.00

Universal Model 1006

Similar to the Model 1005SB with stainless steel finish.
Estimated Value: Excellent: $200.00
Very good: $150.00

Universal Model 2200 Leatherneck

Universal Model 2200 Leatherneck
Similar to the Model 1003 in 22 caliber. Produced from the early 1980's to mid 1980's.
Estimated Value: Excellent: $170.00
Very good: $130.00

Valmet

Valmet Model 412K Double

Valmet Finnish Lion

Valmet Model M-71S

Valmet Finnish Lion
Caliber: 22 long rifle
Action: Bolt action; single shot
Magazine: None
Barrel: Blued, 29″, heavy
Sights: Extended peep rear, changeable front
Stock & Forearm: Free-rifle, pistol grip, with thumb hole, one-piece stock and forearm; palm rest; swivels; Swiss buttplate
Approximate wt.: 15 lbs.
Comments: International Match-type rifle; discontinued in the late 1970's.
Estimated Value: Excellent: $540.00
Very good: $400.00

Valmet Model 412K, and 412S (mid 1980's) Double
Caliber: 243, 308, 30-06
Action: Top lever, break-open, hammerless; extractors
Magazine: None
Barrel: Over and under double barrel; 24″ with space between barrels
Sights: Open rear, blade front; drilled for scope
Stock & Forearm: Checkered walnut Monte Carlo pistol grip stock and forearm; recoil pad; swivels
Approximate wt.: 6½ lbs.
Comments: A double rifle produced in Finland as part of the 412 Shotgun Combination series.
Estimated Value: New (retail): $1,069.00
Excellent: $ 800.00
Very good: $ 600.00

Valmet 412KE Double and 412SE Double
Similar to the Model 412K Double with automatic ejectors. Introduced in early 1980's. Calibers 375 Win. and 9.3x74 only.
Estimated Value: New (retail): $1,119.00
Excellent: $ 840.00
Very good: $ 630.00

Valmet Model M-72S, M-715S, M-71S
Caliber: 223, 5.56mm
Action: Semi-automatic, gas operated
Magazine: 15- or 30-shot, curved detachable box
Barrel: 16½″
Sights: Open tangent rear, hooded post front; both adjustable
Stock & Forearm: Wood or reinforced resin stock; pistol grip; swivels; wood stock and forearm and plastic pistol grip on Model M-71S
Approximate wt.: 8¾ lbs.
Comments: Similar to the M-62/S.
Estimated Value: Excellent: $650.00
Very good: $485.00

Valmet Model M-62 S

Caliber: 7.62 x 39mm Russian
Action: Semi-automatic; gas piston, rotating bolt
Magazine: 15- or 30-shot, curved detachable box
Barrel: 16½″
Sights: Adjustable tangent peep rear, adjustable hooded post front
Stock & Forearm: Fixed metal tube or walnut stock ; pistol grip; ventilated forearm
Approximate wt.: 8¾ lbs.
Comments: A powerful semi-automatic made in the mid 1970's. Add $15.00 for wood stock version.
Estimated Value: Excellent: $600.00
Very good: $450.00

Valmet Model M-76 FS

Similar to the Model M-62 S in 223 and 7.62x39mm Russian caliber.
Estimated Value: New (retail): $649.00
Excellent: $485.00
Very good: $365.00

Walther

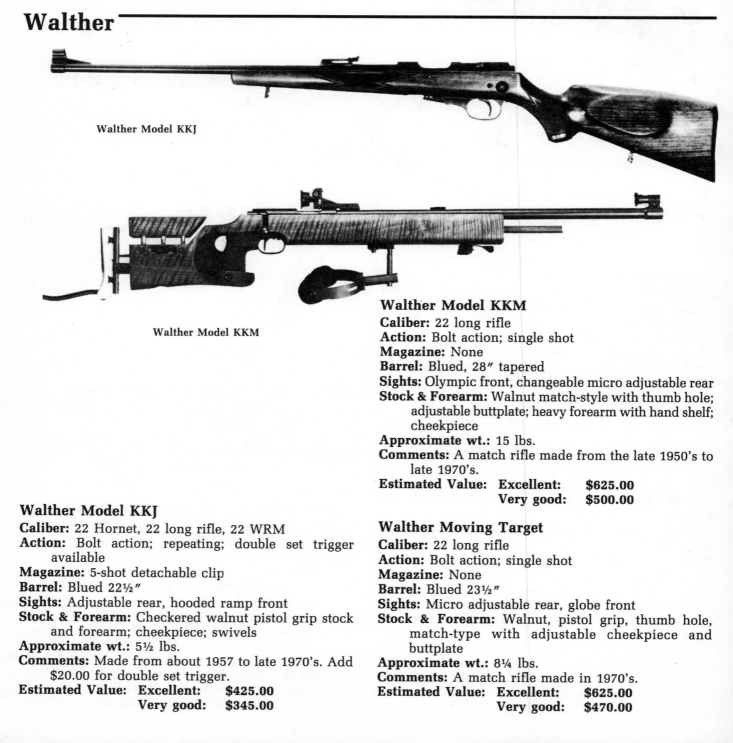

Walther Model KKJ

Walther Model KKM

Walther Model KKM

Caliber: 22 long rifle
Action: Bolt action; single shot
Magazine: None
Barrel: Blued, 28″ tapered
Sights: Olympic front, changeable micro adjustable rear
Stock & Forearm: Walnut match-style with thumb hole; adjustable buttplate; heavy forearm with hand shelf; cheekpiece
Approximate wt.: 15 lbs.
Comments: A match rifle made from the late 1950's to late 1970's.
Estimated Value: Excellent: $625.00
Very good: $500.00

Walther Model KKJ

Caliber: 22 Hornet, 22 long rifle, 22 WRM
Action: Bolt action; repeating; double set trigger available
Magazine: 5-shot detachable clip
Barrel: Blued 22½″
Sights: Adjustable rear, hooded ramp front
Stock & Forearm: Checkered walnut pistol grip stock and forearm; cheekpiece; swivels
Approximate wt.: 5½ lbs.
Comments: Made from about 1957 to late 1970's. Add $20.00 for double set trigger.
Estimated Value: Excellent: $425.00
Very good: $345.00

Walther Moving Target

Caliber: 22 long rifle
Action: Bolt action; single shot
Magazine: None
Barrel: Blued 23½″
Sights: Micro adjustable rear, globe front
Stock & Forearm: Walnut, pistol grip, thumb hole, match-type with adjustable cheekpiece and buttplate
Approximate wt.: 8¼ lbs.
Comments: A match rifle made in 1970's.
Estimated Value: Excellent: $625.00
Very good: $470.00

Walther Model UIT

Walther Prone 400

Weatherby Magnum Deluxe

Weatherby Deluxe

Walther Model UIT

Caliber: 22 long rifle
Action: Bolt action; single shot
Magazine: None
Barrel: 25½"
Sights: Changeable front, micro adjustable rear
Stock & Forearm: Match-style, walnut pistol grip stock and wide forearm
Approximate wt.: 10¼ lbs.
Comments: A match rifle made from the mid 1960's. Super and Special match models still produced.
Estimated Value: **Excellent:** $600.00
       Very good: $450.00

Walther Prone 400

Similar to the UIT with split stock and adjustable cheekpiece; thumb hole; no sights.
Estimated Value: **Excellent:** $500.00
       Very good: $375.00

Weatherby

Weatherby Magnum Deluxe

Caliber: 378 mag., 300 mag., 375 mag., 7mm mag., 270 mag., 257 mag., 220 Rocket
Action: Bolt action; Mauser-type
Magazine: 3-shot
Barrel: Blued 24"; 26" available on some calibers
Sights: None
Stock & Forearm: Checkered wood Monte Carlo one-piece pistol grip stock and tapered forearm; recoil pad; swivels; cheekpiece
Approximate wt.: 7 to 8 lbs.
Comments: Made from the late 1940's to the late 1950's.
Estimated Value: **Excellent:** $450.00
       Very good: $340.00

Weatherby Deluxe

Similar to the Magnum Deluxe but in 270 Win. caliber.
Estimated Value: **Excellent:** $325.00
       Very good: $245.00

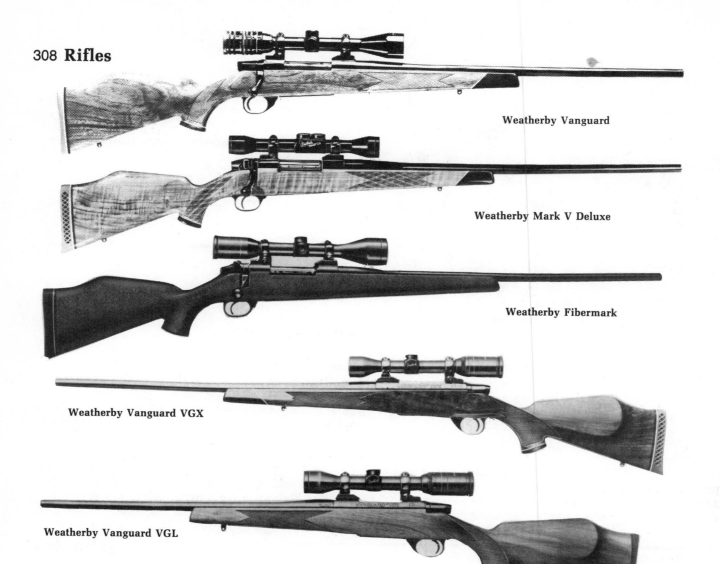

Weatherby Vanguard

Weatherby Mark V Deluxe

Weatherby Fibermark

Weatherby Vanguard VGX

Weatherby Vanguard VGL

Weatherby Mark V Deluxe

Caliber: 30-06, 240, 257, 270, 7mm, 300 mag., 340 mag., 378 mag., 460 mag.

Action: Bolt action; repeating

Magazine: 2-, 3- or 4-shot, depending on caliber

Barrel: 24″ or 26″ blued

Sights: None

Stock & Forearm: Checkered walnut Monte Carlo one-piece pistol grip stock and tapered forearm; cheekpiece; recoil pad; swivels

Approximate wt.: 7¼ to 10½ lbs.

Comments: Made from the late 1950's to present. Right or left hand models available. Also available in Euromark and Lazermark series with custom extras. Add 7% for Euromark; 14% for Lazermark; 2½% for 340 magnum caliber; 21% for 378 Win. caliber; 38% for 460 magnum caliber.

Estimated Value:	New (retail):	$819.95
	Excellent:	$615.00
	Very good:	$460.00

Weatherby Model Varmintmaster

A scaled-down version of the Mark V Deluxe in 22-250 or 224 Weatherby magnum; 24″ or 26″ barrel. Add 15% for Lazermark Series.

Estimated Value:	New (retail):	$798.95
	Excellent:	$600.00
	Very good:	$450.00

Weatherby Fibermark

Similar to the Mark V Deluxe except one-piece black fiberglass stock and forearm; weighs 7½-8 lbs. Introduced in the mid 1980's.

Estimated Value:	New (retail):	$949.95
	Excellent:	$715.00
	Very good:	$535.00

Weatherby Vanguard VGX, VGS, VGL

Caliber: 22-250, 25-06, 243, 264, 270, 30-06, 7mm Rem. mag., 300 Win. mag.

Action: Bolt action; repeating

Magazine: 5-shot (3-shot magnum), box with hinged floor plate

Barrel: 24″ blued

Sights: None

Stock & Forearm: Checkered walnut, Monte Carlo pistol grip, one-piece stock and forearm; recoil pad, swivels; VGX has deluxe finish

Approximate wt.: 8 lbs; 6½ lbs. for VGL

Comments: Made from early 1970's to present. Add 25% for VGX.

Estimated Value:	New (retail):	$399.95
	Excellent:	$300.00
	Very good:	$225.00

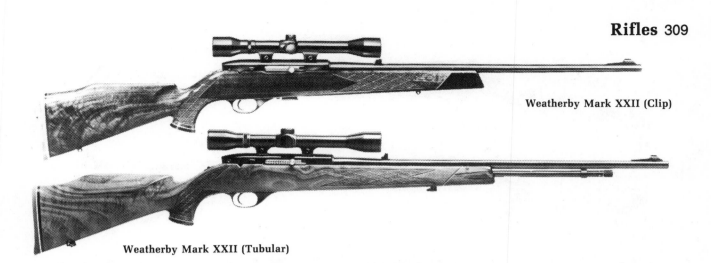

Weatherby Mark XXII (Clip)

Weatherby Mark XXII (Tubular)

Weatherby Vanguard Fiberguard

Caliber: 223, 243, 270, 7mm Rem. magnum, 30-06, 308 Win.
Action: Bolt action; repeating; short action
Magazine: 6-shot in 223; 5-shot in 243, 270, 30-06 and 308; 3-shot in 7mm Rem. magnum
Barrel: 20″ blued
Sights: None
Stock & Forearm: A rugged, all weather fiberglass one-piece semi-pistol grip stock and forearm; forest green wrinkle finish with black butt pad
Approximate wt.: 6½ lbs.
Comments: Made from the mid 1980's to present.
Estimated Value: New (retail): $579.95
Excellent: $435.00
Very good: $325.00

Weatherby Mark XXII Deluxe

Caliber: 22 long rifle
Action: Semi-automatic; hammerless
Magazine: 5- or 10-shot clip; 15-shot tubular
Barrel: Blued 24″
Sights: Open rear, ramp front
Stock & Forearm: Checkered walnut Monte Carlo one-piece pistol grip stock and tapered forearm; swivels
Approximate wt.: 6 lbs.
Comments: Made from the mid 1960's to present.
Estimated Value: New (retail): $369.95
Excellent: $280.00
Very good: $210.00

Western Field

Western Field Model 732

Western Field Model 730

Western Field Model 732

Caliber: 7mm, 30-06
Action: Bolt action; repeating; hammerless
Magazine: 4- or 5-shot tubular, depending on caliber
Barrel: Blued 22″
Sights: Leaf rear, bead front
Stock & Forearm: Checkered walnut Monte Carlo one-piece pistol grip stock and forearm; swivels
Approximate wt.: 8 lbs.
Comments: Manufactured into the late 1970's.
Estimated Value: Excellent: $200.00
Very good: $150.00

Western Field Model 730

Similar to 732. Produced until mid 1970's.
Estimated Value: Excellent: $180.00
Very good: $135.00

Western Field Model 780

Western Field Model 775

Western Field Bolt Action Repeater

Western Field Model 842

Western Field Bolt Action Repeater

Caliber: 22 short, long, long rifle; 22 WMR
Action: Bolt action; repeating
Magazine: 7-shot clip in 22; 5-shot in 22 WMR
Barrel: Blued 24″
Sights: Adjustable rear, ramp front
Stock & Forearm: Walnut one-piece pistol grip stock and forearm
Approximate wt.: 6 lbs.
Comments: Discontinued in the early 1980's. Add $5.00 for 22 WMR.
Estimated Value: Excellent: $50.00
  Very good: $40.00

Western Field Model 780

Caliber: 243, 308
Action: Bolt action; repeating
Magazine: 5-shot tubular
Barrel: Blued 22″
Sights: Adjustable rear, bead front
Stock & Forearm: Checkered walnut Monte Carlo one-piece pistol grip stock and forearm
Approximate wt.: 6½ lbs.
Comments: Manufactured to the late 1970's.
Estimated Value: Excellent: $170.00
  Very good: $130.00

Western Field Model 775, 776

Similar to the 780; produced until mid 1970's.
Estimated Value: Excellent: $160.00
  Very good: $120.00

Western Field Bolt Action

Caliber: 30-06
Action: Bolt action; repeating
Magazine: 4-shot, hinged floorplate
Barrel: Blued 22″ round
Sights: Bead front, adjustable rear
Stock & Forearm: Smooth hardwood one-piece pistol grip stock and forearm with sling swivels
Approximate wt.: 7¾ lbs.
Comments: Made until the early 1980's.
Estimated Value: Excellent: $160.00
  Very good: $120.00

Western Field Model 842

Caliber: 22 short, long, long rifle
Action: Bolt action; repeating
Magazine: Tubular; 18 long rifles, 20 longs, 22 shorts
Barrel: Blued 24″
Sights: Adjustable rear, bead front
Stock & Forearm: Walnut Monte Carlo one-piece pistol grip stock and forearm
Approximate wt.: 6¼ lbs.
Comments: Manufactured until the mid 1970's.
Estimated Value: Excellent: $60.00
  Very good: $45.00

Western Field Model 78 Deluxe

Caliber: 7mm mag., 30-06
Action: Bolt action
Magazine: 3-shot rotary magazine in 7mm, 4-shot in 30-06
Barrel: 24″ in 7mm; 22″ in 30-06
Sights: Bead front, adjustable rear
Stock & Forearm: Checkered walnut pistol grip stock and forearm; swivels
Approximate wt.: 7mm: 8¾ lbs.; 30-06: 7½ lbs.
Comments: Manufactured to the early 1980's.
Estimated Value: Excellent: $180.00
Very good: $140.00

Western Field Model 815

Caliber: 22 short, long, long rifle
Action: Bolt action; single shot; hammerless
Magazine: None
Barrel: Blued 24″
Sights: Adjustable rear, bead front
Stock & Forearm: Wood Monte Carlo one-piece pistol grip stock and forearm
Approximate wt.: 8 lbs.
Comments: Made until the mid 1970's.
Estimated Value: Excellent: $40.00
Very good: $30.00

Western Field 72

Western Field Model 72

Caliber: 30-30
Action: Lever-action; exposed hammer; repeating; side ejection
Magazine: 6-shot tubular
Barrel: Blued 18″, 20″
Sights: Adjustable open rear, ramp front
Stock & Forearm: Walnut two-piece pistol grip stock and forearm; barrel band; fluted comb
Approximate wt.: 7½ lbs.
Comments: Made into the late 1970's.
Estimated Value: Excellent: $125.00
Very good: $100.00

Western Field Model 740

Similar to Model 72 with recoil pad and 20″ barrel. Produced until mid 1970's.
Estimated Value: Excellent: $120.00
Very good: $90.00

Western Field Model 79

Caliber: 30-30
Action: Lever-action; exposed hammer; repeating; side ejection
Magazine: 6-shot tubular, side load
Barrel: Blued 20″ round
Sights: Bead front, rear adjustable for elevation
Stock & Forearm: Smooth hardwood pistol grip stock and forearm
Approximate wt.: 7 lbs.
Comments: Made to the early 1980's.
Estimated Value: Excellent: $120.00
Very good: $90.00

Western Field Model 865

Caliber: 22 short, long, long rifle
Action: Lever-action; hammerless; repeating
Magazine: Tubular; 13 long rifles, 15 longs, 20 shorts
Barrel: Blued; 20″
Sights: Adjustable rear, bead front
Stock & Forearm: Wood Monte Carlo pistol grip stock and forearm; barrel band; swivels
Approximate wt.: 7 lbs.
Comments: Made until the mid 1970's.
Estimated Value: Excellent: $75.00
Very good: $60.00

Western Field Model 895

Western Field Model 895

Caliber: 22 long rifle
Action: Semi-automatic; hammerless
Magazine: 18-shot tubular
Barrel: Blued 24″
Sights: Open rear, bead front
Stock & Forearm: Checkered walnut Monte Carlo pistol grip stock and forearm
Approximate wt.: 7 lbs.
Comments: Made until mid 1970's.
Estimated Value: Excellent: $70.00
Very good: $55.00

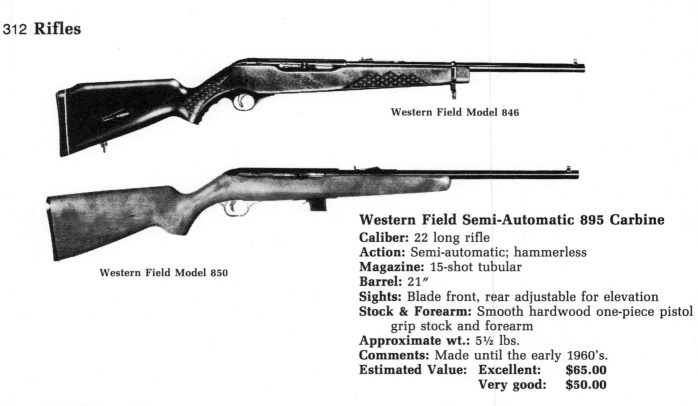

Western Field Model 846

Western Field Model 850

Western Field Semi-Automatic 895 Carbine
Caliber: 22 long rifle
Action: Semi-automatic; hammerless
Magazine: 15-shot tubular
Barrel: 21″
Sights: Blade front, rear adjustable for elevation
Stock & Forearm: Smooth hardwood one-piece pistol
grip stock and forearm
Approximate wt.: 5½ lbs.
Comments: Made until the early 1960's.
Estimated Value: Excellent: $65.00
                      Very good: $50.00

Western Field Model 850
Caliber: 22 long rifle
Action: Semi-automatic; hammerless
Magazine: 7-shot clip
Barrel: Blued 18½″
Sights: Adjustable rear, bead front
Stock & Forearm: Wood one-piece semi-pistol grip stock
and tapered forearm
Approximate wt.: 5½ lbs.
Comments: Made to the mid 1970's.
Estimated Value: Excellent: $60.00
                      Very good: $45.00

Western Field Model 846
Caliber: 22 long rifle
Action: Semi-automatic; hammerless
Magazine: 15-shot tubular, stock load
Barrel: Blued 18½″
Sights: Adjustable rear, bead front
Stock & Forearm: Checkered wood one-piece pistol grip
stock and forearm; barrel band; swivels
Approximate wt.: 5¼ lbs.
Comments: Made until mid 1970's.
Estimated Value: Excellent: $70.00
                      Very good: $55.00

Whitworth

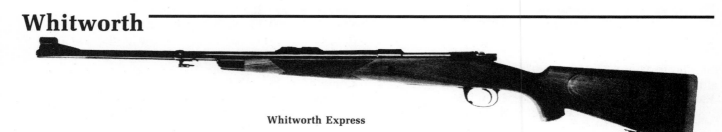

Whitworth Express

Whitworth Viscount
Caliber: 22-250, 243, 25-06, 270 Win., 7x57mm, 308,
30-06, 7mm Rem. magnum, 300 Win. magnum
Action: Bolt action, mauser style; repeating; adjustable
trigger
Magazine: Box magazine with hinged floorplate
Barrel: 24″
Sights: Adjustable rear, hooded ramp front
Stock & Forearm: Hardwood with walnut finish, one-
piece checkered stock and forearm; sling swivels
Approximate wt.: 7 lbs.
Comments: A sporting rifle designed for rough field use;
currently produced.
Estimated Value: New (retail): $425.00
                      Excellent: $320.00
                      Very good: $240.00

Whitworth Express, Safari
Caliber: 375 H & H mag., 458 Win. mag.
Action: Bolt action, Mauser style; repeating; adjustable
trigger
Magazine: 3-shot box with hinged floor plate
Barrel: 24″
Sights: 3 leaf express sights
Stock & Forearm: Checkered European walnut, Monte
Carlo one-piece stock and forearm; cheekpiece;
swivels; recoil pad
Approximate wt.: 7½ lbs.
Comments: Currently produced.
Estimated Value: New (retail): $650.00
                      Excellent: $485.00
                      Very good: $360.00

Whitworth Mannlicher Carbine

Similar to the Whitworth Viscount except: 20″ barrel with full length forearm; available in calibers 243 Win., 270 Win., 7x57mm, 308 Win., 30-06; European walnut stock.

Estimated Value: New (retail): $675.00
Excellent: $500.00
Very good: $380.00

Whitworth Sporting American Field

Similar to the Whitworth Viscount except: European walnut stock; rubber recoil buttplate; receiver is drilled and tapped for scope mounts; also equipped with sights.

Estimated Value: New (retail): $625.00
Excellent: $395.00
Very good: $295.00

Winchester

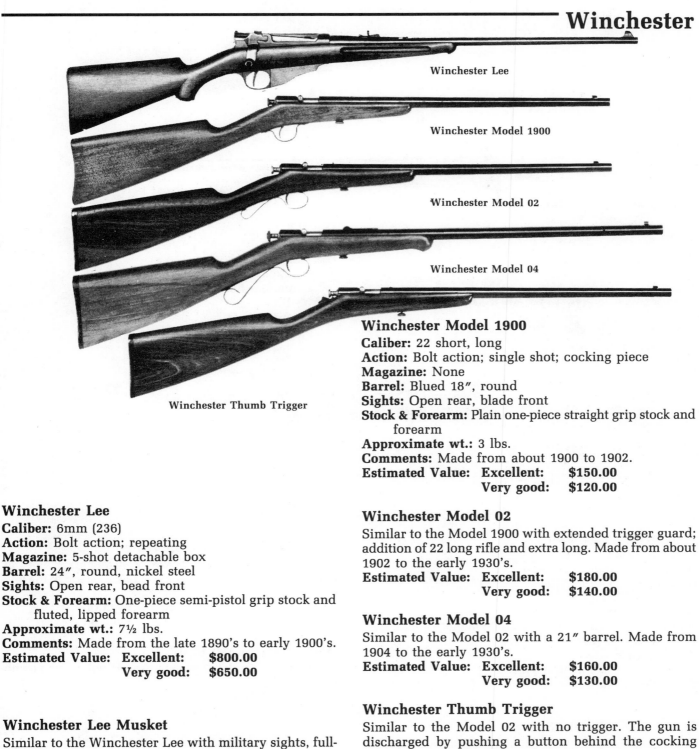

Winchester Lee

Winchester Model 1900

Winchester Model 02

Winchester Model 04

Winchester Thumb Trigger

Winchester Lee

Caliber: 6mm (236)
Action: Bolt action; repeating
Magazine: 5-shot detachable box
Barrel: 24″, round, nickel steel
Sights: Open rear, bead front
Stock & Forearm: One-piece semi-pistol grip stock and fluted, lipped forearm
Approximate wt.: 7½ lbs.
Comments: Made from the late 1890's to early 1900's.
Estimated Value: Excellent: $800.00
Very good: $650.00

Winchester Lee Musket

Similar to the Winchester Lee with military sights, full-length musket forearm, 28″ barrel, swivels.
Estimated Value: Excellent: $700.00
Very good: $550.00

Winchester Model 1900

Caliber: 22 short, long
Action: Bolt action; single shot; cocking piece
Magazine: None
Barrel: Blued 18″, round
Sights: Open rear, blade front
Stock & Forearm: Plain one-piece straight grip stock and forearm
Approximate wt.: 3 lbs.
Comments: Made from about 1900 to 1902.
Estimated Value: Excellent: $150.00
Very good: $120.00

Winchester Model 02

Similar to the Model 1900 with extended trigger guard; addition of 22 long rifle and extra long. Made from about 1902 to the early 1930's.
Estimated Value: Excellent: $180.00
Very good: $140.00

Winchester Model 04

Similar to the Model 02 with a 21″ barrel. Made from 1904 to the early 1930's.
Estimated Value: Excellent: $160.00
Very good: $130.00

Winchester Thumb Trigger

Similar to the Model 02 with no trigger. The gun is discharged by pushing a button behind the cocking piece. Made to the early 1920's.
Estimated Value: Excellent: $240.00
Very good: $185.00

Winchester Model 52

Winchester Model 52 Sporting

Winchester Model 52 Heavy Barrel

Winchester Model 52-B

Winchester Model 52-B Heavy Barrel

Winchester Model 52

Caliber: 22 long rifle
Action: Bolt action; repeating
Magazine: 5-shot box
Barrel: Blued 28″
Sights: Peep rear, blade front
Stock & Forearm: Plain walnut one-piece pistol grip stock and forearm
Approximate wt.: 8½ lbs.
Comments: Made from about 1920 to the late 1930's.
Estimated Value: **Excellent:** $360.00
                       Very good: $285.00

Winchester Model 52 Heavy Barrel

Similar to the Model 52 but with a heavy barrel and special Lyman sights.
Estimated Value: **Excellent:** $370.00
                       Very good: $280.00

Winchester Model 52 Sporting

Similar to the Model 52 except: 24″ barrel; special Lymann sights; checkering; cheekpiece. Made to the late 1950's.
Estimated Value: **Excellent:** $775.00
                       Very good: $580.00

Winchester Model 52-B

Similar to the Model 52 with improved action; high comb stock available. Made from the mid 1930's to late 1940's.
Estimated Value: **Excellent:** $300.00
                       Very good: $230.00

Winchester Model 52-B Heavy Barrel

Similar to the Model 52-B with a heavy barrel.
Estimated Value: **Excellent:** $350.00
                       Very good: $265.00

Winchester Model 52-B Bull Gun

Winchester Model 52-B Sporting

Winchester Model 52-C Bull Gun

Winchester Model 52-C

Winchester Model 52-D Target

Winchester Model 52-B Bull Gun

Similar to the Model 52-B Heavy Barrel with still heavier barrel. Weighs about 12 lbs.

Estimated Value: **Excellent:**   **$400.00**
                    Very good: **$300.00**

Winchester Model 52-B Sporting

Similar to the Model 52 Sporting with a 52-B action. Made to the early 1960's.

Estimated Value: **Excellent:**   **$780.00**
                    Very good: **$585.00**

Winchester Model 52-C

Similar to the 52-B with more improvements on the action; high comb stock. Made from the late 1940's to early 1960's.

Estimated Value: **Excellent:**   **$330.00**
                    Very good: **$250.00**

Winchester Model 52-C Heavy Barrel

Similar to the Model 52 Heavy Barrel with a 52-C action

Estimated Value: **Excellent:**   **$360.00**
                    Very good: **$270.00**

Winchester Model 52-C Bull Gun

Similar to the Model 52-B Bull Gun with a 52-C action.

Estimated Value: **Excellent:**   **$400.00**
                    Very good: **$300.00**

Winchester Model 52-D Target

Similar to the 52-C; single shot; hand stop on forearm. Made from the early 1960's to late 1970's; 22 long rifle caliber; approximate wt. 11 lbs.

Estimated Value: **Excellent:**   **$420.00**
                    Very good: **$315.00**

Winchester Model 54

Winchester Model 54 Sporting (Improved)

Winchester Model 54 Super

Winchester Model 54 Sniper

Winchester Model 54 National Match

Winchester Model 54

Caliber: 270, 7x57, 30-30, 30-06, 7.65x53mm, 9x57mm, 7mm, 250-3000, 22 Hornet, 220 Swift, 257 Roberts
Action: Bolt action; repeating
Magazine: 5-shot box, non-detachable
Barrel: Blued 24″
Sights: Open rear, bead front
Stock & Forearm: Checkered walnut one-piece pistol grip stock and forearm
Approximate wt.: 7½ lbs.
Comments: Made from the mid 1920's to about 1930.
Estimated Value: Excellent: $520.00
 Very good: $390.00

Winchester Model 54 Carbine

Similar to the Model 54 with a 20″ barrel; no checkering on stock.
Estimated Value: Excellent: $525.00
 Very good: $395.00

Winchester Model 54 Sporting (Improved)

Similar to the Model 54 with an improved acton; 26″ barrel; additional calibers. Made from about 1930 for six years.
Estimated Value: Excellent: $530.00
 Very good: $400.00

Winchester Model 54 Carbine (Improved)

Similar to the Model 54 Carbine with improved action. Made from 1930 to the mid 1930's.
Estimated Value: Excellent: $580.00
 Very good: $435.00

Winchester Model 54 Super

Similar to the Model 54 with cheekpiece; select wood; deluxe finish; swivels.
Estimated Value: Excellent: $600.00
 Very good: $450.00

Winchester Model 54 Sniper

Similar to the Model 54 with a 26″ heavy barrel; special Lyman sights; 30-06 caliber only.
Estimated Value: Excellent: $620.00
 Very good: $465.00

Winchester Model 54 Sniper Match

Deluxe version of the Model 54 Sniper with high quality finish.
Estimated Value: Excellent: $670.00
 Very good: $500.00

Winchester Model 54 National Match

Similar to the Model 54 with special Lyman sights and marksman stock.
Estimated Value: Excellent: $525.00
 Very good: $395.00

Winchester Model 54 Target

Similar to the Model 54 with 24″ barrel and special Lyman sights.
Estimated Value: Excellent: $600.00
 Very good: $450.00

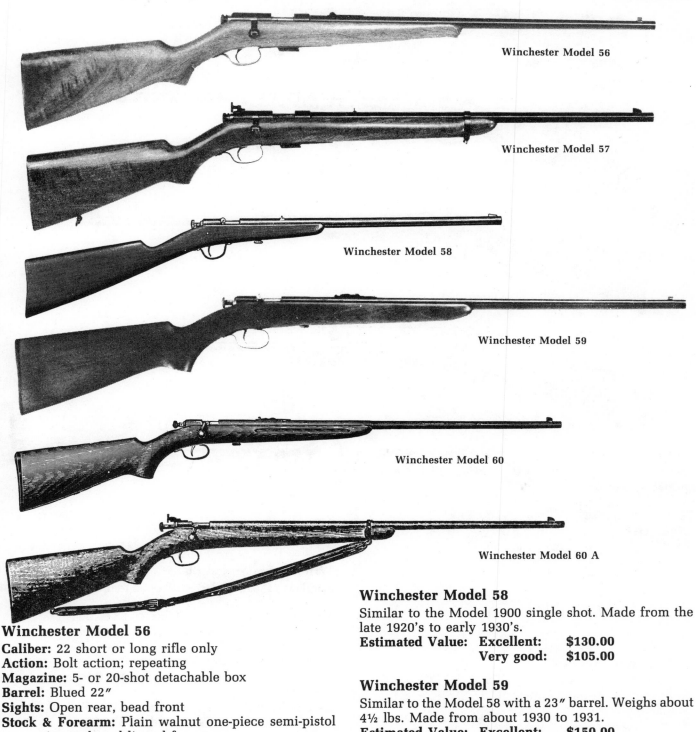

Winchester Model 56

Winchester Model 57

Winchester Model 58

Winchester Model 59

Winchester Model 60

Winchester Model 60 A

Winchester Model 56

Caliber: 22 short or long rifle only
Action: Bolt action; repeating
Magazine: 5- or 20-shot detachable box
Barrel: Blued 22″
Sights: Open rear, bead front
Stock & Forearm: Plain walnut one-piece semi-pistol grip stock and lipped forearm
Approximate wt.: 5 lbs.
Comments: Made from the mid to late 1920's. A fancy version was available with checkered walnut stock and forearm.
Estimated Value: **Excellent:** $175.00
                        Very good: $130.00

Winchester Model 57

Similar to the Model 56 with longer, unlipped forearm; barrel band, swivels; special Lyman sights; target model. Made from the mid 1920's to mid 1930's.
Estimated Value: **Excellent:** $250.00
                        Very good: $190.00

Winchester Model 58

Similar to the Model 1900 single shot. Made from the late 1920's to early 1930's.
Estimated Value: **Excellent:** $130.00
                        Very good: $105.00

Winchester Model 59

Similar to the Model 58 with a 23″ barrel. Weighs about 4½ lbs. Made from about 1930 to 1931.
Estimated Value: **Excellent:** $150.00
                        Very good: $120.00

Winchester Model 60

Similar to the Model 59 with 23″ or 27″ barrel. Made from the early to mid 1930's.
Estimated Value: **Excellent:** $125.00
                        Very good: $100.00

Winchester Model 60 A

Similar to the Model 60 with special Lyman sights; swivels. Made to about 1940.
Estimated Value: **Excellent:** $145.00
                        Very good: $110.00

Winchester Model 67

Winchester Model 67 Boy's

Winchester Model 68

Winchester Model 677

Winchester Model 69

Winchester Model 67

Caliber: 22 short, long, long rifle
Action: Bolt action; single shot
Magazine: None
Barrel: Blued 27″
Sights: Open rear, bead front
Stock & Forearm: Plain walnut one-piece semi-pistol grip stock and fluted forearm
Approximate wt.: 5 lbs.
Comments: Made from the mid 1930's to the early 1960's.
Estimated Value: Excellent: $95.00
Very good: $75.00

Winchester Model 67 Boy's

Similar to the Model 67 with a 20″ barrel and youth stock.
Estimated Value: Excellent: $90.00
Very good: $70.00

Winchester Model 68

Similar to the Model 67 with peep rear sight. Made from the mid 1930's to mid 1940's.
Estimated Value: Excellent: $110.00
Very good: $ 80.00

Winchester Model 677

Similar to the Model 67 with no sights. Made only in the late 1930's.
Estimated Value: Excellent: $100.00
Very good: $75.00

Winchester Model 69

Caliber: 22 short, long, long rifle
Action: Bolt action; repeating
Magazine: 5- or 10-shot detachable box
Barrel: Blued 25″
Sights: Peep or open rear, ramp front
Stock & Forearm: Plain walnut one-piece semi-pistol grip stock and forearm
Approximate wt.: 5½ lbs.
Comments: Made from the mid 1930's to the early 1960's.
Estimated Value: Excellent: $120.00
Very good: $ 90.00

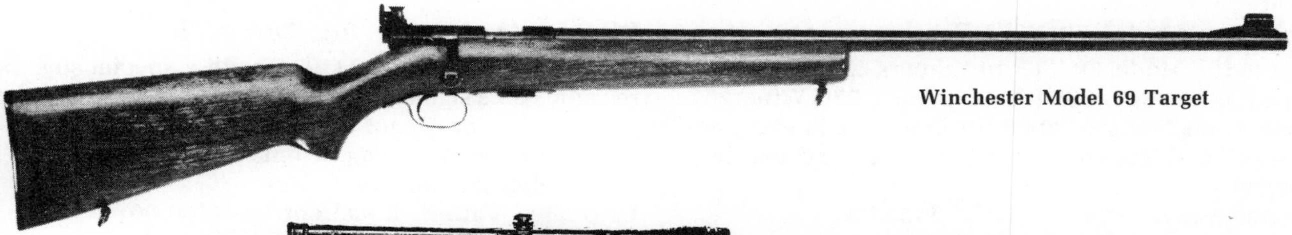

Winchester Model 69 Target

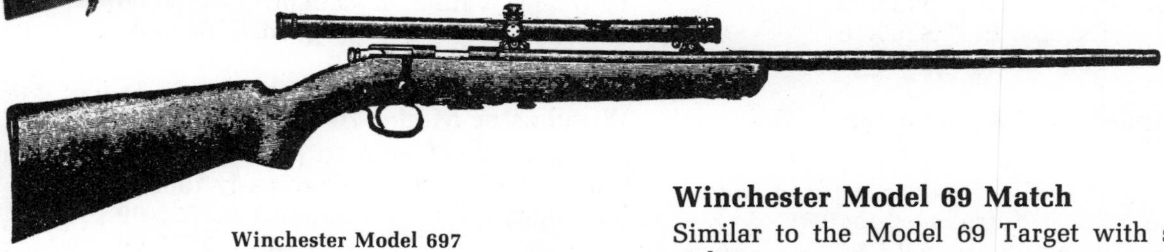

Winchester Model 697

Winchester Model 69 Match

Similar to the Model 69 Target with special Lyman sights.

Estimated Value: Excellent: $150.00
Very good: $110.00

Winchester Model 697

Similar to the Model 69 with no sights. Made from the late 1930's to early 1940's.

Estimated Value: Excellent: $135.00
Very good: $100.00

Winchester Model 69 Target

Similar to the Model 69 with peep sight only; swivels.

Estimated Value: Excellent: $130.00
Very good: $100.00

Winchester Model 70 (1937)

Winchester Model 70 (1964)

Winchester Model 70 XTR

Winchester Model 70 (1937)

Caliber: 375 H&H mag., 300 H&H mag., 308 Win., 30-06, 7x57mm, 270 Win., 257 Roberts, 250-3000, 243, 220, 22 Hornet
Action: Bolt action; repeating
Magazine: 5-shot box; 4-shot box in magnum
Barrel: Blued 24″, 26″
Sights: Open rear, hooded ramp front
Stock & Forearm: Checkered walnut one-piece pistol grip stock and forearm
Approximate wt.: 7¾ lbs.
Comments: Made from about 1937 to 1963. Add $150.00 for mint, unfired condition.
Estimated Value: Excellent: $750.00
Very good: $575.00

Winchester Model 70 (1964)

Similar to the Model 70 (1937) with improvements: Monte Carlo stock; swivels. Made from about 1964 until 1970; calibers 22-250, 222 Rem., 225, 243, 270, 308, 30-06.

Estimated Value: Excellent: $325.00
Very good: $240.00

Winchester Model 70 (1971), 70 XTR, 70 XTR Sporter

Similar to the Model 70 (1964) with improvements. Made from 1971 to present. Calibers 270 Win., 30-06, 25-06 and 308.

Estimated Value: New (retail): $479.95
Excellent: $360.00
Very good: $270.00

Winchester Model 70 XTR Featherweight

Similar to the Model 70 XTR in calibers 22-250, 223 (introduced 1984); 243, 308 (short action); 270 Win., 257 Roberts, 7mm Mauser, 30-06 Springfield (standard action); recoil pad; lipped forearm; decorative checkering; 22″ barrel.

Estimated Value:	New (retail):	$481.95
	Excellent:	$365.00
	Very good:	$275.00

Winchester Model 70XTR European Featherweight

Similar to the Model 70XTR Featherweight in caliber 6.55x55 Swedish Mauser. Introduced in 1986.

Estimated Value:	New (retail):	$481.95
	Excellent:	$365.00
	Very good:	$275.00

Winchester Model 70 Lightweight Carbine

Similar to the Model 70XTR Featherweight with different outward appearance, 20″ barrel; in calibers 270 Win., 30-06 Springfield, or short action version of 22-250 Rem., 223 Rem., 243 Win., 308 Win.; weighs 6-6¼ lbs. Introduced in 1984. 250 Savage caliber introduced 1986.

Estimated Value:	New (retail):	$422.95
	Excellent:	$320.00
	Very good:	$240.00

Winchester Model 70A, 70A XTR

Similar to the Model 70 (1971) with a special steel barrel; adjustable sights. Made from the early 1970's to about 1981; 4-shot or 3-shot (magnum) box magazine. Add $20.00 for 264 Win. mag., 7mm Rem. mag., or 300 Win. mag. Police Model $10.00 less.

Estimated Value:	Excellent:	$300.00
	Very good:	$225.00

Winchester Model 70 Super (1937)

Similar to the Model 70 (1937) with swivels; deluxe finish; cheekpiece. Made to early 1960's.

Estimated Value:	Excellent:	$825.00
	Very good:	$620.00

Winchester Model 70 Super

Similar to the Model 70 Super (1937) with recoil pad; select wood. Made from mid 1960's to mid 1970's.

Estimated Value:	Excellent:	$325.00
	Very good:	$245.00

Winchester Model 70XTR Featherweight

Winchester Model 70 Lightweight Carbine

Winchester Model 70A

Winchester Model 70 Super (1937)

Winchester Model 70 Super

Winchester Model 70 Target (1937)

Winchester Model 70 Target (1964)

Winchester Model 70 National Match

Winchester Model 70 Mannlicher

Winchester Model 70 Varmint (1956) (1964) (1971)

Winchester Model 70 Featherweight Sporter

Winchester Model 70 Target (1937)

Similar to the Model 70 (1937) with 24″ barrel and improved stock. Made until about 1963.
Estimated Value: **Excellent:** **$900.00**
Very good: **$675.00**

Winchester Model 70 Target (1964) & (1971)

Similar to the Model 70 Target (1937) with aluminum hand stop. Model (1971) has minor improvements; calibers 30-06, 308 Win., or 308 Int'l Army. Add $132.00 for Int'l Army.
Estimated Value: **Excellent:** **$375.00**
Very good: **$280.00**

Winchester Model 70 National Match

Similar to the Model 70 (1937) with marksman stock in 30-06 caliber. Made to the early 1960's.
Estimated Value: **Excellent:** **$775.00**
Very good: **$580.00**

Winchester Model 70 Mannlicher

Similar to the Model 70 (1964) with full length forearm; 19″ barrel; calibers 243, 270, 308, 30-06. Made to the early 1970's.
Estimated Value: **Excellent:** **$325.00**
Very good: **$245.00**

Winchester Model 70 Varmint (1956) (1964) (1971) 70 XTR Varmint

Similar to the Model 70 (1937) with heavy 24″ or 26″ barrel. Improvements made along with other Model 70's. Calibers 222 Rem., 22-250 or 243 Win. Add 60% for pre-1964 models.
Estimated Value: **New (retail): $479.95**
Excellent: **$360.00**
Very good: **$270.00**

Winchester Model 70 Featherweight Sporter

A lightweight rifle similar to the Model 70 (1937) with improved stock. Made from the early 1950's to 1960's.
Estimated Value: **Excellent:** **$720.00**
Very good: **$540.00**

Winchester Model 70 Featherweight Super

Similar to the Featherweight Sporter with deluxe finish; cheekpiece; swivels. Made after 1964.
Estimated Value: **Excellent:** **$325.00**
Very good: **$240.00**

Winchester Model 70 African (1956)

Similar to the Model 70 (1937) Super Grade with recoil pad; Monte Carlo stock; 3-shot magazine; 24″ barrel. Available only in 458 caliber. Made to 1963.
Estimated Value: **Excellent:** **$925.00**
Very good: **$695.00**

Winchester Model 70 African (1964)

Similar to the Model 70 African (1956) with improvements. Made to 1970.
Estimated Value: **Excellent:** **$400.00**
Very good: **$300.00**

Winchester Model 70 African (1971)

Similar to the Model 70 African (1964) with floating barrel; caliber 458 Win. mag. Discontinued about 1981.
Estimated Value: **Excellent:** **$450.00**
Very good: **$350.00**

Winchester Model 70 Westerner

Similar to the Model 70 Alaskan. Made in the early 1960's.
Estimated Value: **Excellent:** **$700.00**
Very good: **$550.00**

Winchester Model 70 Westerner (1982)

Similar to the Model 70XTR with a 22″ barrel and 4-shot magazine in calibers 243 Win., 270 Win., 308 Win., and 30-06 Springfield; 24″ barrel and 3-shot magazine in calibers 7mm Rem. mag., 300 Win. mag.; weighs about 7½ to 7¾ lbs.; recoil pad. Introduced in 1982; discontinued in 1984.
Estimated Value: **Excellent:** **$350.00**
Very good: **$260.00**

Winchester Model 70 Featherweight Super

Winchester Model 70 African (1956)

Winchester Model 70 African (1964)

Winchester Model 70 African (1971)

Winchester Model 70 Westerner (1982)

Winchester Model 70 Alaskan

Winchester Model 70 Magnum

Winchester Model 70 Deluxe

Winchester Model 70XTR Sporter Magnum

Winchester Model 70XTR Super Express Magnum

Winchester Model 70 Winlite

Winchester Model 70 Magnum

Similar to the Model 70 (1964) with Monte Carlo stock; recoil pad; swivels; 3-shot magazine. Made to the early 1970's.

Estimated Value: Excellent: $350.00
Very good: $260.00

Winchester Model 70 Alaskan

Similar to the Model 70 (1937) with 24″ or 26″ barrel. Made in the early 1960's.

Estimated Value: Excellent: $725.00
Very good: $550.00

Winchester Model 70 Deluxe

Similar to the Model 70 (1964) with Monte Carlo stock; recoil pad; deluxe features. Made to the early 1970's.

Estimated Value: Excellent: $375.00
Very good: $280.00

Winchester Model 70 Winlite

Caliber: 270, 30-06, 7mm Rem. magnum, 338 Win. magnum
Action: Bolt action, repeating
Magazine: 4-shot in 270 or 30-06; 3-shot in 7mm Rem. magnum or 338 Win. magnum
Barrel: 22″ in 270 and 30-06; 24″ in magnum calibers
Sights: None
Stock & Forearm: Fiberglass reinforced one-piece stock and forearm with thermoplastic bedding for receiver and barrel
Approximate wt.: 6¼ to 6¾ lbs.
Comments: Introduced in 1986.
Estimated Value: New (retail): $629.95
Excellent: $480.00
Very good: $360.00

Winchester Model 70XTR Sporter Magnum

Caliber: 264, 300, 338 Win. mag.; 7mm Rem. mag.
Action: Bolt action; repeating
Magazine: 3-shot box
Barrel: Blued 24″
Sights: Folding leaf rear; hooded ramp front
Stock & Forearm: Checkered walnut Monte Carlo one-piece pistol grip stock and forearm; cheekpiece; recoil pad; swivels
Approximate wt.: 7¾ lbs.
Comments: Introduced in 1982.
Estimated Value: New (retail): $479.95
Excellent: $360.00
Very good: $275.00

Winchester Model 70XTR Super Express Magnum

Similar to the Model 70XTR Sporter Magnum with a 22″ barrel in 458 Win. magnum caliber; 24″ barrel in 375 H & H magnum caliber.

Estimated Value: New (retail): $821.95
Excellent: $620.00
Very good: $470.00

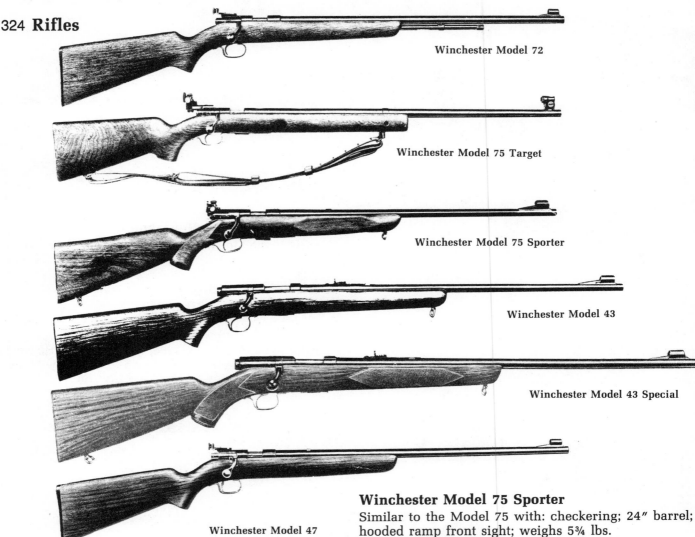

Winchester Model 72

Winchester Model 75 Target

Winchester Model 75 Sporter

Winchester Model 43

Winchester Model 43 Special

Winchester Model 47

Winchester Model 72

Caliber: 22 short, long, long rifle
Action: Bolt action; repeating
Magazine: Tubular; 15 long rifles, 16 longs, 20 shorts
Barrel: Blued 25″
Sights: Peep or open rear, bead front
Stock & Forearm: Plain walnut one-piece semi-pistol grip stock and forearm
Approximate wt.: 5¾ lbs.
Comments: Made from the late 1930's to late 1950's.
Estimated Value: **Excellent:** $120.00
　　　　　　　　　Very good: $ 90.00

Winchester Model 75 Target

Caliber: 22 long rifle
Action: Bolt action; repeating
Magazine: 5- or 10-shot detachable box
Barrel: Blued 28″
Sights: Special target sights
Stock & Forearm: Plain walnut one-piece pistol grip stock and forearm
Approximate wt.: 8¾ lbs.
Comments: Made from the late 1930's to late 1950's.
Estimated Value: **Excellent:** $280.00
　　　　　　　　　Very good: $210.00

Winchester Model 75 Sporter

Similar to the Model 75 with: checkering; 24″ barrel; hooded ramp front sight; weighs 5¾ lbs.
Estimated Value: **Excellent:** $290.00
　　　　　　　　　Very good: $220.00

Winchester Model 43

Caliber: 218 Bee, 22 Hornet, 25-20, 32-30 (25-20 and 32-30 dropped in 1950)
Action: Bolt action; repeating
Magazine: 3-shot detachable box
Barrel: Blued 24″
Sights: Open rear, hooded ramp front
Stock & Forearm: Plain wood one-piece semi-pistol grip stock and forearm; swivels
Approximate wt.: 6 lbs.
Comments: Made from the late 1940's to late 1950's.
Estimated Value: **Excellent:** $275.00
　　　　　　　　　Very good: $210.00

Winchester Model 43 Special

Similar to the Model 43 with checkering and choice of open rear sight or micrometer.
Estimated Value: **Excellent:** $320.00
　　　　　　　　　Very good: $240.00

Winchester Model 47

Similar to the Model 43 in 22 short, long or long rifle single shot; 25″ barrel. Made from the late 1940's to mid 1950's.
Estimated Value: **Excellent:** $100.00
　　　　　　　　　Very good: $ 75.00

Winchester Model 670

Winchester Model 770

Winchester Model 770 Magnum

Winchester Model 770

Caliber: 22-250, 222, 243, 270, 30-06
Action: Bolt action; repeating
Magazine: 4-shot box
Barrel: Blued 22″
Sights: Open rear, hooded ramp front
Stock & Forearm: Checkered walnut Monte Carlo one-piece pistol grip stock and forearm; swivels
Approximate wt.: 7 lbs.
Comments: Made from the late 1960's to early 1970's.
Estimated Value: Excellent: $270.00
Very good: $200.00

Winchester Model 670

Caliber: 243, 270, 30-06, 225, 243, 270, 308, 30-06 mag., 300 Win. mag., 264 Win. mag.,
Action: Bolt action; repeating
Magazine: 4-shot box; 3-shot box in magnum
Barrel: Blued 19″, 22″, 24″
Sights: Open rear, ramp front
Stock & Forearm: Checkered hardwood Monte Carlo one-piece pistol grip stock and forearm
Approximate wt.: 7 lbs.
Comments: Made from the mid 1960's to the late 1970's.
Estimated Value: Excellent: $250.00
Very good: $190.00

Winchester Model 770 Magnum

Similar to the Model 770 in magnum with recoil pad and 24″ barrel, 3-shot magazine.
Estimated Value: Excellent: $290.00
Very good: $220.00

Winchester Model 310

Winchester Model 320

Winchester Model 310

Caliber: 22 short, long, long rifle
Action: Bolt action; single shot
Magazine: None
Barrel: Blued 22″
Sights: Adjustable rear, ramp front
Stock & Forearm: Checkered walnut Monte Carlo one-piece pistol grip stock and forearm; swivels
Approximate wt.: 6 lbs.
Comments: Made from the early to mid 1970's.
Estimated Value: Excellent: $50.00
Very good: $40.00

Winchester Model 320

Similar to the Model 310 in repeating action with a 5-shot clip.
Estimated Value: Excellent: $75.00
Very good: $55.00

Winchester Model 121

Caliber: 22 short, long, long rifle
Action: Bolt action; single shot
Magazine: None
Barrel: Blued 20½″
Sights: Open rear, bead post front
Stock & Forearm: Plain one-piece semi-pistol grip stock and forearm
Approximate wt.: 5 lbs.
Comments: Made from the late 1960's to early 1970's.
Estimated Value: **Excellent:** $50.00
  Very good: $40.00

Winchester Model 121 Deluxe

Similar to the Model 121 with Monte Carlo stock; swivels; slightly different sights.
Estimated Value: **Excellent:** $55.00
  Very good: $45.00

Winchester Model 121 Youth

Similar to the Model 121 with shorter barrel and youth stock.
Estimated Value: **Excellent:** $45.00
  Very good: $35.00

Winchester Model 131

Similar to the Model 121 with semi-Monte Carlo stock; 7-shot clip magazine.
Estimated Value: **Excellent:** $70.00
  Very good: $55.00

Winchester Model 141

Similar to the 131 with tubular magazine.
Estimated Value: **Excellent:** $75.00
  Very good: $60.00

Winchester Ranger

Caliber: 270 Win., 30-06 Springfield
Action: Bolt action; repeating
Magazine: 4-shot
Barrel: 22″ blued
Sights: Beaded ramp front, adjustable rear
Stock & Forearm: Plain one-piece semi-pistol grip wood stock and forearm
Approximate wt.: 7¹⁄₈ lbs.
Comments: Introduced in the mid 1980's.
Estimated Value: **New (retail):** $355.95
  Excellent: $270.00
  Very good: $200.00

Winchester Ranger Youth

A scaled down bolt action (short action) carbine for young or small shooters; caliber is 243 Win., barrel is 20″; weighs 5¾ lbs.; beaded ramp front sight, semi-buckhorn, folding-leaf rear; plain wood, one-piece stock and forearm with swivels. Introduced in the mid 1980's.
Estimated Value: **New (retail):** $365.95
  Excellent: $275.00
  Very good: $205.00

Winchester Model 121

Winchester Model 131

Winchester Ranger Youth

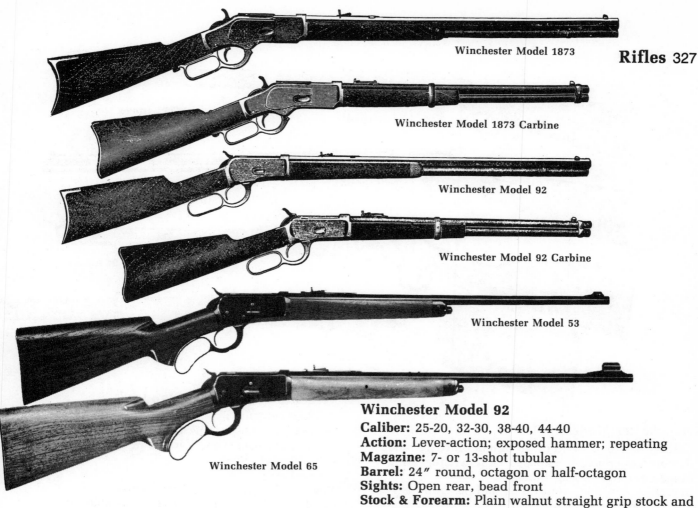

Winchester Model 1873

Winchester Model 1873 Carbine

Winchester Model 92

Winchester Model 92 Carbine

Winchester Model 53

Winchester Model 65

Winchester Model 92

Caliber: 25-20, 32-30, 38-40, 44-40
Action: Lever-action; exposed hammer; repeating
Magazine: 7- or 13-shot tubular
Barrel: 24″ round, octagon or half-octagon
Sights: Open rear, bead front
Stock & Forearm: Plain walnut straight grip stock and forearm
Approximate wt.: 7 lbs.
Comments: Made from about 1892 to early 1930's.
Estimated Value: **Excellent:** $650.00
                      Very good: $490.00

Winchester Model 92 Carbine

Similar to the Model 92 with a 20″ barrel; barrel band; and 5- or 11-shot magazine. Discontinued in the early 1940's.
Estimated Value: **Excellent:** $700.00
                      Very good: $525.00

Winchester Model 53

Similar to the Model 92 with a 6- or 7-shot magazine; 22″ nickel steel barrel; choice of straight or pistol grip stock. Made from the mid 1920's to the early 1930's.
Estimated Value: **Excellent:** $600.00
                      Very good: $450.00

Winchester Model 65

Similar to the Model 53 in 25-20 and 32-20 caliber; semi-pistol grip stock; other minor improvements. Made from the early 1930's to late 1940's.
Estimated Value: **Excellent:** $600.00
                      Very good: $450.00

Winchester Model 65, 218 Bee

Similar to the Model 65 with peep sight and 24″ barrel. Made from the late 1930's to late 1940's.
Estimated Value: **Excellent:** $900.00
                      Very good: $675.00

Winchester Model 1873

Caliber: 32-20, 38-40, 44-40, 22
Action: Lever-action; exposed hammer; repeating
Magazine: 6- or 15-shot tubular
Barrel: 24″ or 26″ round, octagon or half-octagon
Sights: Open rear, blade front
Stock & Forearm: Straight grip stock and forearm
Approximate wt.: 8 lbs.
Comments: Thousands of this model were sold by Winchester until 1920. Add $200.00 to $500.00 for Deluxe engraved models. Price range is for the different models; i.e., 1st, 2nd and 3rd models.
Estimated Value: **Excellent:** $1,000.00 - $1,850.00
                      Very good: $ 650.00 - $1,390.00

Winchester Model 1873 Carbine

Similar to the Model 1873 with a 20″ barrel and 12-shot magazine. Three models made from 1873 to 1920.
Estimated Value: **Excellent:** $800.00 - $1,800.00
                      Very good: $600.00 - $1,350.00

Winchester Model 1873 Musket

Similar to the Model 1873 with a 30″ round barrel, full-length forearm and 17-shot magazine. Three models made from 1873 to 1920.
Estimated Value: **Excellent:** $1,200.00 - $2,500.00
                      Very good: $ 900.00 - $1,875.00

Winchester Model 1886 Carbine

Winchester Model 94

Winchester Model 94 Antique

Winchester Model 94 Trapper

Winchester Model 1886

Caliber: 45-70, 33 Win.; also others on early models
Action: Lever-action; exposed hammer; repeating
Magazine: 4- or 8-shot tubular
Barrel: 26″; round, octagon or half-octagon
Sights: Open rear, blade front
Stock & Forearm: Plain wood straight grip stock and forearm
Approximate wt.: 7½ lbs.
Comments: Made from the mid 1880's to the mid 1930's.
Estimated Value: Excellent: $750.00 - $1,000.00
                 Very good: $560.00 - $ 750.00

Winchester Model 1886 Carbine

Similar to the Model 1886 with a 22″ barrel.
Estimated Value: Excellent: $600.00 - $1,200.00
                 Very good: $450.00 - $ 900.00

Winchester Model 94

Caliber: 25-35, 30-30, 32 Special, 32-40, 38-55
Action: Lever-action; exposed hammer; repeating
Magazine: 4- or 7-shot tubular
Barrel: 22″, 26″, round, octagon or half-octagon
Sights: Open rear, bead front
Stock & Forearm: Straight stock and forearm; saddle ring on some models
Approximate wt.: 6¾ lbs.
Comments: Made from 1894 to the late 1930's. Sometimes referred to as the "Klondike" model.
Estimated Value: Excellent: $450.00 - $750.00
                 Very good: $300.00 - $600.00

Winchester Model 94 Carbine

Similar to the Model 94 with a 20″ barrel; barrel band; saddle ring. 6-shot magazine. Add $200.00 for pre-World War II models. Add $400.00 for pre-1925 Models with saddle ring. Made to mid 1960's.
Estimated Value: Excellent: $300.00
                 Very good: $250.00

Winchester Model 94 Standard

Caliber: 30-30
Action: Lever action, exposed hammer; repeating; Angle-eject feature added in 1984, listed as "Side eject" in 1986
Magazine: 6-shot
Barrel: 20″ round with barrel band
Sights: Hooded or post front, adjustable rear
Stock & Forearm: Plain wood straight stock and forearm; barrel band
Approximate wt.: 6½ lbs.
Comments: Made from the mid 1960's to present; also made in calibers 44 magnum, 45 Colt and 444 Marlin in the mid 1980's.
Estimated Value: New (retail): $289.95
                 Excellent: $220.00
                 Very good: $165.00

Winchester Model 94 Antique

Similar to the Model 94 Standard with case hardened, scroll design frame. Made from the late 1960's to 1984 in 30-30 caliber.
Estimated Value: Excellent: $180.00
                 Very good: $140.00

Winchester Model 94 Trapper

Same as the Mdoel 94 Standard wth 16″ barrel; calibers 44 magnum and 45 Colt added in the mid 1980's. Magazine capacity is 5-shot in 30-30 and 9-shot in 44 and 45; weighs 6 lbs.; made from 1980 to present.
Estimated Value: New (retail): $286.95
                 Excellent: $220.00
                 Very good: $165.00

Winchester Model 94XTR

Similar to the Model 94 Standard with higher grade wood, checkered stock and forearm. Made from 1979 to 1984 in 30-30 and 375 Win.; the 375 model has recoil pad. Add 23% for 375 Win.
Estimated Value: Excellent: $210.00
                 Very good: $160.00

Winchester Model 94XTR Angle Eject

Similar to the Model 94XTR except an "angle Eject" feature was added om 1984; in 186 Winchester called it "side Eject". Made in calibers 30-30, 7x30 Waters, 307, 356 and 375 Win.; 7x30 Waters has 7-shot magazine and 24″ barrel; other models have 6-shot magazines and 20″ barrels; 307, 356 and 357 calibers made from 1984 to 1986; 30-30 and 7x30 Waters made from 1984 to present; add 10% for 7x30 Waters.

Estimated Value: **Excellent:** $312.95
                     Very good: $235.00

Winchester Model 94 Side Eject Standard

Similar to the Model 94 Standard with "Side Eject" feature; calibers 307, 356 and 375 Win.; 6-shot magazine; recoil pad; made from 1985 to present.

Estimated Value: **New (retail):** $316.95
                     Excellent: $240.00
                     Very good: $180.00

Winchester Ranger Lever Action Side Eject

Similar to the Model 94 Standard in 30-30 caliber with 5-shot magazine; blade front sight and semi-buckhorn rear; made for economy and utility; smooth wood stock and forearm with walnut finish; made from the mid 1980's to present.

Estimated Value: **New (retail):** $244.95
                     Excellent: $185.00
                     Very good: $140.00

Winchester Model 94 Classic Rifle or Carbine

Similar to the Model 94 Standard with select walnut stock; scroll engraving. Made from the late 1960's to early 1970's.

Estimated Value: **Excellent:** $210.00
                     Very good: $160.00

Winchester Model 94 Wrangler

Same as the Model 94 Trapper with hoop-type finger lever; roll-engraved receiver; 32 Special caliber with 5-shot magazine; no angle eject feature; made from about 1980 to 1984.

Estimated Value: **Excellent:** $200.00
                     Very good: $150.00

Winchester Model 34 Wrangler II

Similar to the Model 94 Wrangler in 38-55 caliber; has angle eject feature. Made from about 1984 to 1986.

Estimated Value: **Excellent:** $210.00
                     Very good: $160.00

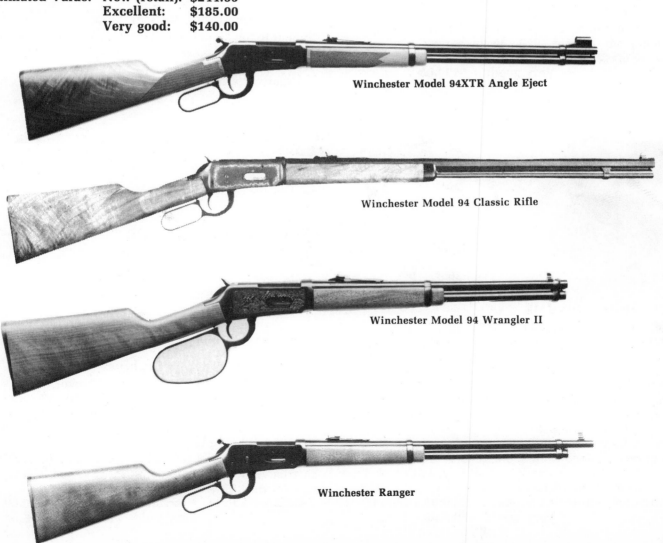

Winchester Model 94XTR Angle Eject

Winchester Model 94 Classic Rifle

Winchester Model 94 Wrangler II

Winchester Ranger

Winchester Model 55

Winchester Model 64

Winchester Model 64 Zipper

Winchester Model 64 Deer

Winchester Model 64

Similar to the Model 94 and 55 with improvements; 20″ or 26″ barrel; available in 25-35, 30-30, 32, 219 Zipper (from 1938-41). Made from the early 1930's to the late 1950's. Add $200.00 for 219 Zipper caliber.
Estimated Value: **Excellent:**   **$300.00**
                       Very good: **$225.00**

Winchester Model 55

Similar to the Model 94 with a 24″ nickel steel barrel. Made from the mid 1920's to the early 1930's.
Estimated Value: **Excellent:**   **$650.00**
                       Very good: **$490.00**

Winchester Model 64 Deer

Similar to the Model 64 in 32 and 30-30 caliber; swivels; checkered pistol grip stock. Made from the the mid 1930's to mid 1950's.
Estimated Value: **Excellent:**   **$425.00**
                       Very good: **$325.00**

Winchester Model 95

Winchester Model 95 Carbine

Winchester Model 95

Caliber: 30-40 Krag, 30-06, 30-30, 303, 35, 405
Action: Lever-action; exposed hammer; repeating
Magazine: 4-shot box
Barrel: 24″, 26″, 28″, octagon, round or half octagon
Sights: Open rear, bead front
Stock & Forearm: Plain wood straight stock and tapered lipped forearm. A limited number was available with a pistol grip
Approximate wt.: 8½ lbs.
Comments: Made from about 1895 to the early 1930's. A few thousand early models were built with a flat receiver; add $200.00.
Estimated Value: **Excellent:**   **$500.00 - $800.00**
                       Very good: **$375.00 - $600.00**

Winchester Model 95 Carbine

Similar to the Model 95 with a 22″ barrel.
Estimated Value: **Excellent:**   **$550.00 - $850.00**
                       Very good: **$410.00 - $640.00**

Winchester Model 1895 Musket

Similar to the Model 1895 with a 28″ or 30″ round nickel steel barrel; full-length forearm; barrel bands; 30-40 gov't caliber. Add $300.00 for U.S. Gov't models.
Estimated Value: **Excellent:**   **$600.00 - $900.00**
                       Very good: **$450.00 - $675.00**

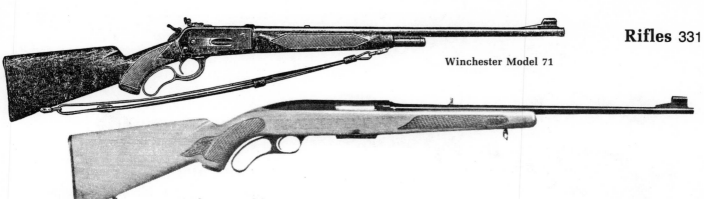

Winchester Model 71

Winchester Model 88

Winchester Model 71

Caliber: 348 Win.
Action: Lever-action; exposed hammer; repeating
Magazine: 4-shot tubular
Barrel: Blued 20″ or 24″
Sights: Open rear, hooded ramp front; peepsights available
Stock & Forearm: Plain or checkered walnut pistol grip stock and forearm; swivels available
Approximate wt.: 8 lbs.
Comments: Made from the mid 1930's to the late 1950's.
Estimated Value: Excellent: $600.00
                        Very good: $450.00

Winchester Model 71 Special

Similar to the Model 71 with checkering and swivels.
Estimated Value: Excellent: $625.00
                        Very good: $470.00

Winchester Model 88

Caliber: 243, 284, 308, 358
Action: Lever-action; hammerless; repeating
Magazine: 4-shot box on late models; 5–shot box on early models; 3-shot box in 284 caliber
Barrel: 22″
Sights: Folding leaf rear, hooded ramp front
Stock & Forearm: Checkered walnut one-piece semi-pistol grip stock and forearm; barrel band
Approximate wt.: 7¼ lbs.
Comments: Made from the mid 1950's to mid 1970's.
Estimated Value: Excellent: $300.00
                        Very good: $225.00

Winchester Model 88 Carbine

Similar to the Model 88 with a plain stock and forearm and 19″ barrel. Made from the late 1960's to early 1970's.
Estimated Value: Excellent: $275.00
                        Very good: $210.00

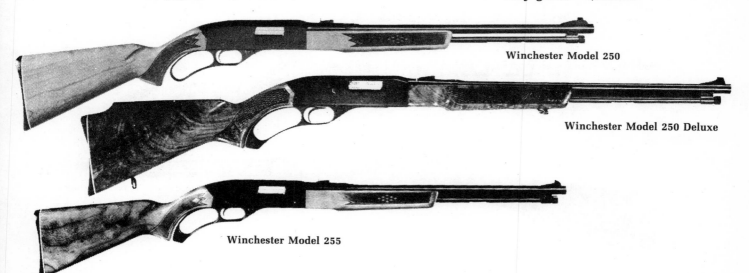

Winchester Model 250

Winchester Model 250 Deluxe

Winchester Model 255

Winchester Model 250

Caliber: 22 short, long, long rifle
Action: Lever-action; hammerless; repeating
Magazine: Tubular; 15 long rifles, 17 longs, 21 shorts
Barrel: Blued 20½″
Sights: Open rear, ramp front
Stock & Forearm: Plain or checkered walnut semi-pistol grip stock and forearm
Approximate wt.: 5 lbs.
Comments: Made from the early 1960's to mid 1970's.
Estimated Value: Excellent: $125.00
                        Very good: $ 95.00

Winchester Model 250 Deluxe

Similar to the Model 250 with Monte Carlo stock and swivels.
Estimated Value: Excellent: $130.00
                        Very good: $100.00

Winchester Model 255

Similar to the Model 250 in 22 magnum caliber; 11-shot magazine. Made from the mid 1960's to early 1970's.
Estimated Value: Excellent: $120.00
                        Very good: $ 90.00

Winchester Model 150

Winchester Model 9422

Winchester Model 9422 and 9422 XTR

Caliber: 22 short, long, long rifle or 22 magnum
Action: Lever-action; exposed hammer; repeating
Magazine: Tubular; 15 long rifles, 17 longs, 21 shorts.
    11 round magazine in 22 magnum
Barrel: 20½"
Sights: Adjustable rear, hooded ramp front
Stock & Forearm: Plain or checkered wood straight grip
    stock and forearm; barrel band
Approximate wt.: 6¼ lbs.
Comments: Made from about 1972 to present. 9422XTR
    has higher grade wood and finish also checkered.
    Introduced in 1979.
Estimated Value: New (retail): $316.95
                     Excellent: $240.00
                     Very good: $180.00

Winchester Model 150

Caliber: 22 short, long, long rifle
Action: Lever-action; hammerless; repeating
Magazine: Tubular; 15 long rifles, 17 longs, 21 shorts
Barrel: Blued 20½"
Sights: Open adjustable rear, blade front
Stock & Forearm: Straight stock and forearm; barrel
    band; alloy receiver
Approximate wt.: 5 lbs.
Comments: Made from the late 1960's to mid 1970's.
Estimated Value: Excellent: $120.00
                  Very good: $ 95.00

Winchester Model 9422XTR Classic Rifle

Similar to the Model 9422XTR with satin-finish walnut
pistol grip stock and forearm, fluted comb and crescent
steel buttplate; curved finger lever; longer forearm; 22½"
barrel; 22 or 22 magnum caliber. Introduced in 1986.
Estimated Value: New (retail): $349.95
                     Excellent: $265.00
                     Very good: $200.00

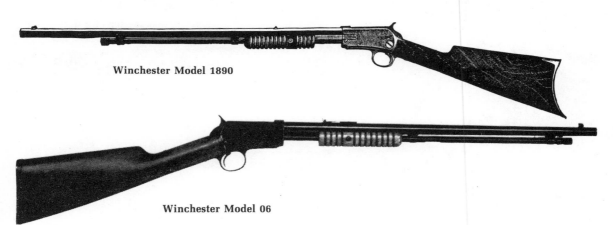

Winchester Model 1890

Winchester Model 06

Winchester Model 1890

Caliber: 22 short, long, long rifle
Action: Slide action; exposed hammer; repeating
Magazine: Tubular; 11 long rifles, 12 longs, 15 shorts
Barrel: 24" octagon
Sights: Open rear, bead front
Stock & Forearm: Plain wood straight grip stock and
    grooved slide handle
Approximate wt.: 5¾ lbs.
Comments: Made from 1890 to the early 1930's.
Estimated Value: Excellent: $375.00
                  Very good: $280.00

Winchester Model 06

Caliber: 22 short, long, long rifle
Action: Slide action; exposed hammer; repeating
Magazine: Tubular; 11 long rifles, 12 longs, 15 shorts
Barrel: Blued 20"
Sights: Open rear, bead front
Stock & Forearm: Plain wood straight stock, grooved or
    plain slide handle; nickel trimmed receiver and
    pistol grip stock available
Approximate wt.: 5 lbs.
Comments: Made from 1906 until the early 1930's.
Estimated Value: Excellent: $380.00
                  Very good: $285.00

Winchester Model 61

Winchester Model 62

Winchester Model 61 Magnum

Similar to the Model 61 in 22 magnum. Made in the early 1960's.

Estimated Value: Excellent: $325.00
Very good: $240.00

Winchester Model 62, 62A

Caliber: 22 short, long, long rifle
Action: Slide action; exposed hammer; repeating
Magazine: Tubular; 14 long rifles, 16 longs, 20 shorts
Barrel: Blued 23″
Sights: Open rear, blade front
Stock & Forearm: Walnut straight grip stock and grooved slide handle
Approximate wt.: 5½ lbs.
Comments: Made from the early 1930's to the late 1950's. A gallery model was available chambered for 22 short only. It became 62A in the 1940's with internal improvements.
Estimated Value: Excellent: $325.00
Very good: $245.00

Winchester Model 61

Caliber: 22 short, long, long rifle
Action: Slide action; hammerless; repeating
Magazine: Tubular; 14 long rifles, 16 longs, 20 shorts
Barrel: Blued 24″; round or octagon
Sights: Open rear, bead front
Stock & Forearm: Plain wood semi-pistol grip stock and grooved slide handle
Approximate wt.: 5½ lbs.
Comments: Made from the early 1930's to early 1960's.
Estimated Value: Excellent: $310.00
Very good: $230.00

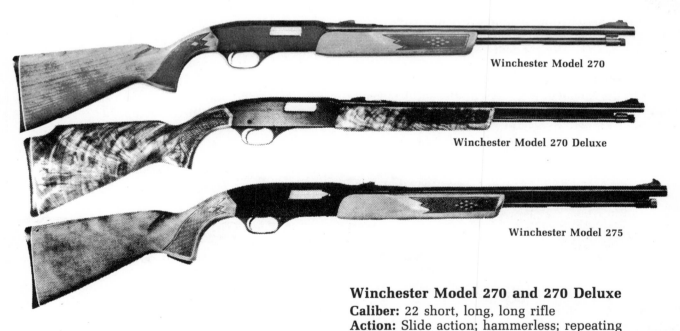

Winchester Model 270

Winchester Model 270 Deluxe

Winchester Model 275

Winchester Model 270 and 270 Deluxe

Caliber: 22 short, long, long rifle
Action: Slide action; hammerless; repeating
Magazine: Tubular; 15 long rifles, 17 longs, 21 shorts
Barrel: 20½″
Sights: Open rear, ramp front
Stock & Forearm: Walnut pistol grip stock and slide handle; plastic available; later models checkered; Model 270 Deluxe has Monte Carlo stock.
Approximate wt.: 5 lbs.
Comments: Made from the mid 1960's to mid 1970's.
Estimated Value: Excellent: $100.00
Very good: $ 75.00

Winchester Model 275 and 275 Deluxe

Similar to the Model 270 and 270 Deluxe in 22 magnum caliber.
Estimated Value: Excellent: $110.00
Very good: $ 85.00

Winchester Model 03

Winchester Model 05

Winchester Model 07

Winchester Model 10

Winchester Model 03

Caliber: 22 short, long, long rifle
Action: Semi-automatic
Magazine: 10-shot tubular, loaded in stock
Barrel: Blued 20″
Sights: Open rear, bead front
Stock & Forearm: Plain wood semi-pistol grip or straight stock; checkering on some models
Approximate wt.: 6 lbs.
Comments: Made from 1903 to the mid 1930's.
Estimated Value: Excellent: $300.00
　　　　　　　　　　Very good: $225.00

Winchester Model 05

Simiar to the Model 03 with a 5- or 10-shot detachable box magazine; 22″ barrel. Made to about 1920.
Estimated Value: Excellent: $350.00
　　　　　　　　　　Very good: $270.00

Winchester Model 07

Caliber: 351
Action: Semi-automatic; hammerless
Magazine: 5- or 10-shot detachable box
Barrel: Blued 20″
Sights: Open rear, bead front
Stock & Forearm: Semi-pistol grip stock and forearm; plain wood
Approximate wt.: 7½ lbs.
Comments: Made from 1907 to the late 1950's.
Estimated Value: Excellent: $425.00
　　　　　　　　　　Very good: $315.00

Winchester Model 10

Similar to the Model 07 except: 401 caliber; 4-shot magazine. Made until the mid 1930's.
Estimated Value: Excellent: $430.00
　　　　　　　　　　Very good: $320.00

Winchester Model 63

Winchester Model 74

Winchester Model 63

Caliber: 22 long rifle, high speed; 22 long rifle Super X
Action: Semi-automatic; hammerless
Magazine: 10-shot tubular, load in stock
Barrel: Blued 20″, 23″
Sights: Open rear, bead front
Stock & Forearm: Plain wood pistol grip stock and forearm
Approximate wt.: 5½ lbs.
Comments: Made from the early 1930's to the late 1950's.
Estimated Value: Excellent: $400.00
　　　　　　　　　　Very good: $300.00

Winchester Model 74

Caliber: 22 long rifle only or 22 short only
Action: Semi-automatic
Magazine: Tubular; 14 long rifles, 20 shorts; in stock
Barrel: Blued 24″
Sights: Open rear, bead front
Stock & Forearm: Plain wood one-piece semi-pistol grip stock and forearm
Approximate wt.: 6¼ lbs.
Comments: Made from the late 1930's to the mid 1950's.
Estimated Value: Excellent: $200.00
　　　　　　　　　　Very good: $150.00

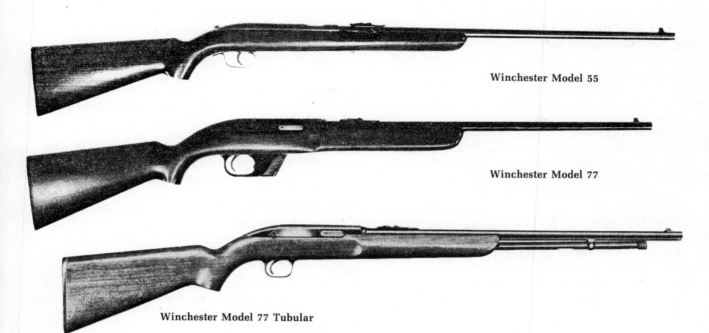

Winchester Model 55

Winchester Model 77

Winchester Model 77 Tubular

Winchester Model 77

Caliber: 22 long rifle
Action: Semi-automatic
Magazine: 8-shot detachable box
Barrel: Blued 22″
Sights: Open rear, bead front
Stock & Forearm: Plain walnut one-piece semi-pistol grip stock and forearm
Approximate wt.: 5½ lbs.
Comments: Made from the mid 1950's to early 1960's.
Estimated Value: **Excellent:** $110.00
  Very good: $ 85.00

Winchester Model 77 Tubular

Similar to the Model 77 with a 15-shot tubular magazine.
Estimated Value: **Excellent:** $120.00
  Very good: $ 90.00

Winchester Model 55

Caliber: 22 short, long, long rifle
Action: Single shot; hammerless
Magazine: None
Barrel: 22″
Sights: Open rear, bead front
Stock & Forearm: Plain wood one-piece semi-pistol grip stock and forearm
Approximate wt.: 5½ lbs.
Comments: Made from the late 1950's to the early 1960's.
Estimated Value: **Excellent:** $80.00
  Very good: $60.00

Winchester Model 100

Winchester Model 100

Caliber: 243, 248, 308
Action: Semi-automatic, gas operated; hammerless
Magazine: 4-shot clip; 3-shot clip in 284
Barrel: Blued 19″, 22″
Sights: Open rear, hooded ramp front
Stock & Forearm: Checkered walnut one-piece stock and forearm; swivels
Approximate wt.: 7 lbs.
Comments: Made from the early 1960's to mid 1970's.
Estimated Value: **Excellent:** $350.00
  Very good: $265.00

Winchester Model 100 Carbine

Similar to the Model 100 with no checkering: 19″ barrel; barrel bands.
Estimated Value: **Excellent:** $325.00
  Very good: $245.00

Winchester Model 190

Caliber: 22 long rifle or 22 long
Action: Semi-automatic; hammerless
Magazine: Tubular; 15 long rifles, 17 longs, 21 shorts
Barrel: 20½", 22"
Sights: Open rear, blade front
Stock & Forearm: Plain semi-pistol grip stock and forearm
Approximate wt.: 5 lbs.
Comments: 22 short dropped in the early 1970's; made from the mid 1960's to the late 1970's.
Estimated Value: **Excellent:**   **$80.00**
                      Very good: **$60.00**

Winchester Model 190 Carbine

Similar to the Model 190 with a 20½" barrel; barrel band and swivels. Discontinued in the early 1970's.
Estimated Value: **Excellent:**   **$85.00**
                      Very good: **$65.00**

Winchester Model 290

Caliber: 22 short, long, long rifle
Action: Single; hammerless
Magazine: Tubular; 15 longs, 17 long rifles, 21 shorts
Barrel: 20½"
Sights: Open rear, ramp front
Stock & Forearm: Checkered walnut pistol grip stock and forearm
Approximate wt.: 5 lbs.
Comments: Made from the mid 1960's to mid 1970's.
Estimated Value: **Excellent:**   **$100.00**
                      Very good: **$75.00**

Winchester Model 490

Caliber: 22 long rifle
Action: Semi-automatic
Magazine: 5-, 10- or 15-shot clip
Barrel: Blued 22"
Sights: Folding leaf rear, hooded ramp front
Stock & Forearm: Checkered walnut one-piece pistol grip stock and forearm
Approximate wt.: 6 lbs.
Comments: Made in the mid 1970's.
Estimated Value: **Excellent:**   **$150.00**
                      Very good: **$115.00**

Winchester Model 190

Winchester Model 290

Winchester Model 490

Handguns

AMT

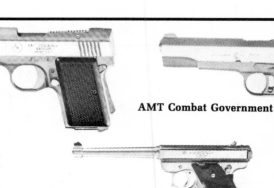

AMT 380 Backup

AMT Combat Government

AMT Lightning Pistol

AMT Backup

Caliber: 380 ACP, 22 long rifle
Action: Semi-automatic; concealed hammer; manual and grip safeties
Magazine: 5-shot clip in 380 ACP; 8-shot in 22LR
Barrel: 2½″
Sights: Fixed
Finish: Smooth wood grips; all stainless steel construction; Lexon grips on later models
Length Overall: 5″
Approximate wt.: 17 oz.
Comments: Made from 1970's to present.
Estimated Value: New (retail): $249.95
Excellent: $190.00
Very good: $140.00

AMT Combat Government

Caliber: 45 ACP
Action: Semi-automatic; exposed hammer; loaded chamber indicator; manual and grip safeties; adjustable target-type trigger
Magazine: 7-shot clip
Barrel: 5″
Sights: Fixed
Finish: Checkered walnut grips; all stainless steel construction
Length Overall: 8½″
Approximate wt.: 39 oz.
Comments: Made from the 1970's to present.
Estimated Value: New (retail): $440.00
Excellent: $330.00
Very good: $250.00

AMT Hardballer

Same as the AMT Combat Government except: adjustable combat type sights: serrated matte slide rib; grooved front and backstraps.
Estimated Value: New (retail): $550.00
Excellent: $415.00
Very good: $310.00

AMT Skipper

Same as the AMT Hardballer except 4″ barrel and 7½″ overall length.
Estimated Value: Excellent: $375.00
Very good: $300.00

AMT Hardballer Long Slide

Same as the AMT Hardballer except: 7″ barrel and 10½″ overall length.
Estimated Value: New (retail): $575.00
Excellent: $430.00
Very good: $325.00

AMT Lightning Pistol

Caliber: 22 long rifle
Action: Semi-automatic, concealed hammer
Magazine: 10 shot clip
Barrel: 5″ bull, 6½″ tapered or bull, 8½″ tapered or bull, 10″ tapered or bull, 12½″ tapered; interchangeable
Sights: Rear adjustable for windage
Finish: Stainless steel; rubber wrap-around grips
Length Overall: 9″ (5″barrel)
Approximate wt.: 38 oz. (5″ bull barrel)
Comments: Introduced in the mid 1980's. Add 5% for 12½″ barrel.
Estimated Value: New (retail): $235.95
Excellent: $175.00
Very good: $130.00

American

American Two Barrel Derringer

Estimated Value: New (retail): $200.00 - $369.00
Excellent: $150.00 - $275.00
Very good: $110.00 - $210.00

American Two Barrel Derringer

Caliber: 22 short, long, long rifle; 22 WMR, 38 Special; other calibers introduced in the early 1980's
Action: Single action; exposed hammer; spur trigger; tip-up barrels
Cylinder: None; cartridges chamber in barrels; 2-shot capacity
Barrel: 3″ double barrel (superposed)
Sights: Fixed
Finish: Stainless steel; checkered plastic grips
Length Overall: 5″
Approximate wt.: 15 oz., 11 oz., or ultra light 7½ oz.
Comments: Made from about 1972 to 1974. Reintroduced in 1980. All stainless steel construction. Current models marked "American Derringer." A variety of calibers is available.

American 25 Automatic

Caliber: 25 ACP; 250 magnum
Action: Semi-automatic; concealed hammer
Magazine: 8-shot clip; 7-shot in magnum
Barrel: 2"
Sights: Fixed
Finish: Blue or stainless steel; smooth rosewood grips; finger extension on clip
Length Overall: 4½"
Approximate wt.: 15½ oz.
Comments: Made from about 1969 to 1974; reintroduced in 1980. Early models (1969-1974) are marked "American Firearms." Current models (after 1980) are marked "American Derringer." Add $35.00 for .250 magnum.

Amerian 25 Automatic

Estimated Value:	Blue	Stainless Steel
Excellent:	$115.00	$125.00
Very good:	$ 85.00	$100.00

American Baby Model

Similar to the 25 Automatic except slightly more compact, 6-shot clip. Produced from 1982 to 1985.

Estimated Value:	Excellent:	$120.00
	Very good:	$ 90.00

Astra

Astra 1911 Model - Patent

Astra 1911 Model - Patent

Caliber: 32 ACP (7.65 mm)
Action: Semi-automatic; concealed hammer
Magazine: 7-shot clip
Barrel: 3¼"
Sights: Fixed
Finish: Blued; checkered hard rubber grips
Length Overall: 5¾"
Approximate wt.: 29 oz.
Comments: A Spanish copy of the Browning blowback action, probably made of trade parts. Not made by Unceta y Compania.

Estimated Value:	Excellent:	$150.00
	Very good:	$120.00

Astra 1915 Model - Patent

Caliber: 32 ACP (7.65 mm)
Action: Semi-automatic; concealed hammer
Magazine: 9-shot clip
Barrel: 3¼"
Sights: Fixed
Finish: Blued; checkered hard rubber grips
Length Overall: 5¾"
Approximate wt.: 29 oz.
Comments: A Spanish copy of the Browning blowback action, probably made of trade parts. Not made by Unceta y Compania.

Estimated Value:	Excellent:	$130.00
	Very good:	$100.00

Astra 1916 Model - Patent

Caliber: 32 ACP (7.65 mm)
Action: Semi-automatic; concealed hammer
Magazine: 9-shot clip
Barrel: 4"
Sights: Fixed
Finish: Blued; checkered hard rubber grips
Length Overall: 6½"
Approximate wt.: 32 oz.
Comments: A Spanish copy of the Browning blowback action, made under several trade names, probably of trade parts. Many were sold in the United States, Central America and South America. Not made by Unceta y Compania.

Estimated Value:	Excellent:	$135.00
	Very good:	$110.00

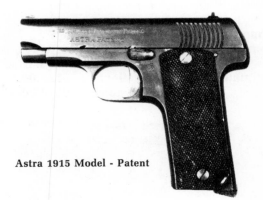

Astra 1915 Model - Patent

Astra 1924 Hope

Caliber: 25 ACP (6.35 mm)
Action: Semi-automatic; concealed hammer
Magazine: 6-shot clip
Barrel: 2″
Sights: Fixed
Finish: Blued; checkered rubber grips
Length Overall: 4⅓″
Approximate wt.: 12 oz.
Comments: Some of these pistols have "HOPE" designation on barrel.
Estimated Value: Excellent: $140.00
Very good: $100.00

Astra Model 2000 Cub Pocket

Caliber: 22 short, 25 ACP (6.35 mm)
Action: Semi-automatic; exposed hammer
Magazine: 6-shot clip
Barrel: 2⅛″
Sights: Fixed
Finish: Blued; chrome and/or engraved, checkered grips
Length Overall: 4½″
Approximate wt.: 13 to 14 oz.
Comments: A well-made pistol of the post-World War II period. Importation to the United States was discontinued in 1968. Add $20.00 for chrome finish.
Estimated Value: Excellent: $150.00
Very good: $115.00

Astra Camper Pocket

Same as Astra Cub (Model 2000) except: 22 caliber short only; 4″ barrel which extends beyond front of slide; laterally adjustable rear sight. Discontinued in 1966. Add $10.00 for chrome finish.
Estimated Value: Excellent: $120.00
Very good: $ 95.00

Astra Model 300

Caliber: 380 ACP (9 mm Kurz)
Action: Semi-automatic; concealed hammer
Magazine: 7-shot clip
Barrel: 4¼″
Sights: Fixed
Finish: Blued; checkered rubber grips
Length Overall: 6½″
Approximate wt.: 21 oz.
Comments: This pistol was a shorter version of the Model 400 and production was started in 1922.
Estimated Value: Excellent: $225.00
Very good: $170.00

Astra 1924 Hope

Astra Model 2000 Cub Pocket

Astra Camper Pocket

Astra Model 300

Astra Model 600

Caliber: 32 ACP (7.65 mm), 9mm Luger
Action: Semi-automatic; concealed hammer
Magazine: 10-shot clip in 32 caliber; 8-shot clip in 9mm
Barrel: 5¼″
Sights: Fixed
Finish: Blued; checkered rubber grips
Length Overall: 8½″
Approximate wt.: 35 oz.
Comments: Made from 1944 to 1945 for military and police use. The 9mm was used as a substitute pistol in German military service, so some will have German acceptance marks.
Estimated Value: Excellent: $225.00
Very good: $170.00

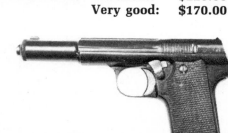

Astra Model 600

Astra Model 400
Caliber: 9mm Bayard long; 38 ACP, 9mm Steyr, 9mm Glisenti, 9mm Luger, 9mm Browning long cartridges can be used due to chamber design
Action: Semi-automatic; concealed hammer
Magazine: 9-shot clip
Barrel: 6″
Sights: Fixed
Finish: Blued; checkered rubber grips
Length Overall: 9″
Approximate wt.: 36 oz.
Comments: Made from 1921 until 1945 for both commercial and military use.
Estimated Value: Excellent: $300.00
Very good: $225.00

Astra Model 400

Astra Model 800 Condor
Caliber: 9mm Parabellum
Action: Semi-automatic; exposed hammer
Magazine: 8-shot clip
Barrel: 5¼″
Sights: Fixed
Finish: Blued; checkered grips
Length Overall: 8¼″
Approximate wt.: 32 oz.
Comments: A post-war version of the Model 600 military pistol. It has a loaded chamber indicator.
Estimated Value: Excellent: $275.00
Very good: $210.00

Astra Model 800 Condor

Astra Model 200 Firecat
Caliber: 25 ACP (6.35mm)
Action: Semi-automatic; concealed hammer; grip safety
Magazine: 6-shot clip
Barrel: 2¼″
Sights: Fixed
Finish: Blued or chrome; plastic grips
Length Overall: 4½″
Approximate wt.: 13 oz.
Comments: A well-machined pistol made from early 1920 to present. It was imported to the United States from World War II until 1968. Add $10.00 for chrome finish.
Estimated Value: Excellent: $150.00
Very good: $120.00

Astra Model 200 Firecat

Astra Model 3000

Astra Model 3000
Caliber: 22 long rifle, 32 ACP, 380 ACP (9mm short)
Action: Semi-automatic; concealed hammer
Magazine: 10-shot clip in 22 caliber, 7-shot clip in 32 caliber; 6-shot clip in 380; clip
Barrel: 4″
Sights: Fixed
Finish: Blued; checkered grips
Length Overall: 6³/₈″
Approximate wt.: 23 oz.
Comments: Made from about 1947 to 1956. Well-machined and well-finished commercially produced pistol. The 380 caliber has loaded chamber indicator.
Estimated Value: Excellent: $175.00
Very good: $130.00

Astra Model 4000 Falcon

Astra Model 4000 Falcon
Caliber: 22 long rifle, 32 ACP (7.65mm), 380 ACP (9mm short)
Action: Semi-automatic; exposed hammer
Magazine: 10-shot clip in 22 caliber; 8-shot clip in 32 caliber; 7-shot clip in 380 caliber
Barrel: 4¼″
Sights: Fixed
Finish: Blued; checkered grips
Length Overall: 6½″
Approximate wt.: 20 to 24 oz.
Comments: A conversion unit was available to fit the 32 caliber and 380 caliber pistols, so that 22 caliber long rifle ammunition could be used.
Estimated Value: Excellent: $190.00
Very good: $145.00

Astra Model 5000 Constable

Astra Model 5000 Constable

Caliber: 22 long rifle, 32 ACP (7.65mm), (32 discontinued), 380 ACP

Action: Double-action; semi-automatic; exposed hammer with round spur

Magazine: 10-shot clip in 22 caliber long rifle, 8-shot clip in 32 ACP; 7-shot clip in 380 ACP

Barrel: 3½″; 6″ on Sport model

Sights: Fixed

Finish: Blued or chrome; grooved grips; checkered on late model; plastic of wood grips

Length Overall: 6⅝″ to 9⅛″

Approximate wt.: 24 to 26 oz.

Comments: The barrel is rigidly mounted in the frame, all steel construction with hammer block safety. Add 40% for factory engraving; 10% for wood grips; 10% for chrome finish; 30% for stainless steel.

Estimated Value: New (retail): $265.00
Excellent: $200.00
Very good: $150.00

Astra Model A-80, A-90

Caliber: 9mm Parabellum, 38 Super, 45 ACP

Action: Double action; semi-automatic; exposed hammer

Magazine: 15-shot clip in 9mm and 38 calibers; 9-shot clip in 45 ACP

Barrel: 3¾″

Sights: Fixed

Finish: Blued or chrome; checkered plastic grips

Length Overall: 7″

Approximate wt.: 40 oz.

Comments: Introduced in 1982. Add 10% for chrome finish.

Estimated Value: New (retail): $395.00
Excellent: $295.00
Very good: $220.00

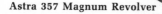

Astra 357 Magnum Revolver

Astra Model 357

Caliber: 357 magnum, 38 special

Action: Double action

Cylinder: 6-shot, swing out

Barrel: 3″, 4″, 6″, 8½″ heavy weight with rib

Sights: Adjustable rear, fixed front

Finish: Blued; checkered walnut grips; stainless steel available after 1982

Length Overall: 8¼″ to 13¾″

Approximate wt.: 38 to 42 oz.

Comments: All steel construction with wide spur hammer and grooved trigger. Currently made. Add 3% for 8½″ barrel; 10% for stainless steel.

Estimated Value: New (retail): $275.00
Excellent: $210.00
Very good: $155.00

Astra Model 41, 44

Similar to the Model 357 except 41 magnum or 44 magnum caliber; 6″ or 8½″ barrel. Introduced in the early 1980's. Add $10.00 for 8½″ barrel; Model 41 discontinued in mid 1980's.

Estimated Value: New (retail): $295.00
Excellent: $225.00
Very good: $170.00

Astra Model 45

Similar to the Model 357 except 45 Colt or 45 ACP caliber; 6″ barrel. Introduced in the early 1980's.

Estimated Value: New (retail): $295.00
Excellent: $225.00
Very good: $170.00

Astra Model 41, 44

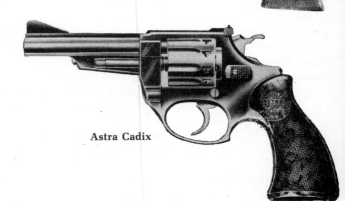

Astra Cadix

Astra Cadix

Caliber: 22 short, long and long rifle, 38 Special

Action: Double action

Cylinder: Swing out 9-shot in 22 caliber; 5-shot in 38 Special

Barrel: 2″, 4″ and 6″

Sights: Adjustable rear on 4″ and 6″ barrel

Finish: Blued; checkered grips

Length Overall: 6½″, 9″, 11″

Approximate wt.: 25 to 27 oz.

Comments: Made from about 1960 to the late 1960's.

Estimated Value: Excellent: $135.00
Very good: $100.00

Auto Mag

Auto Mag.

Caliber: 357 auto magnum or 44 auto magnum custom loaded or hand loaded cartridges (no commerical ammo available)

Action: Semi-automatic; exposed hammer; adjustable trigger

Magazine: 7-shot clip

Barrel: 6½″ ventilated rib (44 auto mag.); 6½″ or 8½″ (.357 auto mag.); no rib on 8½″ barrel

Sights: Ramp front sight and adjustable rear sight

Finish: Stainless steel; black polyurethane grips

Length Overall: 11½″

Approximate wt.: 60 oz.

Comments: The most potent autoloader made. Designed by Harry Sanford, it was made by different factories (Auto Mag Corp., TDE Corp., High Standard & etc.). Requires special ammunition made from the 308 Winchester, .243, or 7.62 NATO cases. Made from about 1970 to late 1970's. All stainless steel construction. Total production was rather small. First model called Pasadena Auto Mag. in .44 caliber only.

Auto Mag.

Estimated Value: **Excellent:** $800.00 - $2,000.00
Very good: $650.00 - $1,800.00

Bauer

Bauer Stainless

Caliber: 25 ACP

Action: Semi-automatic; concealed hammer

Magazine: 6-shot clip

Barrel: 2¹/₈″

Sights: Fixed

Finish: Heat treated stainless steel; plastic grips

Length Overall: 4″

Approximate wt.: 10 oz.

Comments: Manufactured completely in the United States from about 1972 to mid 1980's.

Estimated Value: **Excellent:** $100.00
Very good: $ 75.00

Bauer Stainless

Bayard

Bayard Model 1908

Bayard Model 1923

Bayard Model 1908

Caliber: 25 ACP (6.35 mm), 32 ACP (7.65mm), 380 ACP (9mm short)

Action: Semi-automatic; concealed hammer

Magazine: 6-shot clip

Barrel: 2¼″

Sights: Fixed

Finish: Blued; checkered grips

Length Overall: 5″

Approximate wt.: 15 to 17 oz.

Comments: Made from basic Pieper patents of the 1900's. All calibers appear the same from a side view. Commercially sold throughout the world; one of the most compact pistols made.

Estimated Value: **Excellent:** $160.00
Very good: $125.00

Bayard Model 1923 (25 ACP)

Caliber: 25 ACP

Action: Semi-automatic; concealed hammer

Magazine: 6-shot clip

Barrel: 2¹/₈″

Sights: Fixed

Finish: Blued; checkered grips

Length Overall: 4⅓″

Approximate wt.: 12 oz.

Comments: A Belgian variation of the Browning. This model has better construction that the Model 1908.

Estimated Value: **Excellent:** $175.00
Very good: $130.00

Bayard Model 1923 (32, 380)

Caliber: 32 ACP (7.65mm), 380 ACP (9mm short)
Action: Semi-automatic; concealed hammer
Magazine: 6-shot clip
Barrel: 3³/₈″
Sights: Fixed
Finish: Blued; checkered grips
Length Overall: 5¾″
Approximate wt.: 18 to 19 oz.
Comments: A Belgian variation of the Browning. Better construction than the 1908.
Estimated Value: Excellent: $225.00
Very good: $165.00

Bayard Model 1930

Caliber: 25 ACP (6.35mm)
Action: Semi-automatic; concealed hammer
Magazine: 6-shot clip
Barrel: 2″
Sights: Fixed
Finish: Blued; checkered grips
Length Overall: 4³/₈″
Approximate wt.: 12 oz.
Comments: A modification of the Model 1923.
Estimated Value: Excellent: $200.00
Very good: $160.00

Beretta

Beretta Model 1915

Beretta Model 1919 "Bantam"

Beretta Model 1923

Beretta Model 1915

Caliber: 32 ACP (7.65mm)
Action: Semi-automatic; concealed hammer
Magazine: 8-shot clip
Barrel: 3¼″
Sights: Fixed
Finish: Blued; wood or metal grips
Length Overall: 5⁷/₈″
Approximate wt.: 20 oz.
Comments: The earliest of the Beretta series used for military service during World War I, as well as being sold commercially. Has rigid lanyard loop on left side. Grip safety was added in 1919. Made from about 1915 to 1924.
Estimated Value: Excellent: $250.00
Very good: $185.00

Beretta Model 1919 Bantam

Caliber: 25 ACP (6.35mm)
Action: Semi-automatic; concealed hammer
Magazine: 7-shot clip
Barrel: 2½″
Sights: Fixed
Finish: Blued, wood grips
Length Overall: 4½″
Approximate wt.: 14 oz.
Comments: Basic Beretta patent with addition of a grip safety. The front sight contour was changed prior to World War II. Importation to the United States was discontinued in 1956.
Estimated Value: Excellent: $175.00
Very good: $130.00

Beretta Model 1923

Caliber: 9mm Luger
Action: Semi-automatic; exposed hammer
Magazine: 9-shot clip
Barrel: 4″
Sights: Fixed
Finish: Blued, wood grips
Length Overall: 6½″
Approximate wt.: 30 oz.
Comments: Basically an Italian service pistol, but also sold commercially. A modified version of the 1915, 1919 patents. This was the first model produced with exposed hammer. Lanyard loop on left side.
Estimated Value: Excellent: $300.00
Very good: $225.00

Beretta Model 1931

Caliber: 32 ACP (7.65mm)
Action: Semi-automatic; concealed hammer
Magazine: 7-shot clip
Barrel: 3⁵/₁₆″
Sights: Fixed
Finish: Blued, wood grips
Length Overall: 5¾″
Approximate wt.: 22 oz.
Comments: A modified version of the Model 1923.
Estimated Value: Excellent: $225.00
Very good: $175.00

Beretta Model 1931

Beretta Cougar

Caliber: 380 ACP (9mm short)
Action: Semi-automatic; exposed hammer
Magazine: 7-shot clip
Barrel: 3½″
Sights: Fixed
Finish: Blued or chrome; plastic grips
Length Overall: 6″
Approximate wt.: 22 oz.
Comments: A post-World War II version of the Model 934 (1934). Those imported into the United States have the "Cougar" name on pistol. Some of the later models are marked "P.B. 1966". Add $10.00 for chrome.
Estimated Value: Excellent: $210.00
Very good: $160.00

Beretta Cougar

Beretta Model 948 Plinker

Caliber: 22 long rifle
Action: Semi-automatic; exposed hammer
Magazine: 7-shot clip
Barrel: 3½″, 6″
Sights: Fixed
Finish: Blued; plastic grips
Length Overall: 6″ or 8½″
Approximate wt.: 16 to 18 oz.
Comments: Made from 1948 to 1958. Similar to the 1934/35 series except: 22 caliber; aluminum alloy frame. Replaced by the "Jaguar." The 6″ barrel extends beyond the slide about 3″.
Estimated Value: Excellent: $150.00
Very good: $110.00

Beretta Model 934 (1934)

Beretta Model 934 (1934) 380 and 935 (1935) 32

Caliber: 32 ACP (7.65mm), 380 ACP (9mm short)
Action: Semi-automatic; exposed hammer
Magazine: 8-shot clip in 32; and 7-shot clip in 380
Barrel: 3½″
Sights: Fixed
Finish: Blued; plastic grips
Length Overall: 6″
Approximate wt.: 22 to 24 oz.
Comments: Official pistol of the Italian Armed Forces from 1934 until 1951 in 380 caliber. Still sold commercially and used by Italian police. Lanyard loop on left side. Model 935 was discontinued in 1958.
Estimated Value: Excellent: $225.00
Very good: $175.00

Beretta Model 935 (1935)

Beretta Model 70T

Caption: Beretta Model 70T

Beretta Model 70 Puma

Caliber: 32 ACP (7.65mm); 380 ACP
Action: Semi-automatic; exposed hammer
Magazine: 7-shot clip
Barrel: 3½″
Sights: Fixed
Finish: Blued; plastic wrap-around grip
Length Overall: 6½″
Approximate wt.: 15 oz.
Comments: Post-World War II (1946) version of the Model 935 (1935). Aluminum alloy frame was used to reduce weight. Those imported into the United States have "Puma" designation. Also made with steel frame. Discontinued. Add $15.00 for nickel finish.
Estimated Value: Excellent: $175.00
                   Very good: $130.00

Beretta Model 70T

Caliber: 32 ACP (7.65mm)
Action: Semi-automatic; exposed hammer
Magazine: 9-shot clip
Barrel: 6″
Sights: Adjustable rear; blade front
Finish: Blued; plastic wrap-around grip
Length Overall: 9½″
Approximate wt.: 20 oz.
Comments: Imported from Italy. Target length barrel extends beyond front of slide.
Estimated Value: Excellent: $200.00
                   Very good: $150.00

Beretta Model 101

Same as Model 70T except: 22 caliber long rifle; 10 shot clip.
Estimated Value: Excellent: $200.00
                   Very good: $150.00

Beretta Models 71 & 72 Jaguar

Caliber: 22 long rifle
Action: Semi-automatic; exposed hammer
Magazine: 7-shot clip
Barrel: 3½″ (Model 71) and 6″ (Model 72)
Sights: Fixed
Finish: Blued; wrap-around plastic grip
Length Overall: 6¼″ or 8¾″
Approximate wt.: 16-18 oz.
Comments: Importation to the United States started in 1956. The light weight was obtained by using aluminum alloy receiver. Similar in appearance to the Puma except the 6″ barrel extends about 3″ beyond the slide.
Estimated Value: Excellent: $190.00
                   Very good: $140.00

Caption: Beretta Model 70 Puma

Caption: Beretta Model 71 & 72 Jaguar

Caption: Beretta Model 70S

Caption: Beretta Model 949 Olympic

Beretta Model 70S

Caliber: 380 ACP (9mm short); 22 long rifle
Action: Semi-automatic; exposed hammer
Magazine: 7-shot clip in 380; 8-shot clip in 22
Barrel: 3½″
Sights: Fixed
Finish: Blued; 2-piece wrap-around plastic grip
Length Overall: 6¼″
Approximate wt.: 24 oz.
Comments: All steel compact pistol imported from Italy. Discontinued in mid 1980's
Estimated Value: Excellent: $210.00
                   Very good: $155.00

Beretta Model 949 Olympic, 949C

Caliber: 22 short, 22 long rifle
Action: Semi-automatic; exposed hammer
Magazine: 5-shot clip
Barrel: 8¾″ with compensator muzzle brake
Sights: Rear adjustable for windage; front adjustable for elevation
Finish: Blued; checkered walnut grips with thumb rest
Length Overall: 12½″
Approximate wt.: 38 oz.
Comments: Also called the 949C, it was designed for use in Olympic rapid-fire matches and designed 949LR. Both models have been discontinued.
Estimated Value: Excellent: $360.00
                   Very good: $270.00

Beretta Model 951 (1951)

Caliber: 9mm Parabellum (Luger)
Action: Semi-automatic; exposed hammer
Magazine: 8-shot clip
Barrel: 4½″
Sights: Fixed
Finish: Blued; plastic wrap-around grip
Length Overall: 8″
Approximate wt.: 31 oz.
Comments: First produced in 1950 and adopted by Italian Army and Navy. Basic 1934 model features except it has aluminum alloy receiver. Also known as Brigadier model.
Estimated Value: Excellent: $325.00
Very good: $250.00

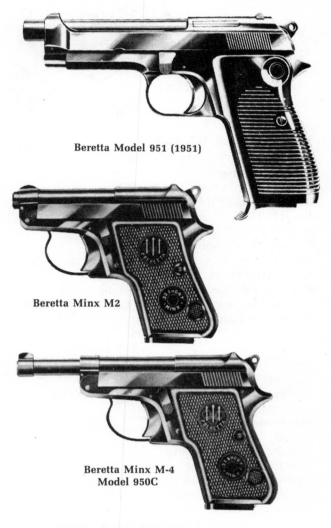

Beretta Model 951 (1951)

Beretta Minx M2

Beretta Minx M-4
Model 950C

Beretta Minx M2, Model 950 B, 950 BS

Caliber: 22 short, 25 ACP
Action: Semi-automatic; exposed hammer
Magazine: 6-shot clip
Barrel: 2½″
Sights: Fixed
Finish: Blued or nickel; plastic grips
Length Overall: 4½″
Approximate wt.: 10 oz.
Comments: Made from 1956 to present. Imported from 1956 to 1968. Aluminum alloy frame with a hinged barrel that tips up at chamber end. Can be used as single shot by removing magazine and tipping up barrel to load. Reintroduced in 1979, manufactured in the United States. Add 10% for nickel finish.
Estimated Value: New (retail): $189.95
Excellent: $145.00
Very good: $100.00

Beretta Minx M-4, Model 950C, 950 BS4

Same as Minx M-2, except: 4″ barrel; overall length 6″; approximate weight 12 oz. Add 10% for nickel finish.
Estimated Value: New (retail): $200.00
Excellent: $150.00
Very good: $110.00

Beretta Jetfire Model 950B

Same as Minx M-2 except: 25 ACP (6.35mm) caliber; 6-shot magazine. Add 7% for nickel finish.
Estimated Value: Excellent: $145.00
Very good: $100.00

Beretta Jetfire Model 950B

Beretta Model 76

Beretta Model 76 Target

Caliber: 22 long rifle
Action: Semi-automatic; exposed hammer
Magazine: 10-shot clip
Barrel: 6″
Sights: Adjustable rear, blade front
Finish: Blued; 2-piece wrap around plastic or wood grip
Length Overall: 9½″
Approximate wt.: 35 oz.
Comments: Imported from Italy. Competition-type heavy barrel. Add 10% for wood grips. Discontinued in mid 1980's.
Estimated Value: Excellent: $280.00
Very good: $210.00

Beretta Model DA 380

Beretta Model DA 380

Caliber: 380 ACP (9mm short)
Action: Double action; semi-automatic; exposed round spur hammer
Magazine: 13-shot clip
Barrel: 3¾"
Sights: Fixed
Finish: Blued; smooth walnut grips
Length Overall: 6½"
Approximate wt.: 23 oz.
Comments: This pistol features magazine release and safety release for either right or left hand.
Estimated Value: Excellent: $300.00
                        Very good: $225.00

Beretta Model 90

Caliber: 32 ACP (7.65mm)
Action: Semi-automatic; straight blow-back; double action; exposed hammer
Magazine: 8-shot clip
Barrel: 3½"
Finish: Blued; contoured plastic grips
Length Overall: 6½"
Approximate wt.: 19 oz.
Comments: Discontinued in mid 1980's.
Estimated Value: Excellent: $290.00
                        Very good: $220.00

Beretta Model 92, 92S

Caliber: 9mm Parabellum
Action: Semi-automatic; double and single action
Magazine: 15-shot clip
Barrel: 5"
Sights: Fixed
Finish: Blued; plastic or smooth wood grips
Length Overall: 8½"
Approximate wt.: 33 oz.
Comments: Made from the late 1970's to early 1980's. Add 5% for wood grips. Loaded chamber indicator.
Estimated Value: Excellent: $410.00
                        Very good: $300.00

Beretta Model 90

Beretta Model 20

Beretta Model 92SB

Caliber: 9mm Parabellum
Action: Semi-automatic; straight blow-back; double action; exposed hammer
Magazine: 15-shot staggered clip
Barrel: 5"
Sights: Fixed
Finish: Blued; walnut or checkered plastic grips
Length Overall: 8½"
Approximate wt.: 34½ oz.
Comments: Introduced in the early 1980's. Add 3% for wood grips.
Estimated Value: Excellent: $450.00
                        Very good: $340.00

Beretta Model 92SB Compact

Similar to the Model 92SB except 4¼" barrel; 13-shot clip; weight 31 oz. Add 3% for wood grips.
Estimated Value: Excellent: $465.00
                        Very good: $375.00

Beretta Model 92F

Similar to the Model 92SB with improved safety features, ambidextrous safety, open slide design, non-glare finish, reversible magazine release button, disassembling latch. Adopted for use by the U.S. military. Add 2% for wood grips.
Estimated Value: New (retail): $685.00
                        Excellent: $515.00
                        Very good: $385.00

Beretta Model 92

Beretta Model 92F

Beretta Model 92F Compact

Similar to the Model 92F with a 4¼" barrel, weighs 31 oz.
Estimated Value: New (retail): $685.00
                        Excellent: $515.00
                        Very good: $385.00

Beretta Model 20

Caliber: 25 ACP
Action: Straight blowback, recoil ejection, double action semi-automatic
Magazine: 8-shot clip
Barrel: 2½" tip-up
Sights: Fixed
Finish: Blued; alloy frame, plastic or walnut grips
Length Overall: 5"
Approximate wt.: 10½ oz.
Comments: Introduced in 1984. Discontinued 1986.
Estimated Value: Excellent: $175.00
                        Very good: $120.00

Beretta Model 21   Beretta Model 81   Beretta Model 86

Beretta Model 21

Caliber: 22 long rifle
Action: Straight blowback, double action semi-automatic
Magazine: 7-shot clip
Barrel: 2½″ tip up
Sights: Fixed
Finish: Blued, alloy frame; wood grips
Length Overall: 5″
Approximate wt.: 12 oz.
Comments: Introduced in 1984.
Estimated Value: New (retail): $230.00
      Excellent: $175.00
      Very good: $135.00

Beretta Model 81

Caliber: 32 ACP
Action: Semi-automatic; double and single action
Magazine: 12-shot clip
Barrel: 3¾″
Sights: Fixed
Finish: Blued; plastic or smooth wood grips; nickel available
Length Overall: 6¾″
Approximate wt.: 23½ oz.
Comments: Produced in the late 1970's to about 1984. Add 3% for wood grips; 15% for nickel finish.
Estimated Value: Excellent: $310.00
      Very good: $230.00

Beretta Model 84

Similar to Model 81 in 380 caliber (9mm short); 13-shot clip. Add 3% for wood grips; 15% for nickel finish.
Estimated Value: New (retail): $495.00
      Excellent: $370.00
      Very good: $280.00

Beretta Model 85

Similar to the Model 82 except 380 caliber (9mm short) and 8-shot clip. Add 10% for nickel.
Estimated Value: New (retail): $460.00
      Excellent: $345.00
      Very good: $260.00

Beretta Model 86

Similar to Model 85 with tip-up barrel for loading without working the slide. Add 20% for wood grips.
Estimated Value: New (retail): $400.00
      Excellent: $300.00
      Very good: $225.00

Beretta Model 87

Similar to the Model 85 but chambered for 22 long rifle.
Estimated Value: New (retail): $435.00
      Excellent: $325.00
      Very good: $245.00

Beretta Model 82

Caliber: 32 ACP (7.65mm)
Action: Semi-automatic; straight blow-back; double action; exposed hammer
Magazine: 9-shot clip
Barrel: 3¾″
Sights: Fixed
Finish: Blued or nickel; walnut grips
Length Overall: 6¾″
Approximate wt.: 17 oz.
Comments: Similar to the Model 81 with a more compact grip size. Add 15% for nickel finish.
Estimated Value: Excellent: $310.00
      Very good: $230.00

Browning Model 1910

Browning

Browning 25 Pocket

Caliber: 25 ACP (6.35mm)
Action: Semi-automatic; concealed hammer
Magazine: 6-shot clip
Barrel: 2¹⁄₈″
Sights: Fixed
Finish: Blued, hard rubber grips; nickel plated, light weight, plastic pearl grips; Renaissance engraved, Nacolac pearl grips available
Length Overall: 4″
Approximate wt.: 8 to 10 oz.
Comments: A post-World War II modification of the FN Browning Baby Automatic pistol, it was lightened and the grip safety removed. Imported into the U.S. from 1954 to 1968. Pistols imported into the U.S. and Canada usually do not have the FN trademark. Add $25.00 for nickel finish; $550.00 for nickel plated Renaissance engraved model (mint).
Estimated Value: Excellent: $225.00
      Very good: $170.00

Browning Model 1910

Caliber: 380 ACP (9mm short), 32 ACP
Action: Semi-automatic; concealed hammer
Magazine: 6-shot clip
Barrel: 3½″
Sights: Fixed
Finish: Blued; hard rubber grips; Renaissance engraved, Nacolac pearl grips available
Length Overall: 6″
Approximate wt.: 21 oz.
Comments: Basic design of the 1900 model FN Browning, with the appearance streamlined and a grip safety added. Imported from 1954 to 1968. Pistols imported into the U.S. and Canada usually do not have the FN trademark. Add $650.00 for Nickel plated Renaissance engraved model (mint).
Estimated Value: Excellent: $235.00
      Very good: $180.00

Browning Model 1935, Hi Power, 9MM

Caliber: 9mm Parabellum
Action: Semi-automatic; exposed hammer
Magazine: 13-shot clip
Barrel: $4^5/_8$"
Sights: Fixed or adjustable rear sight
Finish: Blued; checkered walnut or molded Polymide grips; Renaissance engraved, Nacolac pearl grips available; chrome available 1982 with Packmayr grips; nickel available until 1986; Matte finish with molded grips available after 1985.
Length Overall: $7^3/_4$"
Approximate wt.: 34 oz.
Comments: Imported into the US. from 1954 to present. Some were manufactured in Canada beginning in 1943. These have alloy frames for weight reduction. Pistols imported into the U.S. from Belgium usually do not have FN trademark. Add 10% for adjustable rear sight; 10% for nickel or chrome finish; $850.00 for nickel plated Renaissance engraved (mint); deduct 5% for molded grips; 15% for matte finish.

Estimated Value:	New (retail):	$472.50
	Excellent:	$355.00
	Very good:	$265.00

Browning Renaissance Engraved Cased Set

Contains one each of the following:
Browning 25 Automatic Pistol
Browning Model 1910 380 Automatic Pistol
Browning Model 1935 Hi Power Automatic Pistol
in a special walnut carrying case. Each pistol is nickel plated, Renaissance Engraved with Nacolac pearl grips. Imported into the U.S. from 1954 through 1968. Price includes walnut case.

Estimated Value:	
Mint Condition (unused):	$4,000.00
Excellent:	$1,800.00

**Browning Model 1935
Hi Power**

Browning Challenger

Browning Challenger

Caliber: 22 long rifle
Action: Semi-automatic; concealed hammer
Magazine: 10-shot clip
Barrel: $4^1/_2$" or $6^3/_4$"
Sights: Removable blade front, adjustable rear
Finish: Blued; checkered walnut grips; Gold model (gold inlaid) finely figured walnut grips; Renaissance engraved finely figured walnut grips
Length Overall: $9^3/_{16}$" or $11^7/_{16}$"
Approximate wt.: 36 to 38 oz.
Comments: Blued model made from 1963 to 1974. Gold and Renaissance models introduced in 1971. All steel construction. Add $300.00 for gold model; $350.00 for nickel plated Renaissance engraved model.

Estimated Value:	Excellent:	$300.00
	Very good:	$225.00

Browning Challenger II

Similar to the Challenger except $6^3/_4$" barrel only; made from about 1975 to mid 1980's. Impregnated wood grips.

Estimated Value:	Excellent:	$200.00
	Very good:	$150.00

Browning Challenger III

Caliber: 22 long rifle
Action: Semi-automatic; concealed hammer
Magazine: 10-shot clip
Barrel: $5^1/_2$" bull barrel
Sights: Blade front, adjustable rear
Finish: Blued, smooth impregnated hardwood grips
Length Overall: $9^1/_2$"
Approximate wt.: 35 oz.
Comments: Produced 1982 to 1986.

Estimated Value:	Excellent:	$190.00
	Very good:	$140.00

Browning Challenger III Sporter

Similar to the Challenger III with $6^3/_4$" round barrel. Introduced in 1985.

Estimated Value:	New (retail):	$239.95
	Excellent:	$180.00
	Very good:	$135.00

Browning Challenger II

Browning Challenger III

Browning Buck Mark 22

Caliber: 22 long rifle
Action: Semi-automatic, blow-back; concealed hammer
Magazine: 10-shot clip
Barrel: 5½″ bull barrel with non-glare top
Sights: Adjustable rear, ramp front
Finish: Blued, matte except for lustre barrel sides; checkered black molded composit grips, deer head medallion: brass-plate trigger
Length Overall: 9½″
Approximate wt.: 32 oz.
Comments: Introduced in 1985.
Estimated Value: New (retail): $164.95
Excellent: $125.00
Very good: $ 90.00

Browning Nomad

Browning Medalist

Caliber: 22 long rifle
Action: Semi-automatic; concealed hammer
Magazine: 10-shot clip
Barrel: 6¾″, ventilated rib
Sights: Removable blade front, adjustable micrometer rear
Finish: Blued; checkered walnut grips with thumb rest; Gold model (gold inlaid) finely figured and carved walnut grips with thumb rest; Renaissance Model engraved, finely figured and carved walnut grips with thumb rest
Length Overall: 11¾″
Approximate wt.: 45 oz.
Comments: All steel construction, made from 1963 to 1974. Gold model and Renaissance model introduced in 1971. Add $450.00 for Gold model; $500.00 for nickel plated Renaissance engraved model (mint).
Estimated Value: Excellent: $450.00
Very good: $340.00

Browning Nomad

Caliber: 22 long rifle
Action: Semi-automatic; concealed hammer
Magazine: 10-shot clip
Barrel: 4½″ or 6¾″
Sights: Removable blade front, adjustable rear sight
Finish: Blued, plastic grips
Length Overall: 9″ and 11¼″
Approximate wt.: 26 to 28 oz.
Comments: Made from 1963 to 1973 with an alloy frame.
Estimated Value: Excellent: $250.00
Very good: $190.00

Browning Model BDA

Caliber: 45 ACP, 9mm, 38 Super
Action: Semi-automatic; exposed hammer; built-in safety block; double and single action
Magazine: 7-shot clip in 45 ACP; 9-shot clip in 9mm and 38 Super
Barrel: 4½″
Sights: Adjustable square notch rear, blade front
Finish: Blued; black checkered plastic grips
Length Overall: 7¾″
Approximate wt.: 29 oz.
Comments: A handgun with a built-in safety feature. Introduced in the late 1970's, discontinued 1980's.
Estimated Value: Excellent: $300.00
Very good: $225.00

Browning Model BDA

Browning Model BDA 380

Caliber: 380 ACP
Action: Semi-automatic; exposed hammer; double and single action
Magazine: 12-shot staggered row clip
Barrel: 3¾″
Sights: Adjustable square notch rear, blade front
Finish: Blued, smooth walnut grips, bronze medallion; nickel finish available 1982
Length Overall: 6¾″
Approximate wt.: 23 oz.
Comments: Introduced in the late 1970's. Add 5% for nickel finish.
Estimated Value: New (retail): $384.50
Excellent: $290.00
Very good: $215.00

Browning Model BDA 380

Browning International Medalist

Browning International Medalist

Caliber: 22 long rifle
Action: Semi-automatic; hammerless
Magazine: 10-shot clip
Barrel: 5$^{15}/_{16}$″ heavy, counter weight
Sights: Fixed, non-reflective
Finish: Blued; wide walnut grips, adjustable hand stop
Length Overall: 11¾″
Approximate wt.: 46 oz.
Comments: A target pistol produced in 1980.
Estimated Value: Excellent: $500.00
Very good: $360.00

Browning, FN

FN Browning Model 1900

FN Browning
Model 1903 Military

FN Browning Model 1903 Military

Caliber: 9mm Browning long
Action: Semi-automatic; concealed hammer
Magazine: 7-shot clip
Barrel: 5″
Sights: Fixed
Finish: Blued, hard rubber grips with FN trademark
Length Overall: 8″
Approximate wt.: 33 oz.
Comments: Made from 1903 to 1939. Lanyard ring on
   left grip.
Estimated Value: Excellent: $250.00
                      Very good: $190.00

FN Browning 6.35 mm Pocket

Caliber: 25 ACP (6.35mm)
Action: Semi-automatic; concealed hammer; grip safety
Magazine: 6-shot clip
Barrel: 2″
Sights: Fixed
Finish: Blued; hard rubber grips with FN trademark
Length Overall: 4½″
Approximate wt.: 13 oz.
Comments: Made from 1905 to 1947.
Estimated Value: Excellent: $300.00
                      Very good: $225.00

FN Browning Model 1910

Caliber: 32 ACP (7.65mm), 380 ACP (9mm short)
Action: Semi-automatic; concealed hammer
Magazine: 7-shot clip in 32 ACP, 6-shot clip in 380
Barrel: 3½″
Sights: Fixed
Finish: Blued, hard rubber grips with FN trademark
Length Overall: 6″
Approximate wt.: 21 oz.
Comments: The basic design of the Model 1900 except
   it has streamlined appearance and grip safety.
Estimated Value: Excellent: $220.00
                      Very good: $165.00

FN Browning Model 1900

Caliber: 32 ACP (7.65mm)
Action: Semi-automatic, concealed hammer
Magazine: 7-shot clip
Barrel: 4″
Sights: Fixed
Finish: Blued, hard rubber grips with FN trademark
Length Overall: 6¾″
Approximate wt.: 22 oz.
Comments: John Browning's first commercially suc-
   cessful pistol. This was the beginning for the 32
   automatic cartridge, which is called 7.65 Brown-
   ing pistol cartridge in the rest of the world. The
   1900 was sold commercially throughout the world
   and was also used by police and military in coun-
   tries such as Belgium, Russia, China and France.
   Made from 1900 to 1912.
Estimated Value: Excellent: $250.00
                      Very good: $190.00

FN Browning Model 1910

FN Browning Model 1922

FN Browning
6.35 mm Pocket

FN Browning Model 1922 Military and Police

Caliber: 32 ACP (7.65mm), 380 ACP (9mm short)
Action: Semi-automatic; concealed hammer
Magazine: 9-shot clip in 32; 8-shot clip in 380
Barrel: 4½″
Sights: Fixed
Finish: Blued; hard rubber grips with FN trademark
Length Overall: 7″
Approximate wt.: 24 oz.
Comments: Identical to Model 1910 except it has longer
   grip frame, magazine and barrel. Lanyard ring on
   the left grip.
Estimated Value: Excellent: $200.00
                      Very good: $150.00

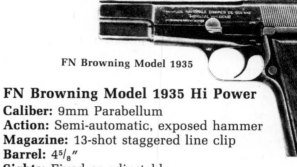
FN Browning Model 1935

FN Browning Baby

Caliber: 25 ACP (6.35mm)
Action: Semi-automatic; concealed hammer
Magazine: 6-shot clip
Barrel: 2¹/₈″
Sights: Fixed
Finish: Blued, hard rubber grips with FN trademark
Length Overall: 4″
Approximate wt.: 10 oz.
Comments: Made from 1940 to present. All steel construction, similar to Browning 25 Pocket Automatic Pistol, imported into U.S. from 1954 to 1968.
Estimated Value: Excellent: $325.00
                Very good: $240.00

FN Browning Model 1935 Hi Power

Caliber: 9mm Parabellum
Action: Semi-automatic, exposed hammer
Magazine: 13-shot staggered line clip
Barrel: 4⁵/₈″
Sights: Fixed or adjustable
Finish: Blued or parkerized; checkered walnut or plastic grips
Length Overall: 7¾″
Approximate wt.: 34 oz.
Comments: Production of this model by John Inglis Co. of Canada began in 1943. Some of these were produced with an alloy frame to reduce weight. Also during World War II Model 1935 was produced under German supervision for military use. The quality of the German pistol was poorer than those made before or after the war. A smaller version was also made from 1937 to 1940 with shorter barrel, slide and 10-shot clip.

Estimated Value	FN	German (superv.)	Canadian
Excellent:	$400.00	$300.00	$360.00
Very good:	$300.00	$225.00	$275.00

FN Browning Baby

Budischowsky

Budischowsky TP-70 Automatic Pistol

Caliber: 22 long rifle, 25 ACP
Action: Double action; semi-automatic; exposed hammer
Magazine: 6-shot clip
Barrel: 2½″
Sights: Fixed
Finish: Stainless steel; checkered plastic grips
Length Overall: 4¾″
Approximate wt.: 12 oz.
Comments: All stainless steel construction. Manual and magazine safeties. Manufactured by Norton Armament Corp. 1973 to 1977.
Estimated Value: Excellent: $150.00
                Very good: $120.00

Budischowsky TP-70

CZ

CZ Model 22 (1922)

Caliber: 380 ACP (9mm short), 25 ACP
Action: Semi-automatic; exposed hammer with shielding on both sides
Magazine: 8-shot clip
Barrel: 3½″
Sights: Fixed
Finish: Blued
Length Overall: 6″
Approximate wt.: 22 oz.
Comments: Made in Czechoslovakia in the 1920's.
Estimated Value: Excellent: $190.00
                Very good: $140.00

CZ Model 22 (1922)

CZ Model 1936 Pocket

Caliber: 25 ACP (6.35mm)
Action: Double action semi-automatic; slide does not cock hammer; (hammer is cocked and released by the trigger) shielded exposed hammer
Magazine: 8-shot clip
Barrel: 2½"
Sights: Fixed
Finish: Blued; plastic grips
Length Overall: 4¾"
Approximate wt.: 14 oz.
Comments: Made from 1936 to present. U.S. importation discontinued in 1968.
Estimated Value: Excellent: $150.00
Very good: $120.00

CZ Model 38 (1938)

Caliber: 380 ACP (9mm short)
Action: Double action; semi-automatic
Magazine: 9-shot clip
Barrel: 3¾"
Sights: Fixed
Finish: Blued; plastic grips
Length Overall: 7"
Approximate wt.: 28 oz.
Comments: Made in the late 1930's
Estimated Value: Excellent: $185.00
Very good: $130.00

CZ Model 1945 Pocket

Same as CZ Model 1936 except for minor modifications.
Estimated Value: Excellent: $165.00
Very good: $125.00

CZ Model 50 (1950)

Caliber: 32 ACP (7.65mm)
Action: Semi-automatic; exposed hammer; double action
Magazine: 8-shot clip
Barrel: 3⅛"
Sights: Fixed
Finish: Blued, plastic grips
Length Overall: 6½"
Approximate wt.: 25 oz.
Comments: No longer imported into the U.S.
Estimated Value: Excellent: $180.00
Very good: $140.00

CZ "Duo" Pocket

Caliber: 25 ACP (6.35mm)
Action: Semi-automatic; concealed hammer
Magazine: 6-shot clip
Barrel: 2⅛"
Sights: Fixed
Finish: Blued, plastic grips
Length Overall: 4½"
Approximate wt.: 15 oz.
Comments: Importation into the U.S. was discontinued in 1968.
Estimated Value: Excellent: $175.00
Very good: $140.00

CZ Model 27 (1927)

Caliber: 32 ACP (7.65mm)
Action: Semi-automatic; exposed hammer with shielding on both sides
Magazine: 8-shot clip
Barrel: 4"
Sights: Fixed
Finish: Blued, plastic grips
Length Overall: 6½"
Approximate wt.: 25 oz.
Comments: This pistol usually bears the CZ mark, but World War II version may have the name Bohmische Waffenfabrik on top of slide
Estimated Value: Excellent: $180.00
Very good: $140.00

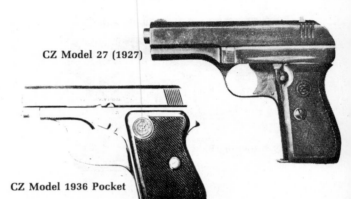

CZ Model 27 (1927)

CZ Model 1936 Pocket

CZ Model 38 (1938)

CZ Model 1945 Pocket

CZ Model 50 (1950)

CZ "Duo" Pocket

CZ Model 70

Caliber: 7.65mm (32)
Action: Semi-automatic; exposed hammer; double action
Magazine: 8-shot clip
Barrel: 3¹/₈″
Sights: Fixed
Finish: Blued; checkered plastic grips
Length Overall: 6½″
Approximate wt.: 25 oz.
Comments: Currently produced in Czechoslovakia. Not readily available in the U.S. due to importation prohibitions on some items produced in Iron Curtain countries.
Estimated Value: Excellent: $185.00
 Very good: $145.00

CZ Model 75

Caliber: 9mm Parabellum
Action: Semi-automatic; selective double action; exposed hammer
Magazine: 15-shot clip
Barrel: 4½″
Sights: Fixed
Finish: Blued; checkered plastic grips
Length Overall: 8″
Approximate wt.: 35 oz.
Comments: Currently produced in Czechoslovakia. Not readily available in the U.S. due to importation prohibitions on some items produced in Iron Curtain countries.
Estimated Value: Excellent: $225.00
 Very good: $180.00

Charter Arms

Charter Arms Model 79K

Charter Arms Model 79K

Caliber: 380 Auto, 32 Auto
Action: Semi-automatic, double action; exposed hammer
Magazine: 7-shot clip
Barrel: 3½″
Sights: Adjustable
Finish: Stainless steel, checkered walnut grips
Length Overall: 6½″
Approximate wt.: 24½ oz.
Comments: Introduced in 1985.
Estimated Value: New (retail): $390.00
 Excellent: $295.00
 Very good: $220.00

Charter Arms Model 40

Similar to the Model 79K in 22 long rifle caliber; 8-shot clip; weighs 21½ oz.
Estimated Value: New (retail): $319.00
 Excellent: $240.00
 Very good: $180.00

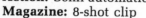

Charter Arms Explorer II

Charter Arms Explorer II

Caliber: 22 long rifle
Action: Semi-automatic
Magazine: 8-shot clip
Barrel: 6″ or 10″ interchangeable
Sights: Blade front, adjustable rear
Finish: Black, semi-gloss textured enamel; simulated walnut grips; extra clip storage in grip; also available in silvertone
Length Overall: 13½″ with 6″ barrel
Approximate wt.: 27 oz.
Comments: A survival pistol styled from the AR-7 rifle; introduced in the late 1970's.
Estimated Value: New (retail): $109.00
 Excellent: $ 80.00
 Very good: $ 65.00

Charter Arms Police Bulldog

Charter Arms Bulldog

Charter Arms Police Bulldog

Caliber: 38 Special, 32 H&R Mag.
Action: Single and double action
Cylinder: 6-shot swing-out
Barrel: 2″ or 4″ tapered or bull barrel
Sights: Fixed
Finish: Blued or stainless steel; checkered walnut bulldog grips, square butt grips or Neoprene grips
Length Overall: 8½″
Approximate wt.: 21 oz.
Comments: Production began in 1976. Add 25% for stainless steel.
Estimated Value: New (retail): $208.00
 Excellent: $155.00
 Very good: $115.00

Charter Arms Bulldog

Caliber: 44 Special, 357 magnum (discontinued in 1980's)
Action: Single and double action
Cylinder: 5-shot swing-out
Barrel: 2½″, 3″, 4″, 6″. 4″ & 6″ discontinued in 1985
Sights: Fixed
Finish: Blued; oil finished, checkered walnut bulldog grips or Neoprene grips; stainless steel added 1982
Length Overall: 7½″ (3″ barrel)
Approximate wt.: 19 oz.
Comments: Made from 1971 to present. Add 30% for stainless steel.
Estimated Value: New (retail): $211.00
 Excellent: $155.00
 Very good: $115.00

Charter Arms Target Bulldog

Similar to the Bulldog with a 4" barrel; shrouded ejector rod; adjustable rear sight. Introduced in the late 1970's. Add 5% for 44 Special.

Estimated Value: New (retail): **$232.00**
Excellent: **$175.00**
Very good: **$130.00**

Charter Arms Bulldog Pug

Similar to the Bulldog with a 2½" shrouded barrel. Introduced in 1986.

Estimated Value: New (retail): **$234.00**
Excellent: **$175.00**
Very good: **$130.00**

Charter Arms Target Bulldog

Charter Arms Bulldog Pug

Charter Arms Undercover

Charter Arms Undercover

Caliber: 38 Special
Action: Single or double action
Cylinder: 5-shot swing-out
Barrel: 2" or 3"
Sights: Fixed
Finish: Blued or nickel; oil finished, plain or hand checkered walnut grips or Neoprene grips; stainless steel available after 1982
Length Overall: 6¼" or 7³/₈"
Approximate wt.: 16 or 17 oz.
Comments: Made from 1965 to present. Add 5% for nickel (discontinued early 1980's); 25% for stainless steel.

Estimated Value: New (retail): **$195.00**
Excellent: **$145.00**
Very good: **$110.00**

Charter Arms Undercoverette

Caliber: 32 S&W long
Action: Single or double action
Cylinder: 6-shot, swing-out
Barrel: 2"
Sights: Fixed
Finish: Blued; oil finished, plain walnut grips
Length Overall: 6¼"
Approximate wt.: 16½ oz.
Comments: Made from 1970 to present. Also called Undercover.

Estimated Value: New (retail): **$195.00**
Excellent: **$145.00**
Very good: **$105.00**

Charter Arms Bulldog Tracker

Charter Arms Undercoverette

Charter Arms Bulldog Tracker

Caliber: 357 magnum
Action: Single and double action
Cylinder: 5-shot swing-out
Barrel: 2½", 4", or 6" bull barrel
Sights: Adjustable rear, ramp front
Finish: Blued; checkered walnut square bull grips
Length Overall: 11"
Approximate wt.: 27½ oz.
Comments: Introduced in 1980.

Estimated Value: New (retail): **$214.00**
Excellent: **$160.00**
Very good: **$120.00**

Charter Arms Pathfinder

Charter Arms Pathfinder

Caliber: 22 long rifle, 22 magnum
Action: Single or double action
Cylinder: 6-shot, swing-out
Barrel: 2", 3" or 6"
Sights: Adjustable rear and partridge-type front on serrated ramp
Finish: Blued; oil finished, plain or hand checkered walnut bulldog grips; stainless steel after 1982
Length Overall: 7¹/₈" (3" barrel)
Approximate wt.: 19 oz.
Comments: Made from 1970 to present. Add 25% for stainless steel; 20% for 6" barrel.

Estimated Value: New (retail): **$204.00**
Excellent: **$150.00**
Very good: **$115.00**

Charter Arms Pocket Target

Charter Arms Pocket Target
Caliber: 22 short, long, long rifle
Action: Single and double action, exposed hammer
Cylinder: 6-shot swing-out
Barrel: 3″
Sights: Adjustable snag-free rear, ramp front
Finish: Blued; plain grips or checkered walnut bulldog
  grips
Length Overall: 7 1/8″
Approximate wt.: 19 oz.
Comments: Made from the 1960's to 1970's.
Estimated Value: **Excellent:** $140.00
  Very good: $110.00

Charter Arms
Police Undercover

Charter Arms Off Duty

Charter Arms Off Duty
Caliber: 38 Special
Action: Single and double
Cylinder: 5-shot swing out, fluted
Barrel: 2″
Sights: Fixed
Finish: Flat black or stainless steel; smooth or checkered walnut or Neoprene grips
Length Overall: 6½″
Approximate wt.: 16 oz.
Comments: Introduced in 1984. Add 30% for stainless steel.
Estimated Value: **New (retail):** $164.00
  Excellent: $125.00
  Very good: $ 90.00

Charter Arms Police Undercover
Caliber: 32 H&R magnum, 38 Special
Action: Single or double, pocket (bobbed) hammer available
Cylinder: 6-shot swing out, fluted
Barrel: 2″ or 4″
Sights: Fixed
Finish: Blued or stainless steel; checkered walnut grips
Length Overall: 6¼″
Approximate wt.: 17½-20 oz.
Comments: Introduced in the 1980's. Add 25% for stainless steel.
Estimated Value: **New (retail):** $198.00
  Excellent: $150.00
  Very good: $110.00

Colt

Colt Model 1900
Caliber: 38 ACP
Action: Semi-automatic; exposed spur hammer
Magazine: 7-shot clip
Barrel: 6″
Sights: Fixed
Finish: Blued; plain walnut grips
Length Overall: 9″
Approximate wt.: 35 oz.
Comments: Combination safety and rear sight. Rear sight is pressed down to block hammer from firing pin. One of the first automatic pistols made in the U.S. and first automatic pistol made by Colt. Made from 1900 to 1902. No slide lock.
Estimated Value: **Excellent:** $650.00 - $1,400.00
  Very good: $490.00 - $1,000.00

Colt Model 1900

Colt Model L (1902) Military

Colt Model L (1903) Pocket

Colt Model L (1902)
Similar to Colt Model 1900 except: no safety; round hammer; hard rubber grips. Made from 1902 to 1907.
Estimated Value: **Excellent:** $650.00
  Very good: $490.00

Colt Model L (1902) Military
Same as Colt Model L (1902) except: longer grips (more square at bottom) with lanyard ring; 8-shot magazine; weigh of 37 oz. Made from 1902 to 1928. Spur-type hammer used after 1907.
Estimated Value: **Excellent:** $500.00 - $1,250.00
  Very good: $375.00 - $ 950.00

Colt Model L (1903) Pocket
Caliber: 38 ACP
Action: Semi-automatic; exposed hammer
Magazine: 7-shot clip
Barrel: 4½″
Sights: Fixed
Finish: Blued; checkered hard rubber grips
Length Overall: 7½″
Approximate wt.: 31 oz.
Comments: Made from 1903 to 1927. Round type hammer to 1908, then changed to spur type hammer; no slide lock or safety.
Estimated Value: **Excellent:** $350.00
  Very good: $275.00

Colt Model M (32) 1st Issue Pocket

Colt Model M (32) 2nd Issue Pocket

Colt Model M (32) 3rd Issue Pocket

Colt Model M (32) 3rd Issue Pocket

Similar to 2nd Issue Model M (32) except: safety disconnector, which prevents cartridge in chamber from being fired if magazine is removed. Made from 1926 to 1941.

Estimated Value: Excellent: $275.00
Very good: $210.00

Colt Model M (380) 1st Issue Pocket

Caliber: 380 ACP (9mm short)
Action: Semi-automatic
Magazine: 7-shot clip
Barrel: 3¾″
Sights: Fixed
Finish: Blued or nickel; hard rubber or checkered walnut grips
Length Overall: 6¾″
Approximate wt.: 24 oz.
Comments: Made from 1908 to 1911. Slide lock safety and grip safety. Barrel lock bushing at muzzle.
Estimated Value: Excellent: $325.00
Very good: $245.00

Colt Model M (380) 2nd Issue Pocket

Similar to 1st Issue Model M (380) except: without barrel lock bushing and other minor changes. Made from 1911 to 1926. Add $200.00 for Military Model.
Estimated Value: Excellent: $300.00
Very good: $250.00

Colt Model M (380)
1st Issue Pocket

Colt Model M (380)
2nd Issue Pocket

Colt Model M (32) 1st Issue Pocket

Caliber: 32 ACP (7.65mm)
Action: Semi-automatic; concealed hammer
Magazine: 8-shot clip
Barrel: 3¾″
Sights: Fixed
Finish: Blued or nickel; hard rubber or checkered walnut grips
Length Overall: 6¾″
Approximate wt.: 25 oz.
Comments: Made from 1903 to 1911. Slide lock safety and grip safety. Barrel lock bushing at muzzle.
Estimated Value: Excellent: $325.00
Very good: $245.00

Colt Model M (32) 2nd Issue Pocket

Similar to 1st issue Model M (32) except: without barrel lock bushing and other minor modifications. Made from 1911 to 1926. Add $200.00 for Military Model.
Estimated Value: Excellent: $280.00
Very good: $215.00

Colt Model 1905 Military

Colt Model M (380) 3rd Issue Pocket

Similar to 2nd Issue Model M (380) except: it has safety disconnector, which precents cartridge in chamber from being fired if magazine is removed. Made from 1926 to 1941.
Estimated Value: Excellent: $290.00
Very good: $225.00

Colt Model 1905 Military

Caliber: 45 ACP
Action: Semi-automatic
Magazine: 7-shot clip
Barrel: 5″
Sights: Fixed
Finish: Blued; checkered walnut grips
Length Overall: 8½″
Approximate wt.: 34 oz.
Comments: Made from 1905 to 1912. Similar to Model 1902 38 caliber automatic pistol. First 45 caliber military automatic pistol made by Colt. Slide stop but no safety except some experimental models with short grip safety. Round hammer 1905 to 1908; after 1908 spur type hammer. Approximately 5,000 produced. Some were fitted and equipped with a short-stock holster. These are scarce collectors items and valued much higher.
Estimated Value: Excellent: $1,000.00
Very good: $ 800.00

Colt Model N Pocket

Caliber: 25 ACP
Action: Semi-automatic; concealed striker instead of hammer
Magazine: 6-shot clip
Barrel: 2″
Sights: Fixed
Finish: Blued or nickel; hard rubber or checkered walnut grips
Length Overall: 4½″
Approximate wt.: 14 oz.
Comments: Made 1908 to 1941. Magazine safety disconnector added in 1916 (about serial number 141,000). All models have thumb safety and grip safety. Add $200.00 for Military Model; $50.00 for nickel finish.
Estimated Value: Excellent: $280.00
                    Very good: $220.00

Colt Model N Pocket

Colt Junior Pocket Model 0-6

Colt Government Model 1911 A1

Same as Government Model 1911 except: the grip safety tang was lengthened (to stop the hammer bite on fleshy hands); the trigger was shortened (to allow stubby fingers better control); the back strap below the grip safety weas arched (for better instinctive pointing); and the sights were made larger and squared (to improve sight picture). Also the grips were made of checkered walnut or plastic. The 1911 A1 was made from 1925 to present. Changed started about serial number 650000 in military model. Also check prices for other manufacturer's and commercial models.
Estimated Value: Excellent: $350.00
                        Very good: $275.00

Colt Commerical Model 1911

Same as Government Model 1911 except: not marked with military markings. The letter "C" is used in serial numbers. Blued or nickel finish. Made from 1911 to 1926 then changed to 1911 A1 about serial number C130000.
Estimated Value: Excellent: $380.00
                        Very good: $290.00

Colt Commecial Model 1911 A1

Same as Commercial Model 1911 except it has same modifications as the Government Model 1911 A1. Made from 1925 to 1970.
Estimated Value: Excellent: $350.00
                        Very good: $275.00

Colt Junior Pocket Model 0-6

Caliber: 22 short, 25 ACP
Action: Semi-automatic; exposed round spur hammer
Magazine: 6-shot clip
Barrel: 2¹/₈″
Sights: Fixed
Finish: Blued; checkered walnut grips
Length Overall: 4½″
Approximate wt.: 13 to 14 oz.
Comments: Made in Spain by Astra (Uneta Y Compania, Guernice, Spain) for Colt as a replacement for the Model N which was discontinued in 1941. Imported from about 1957 to 1973. Colt advertised in 1984 that many of these guns made between 1957 and 1973 were unsafe due to the firing mechanism. Colt offered to modify the pistol free and advised owners of non-modified pistols to carry the pistol with an empty chamber.
Estimated Value: Excellent: $185.00
                        Very good: $140.00

Colt Government Model 1911

Caliber: 45 ACP
Action: Semi-automatic; exposed spur hammer
Magazine: 7-shot clip
Barrel: 5″
Sights: Fixed
Finish: Blued, nickel and parkerized or similar finish, checkered walnut grips
Length Overall: 8½″
Approximate wt.: 39 oz.
Comments: Slide lock, thumb safety and grip safety. Adopted as a military side arm in 1911 in U.S. Made from 1911 to present with some modifications. Changed to Model 1911 A1 in 1925. Military models are marked "U.S. Army," "U.S. Navy," or "U.S. Marines" and "United States Property." Colt licensed other firms to produce this pistol during both World Wars. Check prices under manufacturer's name. Also check commercial model prices.
Estimated Value: Excellent: $450.00
                        Very good: $350.00

Colt Government Model 1911

Colt Government Model 1911A1

Colt 1911 (North American Arms Co.)

Same general specifications as 1911 Colt except made by North American Arms Co., in World War I period. About 100 made; company markings and serial number on slide.

Estimated Value: Excellent: $5,000.00
Very good: $4,000.00

Colt 1911 (by Remington UMC)

Colt Super 38

Same as Colt Commercial Model 1911 A1 except: caliber is 38 Super ACP; magazine is 9-shot clip. Made from about 1928 to 1970.

Estimated Value: Excellent: $360.00
Very good: $275.00

Colt Super 38 Match

Same as Colt Super except: adjustable rear sight; hand honed action; match grade barrel. Made from about 1932 to 1940.

Estimated Value: Excellent: $500.00
Very good: $380.00

Colt National Match

Same as Colt Commercial Model 1911 A1 except: adjustable rear sight; hand honed action; match grade barrel. Made from 1932 to 1940.

Estimated Value: Excellent: $625.00
Very good: $470.00

Colt Service Model Ace

Similar to Colt National Match except: 22 caliber long rifle; 10-shot clip; weighs about 42 oz. It has a "floating chamber" that makes the recoil much greater than normal 22 caliber. Made from 1938 to mid 1940's. See Colt Ace (current).

Estimated Value: Excellent: $800.00
Very good: $600.00

Colt 1911 Springfield Armory N.R.A.

Same general specifications as 1911 Colt except: approximately 200 were made prior to World War I and sold through the Director of Civilian Marksmanship and have N.R.A. markings on frame.

Estimated Value: Excellent: $2,200.00
Very good: $1,800.00

Colt 1911 (Springfield Armory)

Same general specifications as 1911 Colt except approximately 26,000 produced. Eagle motif and flaming bomb on frame and slide. Made in World War I period.

Estimated Value: Excellent: $650.00
Very good: $500.00

Colt 1911 (Remington UMC)

Same genereal specifications as 1911 Colt except approximately 22,000 produced in World War I period. Inspector stamps B or E.

Estimated Value: Excellent: $600.00
Very good: $450.00

Colt 1911 A1 (Singer Manufacturing Co.)

Same general specifications as 1911 A1 Colt except: approximately 500 made; blued finish, slide marked S.M. Co.; JKC inspector marking.

Estimated Value: Excellent: $3,200.00
Very good: $2,600.00

COLT 1911 A1 pistols were also produced during WWII by Union Switch & Signal Company, Remington Rand, Inc., and Ithaca Gun Company, Inc. Generally the estimated values of these pistols are about the same as the 1911 A1 pistol produced by Colt.

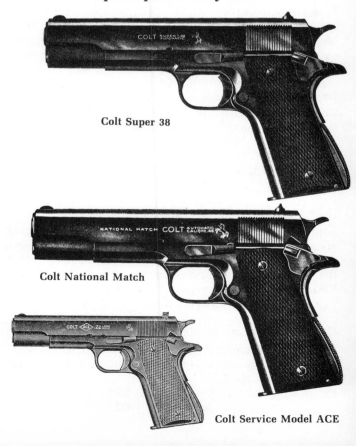

Colt Super 38

Colt National Match

Colt Service Model ACE

Colt Gold Cup National Match

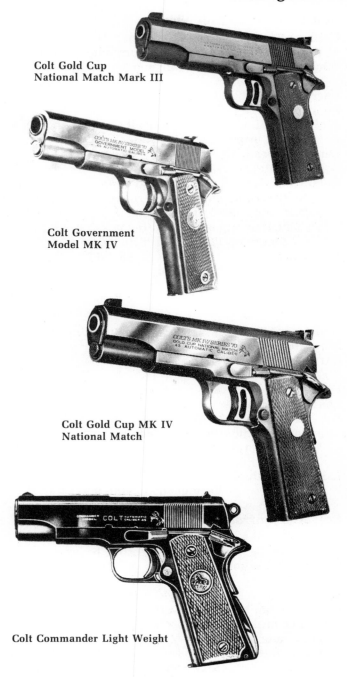

Colt Gold Cup
National Match Mark III

Colt Government
Model MK IV

Colt Gold Cup MK IV
National Match

Colt Commander Light Weight

Colt Gold Cup National Match

Same as the Colt Commercial Model 1911 A1 except: hand fitted slide; enlarged ejection port; adjustable rear sight; adjustable trigger stop; new bushing design; checkered walnut grips; match grade barrel; flat grip below safety like model 1911. Made from about 1957 to 1970.

Estimated Value: Excellent: $450.00
                      Very good: $340.00

Colt Gold Cup National Match Mark III

Similar to Colt Gold Cup National Match except chambered for 38 Special mid-range wad cutter only. Operates with fixed barrel rather than locked breech. Made from 1960 to 1974.

Estimated Value: Excellent: $425.00
                      Very good: $320.00

Colt Government Model MK IV / Series 70

Caliber: 9mm Parabellum, 38 Super APC, 45 APC
Action: Semi-automatic; exposed spur hammer
Magazine: 9-shot clip in 9mm and 38; 7-shot clip in 45
Barrel: 5″
Sights: Fixed
Finish: Blued or nickel; smooth or checkered walnut grips
Length Overall: 8½″
Approximate wt.: 38 to 39 oz.
Comments: Made from about 1970 to mid 1980's. Add $15.00 for 38 Super; $5.00 for 9mm; $25.00 for nickel finish.

Estimated Value: Excellent: $350.00
                      Very good: $275.00

Colt Gold Cup MK IV National Match (Series 70)

Caliber: 38 Special Mid-Range, 45 ACP
Action: Semi-automatic; exposed spur hammer
Magazine: 9-shot clip in 38, 7-shot clip in 45
Barrel: 5″
Sights: Adjustable rear for wind and elevation
Finish: Blued; checkered walnut grips with gold medallion
Length Overall: 8¾″
Approximate wt.: 39 oz.
Comments: Arched or flat housing below grip safety. Adjustable trigger stop, hand fitted slide, and improved barrel bushing. Made from about 1970 to mid 1980's.

Estimated Value: Excellent: $400.00
                      Very good: $300.00

Colt NRA Centennial Gold Cup National Match

Similar to Colt Gold Cup MK IV except: 45 caliber only; inscribed Commemorative Model, 2500 made in 1971. Original price was $250.00 each. Price includes case.
Estimated Value: Mint: $625.00

Colt Commander Light Weight

Caliber: 45 ACP
Action: Semi-automatic; exposed round spur hammer
Magazine: 7-shot clip
Barrel: 4¼″
Sights: Fixed
Finish: Blued; checkered or smooth walnut grips
Length Overall: 7¾″
Approximate wt.: 27 oz.
Comments: Same design as Gov. 1911 A1 model except: shorter and lighter; rounded hammer. Aluminum alloy receiver and frame. Made from 1949 to mid 1980's. An all-steel model was introduced in 1971 known as Combat Commander.

Estimated Value: Excellent: $335.00
                      Very good: $250.00

Colt Combat Commander

Caliber: 9mm Parabellum, 38 Super ACP, 45 ACP
Action: Semi-automatic; exposed round hammer
Magazine: 9-shot clip in 9mm and 38 Super; 7-shot clip in 45 ACP
Barrel: 4¼″
Sights: Fixed
Finish: Blued or nickel (in 45 caliber only); checkered walnut grips
Length Overall: 7⅞″
Approximate wt.: 37 oz.
Comments: Same design as the Government 1911 A1 except: shorter and lighter; round hammer; made from about 1971 to mid-1980's with all steel frame and flat or arched mainspring housing. Add $5.00 for 9mm; $20.00 for nickel finish.
Estimated Value: Excellent: $350.00
Very good: $260.00

Colt Ace Target

Caliber: 22 long rifle
Action: Semi-automatic; exposed spur hammer
Magazine: 10-shot clip
Barrel: 4¾″
Sights: Adjustable rear sight
Finish: Blued; checkered walnut or plastic grips
Length Overall: 8¼″
Approximate wt.: 38 oz.
Comments: Similar in appearance to the 1911 A1 with same safety features. Made from about 1931 to 1941.
Estimated Value: Excellent: $650.00
Very good: $480.00

Colt Ace (current)

Caliber: 22 long rifle
Action: Semi-automatic; exposed spur hammer
Magazine: 10-shot clip
Barrel: 5″
Sights: Fixed rear, ramp style front
Finish: Blued; checkered walnut grips
Length Overall: 8⅜″
Approximate wt.: 42 oz.
Comments: A full-size automatic similar to the Colt Government MK IV/Series in 22 long rifle. Produced from 1979 to mid 1980's. Also see Colt Service Model Ace.
Estimated Value: Excellent: $370.00
Very good: $275.00

Colt Combat Commander

Colt Ace Target

Colt MK IV Series 80 Officer's ACP

Colt MK IV Series 80 Officer's ACP

Caliber: 45 ACP
Action: Semi-automatic: exposed round spur hammer
Magazine: 6-shot clip
Barrel: 3½″
Sights: Fixed with dovetail rear
Finish: Non-glare matte blue or stainless steel (1986); checkered wood grips
Length Overall: 7¼″
Approximate wt.: 24 oz. (lightweight); 34 oz. (steel)
Comments: A compact 45 ACP pistol about 1¼″ shorter than the regular Colt Government models. Available in lightweight aluminum alloy or steel models. Add 2% for lightweight and 10% stainless steel.
Estimated Value: New (retail): $516.50
Excellent: $390.00
Very good: $290.00

Colt Government Model MK IV/Series 80

Similar to the MK IV Series 70 with internal improvements. Introduced in 1983. Add $30.00 for nickel finish; $10.00 for 9mm and 38 Super calibers. Add 12% for stainless steel.
Estimated Value: New (retail): $526.50
Excellent: $395.00
Very good: $295.00

Colt Combat Commander Series 80

Similar to the Combat Commander with internal improvements; introduced in 1983. Add $22.00 for nickel finish; $5.00 for 9mm and 38 Super calibers.
Estimated Value: New (retail): $526.50
Excellent: $395.00
Very good: $295.00

Colt Gold Cup National Match MK IV/Series 80

Similar to the Gold Cup MK IV National Match (Series 70) with internal improvements. Introduced in 1983; 45 caliber only; stainless steel model introduced in 1985; Add 12% for stainless steel.
Estimated Value: New (retail): $687.50
Excellent: $515.00
Very good: $385.00

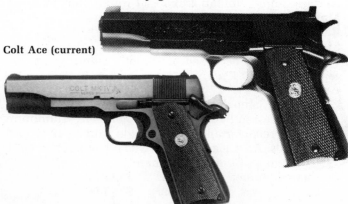

Colt Ace (current)

Colt Government Model MK IV/Series 80

Colt Commander Light Weight Series 80

Colt Combat Government Model/80

Colt 380 Government Model

Colt Commander Light Weight Series 80

Similar to the Light Weight Commander with internal improvements. Introduced in 1983.

Estimated Value: New (retail): $526.50
Excellent: $395.00
Very good: $295.00

Colt Combat Government Model/80

Similar to the Government MK IV/Series 80 with undercut front sight, outline rear sight, Colt Pachmayr grips and other slight variations. Introduced in 1984.

Estimated Value: New (retail): $632.50
Excellent: $475.00
Very good: $355.00

Colt 380 Government Model

A "scaled down" version of the Colt Government Model MKIV Series 80 in 380 ACP caliber; with round spur hammer; 3¼″ barrel, weighs 21¾ oz., overall length 6-¹/₈″. Introduced in 1984. Add 9% for nickel finish.

Estimated Value: New (retail): $340.50
Excellent: $255.00
Very good: $190.00

Colt MK IV Series 80 Mustang 380

Caliber: 380 ACP
Action: Semi-automatic: exposed round spur hammer
Magazine: 5-shot clip
Barrel: 2¾″
Sights: Fixed; with dovetail rear
Finish: Blued; composition grips
Length Overall: 5½″
Approximate wt.: 18½ oz.
Comments: A small, compact pistol introduced in 1986.

Estimated Value: New (retail): $340.00
Excellent: $255.00
Very good: $190.00

Colt Woodsman Sport Model (1st Issue)

Caliber: 22 long rifle
Action: Semi-automatic; concealed hammer
Magazine: 10-shot clip
Barrel: 4½″ tapered barrel
Sights: Adjustable
Finish: Blued; checkered walnut grips
Length Overall: 8½″
Approximate wt.: 27 oz.
Comments: Same as Colt Woodsman Target Model (2nd Issue) except shorter. Made from about 1933 to late 1940's.

Estimated Value: Excellent: $350.00
Very good: $265.00

Colt MK IV Series 80 Mustang 380

Colt Woodman Sport Model (1st Issue)

Colt Woodsman Target Model

Colt Woodsman Target Model

(2nd Issue)

Colt Woodsman Target Model (1st Issue)

Caliber: 22 long rifle (regular velocity)
Action: Semi-automatic; concealed hammer
Magazine: 10-shot clip
Barrel: 6½″
Sights: Adjustable
Finish: Blued; checkered walnut grips
Length Overall: 10½″
Approximate wt.: 28 oz.
Comments: This model was not strong enough for Hi-speed cartridges, until a strong heat treated housing was produced about serial number 83790. Thumb safety only. Made from about 1915 to 1932.

Estimated Value: Excellent: $340.00
Very good: $260.00

Colt Woodsman Target Model (2nd Issue)

Same as Colt Woodsman Target Model 1st Issue except: heavier tapered barrel and stronger housing for using either the 22 long rifle regular or Hi-speed cartridges. Made from about 1932 to 1945. Approximate wt. 29 oz.

Estimated Value: Excellent: $360.00
Very good: $270.00

Colt Woodsman Target Model S-2 (3rd Issue)

Similar to Colt Woodsman Target Model (2nd Issue) except: longer grips with thumb rest, larger thumb safety; slide stop; magazine disconnector; slide stays open when magazine is empty; checkered walnut or plastic grips. Approximate wt. 32 oz. Made from 1948 to late 1970's.
Estimated Value: Excellent: $260.00
                     Very good: $200.00

Colt Woodsman Sport Model S-1 (2nd Issue)

Same as Colt Woodsman Target Model S-2 (3rd Issue) except: 4½" barrel, 9" overall length; approximate wt. 30 oz. Made from about 1948 to late 1970's.
Estimated Value: Excellent: $235.00
                     Very good: $175.00

Colt Model S-4 Targetsman

Similar to Colt Woodsman Target Model (3rd Issue) except: cheaper made adjustable rear sight and lacks automatic slide stop. Made from about 1959 to late 1970's.
Estimated Value: Excellent: $225.00
                     Very good: $170.00

Colt Woodsman Target Model

Colt Woodsman Sports Model S-1 (2nd Issue)

Colt Model S-4 Targetsman

Colt Woodsman Match Target (1st Issue)

Colt Woodsman Match Target (1st Issue)

Caliber: 22 long rifle
Action: Semi-automatic; concealed hammer
Magazine: 10-shot clip
Barrel: 6½"; slightly tapered with flat sides
Sights: Adjustable rear
Finish: Blued; checkered walnut, one-piece grip with extended sides
Length Overall: 11"
Approximate wt.: 36 oz.
Comments: Made from about 1938 to 1942.
Estimated Value: Excellent: $600.00
                     Very good: $475.00

Colt Woodsman Match Target Model S-3

Caliber: 22 long rifle
Action: Semi-automatic; concealed hammer
Magazine: 10-shot clip
Barrel: 4½", 6"
Sights: Adjustable rear
Finish: Blued; checkered walnut grips with thumb rest
Length Overall: 9", 10½"
Approximate wt.: 36 to 39 oz.
Comments: Made from about 1948 to late 1970's. Flat sided weight added to full length of barrel. It has a slide stop and magazine safety.
Estimated Value: Excellent: $300.00
                     Very good: $225.00

Colt Woodsman Match Target Model S-3

Colt Challenger Model

Caliber: 22 long rifle
Action: Semi-automatic; concealed hammer
Magazine: 10-shot clip
Barrel: 4½″, 6″
Sights: Fixed
Finish: Blued; checkered plastic grips
Length Overall: 9″, 10½″
Approximate wt.: 30 to 32 oz. (depending on length)
Comments: Same basic design as Colt Woodsman Target
Model (3rd Issue) except: slide doesn't stay open
when magazine is empty; no magazine safety.
Made from about 1950 to 1955.
Estimated Value: **Excellent:** **$230.00**
Very good: **$175.00**

Colt Huntsman Model S-5

Caliber: 22 long rifle
Action: Semi-automatic; concealed hammer
Magazine: 10-shot clip
Barrel: 4½″, 6″
Sights: Fixed
Finish: Blued; checkered walnut grips
Length Overall: 9″, 10½″
Approximate wt.: 31 to 32 oz.
Comments: Made from about 1955 to 1970's.
Estimated Value: **Excellent:** **$235.00**
Very good: **$180.00**

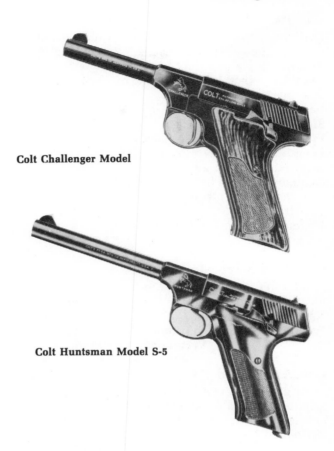

Colt Challenger Model

Colt Huntsman Model S-5

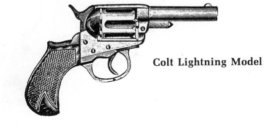

Colt Lightning Model

Colt Double Action Army Model

Colt Lightning Model

Caliber: 38 centerfire, 41 centerfire
Action: Single and double action
Cylinder: 6-shot; ⅔ fluted; side load; loading gate
Barrel: 2½″, 3½″, 4½″, 6″
Sights: Fixed
Finish: Blued or nickel; hard rubber birds-head grips
Length Overall: 7½″ to 11″
Approximate wt.: 26 to 30 oz.
Comments: Made from 1877 to 1912 with and without
side rod ejector. This was the first double action
revolver made by Colt.
Estimated Value: **Excellent:** **$475.00**
Very good: **$375.00**

Colt Double Action Army Model

Caliber: 38-40, 44-40, 45 Colt
Action: Single or double action
Cylinder: 6-shot; ⅔ fluted; side load
Barrel: 3½″ and 4″ without side rod ejector; 4¾″, 5½″
and 7½″ with the side rod ejector
Sights: Fixed
Finish: Blued or nickel; hard rubber or checkered walnut
grips
Length Overall: 8½″ to 12½″
Approximate wt.: 35 to 39 oz.
Comments: Made from 1877 to 1910. Lanyard loop in
butt; also called "Double Action Frontier." Similar
to Lightning Model except larger.
Estimated Value: **Excellent:** **$600.00**
Very good: **$460.00**

Colt Double Action Philippine Model

Same as Colt Double Action Army Model except: larger
trigger guard and trigger. It was made originally for the
Army in Alaska but was sent to the Philippines instead.
Estimated Value: **Excellent:** **$625.00**
Very good: **$475.00**

Colt New Army Model 1892

Caliber: 38 Colt short and long, 41 Colt short and long, 38 Special added in 1904, 32-20 added in 1905
Action: Single and double action
Cylinder: 6-shot; ⅔ fluted; swing out; simultaneous hand ejector
Barrel: 3″, 4½″, 6″
Sights: Fixed
Finish: Blued or nickel; hard rubber or walnut grips
Length Overall: 8¼″ to 11¼″
Approximate wt.: 29 to 32 oz.
Comments: Made from 1892 to 1908. Lanyard swivel attached to butt in 1901. All calibers on 41 caliber frame.
Estimated Value: Excellent: $300.00
Very good: $240.00

Colt New Navy Model 1892

Similar to Colt New Army Model 1892 except: has double cylinder notches and locking bolt. Sometimes called New Army 2nd issue.
Estimated Value: Excellent: $325.00
Very good: $245.00

Colt Army Model 1903

Same as Colt New Army Model 1892 except: modified grip design (smaller and shaped better); bore is slightly smaller in each caliber to increase accuracy.
Estimated Value: Excellent: $250.00
Very good: $190.00

Colt New Pocket

Caliber: 32 short and long Colt
Action: Single and double action
Cylinder: 6-shot; swing out; simultaneous ejector
Barrel: 2½″, 3½″, 6″
Sights: Fixed
Finish: Blued or nickel; hard rubber grips
Length Overall: 6½″ to 10½″
Approximate wt.: 15 to 18 oz.
Comments: Made from about 1895 to 1905.
Estimated Value: Excellent: $290.00
Very good: $220.00

Colt Pocket Positive

Similar to the New Pocket with the positive locking system of the Police Positive; 32 short and long S&W cartridges or 32 Colt Police Positive. Made from the early 1900's to just prior to World War II.
Estimated Value: Excellent: $250.00
Very good: $190.00

Colt Pocket Positive

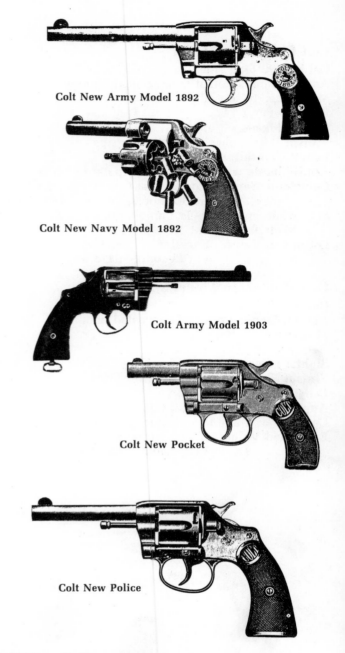

Colt New Army Model 1892

Colt New Navy Model 1892

Colt Army Model 1903

Colt New Pocket

Colt New Police

Colt New Police

Caliber: 32 Colt short and long, 32 Colt New Police (S&W long)
Action: Single or double action
Cylinder: 6-shot; swing out; simultaneous ejector
Barrel: 2½″, 4″, 6″
Sights: Fixed
Finish: Blued or nickel; hard rubber grips
Length Overall: 6½″ to 10″
Approximate wt.: 16 to 18 oz.
Comments: Built on same frame as New Pocket except larger grips. Made from about 1896 to 1905.
Estimated Value: Excellent: $300.00
Very good: $240.00

Colt New Police Target

Same as Colt New Police except: 6″ barrel only; blued finish and target sights. This is a target version of the New Police Model, made from 1896 to 1905.
Estimated Value: Excellent: $350.00
Very good: $270.00

Colt Bisley Flat-Top Model

Colt Bisley Model

Colt New Service

Caliber: 38 special, 357 magnum (introduced about 1936), 38-40, 44-40, 44 Russian, 44 Special, 45 ACP, 45 Colt, 450 Eley, 455 Eley and 476 Eley
Action: Single or double action
Cylinder: 6-shot; swing out; simultaneous ejector
Barrel: 4″, 5″, 6″ in 357 and 38 Special; 4½″, 5½″, 7½″ in other calibers; 4½″ in 45 ACP (Model 1917 Revolver made for U.S. government during World War II)
Sights: Fixed
Finish: Blued or nickel; checkered walnut grips
Length Overall: 9¼″ to 12¾″
Approximate wt.: 39 to 44 oz.
Comments: Made from about 1898 to 1942. The above calibers were made sometime during this period.
Estimated Value: Excellent: $400.00
                          Very good: $300.00

Colt New Service Target

Caliber: Originally made for 44 Russian, 450 Eley, 455 Eley and 476 Eley. Later calibers were made for 44 Special, 45 Colt and 45 ACP
Action: Single or double action
Cylinder: 6-shot; swing out; simultaneous ejector
Barrel: 6″ and 7″
Sights: Adjustable target sights
Finish: Blued; checkered walnut grips
Length Overall: 11¼″ and 12¾″
Approximate wt.: 40 to 42 oz.
Comments: A target version of the New Service revolver with hand finished action. Made from about 1900 to 1939.
Estimated Value: Excellent: $600.00
                          Very good: $490.00

Colt Bisley Model

Caliber: 32 long centerfire, 32-20 WCF, 38 long Colt CF, 38-40 WCF, 41 long Colt CF, 44 S&W Russian, 44-40 WCF, 45 Colt, 455 Eley
Action: Single action
Cylinder: 6-shot; half flute; side load
Barrel: 4¾″, 5½″, 7½″ with side rod ejector
Sights: Fixed
Finish: Blued with case hardened frame and hammer; checkered hard rubber grips
Length Overall: 10¼″ to 13″
Approximate wt.: 36 to 40 oz.
Comments: Developed from the original Single Action Army Revolver by changing the trigger, hammer and grips. Made from 1897 to 1912.
Estimated Value: Excellent: $550.00
                          Very good: $420.00

Colt Bisley Flat-Top Model

Similar to Colt Bisley Model except: frame over the cylinder has a flat top; the longer barrel models were referred to as target models; wood and ivory grips as well as hard rubber; target adjustable sights or regular fixed sights. Short barrel models sometimes referred to as the Pocket Bisley. It usually had fixed sights and no side rod ejector.
Estimated Value: Excellent: $950.00
                          Very good: $700.00

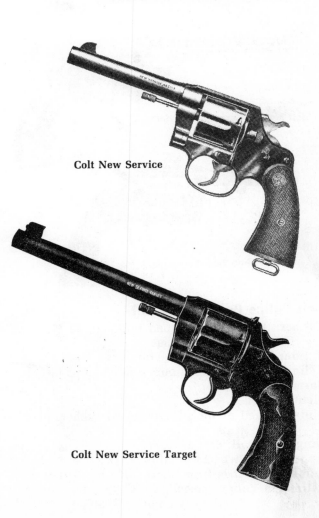

Colt New Service

Colt New Service Target

Colt Police Positive

Colt Police Positive Target

Colt Officers Model Target (1st Issue)

Colt Marine Corps Model 1905

Colt Police Positive Special

Colt Police Positive

Caliber: 32 short and long Colt (discontinued in 1915), 32 Colt New Police (32 S&W long), 38 New Police (38 S&W long)

Action: Single or double action

Cylinder: 6-shot; swing out; simultaneous ejector

Barrel: 2½", 4", 5", and 6"

Sights: Fixed

Finish: Blued or nickel; hard rubber or checkered walnut grips

Length Overall: 6½" or 10½"

Approximate wt.: 18 to 22 oz.

Comments: This is an improved version of the New Police with the Positive Lock feature which prevents the firing pin from contacting the cartridge until the trigger is pulled. Made from 1905 to 1943.

Estimated Value: **Excellent:**   **$250.00**
                    Very good: **$190.00**

Colt Police Positive Target

Same as Colt Police Positive except: 22 caliber long rifle from 1910 to 1932 and 22 long rifle regular or hi-speed after 1932, 22 Winchester rim fire from 1910 to 1935; blued finish; 6" barrel only; adjustable target sights; checkered walnut grips. Approximate wt. 22 to 26 oz.

Estimated Value: **Excellent:**   **$375.00**
                    Very good: **$285.00**

Colt Officers Model Target (1st Issue)

Caliber: 38 special

Action: Single or double action

Cylinder: 6-shot; ⅔ fluted; swing out; simultaneous ejector

Barrel: 6"

Sights: Adjustable

Finish: Blued; checkered walnut grips

Length Overall: 10½"

Approximate wt.: 34 oz.

Comments: Hand finished action. Made from about 1904 to 1908.

Estimated Value: **Excellent:**   **$375.00**
                    Very good: **$290.00**

Colt Marine Corps Model 1905

Caliber: 38 Colt short and long

Action: Single or double action

Cylinder: 6-shot; ⅔ fluted; swing out; simultaneous hand ejector

Barrel: 6"

Sights: Fixed

Finish: Blued or nickel; hard rubber or walnut grips

Length Overall: 10½"

Approximate wt.: 32 oz.

Comments: Made from 1905 to 1908. Lanyard ring in butt; grip is smaller and more rounded at the butt than the Army or Navy Models. Sometimes called Model 1907.

Estimated Value: **Excellent:**   **$750.00**
                    Very good: **$570.00**

Colt Police Positive Special

Caliber: 32-20 (discontinued in 1942), 32 New Police (S&W long), 38 Special

Action: Single or double action

Cylinder: 6-shot; swing out; simultaneous ejector

Barrel: 4", 5", 6"

Sights: Fixed

Finish: Blued or nickel; checkered rubber, plastic or walnut grips

Length Overall: 8¾" to 10¾"

Approximate wt.: 23 to 28 oz.

Comments: Made from about 1907 to 1970's.

Estimated Value: **Excellent:**   **$210.00**
                    Very good: **$160.00**

Colt New Service Model 1909

Caliber: 32-20, 38 Special, 38-40, 42 Colt short and long, 44 Russian, 44-40, 45 Colt
Action: Single or double action
Cylinder: 6-shot; ⅔ fluted; swing out; simultaneous hand ejector
Barrel: 4″, 4½″, 5″, 6″
Sights: Fixed
Finish: Blued or nickel; hard rubber or walnut grips
Length Overall: 9¼″ to 11¼″
Approximate wt.: 32 to 34 oz.
Comments: Made from 1909 to 1928. Adopted by U.S. armed forces from 1909 to 1911 (Automatic became standard sidearm). Also called "Army Special."
Estimated Value: Excellent: $385.00
Very good: $285.00

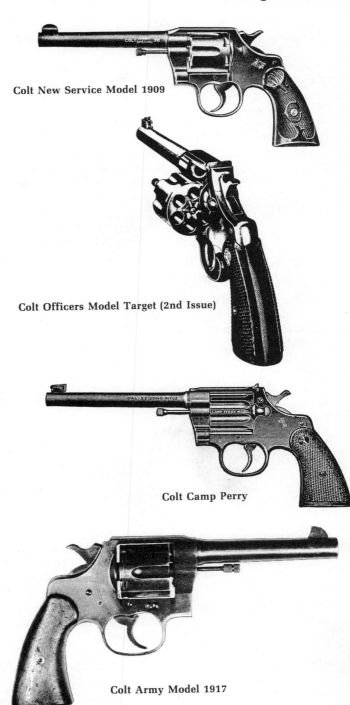

Colt New Service Model 1909

Colt Officers Model Target (2nd Issue)

Colt Camp Perry

Colt Army Model 1917

Colt Officers Model Target (2nd Issue)

Caliber: 22 long rifle (regular) 1930-32; 22 long rifle (Hi-speed) 1932-49; 32 Police Positive 1932-42; 38 Special 1908-49
Action: single or double action
Cylinder: 6-shot; ⅔ fluted; swing out; simultaneous hand ejector
Barrel: 6″ in 22 caliber and 32 Police Positive; 4″, 4½″, 5″, 6″ and 7½″ in 38 Special
Sights: Adjustable rear
Finish: Blued; checkered walnut grips
Length Overall: 9¼″ to 12¾″
Approximate wt.: 32 to 40 oz.
Comments: Hand finished action, tapered barrel. Made from about 1908 to 1949.
Estimated Value: Excellent: $375.00
Very good: $285.00

Colt Camp Perry (1st Issue)

Caliber: 22 short, long, long rifle
Action: Single
Cylinder: 1-shot; swing out flat steel block instead of cylinder with rod ejector
Barrel: 10″
Sights: Adjustable front for elevation and adjustable rear for windage
Finish: Blued; checkered walnut grips with medallion
Length Overall: 14″
Approximate wt.: 35 oz.
Comments: Built on Officers Model frame. Made from about 1926 to 1934.
Estimated Value: Excellent: $750.00
Very good: $575.00

Colt Camp Perry (2nd Issue)

Same as 1st Issue except: 8″ barrel (heavier); shorter hammer fall; overall length 12″; approximate wt. 34 oz., chamber is embedded for cartridge head to make it safe to use 22 long rifle Hi-Speed cartridges. Made from about 1934 to 1941.
Estimated Value: Excellent: $800.00
Very good: $600.00

Colt Army Model 1917

Caliber: 45 ACP or 45 ACP rim cartridges
Action: Single or double action
Cylinder: 6-shot; fluted; swing out; simultaneous hand ejector; used semi-circular clips to hold rimless case of 45 ACP
Barrel: 5½″ round tapered
Sights: Fixed
Finish: Blued; oil-finished walnut grips
Length Overall: 10¾″
Approximate wt.: 40 oz.
Comments: Made from 1917 to 1928.
Estimated Value: Excellent: $400.00
Very good: $300.00

Colt Bankers Special

Caliber: 22 short, long, long rifle (Regular or Hi-Speed);
  38 New Police (S&W long)
Action: Single or double action
Cylinder: 6-shot; swing out; simultaneous ejector
Barrel: 2″
Sights: Fixed
Finish: Blued; checkered walnut grips
Length Overall: 6½″
Approximate wt.: 19 to 23 oz.
Comments: Same as Police Positive except 2″ barrel only
  and rounded grip after 1933. Made from about
  1928-40.

Estimated Value:	22 Cal.	38 Cal.
Excellent:	$800.00	$500.00
Very good:	$600.00	$375.00

Colt Shooting Master

Caliber: 38 Special, 357 magnum (introduced in 1936),
  44 Special, 45 ACP, 45 Colt
Action: Single or double action
Cylinder: 6-shot; swing out; simultaneous ejector
Barrel: 6″
Sights: Adjustable target sight
Finish: Blued; checkered walnut grips
Length Overall: 11¼″
Approximate wt.: 42 to 44 oz.
Comments: A deluxe target revolver based on the New
  Service revolver. Made from about 1932 to 1940.

Estimated Value:	Excellent:	$600.00
	Very good:	$460.00

Colt Official Police (Model E-1)

Caliber: 22 long rifle (regular) introduced in 1930; 22
  long rifle (Hi-Speed) introduced in 1932; 32-20 made
  from about 1928 to 1942; 38 Special made from
  1928 to 1969; 41 long Colt made from 1928 to 1930
Action: Single or double action
Cylinder: 6-shot; fluted; swing out; simultaneous ejector
Barrel: 4″ and 6″ in 22 caliber; 4″, 5″ and 6″ in 32-20;
  2″, 4″, 5″, and 6″ in 41 caliber
Sights: Fixed
Finish: Blued or nickel; checkered walnut or plastic
  grips
Length Overall: 7¼″ to 11¼″
Approximate wt.: 30 to 38 oz.
Comments: 41 caliber frame in all calibers. A refined ver-
  sion of the New Service Model 1909 which was
  discontinued in 1928. Made from about 1928 to
  1970.

Estimated Value:	Excellent:	$300.00
	Very good:	$225.00

Colt Commando

Similar to Colt Official Police (Model E-1) except: made
to government specifications in 38 Special only; sand-
blasted blued finish; produced for the government. Made
from 1942 to 1945.

Estimated Value:	Excellent:	$325.00
	Very good:	$245.00

Colt Detective Special (Model D-1)

Caliber: 32 New Police (S&W long), 38 Special
Action: Single or double action
Cylinder: 6-shot; swing out; simultaneous ejector
Barrel: 2″ or 3″
Sights: Fixed
Finish: Blued or nickel; checkered walnut grips with
  rounded or square butt
Length Overall: 6¾″ or 7¾″
Approximate wt.: 21 oz.
Comments: Made from about 1926 to present. Available
  with or without hammer shroud. Current model 38
  Special only. Add $35.00 for nickel finish.

Estimated Value:	New (retail):	$428.50
	Excellent:	$325.00
	Very good:	$240.00

Colt Bankers Special

Colt Detective Special

Colt Official Police

Colt Shooting M

Colt Commando

Colt Commando Special

Colt Commando Special

Similar to the Detective Special with matte finish and
rubber grips. Introduced in 1984.

Estimated Value:	New (retail):	$299.95
	Excellent:	$225.00
	Very good:	$170.00

Colt Officers Model Special

Caliber: 22 long rifle (regular and Hi-Speed); 38 Special
Action: Single or double action
Cylinder: 6-shot, ⅔ fluted; swing out; simultaneous ejector
Barrel: 6″
Sights: Adjustable for windage and elevation
Finish: Blued; checkered plastic grips
Length Overall: 11¼″
Approximate wt.: 42 oz. in 22 caliber, 38 oz. in 38 caliber
Comments: Replaced the Officers Model Target (2nd issue) as target arm; heavier non-tapered barrel and re-designed hammer. Made from 1949 to 1953.

Estimated Value: Excellent: $300.00
Very good: $225.00

Colt Officers Model Special

Colt Cobra Model D-3

Caliber: 22 short and long rifle; 32 New Police (S&W long); 38 Special
Action: Single or double action
Cylinder: 6-shot; ⅔ fluted; swing out; simultaneous ejector
Barrel: 2″, 3″, 4″ and 5″
Sights: Fixed
Finish: Blued or nickel; checkered walnut grips
Length Overall: 6⅝″ to 9⅝″
Approximate wt.: 16 to 22 oz.
Comments: Frame is made of a light alloy, but cylinder is steel. Made from 1950 to late 1970. Add $25.00 for nickel finish.

Estimated Value: Excellent: $220.00
Very good: $165.00

Colt Cobra

Colt Agent Model D-4

Caliber: 38 special
Action: Single or double action
Cylinder: 6-shot; swing out; simultaneous ejector
Barrel: 2″
Sights: Fixed
Finish: Blued; checkered walnut grips
Length Overall: 6¾″
Approximate wt.: 14 oz.
Comments: Frame made of lightweight alloy. Made from 1955 to late 1970's. Also available with hammer shroud.

Estimated Value: Excellent: $225.00
Very good: $170.00

Colt Agent Model D-4

Colt Agent Light Weight

Similar to the Detective Special with matte finish; 2″ barrel; approx. wt. 17 oz.; introduced in the mid 1980's.

Estimated Value: New (retail): $259.50
Excellent: $195.00
Very good: $150.00

Colt Agent Light Weight

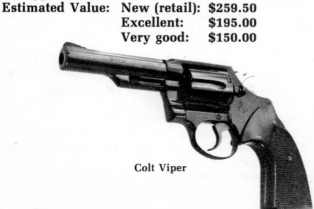

Colt Viper

Colt Aircrewman Special

Caliber: 38 Special
Action: Single or double action
Cylinder: 6-shot; swing out; simultaneous ejector; aluminum alloy
Barrel: 2″
Sights: Fixed
Finish: Blued; checkered walnut grips
Length Overall: 6¾″
Approximate wt.: 14 oz.
Comments: A rare lightweight special revolver developed by Colt at the request of U.S. Air Force during the Korean War. They were recalled in 1960.

Estimated Value: Excellent: $800.00
Very good: $600.00

Colt Viper

Caliber: 38 Special
Action: Single or double action
Cylinder: 6-shot; swing out
Barrel: 4″
Sights: Fixed rear, ramp front
Finish: Blued or nickel; checkered walnut wrap-around grips
Length Overall: 8⅝″
Approximate wt.: 20 oz.
Comments: Lightweight aluminum alloy frame, shrouded ejector rod. Made in the late 1970's. Add $20.00 for nickel model.

Estimated Value: Excellent: $220.00
Very good: $170.00

Colt Border Patrol

Caliber: 38 Special
Action: Single or double action
Cylinder: 6-shot; swing out; simultaneous ejector
Barrel: 4″
Sights: Fixed; Baughman quick draw front sight
Finish: Blued; checkered walnut grips
Length Overall: 8¾″
Approximate wt.: 34 oz.
Comments: In 1952 about 400 were produced for a branch of the U.S. Treasury Dept. The barrel is marked on the left side "Colt Border Patrol."
Estimated Value: Excellent: $800.00
                              Very good: $600.00

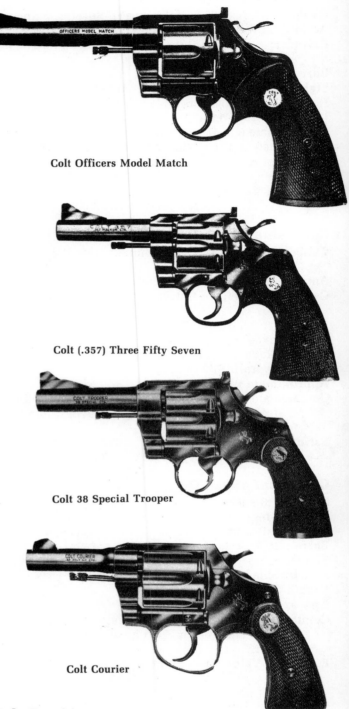

Colt Officers Model Match

Colt (.357) Three Fifty Seven

Colt 38 Special Trooper

Colt Courier

Colt Officers Model Match

Caliber: 22 long rifle, 38 Special
Action: Single or double action
Cylinder: 6-shot; swing out; simultaneous ejector; ⅔ fluted
Barrel: 6″
Sights: Adjustable for windage and elevation
Finish: Blued; checkered walnut grips
Length Overall: 11¼″
Approximate wt.: 22 caliber, 42 oz; 38 caliber 38 oz.
Comments: Has heavy tapered barrel and wide hammer spur. Made from about 1953 to 1970.
Estimated Value: Excellent: $320.00
                              Very good: $240.00

Colt (.357) Three Fifty Seven

Caliber: 357 magnum and 38 Special
Action: Single or double action
Cylinder: 6-shot; swing out; simultaneous ejector
Barrel: 4″ and 6″
Sights: Adjustable rear sight
Finish: Blued; checkered walnut grips
Length Overall: 9¼″ and 11¼″
Approximate wt.: 36 to 39 oz.
Comments: Made from about 1953 to 1962. It was replaced by Trooper Model.
Estimated Value: Excellent: $250.00
                              Very good: $185.00

Colt 38 Special Trooper

Caliber: 22, 38 Special
Action: Single or double action
Cylinder: 6-shot; swing out; simultaneous ejector
Barrel: 4″ or 6″
Sights: Adjustable rear and quick draw front
Finish: Blued or nickel; checkered walnut square butt grips
Length Overall: 9¼″ and 11¼″
Approximate wt.: 36 to 43 oz.
Comments: Made from about 1953 to 1962.
Estimated Value: Excellent: $275.00
                              Very good: $210.00

Colt Courier

Caliber: 22 short, long, long rifle, 32 New Police (S&W long)
Action: Single or double action
Cylinder: 6-shot; swing out; simultaneous ejector; made of lightweight alloy
Barrel: 3″
Sights: Fixed
Finish: Dual tone blue; checkered plastic grips
Length Overall: 7½″
Approximate wt.: 14 to 20 oz.
Comments: Frame and cylinder made of lightweight alloy. Made in 1954 and 1955 only. A limited production revolver.
Estimated Value: Excellent: $725.00
                              Very good: $550.00

Colt Trooper

Colt Trooper MKIII

Colt Trooper MK V

Colt Lawman MKIII

Colt Lawman MK V

Colt Trooper

Caliber: 357 magnum, 38 Special
Action: Single or double
Cylinder: 6-shot swing out; simultaneous ejector
Barrel: 4″ or 6″
Sights: Adjustable rear and quick draw front
Finish: Blue or nickel; checkered walnut, square butt grips
Length Overall: 9¼″ to 11¼″
Approximate wt.: 34 to 38 oz.
Comments: Made from about 1953 to 1969. Replaced by Trooper MKIII.
Estimated Value: Excellent: $235.00
Very good: $180.00

Colt Trooper MK III

Caliber: 357 magnum, 38 Special; 22 long rifle and 22 WMR added in 1979
Action: Single or double action
Cylinder: 6-shot; swing out; simultaneous ejector
Barrel: 4″, 6″ and 8″ in 1980
Sights: Adjustable rear
Finish: Blued or nickel; checkered walnut grips; non-glare electroless plating available after 1981 (Colt-guard)
Length Overall: 9½″, 11½″ and 13½″
Approximate wt.: 39 to 42 oz.
Comments: Made from about 1969 to mid 1980's; wide target-type trigger and hammer. Add $20.00 for nickel; $7.00 for 8″ barrel.
Estimated Value: Excellent: $250.00
Very good: $195.00

Colt Trooper MK V

Caliber: 357 magnum or 38 Special
Action: Single or double action; exposed hammer
Cylinder: 6-shot; swing out; simultaneous ejector
Barrel: 4″ or 6″ ventilated rib
Sights: Red insert front, adjustable rear
Finish: Blued, nickel or non-glare electroless plating (Coltguard); checkered walnut grips
Length Overall: 9½″ to 11½″″
Approximate wt.: 39 to 45 oz.
Comments: A medium frame revolver with inner and outer improvements on the Trooper MK III. Introduced in 1982. Add $30.00 for nickel finish.
Estimated Value: New (retail): $361.50
Excellent: $270.00
Very good: $205.00

Colt Lawman MK III

Caliber: 357 magnum and 38 Special
Action: Single or double action
Cylinder: 6-shot; swing out; simultaneous ejector
Barrel: 2″ or 4″
Sights: Fixed
Finish: Blued or nickel; checkered walnut grips; non-glare electroless plating available after 1981 (Colt-guard)
Length Overall: 7¼″, 9¼″
Approximate wt.: 36 and 39 oz.
Comments: Made from 1970 to early 1980's. Add $20.00 for nickel.
Estimated Value: Excellent: $230.00
Very good: $175.00

Colt Lawman MK V

Similar to the Trooper MK V with a 2″ or 4″ solid rib barrel, fixed sights. Add $20.00 for nickel finish. Discontinued in mid 1980's.
Estimated Value: Excellent: $250.00
Very good: $190.00

Colt Diamondback

Caliber: 22, 22 long rifle, 38 Special
Action: Single or double
Cylinder: 6-shot; swing out; simultaneous ejector
Barrel: 2½″, 4″, 6″ ventilated rib; 2½″ dropped in late 1970's
Sights: Adjustable rear
Finish: Blued or nickel; checkered walnut square butt grips
Length Overall: 7½″, 9″
Approximate wt.: 26 to 32 oz.
Comments: Made from 1967 to present. Add $50.00 for nickel finish.
Estimated Value: New (retail): $460.50
Excellent: $345.00
Very good: $260.00

Colt Model I-3 Python, New Police Python, Python

Caliber: 357 magnum, 38 Special; 22 long rifle and 22 WMR available in 1981 only
Action: Single or double action
Cylinder: 6-shot; swing out; simultaneous ejector
Barrel: 2½″, 3″, 4″, 6″ or 8″ after 1980; ventilated rib
Sights: Blade front, adjustable rear (for windage and elevation). Red insert in front sight in 1980's
Finish: Blued or nickel; checkered walnut target grips; also rubber grips in 1980's; non-glare electroless plating and stainless steel in 1980's
Length Overall: 7¼″ to 13¼″
Approximate wt.: 39 to 44 oz.
Comments: Made from about 1955 to present. Add 14% for bright stainless steel; add 13% for satin stainless steel; add 4% for nickel finish.
Estimated Value: New (retail): $687.50
Excellent: $515.00
Very good: $385.00

Colt Official Police MK III

Caliber: 38 Special
Action: Single or double
Cylinder: 6-shot; swing out; simultaneous ejector
Barrel: 4″, 5″, 6″
Sights: Fixed
Finish: Blued; checkered walnut square butt grips
Length Overall: 9¼″, 10¼″ and 11¼″
Approximate wt.: 34 to 36 oz.
Comments: Made from about 1970 to late 1970's.
Estimated Value: Excellent: $225.00
Very good: $170.00

Colt Single Action Army

Colt Peacekeeper

Caliber: 357 magnum and 38 Special
Action: Single and double action
Cylinder: 6-shot, swing out: simultaneous ejector
Barrel: 4″ or 6″ with ventilated rib and short ejector shroud
Sights: Red-insert front and white-outline adjustable rear
Finish: Non-glare matte blue combat finish with Colt rubber combat grips
Length Overall: 9″ or 11″
Approximate wt.: 38 oz. or 42 oz.
Comments: A medium-frame 357 magnum introduced in the mid 1980's.
Estimated Value: New (retail): $320.50
Excellent: $240.00
Very good: $180.00

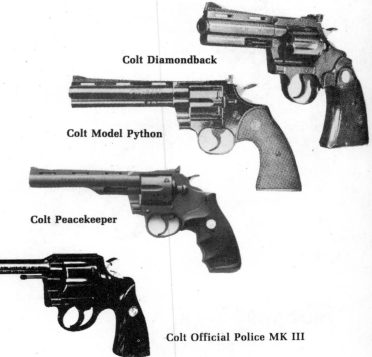

Colt Diamondback

Colt Model Python

Colt Peacekeeper

Colt Official Police MK III

Colt Single Action Army

Caliber: 357 magnum, 38 Special, 44 Special, 45 Colt, 44-40
Action: Single action
Cylinder: 6-shot; side load; loading gate; under barrel ejector rod
Barrel: 4¾″, 5½″ and 7½″
Sights: Fixed
Finish: Blued with case hardened frame; composite rubber grips; nickel with checkered walnut grips
Length Overall: 10⅛″ to 12⅞″
Approximate wt.: 37 to 43 oz.
Comments: A revival of the Single Action Army Revolver, which was discontinued in 1941. The series numbers start at 1001 SA. The letters SA were added to the serial numbers when production was resumed. Made from about 1955 to mid 1980's. Add $15.00 for a 7½″ barrel; $60.00 for nickel.
Estimated Value: Excellent: $430.00
Very good: $325.00

Colt Single Action Buntline Special

This is basically the same revolver as the Colt Single Action Army Revolver (1955 Model) except it is 45 Colt caliber only. The barrel is 12″; the gun has an overall length of 17½″; weighs about 42 oz. It was made from about 1957 until 1975. Available again in 1980. Add $90.00 for nickel finish. 44 Special available after 1981.

Estimated Value: **Excellent:** **$460.00**
Very good: **$350.00**

Colt Single Action Buntline Special

Colt New Frontier

Colt Frontier Scout

Caliber: 22 and 22 WRF (interchangeable cylinder)
Action: Single action
Cylinder: 6-shot side load; loading gate; under barrel ejector rod
Barrel: 4¾″ or 9½″ (Buntline Scout)
Sights: Fixed
Finish: Blued or nickel; plastic or wood grips
Length Overall: 9⁵/₁₆″ to 14¼″
Approximate wt.: 24 to 34 oz.
Comments: Single Action Army replica ¾ scale size in 22 caliber. Made with bright alloy frame and blued steel frame from about 1958 to 1972. Add $10.00 for interchangeable cylinder; $10.00 for nickel finish; $10.00 for Buntline Scout.

Estimated Value: **Excellent:** **$180.00**
Very good: **$135.00**

Colt Peacemaker 22 Single Action

Colt New Frontier

Colt New Frontier, Single Action Army

This is the same handgun as the Colt Single Action Army revolver except frame is flat topped; finish is high polished; ramp front sight and adjustable rear sight (wind and elevation); blued and case-hardened finish; smooth walnut grips. This is a target version of the SA Army, made from about 1961 to mid 1980's in 44-40, 44 Spec., and 45 Colt caliber only. Add $20.00 for 7½″ barrel.

Estimated Value: **Excellent:** **$500.00**
Very good: **$375.00**

Colt New Frontier Buntline Special

This revolver is the same as the Colt New Frontier (1961 Model) except: 45 caliber only; 12″ barrel; 17½″ overall; weighs 42 oz. Made from 1962 until 1967.

Estimated Value: **Excellent:** **$525.00**
Very good: **$395.00**

Colt Frontier Scout

Colt Peacemaker 22 Single Action

Caliber: 22, 22 WRF when equipped with dual cylinder
Action: Single
Cylinder: 6-shot; side load; loading gate; under barrel ejector rod
Barrel: 4¾″, 6″ and 7½″
Sights: Fixed
Finish: Blued barrel and cylinder; case hardened frame; black compositie rubber grips
Length Overall: 9⁵/₈″ to 12¾″
Approximate wt.: 29 to 33 oz.
Comments: All steel, 22 caliber version of the 45 caliber Peacemaker. Made from 1972 to late 1970's. Add $6.00 for 7½″ barrel.

Estimated Value: **Excellent:** **$185.00**
Very good: **$140.00**

Colt New Frontier

This is the same handgun as the Colt Peacemaker 22 SA except: equipped with a ramp front sight and adjustable rear sight; flat top frame. Reintroduced in 1982.

Estimated Value: **New (retail):** **$280.95**
Excellent: **$215.00**
Very good: **$160.00**

Dan Wesson

Dan Wesson Pistol Pack

A carrying case containing revolver, 4 interchangeable barrels (2½″, 4″, 6″, 8″), interchangeable grips, 4 additional colored sight blades and other accessories. The following are retail prices:

Model 8-2 (no 8″ barrel)	$375.85
Model 8-2B (no 8″ barrel)	$395.95
Model 708 (no 8″ barrel)	$430.65
Model 9-2	$507.75
Model 709	$580.15
Model 9-2V	$594.45
Model 709-V	$666.90
Model 9-2VH	$672.05
Model 709-VH	$744.30
Model 14-2 (no 8″ barrel)	$375.85
Model 14-2B	$395.95
Model 714	$430.65
Model 15-2	$507.75
Model 715	$580.15
Model 15-2H	Excellent $415.00
Model 15-2V	$594.45
Model 715-V	$666.90
Model 15-2VH	$672.05
Model 715-VH	$744.30
Model 22	$507.75
Model 22M	$525.95
Model 722	$580.15
Model 722M	$598.85
Model 22-V	$594.45
Model 722-V	$666.90
Model 22M-V	$600.48
Model 722M-V	$704.15
Model 22-VH	$672.05
Model 722-VH	$744.30
Model 22M-VH	$690.05
Model 722M-VH	$782.40
Model 41-V (one 8″, one 6″ barrel)	$560.00
Model 741-V (one 8″, one 6″ barrel)	$617.94
Model 41-VH (one 8″, one 6″ barrel)	$603.70
Model 741-VH (one 8″, one 6″ barrel)	$661.62
Model 44V (two 6″, two 8″ barrels)	$615.40
Model 744V (two 6″, two 8″ barrels)	$675.75
Model 44-VH (two 6″, two 8″ barrels)	$659.15
Model 744-VH (two 6″, two 8″ barrels)	$719.40
Model 32	$507.75
Model 32-V	$594.45
Model 32-VH	$672.05
Model 732	$580.15
Model 732-V	$660.90
Model 732-VH	$744.30

Dan Wesson Model 14

Dan Wesson Model 12

Dan Wesson Model 11

Dan Wesson Model 11

Caliber: 357 magnum or 38 Special (interchangeable)
Action: Double or single; exposed hammer; simultaneous ejector
Cylinder: 6-shot; swing out
Barrel: 2½″, 4″, 6″; interchangeable barrels
Sights: Ramp front; fixed rear
Finish: Blued; one-piece changeable walnut grip
Length Overall: 7¾″ to 11¼″
Approximate wt.: 36 to 40 oz.
Comments: Made from about 1970 to 1974. Barrels and barrel cover (shroud) can be changed quickly by means of a recessed barrel nut; also one-piece grip readily changeable to option styles.
Estimated Value: Excellent: $165.00
　　　　　　　　　　 Very good: $115.00

Dan Wesson Model 12

Same as Model 11 except target model with adjustable rear sight.
Estimated Value: Excellent: $175.00
　　　　　　　　　　 Very good: $125.00

Dan Wesson Model 14, 14-2, 714

Caliber: 357 magnum or 38 Special (interchangeable)
Action: Double or single; exposed hammer; simultaneous ejector
Cylinder: 6-shot swing-out; non-fluted available after 1981
Barrel: 2½″, 4″, 6″ interchangeable barrels
Sights: Ramp front; fixed rear
Finish: Blued; one-piece walnut grip; satin blue available; 714 stainless steel
Length Overall: 7¾″ to 13¼″
Approximate wt.: 36 to 42 oz.
Comments: Made from about 1973 to present. A modified version of the Model 22, presently being called the 14-2 series. Price increases with barrel length. Add $15.00 for bright blue finish (14-2B); $35.00 for stainless steel (714).
Estimated Value: New (retail): $219.50 - $231.25
　　　　　　　　　　 Excellent: $165.00 - $175.00
　　　　　　　　　　 Very good: $125.00 - $130.00

Dan Wesson Model 15

Similar to Model 14 except adjustable rear sight. Made from about 1973 to 1976.
Estimated Value: Excellent: $160.00
　　　　　　　　　　 Very good: $130.00

Dan Wesson Model 8-2, 708

Similar to Model 14 except 38 caliber only. Add $15.00 for bright blue finish (8-2B); $35.00 for stainless steel (708).

Estimated Value: New (retail): $219.50 - $231.25
Excellent: $165.00 - $175.00
Very good: $125.00 - $130.00

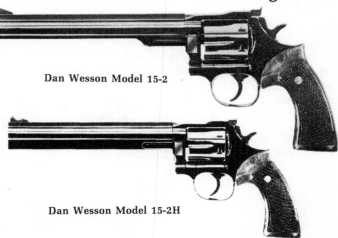

Dan Wesson Model 15-2

Dan Wesson Model 15-2H

Dan Wesson Model 15-2, 715

Caliber: 357 magnum or 38 Special (interchangeably)
Action: Double or single; exposed hammer
Cylinder: 6-shot; swing-out; simultaneous ejector
Barrel: 2½", 4", 6", 8", 10", 12", 15" interchangeable barrels
Sights: Interchangeable colored front sight blade; adjustable rear sight with white outline
Finish: Blued; checkered wood target grips; 715 is stainless steel
Length Overall: 7¾" to 13¼"
Approximate wt.: 32 to 42 oz.
Comments: Made from about 1975 to present. Price increases with barrel length. Add $35.00 for stainless steel (715).

Estimated Value: New (retail): $272.50 - $365.25
Excellent: $205.00 - $275.00
Very good: $155.00 - $205.00

Dan Wesson Model 15-2H

Same as Model 15-2 except it has a heavier bull barrel. A special order item after 1981.

Estimated Value: Excellent: $215.00 - $260.00
Very good: $160.00 - $195.00

Dan Wesson Model 15-2V, 715-V

Same as Model 15-2 except it has ventilated rib. Add $35.00 for stainless steel (715-V).

Estimated Value: New (retail): $291.45 - $396.00
Excellent: $220.00 - $300.00
Very good: $165.00 - $225.00

Dan Wesson Model 9-2, 709

Similar to Model 15-2 except 38 caliber only. No 12" or 15" barrel. Add $35.00 for stainless steel (709).

Estimated Value: New (retail): $272.50 - $297.90
Excellent: $205.00 - $275.00
Very good: $155.00 - $205.00

Dan Wesson Model 15-2V

Dan Wesson Model 9-2V, 709-V

Similar to the Model 9-2 with ventilated rib. Price increased with barrel length. Add $35.00 for stainless steel (709-V).

Estimated Value: New (retail): $291.15 - $324.70
Excellent: $220.00 - $245.00
Very good: $165.00 - $185.00

Dan Wesson Model 9-2VH, 709-VH

Similar to the Model 9-2 with heavier bull barrel and ventilated rib. Prices increases with barrel length. Add $35.00 for stainless steel (709-VH).

Estimated Value: New (retail): $315.20 - $341.15
Excellent: $235.00 - $255.00
Very good: $180.00 - $190.00

Dan Wesson Model 15-2VH

Dan Wesson Model 9-2

Dan Wesson Model 15-2 VH, 715-VH

Same as Model 15-2 except it has a heavier bull barrel with ventilated rib assembly. Add $35.00 for stainless steel (715-VH).

Estimated Value: New (retail): $315.20 - $424.10
Excellent: $235.00 - $320.00
Very good: $180.00 - $240.00

Dan Wesson Model 22, 722

Similar to the Model 15-2 in 22 caliber only. Introduced in the late 1970's. Not available with 10″, 12″ or 15″ barrel. Price increases with barrel length. Add $35.00 for stainless steel (722).

Estimated Value: New (retail): $272.50 - $297.50
Excellent: $205.00 - $225.00
Very good: $155.00 - $170.00

Dan Wesson Model 22M, 722M

Similar to the Model 22 in 22 magnum caliber. Add $35.00 for stainless steel finish (722M).

Estimated Value: New (retail): $281.65 - $307.05
Excellent: $210.00 - $230.00
Very good: $160.00 - $175.00

Dan Wesson Model 22M-V, 722M-V

Similar to the Model 22-V in 22 magnum caliber. Add $35.00 for stainless steel finish (722M-V).

Estimated Value: New (retail): $300.60 - $334.00
Excellent: $225.00 - $250.00
Very good: $170.00 - $190.00

Dan Wesson Model 22M-VH, 722M-VH

Similar to the Model 22-VH in 22 magnum caliber. Add $35.00 for stainless steel finish (722M-VH).

Estimated Value: New (retail): $324.30 - $350.27
Excellent: $245.00 - $265.00
Very good: $185.00 - $195.00

Dan Wesson Model 22-V, 722-V

Similar to the Model 22 with ventilated rib. Price increases with barrel length. Add $35.00 for stainless steel (722-V).

Estimated Value: New (retail): $291.45 - $324.90
Excellent: $220.00 - $245.00
Very good: $165.00 - $185.00

Dan Wesson Model 22-VH, 722-VH

Similar to the Model 22 with heavier bull barrel and ventilated rib. Price increases with barrel length. Add $35.00 for stainless steel (722-VH).

Estimated Value: New (retail): $315.20 - $341.15
Excellent: $235.00 - $255.00
Very good: $175.00 - $190.00

Dan Wesson Model 32, 732

Similar to the Model 15-2 in 32 magnum caliber; 2½″, 4″, 6″ or 8″ barrel. Introduced in the mid 1980's. Add $35.00 for stainless steel (732).

Estimated Value: New (retail): $272.30 - $297.70
Excellent: $205.00 - $220.00
Very good: $155.00 - $165.00

Dan Wesson Model 22V

Dan Wesson Model 32-V, 732-V

Similar to the Model 32 with ventilated rib. Add $35.00 for stainless steel (732-V).

Estimated Value: New (retail): $291.25 - $324.70
Excellent: $215.00 - $245.00
Very good: $160.00 - $180.00

Dan Wesson Model 32-VH, 732-VH

Similar to the Model 32 with ventilated rib, heavy barrel. Add $35.00 for stainless steel (732-VH).

Estimated Value: New (retail): $315.00 - $340.95
Excellent: $235.00 - $255.00
Very good: $175.00 - $190.00

Dan Wesson Model 40-V 357 Super Mag, 740-V

Caliber: 357 Maximum
Action: Single and double, exposed hammer; simultaneous ejector
Cylinder: 6-shot swing-out; fluted; simultaneous ejector
Barrel: 6″, 8″, 10″ interchangeable barrel; ventilated rib
Sights: Interchangeable colored front sight blade, adjustable interchangeable rear
Finish: Blued; smooth walnut grips; stainless steel (740-V)
Length Overall: 14½″ with 8″ barrel
Approximate wt.: 59 to 62 oz.
Comments: Introduced in the mid 1980's. Each model comes with an extra barrel. Price increases with barrel length. Add $50.00 for stainless steel.
Estimated Value: New (retail): $426.35 - $456.10
Excellent: $320.00 - $345.00
Very good: $240.00 - $255.00

Dan Wesson Model 40-V8S, 740-V8S

Similar to the Model 40-V with slotted barrel shroud, 8″ barrel only; extra barrel included; weighs 64 oz. Add $50.00 for stainless steel (740-V8S)

Estimated Value: New (retail): $450.40
Excellent: $340.00
Very good: $255.00

Dan Wesson Model 40-VH, 740-VH

Similar to the Model 40-V with heavy barrel; extra barrel included. Add $50.00 for stainless steel (740-VH)

Estimated Value: New (retail): $437.45 - $482.05
Excellent: $330.00 - $360.00
Very good: $245.00 - $270.00

Dan Wesson Model 41-V, 741-V

Similar to the Model 44V in 42 magnum caliber. Add $35.00 for stainless steel finish (741-V).

Estimated Value: New (retail): $373.50 - $404.50
Excellent: $280.00 - $300.00
Very good: $210.00 - $230.00

Dan Wesson Model 41-VH, 741-VH

Similar to the Model 44VH in 41 magnum caliber. Add $35.00 for stainless steel finish (741-VH).

Estimated Value: New (retail): $393.75 - $431.05
Excellent: $295.00 - $325.00
Very good: $220.00 - $240.00

Dan Wesson Model 44V

Dan Wesson Model 375 Super Mag

Similar to the Model 40V in 375 magnum caliber.
Estimated Value: New (retail): $426.35 - $456.10
Excellent: $320.00 - $340.00
Very good: $240.00 - $255.00

Dan Wesson Model 375-V8S Super Mag

Similar to the Model 375 with slotted barrel shroud, 8" barrel.
Estimated Value: New (retail): $450.40
Excellent: $335.00
Very good: $250.00

Dan Wesson Model 375-VH Super Mag

Similar to the Model 375 with ventilated rib shroud in heavy barrel.
Estimated Value: New (retail): $437.45 - $482.05
Excellent: $325.00 - 360.00
Very good: $245.00 - 270.00

Dan Wesson Model 44-V, 744-V

Caliber: 44 magnum, 44 Special (jacketed only)
Action: Single and double, exposed hammer; wide hammer and trigger
Cylinder: 6-shot swing-out; simultaneous ejector
Barrel: 4", 6", 8", 10" interchangeable barrel; ventilated rib
Sights: Interchangeable colored front sight blade, adjustable rear with white outline
Finish: Blued; smooth or checkered walnut grips with thumb flute; 744V is stainless steel
Length Overall: 12" with 6" barrel
Approximate wt.: 48 to 63 oz.
Comments: Introduced in the early 1980's. Price increases with barrel length. Add $35.00 for stainless steel (744V).
Estimated Value: New (retail): $373.50 - $404.90
Excellent: $280.00 - $300.00
Very good: $210.00 - $225.00

Dan Wesson Model 44-VH, 744-VH

Similar to the Model 44 with heavier bull barrel. Price increases with barrel length. Add $40.00 for stainless steel (744VH).
Estimated Value: New (retail): $393.75 - $431.05
Excellent: $300.00 - $325.00
Very good: $220.00 - $240.00

Dardick

Dardick Magazine Pistol

Dardick 1100 - 11-shot
Dardick 1500 - 15-shot
Dardick 2000 - 20-shot

All models could be convered to a rifle by removing the barrel and fitting the frame into the rifle conversion kit.
Estimated Value:

	Pistol with 22 and 38 caliber barrels
Excellent:	$500.00
Very good:	$375.00
	Pistol, 22 and 38 caliber barrels and rifle conversion kit
Excellent:	$850.00
Very good:	$700.00

Dardick Magazine Pistol

David Dardick developed a handgun, which resembles an automatic pistol, around a new type of cartridge called the "tround." The tround has a triangular case made of plastic. For the 38 caliber, the primer, powder, and bullets are loaded into the tround. The 22 caliber cartridges are simply placed in a plastic tround to adapt them to the feeding system. The firing pin position is changed to rim-fire by manually turning a screw in the frame. Therefore, the basic gun will shoot 22 caliber or 38 caliber by changing the barrel. The feeding system used a three-legged star wheel which moves from magazine to firing position and dumpts trounds through opening on right side. The feeding system is moved 120° with each pull of the trigger. The magazine is loaded by placing trounds in singly or by using 10-shot stripper clips. Production was started in 1959 in Hamden, Connecticut and ceased in 1960. All facilities, guns, and parts were auctioned to Numrich Arms in 1960. Approximately 40 guns were produced. The gun was made in three models and a rifle conversion kit. All models were made with two barrels (22 and 38 caliber.)

Detonics

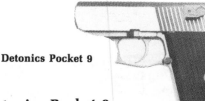

Detonics Combat Master

Detonics Pocket 9

Detonics Mark I, Combat Master
Caliber: 45 ACP; 9mm; 38 Super ACP
Action: Semi-automatic; exposed hammer; single action; thumb safety
Magazine: 6-shot clip
Barrel: 3¼″
Sights: Fixed; some models have adjustable sights
Finish: Polished blue, matte blue; walnut grips
Length Overall: 6¾″
Approximate wt.: 29 oz.
Comments: A lightweight compact combat 45 caliber pistol made from the late 1970's to present.
Estimated Value: New (retail): $610.95
Excellent: $460.00
Very good: $345.00

Detonics Mark V, Combat Master
Similar to the Mark I except matte stainless steel finish. Discontinued 1985.
Estimated Value: Excellent: $500.00
Very good: $375.00

Detonics Mark VI, Combat Master
Similar to the Mark V with polished stainless steel finish.
Estimated Value: New (retail): $685.95
Excellent: $515.00
Very good: $385.00

Detonics Pocket 9
Caliber: 9mm
Action: Double and single action, blow-back; semi-automatic
Magazine: 6-shot clip
Barrel: 3″
Sights: Fixed
Finish: Matte finish stainless steel, hooked and serrated trigger guard
Length Overall: 5¾″
Approximate wt.: 26 oz.
Comments: Introduced in the mid 1980's.
Estimated Value: New (retail): $457.95
Excellent: $340.00
Very good: $255.00

Detonics Scoremaster
Similar to the Combat Master with a 5″ or 6″ barrel, 7 or 8-shot clip; 45 ACP or 451 Detonics magnum. Add $20.00 for 6″ barrel.
Estimated Value: New (retail): $992.95
Excellent: $750.00
Very good: $560.00

Detonics Service Master
Similar to the Combat Master except slightly longer and heavier, Millett sights, dull finish. Add $75.00 for polished stainless steel finish (Service Master II).
Estimated Value: New (retail): $685.00
Excellent: $510.00
Very good: $385.00

Detonics Scoremaster

Fiala

Fiala Single Shot Magazine Pistol
Caliber: 22 short, long, long rifle
Action: Hand operated slide action to chamber cartridge, cock striker and eject empty case
Magazine: 10-shot clip
Barrel: 3″, 7½″, 20″
Sights: Target sight (adjustable rear sight)
Finish: Blued; plain wood grips
Length Overall: 6¾″, 11¼″, or 23¾″
Approximate wt.: 27 to 44 oz.
Comments: Produced from about 1920 to 1923. A rare American pistol which had the appearance of an automatic pistol. A shoulder stock was supplied for use with the 20″ barrel.
Estimated Value:

	Pistol with 3″, 7½″ barrel	Pistol with all 3 barrels & shoulder stock
Excellent:	$400.00	$800.00
Very good:	$300.00	$650.00

Fiala Single Shot Magazine Pistol

Great Western

Great Western Frontier
Caliber: 22 short, long, long rifle, 357 magnum, 38 Special, 44 magnum, 44 Special, 45 Colt
Action: Single, hand ejector
Cylinder: 6-shot
Barrel: 4¾", 5½", 7½" round barrel with ejector housing under barrel
Sights: Blade front; groove in top strap for rear sight
Finish: Blued; imitation stag grips
Length Overall: 10³/₈" to 13¹/₈"
Approximate wt.: 38 to 42 oz.
Comments: Replica of the Colt Single Action revolver. Made from about 1951 to 1962. Values of these revolvers vary due to the poor quality of the early models. After 1955 they were also available in unassembled kit form. Values for factory-made models.
Estimated Value: Excellent: $150.00
  Very good: $115.00

Great Western Double Barrel Derringer

Great Western Frontier

Great Western Double Barrel Derringer
Caliber: 38 Special
Action: Single; double barrel; tip up to eject and load
Cylinder: None; barrels chambered for cartridges
Barrel: Superposed 3" double
Sights: Fixed
Finish: Blued; checkered plastic grips
Length Overall: 4⁷/₈"
Approximate wt.: 14 oz.
Comments: Replica of the Remington Double Derringer. Made from about 1952 to 1962.
Estimated Value: Excellent: $90.00
  Very good: $65.00

Harrington & Richardson

H & R Self Loading 25
Caliber: 25 ACP
Action: Semi-automatic; concealed hammer
Magazine: 6-shot clip; simultaneous ejector
Barrel: 2"
Sights: None
Finish: Blued; hard rubber grips
Length Overall: 4½"
Approximate wt.: 13 oz.
Comments: Approximately 20,000 produced from about 1912 to 1915.
Estimated Value: Excellent: $260.00
  Very good: $195.00

H & R Self Loading 25

H & R Self Loading 32

H & R Self Loading 32
Caliber: 32 ACP
Action: Semi-automatic; concealed hammer; grip safety
Magazine: 8-shot clip
Barrel: 3½"
Sights: Fixed
Finish: Blued; hard rubber grips
Length Overall: 6½"
Approximate wt.: 22 oz.
Comments: A modified Webley & Scott designed pistol. Approximately 40,000 produced from about 1916 to 1939.
Estimated Value: Excellent: $240.00
  Very good: $180.00

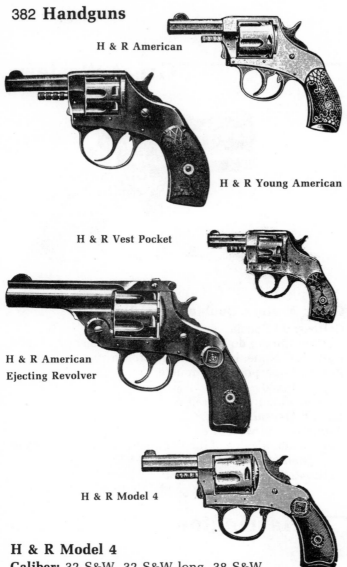

H & R American

H & R Young American

H & R Vest Pocket

H & R American
Ejecting Revolver

H & R Model 4

H & R American

Caliber: S&W, 32 S&W long; 38 S&W
Action: Single or double; exposed hammer; solid frame; side load
Cylinder: 6-shot in 32 caliber; 5-shot in 38 caliber; removable cylinder
Barrel: 2½″, 4½″ or 6″ hexagon barrel
Sights: Fixed
Finish: Blued or nickel; hard rubber round butt grips
Length Overall: 6½″ to 9¾″
Approximate wt.: 14 to 16 oz.
Comments: Made from about 1883 to 1941.
Estimated Value: **Excellent:** **$90.00**
Very good: **$70.00**

H & R Young American

Caliber: 22 short, long, long rifle, 32 S&W short
Action: Single or double; exposed hammer; solid frame; side load
Cylinder: 7-shot in 22 caliber; 5-shot in 32 caliber; removable cylinder
Barrel: 2″, 4½″ or 6″ hexagon barrel
Sights: Fixed
Finish: Blued or nickel; hard rubber round butt grips
Length Overall: 5½″ to 9½″
Approximate wt.: 10 to 12 oz.
Comments: Made from about 1885 to 1941.
Estimated Value: **Excellent:** **$100.00**
Very good: **$ 75.00**

H & R Vest Pocket

Same as H & R Young American except: 1¹/₈″ barrel only; double action only; no spur on hammer; approximate weight 8 oz. Produced from about 1891 to 1941.
Estimated Value: **Excellent:** **$90.00**
Very good: **$70.00**

H & R Automatic Ejecting Revolver

Caliber: 32 S&W, 32 S&W long, 38 S&W
Action: Single or double; exposed hammer; hinged frame; top break
Cylinder: 6-shot in 32 caliber; 5-shot in 38 caliber; simultaneous automatic ejector
Barrel: 3¼″, 4″, 5″, or 6″ round barrel with rib
Sights: Fixed
Finish: Blued or nickel; hard rubber round butt grips
Length Overall: 7¼″ to 10″
Approximate wt.: 15 to 18 oz.
Comments: Manufactured from about 1891 to 1941.
Estimated Value: **Excellent:** **$120.00**
Very good: **$ 95.00**

H & R Model 4

Caliber: 32 S&W, 32 S&W long, 38 S&W
Action: Double and single; exposed hammer; solid frame; side load
Cylinder: 6-shot in 32 caliber, 5-shot in 38 caliber, removable cylinder
Barrel: 2½″, 4½″ or 6″ hexagon barrel
Sights: Fixed
Finish: Blued or nickel; hard rubber round butt grips
Length Overall: 6½″ to 10″
Approximate wt.: 14 to 18 oz.
Comments: Made from about 1904 to 1941.
Estimated Value: **Excellent:** **$100.00**
Very good: **$ 75.00**

H & R Model 5

Similar to Model 4 except: 32 S&W caliber only; smaller frame and cylinder (5-shot); weighs 10-12 oz. Produced from about 1905 to 1939.
Estimated Value: **Excellent:** **$90.00**
Very good: **$70.00**

H & R Model 6

Similar to Model 5 except: 22 short, long, long rifle; 7-shot cylinder; minor change in shape of top of frame at rear of cylinder. Made from about 1906 to 1941.
Estimated Value: **Excellent:** **$100.00**
Very good: **$ 75.00**

H & R Model 5

H & R Model 6

H & R Model 50

Same as Automatic Ejecting Revolver except: double action only; concealed hammer; frame completely encloses hammer area. Made from about 1899 to 1941.

Estimated Value: Excellent: **$125.00**

Very good: **$100.00**

H & R Premier

Caliber: 22 short, long, long rifle, 32 S&W
Action: Single or double; exposed hammer; small hinged frame; top break
Cylinder: 7-shot in 22 caliber; 5-shot in 32 caliber; simultaneous automatic ejector
Barrel: 2″, 3″, 4″, 5″, or 6″ round ribbed barrel
Sights: Fixed
Finish: Blued or nickel; hard rubber round butt grips
Length Overall: 5¾″ to 9¾″
Approximate wt.: 12 to 16 oz.
Comments: Made from about 1895 to 1941.

Estimated Value: Excellent: **$130.00**

Very good: **$105.00**

H & R Model 40

Same as Premier except: double action only; concealed hammer; frame completely enclosed hammer area. Produced from about 1899 to 1941.

Estimated Value: Excellent: **$135.00**

Very good: **$100.00**

H & R Trapper Model

Same as Model 6 except: 6″ barrel, checkered square butt walnut grips. Made from about 1924 to 1942.

Estimated Value: Excellent: **$110.00**

Very good: **$ 85.00**

H & R Hunter Model (1926)

Same as Trapper Model except: 10″ barrel; weighs 18 oz. Made from about 1926 to 1930.

Estimated Value: Excellent: **$100.00**

Very good: **$ 75.00**

H & R Hunter Model (1930)

Similar to Hunter Model (1926) except: larger frame; 9-shot safety cylinder (recessed chambers); weighs 26 oz. Made from about 1930 to 1941.

Estimated Value: Excellent: **$115.00**

Very good: **$ 90.00**

H & R Model 944

Caliber: 22 short, long, long rifle, 22 WRF
Action: Single or double; exposed hammer; heavy hinged frame; top break
Cylinder: 9-shot; simultaneous automatic ejector
Barrel: 6″ round, ribbed barrel
Sights: Fixed
Finish: Blued; checkered square butt walnut grips
Length Overall: 10″
Approximate wt.: 24 oz.
Comments: Produced from about 1925 to 1930.

Estimated Value: Excellent: **$120.00**

Very good: **$100.00**

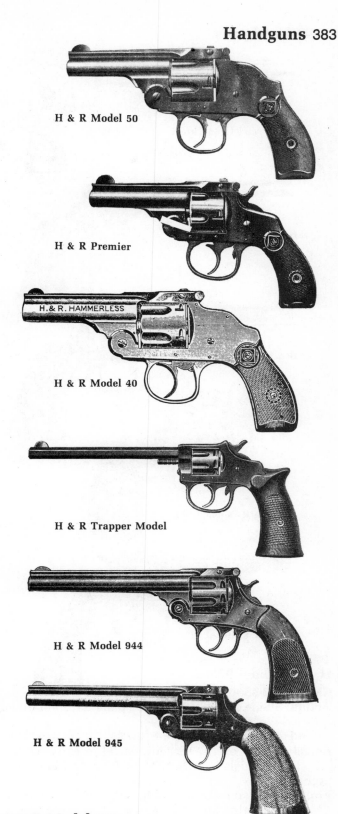

H & R Model 50

H & R Premier

H & R Model 40

H & R Trapper Model

H & R Model 944

H & R Model 945

H & R Model 945

Same as Model 944 except: safety cylinder (recessed chambers.) Made from about 1929 to 1941.

Estimated Value: Excellent: **$125.00**

Very good: **$110.00**

H & R Model 955

Same as Model 945 except: 10″ barrel; approximate weight 28 oz. Made from about 1929 to 1941.

Estimated Value: Excellent: **$130.00**

Very good: **$115.00**

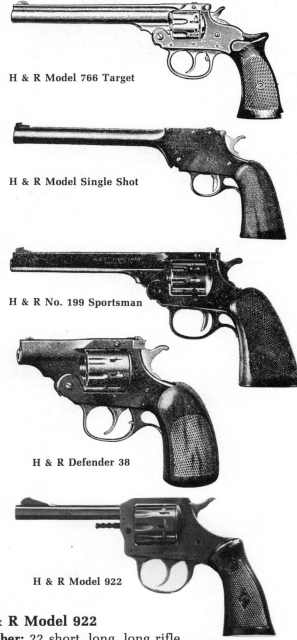

H & R Model 766 Target

H & R Model Single Shot

H & R No. 199 Sportsman

H & R Defender 38

H & R Model 922

H & R Model 922

Caliber: 22 short, long, long rifle
Action: Single or double; exposed hammer; solid frame; side load
Cylinder: 9-shot removable cylinder
Barrel: 4″, 6″, or 10″ octagon barrel in early models; later models had 2½″, 4″ or 6″ round barrel
Sights: Fixed
Finish: Blued; checkered walnut grips on early models; plastic grips on later models
Length Overall: 8¼″ to 14¼″
Approximate wt.: 20 to 26 oz.
Comments: Made from about 1929 to 1970's.
Estimated Value: Excellent: $90.00
Very good: $65.00

H & R Model 923

Same as Model 922 except nickel finish. Made from about 1930 to late 1970's.
Estimated Value: Excellent: $95.00
Very good: $70.00

H & R 766 Target

Caliber: 22 short, long, long rifle, 22 WRF
Action: Single or double; exposed hammer; small hinged frame; top break
Cylinder: 7-shot; simultaneous automatic ejector
Barrel: 6″ round ribbed
Sights: Fixed
Finish: Blued; checkered square butt walnut grips
Length Overall: 10″
Approximate wt.: 16 oz.
Comments: Made from about 1926 to 1936.
Estimated Value: Excellent: $135.00
Very good: $100.00

H & R Ultra Sportsman

Caliber: 22 short, long, long rifle
Action: Single; exposed hammer; hinged frame; top break
Cylinder: 9-shot; simultaneous automatic ejector
Barrel: 6″ round, ribbed
Sights: Adjustable target sights
Finish: Blued; checkered square butt walnut grips
Length Overall: 10″
Approximate wt.: 30 oz.
Comments: Heavy frame; short cylinder; wide hammer spur. Made from about 1928 to 1938.
Estimated Value: Excellent: $145.00
Very good: $120.00

H & R USRA Single Shot

Same as Ultra Sportsman except: single shot only (no cylinder); cartridge chamber in barrel; barrel fills in cylinder space; 7″, 8″ or 10″ barrel lengths; approximate weight 29 to 31 oz. Made from about 1928 to 1943.
Estimated Value: Excellent: $300.00
Very good: $225.00

H & R No. 199 (Sportsman)

Caliber: 22 short, long, long rifle
Action: Single or double; exposed hammer; hinged frame; top break
Cylinder: 9-shot; simultaneous automatic ejector
Barrel: 6″ round, ribbed
Sights: Adjustable target
Finish: Blued; checkered square butt walnut grips
Length Overall: 11″
Approximate wt.: 27 oz.
Comments: Made from about 1931 to 1951.
Estimated Value: Excellent: $110.00
Very good: $ 85.00

H & R Defender 38

Similar to No. 199 Sportsman Model except: 38 S&W caliber; 4″ or 6″ barrel; fixed sights, plastic grips. Made from about 1933 to 1946.
Estimated Value: Excellent: $95.00
Very good: $70.00

H & R Model 299 New Defender

Same as No. 199 Sportsman Model except: 2″ barrel; 6¼″ overall length. Made from about 1936 to 1941.
Estimated Value: Excellent: $100.00
Very good: $ 75.00

H & R No. 999 (Deluxe Sportsman)

Same as No. 199 Sportsman Model except redesigned hammer and barrel rib in 1950's. Made from about 1936 to 1986. 32 caliber (6-shot cylinder) and 4″ barrel available in 1979.

Estimated Value: Excellent: $160.00
Very good: $120.00

H & R No. 999 Deluxe Sportsman

H & R Model 929 Side-Kick

H & R Bobby Model 15

Caliber: 32 S&W, 32 S&W long, 38 S&W
Action: Single or double; exposed hammer; hinged frame; top break
Cylinder: 6-shot in 32 caliber, 5-shot in 38 caliber; simultaneous automatic ejector
Barrel: 4″ round, ribbed
Sights: Fixed
Finish: Blued; checkered square butt walnut grips
Length Overall: 9″
Approximate wt.: 23 oz.
Comments: Made from about 1941 to 1943.
Estimated Value: Excellent: $100.00
Very good: $ 75.00

H & R Model 929 Side-Kick

Caliber: 22 short, long, long rifle
Action: Single or double; exposed hammer; solid frame
Cylinder: 9-shot swing out; simultaneous manual ejector
Barrel: 2½″, 4″ or 6″ round
Sights: 2½″ has fixed sights; 4″ and 6″ have windage adjustable rear sights
Finish: Blued; checkered plastic grips; walnut grips available after 1982
Length Overall: 6¾″ to 10¼″
Approximate wt.: 22 to 28 oz.
Comments: Made from about 1956 to 1986. Add $15.00 for walnut grips.
Estimated Value: Excellent: $ 95.00
Very good: $ 70.00

H & R Model 930 Side-Kick

Same as Model 929 Side-Kick except: nickel finish; 2½″ or 4″ barrel. Add $15.00 for walnut grips.
Estimated Value: Excellent: $100.00
Very good: $ 75.00

H & R Model 632

H & R Model 732 Guardsman

H & R Model 632

Caliber: 32 S&W, 32 S&W long
Action: Single or double; exposed hammer; solid frame; top break; removable
Barrel: 2½″ or 4″ round
Sights: Fixed
Finish: Blued; checkered tenite grips
Length Overall: 6¾″ to 8¼″
Approximate wt.: 19 to 21 oz.
Comments: 2½″ barrel model has round butt grips. Made from about 1946 to 1986.
Estimated Value: Excellent: $ 75.00
Very good: $ 55.00

H & R Model 633

Same as Model 632 except: nickel finish; 2½″ barrel only. Made from about 1946 to late 1970's.
Estimated Value: Excellent: $80.00
Very good: $60.00

H & R Model 732 Guardsman

Caliber: 32 S&W, 32 S&W long
Action: Single or double; exposed hammer; solid frame
Cylinder: 6-shot swing out; simultaneous manual ejector
Barrel: 2½″ or 4″ round
Sights: Fixed
Finish: Blued; checkered plastic grips; walnut grips available after 1982
Length Overall: 6¾″ to 8¼″
Approximate wt.: 23 to 26 oz.
Comments: Made from about 1958 to 1986. Add $15.00 for walnut grips.
Estimated Value: Excellent: $ 95.00
Very good: $ 70.00

H & R Model 622

H & R Model 733 Guardsman

H & R Model 733 Guardsman

Same as Model 732 Guardsman except: nickel finish; round butt grips. Made from about 1958 to 1986. Add $15.00 for walnut grips.
Estimated Value: Excellent: $105.00
Very good: $ 80.00

H & R Model 622

Caliber: 22 short, long, long rifle
Action: Single or double; exposed hammer; solid frame; side load
Cylinder: 6-shot removable
Barrel: 2½", 4" or 6" round
Sights: Fixed
Finish: Blued; checkered plastic grips
Length Overall: 6¾" to 10¼"
Approximate wt.: 24 to 28 oz.
Comments: Made from about 1957 to 1986.
Estimated Value: Excellent: $ 75.00
Very good: $ 55.00

H & R Model 939 Ultra Sidekick & 940

Caliber: 22 short, long, long rifle
Action: Single or double; exposed hammer; solid frame
Cylinder: 9-shot swing out; simultaneous manual ejector
Barrel: 6" ventilated rib target barrel; bull barrel on 940
Sights: Ramp front; adjustable rear sight
Finish: Blued; checkered walnut grips with thumb rest
Length Overall: 10½"
Approximate wt.: 33 oz.
Comments: Made from about 1958 to early 1980's.
Estimated Value: Excellent: $110.00
Very good: $ 90.00

H & R Model 903

Similar to the Model 939 with a solid heavy flat side barrel and adjustable sights. Produced from 1980 to 1984.
Estimated Value: Excellent: $120.00
Very good: $ 95.00

H & R Model 603

Similar to the Model 903 in 22 magnum. Discontinued in 1984.
Estimated Value: Excellent: $120.00
Very good: $ 95.00

H & R Model 904

Similar to the Model 903 with a 4" or 6" heavy round barrel. Blue satin finish available after 1982.
Estimated Value: Excellent: $125.00
Very good: $ 95.00

H & R Model 604

Similar to the Model 904 in 22 magnum.
Estimated Value: Excellent: $125.00
Very good: $ 95.00

H & R Model 642

Similar to the Model 622 in 22 WMR caliber; 2½" or 4" barrel. Discontinued in 1983.
Estimated Value: Excellent: $70.00
Very good: $50.00

H & R Model 623

Same as Model 622 except: nickel finish. Made from about 1957 to late 1970's.
Estimated Value: Excellent: $70.00
Very good: $50.00

H & R Model 939 Ultra Sidekick

H & R Model 905

Similar to the Model 904 with nickel finish. Introduced in 1981. Discontinued 1986.
Estimated Value: Excellent: $135.00
Very good: $100.00

H & R Model 900

H & R Model 900

Caliber: 22 short, long, long rifle
Action: Single or double; exposed hammer; solid frame; side load
Cylinder: 9-shot removable
Barrel: 2½", 4" or 6"
Sights: Fixed
Finish: Blued; checkered plastic grips
Length Overall: 6½" to 10"
Approximate wt.: 23 to 26 oz.
Comments: Made from about 1962 to 1973.
Estimated Value: Excellent: $75.00
Very good: $55.00

H & R Model 901

Same as Model 900 except nickel finish. Made from about 1962 to 1963.
Estimated Value: Excellent: $80.00
Very good: $60.00

H & R Model 949 Forty-Niner

H & R Model 926

H & R Model 925 Defender

Caliber: 38 S&W
Action: Single or double; exposed hammer; hinged frame; top break
Cylinder: 5-shot; simultaneous automatic ejector
Barrel: 2½″ round, ribbed
Sights: Fixed front sight; adjustable rear sight
Finish: Blued; one-piece wrap around grip
Length Overall: 6¾″
Approximate wt.: 22 oz.
Comments: Made from about 1964 to late 1970's.
Estimated Value: Excellent: $120.00
                       Very good: $ 95.00

H & R Model 926

Caliber: 38 S&W
Action: Single or double; exposed hammer; hinged frame; top break
Cylinder: 5-shot; simultaneous automatic ejector
Barrel: 4″
Sights: Adjustable rear sight
Finish: Blued; checkered plastic square butt grips
Length Overall: 8¼″
Approximate wt.: 31 oz.
Comments: Made from about 1972 to late 1970's.
Estimated Value: Excellent: $115.00
                       Very good: $ 90.00

H & R Model 649 Convertible

H & R Model 666 Convertible

H & R Model 666 Convertible

Caliber: 22 short, long, long rifle, 22 magnum (WMR) with extra interchangeable cylinder
Action: Single or double; exposed hammer; solid frame; side load
Cylinder: 6-shot removable; extra interchangeable cylinder so either cartridge can be used
Barrel: 6″ round
Sights: Fixed
Finish: Blued; black cycolac, square butt grips
Length Overall: 10¼″
Approximate wt.: 28 oz.
Comments: Made from about 1975 to late 1970's.
Estimated Value: Excellent: $100.00
                       Very good: $ 75.00

H & R Model 949 Forty-Niner

Caliber: 22 short, long, long rifle
Action: Single or double; exposed hammer; solid frame; side load and ejection
Cylinder: 9-shot
Barrel: 5½″ round; ejector
Sights: Blade front; adjustable rear sights
Finish: Blued; smooth walnut, one-piece, western style grips
Length Overall: 10¼″
Approximate wt.: 31 oz.
Comments: Made from about 1959 to 1986.
Estimated Value: Excellent: $ 95.00
                       Very good: $ 70.00

H & R Model 950 Forty-Niner

Same as Model 949 Forty-Niner revolver except nickel finish.
Estimated Value: Excellent: $100.00
                       Very good: $ 75.00

H & R Model 976

Similar to 949 with 7½″ barrel, case hardened frame. Add $20.00 for nickel finish. Discontinued early 1980's.
Estimated Value: Excellent: $85.00
                       Very good: $70.00

H & R Model 649 Convertible

Caliber: 22 short, long, long rifle, 22 magnum (WMR) with extra interchangeable cylinder
Action: Single or double; exposed hammer; solid frame; side load and ejection
Cylinder: 6-shot removable cylinder; single manual ejector; extra interchangeable cylinder
Barrel: 5½″ or 7½″ round barrel; ejector rod housing under barrel
Sights: Blade front; adjustable rear sights
Finish: Blued barrel; satin finish frame; smooth western style walnut grips
Length Overall: 10¼″
Approximate wt.: 32 oz.
Comments: Western style; made from about 1975 to 1986.
Estimated Value: Excellent: $115.00
                       Very good: $ 85.00

H & R Model 650 Convertible

Same as Model 649 Convertible except nickel finish.
Estimated Value: Excellent: $120.00
                       Very good: $ 95.00

H & R Model 676 Convertible

Similar to Model 649 Convertible except: 4½″, 5½″, 7½″ or 12″ barrel; blued barrel with antique color cased frame; finger rest at back of trigger guard. Discontinued early 1980's. Add $25.00 for 12″ barrel model.
Estimated Value: Excellent: $120.00
                       Very good: $ 95.00

H & R Model 686 Convertible

Similar to the Model 676 with ramp front sight, adjustable rear sight. Add $20.00 for 12″ barrel.
Estimated Value: Excellent: $135.00
                       Very good: $100.00

H & R Model 504

H & R Model 829

H & R Model 532

H & R Model 586

H & R Model 504

Caliber: 32 H&R magnum
Action: Single and double, swing-out cylinder, exposed hammer
Cylinder: 5-shot swing-out
Barrel: 3″, 4″, 6″ target bull
Sights: Blade front, rear adjustable for windage and elevation
Finish: Blued, smooth walnut grips, round or square butt
Length Overall: 7½″ - 10″
Approximate wt.: 29 to 35 oz.
Comments: Introduced in 1984 for the new H&R magnum caliber. Discontinued 1986.
Estimated Value: Excellent: $140.00
Very good: $105.00

H & R Model 586

Caliber: 32 H&R magnum
Action: Single and double, side loading and ejection
Cylinder: 5-shot removeable
Barrel: 4½″, 5½″, 7½″, 10″ round
Sights: Ramp and blade front, rear adjustable for windage and elevation
Finish: Blued, case hardened frame; hardwood grips
Length Overall: 10¼″ (5½″ barrel)
Approximate wt.: 30 to 38 oz.
Comments: Introduced in 1984 for the new 32 H&R magnum caliber. Discontinued 1986.
Estimated Value: Excellent: $145.00
Very good: $110.00

Hartford

H & R Model 829

Caliber: 22 long rifle
Action: Single or double; exposed hammer
Cylinder: 9-shot swing out
Barrel: 3″ bull barrel
Sights: Ramp front, adjustable rear
Finish: Blued; smooth walnut grips
Length Overall: 7¼″
Approximate wt.: 27 oz.
Comments: Produced from 1981 to 1984.
Estimated Value: Excellent: $110.00
Very good: $ 85.00

H & R Model 830

Similar to the Model 829 with nickel finish. Produced from 1982 to 1984.
Estimated Value: Excellent: $120.00
Very good: $ 95.00

H & R Model 826

Similar to the Model 829 in 22 magnum caliber.
Estimated Value: Excellent: $115.00
Very good: $ 90.00

H & R Model 832

Similar to the Model 829 in 32 caliber. Discontinued in 1984.
Estimated Value: Excellent: $100.00
Very good: $ 75.00

H & R Model 833

Similar to the Model 832 with nickel finish. Produced from 1982 to 1984.
Estimated Value: Excellent: $115.00
Very good: $ 90.00

H & R Model 532

Caliber: 32 H&R magnum
Action: Single and double
Cylinder: 5-shot pull-pin removeable
Barrel: 2¼″, 4″ round
Sights: Fixed
Finish: Blued; smooth walnut grips
Length Overall: 6¾″ - 8¼″
Approximate wt.: 20 to 25 oz.
Comments: Introduced in 1984 for the new H&R magnum caliber. Discontinued 1986.
Estimated Value: Excellent: $ 90.00
Very good: $ 65.00

Hartford Automatic Target

Hartford Automatic Target

Caliber: 22 long rifle
Action: Semi-automatic; concealed hammer
Magazine: 10-shot clip
Barrel: 6¾″
Sights: Fixed front; rear sight dovetailed in slide
Finish: Blued; black rubber grips
Length Overall: 10¾″
Approximate wt.: 32 oz.
Comments: Made from about 1929 to 1930. Similar in appearance to Colt Woodsman and Hi Standard Model B Automatic Pistol. Rights and properties of Hartford Arms were sold to High Standard Mfg. Co. in 1932.
Estimated Value: Excellent: $325.00
Very good: $250.00

Hartford Repeating Pistol

Caliber: 22 long rifle
Action: Manual operation of slide after each shot to eject cartridge and feed another cartridge from magazine to chamber; concealed hammer
Magazine: 10-shot clip
Barrel: 6¾″
Sights: Fixed front; rear sight dovetailed into slide
Finish: Blued; black rubber grips
Length Overall: 10¾″
Approximate wt.: 31 oz.
Comments: Made from about 1929 to 1930.
Estimated Value: Excellent: $400.00
Very good: $300.00

Hartford Single Shot

Caliber: 22 long rifle
Action: Single action, hand operated, concealed hammer
Magazine: None
Barrel: 6¾″
Sights: Fixed front; rear dovetailed into slide
Finish: Matte finish on slide and frame; blued barrel; black rubber or walnut grips
Length Overall: 10¾″
Approximate wt.: 37 oz.
Comments: Made from about 1929 to 1930.
Estimated Value: Excellent: $450.00
Very good: $335.00

Heckler & Koch

Heckler & Koch Model P7 (M-8 & M-13)

Caliber: 9mm Parabellum
Action: Recoil operated semi-automatic; concealed hammer; contains a unique system of cocking by squeezing front of grips, uncocking by releasing; double action
Magazine: 8-shot clip (M-8); 13-shot clip (M-13)
Barrel: 4¹⁄₈″
Sights: Fixed
Finish: Blued; black grips
Length Overall: 6½″
Approximate wt.: 33½ oz.
Comments: Made in West Germany. Introduced in 1982. Add $50.00 for M-13.
Estimated Value: New (retail): $612.00
Excellent: $460.00
Very good: $345.00

Heckler & Koch Model P9S

Caliber: 9mm Parabellum; 45 ACP
Action: Semi-automatic; concealed hammer; cocking lever
Magazine: 9-shot clip; 7-shot clip in 45 ACP
Barrel: 4″
Sights: Fixed; blade front, square notch rear
Finish: Blued; black plastic grips; wood combat grips available
Length Overall: 7½″
Approximate wt.: 28 to 31 oz.
Comments: Made in West Germany. Add $65.00 for 45 ACP caliber.
Estimated Value: New (retail): $666.00
Excellent: $500.00
Very good: $375.00

Heckler & Koch Model P9S Competition

Similar to the Model P9S Target with both 4″ and 5½″ barrel, 2 slides, wood competition grips and plastic grips, all packed in a special case. 9mm only.
Estimated Value: New (retail): $1,333.00
Excellent: $1,000.00
Very good: $ 725.00

Heckler & Koch Model P9S Target

Similar to the Model P9S with adjustable trigger, trigger stop and adjustable rear sight; 5½″ barrel available. Add $65.00 for 45 ACP caliber.
Estimated Value: New (retail): $799.00
Excellent: $600.00
Very good: $450.00

Heckler & Koch Model HK4

Heckler & Koch Model P9S

Heckler & Koch Model HK4

Caliber: 380; conversion kits available for calibers 35, 25, and 22 long rifle
Action: Semi-automatic; double action; exposed hammer spur
Magazine: 7-shot clip
Barrel: 3³⁄₈″
Sights: Fixed, blade front, notch rear; non-reflective
Finish: Blued; black plastic grips; grip extension on clip
Length Overall: 6″
Approximate wt.: 17 oz.
Comments: Discontinued in mid 1980's. Add $160.00 for all three conversion kits.
Estimated Value: Excellent: $320.00
Very good: $240.00

Heckler & Koch Model VP70Z

Caliber: 9mm
Action: Semi-automatic, blow back, recoil operated; double action only; hammerless
Magazine: Double stacked 18-shot clip; 2 magazines standard
Barrel: 4½″
Sights: Fixed, ramp front, notched rear
Finish: Blued; black plastic grips; solid plastic receiver
Length Overall: 8″
Approximate wt.: 29 oz.
Comments: A pistol with few moving parts, designed for the outdoorsman. Discontinued in mid 1980's.
Estimated Value: Excellent: $300.00
Very good: $225.00

High Standard

High Standard Model B

High Standard Model B

Caliber: 22 long rifle
Action: Semi-automatic; concealed hammer; thumb safety
Magazine: 10-shot clip
Barrel: 4½″ or 6¾″
Sights: Fixed
Finish: Blued; hard rubber grips
Length Overall: 8½″ and 10¾″
Approximate wt.: 30 to 34 oz.
Comments: Produced from about 1931 to 1942.
Estimated Value: Excellent: $175.00
 Very good: $130.00

High Standard Model HB

Same as Model B except: exposed hammer and no thumb safety. Made from about 1932 to 1942.
Estimated Value: Excellent: $180.00
 Very good: $135.00

High Standard Model A

Caliber: 22 long rifle
Action: Semi-automatic; concealed hammer; thumb safety
Magazine: 10-shot clip
Barrel: 4½″ or 6¾″
Sights: Adjustable target sights
Finish: Blued; checkered walnut grips
Length Overall: 9¼″ or 11¼″
Approximate wt.: 34 to 36 oz.
Comments: Made from about 1937 to 1942.
Estimated Value: Excellent: $175.00
 Very good: $130.00

High Standard Model HA

Same as Model A except exposed hammer spur and no thumb safety.
Estimated Value: Excellent: $185.00
 Very good: $140.00

High Standard Model D

Same as Model A except: heavier barrel; approximate weight 37 to 40 oz., depending on barrel length.
Estimated Value: Excellent: $200.00
 Very good: $150.00

High Standard Model HD

Same as Model D except: exposed hammer spur and no thumb safety.
Estimated Value: Excellent: $210.00
 Very good: $150.00

High Standard Model HDM or HD Military

Same as Model HD except it has thumb safety. Made from about 1941 to 1947, stamped "U.S. Property."
Estimated Value: Excellent: $300.00
 Very good: $225.00

High Standard Model SB

Same as Model B except: 6¾″ smooth bore for shooting 22 long rifle shot cartridges.
Estimated Value: Excellent: $180.00
 Very good: $135.00

High Standard Model C

Same as Model B except: chambered for 22 shot cartridges. Made from about 1932 to 1942.
Estimated Value: Excellent: $185.00
 Very good: $140.00

High Standard Model A

High Standard Model E

High Standard Model HD

High Standard Model HD Military (Post War)

Same as Model HDM except it is not stamped "U.S. Property." Made from about 1946 to 1951 (post World War II model.)
Estimated Value: Excellent: $200.00
 Very good: $150.00

High Standard Model E

Similar to Model A except: extra heavy barrel; thumb rest grips. Approximate weight 39 to 42 oz.
Estimated Value: Excellent: $185.00
 Very good: $140.00

High Standard Model HE

Same as Model E except: exposed hammer spur; no thumb safety.
Estimated Value: Excellent: $195.00
 Very good: $145.00

High Standard G-B

High Standard Model G-B

Caliber: 22 long rifle
Action: Semi-automatic; concealed hammer; takedown
    model; interchangeable barrels; thumb safety
Magazine: 10-shot clip
Barrel: 4½″ and 6¾″
Sights: Fixed
Finish: Blued; checkered plastic grips
Length Overall: 8½″ and 10¾″
Approximate wt.: 34 to 36 oz.
Comments: Made from about 1948 to 1951. Add $20.00
    if pistol has both barrels.
Estimated Value: **Excellent:**   **$175.00**
                Very good: **$130.00**

High Standard Model G-D

Same as Model G-B except: adjustable target sights;
checkered walnut grips; approximate weight 38 to 40 oz.;
length overall about 9¼″ to 11½″. Add $20.00 if pistol
has both barrels.
Estimated Value: **Excellent:**   **$185.00**
                Very good: **$140.00**

High Standard
Model G-D

High Standard Model G-E

Same as Model G-D except: heavy barrel; thumb rest;
walnut grips; approximate weight 42 to 44 oz. Add
$25.00 if pistol has both barrels.
Estimated Value: **Excellent:**   **$190.00**
                Very good: **$145.00**

High Standard
Olympic 1st Model

High Standard Olympic 1st Model

Same as Model G-E except: 22 short caliber; light alloy
slide; made from about 1950 to 1951; approximate weight
38 to 40 oz. Add $25.00 if pistol has both barrels.
Estimated Value: **Excellent:**   **$250.00**
                Very good: **$190.00**

High Standard Olympic 2nd Model

Same as Olympic 1st Model except: thumb safety located
at center top of left grip; plastic grips with thumb rest;
produced from about 1951 to 1958. Add $20.00 if pistol
has both barrels.
Estimated Value: **Excellent:**   **$230.00**
                Very good: **$175.00**

High Standard Olympic 2nd Model

High Standard Olympic ISU

Caliber: 22 short
Action: Semi-automatic; concealed hammer; wide target
    trigger; anti-backlash trigger adjustment
Magazine: 10-shot clip
Barrel: 5½″ bull barrel (1963-1966); 8″ tapered barrel
    (1958-1964); 6¾″ tapered barrel (1958-present); in-
    tegral stabilizer and 2 removable weights
Sights: Ramp front; adjustable rear
Finish: Blued; checkered walnut grips with thumb rests
Length Overall: 11¼″ (6¾″ barrel)
Approximate wt.: 40 to 41 oz.
Comments: Meets International Shooting Union Regula-
    tions; left or right hand grips; regular Hi-Standard
    style grip or the squared military style grip; military
    style has rear sight frame mounted. Made from
    about 1958 to late 1970's.
Estimated Value: **Excellent:**   **$275.00**
                Very good: **$205.00**

High Standard Olympic ISU

High Standard Model G-380

Caliber: 380 ACP
Action: Semi-automatic; exposed hammer spur; thumb
    safety; barrel takedown model
Magazine: 6-shot clip; bottom release
Barrel: 5″
Sights: Fixed; blade front and notched rear
Finish: Blued; checkered plastic grips
Length Overall: 9″
Approximate wt.: 40 oz.
Comments: First of the barrel takedown models produc-
    ed by High Standard. Made from about 1944 to
    1950.
Estimated Value: **Excellent:**   **$300.00**
                Very good: **$225.00**

High Standard Model G-380

High Standard Sport-King 1st Model

High Standard Sport-King
2nd Model

Standard Citation Model

High Standard Sport-King 1st Model

Caliber: 22 long rifle
Action: Semi-automatic; concealed hammer; takedown model with interchangeable barrel; thumb safety at top center of left grip
Magazine: 10-shot clip
Barrel: 4½″ and/or 6¾″
Sights: Fixed
Finish: Blued; checkered plastic grips with thumb rest
Length Overall: 9″; 11¼″
Approximate wt.: 36 to 39 oz.
Comments: Made from about 1951 to 1958. Add $15.00 for pistol with both barrels.
Estimated Value: Excellent: $160.00
Very good: $120.00

High Standard Sport-King 2nd Model

Similar to Sport-King 1st Model except: made from about 1958 to present; interior changes; still has interchangeable barrel; blued or nickel finish; weighs 39 to 42 oz. Add $15.00 for nickel finish. Reintroduced in early 1980's to 1985, slightly different grip style.
Estimated Value: Excellent: $190.00
Very good: $140.00

High Standard Lightweight Sport-King

Same as Sport-King 1st Model except: made from about 1954 to 1965; aluminum alloy frame; weight 28 to 30 oz. Add $15.00 for pistol with both barrels.
Estimated Value: Excellent: $150.00
Very good: $110.00

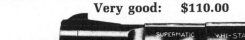

High Standard Supermatic

Standard Tournament Model

Supermatic Standard Citation
and Military Citation Model

High Standard Supermatic Series

Caliber: 22 long rifle
Action: Semi-automatic; concealed hammer; thumb safety; takedown model with interchangeable barrels
Magazine: 10-shot clip
Barrel: 4½″, 5½″, 6¾″, 7¼″, 8″, 10″
Sights: Ramp front, adjustable rear
Finish: Blued; checkered plastic or checkered wood grips with or without thumb rest
Length Overall: 9¼″ to 14¾″
Approximate wt.: 40 to 46 oz.
Comments: The 5¼″ barrels are heavy (bull) barrels and the 7¼″ barrels are heavy (bull) fluted barrels.

Standard Supermatic Model manufactured from about 1951 to 1958; 4¼″ and 6¾″ interchangeable barrels. Add $20.00 for pistols with both barrels.

Excellent: $175.00
Very good: $130.00

Standard Tournament Model made from about 1958 to 1963; 5½″ bull barrel and/or 6¾″ regular barrel with stabilizer and 2 removable weights; adjustable trigger pull. Add $20.00 for pistol with both barrels.

Excellent: $200.00
Very good: $150.00

Standard Citation Model made from about 1959 to 1966; 5½″ bull barrel or 6¾″, 8″ or 10″ tapered barrel with stabilizer and 2 removable weights; adjustable trigger pull.

Excellent: $210.00
Very good: $175.00

Supermatic Standard Citation, Military or Citation II made from about 1965 to 1985; 5½″ heavy (bull) or 7¼″ heavy fluted barrel with military grip or standard grip. 5½″ or 7¼″ slabbed barrel in 1984 (Citation II).

Excellent: $265.00
Very good: $200.00

Supermatic Trophy Military Model

Supermatic Trophy Citation made from about 1959 to 1966; 5½″ bull barrel or 7¼″ fluted barrel.

> Excellent: $250.00
> Very good: $200.00

Supermatic Trophy Military Model manufactured from about 1965 to 1985; 5½″ bull barrel or 7¼″ fluted barrel with square military style grip; adjustable trigger pull. Add $20.00 for 7¼″ barrel.

> Excellent: $285.00
> Very good: $215.00

High Standard Flite-King 1st Model

Same as Sport-King 1st Model except: made from about 1953 to 1958; aluminum alloy frame and slide; weight 24 to 26 oz.; 22 short caliber only. Add $20.00 for pistol with both barrels.

Estimated Value: Excellent: $150.00
                     Very good: $110.00

High Standard Flite-King 2nd Model

Same a Flite-King 1st Model Automatic except: made from about 1958 to 1965; all steel construction; 22 long rifle caliber only. Add $20.00 for pistol with both barrels.

Estimated Value: Excellent: $165.00
                     Very good: $130.00

High Standard Flite-King 1st Model

High Standard Field-King

Same as Sport-King 1st Model except: adjustable target sights; 6¾″ heavy barrel; weight about 44 oz.

Estimated Value: Excellent: $160.00
                     Very good: $120.00

High Standard Dura-Matic

Caliber: 22 long rifle
Action: Semi-automatic; concealed hammer; takedown interchangeable barrel model
Magazine: 10-shot clip
Barrel: 4½″, 6½″
Sights: Fixed
Finish: Blued, checkered plastic grips
Length Overall: 8⅞″, 10⅞″
Approximate wt.: 33 to 35 oz.
Comments: Manufactured from about 1954 to 1969.

Estimated Value: Excellent: $145.00
                     Very good: $110.00

High Standard Field-King

High Standard Dura-Matic

High Standard Plinker

Caliber: 22 long rifle
Action: Semi-automatic; concealed hammer
Magazine: 10-shot clip
Barrel: 4½″, 6½″
Sights: Fixed
Finish: Blued, checkered plastic grips
Length Overall: 9″ to 11″
Approximate wt.: 28 to 30 oz.
Comments: Made from about 1971 to 1974.

Estimated Value: Excellent: $125.00
                     Very good: $ 95.00

High Standard Plinker

High Standard Sharpshooter and Survival Pack

Caliber: 22 long rifle
Action: Semi-automatic; concealed hammer
Magazine: 10-shot clip
Barrel: 5½″ bull barrel
Sights: Ramp front; adjustable rear
Finish: Blued; checkered walnut grips; nickel available after 1982
Length Overall: 10¼″
Approximate wt.: 42 oz.
Comments: Made from about 1971 to 1985. A survival pack consisting of a nickel pistol; extra magazine and canvas case available after 1982. Add $75.00 for complete pack.
Estimated Value: Excellent: $235.00
Very good: $175.00

High Standard Victor

Caliber: 22 long rifle
Action: Semi-automatic; concealed hammer; interchangeable barrel
Magazine: 10-shot clip
Barrel: 4½″ or 5½″ with solid or aluminum ventilated rib and barrel weights
Sights: Ramp front; adjustable rear
Finish: Blued; checkered walnut grips with thumb rest; later models have some parts gold plated
Length Overall: 8¾″, 9¾″
Approximate wt.: 38 to 42 oz.
Comments: Hi-Standard type grip or square military type grip. Made from about 1972 to 1985. 5½″ barrel only in 1980's.
Estimated Value: Excellent: $300.00
Very good: $230.00

High Standard Sharpshooter

High Standard Victor

High Standard 10-X

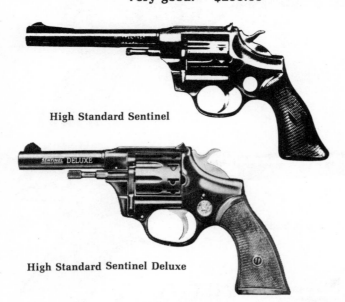

High Standard Sentinel

High Standard Sentinel Deluxe

High Standard Sentinel Deluxe

Same as Sentinel Revolver except: adjustable rear sight; checkered square butt walnut grips; wide trigger; 4″ or 6″ only; made from about 1965 to 1974.
Estimated Value: Excellent: $110.00
Very good: $ 85.00

High Standard 10-X

Caliber: 22 long rifle
Action: Semi-automatic; concealed hammer; adjustable target trigger
Magazine: 10-shot clip; 2 extra standard
Barrel: 5½″ bull barrel
Sights: Blade front, adjustable rear mounted independent of slide
Finish: Non-reflective blue; checkered walnut military grip; components hand picked and fitted by gunsmith; gunsmith's initials located under left grip
Length Overall: 10¼″
Approximate wt.: 42 oz.
Comments: A custom competition gun.
Estimated Value: Excellent: $550.00
Very good: $420.00

High Standard Sentinel

Caliber: 22 short, long, long rifle
Action: Single or double; solid frame
Cylinder: 9-shot swing out; simultaneous manual ejector
Barrel: 3″, 4″, 6″
Sights: Fixed
Finish: Blued or nickel; checkered plastic grips
Length Overall: 8″ to 11″
Approximate wt.: 18 to 24 oz.
Comments: Made from about 1954 to 1974; aluminum alloy frame.
Estimated Value: Excellent: $100.00
Very good: $ 75.00

High Standard Sentinel Imperial

Same as Sentinel revolver except: ramp front sight; black or nickel finish; checkered square butt walnut grips. Made from about 1961 to 1965.

Estimated Value: **Excellent:**   **$105.00**
                     Very good: **$ 80.00**

High Standard Sentinel Imperial

High Standard Sentinel Snub

Same as Sentinel Revolver except: 2³/₈″ barrel only; overall length 7½″; weighs 15 oz.; checkered plastic birds-head grip (rounded butt). Made from about 1956 to 1974. Some were made in pink, turquoise and gold colored finish as well as blue and nickel.

Estimated Value: **Excellent:**   **$110.00**
                     Very good: **$ 85.00**

High Standard Sentinel Snub

High Standard Sentinel Mark I, Sentinel

Caliber: 22 short, long, long rifle
Action: Single or double; solid frame
Cylinder: 9-shot swing out; simultaneous manual ejector
Barrel: 2″, 4″
Sights: Ramp front; fixed or adjustable rear
Finish: Blued or nickel; smooth walnut grips
Length Overall: 7″, 9″
Approximate wt.: 28 to 30 oz.
Comments: A completely redesigned and improved all steel version of the 22 caliber Sentinel. Made from about 1974 to late 1970's. Add $10.00 or nickel finish; $10.00 for adjustable rear sight.

Estimated Value: **Excellent:**   **$160.00**
                     Very good: **$120.00**

High Standard Sentinel Mark IV

High Standard Sentinel Mark IV, Sentinel

Same as Sentinel Mark I except 22 magnum only. Add $10.00 for nickel finish or adjustable rear sight.

Estimated Value: **Excellent:**   **$165.00**
                     Very good: **$125.00**

High Standard Sentinel Mark II

High Standard Sentinel Mark II

Caliber: 38 Special, 357 magnum
Action: Single or double; solid frame
Cylinder: 6-shot swing out; simultaneous manual ejector
Barrel: 2½″, 4″, 6″
Sights: Fixed rear; ramp front
Finish: Blued; checkered walnut grips
Length Overall: 7½″ to 11″
Approximate wt.: 38 to 40 oz.
Comments: Heavy-duty all steel revolver. Made from about 1974 to late 1970's.

Estimated Value: **Excellent:**   **$180.00**
                     Very good: **$135.00**

High Standard Sentinel Mark III

High Standard Sentinel Mark III

Same as Sentinel Mark II except: deluxe trophy blue finish; checkered walnut wrap-around grips; checkered back strap; adjustable rear sight.

Estimated Value: **Excellent:**   **$190.00**
                     Very good: **$140.00**

High Standard Sentinel New Model

High Standard Sentinel New Model

Similar to the Sentinel with 22 caliber cylinder and interchangeable 22 magnum cylinder. Available with 2″ or 4″ barrel. Reintroduced in 1982 to 1985. Add $15.00 for extra cylinder.

Estimated Value: **Excellent:**   **$175.00**
                     Very good: **$135.00**

High Standard Longhorn

Caliber: 22 short, long and long rifle
Action: Double and single; solid frame
Cylinder: 9-shot swing-out; simultaneous manual ejector
Barrel: 4½" or 5½" (1961 to 1966); 9½" (1971 to present); dummy ejector housing under barrel
Sights: Blade front; fixed or adjustable rear
Finish: Blued; plastic grips; walnut grips on 9½" barrel model
Length Overall: 10", 11", 15"
Approximate wt.: 26 to 32 oz.
Comments: Aluminum alloy frame. Made from about 1961 to 1985.
Estimated Value: Excellent: $175.00
Very good: $130.00

High Standard Longhorn Combination

Similar to Longhorn revolver except: extra interchangeable cylinder in 22 magnum caliber; 9½" barrel only; smooth walnut grips. Made from about 1971 to 1985.
Estimated Value: Excellent: $190.00
Very good: $140.00

High Standard Kit Gun

Caliber: 22 short, long, long rifle
Action: Single or double; solid frame
Cylinder: 9-shot swing out; simultaneous manual ejector
Barrel: 4"
Sights: Ramp front; adjustable rear
Finish: Blued; checkered walnut grips
Length Overall: 9"
Approximate wt.: 19 oz.
Comments: Aluminum alloy frame. Made from about 1970 to 1973.
Estimated Value: Excellent: $95.00
Very good: $70.00

High Standard Double Nine

Caliber: 22 short, long, long rifle
Action: Single or double; solid frame
Cylinder: 9-shot swing out; simultaneous manual ejector
Barrel: 5½"; dummy ejector housing under barrel
Sights: Blade front; fixed or adjustable rear
Finish: Blued or nickel; plastic grips
Length Overall: 11"
Approximate wt.: 28 oz.
Comments: Aluminum alloy frame; a western style of the Sentinel revolvers. Made from about 1958 to 1985. Add $10.00 for nickel finish.
Estimated Value: Excellent: $175.00
Very good: $130.00

High Standard Double Nine Combination

Same as Double Nine revolver except: extra interchangeable cylinder in 22 magnum caliber; smooth walnut grip; made from about 1971 to 1985; steel frame; weighs 32 oz. Add $10.00 for nickel finish.
Estimated Value: Excellent: $190.00
Very good: $140.00

High Standard Natchez

Similar to Double Nine revolver except: 4½" barrel only; 10" overall length; weighs 32 oz.; blued finish only; plastic ivory birds-head grips. Made from about 1961 to 1966.
Estimated Value: Excellent: $150.00
Very good: $110.00

High Standard Posse

Similar to Double Nine revolver except: 3½" barrel without dummy ejector housing; 9" overall length; weighs 24 oz.; brass trigger guard and grip frame; blued finish only; smooth walnut grips. Made from about 1961 to 1966.
Estimated Value: Excellent: $140.00
Very good: $110.00

High Standard Longhorn

High Standard Longhorn Combination

Double Nine Combination

High Standard Double Nine

High Standard Natchez

High Standard Posse

High Standard Hombre

Caliber: 22 short, long, long rifle
Action: Single or double; solid frame
Cylinder: 9-shot swing out; simultaneous ejector
Barrel: 4½″
Sights: Blade front, adjustable rear
Finish: Blued or nickel; smooth walnut grip
Length Overall: 10″
Approximate wt.: 26 oz.
Comments: Steel frame; manufactured from about 1972 to 1974. Add $5.00 for nickel finish.
Estimated Value: Excellent: $140.00
　　　　　　　　　Very good: $105.00

High Standard Hombre

High Standard Durango

High Standard High Sierra Combination

High Standard Durango

Caliber: 22 short, long, long rifle
Action: Single or double; solid frame
Cylinder: 9-shot swing out, simultaneous ejector
Barrel: 4½″, 5½″; dummy ejector housing under barrel
Sights: Blade front, adjustable rear
Finish: Blued or nickel; smooth walnut grips
Length Overall: 10″, 11″
Approximate wt.: 25 to 27 oz.
Comments: Made from about 1972 to 1975.
Estimated Value: Excellent: $150.00
　　　　　　　　　Very good: $115.00

High Standard High Sierra Combination

Caliber: 22 short, long, long rifle and .22 magnum
Action: Double and single; solid frame
Cylinder: 9-shot swing-out; two interchangeable cylinders (22 cal. and 22 mag. cal.)
Barrel: 7″ octagonal
Sights: Blade front; adjustable rear
Finish: Blued; smooth walnut grips
Length Overall: 12½″
Comments: Steel frame; gold plated trigger guard and backstrap. Made from about 1973 to 1985.
Estimated Value: Excellent: $190.00
　　　　　　　　　Very good: $140.00

High Standard Camp Gun

High Standard Crusader

High Standard Crusader Medium Frame

High Standard Camp Gun

Caliber: 22 short, long, long rifle, 22 magnum
Action: Single or double; solid frame; simultaneous ejector
Cylinder: 9-shot swing out
Barrel: 6″
Sights: Ramp front; adjustable rear
Finish: Blued; checkered walnut grips
Length Overall: 11″
Approximate wt.: 28 oz.
Comments: Made from about 1975 to late 1970's. Add $3.00 for 22 magnum caliber. Reintroduced in 1982 to 1985.
Estimated Value: Excellent: $190.00
　　　　　　　　　Very good: $140.00

High Standard Crusader

Caliber: 44 magnum, 45 Colt, 357 magnum
Action: Single or double
Cylinder: 6-shot
Barrel: 4½″ in 44 or 45; 6½″ in 44, 45 or 357; 8³/₈″ in 44, 45 or 357
Sights: Adjustable rear, ramp blade front
Finish: Blued; shrouded ejector rod; smooth walnut grips in 44; checkered walnut grips in 45 and 357
Length Overall: 9⁷/₈″ - 14″
Approximate wt.: 43 to 52 oz.
Comments: A large frame handgun made from about the late 1970's to early 1980's. Add $5.00 for 6½″ barrel; $12.00 for 8³/₈″ barrel.
Estimated Value: Excellent: $275.00
　　　　　　　　　Very good: $200.00

High Standard Crusader Medium Frame

Similar to the Crusader in 357 magnum only; 4½″ or 6½″ barrel; weight is 40 to 42 oz.; a smaller version of the Crusader. Add $7.00 for 6½″ barrel.
Estimated Value: Excellent: $200.00
　　　　　　　　　Very good: $150.00

High Standard Derringer

Caliber: 22 short, long, long rifle (1962 to present); 22 magnum rimfire (1963 to present)

Action: Double; concealed hammer; hammer block safety; front of trigger guard cut away

Cylinder: None; 2-shot chambers in barrels.

Barrel: 3½″ double barrel (superposed); duel ejection; cartridge chamber in each barrel

Sights: Fixed

Finish: Blued or nickel; plastic grips (1962 to present); gold plated presentation model in walnut case (1965 to 1966). Electroless nickel finish and walnut grips after 1982.

Length Overall: 5″

Approximate wt.: 11 oz.

Comments: Steel barrels; aluminum alloy frame. Made from about 1962 to 1985.

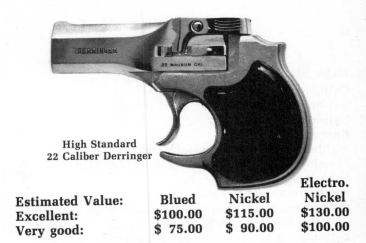

High Standard
22 Caliber Derringer

Estimated Value:	Blued	Nickel	Electro. Nickel
Excellent:	$100.00	$115.00	$130.00
Very good:	$ 75.00	$ 90.00	$100.00

Gold presentation models with case in unused condition: (with consecutive numbers)

1-derringer $225.00
2-derringer $470.00

Iver Johnson

Iver Johnson X300 Pony, PO380, PO380B

Caliber: 380 ACP

Action: Single or double; semi-automatic; exposed hammer

Magazine: 6-shot clip

Barrel: 3″

Sights: Adjustable rear, blade front

Finish: Blued, nickel or military; checkered or smooth walnut grips

Length Overall: 6″

Approximate wt.: 20 oz.

Comments: Add $12.00 for nickel finish.

Estimated Value:	New (retail):	$287.00
	Excellent:	$215.00
	Very good:	$160.00

Iver Johnson X300 Pony

Iver Johnson Model TP22

Iver Johnson Model TP22, TP25, TP22B & TP25B

Caliber: 22 long rifle (TP22), 25 ACP (TP25)

Action: Double action; semi-automatic; exposed hammer

Magazine: 7-shot clip

Barrel: 3″

Sights: Fixed

Finish: Blued; plastic grips; finger extension on clip

Length Overall: 5½″

Approximate wt.: 15 oz.

Comments: Introduced in 1982.

Estimated Value:	New (retail):	$154.00
	Excellent:	$115.00
	Very good:	$ 85.00

Iver Johnson Trailsman

Caliber: 22 long rifle

Action: Semi-automatic, concealed hammer

Magazine: Clip

Barrel: 4½″, 6″

Sights: Fixed

Finish: Blued; checkered plastic or smooth hardwood grips.

Length Overall: 9″ to 11″

Approximate wt.: 28 to 30 oz.

Comments: Introduced in 1984. Add 10% for HiPolish with hardwood grips.

Estimated Value:	New (retail):	$191.00
	Excellent:	$145.00
	Very good:	$107.00

Iver Johnson Safety Hammer

Caliber: 22 short, long, long rifle, 32 S&W, 32 S&W long or 38 S&W

Action: Single or double; exposed hammer; hinged frame; top break style; simultaneous ejector; heavier frame for 32 and 38 caliber

Cylinder: 7-shot in 22 caliber; 6-shot in 32 caliber; 5-shot in 38 caliber

Barrel: 2″, 3″, 3¼″, 4″, 5″, 6″; round barrel with rib on top

Sights: Fixed

Finish: Blued or nickel; hard rubber or wood grips; round or square butt grip

Length Overall: 6¾″ to 10¾″ depending on barrel length

Approximate wt.: 14 to 21 oz. depending on caliber and barrel length

Comments: Made from about 1892 to 1950 with some improvements and minor changes.

Estimated Value:	Excellent:	$120.00
	Very good:	$ 95.00

Iver Johnson Safety Hammer

Iver Johnson Safety Hammerless

Same as Safety Hammer model except: side plates of frame extended to enclose hammer; double action only; concealed hammer. Made from about 1895 to 1950.

Estimated Value: Excellent: $125.00
Very good: $100.00

Iver Johnson Safety Hammerless

Iver Johnson Model 1900

Caliber: 22 short, long, long rifle, 32 S&W, 32 S&W long, 38 S&W
Action: Single or double; exposed hammer; solid frame; side load
Cylinder: 7-shot in 22 caliber; 6-shot in 32 caliber; 5-shot in 38 caliber; removable cylinder
Barrel: 2½″, 4½″, 6″; octagon barrel
Sights: Fixed
Finish: Blued or nickel; hard rubber grips
Length Overall: 7″ to 10¾″ depending on barrel length
Approximate wt.: 11 to 19 oz.
Comments: Made from about 1900 to 1947.
Estimated Value: Excellent: $95.00
Very good: $75.00

Iver Johnson Model 1900

Iver Johnson Model 1900 Target

Same as Model 1900 except: 22 caliber only; 6″ or 9″ barrel length; length overall 10¾″ to 13¾″; approximate weight 22 to 26 oz.; checkered walnut grips; blued finish only. Made from about 1925 to 1942.

Estimated Value: Excellent: $110.00
Very good: $90.00

Iver Johnson Target 9-shot Revolver

Similar to Model 1900 Target except: 9-shot cylinder; 6″ or 10″ barrel; 10¾″ to 14¾″ length overall; weight 24 to 28 oz. Introduced about 1929 and discontinued in 1946.

Estimated Value: Excellent: $115.00
Very good: $95.00

Iver Johnson Supershot

Caliber: 22 short, long, long rifle
Action: Single or double; exposed hammer; hinged frame; top break style; simultaneous ejector
Cylinder: 7-shot; 9-shot
Barrel: 6″; round barrel with solid rib on top
Sights: Fixed
Finish: Blued; checkered walnut grips (one piece)
Length Overall: 10¾″
Approximate wt.: 25 oz.
Comments: Some have adjustable finger rest behind trigger guard. Made from about 1929 to 1949.
Estimated Value: Excellent: $110.00
Very good: $85.00

Iver Johnson Sealed Eight Supershot

Similar to Supershot Revolver except: 8-shot cylinder recessed for cartridge head; 10″ barrel length; 10¾″ to 14¾″ overall lengths; adjustable rear sight. Made from about 1931 to 1957.

Estimated Value: Excellent: $120.00
Very good: $95.00

Iver Johnson Sealed Eight Target

Caliber: 22 short, long, long rifle
Action: Single or double; exposed hammer; solid frame; side load
Cylinder: 8-shot; cylinder recessed for cartridge head; removable
Barrel: 6″, 10″; octagon barrel
Sights: Fixed
Finish: Blued; checkered walnut grips (one piece)
Length Overall: 10¾″; 14¾″
Approximate wt.: 24 to 28 oz.
Comments: Made from about 1931 to 1957.
Estimated Value: Excellent: $100.00
Very good: $75.00

Iver Johnson Model 1900 Target

Iver Johnson Sealed Eight Supershot

Iver Johnson Sealed Eight Target

Iver Johnson Sealed Eight Protector

Caliber: 22 short, long, long rifle
Action: Single or double; exposed hammer; hinged frame; top break style; simultaneous ejector
Cylinder: 8-shot; cylinder recessed for cartridge head
Barrel: 2½″
Sights: Fixed
Finish: Blued; checkered walnut grips
Length Overall: 7½″
Approximate wt.: 20 oz.
Comments: Some had adjustable finger rest behind trigger guards. Made from about 1933 to 1949.
Estimated Value: Excellent: $140.00
Very good: $105.00

Iver Johnson
Sealed Eight Protector

Iver Johnson Champion

Caliber: 22 short, long, long rifle
Action: Single; exposed hammer; hinged frame; top break style; simultaneous ejector
Cylinder: 8-shot; cylinder recessed for cartridge head
Barrel: 6″
Sights: Adjustable target sights
Finish: Blued; checkered walnut grips (one piece)
Length Overall: 10¾″
Approximate wt.: 28 oz.
Comments: Made from about 1938 to 1948. Adjustable finger rest behind trigger guard.
Estimated Value: Excellent: $150.00
Very good: $110.00

Iver Johnson Champion

Iver Johnson
Trigger Cocking Target

Iver Johnson Trigger Cocking Target

Same as Champion Revolver except the trigger cocks the hammer on the first pull, then releases the hammer to fire the revolver on the second pull. Made from about 1940 to 1947.
Estimated Value: Excellent: $160.00
Very good: $120.00

Iver Johnson Armsworth Model 855

Caliber: 22 short, long, long rifle
Action: Single action; exposed hammer; hinged frame; top break style; simultaneous ejector
Cylinder: 8-shot; chambers recessed for cartridge head
Barrel: 6″
Sights: Adjustable front and rear sights
Finish: Blued; checkered walnut grips (one piece)
Length Overall: 10¾″
Approximate wt.: 30 oz.
Comments: Adjustable finger rest behind trigger guard. Made from about 1954 to 1957.
Estimated Value: Excellent: $125.00
Very good: $100.00

Iver Johnson Armsworth Model 855

Iver Johnson Supershot Model 844

Similar to Armsworth Model 855 except: double and single action; 4½″ or 6″ barrel lengths; 9¼″ to 10¾″ overall length. Introduced about 1955, discontinued about 1957.
Estimated Value: Excellent: $110.00
Very good: $ 85.00

Iver Johnson Supershot Model 844

Iver Johnson Model 55S Cadet

Caliber: 22 short, long, long rifle, 32, 38
Action: Single or double; solid frame; exposed hammer; side load
Cylinder: 8-shot in 22 caliber; 5-shot in 32 and 38 caliber; removable cylinder
Barrel: 2½″
Sights: Fixed
Finish: Blued; plastic round butt grips
Length Overall: 7″
Approximate wt.: 24 oz.
Comments: Made from about 1954 to 1961.
Estimated Value: Excellent: $100.00
Very good: $ 75.00

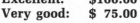

Iver Johnson Model 55S Cadet

Iver Johnson Model 55 S-A Cadet

Similar to Model 55S Cadet except: addition of loading gate about 1962; also in calibers 22 WMR and 38 Special. Made from about 1962 to late 1970's.
Estimated Value: Excellent: $90.00
Very good: $70.00

Iver Johnson Model 55

Caliber: 22 short, long, long rifle
Action: Single or double; exposed hammer; solid frame; side load
Cylinder: 8-shot; chambers recessed for cartridge head; removable cylinder; unfluted cylinder
Barrel: 4½", 6"
Sights: Fixed
Finish: Blued; checkered walnut grips
Length Overall: 9¼" to 10¾"
Approximate wt.: 22 to 24 oz.
Comments: Made from about 1955 to 1961.
Estimated Value: Excellent: $100.00
Very good: $ 75.00

Iver Johnson Model 55A Target

Same as Model 55 Revolver except: fluted cylinder; loading gate; checkered plastic grips. Introduced about 1962. Made to late 1970's.
Estimated Value: Excellent: $85.00
Very good: $65.00

Iver Johnson Model 57

Same as Model 55 Revolver except: adjustable front and rear sights; checkered plastic grips. Made from about 1955 to 1961.
Estimated Value: Excellent: $90.00
Very good: $70.00

Iver Johnson Model 57A Target

Same as Model 55 Revolver except: fluted cylinder; adjustable front and rear sights; checkered plastic grips; loading gate. Made from about 1962 to late 1970's.
Estimated Value: Excellent: $95.00
Very good: $75.00

Iver Johnson
Model 55 S-A Cadet

Iver Johnson Model 50A Sidewinder

Iver Johnson Model 50A Sidewinder

Caliber: 22 short, long, long rifle
Action: Single or double; exposed hammer; solid frame; side load with loading gate; removable cylinder
Cylinder: 8-shot; recessed chambers
Barrel: 4½", 6"; ejector rod under barrel
Sights: Fixed or adjustable
Finish: Blued; plastic grips
Length Overall: 9¾" to 11¼"
Approximate wt.: 32 oz.
Comments: Frontier style double action revolver. Made from about 1961 to late 1970's. Add $20.00 for adjustable sights.
Estimated Value: Excellent: $100.00
Very good: $ 75.00

Iver Johnson Model 50A Sidewinder Convertible

Same as Model 50A Sidewinder except: extra interchangeable cylinder for 22 magnum (WMR) cartridges. Add $10.00 for adjustable sights.
Estimated Value: Excellent: $105.00
Very good: $ 80.00

Iver Johnson Model 66 Trailsman

Caliber: 22 short, long, long rifle; 32 S&W, 38 S&W
Action: Single or double; exposed hammer; hinged frame; top break style; simultaneous manual ejector under barrel; rebounding type hammer
Cylinder: 8-shot in 22 caliber; 5-shot in 32 and 38 caliber; recessed chambers
Barrel: 2¾", 6", rib on top of barrel
Sights: Adjustable
Finish: Blued; checkered walnut or plastic grip; round butt on 2¾" barrel; square butt on 6" barrel
Length Overall: 7", 11"
Approximate wt.: 28 to 32 oz.
Comments: 2¾" barrel snub model made from about 1961 to 1971; 6" barrel made from about 1958 to 1975.
Estimated Value: Excellent: $100.00
Very good: $ 75.00

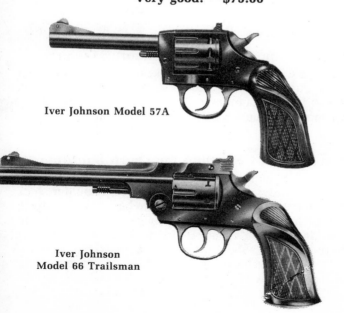

Iver Johnson Model 57A

Iver Johnson
Model 66 Trailsman

Iver Johnson Model 67 Viking

Same as Model 66 Trailsman except: hammer safety device, 4½" or 6" barrel lengths. Made from about 1964 to 1975.

Estimated Value: Excellent: $105.00
Very good: $ 80.00

Iver Johnson Model 67S Viking

Same as Model 67 except: 2¾" barrel length; overall length 7"; approximate weight 25 oz.

Estimated Value: Excellent: $110.00
Very good: $ 85.00

Iver Johnson Bulldog

Caliber: 22 short, long, long rifle; 38 Special
Action: Single or double; exposed hammer; solid frame; side load with loading gate
Cylinder: 8-shot in 22 caliber; 5-shot in 38 caliber; recessed chambers
Barrel: 2½", 4"; heavy duty ribbed
Sights: Adjustable
Finish: Blued; plastic grips; round butt or square butt
Length Overall: 6½", 9"
Approximate wt.: 26 to 30 oz.
Comments: Made from about 1974 to late 1970's. Add $2.00 for 4" barrel; $10.00 for 38 caliber.

Estimated Value: Excellent: $100.00
Very good: $ 75.00

Iver Johnson Cattleman Trail Blazer

Caliber: 22 short, long, long rifle; 22 magnum (WMR)
Action: Single action; solid frame; exposed hammer; side load with loading gate
Cylinder: 6-shot; 2 interchangeable cylinders
Barrel: 5½"; 6"; manual ejector rod under barrel
Sights: Ramp front; adjustable rear
Finish: Blued; case hardened frame, brass backstrap and trigger guard; smooth walnut grip
Length Overall: 11¼" to 12¼"
Approximate wt.: 38 to 40 oz.
Comments: Made from about 1974 to late 1970's. Price include both cylinders.

Estimated Value: Excellent: $150.00
Very good: $110.00

Iver Johnson Model 67S Viking

Iver Johnson Bulldog

Iver Johnson Cattleman Trail Blazer

Iver Johnson Cattleman Buckhorn Buntline

Iver Johnson Cattleman Magnum

Iver Johnson Cattleman Buckhorn Magnum

Iver Johnson Cattleman Magnum

Caliber: 38 Special and 357 magnum, 45 long Colt, 44 Special and 44 magnum
Action: Single; solid frame; exposed hammer; side load with loading gate
Cylinder: 6-shot
Barrel: 4¾", 5½", 7½" (357 magnum & 44 LC); 4¾", 6", 7½" (44 magnum); manual ejector rod under barrel
Sights: Fixed rear; blade front
Finish: Blued, case hardened frame; brass backstrap and trigger guard; smooth walnut grips
Length Overall: 10½" to 13¼"
Approximate wt.: 38 to 46 oz.
Comments: Made from about 1974 to late 1970's. Add $25.00 for 44 magnum.

Estimated Value: Excellent: $175.00
Very good: $130.00

Iver Johnson Cattleman Buckhorn Magnum

Same as Cattleman Magnum except: ramp front sight and adjustable rear sight. Add $25.00 for 12" barrel; $25.00 for 44 magnum.

Estimated Value: Excellent: $190.00
Very good: $145.00

Iver Johnson Cattleman Buckhorn Buntline

Same as Cattleman Buckhorn Magnum except: 18" barrel length only; grip backstrap is cut for shoulder stock attachment; smooth walnut attachable shoulder stock; overall length without shoulder stock 24" and with shoulder stock 36½"; approximate wt. is 56 oz. without shoulder stock; shoulder stock wt. approximately 30 oz. Prices include stock. Add $25.00 for 44 magnum.

Estimated Value: Excellent: $335.00
Very good: $250.00

Iver Johnson Sportsman

Iver Johnson Rookie
Caliber: 38 Special
Action: Single or double
Cylinder: 5-shot, fluted
Barrel: 4″
Sights: Fixed
Finish: Blued or nickel; plastic grips
Length Overall: 9″
Approximate wt.: 29 oz.
Comments: Made from the mid to late 1970's.
Estimated Value: **Excellent:** $120.00
    Very good: $ 90.00

Iver Johnson Deluxe Target
Similar to the Sportsman with adjustable sights.
Estimated Value: **Excellent:** $100.00
    Very good: $ 75.00

Iver Johnson Sportsman
Similar to the Rookie in 22 long rifle caliber; 4¾″ or 6″ barrel; blued finish; made in the mid 1970's.
Estimated Value: **Excellent:** $110.00
    Very good: $ 85.00

Japanese

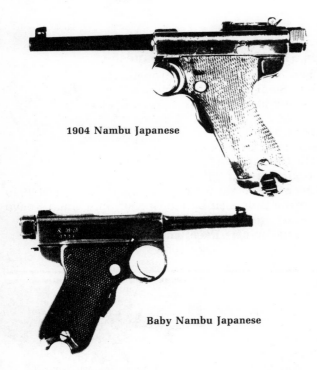

1904 Nambu Japanese

Baby Nambu Japanese

Type 26 Japanese
Caliber: 9mm rimmed pistol
Action: Double only; top break; hammer without cocking spur
Cylinder: 6-shot; automatic ejector
Barrel: 4¾″
Sights: Blade front; "V" notch rear
Finish: Blued; checkered one-piece round grip
Length Overall: 9½″
Approximate wt.: 32 oz.
Comments: Made from about 1893 to 1914.
Estimated Value: **Excellent:** $200.00
    Very good: $150.00

1904 Nambu Japanese
Caliber: 8mm bottle-necked Japanese
Action: Semi-automatic; grip-safety below trigger guard
Magazine: 8-shot clip
Barrel: 4¾″
Sights: Barley corn front; notched tangent rear
Finish: Blued; checkered wood grips
Length Overall: 32 oz.
Comments: Made from about 1904 to 1925. Usually has a slot cut in rear of grip to accommodate shoulder stock holster. Add $75.00 for shoulder stock holster.
Estimated Value: **Excellent:** $800.00
    Very good: $600.00

Nambu Type 14 Japanese
Caliber: 8mm bottle-necked Japanese
Action: Semi-automatic; manual safety
Magazine: 8-shot clip
Barrel: 4¾″
Sights: Barley corn front; undercut notch rear
Finish: Blued; grooved wood grips
Length Overall: 9″
Approximate wt.: 32 oz.
Comments: A modified form of the 1904 Nambu introduced about 1925 and produced until about 1945.
Estimated Value: **Excellent:** $400.00
    Very good: $325.00

Baby Nambu Japanese
Caliber: 7mm bottle-necked Japanese cartridge
Action: Semi-automatic; grip safety below trigger guard
Magazine: 7-shot clip
Barrel: 3¼″
Sights: Barley corn front, "V" notch rear
Finish: Blued; checkered wood grips
Approximate wt.: 24 oz.
Comments: This is a smaller version of the 1904 Nambu.
Estimated Value: **Excellent:** $1,200.00
    Very good: $ 900.00

Modified Nambu Type 14 Japanese

Similar to Nambu Type 14 except it has enlarged trigger guard to allow use of heavy gloves and a spring mounted in lower front of grip to hold magazine more securely.

Estimated Value: Excellent: $425.00
                     Very good: $335.00

Type 94 Japanese

Caliber: 8mm bottle-necked Japanese
Action: Semi-automatic
Magazine: 6-shot clip
Barrel: 3¾"
Sights: Barley corn front; square notch rear
Finish: Blued; checkered grips
Length Overall: 7¼"
Approximate wt.: 28 oz.
Comments: Made from about 1934 to 1945. Made for export but was used as a service pistol during World War II. Most show evidence of poor manufacture.

Estimated Value: Excellent: $300.00
                     Very good: $225.00

Type 57 New Nambu Japanese

Caliber: 9mm Parabellum; 45 ACP
Action: Semi-automatic; recoil operated
Magazine: 8-shot clip
Barrel: 4½"
Sights: Fixed
Finish: Blued; checkered grips
Length Overall: 7¾"
Approximate wt.: 28 oz.
Comments: A modified copy of the U.S. 1911 A1 produced by the firm of Shin Chuo Kogyo K.K. since World War II. Magazine catch at bottom of grip; doesn't have the grip safety.

Estimated Value: Excellent: $200.00
                     Very good: $150.00

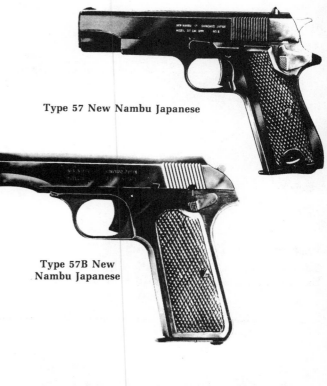

Type 57 New Nambu Japanese

Type 57B New
Nambu Japanese

Type 57B New Nambu Japanese

Caliber: 32 ACP (7.65mm Browning)
Action: Semi-automatic; blow back operated
Magazine: 8-shot clip
Barrel: 3"
Sights: Fixed
Finish: Blued; checkered grips
Length Overall: 6¼"
Approximate wt.: 20 oz.
Comments: A modified copy of the Browning M 1910 pistol produced by the firm of Shin Chuo Kogyo K.K. after World War II.

Estimated Value: Excellent: $175.00
                     Very good: $130.00

Lignose

Lignose Einhand
Model 2A Pocket

Lignose Model 2 Pocket

Caliber: 25 ACP (6.35mm)
Action: Semi-automatic; concealed hammer; thumb safety at top rear of left grip
Magazine: 6-shot clip
Barrel: 2⅛"
Sights: Fixed
Finish: Blued; checkered hard rubber grips
Length Overall: 4¾"
Approximate wt.: 15 oz.
Comments: Operation principle based on the 1906 Browning 25 caliber automatic pocket pistol; production started about 1920. Made in Germany. Early models marked "Bergmann."

Estimated Value: Excellent: $200.00
                     Very good: $150.00

Lignose Model 2 Pocket

Lignose Einhand Model 2A Pocket

Similar specifications as Model 2 except: designed for one-hand operation, hence the name Einhand (one hand). Slide can be retracted to load and cock hammer, by using the trigger finger to pull back the front part of the trigger guard.

Estimated Value: Excellent: $275.00
                     Very good: $210.00

Lignose Einhand Model 3A Pocket

Same as Model 2A except: longer grip and uses 9-shot clip.

Estimated Value: Excellent: $300.00
                     Very good: $225.00

Llama

Llama Model IIIA

Llama Model IX

Llama Model IIIA

Caliber: 380 ACP
Action: Semi-automatic; manual and grip safety; exposed hammer
Magazine: 7-shot clip
Barrel: 3$^{11}/_{16}$″
Sights: Partridge front; adjustable rear
Finish: Blued, chrome, chrome engraved; plastic grips
Length Overall: 6¼″
Approximate wt.: 24 oz.
Comments: Made from about 1951 to late 1970's. Ventilated rib on top of slide. Add $40.00 for chrome; $50.00 for engraved.
Estimated Value: **Excellent:**   **$200.00**
                  Very good: **$150.00**

Llama Model VIII

Caliber: 9mm Luger, 38 Super ACP
Action: Semi-automatic; manual and grip safety; exposed hammer
Magazine: 9-shot clip
Barrel: 5″
Sights: Fixed front; adjustable rear
Finish: Blued, chrome, chrome engraved; checkered wood or simulated pearl grips
Length Overall: 8½″
Approximate wt.: 39 oz.
Comments: Made from about 1953 to late 1970's. Add $40.00 for chrome; $50.00 for engraved.
Estimated Value: **Excellent:**   **$270.00**
                  Very good: **$200.00**

Llama Model XI

Caliber: 9mm Luger
Action: Semi-automatic; manual safety; no grip safety; round exposed hammer
Magazine: 8-shot clip
Barrel: 4$^{7}/_{8}$″
Sights: Fixed
Finish: Blued, chrome; checkered plastic grips with modified thumb rest
Length Overall: 8″
Approximate wt.: 34 oz.
Comments: Made from about 1951 to late 1970's, with some minor modifications. Add $40.00 for chrome.
Estimated Value: **Excellent:**   **$250.00**
                  Very good: **$190.00**

Llama Model IX

Caliber: 45 ACP
Action: Semi-automatic; locked breech; exposed hammer; manual safety
Magazine: 7-shot clip
Barrel: 5″
Sights: Fixed
Finish: Blued; checkered walnut grips
Length Overall: 8½″
Approximate wt.: 39 oz.
Comments: Made from about 1936 to 1952.
Estimated Value: **Excellent:**   **$195.00**
                  Very good: **$145.00**

Llama Model IXA

Similar to Model IX except: ventilated rib on slide; modified and improved version; also in chrome and chrome engraved finish. Made from about 1952 to late 1970's. Add $40.00 for chrome; $50.00 for chrome engraved.
Estimated Value: **Excellent:**   **$225.00**
                  Very good: **$170.00**

Llama Model I

Caliber: 32 ACP (7.65mm)
Action: Semi-automatic; blow back type; exposed hammer
Magazine: 8-shot clip
Barrel: 4″
Sights: Fixed
Finish: Blued; wood grips
Length Overall: 6½″
Approximate wt.: 25 oz.
Comments: Made from about 1935 to 1941.
Estimated Value: **Excellent:**   **$150.00**
                  Very good: **$115.00**

Llama Model II

Similar to Model I except: 7-shot clip; caliber 380 ACP (9mm short). Made from about 1935 to 1941.
Estimated Value: **Excellent:**   **$160.00**
                  Very good: **$125.00**

Llama Model III

A modified version of the Model II. Made from about 1947 to 1954.
Estimated Value: **Excellent:**   **$170.00**
                  Very good: **$135.00**

Llama Model XI

Llama Model VIII

Llama Standard Automatic Small Frame

Similar to the Models XV, XA, and IIIA. Currently produced. Add $50.00 for chrome finish; $75.00 for engraving; $16.00 for 380 caliber.

Estimated Value: New (retail): $209.95
Excellent: $160.00
Very good: $120.00

Llama Standard Automatic Large Frame

Similar to the Model VIII and IXA. Currently produced. Add $60.00 for chrome; $75.00 for engraving.

Estimated Value: New (retail): $263.95
Excellent: $200.00
Very good: $150.00

Llama Model XV

Caliber: 22 long rifle
Action: Semi-automatic; blow back type; exposed hammer; grip and manual safety
Magazine: 9-shot clip
Barrel: $3^{11}/_{16}$″
Sights: Partridge type, fixed
Finish: Blued, chrome, chrome engraved; checkered waood grips
Length Overall: 6¼″
Approximate wt.: 18 oz.
Comments: A smaller version of the 1911 A1 Colt 45 ACP. Made from about 1955 to late 1970's. Add $40.00 for chrome; $50.00 for engraved.

Estimated Value: Excellent: $190.00
Very good: $150.00

Llama Model XA

Same as Model XV except: caliber 32 ACP; 8-shot clip. Add $40.00 for chrome.

Estimated Value: Excellent: $180.00
Very good: $140.00

Llama Omni

Caliber: 9mm Parabellum, 45 Auto
Action: Semi-automatic; double action; exposed hammer
Magazine: 13-shot clip in 9mm; 7-shot clip in 45
Barrel: 5″
Sights: Fixed
Finish: Blued; checkered plastic grips
Length Overall: 7½″
Approximate wt.: 30 oz.
Comments: Introduced in 1982.

Estimated Value: New (retail): $434.95
Excellent: $325.00
Very good: $250.00

Llama Martial

Llama Model XV

Llama Model XVII

Llama Model XVII

Caliber: 22 short
Action: Semi-automatic; exposed hammer with round spur; manual safety
Magazine: 6-shot clip
Barrel: $2^3/_8$″
Sights: Fixed
Finish: Blued, chrome; plastic grips
Length Overall: 4½″
Approximate wt.: 14 oz.
Comments: No longer imported into U.S.A. because of 1968 gun control law. Also known as Executive Model. Add $20.00 for chrome.

Estimated Value: Excellent: $150.00
Very good: $110.00

Llama Model XVIII

Same as Model XVII except: 25 ACP caliber only; no longer imported into U.S.A. Add $20.00 for chrome.

Estimated Value: Excellent: $150.00
Very good: $120.00

Llama Martial

Caliber: 22 short, long, long rifle; 38 Special
Action: Double action; solid frame; simultaneous ejector
Cylinder: 6-shot swing out with thumb latch on left side of frame
Barrel: 6″ in 22 caliber; 4″ and 6″ in 38 Special; ventilated rib
Sights: Target sights
Finish: Blued, chrome, chrome engraved; checkered wood or simulated pearl grips
Length Overall: 9¼″ to 11¼″
Approximate wt.: 35 to 40 oz.
Comments: Made from about 1969 to late 1970's. Add $25.00 for chrome; $25.00 for engraved.

Estimated Value: Excellent: $190.00
Very good: $140.00

Llama Comanche I

Caliber: 22 short, long, long rifle
Action: Double; simultaneous hand ejector; solid frame
Cylinder: 6-shot swing out with thumb latch on left side of frame
Barrel: 6″ with ventilated rib
Sights: Ramp front; adjustable rear
Finish: Blued; checkered walnut target grips
Length Overall: 9¼″
Approximate wt.: 36 oz.
Comments: Made from about 1978 to mid 1980's. Add $75.00 for chrome.
Estimated Value: Excellent: $200.00
Very good: $150.00

Llama Commanche

Llama Comanche II

Similar to the Comanche I in 38 Special with a 4″ or 6″ barrel. Introduced in 1973.
Estimated Value: Excellent: $175.00
Very good: $130.00

Llama Comanche III

Similar to the Comanche II in 357 magnum caliber. Add $75.00 for satin chrome finish.
Estimated Value: New (retail): $244.95
Excellent: $180.00
Very good: $135.00

Llama Super Comanche, Super Comanche IV

A heavier version of the Comanche for 44 magnum cartridges; 6″ barrel, 8½″ barrel available in early 1980's.
Estimated Value: New (retail): $334.95
Excellent: $250.00
Very good: $190.00

Llama Super Comanche V

Similar to the Super Comanche IV except 357 caliber. This heavy frame revolver has 4″, 6″ and 8½″ barrel. Introduced in 1982.
Estimated Value: New (retail): $314.95
Excellent: $235.00
Very good: $175.00

MAB

MAB Model C

MAB Model A

Caliber: 25 ACP (6.35mm)
Action: Semi-automatic; concealed hammer; manual safety; blow back design
Magazine: 6-shot clip
Barrel: 2½″
Sights: Fixed front; no rear
Finish: Blued; checkered hard rubber or plastic grips
Length Overall: 4½″
Approximate wt.: 18 oz.
Comments: Resembles Browning Model 1906 vest pocket pistol. Production started about 1924, imported into U.S.A. as WAC Model A or Le Defendeur. Importation stopped in 1968.
Estimated Value: Excellent: $160.00
Very good: $120.00

MAB Model B

Similar to Model A except; top part of front section of slide cut away for empty cartridges to eject at top. Made from about 1932 to 1966 (never imported into U.S.A.)
Estimated Value: Excellent: $200.00
Very good: $150.00

MAB Model C

Caliber: 32 ACP, 380 ACP
Action: Semi-automatic; concealed hammer; grip safety and manual safety
Magazine: 7-shot clip in 32 ACP; 6-shot clip in 380 ACP
Barrel: 3¼″
Sights: Fixed
Finish: Blued; checkered hard rubber grips
Length Overall: 6¼″
Approximate wt.: 23 oz.
Comments: Production started about 1933. Importation into U.S.A. stopped in 1968.
Estimated Value: Excellent: $190.00
Very good: $145.00

MAB Model D

Caliber: 32 ACP, 380 ACP
Action: Semi-automatic; concealed hammer; grip safety and manual safety
Magazine: 9-shot clip in 32 ACP, 8-shot clip in 380 ACP
Barrel: 4″
Sights: Fixed
Finish: Blued; checkered hard rubber grips
Length Overall: 7″
Approximate wt.: 25 oz.
Comments: Imported into U.S.A. as WAC Model D or MAB Le Gendarme; manufacture started about 1932; importation discontinued in 1968.
Estimated Value: Excellent: $175.00
Very good: $130.00

408 Handguns

MAB Model E

Caliber: 25 ACP (6.35mm)
Action: Semi-automatic; concealed hammer; manual safety and grip safety
Magazine: 10-shot clip
Barrel: 4″
Sights: Fixed
Finish: Blued; checkered plastic grips
Length Overall: 7″
Approximate wt.: 24 oz.
Comments: Production started about 1949; importation into U.S.A. discontinued in 1968. Imported into U.S.A. as WAC Model E.
Estimated Value: Excellent: $180.00
Very good: $135.00

MAB Model F

Action: 22 long rifle
Action: Semi-automatic; concealed hammer; manual safety; blow back design
Magazine: 9-shot clip
Barrel: 4½″, 6″, 7″
Sights: Fixed
Finish: Blued; checkered grips
Length Overall: 8½″ to 11″
Approximate wt.: 23 oz.
Comments: Production began in 1950. Imported into U.S.A. under WAC trademark. Importation stopped in 1968.
Estimated Value: Excellent: $185.00
Very good: $140.00

MAB Model E

Mauser

MAB Model R

MAB Model P-15

Caliber: 9mm Parabellum
Action: Semi-automatic; exposed hammer with round spur; recoil operated with locking breech; manual safety
Magazine: 8-shot clip; 15-shot staggered row clip
Barrel: 4½″
Sights: Blade front; notch rear
Finish: Blued; checkered grips
Length Overall: 8″
Approximate wt.: 25 oz.
Comments: Bears a resemblance to the Browning Model 1935.
Estimated Value: Excellent: $300.00
Very good: $225.00

MAB Model R

Action: 22 long rifle, 32 ACP, 380 ACP, 9mm Parabellum
Action: Semi-automatic; exposed hammer; manual safety
Magazine: 9-shot clip in 22 caliber; 8-shot clip in 32 ACP; 7-shot clip in 380 ACP, 7- or 14-shot clip in 9mm
Barrel: 4½″ or 7½″ (22); 4″ in other calibers
Sights: Fixed
Finish: Blued; checkered grips
Length Overall: 7″ to 10½″
Approximate wt.: 25 oz.
Comments: This model was never imported into U.S.A.
Estimated Value: Excellent: $200.00
Very good: $150.00

Mauser WTP Model 1 Vest Pocket

Caliber: 25 ACP
Action: Semi-automatic; concealed hammer
Magazine: 6-shot clip
Barrel: 2³/₈″
Sights: Fixed
Finish: Blued; hard rubber grips
Length Overall: 4¼″
Approximate wt.: 12 oz.
Comments: Made from about 1923 to 1939.
Estimated Value: Excellent: $300.00
Very good: $225.00

Mauser WTP Model 2 Vest Pocket

Mauser WTP Model 2 Vest Pocket

Similar to Model 1 except: curved back strap and trigger guard; smaller size (2″ barrel, about 4″ overall length); approximate weight 10 oz. Made from about 1939 to 1942 and from about 1950 to present. Importation into U.S.A. discontinued in 1968.
Estimated Value: Excellent: $290.00
Very good: $215.00

Mauser Model HSC Pocket Pistol

Caliber: 32 ACP, 380 ACP
Action: Semi-automatic; double action; exposed hammer
Magazine: 8-shot clip
Barrel: 3³/₈″
Sights: Fixed
Finish: Blued or nickel; checkered wood grips
Length Overall: 6¼″
Approximate wt.: 21 oz.
Comments: Made from about 1938 to World War II and from about 1968 to present. Add $20.00 for nickel finish.
Estimated Value: New (retail): $415.00
Excellent: $310.00
Very good: $235.00

Mauser Model HSC Pocket Pistol

Mauser Automatic Pocket

Caliber: 25 ACP, 32 ACP
Action: Semi-automatic; concealed hammer
Magazine: 9-shot clip in 25 ACP, 8-shot clip in 32 ACP
Barrel: 3″ on 25 ACP; 3½″ on 32 ACP
Sights: Fixed
Finish: Blued; checkered walnut or hard rubber grips
Length Overall: 5½″ on 25 ACP; 6″ on 32 ACP
Approximate wt.: 22 oz.
Comments: 25 ACP model made from about 1910 to 1939. 32 ACP model made from about 1914 to 1934.
Estimated Value: Excellent: $210.00
Very good: $160.00

Mauser Model 1934 Pocket

Similar to Automatic Pocket Pistol except: larger one-piece wooden wrap-around grip which covered the back strap. Made from about 1934 to 1939. 32 ACP only.
Estimated Value: Excellent: $200.00
Very good: $150.00

Mauser Model 1934 Pocket

Mauser Military Model [Broomhandle Mauser]

Caliber: 7.63 Mauser; 9mm Parabellum (during World War I marked with a large figure "9" cut in the wood grip), 9mm Mauser
Action: Semi-automatic; exposed hammer; selective fire introduced in 1930 - selective lever on "N" operated as normal semi-automatic and on "R" operated as a machine pistol with fully automatic fire
Magazine: 5 to 10-shot box magazine standard; 5 to 20-shot magazine on selective fire models
Barrel: 5½″ standard; also manufactured with other barrel lengths
Sights: Adjustable for elevation
Finish: Blued; checkered wood, serrated wood, carved wood, smooth wood, or hard rubber grips
Length Overall: 12″ with 5½″ barrel
Approximate wt.: 43 oz. with 5½₀ barrel
Comments: Made from about 1896 to 1918 and from about 1922 to 1937 with minor changes and improvements. Also produced with a shoulder stock holster (wood).
Estimated Value: Excellent: $1,500.00 - $7,500.00
Very good: $ 850.00 - $4,000.00

**Mauser Military Model
(Broomhandle Mauser)**

North American Arms

North American Arms (Mini Revolver)

Caliber: 22 short; 22 long rifle (1976); 22 magnum (1978)
Action: Single action; exposed hammer; spur trigger; solid frame
Cylinder: 5-shot; removable cylinder; available with two cylinders (22 long rifle and 22 mag.)
Barrel: 1¹/₈″ (22 short); 1¹/₈″ or 1⁵/₈″ (22 long rifle or 22 magnum)
Sights: Blade front, fixed rear
Finish: Stainless steel; polycarbonate round butt (bird head) grips
Length Overall: 3½″ (22 short); 4½″ (22 long rifle); 5″ (22 magnum)
Approximate wt.: 4 to 5 oz.
Comments: Made from about 1975 to present. Add $18.00 for 22 magnum; $42.00 for revolver with both cylinders.
Estimated Value: New (retail): $124.95
Excellent: $ 95.00
Very good: $ 70.00

North American Arms (Mini Revolver)

Remington

Remington 41 Caliber Double Derringer

Caliber: 41 caliber rim fire
Action: Single; visible hammer with safety position; sheath trigger; manual extractors
Cylinder: None; 2-shot double barrels
Barrel: 3″ superposed double barrels; ribbed top barrel; barrels swing up to load and extract cartridges
Sights: Blade front; groove in frame rear
Finish: Blued or nickel plated; plain or engraved; round butt grips made of metal, walnut, rose wood, hard rubber, ivory or pearl
Length Overall: 4⁷/₈″
Approximate wt.: 11 oz.
Comments: Approximately 132,000 were produced from about 1866 to 1935. Serial numbers were repeated on these pistols, so the best way to estimate the age of a pistol is by the markings. They were marked as follows:
1866-1869 no extractors; left side of barrel E. REMINGTON & SONS, ILION, N.Y.; right side of barrel ELLIOT'S PATENT DEC. 12, 1865.
1869-1880 left side of barrel - ELLIOT'S PATENT DEC. 12 1865; right side of barrel - E. REMINGTON & SONS, ILION, N.Y.
1880-1888 barrel rib top - E. REMINGTON & SONS, ILION N.Y. ELLIOT'S PATENT DEC. 12th 1865
1888-1910 barrel rib top - REMINGTON ARMS CO. ILION N.Y.
1910-1935 barrel rib top - REMINGTON ARMS U.M.C. CO. ILION, N.Y.
In 1934 the Double Derringer was called Model No. 95.

Estimated Values:

Plain models	Excellent:	$500.00 - $1,000.00
	Very good:	$400.00 - $ 800.00
Presentation models	Excellent:	$650.00 - $1,200.00
	Very good:	$450.00 - $1,000.00

Remington 41 Caliber Double Derringer

Remington Model 1901, De-Luxe (S-S) Target

Caliber: 22 short, long, long rifle, 44 Russian CF
Action: Single
Cylinder: None; single-shot with rolling breech block for rim fire or center fire cartridges
Barrel: 9″ round; 10″ half-octagon
Sights: Ivory bead front; adjustable "V" rear
Finish: Blued barrel and frame, checkered walnut grips and fore-end
Length Overall: 13″ to 14″
Approximate wt.: 36 to 44 oz.
Comments: Made from about 1901 to 1909. Approximately 700 produced.
Estimated Value: **Excellent:** $1,000.00
Very good: $ 800.00

Remington Experimental 45 Caliber

An estimated value hasn't been placed on this pistol since it is not known how many were produced or how they were marked. They were similar to the Remington Model 51 Automatic Pistol except: in 45 caliber, larger, and had an exposed spur hammer. They were made for the U.S. Government test purposes about 1917.

Remington Model 1891, Single-Shot Target

Remington Model 1901, De-Luxe (S-S) Target

Remington Model 1891, Single-Shot Target

Caliber: 22, 25, 32RF, 32 S&W CF
Action: Single
Cylinder: None; single-shot with rolling breech block for rim fire or center fire calibers
Barrel: 8″, 10″, 12″; half-octagon
Sights: Dovetail, German silver front and adjustable "V" notch rifle rear
Finish: Blued barrel; case hardened frame; oil finished walnut grips and fore-end
Length Overall: 12″ to 16″ depending on barrel length
Approximate wt.: 40 to 45 oz.
Comments: Made from about 1891 to 1900 in light target calibers. Serial number on side of frame under grip. Less than 200 made.
Estimated Value: **Excellent:** $1,200.00
Very good: $ 900.00

Remington Model 51

Caliber: 32 ACP, 380 ACP
Action: Semi-automatic; concealed hammer
Magazine: 8-shot clip in 32 caliber; 7-shot clip in 380 caliber
Barrel: 3¼″
Sights: Fixed
Finish: Blued; hard rubber grips
Length Overall: 6⁵/₈″
Approximate wt.: 20 oz.
Comments: Made from about 1920 to 1934. Approximately 69,000 were produced in 32 and 380 calibers.
Estimated Value: **Excellent:** $350.00
Very good: $275.00

Remington US Model 1911 and 1911 A1

These were pistols made by Remington, on the Colt Patent, for the U.S. Government during World War I & World War II. See "Colt Government Model 1911 and 1911 A1" for prices.

Remington Model XP-100 Long Range

Caliber: 221 Remington "Fire Ball"
Action: Bolt action; single shot; thumb safety
Cylinder: None
Barrel: 10½" round steel with ventilated rib
Sights: Blade front; adjustable rear
Finish: Blued with bright polished bolt and handle; brown checkered nylon (zytel) one-piece grip and fore-end. Fore-end has cavity for adding balance weights
Length Overall: 16¾"
Approximate wt.: 60 oz.
Comments: Made from about 1963 to 1985. Receiver is drilled and tapped for scope mount.
Estimated Value: **Excellent:** $260.00
 Very good: $200.00

Remington Model XP-100 Silhouette

Similar to the Model XP-100 with a 15" barrel and in 7mm Benchrest Remington caliber. Produced from 1980 to present.
Estimated Value: **New (retail):** $448.95
 Excellent: $335.00
 Very good: $250.00

Remington Model XP-100 Silhouette

Remington Model XP-100 Long Range

Ruger

Ruger Standard Automatic

Ruger Mark I Bull Barrell

Ruger Mark I Target

Ruger Standard Automatic

Caliber: 22 long rifle
Action: Semi-automatic; concealed hammer; thumb safety
Magazine: 9-shot clip
Barrel: 4¾" or 6"; tapered round barrel
Sights: Partridge type front; dovetail rear
Finish: Blued; checkered walnut or hard rubber grips
Length Overall: 8¾", 10"
Approximate wt.: 36 to 38 oz.
Comments: Made from about 1949 to 1982. (Sturm Ruger Company was formed about 1949.) Red eagle insignia on grip used until 1951, then changed to black eagle insignia, after death of Alex Sturm. Add $165.00 for red eagle insignia on grip (pre-1951).
Estimated Value: **Excellent:** $135.00
 Very good: $100.00

Ruger Mark I Target

Similar to Ruger Standard Automatic except: adjustable sights; 6⁷/₈" tapered barrel only. Made from about 1950 to 1982.
Estimated Value: **Excellent:** $140.00
 Very good: $105.00

Ruger Mark I Bull Barrel Target

Same as Ruger Mark I Target Pistol except: barrel length 5½"; overall length 9½"; untapered heavier barrel. Made from about 1963 to 1982.
Estimated Value: **Excellent:** $145.00
 Very good: $110.00

Ruger Mark II Standard Automatic

Similar to the Standard Automatic with internal improvements, 10-shot clip; slight difference in rear receiver design. Introduced in 1982. Add 28% for stainless steel.
Estimated Value: **New (retail):** $180.00
 Excellent: $135.00
 Very good: $100.00

Ruger Mark II Target

Similar to the Mark II Standard Automatic with adjustable sights. 6⁷/₈" tapered barrel only. Introduced in 1982. Add 28% for stainless steel.

Estimated Value: New (retail): $215.00
Excellent: $160.00
Very good: $120.00

Ruger Mark II Bull Barrel Target

Similar to the Mark II Target with 5½" bull barrel. Introduced in 1982. Also 10" bull barrel introduced in 1983. Add 28% for stainless steel.

Estimated Value: New (retail): $215.00
Excellent: $165.00
Very good: $125.00

Ruger Stainless Steel Standard 1 of 5,000 Automatic

Similar to the Ruger Standard Automatic except: constructed of stainless steel with the exception of the grips, sights, magazines and a few minor parts; red eagle grip medallion; packed in a "salt cod" wooden box; rollmarked with "1 of 5,000" on the barrel; reproduction of Ruger's signature on the frame; only 5,000 to be produced; made in 1982 only. This will mark the end of the production of the Standard and Mark I Automatic, which will be replaced by the Mark II models.

Estimated Value: New (retail): $435.00 (1982)
Mint condition: $500.00
Excellent: $325.00
Very good: $250.00

Ruger GP-100 Double-Action Revolver

Caliber: 357 magnum and 38 Special
Action: Double and single; solid frame: exposed hammer
Cylinder: 6-shot, swing out: simultaneous ejector
Barrel: 4" heavy barrel or 6" with ejector shroud
Sights: Interchangeable front and adjustable rear
Finish: Blued, with a new Ruger cushioned grip system. A newly designed skeleton-type grip frame is used. The grips are line rubber with polished wood inserts.
Length Overall: 9³/₈" or 11³/₈"
Approximate wt.: 41 oz.
Comments: Introduced in 1986.
Estimated Value: New (retail): $340.00
Excellent: $255.00
Very good: $195.00

In 1982 Ruger announced the production of a Single Action Conversion Kit that could be fitted on any "Old Model" Ruger Single Action revolver. This innovation, fitted at the factory, would give the old model a "transfer bar" type mechanism by replacing a few key parts in the revolver. This would provide a safer handling single action. Unless it can be verified that the conversion has been made at the factory, all "Old Model" Single Action revolvers should be handled as such with caution.

Ruger Mark II Target

Ruger Single-Six

Ruger GP-100 Double-Action Revolver

Ruger Single-Six

Caliber: 22 short, long, long rifle, 22 WMR (after 1959)
Action: Single; solid frame with loading gate
Cylinder: 6-shot half fluted; flat loading gate from 1954 to 1957 then changed to fit the contour of the frame
Barrel: 4⁵/₈", 5½", 6½", 9½"; ejector rod under barrel
Sights: Blade front; rear sight dovetailed and can be tapped to left or right
Finish: Blued; checkered hard rubber or smooth walnut grips
Length Overall: 10", 10⁷/₈", 11⁷/₈", 14⁷/₈"
Approximate wt.: 32 to 36 oz.
Comments: The grip frame is made of aluminum alloy and the frame is made of chrome molybdenum steel; produced from aobut 1953 to 1973. Add $100.00 for flat loading gate.
Estimated Value: Excellent: $150.00
Very good: $115.00

Ruger Lightweight Single-Six

Same as Ruger Single-Six except; made in 22 short, long & long rifle only; 4⁵/₈" barrel; 10" overall length; weighs 23 oz.; cylinder and frame made of lightweight alloy. Produced from about 1956 to 1958.
Estimated Value: Excellent: $200.00
Very good: $170.00

Ruger Convertible Single-Six

Same as Ruger Single-Six revolver except: furnished with two cylinders - one chambered for 22 and the other chambered for 22 WMR. Manufactured from about 1961 to 1973. Prices for guns with both cylinders.
Estimated Value: Excellent: $140.00
Very good: $105.00

Ruger Convertible Super Single-Six

Same as Ruger Single-Six revolver except: ramp front sight; adjustable rear sight with protective ribs on frame to protect rear sight; 5½″ or 6½″ barrel only. Made from about 1964 to 1973. Prices for guns with both cylinders.
Estimated Value: Excellent: $150.00
Very good: $115.00

Ruger New Model Super Single-Six Convertible

Similar to Ruger Convertible Super Single-Six except: improved version feturing wide trigger; heavy stronger lock words; transfer bar firing pin protector; new interlocking mechanism; other improvements. Made from about 1973 to present. 22 LR and 22 WMR cylinders until 1986, when the 22 WMR cylinder was discontinued.
Estimated Value: New (retail): $207.00
Excellent: $155.00
Very good: $115.00

Ruger New Model Super Single-Six Convertible Stainless Steel

Same as Ruger New Model Super Single-Six Convertible Revolver except: all stainless steel construction except sights (blued). 5½″ or 6½″ barrel only. Made from about 1976 to present. Prices for guns with both cylinders.
Estimated Value: New (retail): $278.00
Excellent: $210.00
Very good: $160.00

Ruger New Model Single-Six 32 Mag

Caliber: 32 H&R magnum, also handles 32 S&W and 32 S&W long
Action: Single; solid frame with loading gate
Cylinder: 6-shot, heavy fluted cylinder
Barrel: 4⅝″, 5½″, 6½″ or 9½″; ejector rod under barrel
Sights: Ramp front, adjustable rear
Finish: Blued; smooth walnut grips
Length Overall: 9⅞″ to 14⅞″
Approximate wt.: 32 to 36 oz.
Comments: Introduced in 1986 to bridge the gap between the 22 caliber and 38 caliber revolvers.
Estimated Value: New (retail): $212.00
Excellent: $160.00
Very good: $120.00

Ruger New Model Blackhawk

Ruger New Model Single-Six 32 Mag

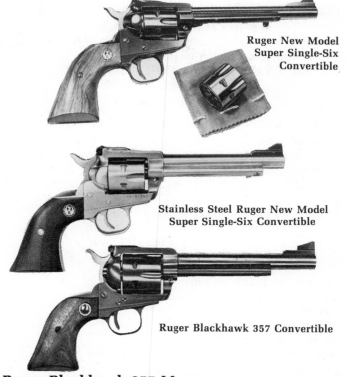

Ruger New Model Super Single-Six Convertible

Stainless Steel Ruger New Model Super Single-Six Convertible

Ruger Blackhawk 357 Convertible

Ruger Blackhawk 357 Magnum

Caliber: 357 magnum and 38 Special interchangeably
Action: Single; solid frame with loading gate
Cylinder: 6-shot
Barrel: 4⅝″; 6½″; round barrel with ejector rod under barrel
Sights: Ramp front and adjustable rear sight
Finish: Blued; checkered hard rubber or smooth walnut wood grips
Length Overall: 10⅛″; 12″
Approximate wt.: 35 to 40 oz.
Comments: Made from about 1955 to 1973. In 1961 the frame was modified to a heavier frame with integral ribs on top to protect rear sight and slight grip alterations to improve the comfort of the "hold".

Estimated Value:	Pre-1961	Post-1961
Excellent:	$150.00	$165.00
Very good:	$115.00	$125.00

Ruger Blackhawk 357 Convertible

Same as Ruger Blackhawk 357 Magnum Revolver except: fitted with extra interchangeable cylinder for 9mm Parabellum cartridges. Manufactured from about 1967 to 1973.
Estimated Value: Excellent: $175.00
Very good: $140.00

Ruger New Model Blackhawk

Similar to Ruger Blackhawk 357 Revolver except: improved version featuring wide trigger; stronger lock works; transfer bar firing pin protector, new interlocking mechanism; other improvements. Made from about 1973 to present in 30 carbine, 357 magnum, 41 magnum and 45 long Colt.
Estimated Value: New (retail): $247.75
Excellent: $185.00
Very good: $140.00

Ruger Stainless Steel New Model Blackhawk 357

Same as Ruger New Model Blackhawk Revolver except: all stainless steel construction except sights (blued). Made from about 1976 to present.

Estimated Value: New (retail): $307.50
Excellent: $230.00
Very good: $175.00

Ruger New Model Blackhawk Convertible

Same as Ruger New Mdoel Blackhawk Revolver except: fitted with extra interchangeable cylinder for 357 magnum and 9mm Parabellum cartridges from about 1973 to present; 45 Colt and 45 ACP cartridges from about 1973 to 1984.

Estimated Value: New (retail): $260.00
Excellent: $195.00
Very good: $145.00

Ruger Blackhawk 44 Magnum

Caliber: 44 magnum and 44 S&W Special interchangeably
Action: Single; solid frame with loading gate
Cylinder: 6-shot, heavy fluted cylinder
Barrel: 6½″; ejector rod under barrel
Sights: Ramp front; adjustable rear sight
Finish: Blued; smooth walnut grips
Length Overall: 12½″
Approximate wt.: 40 oz.
Comments: Produced from about 1956 to 1962.
Estimated Value: Excellent: $300.00
Very good: $250.00

Ruger Super Blackhawk 44 Magnum

Caliber: 44 magnum, 44 S&W Special interchangeably
Action: Single; solid frame with loading gate
Cylinder: 6-shot heavy non-fluted cylinder
Barrel: 7½″; ejector rod under barrel
Sights: Ramp front, adjustable rear sight
Finish: Blued; smooth walnut wood grip; square back trigger guard
Length Overall: 13³/₈″
Approximate wt.: 48 oz.
Comments: Produced from about 1959 to 1973.
Estimated Value: Excellent: $200.00
Very good: $150.00

Ruger New Model Super Blackhawk 44 Magnum

Similar to Super Blackhawk except: improved version, featuring stronger lock works; transfer bar firing pin protector; new interlocking mechanism; blued or stainless steel; 7½″ or 10½″ barrel; other improvements. Made from about 1973 to present. Add 18% for stainless steel.

Estimated Value: New (retail): $276.00
Excellent: $210.00
Very good: $155.00

Ruger New Model Super Blackhawk 44 Magnum

Stainless Steel Ruger New Model Blackhawk 357

Ruger Super Blackhawk 44 Magnum

Ruger Blackhawk 45 Caliber

Caliber: 45 long Colt
Action: Single; solid frame with loading gate
Cylinder: 6-shot
Barrel: 4⁵/₈″; 7½″; round barrel with ejector rod under barrel
Sights: Ramp front and adjustable rear
Finish: Blued; smooth walnut grips
Length Overall: 10¹/₈″; 13¹/₈″
Approximate wt.: 38 to 40 oz.
Comments: Made from about 1970 to 1973. Replaced by New Model Blackhawk in 1973.
Estimated Value: Excellent: $200.00
Very good: $150.00

Ruger Blackhawk 45 Caliber Convertible

Same as Blackhawk 45 Caliber revolver except: fitted with extra interchangeable cylinder for 45 ACP cartridges. Made from about 1970 to 1973. Replaced by New Model Blackhawk in 1973.

Estimated Value: Excellent: $215.00
Very good: $160.00

Ruger Blackhawk 41 Magnum

Ruger Blackhawk 41 Magnum

Caliber: 41 magnum
Action: Single; solid frame with loading gate
Cylinder: 6-shot
Barrel: 4⁵/₈″, 6½″ with ejector rod
Sights: Ramp front; adjustable rear
Finish: Blued; smooth walnut grips
Length Overall: 10¾″; 12¹/₈″
Approximate wt.: 35 to 38 oz.
Comments: Produced from about 1965 to 1973.
Estimated Value: Excellent: $190.00
Very good: $145.00

Ruger Blackhawk 30 Caliber

Caliber: 30 U.S. Carbine (M1)
Action: Single; solid frame with loading gate
Cylinder: 6-shot
Barrel: 7½″ with ejector rod
Sights: Ramp front; adjustable rear sight
Finish: Blued; smooth walnut wood grips
Length Overall: 13¹/₈″
Approximate wt.: 39 oz.
Comments: Made from about 1968 to 1973. A good companion hand gun for the M1 carbine (30 caliber). Replaced by New Model Blackhawk.
Estimated Value: Excellent: $200.00
                             Very good: $150.00

Ruger Redhawk

Caliber: 357 magnum, 41 magnum, 44 magnum
Action: Double and single; solid frame; exposed hammer
Cylinder: 6-shot swing-out; simultaneous ejector
Barrel: 5½″, 7½″, shrouded ejector rod under barrel
Sights: Adjustable rear, blade front
Finish: Stainless steel; blued model added in 1986; checkered or smooth walnut grips
Length Overall: 11″, 13″
Approximate wt.: 52 oz.
Comments: A heavy frame 44 magnum revolver introduced in 1979. 357 magnum and 41 magnum added in 1984. Add 9% for stainless steel. 357 magnum dropped 1986.
Estimated Value: New (retail): $397.00
                             Excellent: $300.00
                             Very good: $225.00

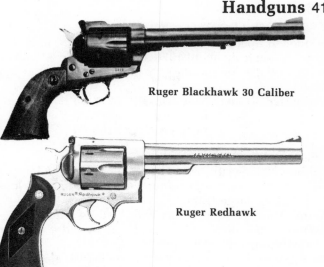

Ruger Blackhawk 30 Caliber

Ruger Redhawk

Ruger Bearcat

Caliber: 22 short, long or long rifle
Action: Single; solid frame with loading gate
Cylinder: 6-shot; non-fluted, engraved
Barrel: 4″ round with ejector rod
Sights: Fixed
Finish: Blued; smooth walnut grips
Length Overall: 8⁷/₈″
Approximate wt.: 17 oz.
Comments: Alloy frame; coil springs and non-fluted engraved cylinder. Manufactured from about 1958 to 1972.
Estimated Value: Excellent: $300.00
                             Very good: $225.00

Ruger Super Bearcat

Same as Ruger Bearcat revolver except: all steel construction and made from about 1971 to 1975.
Estimated Value: Excellent: $250.00
                             Very good: $190.00

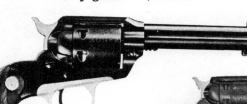

Ruger Bearcat

Ruger Super Bearcat

Ruger Security-Six

Ruger Speed Six

Ruger Security-Six 357 Magnum

Caliber: 357 magnum and 38 Special
Action: Double and single; solid frame; exposed hammer
Cylinder: 6-shot swing out, simultaneous ejector
Barrel: 2¾″, 4″; 6″
Sights: Adjustable sights
Finish: Blued or stainless steel; square butt, checkered walnut grips
Length Overall: 8″; 9¼″, 11¼″
Approximate wt.: 32 to 35 oz.
Comments: Made from 1972 to mid 1980's. A solid frame revolver with swing-out cylinder. Stainless steel model made from about 1975 to mid 1980's. Add $20.00 for stainless steel.
Estimated Value: Excellent: $200.00
                             Very good: $150.00

Ruger Speed-Six

Similar to Security-Six 357 Magnum revolver except: round butt style grips and in calibers 9mm Parabellum, 38 Special and 357 magnum. Fixed sights only. Made from about 1975 to present. Add $16.00 for 9mm; add 9% for stainless steel. 9mm dropped in mid 1980's.
Estimated Value: New (retail): $292.00
                             Excellent: $220.00
                             Very good: $165.00

Ruger Service-Six

Similar to Speed-Six revolver except: square butt style grips. Made from about 1976 to present. Add $16.00 for 9mm; add 8% for stainless steel. 9mm dropped in mid 1980's.

Estimated Value: New (retail): $287.50
Excellent: $215.00
Very good: $160.00

Ruger Hawkeye Single Shot

Ruger Police Service-Six

Ruger New Model Bisley

Caliber: 22 long rifle or 32 H&R magnum in small frame; 357 magnum, 41 magnum, 44 magnum or 45 long Colt in large frame
Action: Single; solid frame with loading gate
Cylinder: 6-shot fluted or unfluted cylinder with or without roll engraving
Barrel: 6½″ small frame, 7½″ large frame; ejector rod under barrel
Sights: Ramp front, adjustable or fixed rear
Finish: Blued: smooth wood grips
Length Overall: 11½″ frame, 13″ large frame
Approximate wt.: 41 oz. small frame, 48 oz. large frame
Comments: Introduced in 1985 and 1986. Based on the Ruger single action design with a longer, different-angle grip similar to the old Colt Bisley revolvers.

Ruger New Model Bisley

Estimated Value:	Small Frame	Large Frame
New (retail):	$258.00	$307.00
Excellent:	$195.00	$230.00
Very good:	$145.00	$175.00

Ruger Hawkeye Single Shot

Caliber: 256 magnum
Action: Single; single shot
Cylinder: None; rotating breech block to load chamber, which is part of the barrel
Barrel: 8½″; chamber in barrel; under barrel ejector rod
Sights: Adjustable target sights
Finish: Blued; smooth walnut grips
Length Overall: 14½″
Approximate wt.: 44 oz.
Comments: The Hawkeye is built on the Ruger 44 magnum frame and resembles a revolver in appearance. Made from about 1963 to 1966.

Estimated Value: Excellent: $550.00
Very good: $420.00

Sauer

Sauer 1913 (Old Model)

Caliber: 32 ACP (7.65mm); 25 ACP (6.35mm)
Action: Semi-automatic; concealed hammer
Magazine: 7-shot clip
Barrel: 3″
Sights: Fixed
Finish: Blued; checkered hard rubber grips
Length Overall: 5⅞″
Approximate wt.: 32 oz.
Comments: Made from about 1913 to 1930.
Estimated Value: Excellent: $200.00
Very good: $150.00

Sauer 1930 Model

Similar to Sauer 1913 (Old Model) except: improved version with main difference being the improved grip design which provides a better hold; some models made with indicator pins to show when they were cocked; some models made with alloy slide and receiver (approximately 15 oz.) Made from about 1930 to 1938.
Estimated Value: Excellent: $190.00
Very good: $140.00

Sauer WTM Pocket

Sauer 1913 (Old Model)

Sauer WTM Pocket

Caliber: 25 ACP (6.35mm)
Action: Semi-automatic; concealed hammer
Magazine: 6-shot clip
Barrel: 2⅛″
Sights: Fixed
Finish: Blued; checkered hard rubber grips
Length Overall: 4⅛″
Approximate wt.: 18 oz.
Comments: Made from about 1924 to 1928. Fluted slide with top ejection port.
Estimated Value: Excellent: $225.00
Very good: $170.00

Sauer 1928 Model Pocket

Similar to Sauer WTM Pocket Pistol except: smaller in size, 2″ barrel and about 3⅞″ overall length. Made from about 1928 to 1938.
Estimated Value: Excellent: $235.00
Very good: $175.00

Sauer 1930 Model

Sauer 1938 Model (Model H)

Caliber: 32 ACP (7.65mm)

Action: Semi-automatic; double action; concealed hammer; lever on left side permitted hammer to be cocked or uncocked by the thumb; also could be fired by pulling trigger in double action style

Magazine: 7-shot clip

Barrel: 3¼″

Sights: Fixed

Finish: Blued; checkered plastic grips

Length Overall: 6¼″

Approximate wt.: 26 oz.

Comments: Some models made with alloy slide (approximately 18 oz. in weight); war time models (WWII) inferior to earlier models. Made from about 1938 to 1944.

Sauer 1938 Model (Model H)

Estimated Value:	pre-War models	War-time models
Excellent:	$250.00	$180.00
Very good:	$185.00	$140.00

Savage

Savage Model 1907

Savage Model 1905 Military Type

Caliber: 45 ACP

Action: Semi-automatic; blow-back design, grip safety; exposed cocking lever

Magazine: 8-shot clip

Barrel: 5¼″

Sights: Fixed

Finish: Blued, checkered walnut grips

Length Overall: 9″

Approximate wt.: 36 oz.

Comments: Approximately 200 were produced from about 1908 to 1911 and sold to U.S. Government Ordnance Dept. for tests, but lost to competition.

Estimated Value:	Excellent:	$2,000.00
	Very good:	$1,500.00

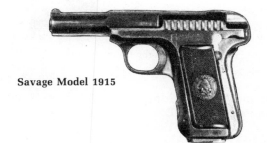

Savage Model 1915

Savage Model 1907

Caliber: 32 ACP, 380 ACP (after 1912)

Action: Semi-automatic; exposed rounded or spur cocking lever

Magazine: 10-shot in 32 caliber, 9-shot in 380 caliber

Barrel: 3¾″ in 32 caliber; 9-shot in 380 caliber

Sights: Fixed

Finish: Blued, metal, hard rubber or wood grips

Length Overall: 6½″ (32 caliber); 7″ (380 caliber)

Approximate wt.: 20 oz.

Comments: Manufactured from about 1908 to 1920, with improvements and some changes in 1909, 1914 and 1918. Some military models with lanyard loop were made of the 1912 variety and sold from 1915 to 1917.

Estimated Value:	Excellent:	$250.00
	Very good:	$190.00

Savage Model 1915

Caliber: 32 ACP, 380 ACP

Action: Semi-automatic; concealed hammer

Magazine: 10-shot in 32 caliber, 9-shot in 380 caliber

Barrel: 3¾″ (caliber); 4¼″ (380 caliber)

Sights: Fixed

Finish: Blued; hard rubber grips

Length Overall: 6½″ (32 caliber), 7″ (380 caliber)

Approximate wt.: 22 oz.

Comments: Manufactured from about 1915 to 1917. Approximately 6,500 were produced in 32 caliber and approximately 2,350 were produced in 380 caliber.

Estimated Value:	Excellent:	$235.00
	Very good:	$175.00

Savage Model 1917

Caliber: 32 ACP, 380 ACP
Action: Semi-automatic; exposed spur cocking lever; thumb safety
Magazine: 20-shot clip in 32; 9-shot clip in 380, wider magazine than previous models to allow for cartridges to be staggered in a double row
Barrel: 3¾″ in 32; 7″ in 380
Sights: Fixed
Finish: Blued; hard rubber grips
Length Overall: 6½″ in 32; 7″ in 380
Approximate wt.: 24 oz.
Comments: Made from about 1918 to 1928. Approximately 28,000 made in 32 caliber and 126,000 in 380 caliber. Wide frame and flared grips and the slide has small verticle gripping serrations.
Estimated Value: Excellent: $250.00
Very good: $195.00

Savage Model 1917

Sheridan

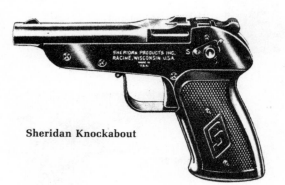

Sheridan Knockabout

Smith & Wesson

Smith & Wesson Model 32 Automatic

Savage Model 101 Single Shot

Savage Model 101 Single Shot

Caliber: 22 short, long, long rifle
Action: Single; single shot
Cylinder: None; the false cylinder is the chamber part of the barrel
Barrel: 5½″ alloy steel; swings out to load; ejector rod under barrel
Sights: Blade front; notched-bar rear
Finish: Blued barrel; painted one-piece aluminum alloy frame; compressed impregnated wood grips
Length Overall: 9½″
Approximate wt.: 20 oz.
Comments: A single shot pistol built to resemble a single action frontier revolver. Made from about 1960 to 1968.
Estimated Value: Excellent: $110.00
Very good: $ 85.00

Sheridan Knockabout

Caliber: 22 short, long, long rifle
Action: Single; exposed hammer
Magazine: None; single shot
Barrel: 5½″; tip up barrel
Sights: Fixed
Finish: Blued; checkered plastic grips
Length Overall: 6¾″
Approximate wt.: 21 oz.
Comments: An inexpensive single shot pistol which resembles an automatic pistol. Made from about 1953 to 1962. Approximately 20,000 produced.
Estimated Value: Excellent: $150.00
Very good: $120.00

Smith & Wesson Model 32 Automatic

Caliber: 32 ACP
Action: Semi-automatic; concealed hammer; grip safety located in front of grip below trigger guard
Magazine: 7-shot clip
Barrel: 3½″; barrel is fixed to the frame; the slide fits into guides on the barrel
Sights: Fixed
Finish: Blued; smooth walnut grips
Length Overall: 6½″
Approximate wt.: 24 oz.
Comments: Serial numbers are a separate series beginning at number 1. Approximately 958 produced from about 1924 to 1937.
Estimated Value: Excellent: $1,000.00
Very good: $ 800.00

Smith & Wesson Model 35 Automatic

Caliber: 35 S&W automatic
Action: Semi-automatic; concealed hammer; grip safety located in front of grip below trigger guard; manual safety at rear of left grip
Magazine: 7-shot clip
Barrel: 3½"; barrel hinged to rear of frame
Sights: Fixed
Finish: Blued or nickel; smooth walnut grips
Length Overall: 6½"
Approximate wt.: 22 oz.
Comments: Serial numbers are a separate series beginning at number 1. Approximately 8,350 were produced from about 1913 to 1921.

Estimated Value: Excellent: $550.00
Very good: $425.00

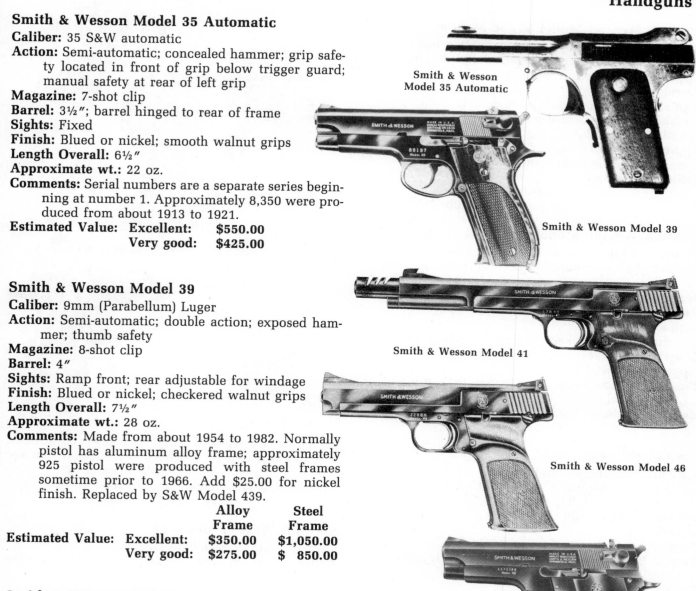

Smith & Wesson
Model 35 Automatic

Smith & Wesson Model 39

Smith & Wesson Model 41

Smith & Wesson Model 46

Smith & Wesson
Model 59 Double Action

Smith & Wesson Model 39

Caliber: 9mm (Parabellum) Luger
Action: Semi-automatic; double action; exposed hammer; thumb safety
Magazine: 8-shot clip
Barrel: 4"
Sights: Ramp front; rear adjustable for windage
Finish: Blued or nickel; checkered walnut grips
Length Overall: 7½"
Approximate wt.: 28 oz.
Comments: Made from about 1954 to 1982. Normally pistol has aluminum alloy frame; approximately 925 pistol were produced with steel frames sometime prior to 1966. Add $25.00 for nickel finish. Replaced by S&W Model 439.

		Alloy Frame	Steel Frame
Estimated Value:	Excellent:	$350.00	$1,050.00
	Very good:	$275.00	$ 850.00

Smith & Wesson Model 41

Caliber: 22 short, 22 long rifle (not interchangeably)
Action: Semi-automatic; concealed hammer; thumb safety
Magazine: 10-shot clip
Barrel: 5½" heavy barrel or 7" regular barrel
Sights: Adjustable
Finish: Blued; checkered walnut grips with thumb rest
Length Overall: 8⅝" to 10½"
Approximate wt.: 40 to 44 oz.
Comments: Made from about 1957 to present. Made for 22 long rifle only at present.

Estimated Value: New (retail): $485.00
Excellent: $365.00
Very good: $275.00

Smith & Wesson Model 46

Similar to Model 41 except: 22 long rifle caliber only; plastic grips with thumb rest. Made from about 1957 to 1966.

Estimated Value: Excellent: $300.00
Very good: $250.00

Smith & Wesson Model 59

Caliber: 9mm (Parabellum) Luger
Action: Semi-automatic; double action; exposed hammer; thumb safety
Magazine: 14-shot staggered column clip
Barrel: 4"
Sights: Ramp front; rear adjustable for windage
Finish: Blued or nickel; checkered high impact molded nylon
Length Overall: 7½"
Approximate wt.: 28 oz.
Comments: Similar to model 39 except back of grip is straight and grip is wider to accommodate the thicker, staggered column magazine. Made from about 1973 to 1982. Add $28.00 for nickel finish. Replaced by S&W Model 459.

Estimated Value: Excellent: $325.00
Very good: $250.00

Smith & Wesson Model 52, 38 Master

Caliber: 38 Special (mid-range wadcutter only)
Action: Semi-automatic; exposed hammer; thumb safety
Magazine: 5-shot clip
Barrel: 5″
Sights: Adjustable rear sights and ramp front
Finish: Blued; checkered walnut grips
Length Overall: 8⁷/₈″
Approximate wt.: 42 oz.
Comments: Made from about 1961 to present.
Estimated Value: New (retail): $657.50
Excellent: $495.00
Very good: $370.00

Smith & Wesson
Model 52

Smith & Wesson
Model 61 Escort

Smith & Wesson Model 459

Smith & Wesson Model 61 Escort

Caliber: 22 long rifle
Action: Semi-automatic; concealed hammer; thumb safety
Magazine: 5-shot clip
Barrel: 2¹/₈″
Sights: Fixed
Finish: Blued or nickel; checkered plastic grips
Length Overall: 4¾″
Approximate wt.: 14 oz.
Comments: Made from about 1970 to 1973. Add $15.00 for nickel finish.
Estimated Value: Excellent: $240.00
Very good: $180.00

Smith & Wesson Model 439

Caliber: 9mm (Parabellum) Luger
Action: Semi-automatic; double action; exposed hammer; thumb safety
Magazine: 8-shot clip
Barrel: 4″
Sights: Serrated ramp front; rear adjustable or fixed
Finish: Blued or nickel; checkered walnut grips with S&W monogram
Length Overall: 7½″
Approximate wt.: 30 oz.
Comments: The frame is constructed of aluminum alloy. It is similar to the Model 39 except with improved extraction system. Made from about 1981 to present. Add 8% for nickel finish; add 5% for adjustable rear sight
Estimated Value: New (retail): $422.00
Excellent: $315.00
Very good: $240.00

Smith & Wesson Model 439

Smith & Wesson Model 539

Similar to the Model 439 except the frame is constructed of steel and the weight is about 36 oz.; made from about 1981 to mid 1980's. Add 8% for nickel finish.
Estimated Value: Excellent: $300.00
Very good: $230.00

Smith & Wesson Model 459

Caliber: 9mm (Parabellum) Luger
Action: Semi-automatic; double action; exposed hammer; thumb safety
Magazine: 14-shot staggered clip
Barrel: 4″
Sights: Serrated ramp front sight; rear adjustable for windage and elevation or fixed
Finish: Blued or nickel; checkered high-impact molded nylon grips
Length Overall: 7½″
Approximate wt.: 30 oz.
Comments: The frame is constructed of aluminum alloy; the grip back is straight; the grip is thick to accommodate the staggered column magazine; it has an improved extraction system. Add 7% for nickel finish. Add 4% for adjustable rear sight. Introduced in 1981.
Estimated Value: New (retail): $459.00
Excellent: $345.00
Very good: $260.00

Smith & Wesson Model 559

Similar to the Model 459 except the frame is steel and the weight approximately 40 oz. Made from about 1981 to mid 1980's. Add 7% for nickel finish.
Estimated Value: Excellent: $335.00
Very good: $250.00

Smith & Wesson Model 469

Smith & Wesson Model 639

Smith & Wesson Model 659

Smith & Wesson Model 645

Smith & Wesson Model 469

Caliber: 9mm (Parabellum) Luger
Action: Double action; semi-automatic; exposed hammer
Magazine: 12-shot clip
Barrel: 3½″
Sights: Serrated ramp front, square notch rear
Finish: Blued; pebble grain molded Delrin grips; aluminum alloy frame
Length Overall: 6⅞″
Approximate wt.: 26 oz.
Comments: Introduced in 1984.
Estimated Value: New (retail): $432.50
　　　　　　　　　　Excellent: $325.00
　　　　　　　　　　Very good: $245.00

Smith & Wesson Model 639

Similar to the Model 439 except satin satinless steel finish. Approx. wt. 36 oz. Introduced in 1984. Add 4% for adjustable rear sight.
Estimated Value: New (retail): $468.00
　　　　　　　　　　Excellent: $350.00
　　　　　　　　　　Very good: $265.00

Smith & Wesson Model 659

Similar to the Model 459 except satin satinless steel finish. Approx. wt. 40 oz. Introduced in 1984. Add 4% for adjustable rear sight.
Estimated Value: New (retail): $509.00
　　　　　　　　　　Excellent: $380.00
　　　　　　　　　　Very good: $290.00

Smith & Wesson Model 669

Same as the model 469 except barrel and slide are stainless steel.
Estimated Value: New (retail): $475.00
　　　　　　　　　　Excellent: $355.00
　　　　　　　　　　Very good: $270.00

Smith & Wesson Model 645

Caliber: 45 ACP
Action: Double action: semi-automatic: exposed hammer
Magazine: 8-shot clip
Barrel: 5″
Sights: Red-ramp front, fixed white-outline rear
Finish: Stainless steel; checkered high-impact molded nylon grips
Length Overall: 8⅝″
Approximate wt.: 38 oz.
Comments: Introduced in the mid 1980's.
Estimated Value: New (retail): $550.50
　　　　　　　　　　Excellent: $415.00
　　　　　　　　　　Very good: $310.00

Smith & Wesson 1891 Single Shot Target Pistol

Caliber: 22 short, long, long rifle
Action: Single; exposed hammer; hinged frame (top break); single shot
Cylinder: None
Barrel: 10″
Sights: Adjutable target
Finish: Blued; hard rubber square butt grips
Length Overall: 13½″
Approximate wt.: 25 oz.
Comments: Made from about 1905 to 1909
Estimated Value: Excellent: $370.00
　　　　　　　　　　Very good: $285.00

Smith & Wesson Perfected Single Shot

Similar to Model 1891 Single Shot except: double and single action; checkered square butt walnut grips; made from about 1909 to 1923; the U.S. Olympic team of 1920 used this pistol, therefore it is sometimes designated "Olympic Model." Add $125.00 for Olympic Models.
Estimated Value: Excellent: $400.00
　　　　　　　　　　Very good: $300.00

Smith & Wesson Straightline

1891 Single Shot

Smith & Wesson Straightline

Caliber: 22 short, long, long rifle
Action: Single; exposed striker (hammer); single shot
Magazine: None
Barrel: 10″; cartridge chamber in barrel; barrel pivots to left to eject and load
Sights: Target sights
Finish: Blued; walnut grips
Length Overall: 11½″
Approximate wt.: 35 oz.
Comments: Pistol resembles automatic pistol in appearance; sold with metal case, screwdriver and cleaning rod. Made from about 1925 to 1937. Add $100.00 for original case and accessories.
Estimated Value: Excellent: $800.00
　　　　　　　　　　Very good: $600.00

Smith & Wesson 32 Double Action

Caliber: 32 S&W center fire
Action: Single and double; exposed hammer; hinged frame (top break)
Cylinder: 5-shot; simultaneous ejector
Barrel: 3″ 1880-1882; 3″, 3½″, 6″, 8″, 10″ 1882-1909; 3″, 3½″, 6″ 1909-1919
Sights: Fixed
Finish: Blued or nickel; round butt, hard rubber grips
Length Overall: 7¼″ to 14¼″
Approximate wt.: 23 to 28 oz.
Comments: Made from about 1880 to 1919 in five modifications or issues; rear of trigger guard is square.

Estimated Value:

Issue	Dates	Quantity	Excellent	Very Good
1st	1880	Less than 100	$2,500.00	$2,000.00
2nd	1880-1882	22,000	$ 230.00	$ 200.00
3rd	1882-1889	21,200	$ 235.00	$ 205.00
4th	1889-1909	239,500	$ 180.00	$ 150.00
5th	1909-1919	44,600	$ 200.00	$ 175.00

Smith & Wesson No. 3 Single Action New Model

Caliber: 44 S&W Russian center fire
Action: Single; exposed hammer; hinged frame (top break); simultaneous automatic ejector
Cylinder: 6-shot
Barrel: 4″, 5″, 6″, 6½″, 7½″ or 8″ ribbed
Sights: Fixed or target
Finish: Blued or nickel; round butt, hard rubber or checkered walnut grips
Length Overall: 9″ to 13″
Approximate wt.: 36 to 40 oz.
Comments: An improved version of the S&W Russian single action revolver. Approximately 36,000 were manufactured from about 1878 to 1908. Sometimes called Single Action Russian Model.

Estimated Value: Excellent: $750.00
Very good: $600.00

Smith & Wesson No. 3 New Model Double Action

Same a No. 3 Single Action New Model except: double and single action; 4″, 5″, 6″ and 6½″ barrel; overall length 9″ to 11½″; sometimes listed as S&W 1881 Navy Revolver; rear of trigger guard is square. Made from about 1881 to 1908.

Estimated Value: Excellent: $450.00
Very good: $350.00

Smith & Wesson Double Action 44 Wesson Favorite

Similar to No. 3 Single Action New Model except: double and single action; 5″ barrel only; lighter barrel and frame. Made from about 1882 to 1883 (approximately 1,200 produced.)

Estimated Value: Excellent: $1,800.00
Very good: $1,200.00

Smith & Wesson No. 3 Single Action New Model

Smith & Wesson No. 3 New Model Double Action

Smith & Wesson 38 Double Action

Smith & Wesson Safety Model Double Action

Smith & Wesson 38 Double Action

Caliber: 38 S&W
Action: Single and double; exposed hammer; hinged frame; top break; back of trigger guard squared
Cylinder: 5-shot; simultaneous ejector
Barrel: 3¼″, 4″, 5″, 6″
Sights: Fixed
Finish: Blued or nickel; round butt; hard rubber grips
Length Overall: 7½″ to 10¼″
Approximate wt.: 20 to 24 oz.
Comments: Made from about 1880 to 1910 with some improvements and minor changes.

Estimated Value: Excellent: $400.00
Very good: $300.00

Smith & Wesson Safety Model Double Action

Caliber: 32 S&W, 38 S&W
Action: Double only; concealed hammer with frame enclosing it; hinged frame; top break style; grip safety on rear of grip frame
Cylinder: 5-shot; simultaneous ejector
Barrel: 2″, 3″, or 3½″ in 32 caliber; 2″, 3¼″, 4″, 5″, or 6″ in 38 caliber; rib on top
Sights: Fixed
Finish: Blued or nickel; hard rubber or checkered walnut grips
Length Overall: 5¾″ to 9¾″
Approximate wt.: 15 to 20 oz.
Comments: Sometimes listed as the Safety Hammerless, New Department Model. Made from about 1887 to 1941. About five changes and improvements were made from 1887 to 1940.

Estimated Value: Excellent: $325.00
Very good: $250.00

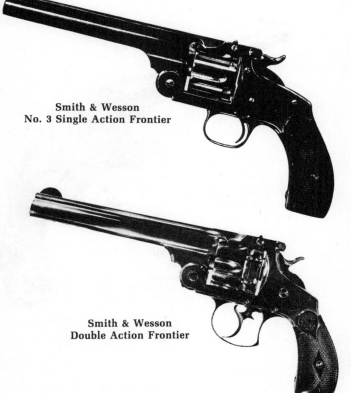

**Smith & Wesson
No. 3 Single Action Frontier**

**Smith & Wesson
Double Action Frontier**

Smith & Wesson No. 3 Single Action Frontier

Caliber: 44-40 Winchester rifle cartridge
Action: Single; exposed hammer; hinged frame (top break)
Cylinder: 6-shot; simultaneous automatic ejector
Barrel: 4″, 5″ and 6½″
Sights: Fixed or target
Finish: Blued or nickel; round butt, hard rubber or checkered walnut grips
Length Overall: 8½″ to 11″
Approximate wt.: 38 to 42 oz.
Comments: Approximately 2,000 manufactured from about 1885 to 1908.
Estimated Value: **Excellent:** $1,000.00
  Very good: $ 800.00

Smith & Wesson Double Action Frontier

Similar to No. 3 Single Action Frontier except: double and single action; rear of trigger guard is square. Made from about 1886 to 1908 (approximately 15,000 were produced.)
Estimated Value: **Excellent:** $500.00
  Very good: $375.00

**Smith & Wesson
1891 Single Action**

Smith & Wesson Perfected 38

Caliber: 38 S&W center fire
Action: Single and double; exposed hammer; hinged frame (top break; but also has side latch)
Cylinder: 5-shot; simultaneous ejector
Barrel: 3¼″, 4″, 5″, and 6″
Sights: Fixed
Finish: Blued or nickel; round butt, hard rubber grip
Length Overall: 7½″ to 10¼″
Approximate wt.: 24 to 30 oz.
Comments: Similar to earlier 38 double action revolvers except: heavier frame; a side latch along with the top latch; improved lock work. Approximately 58,400 were produced from about 1909 to 1920.
Estimated Value: **Excellent:** $350.00
  Very good: $290.00

Smith & Wesson Single Action Target

Caliber: 32-44 S&W, 38-44 S&W
Action: Single; exposed hammer; hinged frame (top break)
Cylinder: 6-shot; simultaneous ejector
Barrel: 6½″
Sights: Target
Finish: Blued or nickel; round butt; hard rubber or checkered walnut grips
Length Overall: 11″
Approximate wt.: 38 to 40 oz.
Comments: One of the first handguns to prove that a short-barrel arm could be a really accurate weapon. Made from 1887 to 1910.
Estimated Value: **Excellent:** $625.00
  Very good: $475.00

Smith & Wesson 1891 Single Action

Caliber: 38 S&W center fire
Action: Single; exposed hammer; hinged frame (top break)
Cylinder: 5-shot; simultaneous ejector
Barrel: 3¼″, 4″, 5″, and 6″
Sights: Fixed
Finish: Blued or nickel; round butt, hard rubber grips
Length Overall: 6¾″ to 9½″
Approximate wt.: 34 to 38 oz. (depending on barrel length)
Comments: This revolver was also available with an accessory single shot target barrel in 22 caliber, 32 caliber or 38 caliber; and 6″, 8″ and 10″ lengths. Made from 1891 to 1911.

Estimated Value:		**Revolver and**
	Revolver	**single shot barrel**
Excellent:	$560.00	$925.00
Very good:	$450.00	$800.00

Smith & Wesson 1899 Hand Ejector

Caliber: 38 long Colt
Action: Double and single; exposed hammer; solid frame
Cylinder: 6-shot; swing-out; simultaneous manual ejector; cylinder release on side of frame
Barrel: 4″, 5″, 6″ or 6½″
Sights: Fixed
Finish: Blued or nickel; checkered hard rubber or walnut round butt grips
Length Overall: 9″ to 11½″
Approximate wt.: 22 to 26 oz.
Comments: Made for police, Army, Navy and commercial use; forerunner of the military and police models. Made from about 1899 to 1902 (approximately 21,000 produced). Army and Navy versions have lanyard swivel in butt and 6″ or 6½″ barrel lengths.
Estimated Value: Excellent: $500.00
                                Very good: $400.00

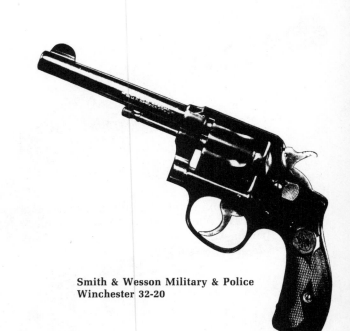

Smith & Wesson Military & Police
Winchester 32-20

Smith & Wesson Military & Police Winchester 32-20

Similar to Model 1899 except: caliber 32-20 only; improvements and changes similar to Model 10 Military & Police revolvers over the years produced from about 1899 to 1940.
Estimated Value: Excellent: $320.00
                                Very good: $250.00

Smith & Wesson Model M Hand Ejector

Caliber: 22 short, long, long rifle
Action: Double and single; exposed hammer; solid frame
Cylinder: 9-shot; swing-out, simultaneous manual ejector
Barrel: 2¼″ (1902-1911); 3″, 3½″ (1906-1911) or 6″ (1911-1921)
Sights: Fixed or adjustable (available after 1911)
Finish: Blued or nickel; checkered hard rubber round butt grips (1902 to 1911); checkered hard rubber square butt grips (1911-1921)
Length Overall: 5¾″ to 10½″
Approximate wt.: 10 to 14 oz.
Comments: Cylinder latch release on left side of frame 1902 to 1906; cylinder latch under barrel 1906 to 1921. Made from about 1902 to 1921, sometimes called Lady Smith.
Estimated Value: Excellent: $725.00
                                Very good: $600.00

Smith & Wesson
Model M Hand Ejector

Smith & Wesson Model 1 Hand Ejector

Caliber: 32 S&W long
Action: Single and double; exposed hammer; first Smith & Wesson solid frame revolver; longer top strap over cylinder than later models
Cylinder: 6-shot; swing out; simultaneous manual ejector
Barrel: 3¼″, 4¼″ or 6″
Sights: Fixed
Finish: Blued or nickel; round butt; hard rubber grips
Length Overall: 8″ to 10¾″
Approximate wt.: 20 to 24 oz.
Comments: First model produced by Smith & Wesson frame. Made from about 1896 to 1903.
Estimated Value: Excellent: $350.00
                                Very good: $275.00

Smith & Wesson Mexican Model

Caliber: 38 S&W center fire
Action: Single; exposed hammer; hinged frame (top break); spur trigger
Cylinder: 5-shot; simultaneous ejector
Barrel: 3¼″, 4″, 5″ and 6″
Sights: Fixed
Finish: Blued or nickel; round butt, hard rubber grips
Length Overall: 7¾″ to 10½″oz.
Comments: Similar to Model 1891 except: it has a spur trigger; doesn't have half-cock notch on the hammer. Approximately 2,000 manufactured from about 1891 to 1911.
Estimated Value: Excellent: $1,200.00
                                Very good: $ 900.00

New Century Triple Lock

Smith & Wesson 44 Hand Ejector

Smith & Wesson Model 30 Hand Ejector

Smith & Wesson Model 22/32 Target

Smith & Wesson Model 34 1953 22/32 Kit Gun

Smith & Wesson New Century Triple Lock

Caliber: 44 S&W Special, 450 Eley, 45 Colt or 455 Mark II British

Action: Single and double; exposed hammer; solid frame

Cylinder: 6-shot swing out; simultaneous hand ejector; called triple lock because of lock on cylinder crane as well as the usual locks under barrel and at rear of cylinder

Barrel: 4″, 5″, 6½″, 7½″ tapered round

Sights: Fixed

Finish: Blued or nickel; checkered square butt walnut grips

Length Overall: 9¼″ to 12¾″

Approximate wt.: 36 to 41 oz.

Comments: Approximately 20,000 made from about 1908 to 1915; about 5,000 of these were made for the British Army.

Estimated Value: Excellent: $675.00
Very good: $575.00

Smith & Wesson 44 Hand Ejector

Similar to New Century Triple Lock except: cylinder crane lock eliminated; 44 Smith & Wesson Special, 44 Smith & Wesson Russian or 45 Colt calibers; 45 Colt caliber made in 6½″ barrel only; other calibers in 4″, 5″, 6″ lengths. Made from about 1915 to 1937.

Estimated Value: Excellent: $450.00
Very good: $375.00

Smith & Wesson Model 30 Hand Ejector

Caliber: 32 S&W and 32 S&W long

Action: Single and double; exposed hammer; solid frame

Cylinder: 6-shot; swing out; simultaneous manual ejector; cylinder release on left side of frame

Barrel: 2″ (1949 to 1975); 3″, 4″, 6″

Sights: Fixed

Finish: Blued or nickel; checkered hard rubber or checkered walnut round butt grips

Length Overall: 6″ to 10″

Approximate wt.: 16 to 20 oz.

Comments: Made from about 1903 to 1975 with many improvements and minor changes over the years.

Estimated Value: Excellent: $225.00
Very good: $170.00

Smith & Wesson Model 35 22/32 Target

Smith & Wesson Model 34 1953 22/32 Kit Gun

Similar to 22/32 Kit Gun except: 2″ or 4″ barrel; round or square butt grips; blued or nickel finish. Made from about 1953 to present. Add 8% for nickel finish.

Estimated Value: New (retail): $307.50
Excellent: $230.00
Very good: $175.00

Smith & Wesson 22/32 Target Revolver

Caliber: 22 short, long, long rifle

Action: Single and double; exposed hammer; solid frame

Cylinder: 6-shot swing out; recessed chamber (1935 to 1953); cylinder release on left side of frame

Barrel: 6″

Sights: Adjustable target sights

Finish: Blued; checkered square butt walnut grips

Length Overall: 10½″

Approximate wt.: 24 oz.

Comments: Frame design similar to Model 30 hand ejector model. Made from about 1911 to 1953.

Estimated Value: Excellent: $280.00
Very good: $225.00

Smith & Wesson Model 35 22/32 Target

Similar to 22/32 target except: newer type adjustable rear sight; S&W magna-type target grips; weight about 25 oz. Made from about 1953 to 1974.

Estimated Value: Excellent: $260.00
Very good: $225.00

Smith & Wesson 22/32 1935 Kit Gun

Same as 22/32 Target except: 4″ barrel; overall length 8″; weight about 21 oz.; round butt grips. Made from about 1935 to 1953.

Estimated Value: Excellent: $270.00
Very good: $210.00

Smith & Wesson Model 43 1955 22/32 Kit Gun

Same as Model 34 1953 22/32 Kit Gun except: 3½″ barrel only; lighter alloy frame; approximately 15 oz. weight; square butt grips. Made from about 1954 to 1974.

Estimated Value: Excellent: $220.00
                  Very good: $165.00

Smith & Wesson Model 51 1960 22/32 Kit Gun

Same as Model 43 1953 22/32 Kit Gun except: chambered for 22 magnum only; all steel construction; approximately 24 oz. weight. Made from about 1960 to 1974.

Estimated Value: Excellent: $210.00
                  Very good: $160.00

Smith & Wesson 1917 Army

Caliber: 45 auto rim cartridge; 45 ACP (by using two 3 round steel half moon clips to hold the cartridge heads)

Action: Single and double; exposed hammer; solid frame

Cylinder: 6-shot swing out; simultaneous manual ejector; release on left side of frame

Barrel: 5½″

Sights: Fixed

Finish: Blued; smooth or checkered square butt walnut grips

Length Overall: 10¾″

Approximate wt.: 37 oz.

Comments: Approximately 175,000 made for U.S. Government from about 1917 to 1919. Then made for commercial sale from about 1919 to 1941. U.S. Government models had a dull blue finish and smooth grips.

Estimated Value:	Military	Commercial
Excellent:	$325.00	$350.00
Very good:	$250.00	$275.00

Smith & Wesson Model 22 1950 Army

Similar to 1917 Army except: made after World War II; minor changes. Made from about 1950 to 1967.

Estimated Value: Excellent: $275.00
                  Very good: $220.00

Smith & Wesson
1926 Model 44 Military

Smith & Wesson
1926 Model 44 Target

Smith & Wesson Model 43
1955 22/32 Kit Gun

Smith & Wesson Model 51
1960 22/32 Kit Gun

Smith & Wesson 1917 Army

Smith & Wesson
Model 22 1950 Army

Smith & Wesson 1926 Model 44 Military

Caliber: 44 S&W Special

Action: Single and double; exposed hammer

Cylinder: 6-shot swing out; simultaneous manual ejector; cylinder release on left side of frame

Barrel: 3¼″, 4″, 5″, 6½″

Sights: Fixed

Finish: Blued or nickel; checkered square butt walnut grips

Length Overall: 9¼″ to 11¾″

Approximate wt.: 40 oz.

Comments: Made from about 1926 to 1941.

Estimated Value: Excellent: $300.00
                  Very good: $250.00

Smith & Wesson 1926 Model 44 Target

Same as 1926 Model Military except: 6½″ barrel only; adjustable target sights; blued finish only. Made from about 1926 to 1941.

Estimated Value: Excellent: $330.00
                  Very good: $280.00

Smith & Wesson Model 21 1950 44 Military

Similar to 1926 Model Military Revolver except: made after World War II; minor changes. Made from about 1950 to 1967.

Estimated Value: Excellent: **$275.00**
Very good: **$210.00**

Smith & Wesson Model 24 1950 44 Target Revolver

Similar to 1926 Model 44 Target except: 4″ or 6½″ barrel; made after World War II; minor changes; ribbed barrel. Made from about 1950 to 1967. A limited edition of 7,500 were made in mid 1980's.

Estimated Value: Excellent: **$280.00**
Very good: **$210.00**

Smith & Wesson Model 624 44 Special

Similar to the Model 24 1950 44 Target Revolver except stainless steel. Introduced in the mid 1980's. Add 3% for 6½″ barrel.

Estimated Value: New (retail): **$449.50**
Excellent: **$340.00**
Very good: **$260.00**

Smith & Wesson Model 25 45 Colt

Caliber: 45 Colt
Action: Single and double; exposed hammer; solid frame
Cylinder: 6-shot swing out; simultaneous manual ejector; cylinder release on left side
Barrel: 4″, 6″, 8³/₈″
Sights: Red ramp front; micrometer click rear adjustable for windage and elevation
Finish: Blued or nickel; checkered Goncolo Alves target grips
Length Overall: 9³/₈″ to 13¾″
Approximate wt.: 44 to 52 oz.
Comments: This revolver is built on the large N frame. Made from about 1955 to present. Add $14.00 for 8³/₈″ barrel, $40.00 for presentation box. Add 4% for nickel.

Estimated Value: New (retail): **$371.00**
Excellent: **$280.00**
Very good: **$210.00**

Smith & Wesson Model 25 1955 Target

Similar to the Model 25-5 except 6″ barrel only; blued finish only; 45 ACP caliber; ⅛″ plain partridge front sight; add $40.00 for presentation box.

Estimated Value: Excellent: **$270.00**
Very good: **$205.00**

Smith & Wesson
Model 21 1950 44 Military

Smith & Wesson
Model 24 1950 44 Target

Smith & Wesson
Model 25 1955 45 Target

Smith & Wesson Model 624

Smith & Wesson Model 20 Heavy Duty

Smith & Wesson Model 20 Heavy Duty

Caliber: 38 Special
Action: Single and double; exposed hammer; solid frame
Cylinder: 6-shot swing out; simultaneous ejector; release on left side of frame
Barrel: 4″, 5″, 6½″
Sights: Fixed
Finish: Blued or nickel; checkered square butt walnut grips
Length Overall: 9³/₈″ to 11⁷/₈″
Approximate wt.: 38 to 41 oz.
Comments: Made from about 1930 to 1967.

Estimated Value: Excellent: **$275.00**
Very good: **$215.00**

Smith & Wesson Model 23 Outdoorsman Revolver

Similar to Model 20 Heavy Duty except; target version; 6½″ barrel only; ribbed barrel after 1950; approximately 42 oz. wt.; blued finish; adjustable target sights. Made from about 1930 to 1967.

Estimated Value: Excellent: **$350.00**
Very good: **$275.00**

Smith & Wesson Model 23 Outdoorsman

Smith & Wesson Model 10 Military & Police

Caliber: 38 Special
Action: Double and single; exposed hammer; solid frame
Cylinder: 6-shot swing out: simultaneous manual ejector
Barrel: 2″, 3″ or 4″
Sights: Fixed
Finish: Blued or nickel: square or round-butt checkered walnut grips
Length Overall: 7″ to 9½″
Approximate wt.: 28 oz. to 34 oz.
Comments: Made from about 1948 to present. Add 7½% for nickel finish.
Estimated Value: New (retail): $282.00
Excellent: $210.00
Very good: $160.00

Smith & Wesson Victory Model

Same as Model 10 Military & Police except: sand blasted or brushed parkerized finish; 4″ barrel; smooth square butt grips with lanyard ring; made from about 1941 to 1946 for the U.S. Government during World War II; 38 Special caliber; Some 38-200 caliber with 5″ barrel were made for the British Forces.
Estimated Value: Excellent: $250.00
Very good: $190.00

Smith & Wesson Model 13 M & P

Similar to the Model 10 Military and Police except 357 magnum caliber and heavy barrel; add $20.00 for nickel.
Estimated Value: New (retail): $282.00
Excellent: $210.00
Very good: $160.00

Smith & Wesson Model 65 M & P

Similar to the Model 13 with a satin stainless steel finish.
Estimated Value: New (retail): $305.00
Excellent: $230.00
Very good: $175.00

Smith & Wesson Model 10

Smith & Wesson Model 13

Smith & Wesson Model 12
Military & Police Airweight

Smith & Wesson Military & Police

Caliber: 38 Special
Action: Single and double; exposed hammer; solid frame
Cylinder: 6-shot swing out; simultaneous ejector; release on left side of frame
Barrel: 2″ (after 1933); 4″, 5″, 6″, 6½″ (1902-1915)
Sights: Fixed
Finish: Blued or nickel; checkered hard rubber or checkered walnut round or square butt grips
Length Overall: 7″ to 11½″
Approximate wt.: 26 to 32 oz.
Comments: Manufactured from about 1902 to 1942 with improvements and minor changes. Basic frame is known as S&W K frame. Add $15.00 for nickel finish. Also known as 1902 Model and 1905 Model M & P.
Estimated Value: Excellent: $190.00
Very good: $145.00

Smith & Wesson Model 64

Smith & Wesson Model 38

Smith & Wesson Model 64 Military & Police

Same as Model 10 Military & Police Revolver except: satin finish stainless steel construction. Made from about 1972 to present.
Estimated Value: New (retail): $305.00
Excellent: $230.00
Very good: $175.00

Smith & Wesson Model 12 Military & Police Airweight

Same as Model 10 Military & Police except: light alloy frame; 2″ or 4″ barrel; approximate wt. 28 oz. Made from about 1952 to present.
Estimated Value: New (retail): $320.50
Excellent: $240.00
Very good: $180.00

Smith & Wesson 38 Military & Police Target

Same as Model 10 Military & Police except: 6″ barrel only; approximate wt. 33 oz.; checkered walnut grips; adjustable target sights. Made from about 1924 to 1941.
Estimated Value: Excellent: $225.00
Very good: $175.00

Smith & Wesson K-32 Target

Similar to S&W 38 Military & Police Target except: caliber 32 S&W, 32 S&W long and 32 Colt New Police; heavier barrel; approximate wt. 34 oz. Introduced about 1940; discontinued about 1941.
Estimated Value: Excellent: $650.00
Very good: $500.00

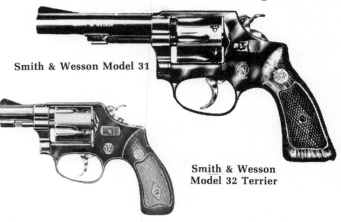

Smith & Wesson Model 31

Smith & Wesson
Model 32 Terrier

Smith & Wesson Model 31 Regulation Police

Caliber: 32 S&W, 32 Colt New Police
Action: Single and double; exposed hammer; solid frame
Cylinder: 6-shot swing out; simultaneous manual ejector; release on left side of frame
Barrel: 2″ (1949-present); 3″, 3¼″, 4″, 4¼″, 6″
Sights: Fixed
Finish: Blued or nickel; checkered square butt walnut grips
Length Overall: 6½″ to 10½″
Approximate wt.: 17 to 20 oz.
Comments: Made from about 1917 to present. Presently made with 2″ and 3″ barrel only. Nickel finish discontinued in early 1980's.
Estimated Value: New (retail): $313.50
                       Excellent: $235.00
                       Very good: $175.00

Smith & Wesson Model Regulation Police Target

Similar to Smith & Wesson Model 31 Regulation Police except: 6″ barrel only; adjustable target sights; blued finish. Made from about 1917 to 1940.
Estimated Value: Excellent: $210.00
                       Very good: $160.00

Smith & Wesson Model 27

Smith & Wesson Model 28
Highway Patrolman

Smith & Wesson Model 28 Highway Patrolman

Similar to Model 27 357 Magnum except: 4″ or 6″ barrel; ramp front sight and adjustable rear sight; blued finish. Made from about 1954 to date. Add $20.00 for target grips.
Estimated Value: New (retail): $305.50
                       Excellent: $230.00
                       Very good: $175.00

Smith & Wesson K-22 Outdoorsman

Smith & Wesson Model 33 Regulation Police Revolver

Same as S&W Model 31 Regulation Police except: 38 caliber S&W and 38 Colt New Police; 5-shot cylinder capacity. Made from about 1917 to 1974.
Estimated Value: Excellent: $215.00
                       Very good: $160.00

Smith & Wesson Model 32 Terrier

Similar to Model 33 Regulation Police except: 2″ barrel only; 6½″ overall length. Made from about 1936 to 1974.
Estimated Value: Excellent: $190.00
                       Very good: $150.00

Smith & Wesson Model 27 357 Magnum

Caliber: 357 magnum and 38 Special
Action: Single and double; exposed hammer; solid frame
Cylinder: 6-shot swing out; simultaneous manual ejector
Barrel: 3½″, 5″, 6″, 6½″, 8⅜″ ribbed
Sights: Adjustable target
Finish: Blued or nickel; checkered walnut grips
Length Overall: 7⅞″ to 14¼″
Approximate wt.: 42 to 49 oz.
Comments: Made from about 1935 to present. Made from 1935 to 1938 on special orders (worth more). Add $25.00 for 8⅜″ barrel. Presently made in 4″, 6″ and 8⅜″ barrel. Add $40.00 for Presentation Box.
Estimated Value: New (retail): $350.00
                       Excellent: $265.00
                       Very good: $200.00

Smith & Wesson Model K-22 Outdoorsman

Caliber: 22 short, long, long rifle
Action: Single and double; exposed hammer; solid frame
Cylinder: 6-shot swing out; simultaneous manual ejector; release on left side of frame
Barrel: 6″
Sights: Fixed or target sights
Finish: Blued or nickel; checkered walnut grips
Length Overall: 11½″
Approximate wt.: 35 oz.
Comments: Made from about 1931 to 1942.
Estimated Value: Excellent: $250.00
                       Very good: $200.00

Smith & Wesson K-22 Masterpiece

Same as K-22 Outdoorsman except: improved version; better adjustable rear sight; short cocking action; antibacklash trigger; made from about 1942 to 1947.

Estimated Value: Excellent: $260.00
Very good: $200.00

Smith & Wesson Model 14 K-38 Masterpiece

Caliber: 38 Special
Action: Single or double; or single action only; exposed hammer; solid frame
Cylinder: 6-shot swing out; simultaneous manual ejector; release on left side of frame
Barrel: 6″ or 8³/₈″
Sights: Partridge front; click adjustable rear
Finish: Blued; checkered square butt walnut grips
Length Overall: 11¹/₈″ or 13½″
Approximate wt.: 36 to 38 oz.
Comments: Made from about 1947 to 1981. Add $10.00 for 8³/₈″ barrel; $40.00 for target accessories.
Estimated Value: Excellent: $225.00
Very good: $170.00

Smith & Wesson Model 14 Single Action

Similar to the Model 14 K-38 Masterpiece in single action; 6″ barrel; blued only.

Estimated Value: Excellent: $210.00
Very good: $160.00

Smith & Wesson Model 15 38 Combat Masterpiece

Same as Model 14 K-38 Masterpiece except: 2″, 4″, 6″ or 8³/₈″ barrel; approximate wt. 30 oz. to 39 oz.; quick draw front sight; blued or nickel finish; double and single action. Made from about 1950 to present. Add 7% for nickel finish; $9.00 for 8³/₈″ barrel.

Estimated Value: New (retail): $321.00
Excellent: $240.00
Very good: $180.00

Smith & Wesson Model 19

Smith & Wesson Model 66

Smith & Wesson Model 16 K-32

Smith & Wesson Model 14

Smith & Wesson Model 14 Single Action

Smith & Wesson Model 15

Smith & Wesson Model 67

Smith & Wesson Model 67 38 Combat Masterpiece

Same as Model 15 38 Combat Masterpiece except: 4″ barrel only; satin finish stainless steel construction. Made from about 1972 to present.

Estimated Value: New (retail): $339.00
Excellent: $255.00
Very good: $190.00

Smith & Wesson 19 357 Combat Magnum

Same as Model 15 38 Combat Masterpiece except: 2½″, 4″ or 6″ barrel; caliber 357 magnum and 38 Special; round butt. Made from about 1956 to present. Add $31.00 for target accessories; $24.00 for target sights.

Estimated Value: New (retail): $310.00
Excellent: $235.00
Very good: $175.00

Smith & Wesson Model 66 357 Combat Magnum

Same as Model 19 357 Combat Magnum except: satin finish stainless steel. Produced from about 1972 to present. Add $41.00 for target accessories.

Estimated Value: New (retail): $352.50
Excellent: $265.00
Very good: $200.00

Smith & Wesson Model 16 K-32 Masterpiece

Same as Model 14 K-38 Masterpiece except: 32 S&W long and 32 Colt Police caliber; 6″ barrel only; double and single action. Made from about 1947 to 1974.

Estimated Value: Excellent: $230.00
Very good: $185.00

Smith & Wesson 17 K-22 Masterpiece

Smith & Wesson Model 48

Smith & Wesson 17 K-22 Masterpiece

Same as Model 14 K-38 Masterpiece except: 22 short, long, long rifle caliber; 4″, 6″ or 8³/₈″ barrel. Made from about 1947 to present; approx. wt. 40 oz. Add $12.00 for 8⅜″ barrel; $50.00 for target trigger and hammer.

Estimated Value:	New (retail):	$313.00
	Excellent:	$235.00
	Very good:	$180.00

Smith & Wesson Model 18 22 Combat Masterpiece

Same a Model 17 K-22 Masterpiece except: 4″ barrel; 9¹/₈″ overall length; approximate wt. 38 oz. Made from about 1950 to mid 1980's. Add $28.50 for target trigger and hammer.

| Estimated Value: | Excellent: | $235.00 |
| | Very good: | $180.00 |

Smith & Wesson Model 48 K-22 Magnum Masterpiece

Same as Model 17 K-22 Masterpiece except: 22 magnum caliber; also available with auxiliary cylinder for 22 short, long and long rifle. Made from about 1948 to present. Add $15.00 for 8⅜″ barrel; $102.00 for auxiliary 22 short, long and long rifle cylinder.

Estimated Value:	New (retail):	$320.00
	Excellent:	$240.00
	Very good:	$180.00

Smith & Wesson Model 57

Smith & Wesson
Model 37 Airweight

Smith & Wesson Model 58

Smith & Wesson Model 36 Chiefs Special

Caliber: 38 Special
Action: Single and double; exposed hammer; solid frame
Cylinder: 5-shot swing out; simultaneous manual ejector; release on left side of frame
Barrel: 2″ or 3″
Sights: Fixed
Finish: Blued or nickel; round or square butt, checkered walnut grips
Length Overall: 6½″ to 7¾″
Approximate wt.: 19 to 20 oz.
Comments: Made from about 1950 to date. Add 8% for nickel finish.

Estimated Value:	New (retail):	$274.50
	Excellent:	$205.00
	Very good:	$155.00

Smith & Wesson Model 57 41 Magnum

Caliber: 41 magnum
Action: Single and double; exposed hammer; solid frame
Cylinder: 6-shot swing out; simultaneous manual ejector; release on left side of frame
Barrel: 4″, 6″ or 8³/₈″ ribbed
Sights: Ramp front, adjustable rear
Finish: Blued or nickel; checkered walnut grips
Length Overall: 9³/₈″ to 13¾″
Approximate wt.: 38 to 42 oz.
Comments: Made from about 1964 to present. Add 3½% for 8⅜″ barrel; $40.00 for presentation box.

Estimated Value:	New (retail):	$371.00
	Excellent:	$280.00
	Very good:	$210.00

Smith & Wesson Model 657 41 Magnum

Similar to the Model 57 41 Magnum except stainless steel; 4″ or 6½″ barrel. Introduced in the mid 1980's. Add 3% for 6½″ barrel.

Estimated Value:	New (retail):	$449.50
	Excellent:	$340.00
	Very good:	$260.00

Smith & Wesson Model 58 41 Military & Police

Similar to Model 57 41 magnum except: 4″ barrel only; fixed sights; no rib on barrel. Made from about 1964 to late 1970's. Add $10.00 for nickel finish.

| Estimated Value: | Excellent: | $250.00 |
| | Very good: | $200.00 |

Smith & Wesson
Model 36 Chiefs Special

Smith & Wesson Model 37 Airweight Chiefs Special

Same as Model 36 Chiefs Special except: light alloy frame; approximate weight, 13 to 14 oz. Made from about 1954 to present. Add 12% for nickel finish.

Estimated Value:	New (retail):	$294.00
	Excellent:	$220.00
	Very good:	$165.00

Smith & Wesson Model 60 Chiefs Special Stainless

Same as Model 36 Chiefs special except: satin finish stainless steel construction 2″ barrel only; round butt grip; approximate wt. 20 oz. Made from about 1965 to present.

Estimated Value: New (retail): $332.00
Excellent: $250.00
Very good: $190.00

Smith & Wesson Model 40 Centennial Hammerless

Same as Model 36 Chiefs Special except: concealed hammer; frame extends over hammer area; 2″ barrel; double action only; grip safety located on rear of grip. Made from about 1952 to 1974.

Estimated Value: Excellent: $250.00
Very good: $190.00

Smith & Wesson Model 42 Centennial Airweight

Same as Model 40 Centennial except: light alloy frame; approximate wt. 13 oz. Made from about 1954 to 1974.

Estimated Value: Excellent: $260.00
Very good: $200.00

Smith & Wesson Model 38 Bodyguard Airweight

Same as Model 36 Chiefs Special except: light alloy frame; shrouded hammer; approximate weight 15 oz.; 2″ barrel only. Produced from about 1955 to present. Add 12½% for nickel finish.

Estimated Value: New (retail): $327.00
Excellent: $245.00
Very good: $185.00

Smith & Wesson Model 49 Bodyguard

Same as Model 38 Bodyguard Airweight except: steel frame; approximate weight 21 oz. Manufactured from about 1959 to present. Add 8% for nickel finish.

Estimated Value: New (retail): $292.00
Excellent: $220.00
Very good: $165.00

Smith & Wesson Model 649

Similar to the Model 49 Bodyguard except stainless steel. Introduced in the mid 1980's.

Estimated Value: New (retail): $346.00
Excellent: $260.00
Very good: $195.00

Smith & Wesson Model 53

Smith & Wesson Model 649

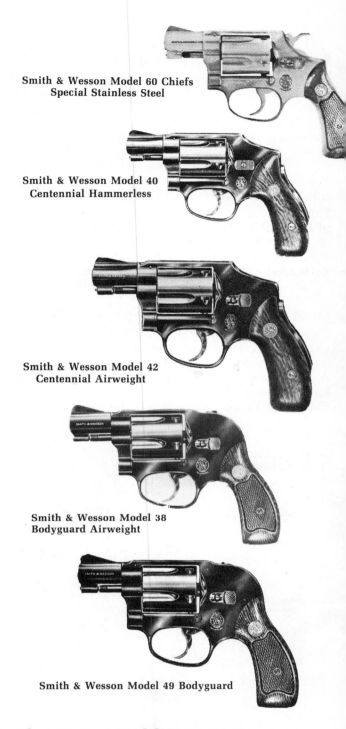

Smith & Wesson Model 60 Chiefs Special Stainless Steel

Smith & Wesson Model 40 Centennial Hammerless

Smith & Wesson Model 42 Centennial Airweight

Smith & Wesson Model 38 Bodyguard Airweight

Smith & Wesson Model 49 Bodyguard

Smith & Wesson Model 53 22 Jet Magnum

Caliber: 22 Rem. Jet center fire and 22 short, long, long rifle by using chamber inserts and repositioning floating firing pin of hammer

Action: Single and double; exposed hammer; solid frame

Cylinder: 6-shot swing out; simultaneous manual ejector; cylinder release on left side of frame

Barrel: 4″, 6″ or 8³/₈″

Sights: Ramp front; adjustable rear

Finish: Blued; checkered walnut target grips

Length Overall: 9¼″ to 13⁵/₈″

Approximate wt.: 38 to 42 oz.

Comments: Made from about 1961 to 1974. Could be fitted with 22 caliber cylinder. Add $100.00 for extra cylinder.

Estimated Value: Excellent: $500.00
Very good: $375.00

Smith & Wesson Model 29

Smith & Wesson Model 29 44 Magnum

Caliber: 44 magnum and 44 Special
Action: Single and double; exposed hammer; solid frame
Cylinder: 6-shot swing out; simultaneous manual ejector; release on left side of frame
Barrel: 4″, 6″, 8⅝″ or 10⅝″ ribbed
Sights: Ramp front; adjustable rear
Finish: Blued or nickel checkered wood grips
Length Overall: 9⅜″ to 13¾″
Approximate wt.: 44 to 49 oz.
Comments: Made from about 1956 to present. Add $14.50 for 8⅝″; Add $46.00 for 10⅝″ barrel; $40.00 for presentation box.
Estimated Value: New (retail): $409.00
   Excellent: $320.00
   Very good: $250.00

Smith & Wesson Model 63 1977 22/32 Kit Gun

Caliber: 22 long rifle
Action: Single and double; exposed hammer
Cylinder: 6-shot swing out
Barrel: 4″
Sights: Adjustable micrometer square notch rear, red ramp front
Finish: Stainless steel, satin finish; checkered walnut grips
Length Overall: 9³/₈″
Approximate wt.: 24½ oz.
Comments: Currently produced.
Estimated Value: New (retail): $355.50
   Excellent: $270.00
   Very good: $200.00

Smith & Wesson Model 581 Distinguished Service Magnum

Caliber: 357 magnum and 38 Special
Action: Single and double; exposed hammer; solid frame
Cylinder: 6-shot swing out; simultaneous manual ejector; release on left side of frame
Barrel: 4″ or 6″ heavy barrel with full length ejector shroud. 4″ barrel only after mid 1980's.
Sights: Serrated ramp front, fixed rear
Finish: Blued or nickel; checkered walnut magna service grips
Length Overall: 9¾″ to 11¾″
Approximate wt.: 42 to 44 oz.
Comments: Smith & Wesson's new "L" frame revolver. It is slightly larger than the K frame which permits it to accommodate a sturdier cylinder. Introduced in 1982. Add 10% for nickel finish.
Estimated Value: New (retail): $313.50
   Excellent: $235.00
   Very good: $175.00

Smith & Wesson Model 681 Distinguished Service Magnum

Similar to the Model 581 except with satin stainless steel finish.
Estimated Value: New (retail): $324.00
   Excellent: $245.00
   Very good: $185.00

Smith & Wesson Model 629

Same as the Model 29 except with a satin stainless steel finish. Add $16.00 for 8³/₈″ barrel; $40.00 for Presentation Box. 10⁵/₈″ barrel not available.
Estimated Value: New (retail): $472.50
   Excellent: $410.00
   Very good: $350.00

Smith & Wesson Model 63

Smith & Wesson Model 586

Smith & Wesson Model 586 Distinguished Combat Magnum

Caliber: 357 magnum and 38 Special
Action: Single and double; exposed hammer; solid frame
Cylinder: 6-shot swing out; simultaneous manual ejector; cylinder release on left side
Barrel: 4″, 6″ or 8³/₈″ heavy barrel with a full length ejector shroud
Sights: Red ramp front, micrometer click rear adjustable for windage and elevation
Finish: Blued or nickel; checkered Goncalo Alves target grips
Length Overall: 9¾″ to 13¾″
Approximate wt.: 42 to 46 oz.
Comments: Smith & Wesson's new "L" frame revolver. It is slightly larger than the K frame which permits it to accommodate a sturdier cylinder; introduced in 1982.
Estimated Value: New (retail): $340.00
   Excellent: $255.00
   Very good: $190.00

Smith & Wesson Model 686 Distinguished Combat Magnum

Similar to the Model 586 except with satin stainless steel finish. Add $20.00 for 8⅜″ barrel.
Estimated Value: New (retail): $374.00
   Excellent: $280.00
   Very good: $210.00

Smith & Wesson Model 547 Military & Police

Caliber: 9mm Parabellum
Action: Single and double; exposed hammer; solid frame
Cylinder: 6-shot swing out; simultaneous manual ejector; release on left side of frame
Barrel: 3″ or 4″ heavy barrel
Sights: Fixed rear, serrated ramp front
Finish: Blued; checkered walnut round butt grips with 3″ barrel and square butt with 4″ barrel
Length Overall: 8¼″ to 9¼″
Approximate wt.: 32 to 34 oz.
Comments: A 9mm revolver built on a K frame that features a unique new extraction system for positive extraction of the 9mm cartridge. Made from about 1981 to mid 1980's.
Estimated Value: Excellent: $235.00
 Very good: $180.00

Smith & Wesson Model 547

Smith & Wesson Model 650 Service Kit Gun

Caliber: 22 magnum
Action: Single and double action, exposed hammer
Cylinder: 6-shot swing out, simultaneous ejector
Barrel: 3″ heavy barrel
Sights: Serrated ramp front, fixed square notch rear
Finish: Satin stainless steel; checkered walnut round butt grips
Length Overall: 7″
Approximate wt.: 23½″ oz.
Comments: A "J" frame revolver introduced in 1984.
Estimated Value: New (retail): $305.00
 Excellent: $230.00
 Very good: $175.00

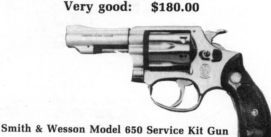

Smith & Wesson Model 650 Service Kit Gun

Smith & Wesson Model 651 Kit Gun

Caliber: 22 magnum
Action: Double and single, exposed hammer
Cylinder: 6-shot swing-out, simultaneous ejector
Barrel: 4″
Sights: Red ramp front, adjustable micrometer click rear
Finish: Satin stainless steel; checkered walnut square butt grips
Length Overall: 8⅝″
Approximate wt.: 24½ oz.
Comments: A "J" frame revolver introduced in 1984.
Estimated Value: New (retail): $345.00
 Excellent: $260.00
 Very good: $195.00

Smith & Wesson Model 651 Kit Gun

Star

Star Model 1919 Pocket

Star Model CO Pocket

Star Model 1919 Pocket

Caliber: 25 ACP (6.35mm)
Action: Semi-automatic; exposed hammer
Magazine: 8-shot clip
Barrel: 2⅝″
Sights: Fixed
Finish: Blued; checkered walnut grips
Length Overall: 4⅞″
Approximate wt.: 16 oz.
Comments: Made from about 1919 to 1934. Distinguished by the safety at the top rear of the slide.
Estimated Value: Excellent: $190.00
 Very good: $140.00

Star Model CO Pocket

Improved version of the 1919 Model; safety in front of left grip rather than top rear of slide; plastic grips; some engraved nickel plated models produced. Made from about 1934 to 1957. Add $20.00 for engraved nickel model.
Estimated Value: Excellent: $190.00
 Very good: $150.00

Star Model H

Similar to Model CO pistol except: caliber 32 ACP; 9-shot clip; approximate wt. 20 oz. Made from about 1934 to 1941.

Estimated Value: Excellent: $150.00
Very good: $115.00

Star Model H

Star Model HN

Same as Model H except: caliber 380 ACP; 6-shot clip.
Estimated Value: Excellent: $160.00
Very good: $130.00

Star Model E Pocket

Caliber: 25 ACP (6.35mm)
Action: Semi-automatic; exposed hammer
Magazine: 6-shot clip
Barrel: 2″
Sights: Fixed
Finish: Blued; checkered grips
Length Overall: 4″
Approximate wt.: 10 oz.
Comments: Small compact pocket pistol; safety located in front of left grip; no longer in production.
Estimated Value: Excellent: $150.00
Very good: $115.00

Star Model F & FR

Star Model A & AS

Caliber: 9mm Luger, 9mm Bergman, 9mm Largo, 38 Super auto
Action: Semi-automatic; exposed hammer
Magazine: 8-shot clip
Barrel: 5″
Sights: Fixed
Finish: Blued; checkered walnut grips
Length Overall: 8″
Approximate wt.: 35 oz.
Comments: This handgun resembles the 1911 A1 Colt. Made from about 1924 to late 1970's.
Estimated Value: Excellent: $175.00
Very good: $135.00

Star Model A

Star Model B

Star Model B

Similar to Model A except: barrel lengths 4¼″ or 6½″; caliber 9mm Parabellum only. Made from about 1924 to 1942.

Estimated Value: Excellent: $180.00
Very good: $140.00

Star Model F & FR

Caliber: 22 long rifle
Action: Semi-automatic; exposed hammer; manual safety at top rear of left grip
Magazine: 10-shot clip
Barrel: 4¼″ (regular); 6″ & 7″ on Sport & Target models
Sights: Fixed; adjustable on Sport & Target models
Finish: Blued, chromed or chromed engraved; plastic grips
Length Overall: 7¼″ to 10″
Approximate wt.: 24 to 32 oz.
Comments: Model F made from about 1942 to 1968. Model FR is improved version made from about 1968 to late 1970's. Add $10.00 for chrome model.
Estimated Value: Excellent: $150.00
Very good: $120.00

Star Model I
(Police Model)

Star Model I (Police Model)

Caliber: 32 ACP
Action: Semi-automatic; exposed hammer
Magazine: 9-shot clip
Barrel: 4¾"
Sights: Fixed
Finish: Blued; plastic grips
Length Overall: 7½"
Approximate wt.: 25 oz.
Comments: Made from abou 1934 to 1945; never imported to U.S.A..
Estimated Value: Excellent: $140.00
　　　　　　　　 Very good: $110.00

Star Model IN

Same as Model I except: caliber 380 ACP; 8-shot clip.
Estimated Value: Excellent: $150.00
　　　　　　　　 Very good: $115.00

Star Model M (Military)

Caliber: 380 ACP; 9mm Luger; 9mm Bergmann, 38 ACP, 45 ACP
Action: Semi-automatic; exposed hammer; manual safety
Magazine: 7-shot clip in 45 caliber, 8-shot clip in all other calibers
Barrel: 5"
Sights: Fixed
Finish: Blued; checkered grips
Length Overall: 8½"
Approximate wt.: 36 oz.
Comments: A modified version of the U.S. Government Colt 1911 45 automatic, made from about 1935 to present. Not imported into U.S.A.
Estimated Value: Excellent: $200.00
　　　　　　　　 Very good: $150.00

Star Model M (Military)

Star Model Super Star

Same as Model M except: 38 Super ACT, 9mm Parabellum and 38 ACP only; addition of disarming bolt; improved sights; magazine safety; indicator for number of unfired cartridges. Made from about 1942 to 1954.
Estimated Value: Excellent: $175.00
　　　　　　　　 Very good: $135.00

Star Model Super Star

Star Model S

Caliber: 38 ACP
Action: Semi-automatic; exposed hammer; manual safety
Magazine: 7-shot clip
Barrel: 4"
Sights: Fixed
Finish: Blued or chromed; engraved; plastic grips
Length Overall: 6½"
Approximate wt.: 20 oz.
Comments: A scaled-down modification of the Colt 1911 45 Automatic. Made from about 1941 to present. Not imported into U.S.A. since 1968.
Estimated Value: Excellent: $150.00
　　　　　　　　 Very good: $110.00

Star Model SI

Same as Model S except: caliber 32 ACP; 8-shot clip.

Estimated Value: Excellent: $140.00
Very good: $100.00

Star Model Super S

Same as Model S except: addition of disarming bolt; improved luminous sights; magazine safety; indicator for number of unfired cartridges. This model was discontinued in 1954.

Estimated Value: Excellent: $170.00
Very good: $130.00

Star Model Super S

Star Model Super SI

Same as Model Super S except: caliber 32 ACP; 8-shot clip.

Estimated Value: Excellent: $160.00
Very good: $120.00

Star Model Super SI

Star Model DK (Starfire)

Caliber: 380 ACP
Action: Semi-automatic; exposed hammer; manual safety at top rear of left grip
Magazine: 6-shot clip
Barrel: 3″
Sights: Fixed
Finish: Blued; checkered plastic grips
Length Overall: 5½″
Approximate wt.: 16 oz.
Comments: Made from about 1958 to present. Never imported into U.S.A.

Estimated Value: Excellent: $175.00
Very good: $135.00

Star Model CU (Starlet)

Caliber: 25 ACP
Action: Semi-automatic; exposed hammer
Magazine: 8-shot clip
Barrel: 2³/₈″
Sights: Fixed
Finish: Blued or chromed slide; black, gray, gold, blue or green receiver; checkered plastic grips
Length Overall: 4¾″
Approximate wt.: 12 oz.
Comments: Made from about 1957 to present. Never imported into U.S.A. Manual safety catch at top rear of left grip. Alloy frame.

Estimated Value: Excellent: $150.00
Very good: $110.00

Star Model HF (Lancer)

Basically same as Model CU Starlet except: caliber 22 long rifle; 3″ barrel; 5½″ overall length.

Estimated Value: Excellent: $175.00
Very good: $140.00

Star Model H F (Lancer)

Star Model Super SM

Star Model Super SM

Caliber: 380 ACP
Action: Semi-automatic; exposed hammer
Magazine: 9-shot clip
Barrel: 4″
Sights: Blade front; rear adjustable for windage
Finish: Blued or chrome; checkered wood grips
Length Overall: 6¾″
Approximate wt.: 21 oz.
Comments: Made from about 1970 to late 1970's. Add $15.00 for chrome model.

Estimated Value: Excellent: $190.00
Very good: $145.00

Star Model PD
Caliber: 45 ACP
Action: Semi-automatic; exposed hammer
Magazine: 8-shot clip
Barrel: 4″
Sights: Ramp front; adjustable rear
Finish: Blued; chrome available until early 1980's; checkered wood grips
Length Overall: 7″
Approximate wt.: 25 oz.
Comments: Made from about 1975 to present. Add $10.00 for chrome model.
Estimated Value: New (retail): $333.00
Excellent: $265.00
Very good: $200.00

Star Model 30PK
An improved version of the Model 28 with alloy frame and slightly shorter length; 15-shot magazine; combat style trigger guard.
Estimated Value: New (retail): $455.00
Excellent: $340.00
Very good: $255.00

Star Model 30M
Similar to the Model 30PK with steel frame and greater sight plane.
Estimated Value: New (retail): $455.00
Excellent: $340.00
Very good: $255.00

Star Model BM

Star Model BK

Sterling

Sterling Model 283

Star Model BK, BKM
Caliber: 9mm Parabellum
Action: Semi-automatic; exposed hammer; manual thumb safety
Magazine: 8-shot clip
Barrel: 4½″
Sights: Fixed
Finish: Blued; chrome; checkered walnut grips
Length Overall: 7¼″
Approximate wt.: 22 oz.
Comments: Made from about 1970 to present. Alloy frame; resembles Colt 1911. Add $15.00 for chrome model.
Estimated Value: New (retail): $305.00
Excellent: $225.00
Very good: $170.00

Star Model BM
Similar to the Model BKM without alloy frame. Add $15.00 for chrome finish.
Estimated Value: New (retail): $305.00
Excellent: $230.00
Very good: $170.00

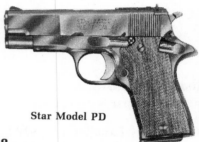

Star Model PD

Star Model 28
Caliber: 9mm Parabellum
Action: Semi-automatic; double action; exposed hammer
Magazine: 15-shot clip
Barrel: 4¼″
Sights: Notched partridge front, adjustable rear
Finish: Blued; checkered plastic grips
Length Overall: 8″
Approximate wt.: 40 oz.
Comments: Made from 1982 to 1985.
Estimated Value: Excellent: $315.00
Very good: $240.00

Sterling Model 283
Caliber: 22 long rifle
Action: Semi-automatic; exposed hammer; adjustable trigger and a rear lock safety
Magazine: 10-shot clip
Barrel: 4½″, 6″ or 8″ heavy bull barrel
Sights: Blade front; click adjustable rear
Finish: Blued; checkered plastic grips
Length Overall: 9″, 10½″ or 12½″
Approximate wt.: 36 to 40 oz.
Comments: All steel construction. Made from about 1970 to 1972. Also known as Target 30 Model.
Estimated Value: Excellent: $140.00
Very good: $105.00

Sterling Model 284

Same as Model 283 automatic pistol except: lighter tapered barrel. also known as Target 300L Model. Made from about 1970 to 1972.

Estimated Value: Excellent: $130.00
Very good: $100.00

Sterling Model 285

Same as Model 283 automatic pistol except: ramp front sight, fixed rear sight; made in 4½″ heavy barrel only; non-adjustable trigger. Made from about 1970 to 1972. Also known as Husky Model.

Estimated Value: Excellent: $125.00
Very good: $100.00

Sterling Model 286

Same as Model 283 automatic pistol except: ramp front sight, fixed rear sight; made in 4½″ and 6″ tapered barrel only; non-adjustable trigger. Also known as Trapper Model. Made from about 1970-1972.

Estimated Value: Excellent: $110.00
Very good: $ 90.00

Sterling Model 285

Sterling Model 286

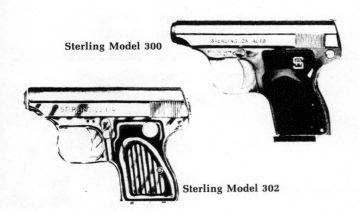

Sterling Model 300

Sterling Model 302

Sterling Model 400 Automatic Pistol

Caliber: 380 ACP
Action: Semi-automatic; double action; exposed hammer; safety locks firing pin
Magazine: 6-shot clip
Barrel: 3½″
Sights: Ramp front, adjustable rear
Finish: Blued or nickel; checkered grips
Length Overall: 6½″
Approximate wt.: 24 oz.
Comments: All steel construction. Made from about 1973 to late 1970's. Replaced by Mark II 400. Add 10% for nickel finish.

Estimated Value: Excellent: $150.00
Very good: $120.00

Sterling MK II 400 & MK II 400S

Similar to 400 except streamlined and lightweight, also 32 ACP. Add 5% for nickel finish; 15% for stainless steel. (400S MK II)

Estimated Value: Excellent: $155.00
Very good: $115.00

Sterling Model 300, 300S

Caliber: 25 ACP
Action: Semi-automatic blowback action; concealed hammer
Magazine: 6-shot clip
Barrel: 2½″
Sights: None
Finish: Blued, nickel or stainless steel (after 1975) with cycolac grips
Length Overall: 4½″
Approximate wt.: 13 oz.
Comments: All steel construction. Made from about 1972 to mid 1980's. Add 10% for nickel finish; 20% for stainless steel.

Estimated Value: Excellent: $ 75.00
Very good: $ 60.00

Sterling Model 302, 302S

Same as Model 300 Automatic Pistol except caliber 22 long rifle. Model 302S is stainless steel; add 20% for stainless steel.

Estimated Value: Excellent: $ 75.00
Very good: $ 60.00

Sterling Model MKII 400

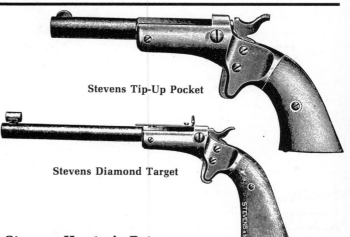

Sterling Model X Caliber

Sterling Model 400S

Similar to Model 400 except constructed of stainless steel. Made from about 1976 to late 1970's.
Estimated Value: Excellent: $200.00
**   Very good: $150.00**

Sterling Model 402 MK II, 402S MK II

Similar to the Model 400 MK II in 32 ACP caliber. Model 402S MK II is stainless steel; add 15%.
Estimated Value: Excellent: $165.00
**   Very good: $125.00**

Sterling Model 402

Similar to Model 400 automatic pistol except: caliber 22 long rifle, 8-shot clip magazine. Made from about 1973 to 1975. Add $10.00 for nickel finish.
Estimated Value: Excellent: $150.00
**   Very good: $110.00**

Sterling Model X Caliber

Caliber: 22 short, long, long rifle, 22 mag., 357 mag., 44 mag.
Action: Single action; single shot
Magazine: None
Barrel: 8″ or 20″ heavy octagonal; a caliber change is made by changing barrel
Sights: Ramp front, adjustable rear; tapped for scope mounts
Finish: Blued; smooth wood, finger-grooved grips and small lipped forearm
Length Overall: 13″ with 8″ barrel
Approximate wt.: 54 to 62 oz.
Comments: A silhouette style single shot pistol with interchangeable barrels for caliber change. Add 50% for each additional barrel.
Estimated Value: Excellent: $160.00
**   Very good: $120.00**

Stevens

Stevens Tip-Up Pocket

Caliber: 22 short, 30 RF (to 1902)
Action: Single with sheath trigger (spur)
Cylinder: None; single shot with tip-up barrel
Barrel: 3½″; part octagon
Sights: Blade front; notch in frame rear
Finish: Blued barrel; nickel plated frame to 1912; blued frame after 1912; varnished walnut square butt grips
Length Overall: 6¼″
Approximate wt.: 10 oz.
Comments: Made from about 1888 to 1915. Marked "J Stevens A. & T. Co."
Estimated Value: Excellent: $175.00
**   Very good: $135.00**

Stevens Tip-Up Pocket

Stevens Diamond Target

Stevens Diamond Target

Caliber: 22 RF long rifle (black power 1888-1912); 22 long rifle (smokeless powder 1912-1915)
Action: Single; sheath trigger (spur)
Cylinder: None; single shot with tip-up barrel
Barrel: 6″, 10″; part octagon
Sights: Globe or bead front; peep or adjustable rear
Finish: Blued barrel; nickel plated iron frame to 1912; varnished long walnut square grips
Length Overall: 9½″ to 13½″
Approximate wt.: 10 to 13 oz.
Comments: Made from about 1888 to 1915. Marked "J. Stevens A. & T. Co." Approximaely 132,000 produced.
Estimated Value: Excellent: $225.00
**   Very good: $170.00**

Stevens Hunter's Pet

Caliber: 22 long rifle, 25 RF, 32 RF, 38 long RF, 44 long RF, 38-40, 44-40, 38-35, 44-50, 24 guage
Action: Single with sheath trigger (spur)
Cylinder: None; single shot with pivoted barrel
Barrel: 18″, 20″, 22″ or 24″ octagon and half octagon
Sights: Adjustable for elevaton; also some had Steven's Vernier peep sight attached to back strap
Finish: Blued barrel; nickel plated frame and detachable skeleton stock; smooth, varnished walnut, square butt grips
Length Overall: 22″ to 28″
Approximate wt.: 5¾ lbs.
Comments: Serial numbers in 4,000 to 13,000 range. Approximately 8,000 produced from about 1888 to 1907.

**   With Stock**
Estimated Value: Excellent: $450.00
**   Very good: $350.00**

Stevens Lord Gallery

Caliber: 22 long rifle, 25 RF (smokeless powder)
Action: Single; tip up barrel
Cylinder: None; single shot
Barrel: Octagon breech; 6″, 8″, 10″
Sights: Bead front; stepped elevator rear
Finish: Blued barrel; plated frame; varnished walnut
   grips with base butt cap; blued frame after 1912
Length Overall: 9¼″ to 13¼″
Approximate wt.: 24 to 28 oz.
Comments: Made from about 1907 to 1915. Marked "J.
   STEVENS A. & T. CO."
Estimated Value: **Excellent:** **$235.00**
                    Very good: **$180.00**

Stevens Lord Gallery

Stevens "Off-Hand" 1907-1915

Caliber: 22 long rifle, 25 RF, smokeless powder
Action: Single, tip up barrel
Cylinder: None; single shot
Barrel: Octagon breech; 6″, 8″, 10″
Sights: Bead front; stepped elevator rear
Finish: Blued barrel; plated frame; varnished walnut
   grips with base butt cap; blued frame after 1912
Length Overall: 9¼″ to 13¼″
Approximate wt.: 24 to 28 oz.
Comments: Made from about 1907 to 1915. Marked "J.
   Stevens A. & T. Co."
Estimated Value: **Excellent:** **$275.00**
                    Very good: **$220.00**

Stevens "Off-Hand" 1907-1915

Stevens Off Hand 1923-1939

Caliber: 22 long rifle
Action: Single; tip up barrel
Cylinder: None; single shot
Barrel: Octagon breech; 6″, 8″, 20″, 12¼″
Sights: Bead front; rear adjustable for elevation
Finish: Blued barrel and frame, also plated frame; walnut
   grips with butt cap
Length Overall: 9¼″ to 15½″
Approximate wt.: 24 to 34 oz.
Comments: Made from about mid 1920's to late 1930's.
Estimated Value: **Excellent:** **$260.00**
                    Very good: **$200.00**

Stevens Off Hand 410

Stevens Single-Shot Target

Stevens Off Hand 410

Caliber: 410 gauge (2½″)
Action: Single; tip-up barrel
Cylinder: None; single shot
Barrel: Octagon breech; choked 8″ or 12¼″ barrel
Sights: Shot gun front sight
Finish: Blued barrel and frame, also plated frame; walnut
   grips with butt cap
Length Overall: 11¼″ to 15½″
Approximate wt.: 23 to 25 oz.
Comments: Made from about 1925 to 1935. Marked "J.
   Stevens Arms Company."
Estimated Value: **Excellent:** **$250.00**
                    Very good: **$190.00**

Stevens Single-Shot Target

Caliber: 22 long rifle
Action: Single; tip up barrel; round knurled cocking
   piece
Cylinder: None; single shot
Barrel: Round, 8″
Sights: Partridge front; adjustable windage rear
Finish: Blued (blackish blue color); black composition
   checkered grips
Length Overall: 11½″
Approximate wt.: 37 oz.
Comments: A single shot target pistol with configura-
   tion of an automatic pistol. Made from about 1919
   to 1942. Approximately 10,000 produced. The 1919
   pistols had serial numbers from 1 to approximate-
   ly 5,000 range with "Pat. App'd For" on barrel.
   After 1920 marked "Pat'd April 27, 1920". All
   pistols marked "J. Stevens Arms Company."
Estimated Value: **Excellent:** **$265.00**
                    Very good: **$200.00**

Steyr

Roth-Steyr Self-Loading Pistol

Caliber: 8mm Roth-Steyr
Action: Semi-automatic; concealed striker; locked breech design uses rotation of barrel by cam action to unlock barrel when fired; the striker is cocked by the recoil, but the trigger action has to pull it further back before it will release to fire
Magazine: 10-shot non-detachable; usually loaded by a charger from the top
Barrel: 5¹/₈″
Sights: Fixed
Finish: Blued; checkered wood grips
Length Overall: 9¹/₈″
Approximate wt.: 36 oz.
Comments: Adopted by the Austro-Hungarian Cavalry in 1907. This is one of the earliest forms of succesful locked-breech pistols.
Estimated Value: Excellent: $150.00
Very good: $120.00

Steyr Model 1909 Pocket Automatic Pistol

Caliber: 32 ACP
Action: Semi-automatic; concealed hammer; blow-back action; early models have no extractor (empty case is blown out by gas after the breech-block is pushed open by firing); barrel can be tipped down for cleaning, using as single shot pistol, or for removing unfired cartridge
Magazine: 7-shot clip
Barrel: 3½″
Sights: Fixed
Finish: Blued; checkered wood grips
Length Overall: 6½″
Approximate wt.: 23 oz.
Comments: Made in both Austria and Belgium. The Austrian variety was a finer pistol from the standpoint of manufacture and reliability. Add $30.00 for later model with extractor.
Estimated Value: Excellent: $175.00
Very good: $135.00

Steyr-Solothurn Pocket Model Automatic Pistol

Similar to the Steyr model 1909 except: a modified version; uses extractors to remove empty cases; production started about 1934 from Solothurn factory in Switzerland.
Estimated Value: Excellent: $180.00
Very good: $140.00

Steyr Vest Pocket (Baby) Automatic

Steyr Vest Pocket (Baby) Automatic Pistol

Caliber: 25 ACP
Action: Semi-automatic; concealed hammer; blow-back action; early models have no extractor (empty case is blown out by gas after the breech block is pushed open by firing); barrel can be tipped down for cleaning, using as a single shot pistol or for removing unfired cartridges
Magazine: 6-shot clip
Barrel: 2″
Sights: Fixed
Finish: Blued; hard rubber checkered grips
Length Overall: 4½″
Approximate wt.: 12 oz.
Comments: First manufactured about 1908. Add $10.00 for later model with extractor.
Estimated Value: Excellent: $160.00
Very good: $120.00

Steyr Model 1912 Military

Caliber: 9mm Steyr
Action: Semi-automatic; exposed hammer; short recoil; locked breech action (barrel rotates to unlock breech when gun is fired)
Magazine: 8-shot non-detachable; loaded from top singly or by using a strip clip
Barrel: 5″
Sights: Fixed
Finish: Blued; checkered wood grips
Length Overall: 8½″
Approximate wt.: 33 oz.
Comments: Made from about 1911 until after World War I; also referred to as Model 1911 or Steyr-Hahn; adopted by the Austro-Hungarian Army in 1912.
Estimated Value: Excellent: $250.00
Very good: $200.00

Steyr Nazi-Proofed

Same as Steyr Model 1912 except: converted to fire the 9mm Luger cartridge during World War II and marked "P-08."
Estimated Value: Excellent: $300.00
Very good: $225.00

Steyr Model GB

Caliber: 9mm Parabellum
Action: Gas delayed blowback action, semi-automatic, double action
Magazine: 18-shot clip
Barrel: 5½″
Sights: Fixed
Finish: Black crinkled with blued slide; plastic checkered grips and trigger guard
Length Overall: 8½″
Approximate wt.: 39 oz.
Comments: A new Steyr pistol introduced in the mid 1980's.
Estimated Value: New (retail): $595.00
Excellent: $445.00
Very good: $335.00

Thompson Center

Thompson Center Contender

Caliber: 22 short, long, long rifle; 22 WMR, 5mm Rem., 22 Hornet, 22 Rem. Jet, 221 Fireball, 222 Rem., 256 Win. mag., 30 M1 carbine, 30-30 special, 357 mag., 9mm Luger, 45 ACP, 45 Colt, 44 mag. and other wildcat calibers

Action: Single; frame accommodates any caliber barrel; hammer adjusts to rim fire or center fire; adjustable trigger pull

Cylinder: None; single shot

Barrel: 8¾″, 10″, 14″; the 357 magnum, 45 Colt and 44 magnum barrels have detachable chokes for use with shot shells; ventilated rib available; bull barrel available

Sights: Ramp front, adjustable rear

Finish: Blued; checkered or smooth walnut grips and fore-end

Length Overall: 12½″ to 17¾″

Approximate wt.: 38 to 60 oz.

Comments: Made from about 1967 to present; add 5% for ventilated rib; 3% for Super "14".

Estimated Value:	**New (retail):**	$305.00
	Excellent:	$230.00
	Very good:	$170.00

Thompson Center Contender

Thompson Center Contender Armour Alloy II

Similar to the Contender with a special Armour Alloy II, non-glare satin finish. These parts are not interchangeable with the standard model. Introduced in 1986. Available in 22 long rifle, 223 Rem., 357 mag., 357 Rem. max., 44 mag., 7mmTCU, 30-30 Win., 45 Colt/410 internal choke; ventilated rib available in 45/410; Super 14″ model available.

Estimated Value:	**New (retail):**	$365.00 - $380.00
	Excellent:	$275.00 - $285.00
	Very good:	$205.00 - $215.00

Walther

Walther Model 1 Vest Pocket

Caliber: 25 ACP

Action: Semi-automatic; concealed hammer

Magazine: 6-shot clip

Barrel: 2″

Sights: Fixed

Finish: Blued; checkered hard rubber grips

Length Overall: 4¼″

Approximate wt.: 10 oz.

Comments: Top section of slide is cut away from behind top sight to breech block face. Made from about 1908 to 1912.

Estimated Value:	**Excellent:**	$300.00
	Very good:	$240.00

Walther Model 5 Vest Pocket Pistol

Walther Model 2 Vest Pocket

Similar to Model 1 except: slide fully encloses the barrel; ejector port right side of slide; overall length 4¼″; approximately wt. 12 oz. Made from about 1909 to 1915.

Estimated Value:	**Excellent:**	$275.00
	Very good:	$210.00

Walther Model 4 Pocket

Walther Model 3 Pocket

Caliber: 32 ACP

Action: Semi-automatic; concealed hammer

Magazine: 6-shot clip

Barrel: 2⅝″

Sights: Fixed

Finish: Blued; checkered hard rubber grips

Length Overall: 5″

Approximate wt.: 17 oz.

Comments: Made from about 1910 to 1918; ejector port on left side of slide.

Estimated Value:	**Excellent:**	$325.00
	Very good:	$245.00

Walther Model 4 Pocket

Similar to Model 3 except: larger in overall size; 3½″ barrel; 6″ overall; longer grip; 8-shot clip; a slide extension connected to forward end of the slide. Made from about 1910 to 1918.

Estimated Value:	**Excellent:**	$280.00
	Very good:	$220.00

Walther Model 5 Vest Pocket Pistol

Similar to Model 2 except: improved version with a better finish. Made from about 1913 to 1920.

Estimated Value:	**Excellent:**	$260.00
	Very good:	$200.00

Walther Model 6

Caliber: 9mm Parabellum
Action: Semi-automatic; concealed hammer
Magazine: 8-shot clip
Barrel: 4¾″
Sights: Fixed
Finish: Blued; hard rubber grips
Length Overall: 8¼″
Approximate wt.: 33 oz.
Comments: Made from about 1915 to 1917; ejection port on right side of slide.
Estimated Value: **Excellent:** $450.00
                                Very good: $340.00

Walther Model 7 Pocket

Caliber: 25 ACP
Action: Semi-automatic; concealed hammer
Magazine: 8-shot clip
Barrel: 3″
Sights: Fixed
Finish: Blued; checkered hard rubber grips
Length Overall: 5¼″
Approximate wt.: 13 oz.
Comments: Introduced in 1917, discontinued in 1918. Ejection port on right side of slide.
Estimated Value: **Excellent:** $350.00
                                Very good: $250.00

Walther Model 8 Pocket

Caliber: 25 ACP
Action: Semi-automatic; concealed hammer
Magazine: 8-shot clip
Barrel: 2⅞″
Sights: Fixed
Finish: Blued; checkered plastic grips
Length Overall: 5⅛″
Approximate wt.: 13 oz.
Comments: Made from about 1920 to 1945. Earlier models had takedown catch but later models used trigger guard as slide lock; a variety of special styles were made such a nickel or gold plated, engraved finishes with pearl or ivory grips. Special plated and engraved styles worth more.
Estimated Value: **Excellent:** $300.00
                                Very good: $230.00

Walther Model 9 Vest Pocket

Caliber: 25 ACP
Action: Semi-automatic; concealed hammer
Magazine: 6-shot clip
Barrel: 2″
Sights: Fixed
Finish: Blued; checkered plastic grips
Length Overall: 4″
Approximate wt.: 9½ oz.
Comments: Made from about 1921 to 1945; a variety of special styles were made such as nickel or gold plated engraved finishes with pearl or ivory grips; top section of slide from front sight to breech block face is cut away. Special plated and engraves styles worth more.
Estimated Value: **Excellent:** $280.00
                                Very good: $220.00

Walther Model 7 Pocket

Walther Model 9 Vest Pocket

Walther Model PP

Walther Model 8 Lightweight Pocket

Same as Model 8 except: aluminum alloy used for frame, making it lighter; approximately wt. 9 oz.
Estimated Value: **Excellent:** $325.00
                                Very good: $245.00

Walther Model PP

Caliber: 22 long rifle, 25 ACP, 32 ACP or 380 ACP
Action: Semi-automatic; double action; exposed hammer; thumb safety that drops the hammer on blocked firing pin
Magazine: 8-shot clip
Barrel: 3¾″
Sights: Fixed
Finish: Blued; checkered plastic or checkered wood grips; steel back strap
Length Overall: 6⁹⁄₁₆″
Approximate wt.: 24 oz.
Comments: Made from about 1929 to 1945; also nickel, silver and gold plated engraved models with ivory and pearl grips were produced; first commercially successful double action automatic pistol; initially made in 32 ACP but later made in 22, 25 and 380 calibers; the center fire calibers were made with and without a signal pin to indicate a round in the chamber; World War II models had poorer finish and workmanship. Special plated and engraved models worth more.

Estimated Value:	**Regular Model**	**WWII Model**
Excellent:	$460.00	$360.00
Very Good:	$350.00	$270.00

Walther Model PPK

Same a Model PP except: 3¼″ barrel; 5¹⁵⁄₁₆″ overall length; 7-shot magazine; approximately wt. 19 oz.; one-piece wrap around grip. Made from about 1931 to 1945.

Estimated Value:	Regular Model	WWII Model
Excellent:	$450.00	$350.00
Very good:	$340.00	$265.00

Walther Model PPK

Walther Models PP & PPK Lightweight

Same as Models PP & PPK except: lighter in weight due to aluminum alloy frame.

Estimated Value:	Excellent:	$425.00
	Very good:	$325.00

Walther Presentation Models PP & PPK

Same size as regular Models PP & PPK in 32 caliber; not made to be fired because they were construction of soft aluminum alloy.

Estimated Value: Excellent: $500.00 - $1,200.00

Walther Model PP

Walther Model PPK/S

Same as Model PPK except: larger size to meet U.S.A. Treasury Dept. specifications in 1968; uses the slide and barrel of PPK Model mounted on the PP Model frame; overall length of about 6″; 8-shot magazine. Add $20.00 for 22 long rifle.

Estimated Value:	New (retail):	$500.00
	Excellent:	$380.00
	Very good:	$290.00

Walther Model PPK/S

Walther Model PP Auto

Same as pre-World War II Model PP except for being produced in West Germany from about 1955 to present. Add $20.00 for 22 caliber.

Estimated Value:	New (retail):	$550.00
	Excellent:	$410.00
	Very good:	$310.00

Walther Model PPK American

Similar to the Model PPK except manufactured in the United States in stainless steel. Introduced in 1986.

Estimated Value:	New (retail):	$515.00
	Excellent:	$385.00
	Very good:	$290.00

Walther Model PPK Auto

Same as pre-World War II Model PPK except for being produced in West Germany from about 1955 to date. Importation into U.S.A. discontinued in 1968 due to restrctions imposed by the U.S. Treasury Dept.

Estimated Value:	Excellent:	$400.00
	Very good:	$300.00

Walther Model PPK/S American

Caliber: 380 ACP
Action: Semi-automatic; double action; exposed hammer
Magazine: 7-shot clip
Barrel: 3¼″
Sights: Fixed
Finish: Blued or stainless steel; plastic grips
Length Overall: 6″
Approximate wt.: 23 oz.
Comments: An American-built model of the Walther PPK/S, introduced in the late 1970's. Add 10% for stainless steel.

Estimated Value:	New (retail):	$459.00
	Excellent:	$345.00
	Very good:	$260.00

Walther Model PPK Lightweight

Same as Model PPK except: lighter in weight due to use of aluminum alloy frame and not made in 380 caliber. Importation discontinued in 1968.

Estimated Value:	Excellent:	$450.00
	Very good:	$340.00

Walther Model P-5

Caliber: 9mm Parabellum
Action: Semi-automatic; double action; exposed hammer
Magazine: 8-shot clip
Barrel: 3½″
Sights: Adjustable rear, blade front
Finish: Blued; plastic grips
Length Overall: 7″
Approximate wt.: 28 oz.
Comments: Introduced in 1980.

Estimated Value:	New (retail):	$750.00
	Excellent:	$560.00
	Very good:	$420.00

Walther Model P-5

Walther Model HP

Caliber: 9mm Parabellum
Action: Semi-automatic; double action; exposed hammer
Magazine: 8-shot clip
Barrel: 5″
Sights: Fixed
Finish: Blued; checkered walnut or plastic grips
Length Overall: 8⅜″
Approximate wt.: 35 oz.
Comments: Well-made pistol, produced from about 1937 to 1945.
Estimated Value: Excellent: $900.00
                       Very good: $700.00

Walther Model HP

Walther P-38

Walther Model P-38 IV

Walther P-38 Military

Similar to Model HP except: modified version of the Model HP adopted as the Offical German service arm in 1938 and produced until about 1945. A poorer quality mass-produced military pistol; some of the war time models were of very loose fit and very rough finish.
Estimated Value: Excellent: $425.00
                       Very good: $320.00

Walther P-38

Same as P-38 Military Model except: improved workmanship; use of aluminum alloy in construction of frame; calibers 22 long rifle, 30 Luger and 9mm Parabellum; approximate wt. 28 oz.; add $40.00 for 22 caliber.
Estimated Value: New (retail): $640.00
                       Excellent: $480.00
                       Very good: $360.00

Walther Model P-38 IV

Similar to the P-38 with strengthened slide, no dust cover and steel reinforced frame; adjustable rear sight.
Estimated Value: Excellent: $470.00
                       Very good: $350.00

Walther Model P-38 K

Similar to the Model P-38 IV with a 2¾″ barrel.
Estimated Value: Excellent: $475.00
                       Very good: $345.00

Webley

Webley 1906 Model Vest Pocket

Caliber: 25 ACP
Action: Semi-automatic; exposed hammer; grip safety in front of grip
Magazine: 6-shot clip
Barrel: 2⅛″
Sights: None
Finish: Blued; checkered hard rubber grips
Length Overall: 4¾″
Approximate wt.: 12 oz.
Comments: Made from about 1906 to 1940.
Estimated Value: Excellent: $190.00
                       Very good: $145.00

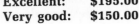

Webley 1906 Model
Vest Pocket

Webley & Scott 1906 Model Police

Caliber: 32 ACP; 380 ACP
Action: Semi-automatic; exposed hammer
Magazine: 8-shot clip in 32 ACP, 7-shot clip in 380 ACP
Barrel: 3½″
Sights: Fixed; police version has rear sight and civilian model has a groove for rear sight
Finish: Blued; checkered hard rubber grips
Length Overall: 6¼″
Approximate wt.: 20 oz.
Comments: Made from about 1905 to 1940; with or without grip safety.
Estimated Value: Excellent: $200.00
                       Very good: $150.00

Webley & Scott 1909 Model Vest Pocket

Similar to 1906 Model except: ejection port in top of slide; concealed hammer; has fixed front and rear sights mounted on slide. Made from about 1909 to 1940.
Estimated Value: Excellent: $195.00
                       Very good: $150.00

Webley & Scott 9mm Military & Police

Caliber: 9mm Browning long
Action: Semi-automatic; exposed hammer; grip safety
Magazine: 8-shot clip
Barrel: 5¼″
Sights: Fixed
Finish: Blued; checkered plastic grips
Length Overall: 8″
Approximate wt.: 32 oz.
Comments: Made from about 1909 to 1930.
Estimated Value: Excellent: $500.00
Very good: $375.00

Webley & Scott 9mm Military & Police

Webley & Scott Mark I

Caliber: 455 Webley self-loading
Action: Semi-automatic; exposed hammer; grip safety
Magazine: 7-shot clip
Barrel: 5″
Sights: Fixed front; movable rear
Finish: Blued; checkered hard rubber or checkered walnut grips
Length Overall: 8½″
Approximate wt.: 39 oz.
Comments: Adopted by British Royal Navy and Marines in 1913. Made from about 1911 to 1931.
Estimated Value: Excellent: $350.00
Very good: $265.00

Webley & Scott Mark I

Webley & Scott Mark I No. 2

Similar to Mark I except: a slightly different version with fitted shoulder stock and adjustable rear sight; issued to the British Royal Flying Corps in 1915. Prices for gun with shoulder stock.
Estimated Value: Excellent: $750.00
Very good: $560.00

Webley & Scott 38

Similar to Mark I except: a smaller modified version with concealed hammer; 8-shot magazine; 38 ACP caliber. Made from about 1910 to 1930.
Estimated Value: Excellent: $300.00
Very good: $225.00

Webley & Scott 1909 Model Single Shot Target

Caliber: 22 short, long, long rifle
Action: Single action; exposed hammer; hinged frame; tip-up barrel; trigger guard also barrel release
Cylinder: None; single shot; chamber in barrel
Barrel: 10″ round
Sights: Fixed; later models have adjustable rear sight
Finish: Blued; hard rubber or wood grips
Length Overall: 15″
Approximate wt.: 35 oz.
Comments: Target pistol. Made from about 1909 to 1965 with improvements.
Estimated Value: Excellent: $260.00
Very good: $210.00

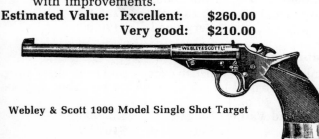

Webley & Scott 1909 Model Single Shot Target

Webley & Scott 1911 Model Single Shot

Caliber: 22 short, long, long rifle
Action: Manually operated slide to chamber cartridge; exposed hammer
Magazine: None; single shot
Barrel: 4½″ or 9″
Sights: Adjustable
Finish: Blued; checkered hard rubber grips
Length Overall: 6¼″ to 10¾″
Approximate wt.: 20 to 24 oz.
Comments: Has the appearance of automatic pistol; built on the 32 caliber frame; made for police training arm; some had removable wooden shoulder stocks. Made from about 1925 to 1927 with only a few hundred being produced.
Estimated Value: Excellent: $400.00
Very good: $300.00

Webley & Scott Match Invader Single Shot Target

Similar to 1909 Model Single Shot Target except: also in caliber 32 S&W long, 38 S&W or 38 Special; approximate wt. 33 oz. Made from about 1952 to 1965.
Estimated Value: Excellent: $200.00
Very good: $150.00

Webley & Scott Mark III Police

Caliber: 38 S&W
Action: Single or double; exposed hammer; hinged frame; top break simultaneous ejector
Cylinder: 6-shot
Barrel: 3″, 4″, 5″
Sights: Fixed or adjustable rear
Finish: Blued; checkered hard rubber or walnut grips
Length Overall: 8¼″ to 10¼″
Approximate wt.: 19 to 22 oz.
Comments: Made from about 1897 to 1945.
Estimated Value: Excellent: $190.00
Very good: $150.00

Webley & Scott Mark III Government Model

Caliber: 450, 455 or 476 Webley
Action: Single or double; exposed hammer; hinged frame; top break; simultaneous ejector
Cylinder: 6-shot
Barrel: 4″, 6″, 7½″
Sights: Fixed, also adjustable rear
Finish: Blued; hard rubber or wood grips
Length Overall: 9¼″ to 12¾″
Approximate wt.: 36 to 40 oz.
Comments: Made from about 1896 to 1928.
Estimated Value: Excellent: $200.00
Very good: $150.00

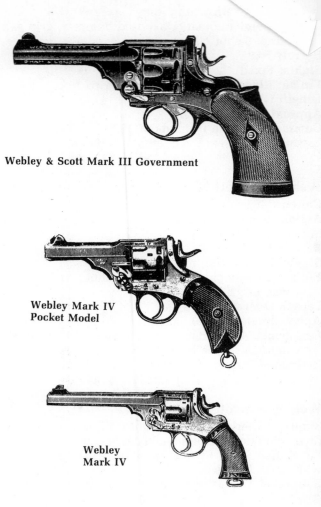

Webley & Scott Mark III Government

Webley Mark IV Pocket Model

Webley Mark IV

Webley & Scott Pocket Model Hammerless

Caliber: 32 S&W
Action: Double action; concealed hammer; hinged frame; top break; simultaneous ejector
Cylinder: 6-shot
Barrel: 3½″
Sights: Fixed
Finish: Blued; hard rubber or wood grips
Length Overall: 6½″
Approximate wt.: 18 oz.
Comments: The hammer is enclosed by the frame. Made from about 1898 to 1940.
Estimated Value: Excellent: $190.00
Very good: $145.00

Webley & Scott Police & Civilian Pocket

Similar to Pocket Model Hammerless except: exposed hammer; double and single action. Made from about 1901 to 1940.
Estimated Value: Excellent: $180.00
Very good: $135.00

Webley Mark IV Police Model

Caliber: 38 S&W
Action: Single or double; exposed hammer; hinged frame; top break; simultaneous ejector
Cylinder: 6-shot
Barrel: 4″, 5″, 6″
Sights: Fixed or adjustable
Finish: Blued; checkered walnut or plastic grips
Length Overall: 8⅛″ to 10⅛″
Approximate wt.: 24 to 29 oz.
Comments: Made from about 1927 to present.
Estimated Value: Excellent: $185.00
Very good: $140.00

Webley Mark IV War Model

Similar to Mark IV Police Model except: made during World War II (from about 1940 to 1945); poor finish and fitting.
Estimated Value: Excellent: $200.00
Very good: $150.00

Webley Mark IV Pocket Model

Similar to Mark IV Police Model except: calibers 32 S&W, 32 S&W long or 38 S&W; barrel length 3″; approximate wt. 24 oz.; overall length 7⅛″.
Estimated Value: Excellent: $180.00
Very good: $140.00

Webley Mark IV Target Model

Similar to Mark IV Police Model except: caliber 22 short, long, long rifle only; adjustable rear sight; barrel length 6″; approximate wt. 32 oz. Made from about 1931 to 1968.
Estimated Value: Excellent: $230.00
Very good: $175.00

Webley Mark VI British Service

Caliber: 455 Webley
Action: Single or double; hinged frame; top break; simultaneous ejector
Cylinder: 6-shot
Barrel: 4″, 6″, 7½″
Sights: Fixed
Finish: Blued; checkered hard rubber or wood grips
Length Overall: 9¼″ to 12¾″
Approximate wt.: 34 to 39 oz.
Comments: Made from about 1915 to 1928
Estimated Value: Excellent: $220.00
Very good: $170.00

Webley Police Mark VI Target

Similar to Mark VI British except: caliber 22 short, long, long rifle; barrel length 6″ only; target sights; approximate wt. 40 oz.
Estimated Value: Excellent: $225.00
Very good: $180.00